SUMMARY of CHANGE

AR 12–15/SECNAVINST 4950.4B/AFI 16–105
Joint Security Cooperation Education and Training

I0438972

This major revision, dated 3 January 2011--

o Changes the title of the regulation from Joint Security Assistance Training to Joint Security Cooperation Education and Training (cover).

o Adds the Regional Defense Combating Terrorism Fellowship Program as one of the training programs managed under the Security Cooperation Education and Training Program (para 1-5*b*(13)).

o Moves HQDA security cooperation responsibility from Deputy Under Secretary of the Army (International Affairs) to Deputy Assistant Secretary of the Army for Defense Exports and Cooperation (para 2-15*b*).

o Adds policy for medical requirements and healthcare (chap 8).

**Headquarters
Departments of the Army,
the Navy,
and the Air Force
Washington, DC
3 January 2011**

***Army Regulation 12–15
*SECNAVINST 4950.4B
*AFI 16–105**

Effective 3 February 2011

Security Assistance and International Logistics

Joint Security Cooperation Education and Training

By Order of the Secretary of the Army, and the Navy:

GEORGE W. CASEY, JR.
*General, United States Army
Chief of Staff*

Official:

JOYCE E. MORROW
*Administrative Assistant to the
Secretary of the Army*

RAY MABUS,
Secretary of the Navy

BRUCE S. LEMKIN,
DCS/International Affairs

History. This publication is a major revision.

Summary. This regulation revises several regulations that cover the education and training of foreign personnel, and implements DOD 5105.38–M. It prescribes policies, responsibilities, procedures, and administration for the education and training of international military students by the Departments of the Army, the Navy, and the Air Force as authorized by the U.S. security assistance legislation. This regulation deals specifically with training under the International Military Education and Training Program, the Foreign Military Sales Program, and related programs; and contains instructions on the U.S. Field Program.

Applicability. This regulation applies to the active Army, the Army National Guard/Army National Guard of the United States, and the U.S. Army Reserve, unless otherwise stated. It also applies to the Reserve Components of the Army, the Navy, the Air Force, the Marine Corps, the Air National Guard, the Coast Guard, and DOD agencies.

Proponent and exception authority. The proponent of this regulation is the Assistant Secretary of the Army for Acquisition, Logistics, and Technology. The

proponent has the authority to approve exceptions or waivers to this regulation that are consistent with controlling law and regulations. The proponent may delegate this approval authority, in writing, to a division chief within the proponent agency or its direct reporting unit or field operating agency, in the grade of colonel or the civilian equivalent. Activities may request a waiver to this regulation by providing justification that includes a full analysis of the expected benefits and must include formal review by the activity's senior legal officer. All waiver requests will be endorsed by the commander or senior leader of the requesting activity and forwarded through their higher headquarters to the policy proponent. Refer to AR 25–30 for specific guidance.

Army internal control process. This regulation contains internal controls and provides an Internal Control Evaluation for use in evaluating key internal controls (see appendix C).

Supplementation. Supplementation of this regulation and establishment of command and local forms are prohibited without prior approval from the Assistant Secretary of the Army for Acquisition, Logistics, and Technology (SAAL–NP),

Suite 8200, 1777 North Kent Street, Suite 8200, Arlington, VA 22209.

Suggested improvements. Users are invited to send comments and suggested improvements on DA Form 2028 (Recommended Changes to Publications and Blank Forms) directly to the Assistant Secretary of the Army Acquisition, Logistics, and Technology (SAAL–NP), 1777 North Kent Street, Suite 8200, Arlington, VA 22209. Navy, Marine Corps, and Coast Guard users should send comments directly to Navy IPO (02C2T), 2521 South Clark Street, Suite 800, Arlington, VA 22202–3528. Air Force users should send comments directly to the Secretary of the Air Force/International Affairs, 1080 Pentagon, Washington, DC 20330–1080.

Distribution. This publication is available in electronic media only and is intended for command levels D and E for the active Army, the Army National Guard/Army National Guard of the United States, and the U.S. Army Reserve; Navy: SNDL–Parts I (less 29N); and Air Force: F.

---

*This regulation supersedes AR 12–15/SECNAVINST 4950.4A/AFI 16–105, dated 5 June 2000.

AR 12–15/SECNAVINST 4950.4B/AFI 16–105 • 3 January 2011

i

UNCLASSIFIED

Contents (Listed by paragraph and page number)

Contents—Continued

Chapter 3
Planning and Programming, *page 18*

Contents—Continued

Contents—Continued

Contents—Continued

Chapter 5
English Language Training (Policy, Planning, Programming, and Implementing English language training), *page 81*

Contents—Continued

Contents—Continued

Contents—Continued

Chapter 8
Medical Requirements and Healthcare, *page 125*

Contents—Continued

Contents—Continued

Contents—Continued

Contents—Continued

Contents—Continued

Contents—Continued

Contents—Continued

Chapter 13
Exchange Training, *page 235*

Contents—Continued

Contents—Continued

Contents—Continued

Glossary

Chapter 1
Introduction

1-1. Purpose
The Joint Security Cooperation Education and Training regulation prescribes policies, procedures, and responsibilities for training international personnel in the categories described, below. Also, it applies to the entire security cooperation education and training process from congressional and State or Defense Department authorization, through the country's identification (ID) of its training needs, through the programming and financial management process, and through all aspects of education and training. It applies to—

a. Training formulated under the Security Cooperation Education and Training Program (SCETP).

b. Individual training attachment of international personnel on temporary duty (TDY).

c. Orientations and observer visits by international military personnel performed at no expense to the U.S. Government.

1-2. References
Required and related publications and prescribed and referenced forms are listed in appendix A.

1-3. Explanation of abbreviations and terms
Abbreviations and special terms used in this regulation are explained in the glossary.

1-4. Responsibilities
Responsibilities are listed in chapter 2.

1-5. Security Cooperation Education and Training Program
The SCETP consists of U.S. military education and training conducted by DOD for international personnel from eligible countries in order to effectively advance U.S. security interests and build defense partnerships for the future. This education and training is conducted within the continental United States (CONUS), primarily at military training facilities, and outside the continental United States (OCONUS) by mobile education or training teams and at selected U.S. facilities overseas. The SCETP is described in DOD 5105.38–M, C10.5–C10.7, and in paragraphs 3–3 through 3–6 in this regulation. The SCETP includes—

a. Major training programs.

(1) International Military Education and Training (IMET) is authorized by the Foreign Assistance Act (FAA) of 1961, as amended. The IMET includes education and training for which military departments (MILDEPs) are reimbursed from foreign assistance appropriations.

(2) Foreign military sales (FMS) is authorized by the Arms Export Control Act (AECA), as amended. The FMS covers the sale of defense articles, services, and training to eligible foreign governments and international organizations. These sales are reimbursed to the MILDEPs as required by law.

b. Other training programs.

(1) African Contingency Operations Training and Assistance.

(2) Aviation Leadership Program.

(3) Bilateral or regional cooperation programs.

(4) Combatant commander initiative funds.

(5) Disaster Response (Humanitarian Assistance).

(6) Drawdowns of training.

(7) Enhanced international peacekeeping capabilities.

(8) Exchanges (professional military education (PME), exchange of training and related support, and flight training exchanges).

(9) International Narcotics Control and Law Enforcement.

(10) Joint combined exchange training (JCET).

(11) Mine action.

(12) Regional Centers for Security Studies.

(a) Africa Center for Strategic Studies.

(b) Asia-Pacific Center for Security Studies.

(c) Center for Hemispheric Defense Studies.

(d) Marshall Center.

(e) Near East South Asia Center for Strategic Studies.

(13) Regional Defense Combating Terrorism Fellowship Program (CTFP).

(14) Section 1004–Counter-Drug Training Support.

(15) Service Academy Programs.

(a) Cadet Semester Exchange Abroad Program.

(b) Military Services Academies International Student Program.

(16) United States Coast Guard (USCG) Academy Foreign Cadet Program.

(17) USCG Caribbean Support Tender.

(18) National Geospatial-Intelligence Agency International Program.

1–6. Objectives of the Security Cooperation Education and Training Program

The objectives of the SCETP are to—

a. Assist the foreign country in developing expertise and systems needed for effective management and operation of its defense establishment.

b. Foster the foreign country's development of its own professional and technical training capability.

c. Promote U.S. military rapport with the armed forces of foreign countries to operate in peacekeeping missions and in coalition environments.

d. Promote better understanding of the United States, its people, political system, institutions, democratic values, and way of life.

e. Increase the international military student (IMS) awareness of the U.S. commitment to the basic principles of internationally recognized human rights.

f. Develop skills needed for effective operation and maintenance of equipment acquired from the United States.

Chapter 2
Responsibilities

Section I
General

2–1. Purpose

This chapter outlines the responsibilities of the various departments, organizations, and elements involved in security cooperation education and training, planning, management, and execution.

2–2. Secretary of State

The Secretary of State is responsible for continuous supervision and general direction of security assistance programs. This includes determining whether (and when) there will be a program or sale for a particular country or activity (to include IMET) and, if so, its size and scope. It also includes the determination of budget requests and allocation of funds for military assistance. The Department of State (DOS) prepares the Security Cooperation Organization Mission Performance Plan.

2–3. Secretary of Defense

The SECDEF establishes military requirements and implements programs to transfer defense articles and Services to eligible foreign countries and international organizations. Within DOD, the principal planning agencies for security cooperation are the Defense Security Cooperation Agency (DSCA), the commanders of combatant commands, the joint staff, the Security Cooperation Office, the MILDEP, and Service international organizations. Department of Defense Directive (DODD) 5132.03 establishes policies and assigns DOD responsibilities relating to security cooperation.

2–4. Under Secretary of Defense for Policy

Under direction of the SECDEF, the Under Secretary of Defense for Policy (USD(P)) is the principal staff assistant and advisor to the SECDEF and Deputy Secretary of Defense for all matters concerning the formation of national security and defense policy and the integration and oversight of DOD policy and plans to achieve national security objectives. USD(P) is the SECDEF's principal security cooperation representative. USD(P) Assistant Secretaries with regional responsibilities coordinate on security cooperation matters that directly affect their regions.

2–5. Assistant Secretary of Defense (International Security Affairs)

The ASD (ISA) under the authority, direction, and control of the USD(P) is responsible for supervising security assistance programs with all foreign governments, with the exception of those of the New Independent States of the former Soviet Union. This office is concerned with much more than just security assistance and includes a specific DOD agency that interprets executive policy and develops Defense Department security assistance policies and programs. The ASD (ISA) designated the DSCA, to administer and supervise the execution of all security cooperation programs for the DOD.

2–6. Deputy Assistant Secretary of Defense (Partnership Strategy and Stability Operations)

Under the authority, direction, and control of the Assistant Secretary of Defense (Global Security Affairs) and the USD(P) are responsible for providing security cooperation policy guidance in close collaboration with the regional Deputy Assistant Secretaries of Defense (Policy). Under the direction of the Assistant Secretary of Defense (Global Security Affairs), the DSCA administers and supervises the execution of many security cooperation programs for the DOD.

2–7. Assistant Secretary of Defense (Special Operations/Low Intensity Conflict)

The Assistant Secretary of Defense (Special Operations/Low Intensity Conflict) is the principal staff assistant and civilian advisor to the USD(P) and the Secretary of Defense on Special Operations and Combating Terrorism. The office of the Assistant SECDEF (Special Operations/Low Intensity Conflict) runs the Regional Defense Counterterrorism Fellowship Program.

2–8. Assistant Secretary of Defense (Strategy and Threat Reduction)

The Assistant SECDEF (Strategy and Threat Reduction) is the principal staff assistant and advisor to the USD(P) and the principal staff assistant to the Secretary and Deputy Secretary of Defense on national security and defense strategy and the forces and contingency plans necessary to implement defense strategy. This office is responsible for the publication of security cooperation guidance.

2–9. Director, Defense Security Cooperation Agency

Under the direction of the USD(P), Director, DSCA directs, administers, and supervises the execution (to include closure) of all security assistance programs for DOD. The Director, DSCA is the DOD focal point for government arms transfers, budgets, legislative, projections, forecasting, and other security assistance matters (including IMET). The Director, DSCA conducts international logistics and sales negotiations with foreign countries, provides financial management, develops and implements security assistance policies, and assists U.S. industry in exporting military equipment and services. All authorities conferred on the SECDEF by the FAA and AECA pertaining to security assistance and all authorities under those acts delegated by the President to the SECDEF are redelegated to the Director, DSCA. The Director, DSCA is not in the Security Cooperation Organization direct chain of command, but funds Security Cooperation Organization program management. The Director, DSCA provides USD(P) staff support for security assistance matters. The Director, DSCA also provides management oversight to a number of DOD schools that provide security cooperation education and training both to the community itself and to international customers. These include the Defense Institute for Security Assistance Management (DISAM) and the Defense Institute for International Legal Studies. In addition to these institutions, there are a number of other DOD schools that fall under the implementing agency of one of the MILDEPS that also provide education and training to international students. These include the Defense Language Institute English Language Center (DLIELC) and the Defense Resources Management Institute (DRMI).

2–10. Director, Defense Finance and Accounting Service

The Director, Defense Finance and Accounting Service (DFAS) performs accounting, billing, disbursing, and collecting functions for the Security Cooperation Program. The DFAS also issues accounting procedures. The Defense Finance and Accounting Service–Denver (DFAS–DE) is the primary office for security cooperation funding accountability.

2–11. Chairman of the Joint Chiefs of Staff

The Chairman of the Joint Chiefs of Staff (CJCS) consists of the Chairman, the Vice Chairman, the Chief of Staff of the Army, the Chief of Naval Operations (CNO), the Chief of Staff of the Air Force, and the Commandant of the Marine Corps (CMC). The Joint Staff has the responsibility for the unified strategic direction of the combatant forces, their operation under unified command, and their integration into an efficient team of land, naval, and air forces.

2–12. Commanders of combatant commands

   a. The commanders of combatant commands have security cooperation responsibilities that include correlation of programs with regional plans, military advice, command, and support of the Security Cooperation Organization, and supervision of budgets. They provide military assessments and Security Cooperation Program impacts within their respective areas of responsibility to the CJCS.

   b. In accordance with DOD security cooperation guidance, each geographic commander of combatant commands develops and publishes a Theater Security Cooperation Plan (TSCP) that outlines security cooperation efforts within their assigned area of responsibility. These plans address all aspects of security cooperation including education and training.

   c. The COCOMs conduct initiatives that include joint exercises (including activities in participating foreign countries), and humanitarian and civil assistance to military and related civilian personnel of foreign countries. These initiatives are an important part of the commanders of combatant commands TSCPs.

   d. Military personnel assigned to Security Cooperation Organization within a geographic area are in the chain of command personnel. The commander (CDR) of a commanders of combatant commands rates Security Cooperation Organization personnel, provides technical assistance, and administrative support, allocate funds made available by DSCA and supervises the preparation and execution of Security Cooperation Organization budgets. The commanders of combatant commands commander commands and supervises the Security Cooperation Organization in matters that are not functions or responsibilities of the Chief of the U.S. Diplomatic Mission.

e. Geographic commanders of combatant commands include the Africa Command (AFRICOM), Central Command (CENTCOM), European Command, Northern Command, Pacific Command, and Southern Command.

2–13. Commanders of component commands

As directed by their commanders of combatant commands and commanders of Service component commands—

a. Provide input into the development of the commanders of combatant commands TSCP.

(1) Ensure that their Service capabilities are considered in the development of the TSCP.

(2) Coordinate their Service's participation in their commanders of combatant commands TSCP Regional Working Groups. Service participants may include, but are not limited to—

(a) Component representatives.

(b) Service headquarters representatives.

(c) Service security cooperation education and training execution agencies.

(3) Participate in other security cooperation conferences sponsored by their commanders of combatant commands.

(4) Recommend priorities for country invitations to Service PME courses.

b. Execute designated portions of their commanders of combatant commands's TSCP within capabilities and resources.

(1) Coordinate, plan, and execute assigned commanders of combatant commands initiatives that can be supported from assigned component resources.

(2) For those commanders of combatant commands initiatives that cannot be supported from assigned component resources, formally forward or coordinate formal forwarding of request for support (resources) via the appropriate chain of command to their Service headquarters.

(3) Provide personnel to deploy to countries in support of security cooperation missions when tasked by appropriate authority.

c. In coordination with their Service security cooperation education and training execution agency, they will maintain situational awareness of all Service security cooperation education or training assistance teams and personnel deployed within their commanders of combatant commands' geographic region.

2–14. Chiefs of security cooperation organizations

a. The FAA authorizes the President to assign U.S. personnel overseas to manage security cooperation programs administered by DOD. The generic term Security Cooperation Organization encompasses all DOD elements, regardless of actual title, located in a foreign country to carry out security cooperation management functions. The programs include grant military assistance, IMET, FMS, and other security cooperation programs.

b. The Security Cooperation Organization personnel serve under the direction and supervision of the Chief of the U.S. Diplomatic Mission to ensure that DOD security cooperation management responsibilities are properly executed. The commanders of combatant commands command and supervise the Security Cooperation Organization in matters that are not Chief of the U.S. Diplomatic Mission functions, including the provision of technical assistance and administrative support. The Security Cooperation Organization Chief ensures that all Security Cooperation Organization activities are fully coordinated with the Chief of the U.S. Diplomatic Mission.

c. The SCOs communicate directly with DSCA, MILDEP, and Service security cooperation elements and activities as appropriate and provide information copies of communications of record to the commanders of combatant commands for evaluation and comment as specified by the commanders of combatant commands.

d. The Security Cooperation Organization personnel perform the following security cooperation functions:

(1) Security cooperation program management and oversight.

(a) Assist foreign countries in—

1. Planning and programming security cooperation education and training requirements.

2. Submitting requirements to appropriate agencies.

3. Administering approved programs in country.

(b) Make recommendations concerning security cooperation education and training for their host country, assist in development of security cooperation education and training programs, and submit appropriate program data.

(c) Observe and report on the use of IMS trained under security cooperation.

(d) Assist in the selection of IMS and ensure that IMS meet security, medical, English language, and technical requirements for security cooperation education and training provided.

(e) Ensure all IMS are briefed before their departure from the home country, to include information on required

physical fitness participation and level of fitness, swimming requirements, clothing, and equipment that must be brought with the student, and other information peculiar to the student's course of training.

(f) Prepare necessary administrative documents related to education and training as required within this regulation.

(g) To the maximum extent possible, obtain returning IMS feedback concerning the education or training and support provided.

(h) Provide appropriate IMS records to the initial training installation.

(i) Release information in the IMS education/training and medical records to country personnel when appropriate. However, records should be screened carefully to ensure that information of a sensitive nature is removed.

(j) Provide administrative support for and country team supervisory control of deployed security cooperation education or training teams in host country.

(2) *General advisory and training assistance.* The Security Cooperation Organization personnel may provide advisory and training assistance to the host country military establishment; however, this assistance must be minimal and cannot interfere with the Security Cooperation Organization performance of security cooperation management responsibilities.

(3) *Administrative support.* The Security Cooperation Organization can provide normal administrative support for personnel assigned in country to perform non-security cooperation functions so long as such support does not reach a level that would require additional administrative personnel.

(4) *U.S. Defense Representative.* When designated as the U.S. Defense Representative (USDR), the Security Cooperation Organization Chief complies with Department of Defense instruction (DODI) 5105.57.

(5) *Safeguarding classified material.* The Security Cooperation Organization safeguards U.S. security-cooperation related classified information located in foreign countries. Except for classified information authorized for release to a foreign government or international organization and under the control of that government or organization, the retention of U.S. classified material is authorized only if it is necessary to satisfy U.S. Government (USG) mission requirements.

Section II
Department of the Army

2–15. Assistant Secretary of the Army (Acquisition, Logistics, and Technology)

a. The Assistant Secretary of the Army (Acquisition, Logistics, and Technology) (ASA (ALT)), acts for the Secretary of the Army and will—

(1) Serve as the organization responsible for all Department of the Army (DA) matters and policy related to acquisition, logistics, technology, procurement, the industrial base, and security cooperation (security assistance and armaments cooperation).

(2) Serve as the organization responsible for resourcing and overseeing the development, coordination, and implementation of policy and programs, associated with the Army's security cooperation activities (FMS, foreign military training, allocation of excess defense articles to foreign countries, armaments cooperation, technology transfer, direct commercial sales, and munitions case processing).

b. Deputy Assistant Secretary of the Army for Defense Exports and Cooperation. The Deputy Assistant Secretary of the Army for Defense Exports and Cooperation (DASA (DE&C)) discharges ASA (ALT) responsibilities for Security Cooperation activities. The DASA (DE&C) is the U.S. Army lead for Security Assistance exports, technology transfer, armaments cooperation, and for equipping and training our international partners. The DASA (DE&C) also manages, leads, directs policy, resources, and strategy for the conduct of the Army's global security cooperation programs with direct tasking authority over the Army's designated lead commands for the execution of their delegated security cooperation responsibilities. Regarding security assistance/international training and Security Assistance Teams (SAT), DASA (DE&C) will—

(1) Develop, coordinate, and promulgate Armywide Secretary of the Army policy, including the development of Army input to specific country security cooperation (SC) programs in support of the Headquarters, Department of the Army (HQDA) missions.

(2) Exercise policy responsibility for security cooperation team under the IMET; FMS; foreign military financing (FMF), and other applicable authority as directed by DOD.

(3) Receive, staff, and serve as final HQDA decision authority for resourcing requests for Army SAT from authorized command and agencies.

(4) For approved SAT requests, coordinate with the Deputy Chief of Staff, G–3/5/7 (DCS, G–3/5/7) for tasking responsible Army agencies and commands for execution.

(5) Return disapproved requests to the requesting command or agency.

(6) Be the final decision authority on discrepancies that occurs between the Training and Doctrine Command (TRADOC) and Army Materiel Command (AMC) on contractor issues.

c. Commanding General, Training and Doctrine Command. The CG, TRADOC will—

(1) Serve as the Army lead command for the operation, development, offer and execution of Security Cooperation training letters of offer and acceptance (LOA) which are also called cases).

(2) Serve as the Army lead for the management and mission execution of HQDA-approved SATs.

(3) Task TRADOC, CONUS, Army commands (ACOMs) (less United States Army Special Operations Command (USASOC)), and other direct reporting units (DRUs) to provide personnel, supplies and equipment to countries and/or to task training support materiel, program of instruction, and foreign disclosure in accordance with HQDA taskings.

(4) Provide centralized financial management and distribution of FMS and IMET program training funds for all operating agencies and training providers.

(5) As required, provide case/program funding to commanders of combatant commands or Army service component commands (ASCCs) that resource SAT from their internal assets.

(6) Maintain security cooperation training execution data sufficient to reply to standard requests for information (RFI).

(7) Maintain a capability to contract Army SAT.

(8) Comply with HQDA tasking suspenses and requirements.

d. Commanding General, U.S. Army Materiel Command. The CG, AMC will—

(1) Serve as the Army lead for the operation and execution of Security Cooperation materiel LOA.

(2) Coordinate and advise TRADOC for training request to support U.S. Army-procured equipment.

(3) Serve as the Army central manager for all approved Army SC cases and exercises sole source approval for contracted Army SC training requirements.

(4) Develop, plan, deploy, and support all new equipment training, quality assurance teams, calibration teams, repair and return teams.

(5) Coordinate all Army SAT requirements with TRADOC during LOA development, except as listed in paragraph (4), above.

(6) Before conducting training, provide Air Worthiness assessment and certification for SC flight training when host nation aircraft will be flown by U.S. DOD/contractor personnel. Provide funding by case or other Government sources.

(7) Provide timely response, and comply with tasking suspense and requirements from DCS, G–3/5/7 designated SAT lead. If unable to support OCONUS SAT missions under this regulation, must respond to lead agent by memorandum over a general officer signature.

(8) Comply with HQDA tasking suspense and requirements.

e. Deputy Chief of Staff, G–3/5/7. The DCS, G–3/5/7 will—

(1) Receive, assess, and provide DCS, G–3/5/7 position for Army SAT requests.

(2) Task HQDA, ACOMs, and DRUs, as appropriate, for the sourcing and support to TRADOC for execution of approved Army SAT, at the request of DASA (DE&C).

(3) Coordinate temporary tour of active duty (TTAD) funding for non-FMS (cash) SAT, for HQDA-approved Reserve Component and National Guard sourced teams.

f. Deputy Chief of Staff, G–1. The DCS, G–1 will—

(1) Participate in the HQDA review and approval process for Army SAT requests.

(2) Provide guidance throughout the Army on the availability and provision of military (except Army Medical Department officers) and DOD civilians to support permanent change of station (PCS) SAT.

(3) Comply with HQDA tasking suspense and requirements.

g. Chief, Army Reserve. The Chief, Army Reserve will—

(1) Identify and activate United States Army Reserve (USAR) Soldiers to execute SAT missions in accordance with AR 135–210, as directed by DCS, G–3/5/7.

(2) Coordinate with TRADOC G–3/Security Assistance Training Field Activity (SATFA) and other Army agencies to fund TTAD and travel costs.

(3) Comply with HQDA tasking suspense and requirements.

h. Chief, National Guard Bureau. The Chief, National Guard Bureau will—

(1) Identify and activate National Guard Soldiers to execute SAT mission in accordance with AR 135–210, as directed by DCS, G–3/5/7.

(2) Coordinate with TRADOC G–3/SATFA and other Army agencies to fund TTAD and travel costs.

(3) Comply with HQDA tasking suspense and requirements.

i. The Surgeon General. The Surgeon General will—

(1) Participate in the HQDA review and approval process for Army medical SAT requests.

(2) Assist and provide guidance to TRADOC regarding HQDA-approved medical team missions, composition, and training support requirements based on the SAT request.

(3) Comply with HQDA tasking suspense and requirements.

j. U.S. Army Corps of Engineers. The U.S. Army Corps of Engineers (COE) is the overall supervisor and coordinate for all engineering activities associated with, and in support of, assigned security cooperation programs and projects.

k. Army service component commands. Army service component commands (ASCC) will—

(1) Receive, review, and assess requests for Army SAT and recommend to the commanders of combatant commands approval, disapproval, or execution within ASCC assets.

(2) Coordinate any requirements external to the ASCC, if the commanders of combatant commands approves internal ASCC execution. Coordinate with the Security Cooperation Organization and TRADOC, for external funding.

(3) Be responsible for all team preparation, pre-deployment, team support, and redeployment requirements, for ASCC-executed teams.

l. Other Army commands, Army staff agencies, and direct reporting units. Other ACOMs, Army staff agencies, and DRU, for DCS, G–3/5/7 designated SAT lead tasking, will—

(1) Provide military and Department of the Army (DA) civilian SAT members who meet qualifications specified in the taskings, and afford them sufficient time, guidance, and support to prepare for their OCONUS missions.

(2) Comply with HQDA tasking suspenses and requirements.

2–16. Deputy Chief of Staff, G–3/5/7

The DCS, G–3/5/7 will—

a. Support DASA (DE&C) in reconciling Army Security Cooperation Program issues and foreign requests for defense articles and services with the U.S. Strategic Plan and policy objectives.

b. Program IMET and FMS CONUS training requirements in the Army Program for Individual Training; task Army trainers to accomplish the training.

c. Serve as the DA proponent for unit exchange training.

d. Serve as the DA proponent for the Professional Military Exchange Program.

e. Coordinate with the U.S. Army Staff and develop priorities for seat allocation which establishes international participation at the U.S. Army War College (AWC), intermediate level education (ILE), and United States Army Sergeants Major Academy (USASMA) in accordance with the U.S. Army Security Cooperation Strategy (USASCS).

f. Coordinate with the ACOMs and the commanders of combatant commands Security Cooperation Training Program managers and provide recommendations to the Chief of Staff, Army (CSA) for foreign military attendees to the AWC. Generate the invitation letters and provide them to the country counterparts.

g. Coordinate with the ASCCs and the commanders of combatant commands\Security Cooperation Training Program managers and provide recommendations to the CSA for foreign military attendees ILE and USASMA. Generate and send out a message inviting the recommended countries.

h. Resolve foreign training problems between two or more ACOMs, or between the TRADOC, and foreign government representatives.

2–17. Deputy Chief of Staff, G–1

The DCS, G–1 will recommend policies to procure, distribute, manage, retain, and separate U.S. military and civilian personnel in support of security cooperation.

2–18. Assistant Secretary of the Army (Financial Management and Comptroller)

The Assistant Secretary of the Army (Financial Management and Comptroller) will—

a. Establish financial management procedures for SC programs within the framework of requirements prescribed by higher authority.

b. Establish and issue policy, principles, and systems for financing, funding, accounting, and financial reporting for FMS, IMET, and related programs.

c. Make and issue uniform policy and principles for use in setting up and maintaining uniform application of pricing and cost criteria. These criteria are for sales of defense articles, services, and training furnished to foreign governments and international organizations under IMET, FMS, and related programs.

d. Receive IMET funds from DSCA.

2–19. Deputy Chief of Staff, G–2

The DCS, G–2, as the principal disclosure authority for the Army, exercises executive level oversight of foreign disclosure activities across the Army. AR 380–10 provides Army policy with regard to the disclosure of classified military information (CMI) and controlled unclassified information (CUI) to foreign nationals. This regulation also assigns responsibilities with respect to the sharing of information and control of foreign visitors, liaison officers, exchange personnel, cooperative program personnel, and other representatives of foreign governments or international organizations. The DCS, G–2 will—

a. Approve disclosure of CMI to foreign governments for the following:

(1) Sale, grant, or loan of equipment.

(2) Training of IMS.

(3) Tours and visits.

(4) Requests for documentary data.

(5) Foreign representatives accredited to DA.

b. Process exceptions to the National Disclosure Policy (NDP).

c. Monitor unit exchanges and advise the Army staff and major subordinate commands (MSCs) on security implications.

d. Oversee and monitor all intelligence related SC missions.

e. Coordinate with SATFA in performing scheduling, administrative and protocol functions for Washington, DC field trips for selected IMS.

2–20. Commanding General, U.S. Army Training and Doctrine Command

a. The CG, TRADOC is the implementing agent for development and implementation of the Security Cooperation Training Program and related training programs under the DOS and Defense. TRADOC is responsible for the central financial management and distribution of decentralized IMET and FMS training funds for all operating agencies as required by HQDA. The CG, TRADOC will oversee, through the Commander, United States Army Combined Arms Center, the operation of the Western Hemisphere Institute for Security Cooperation (WHINSEC). The CG, TRADOC operates and administers the Security Cooperation Training Program through the DCS, G–3/5/7. The Director, Security Assistance Training Directorate is dual-hatted as Director, SATFA. The Director, SATFA, will—

(1) Implement, supervise, and administer the Army Security Cooperation Training Program within established policies, directives and guidance provided by DOD and DA.

(2) Review international training requirements, determine which agencies will fulfill the requirements, and identify costs of the training programs involved. Maintain training requirements via the Standardized Training List (STL).

(3) Expedite training requirements for approved programs.

(4) Task lateral U.S. Army CONUS commands and coordinate with U.S. Army overseas commands on Security Cooperation Training Program requirements.

(5) Develop training plans to support equipment purchases or transfer; ensure training is provided under the total package approach (TPA) by coordinating with U.S. Army Security Assistance Command (USASAC); develop special unique training to support international customers.

(6) Provide guidance and task U.S. Army Security Assistance Training Management Organization (SATMO) for OCONUS SAT.

(7) Manage all SAT FMS cases in the Defense Security Assistance Management System (DSAMS) to include those for OCONUS SAT, except for those listed in paragraph 2–14*d*(4).

(8) Act as point of contact with all foreign attaches, Security Cooperation Organization, and U.S. country representatives for established SCETP to include—

(a) Program changes.

(b) IMS disposition.

(c) IMS administrative and personal problems.

(d) Serious incident reporting.

(9) Develop and maintain information to evaluate the magnitude, trends, and effects of SCETP.

(10) Develop TRADOC course costs for inclusion in the Training Military Articles and Services Listing; consolidate other MSCs tuition data, and include in the Training Military Articles and Service List.

(11) Act as the U.S. Army IMET appropriation manager. Prepare and submit to DSCA the Army requirement for, and administer, nonregional IMET funds (N6A and N7B) and country IMET funds (N7B) designated for CONUS orientation tour (OT) escort officers.

(12) Serve as financial point of contact for distribution/management, billing, collection, and reimbursement of the Army SCETP.

(13) Review and approve all CONUS Army Field Studies Program plans, budgets, and reimbursements.

(14) Determine releasability of country requests for training, in coordination with DCS, G–2.

(15) Develop and maintain the U.S. Army Secretary of the Army Training Web site and Secretary of the Army training resource material for international military student officer (IMSO) personnel.

(16) Program necessary changes to IMET Program received from SCOs and submit them to DSCA via the Security Assistance Network (SAN) Web.

(17) Support DA and represent TRADOC at OCONUS and CONUS international military training workshop and conferences. Project out-year SC training requirements, reserving wholesale seats in Army courses in anticipation of demand.

(18) Plan, coordinate and fund Washington, DC field trip.

(19) Ensure that an IMSO is appointed on every Army installation where IMS are trained. The IMSO will perform IMS administrative functions, monitor training and plan, and implement the Field Studies Program.

(20) Develop temporary living allowance (TLA) estimates for the IMET Program. Provide fund cites for inclusion in the invitational travel order (ITO). Perform TLA accounting for all Army-sponsored international students.

b. The Commander, U.S. John F. Kennedy Special Warfare Center and School, as delegated by CG, TRADOC through Commander, USASOC, will provide administrative support (facilities, training, legal, awards, and so forth), for SATMO. The SATMO will—

(1) Serve as the TRADOC implementing agency (IA) for the OCONUS portion of the TRADOC SC training mission.

(2) Task lateral CONUS commands and other U.S. Army CONUS activities to field training teams or to provide training support material for teams, as required.

(3) Coordinate with other MILDEP, DA, overseas commands, and OCONUS SC elements on training team matters.

(4) Maintain direct communication with and conduct liaison visits to CONUS and OCONUS United States SC agencies, to include commanders of combatant commands/component command Headquarters (HQ), MSCs, civil government agencies, nongovernment civilian activities, and other TRADOC elements.

(5) Develop, plan for, and deploy OCONUS SAT except for quality assurance team, new equipment training, calibration, repair, return, and non-standard items, which are managed by the AMC.

(6) Coordinate requirements for OCONUS teams among security assistance elements. SATMO in conjunction with SATFA, manages financial transactions associated with team deployments.

(7) Coordinate responses to requests received from Security Cooperation Organization or foreign countries for training literature, programs of instruction, lesson plans, and other training materials.

(8) Provide representation at CONUS and OCONUS international military training conferences.

(9) Maintain central training records and status of requests and monitor training completed in relation to forecasts.

2–21. Commanding general, U.S. Army Materiel Command
The CG, AMC, will—

a. Serve as the DA implementing agent for the operation of approved materiel FMS/Foreign Military Financing Program cases. The SC implementing agent responsibilities are discharged primarily through USASAC. AMC responsibilities are in AR 12–1.

b. Coordinate the releasability of materiel, publications, training aids, and training devices.

c. Ensure foreign disclosure guidance on materiel items is provided to TRADOC, foreign disclosure officer (FDO), in sufficient detail to support training course development for foreign government trainees, as required.

2–22. The Surgeon General
The Surgeon General directs, controls and oversees all Army medical training. The Office of the Surgeon General International Programs will—

a. Receive and process all U.S. Army Medical Department (AMEDD) international training requirements via SATFA.

b. Represent The Surgeon General at Security Cooperation Education and Training Working Group meetings; review all foreign country medical training requirements for CONUS command (to include Alaska and Hawaii) AMEDD activities; determine the AMEDD capability and which AMEDD activity will fulfill the requirement; ensure compliance with DA and DOD policies and directives.

c. Develop and refine the AMEDD training program, allocate AMEDD quotas, develop individual medical observer training (OBT) and on-the-job-training (OJT) programs, develop course costs, as appropriate, and advise SATFA for inclusion in the Training Military Articles and Service List, and approve English Comprehension Level (ECL) waivers for AMEDD training.

d. Act as the point of contact between SATFA and AMEDD activities for all AMEDD training matters to include—

(1) Program changes.

(2) IMS disposition.

(3) IMS administrative and personal problems that will affect student status.

(4) Serious incident reporting.

e. Serve as the point of contact for all Army activities for student and Family member healthcare issues.

2–23. Heads of other Army commands and U.S. Army staff agencies
Based on guidance furnished by HQDA, heads of other MSCs, and Army staff agencies, within their respective functional areas, will—

a. Support and supervise the administration and training of IMS, including—

(1) Upon formal tasking, provide training, including OBT and OJT as required to support the SCETP.

(2) Administer SCETP funds and submit financial and training reports according to governing regulations and standing operating procedures.

(3) Monitor the progress of training and the welfare of IMS to include administration of the Field Studies Program.

(4) Conduct training in cultural awareness of personnel responsible for administration and training of IMS.

(5) Participate as required in OT at Army Service schools and installations under their jurisdiction.

b. Develop course costs as appropriate and advise SATFA for inclusion in the Training Military Articles and Service List.

c. Review, process, and forward proposed unit exchange programs annually to HQDA (DAMO–TRF), 450 Army Pentagon, Washington, DC 20130–0450, for Chief of Staff approval.

2–24. Commandant, Western Hemisphere Institute for Security Cooperation

a. The Commandant, WHINSEC operates a DOD school under the executive agency leadership of the U.S. Army. Title 10, United States Code (10 USC), charges WHINSEC to—

(1) Provide professional education and training, primarily in the Spanish language, to military, law enforcement, and civilian personnel of the Western Hemisphere within the context of the democratic principles of the Organization of American States.

(2) Foster mutual knowledge, transparency, confidence, and cooperation among the participating nations.

(3) Promote democratic values, respect for human rights, and knowledge and understanding of U.S. customs and traditions.

b. Commandant, WHINSEC supports a federal advisory committee called the Board of Visitors, which maintains independent review, observation, and recommendations regarding operations of the institute. It was chartered in accordance with the law that established WHINSEC.

c. To enhance the mission of WHINSEC, the Commandant will—

(1) Develop and manage a Guest Instructor Program.

(2) Develop and manage a Fellows Program.

(3) Recognize leaders in the promotion of democracy and human rights throughout the Western Hemisphere through an annual Lecture Series and Awards Program.

(4) Develop and manage an intern program to involve U.S. university students in hemispheric relations through an understanding of the value of security cooperation.

(5) Hire Title 10, USC, civilian professors to develop courses and instruct at WHINSEC as an adjunct campus of U.S. Army Command and General Staff College.

(6) Conduct conferences, seminars and symposia to enrich the curriculum and expand student learning.

(7) Develop and conduct relevant courses that meet the challenges of the 21st Century in the primary languages of the hemisphere.

2–25. Overseas Army commanders

Overseas Army commanders will conduct IMS training programs in accordance with policies and regulations prescribed by their unified commander, using this regulation as a guide.

Section III
Department of the Navy (U.S. Navy, U.S. Marine Corps, and U.S. Coast Guard)

2–26. Secretary of the Navy

The Secretary of the Navy (SECNAV) is responsible for the overall policy direction, coordination, planning, programming, and supervision of security cooperation matters for the Department of Navy (DON).

2–27. Assistant Secretary of the Navy for Research, Development, and Acquisition

The responsibilities of the Assistant Secretary of the Navy for Research, Development, and Acquisition include the development of policy and provision of management oversight for the DON international research, development, and acquisition efforts.

2–28. Deputy Assistant Secretary of the Navy for International Programs/Director of Navy International Programs

The Deputy Assistant Secretary of the Navy for International Programs (DASN/International Program)/Director of Navy International Programs Office (IPO) Navy is a dual hatted-position. As the DASN/International Program, formulates and manages international policy for the ASN (RDA). As the Director, Navy IPO has overall responsibility for development of policy, implementation, and management oversight of the SCETP. In addition, Navy IPO implements and manages approved DON SCETP and is the implementing agent for DON SCETP matters with foreign countries. The Director, Navy IPO, will—

a. Establish implementation policies governing DON training furnished under SC to international students.

b. Implement and direct execution of approved programs according to policies, instructions, and procedures established by or on behalf of Defense Security Cooperation Agency (DSCA).

c. Monitor execution of the DON SCETP.

d. Coordinate with Commandant, USCG International Affairs (G–CI) and other U.S. Government agencies on matters relating to DON SCETP.

e. Negotiate LOAs with foreign governments and monitor FMS training cases. Coordinate all LOAs to ensure adherence to congressional, DOD and DON policies.

f. Establish policies relating to financial management of DON SCETP. Coordinate with the Office of the Secretary of Defense (OSD) on financial issues relating to DON SCETP.

g. Establish English language proficiency levels required for Naval Command College, Naval Staff College, Naval Postgraduate School (NPS), and Systems Commands (SYSCOMs). Approve ECL and rank waivers for Naval Command College and Naval Staff College, and SYSCOMs.

h. Authorize disclosure and releasability for USN/USCG SC training with classified military information and controlled unclassified information.

i. Establish policy for, implement, and supervise execution of the DON portion of the Field Studies Program and extraordinary expense (N6) and supervise execution. Review and approve command Field Studies Program for Naval Command College and Naval Staff College, Naval Postgraduate School, and SYSCOMs.

j. Prepare SECNAV instructions pertaining to DON SC matters.

k. Coordinate the DON portion of SCETWGs.

l. Coordinate medical waivers for international students attending U.S. Navy courses.

m. Coordinate, as appropriate, Secretary of the Army sponsored distinguished visitor orientation tour within CONUS foreign CNO or higher level visits involving DOD (OSD/DSCA) SECNAV, CNO, and U.S. Navy commands and activities.

2–29. Chief of Naval Operations

The Chief of Naval Operations (CNO) will—

a. Provide guidance on the strategic role that international training and education plays in the overall defense strategy of the U.S. Navy.

b. Ensure that U.S. Navy major claimants execute the Navy portion of DON SCETP in accordance with appropriate SECNAV policies and procedures.

c. Ensure foreign training requirements are included in development of the U.S. Navy Training Plan. This includes the requirements from other services for international training.

d. Ensure that international training is considered and identified as appropriate in the development of Navy Training Plans for weapons systems and equipment.

e. Coordinate ship transfer, overhaul, and refresher training portion of U.S. Navy SCETP.

f. Manage and allocate international quotas for Naval Command College and Naval Staff College, and issue invitations to countries selected for attendance.

g. Execute the PME and unit training and related support exchange programs for the U.S. Navy. Manage the U.S. Navy PME and staff the U.S. Navy Service Appendix to the DOD PME Exchange Agreements (see fig 13–2) for signature within U.S. Navy Education and Training chain of command and foreign embassies.

h. Provide political-military guidance as necessary to Navy IPO to resolve distribution of limited training quotas.

2–30. Commandant of the Marine Corps

The CMC will implement the Marine Corps portion of the DON SCETP. The Commandant's implementing agent for all security cooperation is the Deputy Commandant, Plans, Policies, and Operations. This responsibility is executed by the International Issues Branch of the Strategy and Plans Division (Code: PLU).

2–31. Commanding General, Training and Education Command

The Commandant's responsibility for the management and implementation of the Marine Corps portion of the DON SCETP is executed by the Commanding general, Training and Education Command (CG, TECOM). This is accomplished through the Director, Security Cooperation Education and Training Center. Director, Security Cooperation Education and Training Center will—

a. Plan, coordinate, administer, and track Marine Corps security cooperation education and training programs for international students.

(1) Serve as the focal point for all Marine Corps security cooperation education and training matters, coordinating as required with customer country representatives, Security Cooperation Organization, DOD office, and staff agencies, other government departments and agencies, the geographic commanders of combatant commands, and their security cooperation offices and agencies, and other Marine Corps commands, activities, or staff agencies relating to the United States Marine Corp (USMC) SCETP.

(2) In coordination with Security Cooperation Organization or other security cooperation personnel assigned to the U.S. Country Team within a customer country, Deputy Commandant, Plans, Policy and Operations and the appropriate Marine Component Command, review country requests for Marine Corps education and training and determine suitability, availability, and supportability.

(3) Represent the Marine Corps at the various commanders of combatant commands SCETWGs by coordinating participation by personnel from Marine Component Commands and other Marine Corps personnel, as required.

(4) In coordination with the appropriate Marine Component Command, participate in the various commanders of combatant commands TSCP regional working groups.

(5) Participate in other DOD, commanders of combatant commands, MILDEP, or Military Service sponsored security cooperation conferences, workshops, or meetings, as required.

(6) In coordination with Marine Corps Systems Command, develop training plans to support equipment, or weapons systems purchases, or transfer ensuring training is provided under the TPA.

(7) In coordination with Deputy Commandant, Plans, Policy and Operations, establish appropriate policies and procedures for the execution of the USMC SCETP.

(a) Develop USMC SCETP course costs for the military articles and services list (MASL).

(b) Establish prerequisites for international students attending Marine Corps education and training. Prerequisites include, but are not limited to, ECL and oral proficiency interview (OPI) requirements, rank requirements, physical fitness (to include swimming qualification) requirements and education or training that must be completed prior to enrollment.

(c) Approval authority for customer country requests for waivers for established prerequisites.

(8) Manage and administer USMC SCETP in accordance with established law, regulations, policies and procedures.

(a) Determine international requirements for Marine Corps education and training, including requirements requested through other Services, and coordinate inclusion of these requirements in the development of the Marine Corps Training Input Plan; serve as sponsor and quota manager for international quotas for Marine Corps education and training.

(b) On behalf of the commandant, issue invitations to countries selected for attendance at Command and Staff College and other designated professional military education schools.

(c) Ensure all Marine Corps commands and activities providing education and training to international students appoint an IMSO to coordinate the education and training of internationals at their command or activity. Conduct direct liaison with TECOM elements and their designated IMSO, as well as other Marine Corps commands and activities and their designated IMSO, to provide guidance and direction on the execution of security cooperation education and training.

(d) Conduct the Marine Corps portion of the DON IMSO Workshop and coordinate Marine Corps IMSO participation.

(e) Coordinate with Marine Corps Systems Command (International Programs) to ensure the contractor provided training for international is administered and reported in accordance with current regulations, policies, and procedures governing such training.

(f) Ensure that all Marine Corps commands and activities providing education or training to international military students submit all required reports documenting the education or training presented.

(g) Coordinate with Deputy Commandant, Plans, Policy and Operations on disclosure and releasability of Marine Corps CMI and CUI associated with the provision of security cooperation education and training; coordinate annual disclosure review of currently approved course containing CMI and CUI.

(h) Develop, maintain, and promulgate the Marine Corps Security Cooperation Education and Training Desktop Guide, and other informational publications as required; develop and maintain an appropriate site on the world wide web for Marine Corps security cooperation education and training information.

(9) Under the FMS Program, act as case administering office (CAO) for FMS cases that support deployed Marine Corps training assistance teams or personnel as well as other FMS training related cases as designated by Navy IPO.

(a) Develop price and availability data, or LOA data for FMS cases involving Marine Corps education and training.

(b) Coordinate with Navy IPO on CAO matters.

(c) Coordinate with Navy IPO and Naval Education and Training Security Assistance Field Activity (Naval Education and Training Security Assistance Field Activity) on FMS cases written by that field activity that include Marine Corps education and training.

(d) Coordinate with Marine Corps Systems Command (International Programs) on FMS cases written by that Command that includes Marine Corps education and training.

(e) Coordinate all LOA, regardless of CAO, that include Marine Corps education and training.

(f) In coordination with the appropriate CAO, maintain program management, to include fiscal control, of all FMS cases that have a preponderance of Marine Corps education and training.

(10) Coordinate, as appropriate, Secretary of the Army sponsored within CONUS, foreign CNO, or higher level visits involving Marine Corps commands, or activities, as required.

(11) In coordination with Deputy Commandant, Plans, Policy and Operations, coordinate provision of Marine Corps education or training under Presidential drawdown authority.

(12) In coordination with Deputy Commandant, Plans, Policy and Operations, negotiate and execute Marine Corps annex to DOD Professional Military Education Exchange Program.

(13) Coordinate the Marine Corps Professional Military Education Exchange Program and staff the service appendix to the DOD PME Exchange Agreements (see fig 13–2) for signature.

b. Plan, prepare, deploy, sustain, and redeploy Marine Corps security cooperation teams and personnel to execute advisory, education, or training missions not executed by Marine Corps component commands. Direct liaison is authorized for all phases of planning, deployment, sustainment, and redeployment.

(1) Upon receipt of a validated request for the deployment of Marine Corps security cooperation teams or personnel from D/C PP&O, to include identification of and sourcing of personnel to be deployed, initiate planning for deployment.

(a) Conduct/validate mission analysis.

(b) Conduct pre-deployment site survey.

(c) Prepare budget and support requirements and coordinate receipt of funding.

(d) Coordinate approval of deployment plan, as required.

(e) Verify vetting of personnel to be trained.

(2) Upon identification of personnel, prepare, and deploy team/personnel.

(a) Coordinate all administrative actions, as required.

(b) Coordinate all support/logistical actions, as required.

(c) Coordinate all fiscal/financial actions, as required.

(d) Prescribe, coordinate, and provide, or coordinate provision of, all required pre-deployment training assuring that all external requirements are met.

(e) Deploy team/personnel in accordance with approved deployment plan.

(3) Upon deployment, coordinate sustainment of team/personnel, as required.

(4) Upon completion of mission, or as otherwise directed, coordinate redeployment of team/personnel.

(a) Ensure all administrative actions are concluded, as required.

(b) Ensure all support/logistical actions are concluded, as required.

(c) Ensure all fiscal/financial actions are concluded, as required.

(d) Ensure all reporting requirements are met.

c. Serve as financial point of contact for billing, collecting, and reimbursement of Marine Corps security cooperation education and training.

d. In coordination with Deputy Commandant, Plans, Policy and Operations and Deputy Commandant for Manpower and Reserve Affairs, as required, prescribe and coordinate required training for all Marine Corps personnel involved in the management or execution of security cooperation.

(1) Manage and allocate Marine Corps quotas for the DISAM.

(2) Manage the DON International Affairs Workforce Education, Training, and Certification Program for all Marine Corps personnel, military and civilian, involved in the management of security cooperation education and training.

e. Provide a link to governmental and nongovernmental organizations in support of Marine Corps efforts in Humanitarian Assistance and Civil Military Operations.

2–32. Commander, Marine Corps Systems Command

The Commander, Marine Corps Systems Command serves as the Commandant's principal agent for acquisition and sustainment of systems and equipment used by Marine Corps Operating Forces to accomplish their warfighting mission. The execution of those functions relating to international programs is the responsibility of Director, International Program. Director, International Program plans, coordinates, implements, and executes all Marine Corps related SC acquisition and logistics matters as well as certain cooperative programs. Director, International Program acts as office of primary responsibility (OPR) for unilateral or combined exercises involving USMC installations, facilities, or personnel where the costs are captured via FMS. Director, International Program is the SYSCOM Security Cooperation Office (SSCO) for all Maine Corps acquisition, logistics support, and exercise related FMS cases. In support of SCETP, Director, International Program will—

a. Carryout OJT, contractor training, factory training, and nonstandard training provided in support of Marine Corps acquisition, or logistics FMS cases.

b. Direct the project management effort for the integration of training and material in major weapons systems transfers and, in concert with Security Cooperation Education and Training Center for Marine Corps weapons systems, integrate initial and life cycle training requirements to support the TPA in material transfers.

c. For contractor provided training, ensure that the applicable statement of work (SOW) provides students scheduled for such training the same basic student support afforded IMS attending education or training at a U.S. Service school and that all required reports are submitted as required by this regulation.

2–33. Commandant, U.S. Coast Guard, International Affairs

The Coast Guard, even though not part of the Department of Defense or the Department of the Navy, is one of the five Armed Forces as reflected in the Foreign Assistance Act and the Arms Export Control Act. As such, the Coast Guard plays an important role in the SCETP and holds a unique place in the Department of the Navy (DON) SCETP. The International Affairs (G–CI) Staff is responsible for the management and direction of overall USCG participation in the SCETP, as well as, international training and technical assistance activities. The SCETP responsibilities include—

a. Formulation of USCG SCETP strategy, policy, and procedures for execution and financial management of the USCG SCETP.

b. Coordination of USCG personnel assigned to Security Cooperation Organization staffs.

c. Correlation of training and technical assistance requirements of foreign nations to the capabilities of USCG activities.

d. Coordination and liaison with the military services and other DOD agencies, Department of State, SC organizations, international organizations, and all components of the USCG.

e. Coordinate disclosure and releasability of USCG training and training materials prior to responding to foreign request.

f. Evaluate, approve and assign all requests for USCG security assistance training teams, assessment teams, training surveys and maritime advisors.

g. Conduct and coordinate SC-sponsored OT, unit exchanges and visits involving USCG commands and activities.

h. Program and manage USCG international training within the DON standardized training list (STL).

i. Management, planning, scheduling, and allocation of international training quotas.

j. Coordination of LOA relating to USCG training.

k. Development of price and availability data, formulate procedures for and conduct course costing and coordinate financial procedures for reimbursable billings.

l. Establishment of ECL required for all USCG international training, and approves ECL waivers for USCG international training.

m. Provide USCG portion of the MASL in the DON Programming Guide.

n. Develop, maintain, and promulgate the USCG International Training Handbook and the USCG International Military Student Officer (IMSO) Guide.

o. Conduct the USCG portion of Security Cooperation Education and Training Working Group and participate in other conferences or workshops related to SCETP issues.

p. Coordination of IMSO assignments and provision of IMSO and IMS administrative policy and guidance.

q. Develop procedures for and administer the USCG Field Studies Program including review and approval of USCG Field Studies Program budgets and plans.

2–34. Assistant Secretary of the Navy Financial Management and Comptroller

The SECNAV Financial Management and Comptroller will—

a. Establish financial management procedures for DON SC programs within the framework of requirements prescribed by higher authority.

b. Establish and promulgate principles and systems for financing, funding, accounting, and financial reporting for FMS and FMF (to include IMET and Expanded International Military Education and Training (E–IMET)).

c. Make and issue uniform procedures for setting up and maintaining uniform application of pricing and cost criteria for sales of defense articles and services including training courses provided under FMF and FMS.

d. Receive DON FMS and military assistance program (MAP) administrative funds from DSCA and allocate to the appropriate users.

2–35. Navy Surgeon General

a. Receive and coordinate the medical and dental training portion of USN Security Cooperation Education and Training.

b. Coordinate request of medical waivers.

c. Provide resource information, guidance, and assistance in repatriating deceased IMS.

2–36. Commanders of Naval Systems Commands

Commanders of Naval Systems Commands (SYSCOMS) will—

a. Carryout OJT, contractor training, factory training, and nonstandard training provided by the SYSCOMS and any formal courses provided at the Naval Sea Systems Command, Naval Air Systems Command, Naval Supply Systems Command (NAVSUP), and Space and Naval Warfare Systems Command activities.

b. Direct the project management effort for the integration of training and material in major weapons systems transfers and, in concert with the Naval Education and Training Security Assistance Field Activity, (for Navy weapons systems) or the Security Cooperation Education and Training Center (for Marine Corps weapons systems) integrate initial and life cycle training requirements to support the TPA in material transfers.

c. Ensure that subordinate activities appoint an IMSO. The IMSO will monitor and coordinate activities for the IMS' training including implementation of the Field Studies Program. IMSO will be assigned for a minimum of 2 years, when possible, and will receive the necessary training to perform this important function. Training of U.S. Navy IMSO will be coordinated with NETSAFA, training of USMC IMSO will be coordinated by Director, Security Cooperation Education and Training Center.

d. Ensure that subordinate activities provide foreign trainee status reports for all SCETP training conducted.

2–37. Fleet commanders

The Commander, United States Fleet Forces Command and Commander, Pacific Fleet (COMPACFLT), will—

a. Carry out the fleet SC Program provided in connection with assigned units, ships, and aircraft.

b. Carry out fleet training for IMS.

c. Provide price and availability for training at subordinate commands when tasked by competent authority.

d. Provide mobile training team (MTT) and Extended training service specialist (ETSS) as required when tasked by competent authority.

e. Ensure that subordinate commands appoint an IMSO. The IMSO will monitor and coordinate activities for the IMS training, including implementation of the Field Studies Program. IMSO will be assigned for a minimum of 2 years, when possible, and will receive the necessary training to perform this important function. Training of command IMSO will be coordinated with NETSAFA.

2–38. Naval Education and Training Center

The Naval Education Training Center will—

a. Serve as a U.S. Navy systems command for SC education and training.

b. Conduct formal schools training for IMS in Naval Education and Training Command schools.

c. Provide MTT and ETSS as required when tasked by competent authority.

d. Ensure that the Naval Education Training Center appoint an IMSO. The IMSO will monitor and coordinate activities for the IMS training, including implementation of the Field Studies Program. IMSO will be assigned for a minimum of 2 years, when possible.

e. Execute, operate, and administer designated portions of SCETP through the Commanding Officer, NETSAFA.

2–39. Commanding Officer, Naval Education and Training Security Assistance Field Activity

The Commanding Officer, NETSAFA, will—

a. Function as Naval Education Training Center implementing agent for execution of the USN SCETP according to appropriate SECNAV policies.

b. Function as CAO and case manager for all DON FMS training cases unless otherwise directed by Navy IPO.

c. Function as fund administrator for the DON IMET/E–IMET and Regional Defense Counterterrorism Fellowship Program including management of medical funds and payment of medical bills.

d. Function as the administrative and automatic data processing support activity for the execution of DON SCETP. Coordinate provision of this support with Navy IPO, CG, Security Cooperation Education and Training Center Marine Corps Combat Development Command (MCCDC), USCG (GC–I), and appropriate U.S. Navy major claimants, and MILDEP SCETP organizations. Coordinate the release of data contained in the DON database and upload information to the SAN IMSO/Security Cooperation Organization Training Web site.

e. Establish procedures for the execution of U.S. Navy's SCETP.

f. Prepare and submit data required by Navy IPO for preparation of LOAs for all DON sponsored SC education and training.

g. Develop training plans for the support for U.S. Navy equipment sales in concert with Navy IPO and the appropriate SYSCOM, and warfare sponsor. Ensure that training plans are coordinated with Navy IPO for disclosure and releasability of U.S. Navy education and training materials prior to making commitments or programming training. Ensure that training is time-phased with equipment delivery schedules for a TPA.

h. Review requested U.S. Navy SC education and training to determine the appropriateness of the request and availability of training. Determine annual and out-year IMS education and training requirements and coordinate with Bureau of Naval Personnel (BUPERS) and warfare sponsors for quotas in U.S. Navy Training Operations Plans and/or schools. Act as the quota allocation authority for all U.S. Navy IMS quotas.

i. Perform the financial management functions necessary to the administration of FMS training cases and necessary to the financial integrity of case closure including management of medical lines and payment of medical bills, when applicable.

j. Formulate course-costing procedures according to Assistant Secretaryof the Navy (Financial Management and Comptroller) guidance.

k. Develop, maintain, and promulgate the USN SC International Military Student Officer (IMSO) Guide.

l. Participate in conferences or workshops sponsored by DON, other military Services or combatant commands where education and training issues are involved.

m. Review, coordinate and implement the deployment of U.S. Navy MTT, Mobile Education Team, ETSS, and training surveys.

n. Coordinate the establishment of English language proficiency levels required for all categories of U.S. Navy SC education and training.

o. Develop procedures for and administer the Naval Education Training Center Field Studies Program and extraordinary expenses (EE) (N3/8) as they pertain to the SCETP. Review and approve Naval Education Training Center activities Field Studies Program plans.

p. Conduct liaison with Naval Education Training Center units and designated IMSO, as well as elements and IMSO of other U.S. Navy activities, to provide guidance to and respond to queries regarding SCETP.

q. Coordinate foreign training spaces in the Naval Command College, Naval Staff College with (N52), and Navy IPO (02C2T). Provide quota management of IMS at NPS and Defense Resource Management Institute.

r. Approve ECL rank waivers for U.S. Navy SC education and training, coordinating with Navy IPO (02C2T).

s. Review initial IMET, E–IMET, Regional Defense Counterterrorism Fellowship Program and FMS foreign country education and training request and program changes for U.S. Navy SC education and training. Consolidate all DON programming inputs for submission to DSCA and copy to Navy IPO (02C2T).

t. Host the DON SCETP IMSO workshop for Navy IPO. Coordinate the IMSO workshop agenda, schedule, format, and so forth, with Navy IPO, Security Cooperation Education and Training Center, Coast Guard (G–CI), and appropriate U.S. Navy major claimants.

u. Ensure that Naval Education Training Center activities provide commencement and completion reports through the SAN Web, provide academic evaluations, and other required reports for all SC education and training conducted.

v. Coordinate IMSO and SCETP for the U.S. Navy.

w. Coordinate SCETP-sponsored and funded orientation visits to and within CONUS for which the U.S. Navy is the implementing agent, not including foreign CNO or higher level visits.

x. Develop, coordinate, submit, and distribute the DON portion of the DOD Training MASL according to the Security Assistance Management Manual (SAMM).

y. Provide annual USN DISAM quota requirement data to Navy IPO.

Section IV
Department of the Air Force

2–40. General
Guidance in this regulation applies to all international personnel attending United States Air Force (USAF) training and educational institutions (to include USAFA).

2–41. Deputy Under Secretary of the Air Force, International Affairs
The Deputy Under Secretary of the Air Force, International Affairs (SAF), and Deputy Under Secretary of the Air Force, Security Assistance Policy and Education and Training Division is responsible for the policy direction, integration, guidance, management, and supervision of international programs and activities affiliated with the Department of the Air Force. The responsibilities for international training programs include the following:

a. Develop, coordinate, and issue AFwide SC training policy and procedures. Act as point of contact on all SCETP and other cooperative programs policy and procedural matters.

b. Direct implementation of approved programs in accordance with policies, instructions, and procedures established by or on behalf of DSCA. Act as the principal Air Staff representative and focal point within the Air Staff for the SCETP and other cooperative programs.

c. Monitor the execution of approved training programs.

d. Comment on and make recommendations to the USAF position on international training programs that affect United States Air Force (USAF) resources.

e. Prepare a memorandum of understandings (MOUs) and/or memorandum of agreements (MOAs) as/if required for SCETP and other cooperative programs (SAF/International Affairs regional divisions).

f. Act as Air Staff focal point for policy matters involving the Inter-American Air Forces Academy (IAAFA) Deputy Under Secretary of the Air Force, International Affairs, Americas Division.

g. Provide HQ USAF representation at Security Assistance Training conferences and meetings.

h. Provide Air Force policy and procedures for the DOD Field Studies Program, Deputy Under Secretary of the Air Force, International Affairs Airmen Division.

i. Correlate costing information and guidance with the Secretary of the Air Force, Budget Management and Execution Security Assistance Division relating to IMET and FMS security assistance training.

j. Serve as the AF focal point for PME and unit exchange training.

k. Process self-invited visit requests and approve visits to USAF installations proposed under orientation training tours.

l. Advise Major Army Command (USAF) (MAJCOM) on technology transfer and information disclosure implications inherent in proposed SCETP and other cooperative programs.

m. Approve requests to disclose classified and controlled unclassified training and training materials provided to foreign personnel under SCETP and other cooperative programs.

2–42. Director of Budget Investment

The Director of Budget Investment (SAF/Budget Management and Execution Security Assistance Division) will—

a. Establish policies and procedures relating to financial management of the USAF SCETP and other cooperative programs.

b. Validate training tuition rates for security assistance training requirements.

c. Coordinate with OSD on financial issues relating to AF SCETP and other cooperative programs.

d. Establish and direct implementation of financial policies and procedures used by the USAF to manage and control SCETP and other cooperative programs.

e. Coordinate all training LOA for PCS teams, for joint and dedicated training programs, and all LOA on which the FMS Administrative Surcharge is waived to ensure adherence to congressional, DOD, and AF policies.

f. Evaluate the DOD Field Studies Program costs to determine the amount to be included in Air Force tuition rates for creation of a Field Studies Program fund.

g. Establish reporting systems to ensure that all appropriate training costs are identified and billed.

2–43. Deputy Chief of Staff, Manpower and Personnel

The Deputy Chief of Staff, Manpower and Personnel (AF/A1) is overall responsible for all AF education and training programs. The responsibilities for international training programs include the following:

a. The Director, Force Development, Deputy Chief of Staff, Manpower and Personnel (AF/A1D) will—

(1) Be the AF Senior Language Authority.

(2) Have the DLIELC Executive Agent responsibilities on behalf of the Air Force.

(3) Establish the Air Force policy for PME, developmental education programs, and technical training.

b. The Director, Force Management, Deputy Chief of Staff, Manpower and Personnel (AF/A1P) acts as the focal point for submission of approved requests into the Planning, Programming, Budgeting and Execution System.

2–44. Heads of other Air staff organizations

Heads of these organizations will serve as functional proponents for unit exchanges and other security assistance programs within their respective functional areas.

2–45. Commanders of major commands

a. All commanders of MAJCOM will—

(1) As available, provide training to support the SCETP and other cooperative programs, as required.

(2) Ensure that current security assistance training capabilities are accurately reflected in applicable programming documents.

(3) Assist Air Force Security Assistance Training Squadron in developing and reviewing training programs.

(4) Implement approved and funded IMET and FMS programs as requested by HQ SAF/International Affairs or the Air Force Security Assistance Training Squadron.

(5) Submit financial and training reports.

(6) Monitor the progress of training and the welfare of IMS.

(7) Ensure compliance with Field Studies Program, chapter 11, and support actions necessary to ensure effectiveness of the Field Studies Program at pertinent installations within the command.

(8) Process, implement, and report on unit exchange programs once approval is received from SAF/International Affairs.

b. The following commands have these additional responsibilities:

(1) The AETC/International Affairs has oversight of the Air Force Security Assistance Training Squadron and functional oversight of AETC' international training and education providers. The AETC/International Affairs is the focal point for all international training and education action items, projects, policy implementation, and procedures for, or impacting the command, or the command's international training, and education implementing agency responsibilities.

(2) The Commander of Air Force Security Assistance Training Squadron, the central management agency for USAF-sponsored security assistance training, will—

(a) Serve as training consultant to SAF/International Affairs and AETC/International Affairs.

(b) Prepare price and availability (P&A), LOA data, and FMS planning directives (2061s). Prepare and negotiate LOA ("T" cases) for training.

(c) Furnish planning, programming, funding, and implementation guidance to security assistance agencies worldwide

based on established DOD and HQ USAF policies, including guidance to International Military Student Officers (IMSO) in CONUS.

(d) Provide the necessary administrative support for country liaison officers (CLO).

(e) Determine the suitability and staff availability of training with the appropriate MAJCOM and develop training schedules as requested by SAF/International Affairs.

(f) Implement and manage approved and funded SCETP and other cooperative programs.

(g) Negotiate contracts for security assistance-sponsored formal and OJT to be conducted in CONUS or overseas.

(h) Maintain and update the AF training MASL.

(i) Manage and administer the Field Studies Program for AF based on established DOD and HQ USAF policies; provide guidance to all participating agencies, approve funding of routine Field Studies Program, and extraordinary expenses; budget for and host an IMSO Workshop.

(j) Provide quarterly and annual update and input to programmed flying training and programmed technical training documentation for SCETP and other cooperative programs requirements.

(k) Provide administrative assistance pertaining to IMS transportation.

(l) Administer and account for SCETP and other cooperative programs funds allocated for the training, administration, and support of IMS and for MTT, ETSS, language training detachments (LTD), and technical assistance field teams (TAFT) provided from resources.

(m) Maintain data on IMET and FMS training programs implemented in CONUS or overseas, security assistance training teams and TAFT.

(n) Implement and react to N90 English Language Training ((ELT) books/maps/pubs) requirements approved and funded under IMET.

(3) The Commander of the Materiel Command will—

(a) Establish charges for Depot Maintenance Industrial Funding training.

(b) Procure N90 items approved and funded under IMET that are not available from DLIELC resources.

Chapter 3
Planning and Programming

Section I
Planning

3–1. Purpose
This chapter delineates the policies and procedures to be followed for the planning and programming of the Security Cooperation Education and Training Programs. Training may include formal and informal training, exchange training, correspondence courses, and distance learning. Training may also include team training, which is discussed in chapter 4.

3–2. Requirements
a. Training assistance will be provided in response to specific requests presented through appropriate channels by an authorized representative of the foreign government or international organization concerned. The Security Cooperation Organization may advise the foreign country on needed training that is available from U.S. sources but must ensure that no U.S. commitment is made or implied by such recommendations. Training of IMS in Military Service schools should not have a significant adverse effect on the combat readiness of the Armed Forces of the United States.

b. Where practical, the foreign government will assist in supervising and administering its training program.

c. Foreign countries authorized participation in SCETP through IMET are to be encouraged to participate in cost sharing to pay travel and living allowances to IMS and use IMET to cover only tuition costs. This will allow countries to maximize training opportunities.

d. Consideration should be given to the quantity and complexity of equipment in country, the level of education, and the technical aptitude of foreign country military organization to assimilate and maintain modern equipment. Equipment specific training should not be requested unless the Security Cooperation Organization can verify that the equipment is in the respective country's inventory or a letter of request has been submitted to either SATFA or USASAC.

e. Training in support of an initial system sale will be included in a LOA (see para 3–5, below) written and administered by the MILDEP preparing the system sale LOA, regardless of the MILDEP providing the training. This MILDEP will not commit the resources of another MILDEP without prior staffing and approval. For follow-on and annual training requirements, training will be included in the program of and administered by the Military Service providing the training.

3–3. International military education and training

The United States may provide International Military Education and Training (IMET) funds to foreign governments to train and professionalize their militaries. The Department of State has overall responsibility for the IMET program. Congress appropriates IMET funds each year and country allocations are documented in the Congressional Budget Justification Foreign Operations. Based on Congressional guidance and DOS approved country allocations, DSCA (Business Operations/Comptroller and Policy, Plans, and Programs Directorates) manages and issues the IMET funds to the MILDEP, who disperses the funds to individual countries and/or schools.

a. The training must support U.S.-approved programs, plans, and objectives for the country concerned.

b. The country must make optimum use of personnel previously trained under SCETP.

c. The country must make maximum use of its own training resources.

d. Emphasis must be placed on the training of instructor and career personnel.

e. Training must be in skills where actual deficiencies exist and to further overall objectives; the ability to meet the requirement must be clearly beyond the capability of the country.

f. Training requiring a policy waiver from DSCA or another type of waiver will be approved on a case-by-case basis.

g. The IMET programs are developed and funded on an annual basis, so the start date of the course (or initial course if they are attending multiple courses) will determine the program year. The IMET students beginning training in the CONUS from 1 October of a fiscal year (FY) through 31 December of the following calendar year may be included in one annual program. A 5th quarter concept was developed to maximize utilization of IMET funds between countries at the end of each FY and to advantage 1st quarter training opportunities.

h. All requirements for OT, MTTS, and ETSS personnel will be programmed on the basis of the U.S. FY (1 October/30 September) and not implemented under the 5th quarter concept. Noncontract OCONUS teams must return to CONUS no later than (NLT) 30 September.

i. Contract field services (CFS) may be programmed on a 1–year basis for total man-months, including costs, regardless of whether the duration extends into the next FY; however, justification must be forwarded and approval received from DSCA before programming.

j. The IMET training will not be programmed to support FMS equipment purchase unless specifically identified as part of the FMS agreement or approved by DSCA.

k. Training benefits must warrant the high cost of the travel involved. When overseas transportation costs to and from the United States are borne by the IMET program, training in the United States will be arranged only when the total training in formal school courses or in a combination of formal school and OJT is a minimum of 5 weeks exclusive of ELT. An exception to policy must be obtained by the Security Cooperation Organization from DSCA for training of less than 5 weeks. All training at the WHINSEC and the IAAFA is exempt from the 5–week minimum duration.

3–4. Expanded international military education and training

The E–IMET Program is part of the IMET Program. Under E–IMET, personnel are trained in managing and administering military establishments and budgets, in promoting civilian control of the military, and in creating and maintaining effective military justice systems and military codes of conduct, in accordance with internationally recognized human rights.

a. The E–IMET training is exempt from the 5–week minimum duration.

b. Civilians who work in the country's Ministry of Defense (MOD), civilian personnel of ministries other than the MOD, legislators and individuals who are not members of the Government may be trained under the E–IMET Program if the military education and training would contribute to the E–IMET objectives.

c. Training of defense civilians for the express purpose of teaching, developing, or managing in-country English language training programs (ELTP) is also authorized.

d. Defense civilians in Counter Narcotics related positions may also be trained under the E–IMET Program.

e. Maritime law enforcement and other maritime skills training for agencies which are nondefense, or agencies which perform a maritime law enforcement mission, and other maritime skills training provided to a country which does not have a standing armed forces is authorized.

f. Courses may be evaluated by DSCA and be added to the list of approved E–IMET courses if they meet established criteria. Courses currently designated as approved E–IMET courses must be reviewed and recertified every five years if 100 percent E–IMET and taught at 100 percent E–IMET schools; and every 3 years if not 100 percent E–IMET.

g. Military members of foreign governments may also participate in training courses designated as E–IMET.

3–5. Foreign Military Sales Program

a. The FMS Program is that part of Security Cooperation authorized by the AECA and is conducted using formal contracts or agreements between the USG and an authorized foreign purchaser. These contracts, called LOA, are signed by both the USG and the purchasing Government or international organization; and provide for the sale of defense articles and/or defense services (to include training) usually from DOD stocks or through purchase under DOD managed contracts. Further information regarding LOA can be found in paragraph 3–14. As with all security cooperation, the FMS program supports U.S. foreign policy and national security objectives.

b. The FMS training requirements pursuant to the sale of major equipment and weapon systems (ships, aircraft, missiles) should be made a part of sale negotiations. Organizations involved in FMS sales must inform the respective Service training organizations Army SATFA, Navy NETSAFA, Air Force AFSAT, Marine Corp Security Cooperation Education and Training Center, and Coast Guard (G–CI) of training requirements. The same general initial and annual programming process applies to both FMS and IMET. Eligible foreign purchasers may initiate training requests through several channels; for example, designated Security Cooperation Organization, foreign embassies, or purchasing missions located in the United States. Foreign purchasers, with the assistance of Security Cooperation Organization, are encouraged to develop annual FMS training programs. The IMET fifth quarter planning and programming concept does not apply to FMS training.

c. For annual FMS training programs, blanket order (BO) FMS LOA will normally be used. The program presented by the Security Cooperation Organization should be fully coordinated with the requesting government and reflect the country's annual training requirements. The FMS training programs will be accepted for planning, determining capabilities, and allocating quotas.

d. Upon determining capabilities, the MILDEP will assign an FMS case identifier, prepare the LOA, and submit it to the appropriate country representative for customer acceptance and deposit of funds, as required. The MILDEP will implement training only after the case has been accepted and obligation authority has been issued by DFAS.

3–6. Other security cooperation education and training programs

The following list of programs is not all-inclusive; however, the Security Cooperation Organization and Military Service personnel should be aware that these programs exist since they may play an instrumental role:

a. *African Contingency Operations Training and Assistance.* This program provides training of African troops in peacekeeping and humanitarian crisis response. The European Command is the coordinating agent for the Combatant Commands.

b. *Aviation Leadership Program.* The Aviation Leadership Program provides undergraduate pilot training to a small number of selected international students from friendly, less-developed countries. In accordance with 10 USC Chapter 9381–9383, Secretary of the Air Force (SECAF) may fund Aviation Leadership Program.

c. *Bilateral or Regional Cooperation Programs.* Under 10 USC 1051, the SECDEF may pay travel, subsistence, and similar personal expenses of defense personnel of developing countries in connection with attendance at bilateral or regional conferences, seminars or similar meetings if the SECDEF deems attendance is in the U.S. national interest. Also, see 10 USC 1050 for payment of personnel expenses in connection with Latin American Cooperation.

d. *Combatant commander initiative funds.* Under 10 USC 166a, the CJCS may provide funds to combatant commanders for military education and training of military and related civilian personnel of foreign countries (to include transportation, translation, and administrative expenses). This authority provides funding for activities such as force training, contingencies, selected operations, command and control, joint exercises (including activities of foreign countries), humanitarian and civil assistance, military education and training, bilateral or regional cooperation programs, and force protection. An annual dollar limitation is legislated each year. Training falling under combatant commander initiative funds is not managed by MILDEP Security Assistance offices.

e. *Disaster Response (Humanitarian Assistance).* The Humanitarian Assistance, including training in disaster response and/or disaster preparedness, is authorized by 10 USC 2561. Normally, Humanitarian Assistance and training conducted under Title 10 is not provided to foreign militaries. However, selected military members of the host nation are occasionally included in the training so that the military understands the role in supporting the civilian government during emergencies. The ultimate goal of disaster response training is to improve host nation capability to effectively respond to disasters, thereby reducing or eliminating the need for U.S. military response. The training is conducted in the foreign country at no charge. The foreign country pays foreign student TLA expenses.

f. *Drawdowns of training.* Under the FAA, Section 506(a)(1), the President may direct the drawdown of defense services education and training from the DOD if they determine and report to Congress that an unforeseen emergency exists which requires immediate military assistance to a foreign country or international organization; and that such emergency requirement cannot be met under the AECA or any other law except this section. Under the FAA, Section 506(a)(2), the President must determine and report to Congress in accordance with FAA, Section 652 that it is in the national interest of the United States to drawdown articles and services from the inventory of any USG agency and military education and training from the DOD. The FAA, Section 552 provides for drawdown of commodities and services from inventory and resources of any agency of the USG of an aggregate value not to exceed (NTE) $25M in any FY. Under the FAA, Section 506(a)(1) and (2), tuition for military education and training is provided at no cost to the foreign government. Student travel may be funded from the MILDEP operation and maintenance funds if foreign recipient is not able to assume the cost. Students may stay in visiting officers quarters (VOQ) or visiting enlisted quarters (VEQ) and use dining facilities operated by DOD funds, and living allowance is not provided to the student. See SAMM, chapter 11 for additional information on drawdowns.

g. Enhanced - International Peacekeeping Capabilities. The Enhanced International Peacekeeping Capabilities promotes burden sharing and enhances national and regional capability to support peacekeeping operations using a core curriculum for peacekeeping operations education and training and procurement of nonlethal defense-related training equipment. An FMS case is used to purchase this type of training with the Enhanced International Peacekeeping Capabilities funding identified.

h. Foreign Assistance Act, Section 544 - Exchange Training. The FAA, Section 544, authorizes reciprocal PME exchanges. The President may provide for the attendance of foreign military personnel at PME institutions in the United States (other than Service academies) without charge, if such attendance is part of an international agreement. These international agreements provide for the exchange of students on a one-for-one reciprocal basis each FY between the two military services participating in the exchange. Each country is responsible for paying for their student's TLA. Institutions specifically included are the U.S. Military Service Command and Staff Colleges, Joint Forces Staff College, U.S. Military Service War Colleges, Navy Postgraduate School, and the Air Force Institute of Technology. The Military Service is authorized to designate additional schools as PME institutions for security assistance training. Requests for new PME exchanges should be sent to DSCA (Operations Directorate) in coordination with DSCA (Programs Directorate) so that an umbrella (DOD and/or MOD) level exchange agreement is negotiated and completed. Specific Service-level requests are sent to the Implementing Agency after the DOD-level agreement is in place. Chapter 13 of this regulation provides the prescribed MOA format for this purpose.

i. Arms Export Control Act, Section 30A - Exchange of Training and Related Support The AECA, Section 30A authorizes the President to provide training and related support (for example, transportation, food services, health services, logistics, and the use of facilities and equipment) to military and civilian defense personnel of a friendly foreign country or international organization. Such training and related support are provided through the MILDEP (as opposed to the combatant commands). Unit exchanges conducted under this authority are arranged under international agreements negotiated for such purposes, and are integrated into the TSCP of the relevant combatant commander. Recipient countries provide, on a reciprocal basis, comparable training and related support; however, each country is responsible for paying their students' TLA. The related reciprocal training and support must be provided within 1 year. Should the foreign country or international organization not provide comparable training and support, the United States must be reimbursed for the full costs of training and support provided by the United States. Chapter 13 of this regulation provides detailed implementing instructions, to include the prescribed international MOA used for this purpose. Requests for unit exchanges are forwarded to the appropriate MILDEP for action with an information copy to DSCA (Policy, Plans, and Programs Directorate). Pricing guidelines and conversion to reimbursable training when reciprocal training or related support is not provided or not received, is included in DOD 7000.14–R, Volume 11A, Chapter 10.

j. Flight training exchanges. The FAA, Section 544 authorizes the exchange of comparable flight training. The flight training exchange must be pursuant to an international agreement, which provides for the exchange of students on a one-for-one basis during the same U.S. FY. Chapter 13 of this regulation provides the prescribed MOA used for this purpose. The flight training exchanges requests are forwarded to the Implementing Agency for action with an information copy to DSCA (Programs Directorate). The flight training exchange with the United Arab Emirates (UAE) Air Warfare Center are separately authorized.

k. International Narcotics Control and Law Enforcement. The International Narcotics Control and Law Enforcement has two strategic goals: minimize the impact of international crime on the United States and reduce the entry of illegal drugs into the United States. The International Narcotics Control and Law Enforcement training programs strengthen foreign criminal justice sectors and promote international cooperation. Training provided through the FMS system using International Narcotics Control and Law Enforcement funds is governed by the same laws and policies as those outlined for FMF.

l. Joint combined exchange training. The JCET Program permits special operations forces (SOF) to train in a foreign country through interaction with foreign military forces and is authorized by 10 USC 2011. It enhances SOF skills, such as instructor skills, language proficiency, and cultural immersion, critical to required missions generated by either existing plans or unforeseen contingencies. The primary purpose of JCET activities is the training of U.S. SOF personnel, although incidental training benefits may accrue to the foreign friendly forces at no cost. The foreign government pays foreign student TLA expenses. The United States may pay the incremental expenses incurred by a foreign country as the direct result of this training. Incremental expenses include the reasonable and proper cost of rations, fuel, training, ammunition, transportation, and other goods and services consumed during the training. Pay, allowances, and other personnel costs are excluded.

m. Mine action. Mine action programs provide training to foreign nations in mine clearance operations, mine awareness education and information campaigns, assistance in the establishment of mine action centers, emergency medical care, and leadership and management skills needed to successfully conduct a national level mine action program (10 USC 401). The combatant commanders execute the mine action programs. The training is conducted in the foreign country at no charge. The foreign country pays foreign student TLA expenses.

n. Regional Centers for Security Studies. The regional centers provide a forum for bilateral and multilateral communication and military and civilian exchanges within a region. Each center has a different set of legal authorities based on when and how it was established. Some centers have authorities that allow cost waivers with no limits on course length; other centers' authorities are more limited. Some centers can accept foreign gifts to defray operating costs; other centers cannot accept gifts. The payment of foreign student travel and supplemental living allowance varies by center and circumstance. In general, students from developing countries may have these expenses funded, whereas developed countries may be expected to pay these expenses. Each center determines the exceptions. The centers are: Africa Center for Strategic Studies; Asia-Pacific Center for Security Studies; Center for Hemispheric Defense Studies; Marshall Center; and Near East South Asia Center for Strategic Studies.

o. Regional Defense Combating Terrorism Fellowship Program. This program enables the DOD to assist key countries in the war on terrorism by providing training and education on counterterrorism activities. Global Security Affairs Partnership Strategy Office is the administering agency. The Security Cooperation Organization must have the approval of the respective combatant commander before requesting courses under Counterterrorism Fellowship Program. Training under Counterterrorism Fellowship Program will follow the same procedures as IMET with the following exceptions: the fifth quarter planning and programming concept does not apply to Counterterrorism Fellowship Program; living allowance funds for courses that begin in one FY and end in the next FY will be split between the 2 FYs.

p. Counter-Drug Training Support. The Counter-Drug Training Support includes deployments for training of foreign forces at the request of an appropriate law enforcement agency official as defined in Section 1004 of Public Law 101–510 (the National Defense Authorization Act for FY 1991). The purpose of the Counter-Drug Training Support is to conduct counter narcotics-related training of foreign military and law enforcement personnel. DOD schools are reimbursed for the additional costs incurred in providing training. Travel and supplemental living allowance for foreign students based on the established IMET rate may be paid using Counter-Drug Training Support funds.

q. Service Academy Programs. Department of Defense's 3 Service Academies conduct traditional academic exchange programs of varying length and content. Up to 40 foreign students may attend each Service Academy at any one time as actual members of an Academy class. Countries reimburse all or a portion of the program cost (to include the living allowance) to the Service Academy.

r. U.S. Coast Guard Academy Foreign Cadet Program. 14 USC 195 authorizes a limited number of foreign national appointments (maximum of 36) to the USCG Academy. Cadets can earn a Bachelor of Science degree in: marine engineering and naval architecture; electrical engineering: civil engineering; mechanical engineering; marine and environmental sciences; management; or government. The foreign government must agree in advance to reimburse the USCG for all costs incurred for a cadet's training at the Coast Guard Academy, except when a waiver is granted by the Commandant, USCG. Countries must agree that upon graduation, the cadet will serve in the comparable maritime Service of their country for an appropriate period of time.

3–7. General constraints

a. Foreign military sales training will be provided at no cost to the USG except as authorized by law. All costs, as specified in the AECA and DOD 7000.14–R, will be identified and included in tuition pricing.

b. Training listed in the Training Military Articles and Service List is currently provided to eligible foreign governments. In cases where training not listed in the Training Military Articles and Service List is required by the foreign government, the Security Cooperation Organization must submit the request with justification to the cognizant Military Service. Direct or indirect contact with any prospective training activity by country personnel to coordinate and/or commit SC training is strictly prohibited.

c. Courses containing CMI or CUI will be offered to foreign governments on a "need-to-know" basis. Prior to programming, approval must be obtained from the Military Service.

d. The IMS must meet the course prerequisites set by the Military Service for training provided in CONUS or overseas.

e. All training requirements will be reviewed by the Military Service. Where training requirements are potentially sensitive, approval of DSCA will be obtained.

f. Technical skills and information acquired through U.S. training may not be used by the purchasing country to train IMS from a third country unless approved in advance. Countries should submit requests for USG consent to the transfer of training to third parties via diplomatic note to the Department of State. If such requests are received by the Military Service, they should be referred to DSCA for forwarding to the Department of State.

g. The FAA, Section 660, places restrictions on police, internal intelligence or surveillance, or civilian law enforcement training conducted in a foreign country or in the United States. "Police" as used in this prohibition includes military as well as civilian police if the military police perform civilian law enforcement functions. Neither the name given to a unit by the foreign government nor the ministerial authority under which it operates is sufficient in and of itself to determine whether a particular force is a police unit. The determining factor is the nature of the function performed by that unit. Certification is required from the country that students attending military police training will not be involved with or assigned to a unit performing in any civilian law enforcement functions for at least 2 years. Similar certification is required for any training provided on an individual rather than a unit basis, if the individual is from a unit that performs ongoing civilian law enforcement functions. The certification must be maintained by the Security Cooperation Organization until 2 years following completion of training. Military police courses purchased under FMS must have prior approval from DSCA if the IMS is a member of a country unit having civilian police functions. Exceptions are—

(1) Training of law enforcement personnel at WHINSEC, authorized under 10 USC 2166.

(2) Maritime Law Enforcement and training in maritime related skills and training provided by the U.S. Coast Guard, authorized by 22 USC 2420(b)(3).

h. The scope of intelligence training normally available is limited to that which is directly related to combat, operational, or joint staff intelligence.

i. Follow-on training in civilian agencies constitutes termination of SC sponsorship unless DSCA grants a waiver.

j. Section 620(q), FAA, and "The Brooke Amendment" to the FAA of 1961, as amended, imposes sanctions by which security assistance provided to countries ceases when a country is in default in the payment of loans to the United States. Accordingly, Security Cooperation Organization will not request training on weapon systems or equipment that is not in or scheduled for delivery to the country.

(1) Prospective IMET students may not travel to the U.S. or other locations to start training. IMET students outside their countries of origin whose course of study or training program began before the effective date of the sanctions may complete such courses, including already funded sequential courses. However, no additional sequential courses may be added on or after the effective date of the sanctions. IMET students outside their countries of origin whose course of study or training program did not begin before the effective date of the sanctions should normally be returned to their home countries as soon as possible. For the purposes of the Brooke Amendment, an IMET funded course is deemed to begin on the report date specified in the STL. If sanctions are lifted, these students will be considered for late admittance or admittance to the next available course or training program.

(2) The IMET funded MTT and LTD may not be dispatched or extended beyond their scheduled termination date.

(3) The IMET funded training aids may not be issued from supply nor placed on contract by the supplying agency. Section 620(q) does not affect the use of FMS credit funds.

3–8. Total package approach

The TPA outlines training requirements related to the purchase of major equipment or systems. (See fig 3–1 for a training plan checklist for new equipment.)

a. When a country plans to add a new item of equipment to its inventory, a TPA must be used rather than focusing only on the item of equipment. Components of the TPA include the following:

(1) Quantity of end items required for operational elements, training base, and maintenance support.

(2) Training requirements including training aids, training ammunition, and such necessary additional facilities as ranges, airfields, and port facilities.

(3) Publications.

(4) Foreign country facilities and available manpower.

(5) Initial logistics support includes those items required to field the item or system, such as communications and electronic equipment; basic issue items; and technical assistance and technical manuals. Sustaining support consists of those items required to maintain the item or system in operational condition and includes replenishment repair parts, overhaul requirements, and ammunition requirements.

b. The time required to conduct adequate training as well as to develop an in-country maintenance or support capability often becomes the pacing factor and must be considered in relationship to delivery dates of equipment in developing a training plan for a particular end item of equipment or weapon system. Each country must be considered individually. While general training requirements can be determined for any item, the exact composition and duration of the training program will vary based on the individual requirements and capabilities of each country.

c. A comprehensive training support package cannot be developed by Military Service trainers without knowledge of the country specifics. Thus, the important role of the Security Cooperation Organization and survey teams cannot be overemphasized. The Security Cooperation Organization and Military Service must begin planning when the country initially expresses an interest in a weapon system or equipment. This will require close and continuous coordination between the training and material personnel of the various organizations involved, both in the United States and in the purchasing country. Essential information should be included in the initial request for P&A and LOA data on the major item. In-country information on items such as existing facilities, training software, and hardware items in inventory, and levels of experience and training of the IMS is essential to the TPA concept. Using this information as a point of departure, the training support package would reflect the P&A of those additional software and hardware items required to support the end items, as well as an appropriate training plan. A survey team may be required. A trainer should routinely be included as a member of the team.

d. Training programs must be planned realistically, taking into account the skills that must be developed, the background and experience of the individuals selected for the training, and the time required to plan, implement, and complete the program. In the final analysis, the success of any training program will depend upon IMS capability and potential for success. The individual and collective performance of the IMS will set the pace for and measure the true progress of a program.

e. Training in support of FMS equipment purchases should be coordinated with the equipment sales case. Training under the International Military Education and Training Program (IMETP) will not be provided to support FMS equipment purchases. Request for exceptions to this policy should be referred to DSCA with appropriate justification for consideration on a case-by-case basis.

f. Suggested guidance concerning development of comprehensive training plans for new equipment is contained in figure 3–1.

TRAINING PLAN CHECKLIST

Step 1. Organizational analysis.
    a. Will the organization be similar to U.S. Organizations?
    b. Will the organization have a specialized mission?
    c. Is this a new organization or one being upgraded with new equipment?
    d. What is the general organizational structure?
    e. What is the desired initial operational capability date?

Step 2. Service support analysis.
    a. Does the country's logistical system reflect U.S. defense systems?
    b. What is the present maintenance philosophy and capability?
    c. What level of maintenance capability is to be developed? Is this level practical with regard to weapons density and facilities or personnel available?
    d. What is the country's experience with similar weapons systems or end items (United States and foreign)?
    e. Are contractor services available in-country?
    f. Should contractor maintenance, technical assistance field teams (TAFTs), or technical assistance teams (TATs) be considered?

Step 3. Training plan preparation.
    a. What are the total skill requirements to support steps 1 and 2 and density of each skills? (Total requirement less number available in-country equals training requirements.) Training requirement can generally be best staffed by training cadre, which will in turn accomplish the majority of the required training in-country.
    b. Has the country expressed its intended approach to training? If not, try to obtain the information. For example, does the customer want the training to be conducted in CONUS, in-country, or a combination, does the country object to contractor training?
    c. What is the current in-country training capability to produce the needed skills?
    d. Can in-country training be upgraded to support the new equipment? If so, what is required?
    e. What is the in-country English language training capability?
    f. What is the availability of English speaking personnel? Do these people have the necessary technical or education background?
    g. Where can the required skills best be developed, in-country or in CONUS? If U.S. training is desired, first consideration should be CONUS cadre training, which will provide best quality training in a formal classroom environment.
    h. What specialized facilities (for example, ranges, structures, air-fields, and port facilities) will be required in-country?
    i. What is the availability of qualified interpreters and translators?
    j. Are there constraints on CONUS training?
    k. Should contractor training be considered from in-country or CONUS sources?
    l. Is an in-country training requirements or pre-deployment team required?

Figure 3–1. Sample training plan checklist for new equipment-total package approach

Step 4. Concept requirements refinement.

    a. Have all requirements been considered? These requirement include--

        (1) Major end items

        (2) Support items and ammunition to include training ammunition

        (3) Tool sets, tool kits, and shop sets.

        (4) Publications

        (5) Repair parts and services

        (6) Training aids and devices (Lead time frequently exceeds equipment delivery schedules)

        (7) Ranges, classrooms, airfields, and port facilities

        (8) Maintenance facilities and warehouses

        (9) Support of U.S. personnel

    b. Will equipment list support--

        (1) Organization being developed?

        (2) Maintenance and support capability being developed?

        (3) Initial and subsequent training?

    c. Are training plan and equipment delivery dates compatible?

    d. Is a survey required?

Figure 3–1. Sample training plan checklist for new equipment-total package approach–Continued

3–9. References used for security cooperation education and training

The principal references used in planning and programming SC education and training are listed in paragraphs *a* through *m*, below.

a. The SAMM (DOD 5105.38–M) published by DSCA, provides guidance and information for programming, costing, and funding of security cooperation training (http://www.dsca.mil/samm).

b. DOD 7000.14–R, Volume 15, published by Office of the Assistant Secretary of Defense (OASD) (Comptroller), established the pricing and costing criteria for FMS sales of defense articles and services (including training) under the AECA (http://comptroller.defense.gov/fmr/15/index.html).

c. International Military Student Officers (USAF), (http://www.aetc.af.mil/afsat/afsat_fr.htm).

d. The Navy International Training and Education Catalog (NETSAFA) (https://www.netsafa.navy.mil).

e. Security Assistance and Training Desktop Guide (USMC/Security Cooperation Education and Training Center) (http://scetc.tecom.usmc.mil/).

f. International Training Handbook (USCG G–CI) (http://www.uscg.mil/hq/atcmobil/tradiv/IMS/IMSO_Main.htm).

g. Planning and Programming Security Assistance English Language Training (DLIELC Instruction 1025.7).

h. Field Studies Program for International Military and Civilian Students and Military Sponsored Visitors (DODI 5410.17).

i. Expanded IMET Handbook.

j. The Training Military Articles and Service List is a MILDEP database of training that can be provided. It is available as a data download from the SAN to all Security Cooperation Organization (through the TMS) and selected international users (through the international security assistance network (ISAN). The Training Military Articles and Service List provides data on courses available from all Military Service to eligible foreign countries under the SCETP. Associated data provided with the Training Military Articles and Service List are course descriptions, training location, point of contacts (POCs), detailed training location information, and international notes and prerequisites.

k. The STL is a MILDEP database of all training that has been approved and programmed in a country's training program, regardless of source of funding. It is available as a data download from the ISAN to all Security Cooperation Organization and selected U.S. and international users. The STL provides data on all training that has been programmed by the Military Service training agencies. It not only identifies the selected training course, but also identifies the cost of that course and any programmed travel and living allowance expense. The STL also provides scheduling data (report, start, and end dates) of all selected training courses.

Section II
Programming

3–10. Programming cycle

a. The State Department Mission Performance Plan and the Combined Education and Training Program Plan comprise the U.S. country team document that supports the proposed program for the foreign country concerned. These plans provide the level of detail of the proposed requirements for IMET and for FMS credit and Counterterrorism Fellowship Program recommended by the country team. Training is categorized by an analysis code and dollar level. It is submitted through State Department channels and provides the details to support the annual Congressional Budget Justification for foreign operations. The Congressional Budget Justification for Foreign Operations is the supporting document submitted to Congress with the annual legislative proposal for the Security Assistance Program authorization and appropriations. IMET programming data will be forwarded to the Military Service not later than September in support of the Congressional Budget Justification. The Mission Performance Plan also includes all known FMS requests for the budget year (BY).

b. Based on projected IMETP dollar ceilings, Security Cooperation Organization should prepare the Combined Education and Training Program Plan for presentation to combatant commands and Military Service at least 30 days before the annual SCETWGs or as directed by the appropriate MILDEP.

c. Program submission will be by markup of the existing Combined Education and Training Program Plan made available by the Military Service. Desired deviations to the program listing will be forwarded to the Military Service.

d. Annual SCETWGs are hosted by the combatant commands.

(1) The Security Cooperation Education and Training Working Group schedules are based on coordination between combatant commands and Military Service.

(2) The Security Cooperation Organization representative must be prepared to present, discuss, and justify each training line in the proposed program. In this regard, each request for OJT, OBT, and familiarization training will be submitted as shown in figure 3–2. Written justification must be submitted for all programmed OT, LTD, and SAT. If no justification is included, the Security Cooperation Organization representative will be required to prepare one before departure from the working group. Failure to submit proper justification will result in deletion of training from the program.

(3) The Security Cooperation Organization must stipulate factors to be used in IMET costing for travel and living allowances to be paid by the USG or by the foreign government (cost-sharing).

(4) The purpose of the Security Cooperation Education and Training Working Group is to accept, reject, change, or add training lines and training teams to country programs within approved policy guidelines. Training is accepted by the Military Service for programming only, subject to determining the capability to furnish that training in relation to total worldwide requirements.

(5) On completion of the Security Cooperation Education and Training Working Group, each Military Service will have a complete copy of the refined country program.

(6) Based on a refined country program, Military Service will process requirements. After the Security Cooperation Education and Training Working Group, the Security Cooperation Organization will submit program deviations to the Military Service with accompanying backup documents.

e. Unprogrammed training requirements not included in the annual program will be handled on an exception basis. Unscheduled requirements often have an adverse impact on the total training effort. This is particularly true in training courses where quota availability is constrained. It also happens in those cases involving short-notice deployment of MTT personnel from operational units for specialized requirements and preparation of tailored curricula. In addition, unprogrammed training requirements distort planning and make forecasting ineffective. Every reasonable effort should be made to develop programs that will not require revision after review at the Security Cooperation Education and Training Working Group.

f. Deferred items requiring special authorization will not be approved until DSCA has obtained the necessary certification or a waiver has been granted.

g. Upon receipt of funding authority, the Military Service will authorize the Security Cooperation Organization to prepare ITO to send IMS to training.

OJT, OBSERVATION, OR FAMILIARIZATION TRAINING REQUEST FORMAT

A. Requesting country
B. Service branch
C. FMS case or IMET FY
D. WCN
E. TMASAL number
F. Duration (weeks)
G. Course description:
   1. TMASL title or chart narrative of desired course (If no TMASL number)
   2. Specific objective to be accomplished by training
   3. Specific individual task or skills expected to be accomplished by student or knowledge to be acquired.
   4. Specific items of equipment t on which training emphasis is to be used
H. Timeframe desired (if stand-alone request) or list of preceding formal training courses.
I. Latest acceptable graduation date (if established by country)
J. Student information:
   1. Full name (if known) and current duty position
   2. Rank/rate and U.S. equivalent grade
   3. Background/experience by weapon system and still level
   4. Prior CONUS training (or other known formal training)
   5. Expected duty assignment following training
   6. Required level of security clearance of individual
K. Additional comments or amplifying information

Notes:
   A. This formation will be used in all submitted requests for OJT/observation/familiarization training, both at the country program presentation at the Combatant Command Security Cooperation Education and Training Working Groups and for out-of-cycle requests. The more details presented in this format will permit the MILSVC to determine the capability of accomplishing and scheduling the training requirement.
   B For familiarization training following formal USAF courses, this format need not be submitted if country desired the standard familiarization training program developed for international students. Submit this format only if country identifies specific training tasks for a student.

Figure 3–2. Sample format for an OJT, observation, or familiarization training request

3–11. Programming procedures

Strict programming procedures are necessary to achieve training objectives and to account for expenditures.

a. International military education and training.

(1) The IMET program provides training in the United States and, in some cases, in overseas U.S. military facilities to selected foreign military and related civilian personnel on a grant basis.

(2) Congressional scrutiny of the IMETP requires an indication of the relative priority of the training requirements within each country program. These priority indicators are used in responding to Congressional queries, selecting requirements for continuing resolution authority (CRA) funding, and adjusting programs to conform to executive branch decisions and legislative actions when response time will not permit consultation with Security Cooperation Organization or combatant commands. Accordingly, a training requirement priority code system has been established according to the following standardized designations—

(a) Priority Code A. (highest priority). Prime training requirements considered most essential for meeting an in country training objective.

(b) Priority Code B. Used only to indicate training the Security Cooperation Organization wants funded by end of year funds (if available) and should only be used in execution year IMET Programs.

(c) Priority Code D. Valid training requirement above the budget level but within the dollar amount that an Security

Cooperation Organization could reasonably expect to receive at mid-year or end of year. Priority D is an unbudgeted amount and will not normally exceed 10 percent of the budget. Military Service will not obtain quotas for D lines.

b. Foreign military sales. All foreign military sales of defense articles and defense services including training are handled through the use of a LOA. The LOA lists the items, services, estimated costs, terms, and conditions of the sale, and requires the signature of a representative of the foreign country or international organization to indicate acceptance. Receipt of the initial deposit and copies of the signed LOA by DFAS–DE and the MILDEP denotes acceptance on the part of the purchaser of the terms and conditions.

c. Combating Terrorism Fellowship Program.

(1) The Counterterrorism Fellowship Program is to be included in the Combined Education and Training Program Plan.

(2) The combatant command Counterterrorism Fellowship Program coordinators will provide procedural guidelines for coordination on Counterterrorism Fellowship Program plans/STL prior to the Security Cooperation Education and Training Working Group.

(3) Only after Global Security Affairs Partnership Strategy Office has formally approved a country's planning year Counterterrorism Fellowship Program STL is the program considered to be final.

(4) Unlike the IMET program, there will be no additions, changes or deletions made by the Security Cooperation Organization or MILSVCs to the country's current year or approved planning year Counterterrorism Fellowship Program STL without coordination and written approval from the commanders of combatant commands Counterterrorism Fellowship Program coordinator and Global Security Affairs Partnership Strategy Office.

d. The Counter Drug Program.

(1) The program is DOD funded and must comply with requirements contained in CJCSI 3710.01.

(2) The MILDEPS establish pseudo-FMS case designators for DOS and OSD training and prepare separate STL/International Standardized Training Listing.

e. Work sheet control number. This number is the most important element identifier used in the SCETP. The most important use is to track the IMS. Normally, one worksheet control number (WCN) will be assigned per IMS. This procedure reduces administrative effort on the part of the scheduling commands and training installations and allows effective tracking and billing.

f. Cross-Service training. The policy for cross-Service training is as follows:

(1) When an IMS from one Military Service is selected for training exclusively within schools of another Military Service, such training will be made part of the program of the Military Service providing the training.

(2) When an IMS is selected for training involving courses of more than one Military Service, the training will be programmed by the Military Service providing the greater number of total training weeks, exclusive of ELT.

(3) When OT are for IMS assigned to organizations equivalent to the U.S. DOD or when such tours are not clearly identifiable to a particular Military Service, the Security Cooperation Organization will include the tour in the program of the Military Service having predominant interest, or DSCA will designate the Military Service.

(4) Joint courses will be included in the program of the Military Service having implementing agency responsibility for the course. (See table 3–1.)

Table 3–1
Implementing agency for DOD schools

School	Location	Implementing agency
American Forces Information Services	Fort Meade, MD	Army
Center for Civil Military Relations	Monterey, CA	Navy
Defense Acquisition University	Fort Belvoir, VA	Army
Defense Ammunition Center	McAlester, OK	Army
Defense Equal Opportunity Management Institute	Patrick Air Force Base (AFB), FL	Air Force
Defense Geospatial Intelligence School	Fort Belvoir, VA	Army
Defense Information School	Fort Meade, MD	Army
Defense Institute for Medical Operations	San Antonio, TX	Air Force
Defense Institute of International Legal Studies	Newport, RI	Navy
Defense Institute of Security Assistance Management	Wright-Patterson AFB, OH	Air Force
Defense Intelligence College	Bolling AFB, Washington, DC	Air Force

Table 3–1
Implementing agency for DOD schools—Continued

Defense Language Institute English Language Center	Lackland AFB, TX	Air Force
Defense Language Institute Foreign Language Center	Monterey, CA	Army
Defense Logistics Agency Training Center	Columbus, OH	Army
Defense Logistics Information Service	Battle Creek, MI	Army
Defense Resources Management Institute	Monterey, CA	Navy
Defense Systems Management College	Fort Belvoir, VA	Army
Joint Forces Staff College	Norfolk, VA	Navy
National Defense University	Fort McNair, Washington, DC	Army
Western Hemisphere Institute for Security Cooperation	Fort Benning, GA	Army

3–12. Distributive/distance learning

Distributive/distance learning (DL) courses are delivered through a variety of formats that include the Internet or an Intranet, compact disk-read only memory (CD–ROM) or digital video disc (DVD). Military Service will ensure course descriptions and course locations reflect the most current methods of delivery as courses are revised to nontraditional classroom methods. Updated Training Military Articles and Service List information will facilitate selection of IMS with the proper computer background and experience, as well as management of IMS expectations for course delivery. The course delivery location will be included in the MASL description, but could be at the traditional training location, or at a distance learning center. IMET IMS may attend DL courses in CONUS, but require DSCA waiver for OCONUS delivery. FMS IMS may attend courses in CONUS or OCONUS. Distance learning courses delivered OCONUS will have a Training Military Articles and Service List beginning with "B4, "D4," or "P4" per DSCA guidance. Prerequisites and procedures for course attendance generally mirror processes for all other courses; however, each Military Service will provide Service unique procedures.

3–13. Civilian international military students

a. Defense civilians, non-defense ministry civilians, legislators, and individuals who are not members of the government may be trained under the E–IMET program if the military education and training would contribute to the E–IMET objectives.

b. Training of defense civilians for the express purpose of teaching, developing, or managing in-country ELT programs is also authorized.

c. Defense civilians in counter narcotics related positions may also be trained under the E–IMET program.

d. Maritime law enforcement and other maritime skills training for agencies which are nondefense, or agencies which perform a maritime law enforcement mission, and other maritime skills training provided to a country which does not have a standing Armed Forces is authorized.

e. The foreign government must agree to the same administrative control over civilians in training as applies to military personnel. Equivalent grade civilians will be afforded the same status and privileges as military personnel.

f. The military services may provide training to non-MOD personnel under the following authorities.

(1) Training provided directly to non-MOD organizations of friendly countries, international organizations, or voluntary nonprofit relief agencies registered with and approved by the U.S. Agency for International Development (USAID), as authorized by FAA, Section 607, Part I. The military Service must obtain a determination from the International Development Cooperation Agency, through DSCA, that the proposed training is consistent with and furthers the purposes of part I, of the Foreign Assistance Act. The military Service must forward the request for determination to DSCA with the following information:

(a) Name of the international agency.

(b) Number of students to be trained.

(c) Type training, proposed dates, and estimated cost.

(2) Upon receipt of the determination approval from International Development Cooperation Agency, the military department will prepare an LOA for the training and forward to the Security Cooperation Organization for presentation to the international agency. The LOA will include a copy of the determination as an attachment and a supplemental condition as follows: "This sale is made under the authority of Section 607 of the Foreign Assistance Act of 1961, as amended, and the determination there under made by the Director, Trade and Development Program, International Development Cooperation Agency, on (date) (copy attached). Any reference to the Arms Export Control Act herein will be construed to be a reference to FAA, Section 607, 1961, as amended. All other terms, conditions, and procedures under this LOA will apply to this transaction."

(3) A report will be provided directly to Director, U.S. Trade and Development Program, International Development

Cooperation Agency, upon completion of the training to include the completion or termination date of the training and any changes in the original request concerning actual course and or type training, length, and cost.

(4) Training provided in support of other U.S. government sponsored programs, provided in support of other U.S. government programs authorized under the FAA, and financed by USG appropriations. Section 632(a) of the FAA authorizes the transfer of funds from one agency to another to carry out the purposes of the FAA. This training support will be provided under an interagency agreement.

(5) Training provided to international students sponsored by another government agency, financed by the foreign country. The Economy Act authorizes a government agency to render services for another on a reimbursable basis. This training support will be provided under an interagency agreement. Guidance for determining tuition rates for non-DOD-sponsored personnel is contained in DOD 7000.14–R; in all cases the established administrative surcharge will be applied. Student support costs, such as TLA and medical services, are the responsibility of the student's government or the sponsoring agency.

3–14. Education and training provided by contractors or at civilian institutions

a. Contractor-provided training under foreign military sales. Training conducted by contractors, either at DOD contracted or USG facilities, will be conducted under the same procedures and regulations outlined for DOD provided training, to include vetting of students, ITO, administrative support, and reporting in the SAN. When the training is provided by a contractor in non-USG facilities, the contract SOW must include requirements to provide students the same basic student management and life support afforded international students attending training on a USG installation to include payment of TLA (when applicable); travel arrangements, lodging, dining facilities, daily transportation between International Military Students (IMS) quarters, training facility, dining facility, student reporting, medical support, general administration, and a Field Studies Program if training is 4 weeks or longer. The cost of these administrative services will be included in the cost of the contract. Figure 3–3 provides a price and availability checklist for contractor-provided training.

CONTRACTOR-PROVIDED TRAINING CHECKLIST

Course Title: _____ **TMASAL:** _____
Course Location: _____
Desired Dates: _____ **Total Number of Students:** _____

General Requirement: The contract Statement of Work (SOW) will provide IMS with the same basic student management and life support afforded to IMS attending training on a US government installation. The following elements must be included in the SOW, and agreed to as part of the contract, prior to issuance of an ITO. The Checklist should be used as a guide in requesting contractor -provided training under Security Cooperation programs. Include the Checklist with the initial request for P&A. The following references should be review when preparing this Checklist:
DOA - AMSAC-MP Memo of 7 Mar 2003 and NAVYIPOINST 4950.1 of 6 Apr 2004

✓	ITEM	COMMENTS
	Student Data	For each IMS: • Rank/date • Summary of prior training • English Comprehension Level
	TLA	Confirm home country responsibilities in funding travel to the training site and living allowances in addition IMS normal pay.
	Travel	Confirm contractor's responsibility in arranging travel to the US and return to home country.
	Lodging	Contractor will provide suitable lodging for duration of training.
	Meals and Incidentals	Contractor will provide or arrange suitable meals for IMS for the duration of training.
	General Administration	Includes: • In-processing • Student Records, including Academic Reports and Academic/Disciplinary incidents • Receipt of pay and allowances • Transportation from lodging to training • Out-processing
	Facilities	Contractor will identify the training site and ensure it is suitable for the training and anticipated number of IMS
	Equipment and Training Aids	Identify and specific items that will be use in the training. Include procurement requirements, shipment, accountability, anticipated expendable items, and disposition of the end of training.
	Medical	Confirm contractor's responsibilities for ensuring that IMS have adequate medical support for the duration of the training.
	Field Studies Program	For training that exceeds four weeks in duration, contractor will develop and execute an FSP event that conforms to the requirements of the JSCET.
	Student Support Costs	Contractor's cost estimate should include a confirmation of whether or not the funding for the above items will be accomplished through the contract.
	Administrative Costs	Contractor's proposal should also include the cost estimate for the administrative support for the international student(s).
	Sole-source Justification	Describe if required.

Figure 3–3. Sample format of checklist for contractor training

b. Support for direct contractor-provided training. Administrative support for direct contractor training is NOT provided through an FMS case. Room, board, medical care, and related support arrangements for students undergoing commercial contractor training must be arranged between the contractor and the purchaser.

c. Education and training of international military students at civilian institutions.

(1) Training is authorized under the IMET only if equivalent training is not available from U.S. military installations. DSCA approval is required prior to offer or programming.

(2) The requirement to educate or train an IMS at a civilian institution under FMS is more appropriately handled by direct negotiation between the civilian institution and the purchasing country. Security cooperation training at civilian institutions, therefore, generally will not be accomplished under FMS. Requests for exceptions to this policy should be addressed to DSCA Comptroller.

(3) Training at civilian institutions under ongoing Military Service contracts may be requested from the Military Service.

(4) Contract training in support of DCS, that is, foreign government to defense contractor without DOD intervention, is not managed under SC/security assistance training programs.

3–15. Letters of offer and acceptance for the sale of U.S. military training

The LOA, when signed, is an international binding agreement used by the USG to offer to sell defense articles and defense services (training) to a foreign country or international organization. The LOA lists the items, services, estimated costs, terms, and conditions of the sale, and requires the signature of a representative of the foreign country or international organization to indicate acceptance. Detailed guidance on the use and processing of LOA, Amendments and Modifications is in the SAMM, chapter 5.

a. Purpose of the letter of offer and acceptance. The LOA will be used for all foreign military sales of defense articles and defense services, which includes training. Also, when authorized for release to the foreign purchaser, the LOA becomes the official offer by the USG.

(1) The following denote acceptance on the part of the purchaser of the terms and conditions:

(a) Signature by an authorized representative of the purchasing country.

(b) Receipt of the initial deposit and signed copies of the LOA by DFAS and the MILDEP.

(2) Additional terms and conditions as may be appropriate for a particular sales case will be set forth in one or more attachments or continuation sheets to the LOA. All attachments, including notes, annexes, and appendices, are an integral part of the LOA.

b. Letter of offer and acceptance development. Development of an LOA may involve one or more of the statutes that authorize FMS.

(1) Those AECA and FAA sections that pertain to FMS training cases are as follows:

(a) Section 21, AECA. Sale from stock.

(b) Section 22, AECA. DOD Procurement for cash sales.

(c) Section 23, AECA. DOD Credit sales.

(d) Section 24, AECA. DOD guaranties.

(e) Section 503(a)(3), FAA. Use of Foreign Military Financing Program funds for obligation authority.

(2) The SAMM, chapter 5, lists in detail the requirements for preparation of LOA.

3–16. Letters of offer and acceptance for training

a. Training in support of major equipment sales can include the development of operator, maintenance, logistical, and other support skills. In support of such sales, accurate and early planning must be accomplished to complete the following before equipment arrival:

(1) Conduct a training assessment survey.

(2) Determine both CONUS and OCONUS training requirements.

(3) Develop training P&A information for country approval via FMS planning case.

(4) Request, process, and accept LOA and complete financial requirements.

(5) Screen and select IMS for required ELT and other preparatory training.

(6) Conduct training required to operate and maintain equipment.

b. Include in each LOA the date upon which the offer expires.

c. Requests by the purchaser for extensions to expiration dates must be in writing. These requests will be granted only after a full review by the preparing agency to ensure that all data included in the LOA remain valid. The purchaser will be advised by message of the new expiration date, along with the authorization to make a pen and ink change to the expiration date listed on the LOA or amendment. DFAS–DE and DSCA must be provided an information copy of the message.

d. It is not FMS practice to provide a detailed description of the components of costs included in estimated prices for line items on LOA. When such queries are received from the purchaser, the elements of tuition cost, as outlined in DOD 7000.14–R, volume 15, may be provided. Detailed information on tuition computation will not be provided unless specifically authorized on a case-by-case basis by DSCA.

e. The obligation authority will be issued by DFAS–DE only after the receipt of the duly executed LOA and initial deposit if required.

f. To ensure uniformity of LOA for training, certain notes, or supplemental conditions must be included in the LOA. These various notes or conditions are published by each Military Service. Special training cases involving long lead-time and special training assets will necessarily require various caveats, notes, and explanations to legally and administratively define the case. These notes will be prepared to adequately protect the interests of the USG and the purchaser.

g. The LOA must specify the purchasing government's responsibilities; for example, providing pay and allowances, funds for housing, qualified IMS, and any required supervision of these IMS.

h. The LOA for defined training should, wherever possible, include firm scheduling of IMS into specific training courses. When this is not feasible, a statement will be included in the LOA to the effect that the convening date and scheduling information will be provided when available.

3–17. Letters of offer and acceptance amendments
Amendments should be used to meet only minimum essential administrative needs. They may be used for minor changes in scope when such use is essential for administrative reasons. Detailed guidance on the use and processing of amendments is in the SAMM.

3–18. Letters of offer and acceptance modifications
Modifications are used to record modifications to an existing LOA which do not constitute a change in scope. Detailed guidance on the use and processing of modifications is in the SAMM, chapter 5.

3–19. Foreign military sales price increases
For price increase notifications, the following information, if applicable, will be included:

a. Reason for the increase.

b. Options the purchaser has, if any, with respect to avoiding the price increases, for example, contract termination or reduction of quantities.

c. Estimated financial consequences of selecting such options.

d. Time limits, if any, for notifying the USG of the purchaser's desire to cancel or reduce quantities.

3–20. Liability for damages
Training cases which involve the use of U.S. equipment (for example, aircraft and trucks), and which, due to special pricing requirements, do not include an attrition factor, will include a statement on liability for damages. It will state that the foreign government will be liable for any damage to such equipment due to negligence on the part of the student.

Section III
Training Support (Other Media)

3–21. General
Publications necessary to support Security Cooperation cover a wide range of material, in print or other media (such as microfiche, CD and so forth) including technical orders, compendiums/indexes, software, technical manuals, supply catalogs, training publications, administrative publications, engineering drawings, and associated documents, Integrated Logistics Support publications and associated documents, equipment component lists, special file extracts, decals, forms, and audiovisual products. A publication may be bound or loose-leaf, imprinted form, automatic data processing listing, operator's card, microfilm, slide, motion picture film, CD–ROM, and so forth. In most cases, as with other aspects of the FMS Program, no special system has been developed to requisition publications to support the FMS customer. The systems already used by each of MILDEP and other DOD organizations to meet internal requirements have all been adapted for the FMS customer. The U.S. Air Force Security Assistance Technical Order Data System was developed to support the FMS program. However, the systems used by the Army, Air Force, Navy, and Defense Logistics Agency are very different from one another, unlike the processes used to obtain spare parts.

3–22. English language training media
a. Training aids, devices, equipment, books, tapes, and publications used in establishing or supporting in-country ELTP may be programmed and funded in the country IMETP. The dollar value of items obtained under IMETP will be applied against the country's training dollar ceiling. Training materials programmed under Budget Project N90 will be

identified to DSCA when requesting funding and will include an indication that the materials support the in country ELTP.

(1) Training aids, devices, and equipment in support of ELTP will be in the U.S. Army IMETP (N9A).

(2) Books, tapes, and publications in support of ELTP will be in USAF IMETP (N9B).

(3) Packing, crating, and handling costs of the items in paragraphs (1) and (2), above, will be in the respective MILDEP program (N9X).

b. Training aids, devices, equipment, films, books, tapes, and publications not in support of in country ELTP will be obtained through FMS channels. Requests for exceptions to obtain these items through programming and funding under IMETP must be addressed on a case-by-case basis to DSCA. The DSCA exceptions will be granted on a one-time basis and will not apply automatically to similar future requirements. Requests for training aids and support material should be included in IMET waiver requests for SATs. Requests must be completely justified, in writing, and include the following:

(1) Why provisioning of training materials under IMETP is necessary?

(2) Why it is in the U.S. interest?

(3) The impact on the country training program (for example, specific courses and training to be deleted and how this training will be accomplished).

c. In view of the long lead time required in programming, procurement, and delivery, items must be programmed sufficiently in advance to be available in-country when needed. After funding, timely requisitioning is essential to allow Military Service obligations before 1 August of each year.

3–23. Constraints

Training media will not be provided to foreign countries on a loan or non-reimbursable basis. The term "loan" does not apply to SCETP. Foreign governments should be encouraged to purchase training media for their training requirements. However, training media may be leased under the provision of AECA, chapter 6. Under the terms of a lease, the foreign government incurs an obligation to rent the training film and maintain it in an original condition. Lease arrangements present cost-recoupment problems. The costs of cleaning and repairing damaged training media, producing additional film prints to meet foreign demands, and packing, crating, handling, and postage are difficult to factor into the low cost of single training-film lease arrangements. These costs must, however, even though minimal, be recouped by the USG. The following policy applies when providing training media to SC activities, foreign governments, and international organizations:

a. Training media will not be leased to foreign governments without the authorization of DSCA.

b. The SC activities receiving foreign government requests to lease training media will screen the requests carefully to ensure that full justification is provided with the request. The SC activities are authorized to state that the lease, if approved, will be on an exception basis only.

c. The SC activities borrowing media will retain physical custody of the media at all times. The media will not be given to foreign governments while in custody of the SC activity. The media may be shown to foreign government representatives according to authorized disclosure but must be retained at all times by the borrowing SC activity.

Section IV
Department of the Army

3–24. Training references

a. Courses. This document lists CONUS training activity, course number and title, duration (peacetime and mobilization), purpose, scope, prerequisites, and special instructions. Many of these courses are not available to all countries; however, references to this pamphlet and the Training Military Articles and Service List should give the Security Cooperation Organization all necessary data to assist the host country in requesting the training that best meets requirements.

b. Catalog. Most MSCs, schools, and training activities publish printed and online catalogs on available training.

c. The Training Military Articles and Service List.

(1) *Distribution.* The Training Military Articles and Service List are distributed as required by SATFA to commanders of combatant commands, Security Cooperation Organization, and DA.

(2) *Changes.* Changes are made when needed (for example, entering new courses, eliminating courses, and changing course location, length, and cost). The IMSO is encouraged to notify SATFA Policy, Plans, Programs, and Projects (P4)/Regional Operations when new training or courses having potential applicability to IMS have been developed. The SATFA will determine if international interest exists, and if so, will assign a Training Military Articles and Service List number and a cost to the training.

(3) *Updates.* An update of the Training Military Articles and Service List is required annually to reflect available courses, applicable changes and associated tuition costs for the next FY. SATFA will request an annual update of the

Training Military Articles and Service List, to include aforementioned information, from non-TRADOC training activities and schools and ensure inclusion in the Training Military Articles and Service List.

3–25. General course prerequisites, training requirements, and standards

a. The IMS must meet all course prerequisites, except service retainability and U.S. security clearances as prescribed for U.S. personnel and reflected in the Training Military Articles and Service List, the school catalog, or other prerequisites established by the U.S. Army component commander providing the training. IMS must also meet the age requirements established in the SAMM.

b. If IMS selected for Army training do not meet grade prerequisites, biographical data and complete justification to waive grade prerequisites will be submitted to Director, SATFA and the concerned school for approval of course attendance before preparing an ITO. Approvals will be granted by Director, SATFA in coordination with the affected school.

c. The IMS are expected to complete the same course requirements as their U.S. counterparts unless substitute requirements have been approved by the school commandant and Director, SATFA, or unless the material is restricted. IMS are expected to participate in physical training (PT), field training exercises, staff rides, and blocks of instruction dealing with U.S. Army unique material.

d. The IMS in training with U.S. personnel will not be routinely excused from class for prayer or holidays. However, schools are encouraged to permit IMS in good academic standing to observe the two holidays per year selected by their countries provided critical training or testing is not scheduled. The two holidays are chosen by the countries, and published in the Combined Education and Training Program Plan. The DISAM places the complied list on the IMSO Web.

3–26. Special courses

a. Applicants for aviation, Airborne, Ranger, Special Forces, and other courses involving potentially hazardous training will be carefully screened to ensure they meet the prerequisites, USASOC directives and/or the Training Military Articles and Service List. These courses entail "danger to life and limb" activities and have the potential to endanger not only the IMS, but also instructors and fellow students. In addition to meeting rigid physical requirements, applicants must be highly motivated and possess an excellent understanding of and ability to communicate in English.

b. The IMS taking other than airborne training, but who are airborne qualified, may be placed on airborne status for the duration of CONUS training to maintain proficiency. Such status must be approved by the IMS' government. Specific authority must be included in the ITO. Implementation of this authority will depend on the school's capability to conduct airborne jumps.

c. Candidates for initial entry rotary wing course flight training must have a proven aptitude for flight training before reporting to the primary rotary wing course.

d. The IMS that are scheduled for flight training in U.S. Army Service schools will be required to meet class I, International Affairs, or II medical standards. (See AR 40–501, chap 4.) IMS who possess a current, valid aviator rating in the armed forces of their respective countries will be considered the same as U.S. Army aviators and will be required to pass a class II flight medical examination and possess a dental panorex. See paragraph 8–20*b* for additional medical screening information.

e. A U.S. Army aviation medical examination will be given to IMS selected for pilot training by a qualified U.S. Army flight surgeon, U.S. Air Force flight surgeon, or U.S. Navy flight surgeon before the IMS departs from their home area. If the country does not have a U.S. Armed Forces aviation medical officer, the IMS candidate, upon approval of the Security Cooperation Organization, will report to the closest U.S. Armed Forces flight surgeon for examination. The Security Cooperation Organization will issue the ITO and fund cite. The predeparture medical examination will be performed as early as possible to prevent cancellation of training because of physical non-qualification. The examining officer will determine the individual's physical qualification for the flying course. Requests for waivers will be sent to the Dean, U.S. Army School of Aviation Medicine, (MCCS–HAO), Building 301, Fort Rucker, AL 36362–5377, for advice and recommendation (see para 8–11).

f. Flight physical examination records will be hand-carried by the IMS and will accompany the individual through-out aviation training. These records included but are not limited to DD Form 2808 (Report of Medical Examination) and DD Form 2807–1 (Report of Medical History) and a dental panorex.

g. The IMS undergoing physical re-examination in the United States prior to beginning flight training will be required to meet class II medical standards for flying (see AR 40–501).

h. An individual selected for flight training in CONUS must attend the Specialized English Training course at DLIELC before attending flight courses. The Security Cooperation Organization may request exceptions from SATFA only when the IMS has recent experience in an English language flight or navigational environment.

3–27. Senior professional military education

The IMS attend senior PME courses by invitation only. The commanders of combatant commands and the SATFA operations division will be informed by the Security Cooperation Organization on acceptance or declination of invitations. Prerequisites are located on the respective schools' Web pages. Each course is preceded by required preparatory courses.

a. Senior international military officers may participate in the International Fellows Program at the National War College and the Industrial College of the Armed Forces at the National Defense University, Fort McNair, Washington, DC. Invitations are issued by the CJCS.

b. Senior international Army officers may participate in the International Fellows Program at the Army War College (AWC), Carlisle Barracks, Pennsylvania. Invitations are issued by the Chief of Staff of the Army (CSA). The AWC offers a distance education course, also by invitation, in addition to the resident program. This course includes 2-week resident phases.

c. Mid-level international Army officers may participate in the ILE Program at the Command and General Staff College (CGSC), Fort Leavenworth, Kansas. Invitations are issued on behalf of the CSA. The school of advanced military studies at CGSC accepts a limited number of international officers. Desire for possible SAMS attendance must be expressed upon reporting to CGSC for ILE.

d. International noncommissioned officers (NCO) in grades equivalent to master sergeant or above may participate by invitation in the Sergeants Major Course at the U.S. Army USASMA, Fort Bliss, TX.

3–28. Western Hemisphere Institute for Security Cooperation

Western Hemisphere Institute for Security Cooperation is a DOD school operating under the executive agency of the U.S. Army at Fort Benning, Georgia. Instruction is primarily in the Spanish language, with selected courses offered in English.

a. The WHINSEC educates and trains rising civilian, military and law enforcement leaders from throughout the Western Hemisphere. Its goals explicitly include strengthening democracy, instilling a respect for the rule of law and honoring human rights. It educates an array of military and civilian students to solve regional problems, including peacefully resolving border conflicts; fighting terrorism, the illegal drug trade and organized crime; responding to natural disasters; and supporting peacekeeping efforts.

b. The WHINSEC offers an ILE course (in Spanish) that is equivalent to the course at CGSC, Fort Leavenworth, Kansas.

c. Additional information on WHINSEC is provided in appendix B of this regulation.

3–29. On-the-job training and observer training

a. In OJT the IMS learns by actually doing a specific task. In OBT the IMS trains beside U.S. personnel and learns by observation. Neither escorts nor interpreters are authorized for this training.

b. Current assets at U.S. Army training activities and units often prevent offering OJT or OBT. Training should be requested only when completely justified as a definite requirement to accomplish the country training goals. It will not be used to acquire minimum training time to satisfy SAMM requirements or country regulations.

c. Neither OJT nor OBT at HQDA or major Army commands is authorized.

d. The OJT and OBT will normally be conducted on an unclassified basis. If classified information is to be disclosed during the training, SATFA must be provided a detailed narrative of the information in advance of the proposed training so that disclosure authority can be requested in accordance with AR 380–10.

e. Activities should use the standard weekly OJT or OBT rates provided by SATFA unless actual costs are captured and exceed those rates. Training for any portion of a week will be charged this full weekly rate (for example, OJT lasting 4 weeks and 3 days will be charged for 5 weeks at the standard rate).

f. OJT and OBT training with Army National Guard of the United States and U.S. Army Reserve units will be conducted under normal SC training (for example, IMET, FMS) programs.

g. If OJT is requested at a Forces Command (FORSCOM) installation or a unit, HQ, FORSCOM requires that the request be submitted at least 120 days prior to the start of the desired OJT or OBT. Requests for OJT received after the 120 day cutoff may be rejected.

3–30. Limitations of on-the-job training and observer training

Both OJT and OBT may be provided to IMS at CONUS Army installations under the following conditions:

a. On-the-job-training.

(1) The IMS is scheduled to attend two or more courses at the same school with an interval of more than 5 working days between the end of one course and the beginning of the next. The type of training to be furnished will be decided by the school commandant.

(2) The IMS is scheduled to attend two or more courses at separate Service schools with an interval between schools of more than 5 working days, exclusive of processing and travel time. In this scenario, school commandant at the losing school will conduct OJT before the IMS travels to the gaining school.

(3) The IMS is removed from classroom instruction during classified portions of courses because access to the classified information has not been granted. The type of training to be furnished will be decided by the school commandant.

(4) The IMS requires OJT to develop a specific skill for which training was not covered during the formal course of instruction. This training must be directly related to home country duty assignment, must be planned in advance, and must be included in the country's training program. Detailed requirements for the training which include specific areas of interest and type of materiel used by country (if applicable) will be furnished in advance by the Security Cooperation Organization to the country program manager who forwards to the school commandant to determine capability to execute requested OJT unless training with a FORSCOM unit is desired (see para 3–29g).

(5) The OJT will not exceed 2 weeks except when strong justification is furnished by the country and approved by Director, SATFA and the school commandant.

(6) Requests for unprogrammed OJT will be forwarded by the Security Cooperation Organization to SATFA country program manager NLT 120 days before requested start date. Requests will include the information contained in figure 3–2.

b. Observer training.

(1) The OBT will be authorized only when no course covering the desired training is available. The duration will be determined by the school commandant as to how long it will take to cover stated training objectives. Continental United States OBT normally will be scheduled for a minimum of 2 weeks and not more than 6 months.

(2) The OBT will be planned in advance and included in the country's training program. Detailed requirements for training and specific areas of interest will be furnished, as outlined in figure 3–2.

(3) Requests for unprogrammed OBT will be forwarded by the Security Cooperation Organization to SATFA country program manager NLT 120 days before requested start date.

3–31. Administration of on-the-job training and observer training

a. The OJT or OBT programmed according to paragraph 3–27 will be included in the basic ITO (see fig 9–2).

b. The OJT or OBT included in the ITO, but not requested according to procedures in paragraph 3–27, will not be arranged.

c. The OJT or OBT will not be scheduled at CONUS schools, installations, and units during the winter holidays. This period, commonly known as Exodus, is usually the last 2 weeks of December through the New Year's Day holiday.

d. Requests for medical OBT will be accompanied by one copy of the complete biographical data for each IMS and will include specific data as follows:

(1) Prior training, including all medical schools and hospitals where training was received.

(2) Actual professional experience to include past, current, or future positions.

(3) English language proficiency, both written and oral.

(4) Other pertinent available data and any medical certifications and affiliations.

e. Medical internships, residencies, and fellowships are not available in the United States.

f. The OJT and OBT at overseas schools and installations will be provided according to the policies established by the commanders of the commanders of combatant commands.

g. For those IMS attending OBT, prior exposure to the Field Studies Program might be nonexistent or they may have already fully participated in the program. Regardless of level of Field Studies Program exposure, more emphasis should be placed on the specific type of technical training for which they have been programmed. However, in the off-duty time available, IMS will be encouraged to participate in available Field Studies Program events.

3–32. Contractor provided training

a. Specific training may only be available by agencies or civilian (contract) companies outside the military training base. This training may be provided to IMS by requesting the training through SATFA country program manager provided there is an existing USASAC contract vehicle in place. It is programmed and students placed on an ITO.

b. Enough lead time must be given USASAC to establish administrative information such as prices for the training to be included in the Training Military Articles and Service List. Security Cooperation Organization should be aware of available student life support. Many contractor locations do not have IMSO support, VOQ/VEQ or installation transportation; therefore students must arrive with sufficient funds (TLA if applicable) to sustain them during the training period.

3–33. Distributed learning

a. The IMS may take DL courses offered by the U.S. Army and other agencies. In pure DL courses, IMS may access course material from their home countries via internet or CDs. The IMS are screened and vetted in the same manner as IMS coming to CONUS for training. Many resident courses require a DL module or phase to be completed prior to enrolling in the resident course. The IMS students will take the DL portion in residence as a stand alone phase prior to joining the principal resident course. This phase will be scheduled and programmed like other prerequisite courses. The IMSO will coordinate efforts for conducting this training for IMS in residence. Also offered are hybrid courses in which the students take a portion of the course as DL at their home station and one or more resident sessions at a U.S. location.

b. The IMET funding may not be used for home station DL instruction unless a waiver is granted by DSCA. Security Cooperation Organization should forward request for waiver to DSCA for action with a copy furnished to SATFA country program manager. All DL students will be programmed and tracked like other students that are training in CONUS.

3–34. Training literature

a. The Army Publishing Directorate is the Army POC for requisitioning all DA-approved paper and CD–ROM publications and forms. Electronic training publications may be found on the Army Doctrinal and Training Digital Library on the Internet. This site is available at www.apd.army.mil.

b. The Commander, USASAC, is the Army POC for requisitioning training aids, devices, and equipment.

3–35. Programming cycle

a. Security cooperation officer or commanders of combatant command. The Security Cooperation Organization will submit their commanders of combatant commands-approved annual training programs to SATFA and other agencies as directed by the published suspense date.

b. Security Assistance Training Field Activity. The SATFA will request training seats from TRADOC, other MSCs, DOD Schools, and Services as soon as the school schedules and seat availability are published.

c. Senior professional military education.

(1) The SATFA will allocate spaces to the Security Cooperation Organization as soon as they are obtained, provided an invitation has been extended and country has accepted. Security Cooperation Organization will accept or decline invitation to extending agency with copy furnished to SATFA country program manager. Once country has accepted invitation and SATFA country program manager is notified, training will be programmed in the STL. Acceptance or declination messages must include—

(a) The SCETP program vehicle, that is, IMET, FMS, Counterterrorism Fellowship Program, and so forth.

(b) The Training Military Articles and Service List ID.

(c) Course title.

(d) Other information as directed by SATFA.

(2) When a program change is required, the Security Cooperation Organization should send an electronic mail message or fax to SATFA (ATTG–TRI–SR) with an information copy to the commanders of combatant commands and to DA for AWC, CGSC, and USASMA. When a program change is required for NDU, the Security Cooperation Organization should send an electronic mail message or fax directly to National Defense University (NDU) International Student Management Office. Since quotas are much more difficult to obtain after the initial distribution, Security Cooperation Organization should keep declinations and changes to a minimum.

d. Data on confirmed and projected IMS load for current and future FYs are available from STL reports on the IMSO Web. IMSO will provide copies of STL reports to installation resource management personnel to facilitate budget projection, submit earnings to SATFA, and track actual execution.

e. Training requirements are considered to be "confirmed" when dates have been in the STL for a period of at least 30 days.

f. The SATFA will be notified of the cancellation of programmed CONUS training a minimum of 61 days before the class start date to avoid application of a forfeiture charge. It will also identify the WCN, FMS case designator (if applicable), and courses being canceled by starting dates. If medical training is involved, the Commander, U.S. Army Medical Department Center and School (AMEDDC&S) will be included. Forfeiture charges do not apply to training programmed in the STL less than 30 days unless confirmed in writing by the Security Cooperation Organization.

3–36. Letter of offer and acceptance functions

a. The FMS Control Division of DSCA will submit FMS cases to Congress, as required. No implementing agency is authorized to release LOA without DSCA countersignature review and approval.

b. The SATFA provides FMS case load data that results in an initial draft of LOAs for CONUS training and prepares LOA for CONUS training and CONUS-furnished security assistance teams, obtaining any additional necessary data from the training agency, if other than TRADOC, or from SATMO in the case of security assistance team cases.

(1) The SATFA maintains the LOA training case designator file.

(2) The SATFA assigns case designators for all Army FMS training cases to include those prepared overseas. (Designators consist of three letters starting with the letter "O" in alphabetic sequence; for example, OAA, OAB ... OBA, OBB ... OCA, OCB.) Once a case designator is assigned and entered into the DSCA 1200 system, it is important that SATFA be notified of any later cancellation of the case, so that it may be transferred to an inactive or canceled status.

(3) The SATFA provides LOAs, amendments and modifications load data and related forms for CONUS training and OCONUS training teams furnished from CONUS sources by the U.S. Army.

(4) Following SATFA receipt of an implemented FMS case, obligational authority-customer order is issued to each CONUS school and/or SATMO.

(5) SATFA obtains from each CONUS school or training activity all required bills, using SF 1080 (Voucher for Reimbursement for Expenditures on Official Business), supported by copies of each IMS's ITO or other obligating documents.

(6) Reimburse each CONUS school or training installation or command for training and services. No training may occur on an FMS case without sufficient funds available in the case to reimburse the training school or activity.

(7) The FMS purchaser/customer will forward the required data to SATFA to facilitate preparation of the LOA. SATFA will input case data and forward it to the Case Writing Division for further case writing and counter signature review/approval before release to the country according to prescribed procedures.

3–37. Blanket order foreign military cases

a. Training cases will normally be prepared as BO. Defined-line training cases can be written, but should be kept to a minimum because of inherent administrative difficulties.

b. The BO FMS cases are prepared in an estimated dollar amount. (When the country accepts a BO FMS case and deposits funds and DFAS issues the obligation authority, execution of the program is authorized. As the training program develops, SATFA will forward the STL to the Security Cooperation Organization.)

c. The following policies and procedures govern BO FMS cases:

(1) The earliest training date on a BO case should be far enough in the future to allow implementation of the case prior to the first training report date. Exceptions will be properly coordinated by SATFA among involved agencies.

(2) The BO FMS cases are normally prepared in one of two ways.

(a) For a dollar amount specified by the country, with the detailed list of required courses to be developed as required throughout the life of the case.

(b) For a dollar amount or a specific time period in excess of the training requirement known at the time of preparation.

Section V
Department of the Navy (U.S. Navy, U.S. Marine Corps, and U.S. Coast Guard)

3–38. Acceptance of training

When quotas are confirmed, dates will appear in the Security Assistance Network IMSO and Security Cooperation Organization Training Web. If no program changes are requested by the Security Cooperation Organization, training dates are considered to be accepted. Naval Education and Training Security Assistance Field Activity will provide ITO authority by a formal message for each WCN under IMET and Counterterrorism Fellowship Program. Naval Education and Training Security Assistance Field Activity will provide ITO authority by formal message for all training under an FMS case at the time the case is implemented.

3–39. Programming training under foreign military sales

a. Annual FMS training requirements should be submitted at the commanders of combatant commands annual Security Cooperation Education and Training Working Group; however, FMS training may also be arranged directly between the Washington, DC, country representative and Navy IPO/Naval Education and Training Security Assistance Field Activity, or directly between the Security Cooperation Organization and Navy IPO/Naval Education and Training Security Assistance Field Activity. Requests for FMS training for USMC training should be submitted at the commanders of combatant commands annual Security Cooperation Education and Training Working Group; however, they requests may be forwarded directly to CG, Security Cooperation Education and Training Center MCCDC. Such requests are subsequently coordinated with Navy IPO and Naval Education and Training Security Assistance Field Activity for support in the preparation or management of the required FMS training case. USCG (G–CI) will act as central authority for planning and programming all USCG training. Policy and procedural differences will exist for Coast Guard training with regard to OJT, Family members, ship transfers, and so forth. USCG requests are also coordinated with Navy IPO and Naval Education and Training Security Assistance Field Activity for support in the preparation or management of the required FMS training case.

b. Once a case has been signed and the purchaser has submitted any required initial deposit the implementing agency will take action to implement the case. The FMS case must be implemented in all applicable data systems (for example, DSAMS, Defense Integrated Financial System, DSCA 1200 System, and the MILDEP legacy systems before case execution occurs. Naval Education and Training Security Assistance Field Activity will send a message to the Security Cooperation Organization authorizing ITO issuance under the new case.

3–40. Course prerequisites and standards

The Security Cooperation Organization must ensure students meet prerequisites for all scheduled training. The prerequisites are often included in the course catalog for the providing Service and in the Training Military Articles and

Service List. Naval aviation, diving, swimming, explosive ordnance disposal, mountain warfare and reconnaissance training are considered high-risk courses and candidates must be prescreened to meet specific physical and medical requirements prior to enrollment. All international students must have at least the minimum ECL required for the course of instruction and take Specialized English Training if required (unless country is exempt). Information to prepare the students prior to enrollment in each unique area can be found in the U.S. Navy International Training & Education Catalog, the USMC Desktop Guide and the USCG International Training Handbook. See also the DON section of chapter 8.

3–41. Military information/controlled unclassified information
The SECNAVINST 5510.34A requires a disclosure determination by Navy IPO prior to foreign participation in all classified courses. This must be done before training can be programmed. Classified training is provided on a need-to-know-basis only. All requests for courses not previously attended by the country must include justification; this is, explanation of circumstances facts supporting the request. See chapter 10, paragraph 10–39 for further information.

3–42. Additional training requests for International military student after arrival in the United States
Training for IMS at DON installations should be scheduled well in advance to assure proper programming. This assures that the desired training is available when required. For purposes of this regulation and the administration of students, the term "CONUS" includes U.S. Navy and U.S. Marine Corps schools in Hawaii, unless otherwise specified.

a. Occasionally, situations arise where changes in programmed training are necessary. Every attempt must be made to keep these to a minimum and to reduce their impact. The addition of extra lines of training to that initially scheduled for an IMS must have the concurrence of the IMS government, the Security Cooperation Organization, the commanders of combatant commands, Navy IPO, and either Naval Education and Training Security Assistance Field Activity for Navy training, CG, SCETC MCCDC for USMC training, or Coast Guard Headquarters, International Affairs (G–CI) for USCG training. If the IMS is under the sponsorship of another Service, approval must also be obtained from that Military Service security cooperation activity.

b. Requests by IMS for additional training should be discouraged. IMS will be advised that additional training should be requested through their own military Service, via their naval or military attaché or other official representative, a minimum of 60 days before completion of the current training course.

3–43. Training at nonmilitary institutions
This training for IMET/CT IMS is discouraged; however if circumstances dictate and training is not available from U.S. military facilities, training may be authorized with prior approval by DSCA. If a country eligible for FMS training only desires training at a civilian institution, this training can be negotiated directly by the country with the civilian institution concerned or on a case-by-case basis training can be funded using an FMS LOA. In these cases, issuance of ITO will be authorized, as training will be within the purview of the DON SCETP.

3–44. Contracting for foreign military sale training
In fulfillment of DON responsibilities to provide training for IMS in connection with the sale of equipment, weapons systems, or services, situations will arise that preclude training in DON schools as they are presently organized. Contractor services may have to be obtained to provide the desired training.

a. When international training is conducted in Naval Education Training Center schools but requirements cannot be met because of a shortage of instructors, Naval Education Training Center is responsible through the appropriate Navy Field Procurement Activity for contracting civilian instructors. Naval Education Training Center will then prepare the statement of work and will monitor performance of the contractor.

b. When international training is conducted in Naval Education Training Center schools but requirements cannot be met because of limited capacity, availability of training equipment, or national disclosure policy, Naval Education Training Center is responsible through the proper Navy Field Procurement Activity for contracting training services to be conducted at a contractor's site. Naval Education Training Center will then prepare the statement of work and monitor performance of the contractor.

c. When a Navy or Marine Corps SYSCOM is adding new equipment or systems to the U.S. Fleet or Marine Force, or is procuring new equipment peculiar to the international customer (non Service-approved or supported by the DON system), the SYSCOM is responsible for contracting factory training.

3–45. Professional military education
a. Naval Command College.
(1) The Naval Command College is a graduate-level course for senior naval officers of allied and friendly nations. It provides 10 months of intensive study in Strategy and Policy, National Security Decision Making and International Maritime Operations in conjunction with the College of Naval Warfare at the Naval War College in Newport, Rhode Island. Class size is limited to encourage personal interaction with classmates. For this reason, CNO controls the frequency of invitations to any given country to ensure mix of larger and smaller navies, thus providing the optimum avenue for the exchange of maritime concepts. CNO will issue invitations by message via the Security Cooperation

Organization. Naval Education and Training Security Assistance Field Activity will confirm quotas after receipt of formal acceptance by message via the Security Cooperation Organization. Candidates should hold the rank of Commander or Captain U.S. Navy equivalent (O–5/O–6); have ECL of 80 or higher, and have demonstrated high leadership and academic potential during career thus far. The objectives of the Naval Command College are to—

(a) Develop mutual perspectives of international situations among allied and friendly navies, and between those navies, and the U.S. Navy.

(b) To provide instruction, at the post-graduate level, for those senior officer of allied and friendly navies who have shown the clear potential to be chiefs of their services.

(c) To enrich the academic environment of the Naval War College.

(d) To provide an environment which showcases U.S. culture, institutions, and values.

(2) Prerequisites for candidates for Naval Command College should—

(a) Hold the rank of commander or captain U.S. Navy equivalent. Waivers will not be granted.

(b) Score 80 or higher on the in-country screening ECL tests unless exempt by other statutes. Waivers will not be granted.

(c) Have demonstrated high leadership and academic potential during career thus far.

(d) Have been extended a personal invitation by CNO via appropriate in-country Service chief. No alternate invitation procedures are acceptable.

b. *Naval Staff College* The Naval Staff College is a graduate level international program, designed for mid-career naval officers, which is vital in expanding understanding and cooperation among the world's navies. As coalition forces are increasingly summoned to respond to conflicts and promote peace around the world, the role of Naval Staff College gains significance. The Naval War College's academic departments have adapted course studies to reflect the mission confronting the naval forces of today. For example, the course incorporates studies of security assistance, combating terrorism, insurgency and counterinsurgency, low intensity conflict, multilateral peacekeeping, human rights, and drug control and interdiction. The course provides its students who are the future leaders in their respective navies with a unique and unmatched opportunity to come together as a team to gain a respect and appreciation of other cultures, and provides a place for individual professional study in order to realize each student's potential. CNO will issue invitations by message. Naval Education and Training Security Assistance Field Activity will confirm quotas after receipt of formal acceptance by the Security Cooperation Organization.

(1) The Naval Staff College 10-month course (Naval Staff College –10) is conducted annually in the FY 4th quarter, commencing in July, and is open to a maximum of 20 Naval, Coast Guard, or Maritime Service officers, grades 0–3 and 0–4 (senior Lieutenants and Lieutenant Commanders). This program is a separate resident college within the U.S. Naval War College; however, the academic programs of Naval Staff College –10 and its U.S. counterpart, the College of Naval Command and Staff, are almost identical insofar as disclosure restrictions allow. Students pursue the prescribed studies over three trimesters in Strategy and Policy, National Security Decisionmaking, and Joint Military Operations. They follow the same basic schedule and are integrated into the seminars and lectures of their U.S. counterparts. On an optional basis they may participate in the Electives Program during two trimesters. Their studies differ from their U.S. counterparts in the addition of a preliminary orientation study, a course in Operational Law conducted during one trimester, and a series of Curriculum field trip/Informational Program Visits designed to familiarize them with U.S. Navy organization, methods, and doctrines, as well as the government, economy, culture and geography of the United States.

(2) The Naval Staff College five and one-half month course is conducted annually in the FY 2nd quarter, commencing in January, and is open to a maximum of 48 Naval, Coast Guard or Maritime Service officers, grades O–3 and O–4 (senior Lieutenants and Lieutenant Commanders). The program is a condensed version of the 10-month U.S. College of Naval Command and Staff/Naval Staff College 10-month programs.

c. *United States Marine Corps Command and Staff College.* The USMC Command and Staff College is an intermediate professional military education course designed to prepare military officers for command and staff duties with Marine air - ground task force with emphasis on amphibious operations, and for duty assignments with joint and combined organizations. The intent of the curriculum is to provide officers with an understanding of the interrelation of the strategic, operational and tactical levels of war within a joint and/or a combined environment. Attendance at this course is by invitation of the Commandant of the Marine Corps. This course is for officers in the rank of O–4. Waivers may be requested for officers in the rank of O–5. Waivers will not be provided for the rank of O–6. The ECL for this course is 80, Specialized English Training Advised. Duration is 47 weeks and dependents are encouraged to accompany IMS.

d. *Joint Forces Staff College.* The Joint Forces Staff College is a joint school under the National Defense University and the Joint Chiefs of Staff. The Chief of Naval Operations is responsible for the operations and maintenance of the College facilities. The Joint Chiefs of Staff establishes student quotas; IMS quotas are administered by Naval Education and Training Security Assistance Field Activity. Courses are offered in joint and combined organization, planning and operations, and in related aspects of national and international security, to enhance the preparation of selected military officers for duty in all echelons of joint and combined commands. Entrance requirements for the Intermediate Phase II Joint and Combined staff Officers School are: O–4/O–5 equivalent, ECL 85 Specialized English

Training advised; graduate of resident U.S. intermediate level Service college or PME Phase I equivalent program approved by JCS. Requests for programming should be directed to Naval Education and Training Security Assistance Field Activity. The foreign country must then send a biography giving the background of the individual selected. If the individual meets the entrance requirements, Naval Education and Training Security Assistance Field Activity will confirm the quota. IMS will always be scheduled for a one week Joint Transition Course prior to the Joint Forces Staff College.

e. Naval Postgraduate School. The NPS, founded in 1909, is a fully accredited university offering over 35 unique academic masters curricula to military and civilian members of the Department of Defense and allies around the world. These graduate level programs are focused on increasing the combat effectiveness of U.S. and allied armed forces, and fully support the unique needs and interests of the defense establishment. All programs contain a military application and are not duplicated at civilian colleges and universities. NPS confers Master's, Engineer's, or Doctorate degrees upon qualified graduates of the school, subject to U.S. Navy regulations and accreditation criteria. The academic programs are administered through a unique organization composed of curricular offices and academic departments. Each officer student is assigned to a military programs officer for military counseling and supervision, and an academic associate for academic counseling. Naval Education and Training Security Assistance Field Activity will program a country's desired courses under the proper FMS or IMET Program. Security Cooperation Organization must then forward candidate's transcripts and Test of English as a Foreign Language (TOEFL) results (if candidate is from a non-English speaking country) directly to the NPS for evaluation. Quotas will be confirmed by Naval Education and Training Security Assistance Field Activity after review and acceptance by NPS.

f. U.S. Marine Corps Expeditionary Warfare School. The Expeditionary Warfare School is a career-level professional military education school. Expeditionary Warfare School prepares Captains (O–3) to function as commanders and staff officers at the appropriate level of the Operating Forces by providing instruction emphasis on command and control, combined arms operations, warfighting skills, tactical decisionmaking, Marine air - ground task force expeditionary operations, and naval operations. This course is for officers in the rank of O–3. Rank waivers may be requested for the rank of O–4. The ECL for this course is 80, Specialized English Training Advised. Duration is 42 weeks and dependents are encouraged to accompany IMS.

g. U.S. Marine Corps School of Advanced Warfighting. The School of Advanced Warfighting is a graduate level, military education tailored to amplify and complement the comprehensive foundations in Warfighting experienced during the 47-week Command and Staff College curriculum for officers in the rank of O–4/O–5. This follow-on course for selected graduates of the CSC focuses on the link between Warfighting and Warplanning, or preparation for war. Utilizing a dynamic curriculum and an active methodology, School of Advanced Warfighting prepares its students for significant roles in the future preparation of armed forces for success in war, should the nation require that end. The course is held at the Marine Corps University. Participation in School of Advanced Warfighting is by invitation extended to the specific individual based on performance in the USMC Command and Staff College, or an equivalent course of instruction. The ECL for this course is 80, Specialized English Training Advised. Duration is 48 weeks and dependents are encouraged to accompany IMS.

3–46. Accompaniment by dependents

a. Although the practice of IMS bringing their dependents to CONUS while attending courses is generally not encouraged, they are encouraged to bring their dependents while attending the following courses:

(1) Naval Command College.

(2) Naval Staff College for International Officers.

(3) Marine Corps Command and Staff College.

(4) Marine Corps Expeditionary Warfare School.

(5) School of Advanced Warfighting (USMC).

(6) Long-term resident postgraduate courses at NPS (excludes those in the curriculum at Defense Resources Management Institute (DRMI).

(7) NOTE: Joint Forces Staff College (while PME) does NOT encourage dependents.

b. The IMET IMS bringing their dependents to the courses in paragraphs *a*(1) through (6), above, will receive the full IMET living allowance allowable in accordance with the Joint Travel Regulation (JTR); for example, that living allowance based on the non-availability of government quarters and messing facilities.

3–47. Visiting individuals or units

In the absence of statutory or other legal authority to the contrary, any training (or other Service) provided foreign nationals or units (including air crews, explosive ordnance disposal units, sea, air, land teams, and so forth) visiting DON activities will be subject to the AECA or the FAA, as applicable. SECNAVINST 5510.34A provides details on approval procedures for visits.

3–48. Ship transfer, overhaul, and refresher training

Subject to appropriate congressional approval or notification, it is the policy of the U.S. Navy to transfer ships under

SC to eligible foreign governments or international organizations with a minimum use of U.S. Navy personnel. An adequate degree of training in general operational readiness is expected. Training of crews incident to the transfer of a U.S. Navy ship by sale, grant, lease, or loan to the foreign government is coordinated by Navy IPO under the SC program.

a. Guidelines. Guidelines for disclosure of CMI or CUI relating to international military training procedures incident to the transfer of sale, loan, lease, or grant of ships under SCETP are set forth in SECNAVINST 5510.34A. The SECNAVINST 4900.48 provides information and instruction pertinent to implementing the transfer of U.S. Navy ships to foreign governments.

b. Ship overhaul training. When the Security Cooperation Organization requests an overhaul for a foreign naval vessel, it will also prepare, as a portion of the basic program, a request for suitable training to be given to the crew of the foreign naval vessel during the overhaul period.

c. Classified material related to ship turnover. The release of classified material in connection with a ship turnover will be processed according to SECNAVINST 5510.34A.

d. Authorization for transfer crew training. All requests for foreign transfer crew training, classified or unclassified, will be submitted through the chain of command to Navy IPO, with copy to the cognizant offices, for determination of feasibility. Upon receipt of approval, it is the responsibility of the requester to ensure that such training, if classified, is authorized by competent authority. This can be accomplished as follows:

(1) When it has been positively established that the training uses no classified information other than those manuals or publications that have been authorized for release in conjunction with turnover of the ship, U.S. Navy commands may provide ship transfer crew training without additional training disclosure authorization from higher authority. If any doubt exists, a request for authorization will be submitted to Navy IPO with a list of classified material proposed for release. SECNAVINST 5510.34A applies.

(2) If classified information exceeds that turned over with the ship, disclosure authorization must be requested from higher authority as follows:

(a) If the training is to be accomplished at U.S. Navy commands or activities subordinate to the Fleet the disclosure authorization should be requested from the pertinent Fleet who has authority to authorize disclosure according to SECNAVINST 5510.34A.

(b) All other cases must be submitted to Navy IPO for disclosure authorization.

(c) All training, classified or unclassified, to be conducted in a naval shipyard requires the prior approval of Commander, Naval Sea Systems Command.

(3) In certain instances, a country or international organization will require refresher-type training in which its own ships are used. Some of this training involves ships built in the U.S. for a foreign government or international organization or transferred under the SC Program. In almost all instances, the ship has U.S. equipment in varying quantities. Security Cooperation Organization desiring this type of training for a country should follow the procedures below:

(a) As far in advance as possible, submit total requirements to Navy IPO, with information copies to all concerned and with minimum distribution being, commanders of combatant commands, COMFLTFORCOM/COMPACFLT, Naval Education and Training Security Assistance Field Activity, Commander, Naval Supply Systems Command, Commander, Naval Sea Systems Command, Commander, Naval Air Systems Command, and all others involved.

(b) These requirements will be in as complete detail as possible. The types of training desired, length of training, dates of commencement and termination, and method of funding formal training courses envisioned for members of the crew must be provided. MTT or technical assistance requirements for such things as weapons systems and communications systems, and level of competence of the crew, must be addressed.

(c) Navy IPO will task the appropriate command to provide feasibility of the training requested, recommendations as to alternate dates and training arrangements, and cost of the training. Navy IPO will authorize direct liaison as appropriate.

(d) The selected command may recommend that minimum safety-related training (for example, fire fighting and damage control) be conducted before underway training to provide assurance of safety of observers.

(e) Countries or international organizations eligible for IMET may, if they deem feasible, program such training using IMET funds, provided that such program is submitted via the commanders of combatant commands according to existing directives. An LOA will be prepared for countries using FMS funds to cover the cost of the training cruise. In some instances, a training cruise may involve the issuance of both material and training LOA, or may provide for the training as a line item in a material LOA. Navy IPO will be the focal point for all queries concerning the training cruise. Countries and or international organizations should be thoroughly briefed by the Security Cooperation Organization on all points contained in the LOA.

(f) It is usually helpful to all concerned if a preliminary meeting is convened at which the country or international organization and U.S. representatives have the opportunity to discuss in detail the aspects of the training cruise.

3–49. On-the-job training or observership training
OJT or observership training is conducted on a planned program of supervised instruction devoted to practical

application of previously achieved skills usually related to a formal course of instruction. All requests for OJT or observership must include specific objectives.

a. OJT or observership with USN shore activities—

(1) Programmed OJT or observership will normally supplement formal training received at a school. This training will be planned in advance in the country's training program. It will include detailed requirements for training in specific areas of interest and on types of material used by the country concerned. OJT or observership training conducted independently and not in conjunction with formal courses of instruction will be authorized in CONUS only when no course covering the desired training is available. Detailed objectives must be submitted at the time of the initial request.

(2) Medical and dental observation must include specific training objectives with the submission. Naval Education and Training Security Assistance Field Activity will forward the objectives to Bureau of Medicine and Surgery (BUMED) for details as to convening dates and location. Such observership will normally be scheduled for periods of either 12 or 26 weeks. Certain observer training explicitly excludes "hands-on" training. For example, IMS enrolled under medical and dental observer Training are prohibited from hands-on patient care.

(3) OJT or observership on board U.S. installations, afloat or ashore, regardless of duration, is fully reimbursable, either from IMET or FMS funds.

(4) OJT or observership provided to a U.S. Navy employee (direct or indirect hire, regardless of nationality or location) will be paid from MILDEP appropriate funds and is not part of the SCETP.

(5) Any training provided to an IMS that results in identifiable expenses to the USG is fully reimbursable. In some instances these expenses may be minimal, such as OJT or observership for an FMS IMS aboard a fleet unit when the only identifiable expense is the dedicated Service of U.S. military personnel or transportation of an IMET IMS to and from a unit using U.S. resources. Regardless of the amount, identifiable expenses must be recouped.

b. OJT or observership with fleet units.

(1) Requests for OJT or observership aboard COMSIXTHFLT units will be coordinated directly by the Security Cooperation Organization with COMUSNAVEUR, with an information copy to the commanders of combatant commands, Naval Education and Training Security Assistance Field Activity, and others, as appropriate.

(2) Requests for OJT or observership aboard COMSEVENTHFLT units will be coordinated directly by the Security Cooperation Organization with COMPACFLT, with an information copy to the commanders of combatant commands, Naval Education and Training Security Assistance Field Activity, and others, as appropriate.

(3) Requests for OJT or observership aboard fleet units other than specified in paragraphs (1) and (2), above, will be directed to Naval Education and Training Security Assistance Field Activity, with an information copy to the cognizant combatant command and all concerned.

(4) As indicated in paragraph *a*(1) above, OJT or observership will normally be included in the country's planned FY training program. Requests submitted after the Security Cooperation Education and Training Working Group will be directed to Naval Education and Training Security Assistance Field Activity, with an information copy to the appropriate U.S. Navy Command. Naval Education and Training Security Assistance Field Activity will coordinate with the appropriate U.S. Navy command to determine feasibility and cost. An update to the country program will be made if required.

c. OJT or observership with Marine Corps units or activities—

(1) Requests for OJT or observership with Marine Corps units or activities should be submitted to CG, Security Cooperation Education and Training Center MCCDC with the initial request for training. Programmed OJT or observership will normally supplement formal training received at a Marine Corps school. Marine Corps OJT or observership will not be scheduled unless the IMS has completed adequate Marine Corps or Marine Corps-related training prior to enrollment in OJT or observership.

(2) Requests for OJT or observership submitted after the training program management review must be received by CG, Security Cooperation Education and Training Center MCCDC not later than 90 days prior to the proposed commencement of training.

(3) The USMC OJT or observership training must be scheduled for a minimum duration of 1 week. No more than three OJT or observership training periods can be scheduled consecutively.

(4) Country must provide specific training objectives.

3–50. Distributive/distance learning

Many courses have transitioned, or will be converted, from traditional classroom delivery methods to more efficient and effective distance learning (DL) formats that include the Internet or an Intranet, CD–ROM, and DVD. The training location may be at the traditional training location, or at a Distance Learning Center. MASL notes will reflect the most current course delivery method as well as the course location. IMET IMS may attend DL courses in CONUS, but will require DSCA waiver for OCONUS delivery. FMS IMS may attend DL courses in CONUS or OCONUS. DL courses delivered OCONUS will have a "P4" MASL per DSCA guidance.

a. Programming. The DL courses may be requested and programmed like a traditional classroom course. However, Security Cooperation Organization should pay special attention to the following:

(1) *English comprehension level.* The IMS must meet the established ECL for all DL courses. In fact, English *reading comprehension* is vital to successful completion of DL courses.

(2) *Prerequisite basic computer skills.* The IMS must be proficient in basic computer and internet navigation skills, including keyboard and mouse familiarization, start menu, minimize/maximize/close buttons, copy/cut and paste text, save and/or save as, print command, Web browser navigation. Management Information Systems (PDET002) is a prerequisite for all DL courses unless IMS has a requisite level of proficiency.

(3) *Minimum computer requirements for OCONUS courses.*

(a) An IBM-compatible PC which runs Windows 95/98/ME with 64 Mb RAM, or which runs Windows 2000/NT with 128Mb RAM.

(b) An internet connection of at least 56 Kb.

(c) Internet Explorer 4.0 or later.

(d) A 256-color monitor capable of a resolution of 800 x 600.

(e) A current version of Apple QuickTime and Adobe Acrobat Reader.

b. Navy designated point of contact. The Navy designated POC for DL registration will establish IMS access to authorized course(s) after proper ITO authorization. The IMSO at the traditional training site or at the Distance Learning Center will request IMS access by submitting IMS full name, foreign identification number, and date of birth to the Navy designated POC who will then proceed with the registration process.

c. Student administration If course is locally managed by a Facilitator or Instructor, all student administration functions will be performed at the training location. If course is delivered at a Distance Learning Center, the Navy designated POC will be responsible for the student administration functions. DL student administrative functions include the following tasks in the Navy's Learning Management System:

(1) Finding and moving learner from a waitlist to a roster.

(2) Assigning a "job" (content).

(3) Assigning a seat if tracking seats.

(4) Creating transcripts for any labs/tests that are not computer based training (CBT).

(5) Creating and/or editing transcripts for CBT under special circumstances.

(6) Verifying all content, labs, and tests required for curriculum completion are completed, and transcripts are in the system.

(7) Removing the seat assignment and job from learner.

(8) Dropping the learner from a roster and creating a roster transcript that indicates the number of days the learner was on the roster going through training.

d. Cancellation penalty. A cancellation penalty will be applied if course is cancelled after establishment of the IMS Learning Account.

3–51. Correspondence or self-study courses

The OSD policy precludes programming of correspondence of self-study courses under IMET. There is no objection; however, to programming this type of training under FMS, provided the established criteria for enrollment are met. The FMS case must be requested from Navy IPO. Classified correspondence or self-study courses are not available to IMS. Correspondence courses are available from Naval Education Training Center, Pensacola, FL; NPS, Monterey, CA; NAVWARCOL, Newport, RI; Marine Corps Institute, Washington, DC; and BUMED, Washington, DC. Catalogs listing courses in detail are available from the foregoing activities upon direct request. Direct liaison is authorized as necessary to obtain these publications.

a. Programming procedure.

(1) Requests for a correspondence or self-study course, once the particular course is determined, will be submitted to Naval Education and Training Security Assistance Field Activity (for all Navy courses) or to CG, Security Cooperation Education and Training Center MCCDC (for all USMC courses) with all available data to expedite processing. The Security Cooperation Organization or other official requester should use the appropriate MASL ID when programming or requesting these courses. The name and grade of the student, as well as a complete Army/Air Force Post Office (APO) mailing address, is required prior to shipment of any correspondence or self-study courses. Naval Education and Training Security Assistance Field Activity or CG, Security Cooperation Education and Training Center MCCDC, as applicable, will authorize the cognizant activity to provide the course to the country via the Security Cooperation Organization. Naval Education and Training Security Assistance Field Activity or CG, Security Cooperation Education and Training Center MCCDC will advise all concerned of the cost involved and the amount to be charged against the case. The request will be an integral part of the training program.

(2) A WCN will be assigned to each request. For Navy courses only, at the option of the Security Cooperation Organization or requesting country, a WCN may cover one course or a number of courses. This option is not available for USMC courses. As courses are ordered and provided, the appropriate case will be billed. The country will pay only for those courses received, as in the case of formal training courses.

(3) Naval Education and Training Security Assistance Field Activity or CG, Security Cooperation Education and

Training Center MCCDC is responsible for tracking this training as with other FMS training. Naval Education and Training Security Assistance Field Activity is responsible for all billing for this training.

b. Pricing. The Naval Education and Training Security Assistance Field Activity is responsible for coordinating course costs for correspondence and self-study courses. Each course will be assigned all appropriate course costs. In developing these prices, the cost of printed matter will be computed in addition to other appropriate factors. Billing and collecting procedures prescribed for FMS training will be used in connection with recovery costs for correspondence and self-study courses. These costs will be revised on an annual basis as part of the general MASL update. However, once these costs are established for a particular FY, they will remain unchanged for the duration of that year.

c. Self-study courses at NPS. It is advantageous to the NPS and to officer IMS entering its curricular programs to have completed graduate preparatory studies before entry. Self-study materials prepared in English can be made available on a loan basis to specific IMS who have an assigned entry date at the NPS. A Publication entitled "Catalogue of Off-Campus Self-Study Credit Courses," prepared by the Office of Continuing Education, Code 500, Naval Postgraduate School, Monterey, CA 93943–5000, is available upon request. Direct liaison is authorized between Security Cooperation Organization and the NPS for administrative queries concerning the courses available. For programming, however, the requests must be submitted to Naval Education and Training Security Assistance Field Activity. Any specific programming requests received by the NPS from an Security Cooperation Organization or foreign country will be referred to Naval Education and Training Security Assistance Field Activity for official processing.

d. Constraints Correspondence or self-study courses will not be provided to IMS (either military or civilian) unless they are officially requested by an appropriate representative from the customer country. Requests from individual IMS will be returned with a statement that only requests submitted through the Security Cooperation Organization will be honored and given consideration. Requests received by telephone will not be accepted.

e. Sales of course materials. Countries desiring to purchase correspondence or self-study course materials, but not for enrolling a trainee, will do so under current procedures involving the sale of material. These materials will be purchased through a direct requisitioning procedures case or through a material FMS case established specifically for this purpose. Questionable situations. In instances where a Security Cooperation Organization is doubtful as to how to proceed in a case involving the courses and materials discussed in paragraph *e*, above, Naval Education and Training Security Assistance Field Activity should be queried.

3–52. Commanding officer, Naval Small Craft Instruction and Technical Training School

Commanding officer, Naval Small Craft Instruction and Technical Training School operates a dedicated international U.S. Navy Service School, and will—

a. Foster increased levels of maritime security, professionalism and readiness in all Navy and Coast Guard Forces throughout the world through the SCETP by conducting formal courses and Mobile Training Teams in Spanish and/or English. Also provide translation services, if required, when conducting training in non English or Spanish speaking countries. Translate all materials used in training into the required language when conducting MTT.

b. Develop close working relationships with the USMC, USCG, and other governmental and nongovernmental organizations to support CNO guidance and national security policy, enhance homeland defense and improve maritime domain awareness.

c. Conduct international maritime security training and curricula development surveys.

d. Maintain liaison with Naval Education and Training Security Assistance Field Activity and Security Assistance Office staffs on host national training needs.

e. Administer a guest instructor program, to include USMC and USCG instructors.

f. Develop and conduct new courses and modify existing courses in response to user country needs. All such requests will be forwarded for approval to Naval Education and Training Security Assistance Field Activity via chain of command.

g. Appoint an IMSO to monitor and coordinate activities for IMS training, including implementation of the Field Studies Program.

Section VI
Department of the Air Force (Planning and Programming General)

3–53. Training standards

a. The IMS will attend classes with their USAF counterparts except for courses specifically established for them. The IMS enrolled in formal training courses will be required to achieve the same standards of proficiency established for USAF students as far as possible. Special training methods, individual attention, additional training time, and oral or practical tests may be employed to maintain class standards. Actions taken in this respect will be reported to the Air Force Security Assistance Training Squadron, info the appropriate air component command (U.S. Air Forces in Europe (USAFE)/PACAF/12AF) immediately by electrical transmission or AF Form 1761 (International Student Status Report), identifying the IMS country project and line number, WCN, and new graduation date.

b. Flying IMS may be held over one class when necessary to overcome either flying or academic deficiency. These IMS will be credited with the skill level equivalent to the average flying hours of the class to which they are being held over. When it becomes apparent that additional flying hours are required, the MAJCOM will advise the Air Force Security Assistance Training Squadron, with an information copy to SAF/Budget Management and Execution Security Assistance Division. Cost data will be identified, the Security Cooperation Organization/country advised, and the training line adjusted, as appropriate.

c. Physiological training provided by foreign countries can be recognized by HQ, USAF/SGPA on a case-by-case basis. Countries requesting evaluation of its physiological training must forward a request to the Air Force Security Assistance Training Squadron with full details of standards, course outline, altitude chamber training, and overall program.

d. Professional and technical IMS may be held over not to exceed 30 days when it appears reasonably certain that the additional training will enable them to complete the course successfully.

e. Proficiency advancement is used in instances when an IMS is fully qualified and can complete scheduled formal training, familiarization, or qualification in less than the scheduled time.

f. Holdover actions for CONUS IMS in excess of those authorized in d above are subject to prior approval from the Air Force Security Assistance Training Squadron, the Security Cooperation Organization, or country. All advancement and holdover sections will be reported to the Air Force Security Assistance Training Squadron as stated in paragraph *a*, above.

3–54. Military assistance articles and services list items
The training items listed in the military assistance articles and services list (MASL) are not necessarily restrictive. Full consideration will be given to providing other training when required, if requests are accompanied by justification and sufficient detail to identify the requirement when forwarded to the Air Force Security Assistance Training Squadron.

3–55. Classified training
Dates or availability of classified training will not be provided unless disclosure has been authorized through foreign disclosure channels.

3–56. International military student training
Interpreters will not normally be used to conduct USAF training, use of interpreters requires approval by SAF/IAPX.

3–57. United States Air Force training of non-Ministry of Defense personnel
The USAF training of non-MOD personnel will be according to the procedures in paragraph 3–4.

3–58. Contractor training
a. The Air Force Security Assistance Training Squadron is the focal point for all contractor-provided training whether in CONUS or in the territory of the purchaser. Assistance may be required from other major commands in preparing the SOW or the contracting process may be delegated to another major command when deemed appropriate. However, all requests for contractor-provided training will be forwarded to and monitored by the Air Force Security Assistance Training Squadron.

b. The P&A or LOA requests will be processed according to current guidance under AFMAN 16–101, DOD 7000. 14–R, Volume 15, and DOD supplement to part 25 of the Federal Acquisition Regulation. See figure 3–3 for the checklist for contractor (type 1) training.

c. Foreign military sales programs should be structured to utilize customer country's aircraft for contractor training. If necessary, acceleration of initial aircraft deliveries should be explored to meet early training requirements if delayed delivery to country is unacceptable.

3–59. Foreign military sales training programs
Eligible countries interested in USAF training which is not related to the provision of major defense equipment will forward their request for P&A or LOA to the Air Force Security Assistance Training Squadron, with information copy to the appropriate SAF/International Affairs regional division. Usually, such requests are for P&A for a certain course or a number of courses for a number of IMS.

3–60. Implementation of Foreign military sales training cases
Upon receipt of the signed LOA, the Air Force Security Assistance Training Squadron prepares an Implementation Program Directive to direct the appropriate commands to implement the FMS training case. The International Program Directive is issued by message or letter.

a. The Air Force Security Assistance Training Squadron receives obligation or expenditure authority and develops and issues a training project or instruction to the Security Cooperation Organization or designated FMS representative. The implementing instruction generally authorizes the issuance of ITO.

Note. Implementing agent is not required to issue an ITO authorization.

   b. Tuition rates indicated on the FMS cases are estimates only.

3–61. Medical requirements

For a rated IMS, the Security Cooperation Organization must ensure that all available medical and dental records, in English, arrive at the flying training installation 30 days before training start date. This is required so that the Director of Base Medical Services can determine if the IMS has had an adequate physical examination for flying within the preceding 3 months and is qualified under class II standards (Air Force Instruction (AFI) 48–123)). If the IMS does not meet both conditions, the IMS will be further examined and processed according to AFI 48–123. If they qualify, the Director of Base Medical Services clears the individual without further examination. If the rated IMS does not meet the physical qualifications when the records are screened by the Director of Base Medical Services, ITO should not be issued.

3–62. International military student selection

   a. International military student (IMS) selected for training under security assistance must meet the ECL requirements for their particular training. Waiver of ECL requirements for entry into courses other than language will be considered on a case-by-case basis. In addition, IMS must meet the prerequisite qualifications for CONUS formal training set by the MAJCOM as outlined in the AF education and training course announcements (ETCA). Requests for waiver of prerequisites outlined in AF ETCA and ECL will be submitted to the Air Force Security Assistance Training Squadron for staffing with the MAJCOM, with information copies to the major command providing the training and to SAF/IAPX.

   b. The IMS are classified as officers, warrant officers, officer candidates, NCOs, airmen, or USAFA cadets according to their equivalent USAF military grade as specified in their original ITO.

3–63. Correspondence courses

The IMS attending training in CONUS under SCETP and other cooperative programs sponsorship may be enrolled in correspondence courses offered by the AF Institute for Advanced Distributive Learning if funded under a FMS training case or line.

   a. Correspondence courses, or any other off-duty education or training, must not be in conflict with security assistance training.

   b. Correspondence course requirements for IMS not attending CONUS training should be processed according to provisions in the AF Institute for Advanced Distributive Learning Catalog, with the exception of PME correspondence courses.

   c. The AF Institute for Advanced Distributive Learning Catalog and Guide and changes to this publication may be obtained online at www.au.af.mil/au/afiadl/.

3–64. Professional military education correspondence courses

Requests for PME correspondence courses for international students are forwarded to the Air Force Security Assistance Training Squadron through the country Security Cooperation Organization or country embassy. The request must identify an existing source of funding (for example, FMS training case) or request preparation of a new training case; provide the name, address, email, and phone number for the U.S. military officer or U.S. civilian employee who will sponsor the student; and include written verification by the U.S. sponsor that the student meets the rank prerequisite for the desired program and is proficient in the English language to complete the program successfully. The Air Force Security Assistance Training Squadron country manager reviews the request to insure all required information is provided, adds the requirement to the identified FMS training case or prepares a new case, if required. After the availability of funds is confirmed, the Air Force Security Assistance Training Squadron country manager forwards the request to Air University/CFRR and directs them to enroll the student. Air University/CFRR enrolls the student and provides the Air Force Security Assistance Training Squadron country program manager the date of enrollment and the deadline for completion of the program, and mails the materials directly to the U.S. sponsor. The Air Force Security Assistance Training Squadron country manager enters the enrollment date and deadline for completion as the start and projected graduation date in the training database. Air University/CFRR will notify the Air Force Security Assistance Training Squadron country manager of graduates and completion dates monthly and the Air Force Security Assistance Training Squadron country manager updates the training database accordingly. If the sponsor changes during the enrollment period, the Air Force Security Assistance Training Squadron country manager will provide Air University/CFRR with required information on the new sponsor. Air University/CFRR forwards the student's diploma to the USAF sponsor when the international student successfully completes the program.

3–65. Professional Military Education Seminar Program

International students stationed at USAF installations or under SCETP and other cooperative programs sponsorship may attend PME seminar programs. Applications should be submitted to SAF/International Affairs through FMS channels and should cite a FMS training case or line.

3–66. Publications

a. Country requests for English language publications under IMET will include these requirements in the USAF IMET program (N9B) according to the instructions in chapter 5. Countries not eligible for IMET will process requirements or requisitions through AFSAC/COMV under an FMS training case or line.

b. Country requests for training publications (for example, course charts, plans of instruction, student training specifications) not in support of their in-country ELT Program will be processed through AFSAC/COMV under an FMS training case or line.

c. Countries requiring large quantities of USAF directives will process requests through AFSAC under an FMS training case or line.

d. Air Force manuals (AFM), regulations, forms, and pamphlets for Security Cooperation Organization use are ordered through the publishing distribution office (PDO) of the Security Cooperation Organization.

3–67. Training aids

Country requests for English language equipment under IMET will include requirements in the Army IMETP (N9A). Air Force training aids must be requested under a FMS training case or line.

3–68. Training films and film strips

Available films are listed in DOD 5040.2C. Guidance for processing requests is in AFMAN 16–101. Request should be sent to AFSAC, 1822 Van Patton Drive, Wright-Patterson AFB, OH 45443–5337. Training films and film strips are provided under an FMS training case or line.

3–69. Scheduling and implementation

a. The Air Force Security Assistance Training Squadron, in coordination with other functional commands, will tentatively schedule training to meet requested requirements. Details on the training will be included in the STL, which will be forwarded to the Security Cooperation Organization or designated FMS representative at the earliest possible date. Upon receipt, the Security Cooperation Organization or designated FMS representative will review class starting dates and advise the Air Force Security Assistance Training Squadron of dates that cannot be met so rescheduling may be accomplished or spaces deleted from the existing documents. Rescheduling or cancellation of line items must be submitted to the Air Force Security Assistance Training Squadron at least 60 days before class entry dates to preclude a forfeiture charge. To preclude a cancellation, action should be taken by the Security Cooperation Organization or county representative to select and process alternate IMS as backups (complete in-country language training and briefings).

b. The IMS will be enrolled only in the training indicated in the applicable ITO and in the STL. Requests for additional training must originate with the country concerned and be forwarded through established deviation channels.

3–70. Acceptance of training

Upon receipt of authority to publish ITO, which constitutes a commitment of funds, Security Cooperation Organization or the FMS designated representative will advise the Air Force Security Assistance Training Squadron/FM by project line number or WCN on acceptance or nonacceptance of training. Acceptance of training by line or WCN numbers constitutes an obligation. The acceptance must be forwarded before the ITO are published. Deviation action is necessary to delete any line items that the country does not accept. Nonacceptance or cancellation of training must be processed to arrive at least 60 days before scheduled class start date to avoid a forfeiture charge, regardless of when authority to publish the ITO is received.

3–71. Familiarization and qualification training

Qualification training is a portion of a dual channel OJT Program designed to provide the performance skills required for the job. Qualification training for IMS can be provided by USAF or contractor personnel in conjunction with the establishment of an in-country OJT Program. Familiarization training provides practical experience and job-related training for specific systems, functional areas, or operations that require hands-on experience but does not provide for skill-level upgrading. Familiarization training can be provided in the CONUS for a period of not less than 1 week at each location. Familiarization training involving more than one location for a short duration must be considered as an orientation tour (OT) since planning, scheduling, and arrangements are the same as an OT.

a. For all familiarization training, the Security Cooperation Organization will forward the request to the Air Force Security Assistance Training Squadron for evaluation of training capability. (The format for this request is in fig 3–2.) When requesting this type of training, the requirements must be as specific as possible. To estimate the duration of training, the Security Cooperation Organization must consider the complexity of the training desired, level of proficiency, and the individuals' prior experience.

b. The Air Force Security Assistance Training Squadron will review the request for validity and forward the requests to the applicable MAJCOM or separate operating agency for determination of training capability and location. The implementing command will—

(1) Process the request.

(2) Advise the Security Cooperation Organization of training dates, location, and security requirements.

(3) Provide an information copy of the request to the base IMSO after MAJCOM or separate operating agency approves the training.

(4) Notify host MAJCOM by message or letter of training to be conducted by a tenant unit.

(5) Coordinate with the Security Cooperation Organization if additional information is required by the MAJCOM or separate operating agency.

(6) Ensure that all deviations are coordinated with the MAJCOM or separate operating agency and the base IMSO.

c. The MAJCOM or separate operating agency will—

(1) Review requests for training received by the Air Force Security Assistance Training Squadron to determine capability.

(2) Determine the disclosure of classified information or access to secure areas according to AFI 16–201 and MAJCOM determination of training capability.

(3) Monitor the training program of all IMS.

(4) Inform the Air Force Security Assistance Training Squadron of any changes in training capability.

(5) Provide copy of the request to the base IMSO and or the project NCO.

3–72. Documentation for familiarization and qualification training

The following AF forms are used to plan, request, and document familiarization and qualification training for IMS.

a. AF Form 623 (Individual Training Record Folder). This form will be initiated and maintained for all IMS engaged in either familiarization or qualification training. Because of special requirements, OJT upgrade skill levels may be required. The following procedures will be used.

(1) *Section I (Identification Data).* Enter only the IMS name and USAF equivalent grade. Enter the project and line number or WCN in the Social Security Account Number block.

(2) *Section II (Orientation and Certification).* Leave blank.

(3) *Remarks.* Enter each supervisor and all trainers by name, rank, and organization, with dates of supervision or training. Enter on AF Form 623a (On-the-Job Training Record-Continuation Sheet) other appropriate data as required. Do not record unfavorable comments about the IMS.

b. AF Form 797 (Job Qualification Standard Continuation/Command JQS). This form, strictly for AF use, will be used for familiarization and qualification training in excess of 4 weeks. The Security Cooperation Organization will list all tasks and knowledge items to be accomplished during the training. In addition, the IMS' name, project number, line number, or WCN will be entered in the trainee name and Social Security Account Number block. The date started, date completed, IMS initials, and trainer's initials will be entered on the upper line of each tasks block by the training installation.

c. AF Form 1098 (Special Task Certification and Recurring Training). This form will be used to record all training requiring special certification, such as Class A welder certification, egress familiarization, engine run, and flight control rigging. This form will be attached to the AF Form 797. The identification section will reflect only the IMS' name, project, line number, and WCN.

3–73. Air Force Institute of Technology programs

a. The IMS attendance at the Air Force Institute of Technology (AFIT) programs is as follows:

(1) *Nonresident courses.* These courses are not available to IMS under the SCETP and other cooperative programs. The country must negotiate directly with the civilian institution concerned.

(2) *Air Force Institute of Technology resident courses.*

(a) The availability of quotas in AF Institute of Technology graduate programs is provided by the Air Force Security Assistance Training Squadron after AFIT has determined the candidate is qualified for the program. Acceptability of the candidate is the sole prerogative of AFIT. The candidate's application should be forwarded to AFIT/ENES, 2950 Hobson Way, Wright-Patterson AFB, Dayton, Ohio 45433–7765 (Student Services) no later than 31 March for proposed entry in the following August timeframe. Earlier submission is highly encouraged. The candidate's application for Master's programs should include transcripts from all institutions previously attended and the TOEFL score, if applicable. Additionally, graduate record examination (GRE) scores for technical programs or graduate management admission test (GMAT) scores for nontechnical programs are highly encouraged and are required if admission waivers are necessary. Admission applications will be processed by AFIT if GRE and/or GMAT scores are not available, but the applicant's academic record and TOEFL scores must be exceptionally strong to make up for the lack of GRE and/or GMAT scores. Doctoral applications should include transcripts from all institutions previously attended, GRE scores, TOEFL scores, if applicable, and a clear and concise statement describing the area in which the student intends to concentrate on their studies.

(b) Recommend country send more than one application package per graduate program quota request. The AFIT will evaluate all applications and rank order eligible applicants according to academic potential at AFIT.

b. The DSCA must approve funding of degree-granting programs under IMET.

c. The AFIT Graduate School of Engineering and Management Department Heads reserve the right to conditionally accept IMS pending their completion of the 9-week Specialized English Training Program at DLIELC.

d. The cost of the TOEFL, GRE, or GMAT may also be funded by IMET. Test scores are usually valid for 5 years. The Security Cooperation Organization will advise if these test costs will be assumed by IMET when requesting approval of the program. The Air Force Security Assistance Training Squadron will provide voucher cards to the Security Cooperation Organization each summer. These voucher cards will be used by the candidates in lieu of money when registering for the tests. Unused voucher cards should be returned to the Air Force Security Assistance Training Squadron/FM so that the IMET program may be adjusted accordingly.

3–74. Air Force institute of technology short courses

Quotas for short courses taught at the AFIT School of Systems and Logistics (AFIT/School of Systems and Logistics) and School of Civil Engineering and Services (AFIT/CE) are requested by the Air Force Security Assistance Training Squadron from the appropriate school at least 1 year in advance of the course starting date. Therefore, identify requirements to the Air Force Security Assistance Training Squadron with sufficient lead-time. Requirements for AFIT courses should be included in the program submission for the annual Security Cooperation Education and Training Working Group.

a. Once a quota in an AFIT short course has been obtained, the appropriate Security Cooperation Organization will provide AFIT with a complete itinerary of the IMS travel plans. Travel should provide for arrival of the IMS at AFIT at least 3 days before the course starting date. Arrival notice must arrive at AFIT not later than 2 weeks in advance of the planned departure date. Include the following information:

(1) Foreign Service rank and its equivalent to U.S. grade structure.

(2) Date and time of departure en-route to the United States.

(3) Planned or anticipated delays en-route.

(4) Anticipated date and time of arrival at Wright-Patterson AFB.

b. IMS programmed for AFIT/CE and AFIT/School of Systems and Logistics short courses must have achieved an 80 ECL test score before departure for direct entry into training.

3–75. Air Force institute of technology eligibility for attendance

It is the responsibility of the country concerned to provide the necessary credentials for review by AFIT when the IMS is seeking admission. Complete academic records and the TOEFL scores are required for all degree programs. Should candidate's undergraduate work not meet or exceed a grade point average of 3.0 on a 4.0 scale, a GRE or GMAT must accompany the application.

a. The AFIT admission requirements state that Master degree candidates are required to take the GRE or GMAT. GRE and/or GMAT scores can be waived during the initial admissions process; however, the absence of this data could affect the individual's unconditional admissibility into a requested program. The GRE and/or GMAT score are needed to accurately determine the best course of action to ensure the student can successfully complete the requested AFIT Program. If a student is admitted without GRE and/or GMAT scores, AFIT will make the necessary arrangements for the student to take the appropriate examination after they arrive. Admission applications submitted without GRE and/or GMAT scores should be sent to AFIT for consideration no later than 31 December in case it is necessary for the student to arrive early to take preparatory courses. All transcripts for institutions previously attended, TOEFL scores, and GMAT and/or GRE scores if available will be forwarded to AFIT/ENES, 2950 Hobson Way, Wright-Patterson AFB, OH 45433–7765, Attention: Student Services.

b. Admission by AFIT is not a commitment. If AFIT accepts a candidate, the Air Force Security Assistance Training Squadron will then determine availability.

c. The AFIT will provide an estimate of the duration of the course when the IMS is determined eligible; however, the exact number of transfer credits AFIT will accept and how rapidly the IMS will progress cannot be determined until the IMS is enrolled. AFIT, therefore, will quote the maximum estimated course duration.

3–76. Inter-American Air Force academy

The IAAFA provides professional and technical training to students from partner nations eligible to receive Security Assistance. While its primary mission is to train personnel from Latin America and the Caribbean Air Forces, IAAFA offers selected training to Latin American and the Caribbean Army, Navy, and National Security Forces as well. The curriculum is reviewed annually to ensure it meets overall U.S. and DOD security assistance interests. IAAFA conducts training requirements assessment visits to partner nations on a regular basis and also provide Mobile Training Teams (MTTs), when possible, upon request. Depending on the assessed need, IAAFA may propose course changes, deletions, or additions. These proposed changed are submitted to the Curriculum Review Board. The Curriculum Review Board brings together representatives of pertinent security assistance agencies (SAF/International Affairs, AFSOUTH, AF-NORTH, and AETC to approve the curriculum to be offered over the following 2 years. Following the Curriculum Review Board and USSOUTHAF/CC approval, IAAFA implements the approved curriculum.

a. No later than 3 months prior to the Curriculum Review Board, a Strategy Coordination Panel (SCP), using established strategic planning documents and guidance, in order to prioritize and de-conflict IAAFA training requirements and to make recommendations to the Curriculum Review Board will convene.

b. The following information will be provided at the SCP at the Curriculum Review Board for proposed new courses:

(1) The need the course was designed to meet, including countries interested in the training and estimated annual requirements.

(2) Resources (manpower, equipment, and so forth) impact of providing the training.

(3) Impact on current curriculum.

(4) Estimated tuition cost to the country.

(5) Proposed frequency of courses.

(6) Language in which the course will be conducted.

(7) Any other information pertinent to the request.

c. The SCP will also identify low usage courses for possible deletion by the Curriculum Review Board.

3–77. Letter of offer and acceptance notes

The LOAs will include appropriate supplemental conditions for training. Approved LOA notes are included in the Defense Security Assistance Management System (DSAMS). Requested or recommended changes to LOA notes must be forwarded to SAF/IAPX for review, coordination, and approval.

3–78. Blanket order foreign military sales training cases

a. The Air Force Security Assistance Training Squadron will prepare and coordinate training "T" cases according to DSCA and SAF/IAPX prescribed procedures.

b. The Air Force Security Assistance Training Squadron case managers will prepare blanket order (BO) training cases unless the purchaser justifies and is granted approval for a defined order training case by SAF/IAPX. This will allow the Air Force to be more responsive to changing purchaser's training needs and is in the interest of saving time, manpower, and costs involved in amending defined order cases.

c. Foreign military sales training cases will be prepared for a minimum of $20,000 unless the requesting Service's annual training requirements have been for a lesser amount.

d. An International Program Directive is required for each FMS case. The AFM 16–101 provides necessary guidance and examples.

3–79. Security Cooperation Education and Training Working Groups

The 2ndAir Force and AETC/International Affairs participation in the annual SCETP and other cooperative program management review are necessary for long-range forecasting, programming, and coordination of required international training positions. HQ/DPLTS and AETC/DOPZ involvement provides input and analysis of the anticipated training allocations.

Chapter 4
Security Cooperation Education and Training Teams

Section I
General

4–1. Purpose/Introduction

This chapter provides policy guidance on Security Cooperation Education and Training teams. The chapter defines types of teams, discusses the process for requesting, programming, and deploying teams, and highlights quality of life (QOL) and mission sustainment (MS) issues associated with team deployment. Security Cooperation Education and Training teams consist of U.S. Military, DOD civilian, or contractor personnel, deployed to a foreign country on TDY (less than 180 days) or permanent change of station (PCS, more than 179 days) status. These teams provide advice, training, technical assistance, or support to personnel of the hosting country. This assistance is provided to meet specific objectives in connection with development of a country's capability. The deployment of these teams should be based on consideration of all of the advantages and disadvantages inherent in the use of this type of assistance, at a particular time, in a particular country, and should be consistent with DOD, Combatant Command, and Service security cooperation guidance or strategy. The teams support many of the programs and authorities associated with security cooperation. The DOD 5105.38–M, table C10.T1, provides a listing of the various authorities for deploying teams.

4–2. Command relationships

a. Chief of the U.S. Diplomatic Mission. The Chief of the U.S. Diplomatic Mission exercises general supervision over the in-country operations and activities of Security Cooperation Education and Training teams through the Security Cooperation Organization Chief. The regional combatant commander provides necessary technical assistance and administrative support to Security Cooperation Organization to facilitate the efficient and effective oversight of team activities, including quality of life for personnel. The level of support provided to team members varies depending on the duration of their deployment and the program that funds that deployment. Support under an FMS case will not exceed that authorized for other in-country DOD personnel of equivalent grade who are funded by U.S. appropriations. Oversight of security assistance teams by regional combatant commander or their designated component command through Security Cooperation Organization shall not usurp MILDEP authority in issues of case management, contract administration, or the technical execution of the team mission as described in the individual LOA terms of reference.

b. Security cooperation organization chief. The Security Cooperation Organization chief provides operational oversight and local administrative support over in-country teams and is responsible for coordinating team activities to ensure compatibility with other DOD elements in or directly related to the U.S. diplomatic mission. The Security Cooperation Organization chief ensures compliance with directives and keeps the Service International Affairs, team management agency, the combatant commander, and/or the designated component command informed of team activities and progress.

c. Team chief. The team chief is the senior team member and assigns duties and responsibilities to team personnel. The team chief is under the administrative and operational oversight of the Security Cooperation Organization while in country and is an integral part of the Security Cooperation Organization in support of the overall security cooperation mission. The team chief is responsible to the Service International Affairs, team management agency, the combatant commander, and/or the designated component command for the accomplishment of the education or training mission. Team chief responsibilities include, but are not limited to, DOD 5105.38–M, table C4.T1 and paragraph 4–25*c* of this regulation.

d. Security cooperation education and training organization. The Security Cooperation Organization has responsibility for oversight of team personnel and activities and identifies problems to the Service International Affairs, team management agency, the combatant commander, and/or the designated component command for resolution. The Security Cooperation Organization ensures fair and equitable treatment in the level and quality of support provided to all DOD personnel in country. Security Cooperation Organization support of the Service International Affairs, team management agency, the combatant commander, and/or the designated component command includes, but is not limited to, DOD 5105.38–M, table C4.T2 and paragraph 4–25*b* of this regulation.

e. Military justice jurisdiction. The combatant commander has general courts martial convening authority over all military personnel under their command, that is, personnel assigned to the command's Joint Manning Document or attached for Uniform Code of Military Justice (UCMJ) purposes. However, since disciplinary action is normally administered by a commander of the same Service as the offender, the combatant commander should direct the component commander of the member's Service, or that commander's designee, to take courts-martial jurisdiction over PCS team personnel. If the component commander believes a case within their discretion should be referred to a court-martial at a level that is not authorized to convene, they should inform the combatant commander. In these situations, the combatant commander will have the authority to take disciplinary action or return the case back to the component commander for disposition. The combatant commander reserves the right to exercise military justice jurisdiction in those cases impacting the mission, or affecting external relations. Personnel assigned PCS orders and carried on the authorization document (table of distribution and allowances (TDA)), modified table of organization and equipment, and so forth) of the team management agency will remain under the military jurisdiction of that agency unless attached to the combatant command. UCMJ jurisdiction over TDY team members resides with their parent organization commander. Article 15 jurisdiction for all personnel (both TDY and PCS) will be exercised in accordance with Service directives.

4–3. Constraints

Teams will not serve as an integral part of the Armed Forces of the country being served. Teams deploy under authority of the relevant section of either Title 10, USC or Title 22, USC and are subject to such procedures and constraints as the authorizing legislation and or established policy applicable to that type of team may mandate. Procedures and constraints vary greatly from one legislative authority to another and all concerned with a particular team's deployment must fully understand those differences.

a. Prohibited team activities Teams deploying under security assistance authorities (22 USC) will not engage in or provide assistance or advice to foreign forces in a combat situation. Additionally, such teams shall not perform operational duties of any kind except as may be required in the conduct of OJT in the operation and maintenance of equipment, weapons, or supporting systems. Teams deploying under security assistance authorities shall not perform Security Cooperation Organization functions, augment the Security Cooperation Organization or U.S. forces in country, except where specifically authorized by the host country in the LOA. The SCO will inform teams deployed under one of the 10 USC authorities on the rules of engagement or other constraints applicable to the particular section of the law that authorizes their deployment before deploying or upon arrival in country. The Security Cooperation Organization will refer any questions to the combatant commander's staff judge advocate for resolution prior to deployment.

b. Acts of misconduct by host country personnel. All members of Security Cooperation Education and Training must understand their responsibilities concerning acts of misconduct by foreign country personnel. The team management agency will brief team members prior to deployment on what to do if they encounter or observe such acts.

(1) Common article three to the four Geneva conventions of August 12, 1949, provides a list of prohibited acts by parties to the conventions as follows:

(a) Violence to life and person-in particular, murder, mutilation, cruel treatment, and torture.

(b) Taking of hostages.

(c) Outrages upon personal dignity - - in particular, humiliating and degrading treatment.

(d) Passing of sentences and carrying out of executions without previous judgment by a regularly constituted court, affording all the judicial guarantees that are recognized as indispensable by civilized people.

(2) The provisions in paragraph (1), above, represent a level of conduct that the United States expects each foreign country to observe.

(3) If team members encounter prohibited acts, they will disengage from the activity, leave the area if possible, and report the incidents immediately to the proper in-country U.S. authorities. The Chief of the U.S. Diplomatic Mission through the Security Cooperation Organization will identify proper U.S. authorities during the team's initial briefing. Team members will not discuss such matters with non-USG authorities such as journalists or civilian contractors.

4–4. Selection of personnel

a. Agencies providing personnel for assignment to a SAT shall ensure that they have the experience, technical ability, maturity, and personality to accomplish their duties in the best interests of the United States.

(1) Maximum effort should be made to select team members who meet the desirable as well as the mandatory qualifications.

(2) Team members should be highly qualified in their respective fields. They should be the best available who meet all other qualifications.

(3) Team members should be capable of working with others and should have demonstrated their abilities to supervise effectively and conscientiously.

b. Personnel assigned to Security Cooperation Education and Training perform a mission of the highest importance. They will serve as goodwill ambassadors of the United States. Foreigners will consider their behavior to be "typically American." Good or bad, the impressions will endure. Accordingly, selecting the best-qualified team members serves the best interests of the United States.

c. The Security Cooperation Organization requesting a Security Cooperation Education and Training will identify the expertise and qualifications that the team members should possess. Any special requirements, considerations, or restrictions should also be identified.

d. Team members must be medically fit to perform duty with a Security Cooperation Education and Training in the designated country. Physical disorders that may require medical attention or hospitalization disqualify a candidate. Medical expenses incurred for nonmilitary team members will be charged to the program supporting the team.

e. Personnel selected for Security Cooperation Education and Training must have enough time remaining in the Service before separation or retirement to complete the required period of deployment.

f. Refer to paragraph 8–6 for guidance on in-country healthcare.

Section II
Types of Teams

4–5. Extended training service specialist

The ETSS are PCS teams that are technically qualified to provide advice, instruction, and training in the installation, operation, and maintenance of weapons, equipment, and systems. The ETSS deploy under one of the security assistance authorities in 22 USC. They are not used for follow-on retraining or advisory roles, except in rare instances when the recipient country cannot provide qualified personnel from its own resources or hire qualified personnel from non-indigenous sources and the Security Cooperation Organization recommends it as in the interest of the United States. The ETSS provided as English language instructors, supervisors, or advisors on detached duty status from DLIELC are also attached to the Security Cooperation Organization. The English language technical Service provided by DLIELC is referred to as a LTD. The ETSS may perform for periods up to 1 year under IMET; only DSCA (Programs (flight training exchanges) Directorate) can approve longer periods.

4–6. Contract field services

The CFS personnel are civilian personnel under contract from private industry who perform the same functions as

ETSS. Like ETSS, CFS personnel deploy under one of the security assistance authorities in 22 USC. The CFS personnel are used only when the Service International Affairs determines that services by DOD personnel are not practical. Only DSCA (Policy, Plans, and Programs Directorate) can approve use of CFS personnel under IMET. Estimated contract cost covers the total training service costs.

4–7. Mobile education team/mobile training team

a. Mobile education team. The Mobile Education Team provide training developed primarily in response to the Expanded IMET Program (22 USC 2347) in a seminar and/or educational forum. DSCA waiver is not required for E–IMET certified Mobile Education Team. Refer to figure 4–1 for format to request a Mobile Education Team.

Request for Mobile Education Team (MET)

SAO submits requests for MET (120-day lead time required) in the following format to the MILSVC, copy to DSCA, the Unified Command and the MET provider

1. MET identification, Name of MET provider and phase of training requested.
2. Duration. Indicate duration of the mission in weeks,
3. Team restrictions. Reflect any required limitations or exclusion on the type of personnel, uniforms, equipment or methods of instruction.
4. Mission. Provide in detail the scope of instruction of the team is to conduct.
5. Training goal. Include a statement of the results the team effort is expected to achieve. Provide justification for the team in terms of the effect on the security assistance objective. Do not restate the team mission.
6. Personnel to be trained. Indicate number of international Military Students (IMS) by officers, enlisted personnel and civilians.
7. Summary of the host capabilities.
8. Availability of training aids/technical support
9. Interpreter support.
10. Training location.
11. Desired in-country arrival date.
12. Type of facilities available for training and billeting.
13. In-country transportation. Indicate the means of in-country transportation to be provided.
14. To or from billeting, duty location, and dining facilities or specify rental car requirement/availability.
15. In-country cost estimate for authorized expenses.
16. Facilities. Indicate the availability of medical, dental, shopping and laundry facilities.
17. Confirmation of country team approval.
18. Additional information. Include any important data requiring more emphasis or containing information useful to the MET provider. When applicable, data should be included such as sensitive areas, subject to avoid, taboos, and personalities involved. If this data requires classification or special handling, it may be attached to the request as an annex. Include additional data such as availability of monetary facilities in the foreign country for converting personal funds, procedures, and number to be used for telephone contacts. Include reference to any previous team effectiveness evaluations that contain data pertinent to this request.
19. SAO point of contact. Indicate name, grade, DSN and commercial telephone numbers, e-mail address, message and mailing addresses for the SAO.
20. Additional information as applicable.
21. MET indication. Name of MET provider and phase of training requested.
22. Duration. Indicate duration of the mission in weeks.
23. Team restrictions. Reflect any required limitations or exclusion on the type of personnel, uniforms, equipment or methods of instruction.
24. Mission. Provide in detail the scope of instruction the teams is to conduct.
25. Training goal. Include a statement of the results the team effort is expected to achieve. Provide justification for the team in terms of the effort on the security assistance objective. Do no restate the team mission.
26. Personnel to be trained. Indicate number of international Military Students (IMS) by officers, enlisted personnel and civilians.
27. Summary of the host capabilities.
28. Availability of training aids/technical support
29. Interpreter support.
30. Training location.
31. Desired in-country arrival date.
32. Type of facilities available for training and billeting.
33. In-country transportation. Indicate the means of in-country transportation to be provided to or from billeting, duty location, and dining facilities or specify rental car requirement/availability.
34. In-country cost estimate for authorized expenses.

Figure 4–1. Format for submitting request for Mobile Education Team

35. Facilities. Indicate the availability of medical, dental, shopping and laundry facilities.
36. Confirmation of country team approval.
37. Additional information. Include any important data requiring more emphasis or containing information useful to the MET provider. When applicable, data should be included such as sensitive areas, subject to avoid, taboos, and personalities involved. If this data requires classification or special handling, it may be attached to the request as an annex. Include additional data such as availability of monetary facilities in the foreign country for converting personal funds, procedures, and number to be used for telephone contacts. Include reference to any previous team effectiveness evaluations that contain data pertinent to this request.
38. SAO point of contact. Indicate name, grade, DSN and commercial telephone numbers, e-mail address, message and mailing addresses for the SAO.
39. Additional information as applicable.

Figure 4–1. Format for submitting request for Mobile Education Team–Continued

b. Mobile training team. The MTT are Military Service or contract personnel on temporary duty for the purpose of training foreign personnel in the operation, maintenance, or support of weapon systems and support equipment or for specific training requirements and specific capabilities that are beyond in-country U.S. resources. The MTT deploy under one of the security assistance authorities in 22 USC or under one of the 10 USC authorized programs that follow security cooperation procedures. The MTT may be authorized for CONUS or overseas deployment when it is more practical to bring the training capability to country personnel. This includes in-country training surveys to determine specific country training needs; quantity requirements that are beyond the country capability to assess, and that are associated with equipment deliveries; and assistance leading to self-sufficiency. The MTT should be considered when training must be accomplished quickly in response to a threat or adverse condition affecting the security of the country; training is of relatively short duration, must reach a large number of trainees, and entails extensive use of interpreters; or language qualified team members; or training can be conducted only on equipment; or in facilities located in the foreign country. The format to request MTT is found in figure 4–2.

FORMAT FOR SECURITY ASSISTANCE TEAM (SAT) REQUEST/CALL-UP

For the purpose of this format, the term "training" is used; however, requests must specifically state whether training or technical assistance (or both) will be required.

1. SAT identification. See paragraph 4-30.
2. Mission. Provide in detail the scope of instruction the team is to conduct.
3. Training goal. Include a statement of the results the team effort is expected to achieve. Provide justification for the team in terms of the effect on the security assistance objective. Do not restate the team mission.
4. Objectives. State any actions or steps the team will take to accomplish the mission.
5. End state. List the expected results from this training that can be quantified and measured. The measure of these results following training will provide an indicator of mission success.
6. Team composition. List the envisioned quantity, rank, MOS and title of each team member.
7. Duration. Indicate the proposed duration of a PCS mission in months and of a TDY mission in weeks.
8. Personnel to be trained. Indicate number of IMS by officers, enlisted personnel and civilians.
   a. Technical qualifications of prospective foreign military trainees, to include relevant training and educational level(s).
   b. Number of foreign military trainees by officers, enlisted personnel, and/or civilians.
9. Security clearance. Indicate the type of security clearance required for the mission.
10. Team restrictions. List any required limitations or exclusions on the type of personnel, uniforms, equipment or methods of instruction.
11. Summary of host nation capabilities.
12. Equipment on which training is to be conducted and availability of equipment. List tools and equipment required for the mission, and their availability in country.
13. Availability of training aids/technical support. List required training aids and indicate their availability.
14. Interpreter support.
15. Training location(s). If more than one, indicate distance between locations, time requirements for travel and modes of anticipated transportation.
16. Desired in-country arrival date.
17. Type of facilities available for training and quarters.
18. Uniforms and clothing. Describe requirements for on and off-duty uniforms and civilian clothing.
19. In-country transportation. Indicate the means of in-country transportation to be provided to or from quarters, duty location, and dining facilities or specify rental car requirement/availability.
20. In-country cost estimate for authorized expenses.
21. Facilities. Indicate the availability of medical, dental, shopping and laundry facilities.
22. Confirmation of country team approval. Validate the SAT mission; verify that the COCOM and country team support the mission (NSDD38) ICASS, etc., and that it supports the COCOM theater strategy and the country team MPP.
23. PDSS. State, if needed, the requirement for the team chief to conduct a PDSS to visit the training site; SCO and host nation determine requirements prior to team deployment.
24. Additional information. Include any important data requiring more emphasis or containing information useful to the SAT provider and/or team chief.
   a. Include, if applicable, information on sensitive areas, subjects to avoid, taboos and personalities involved.

Figure 4–2. Format for security assistance team request/call-up

b. Include data on availability of monetary facilities in country for converting personal funds, cashing checks, using USG or personal credit cards, etc.

c. Refer to any previous team effectiveness evaluations that contain data pertinent to this request.

d. Indicate the type of passport, if any, that is required and whether a visa is required.

e. When requesting PCS SAT, include estimates for in-country expenses for anything required by the PCS SAT (housing, transportation, security, medical/dental care, maintenance, telephones, schooling costs for family members, TDY, emergency leave, quality of life, ICASS, mailing address for SAT, etc.

f. If any data requires classification or special handling, attach to the request as an annex.

g. Force protection. Address force protection provided to the SAT by the host country/U.S. Embassy. State whether SAT is required to bring weapons, and type of security for weapons/ammunition if required.

h. Civilian contractors. Indicate if country will accept civilian contractors if DOD personnel are not available. If contractors are requested or acceptable, attach a statement of work or performance work statement.

i. ARSOF SAT. If applicable; SATs including ARSOF personnel must be coordinated with the respective theater SOC in accordance with AR 12-7.

25. Type of funding and supporting case data.

26. SCO point of contact. Include name, grade, DSN and commercial telephone numbers, e-mail address, message and mailing addresses for the SCO.

—

Figure 4–2. Format for security assistance team request/call-up–Continued

c. Funding constraints The Security Cooperation Organization may request programming of MTT as follows:

(1) *Foreign military sales.* The MTT and Mobile Education Team may be programmed under FMS cases at the request of the Security Cooperation Organization regardless of whether the FMS case is funded by country funds or FMF, if it is within the scope of the case.

(2) *International military education and training.* Although Expanded IMET Mobile Education Team does not require a DSCA waiver, IMET MTT may be programmed only upon receipt of DSCA waiver. A fundamental IMET objective is to reach foreign military personnel who are likely to be influential in their Services and/or countries. By attending CONUS training, the students are exposed to the American people, their way of life, institutions, beliefs, and aspirations. This must be considered when proposing an MTT versus CONUS training. Every attempt should be made to provide MTT through FMS rather than IMET. The MTT requests under IMET must demonstrate that an MTT is the best approach and IMET is the only available funding option. Subsistence expenses, or per diem allowance in lieu thereof, obligated in one FY for IMET MTT cannot be extended into the succeeding FY. Therefore, personnel on MTT duty must terminate temporary duty and return to home station prior to 30 September unless action has been taken to reprogram the team in the new FY, subject to the 179 day restriction discussed in paragraph d below, receipt of CRA or other budget authority in the new FY, and DSCA approval. Transportation costs for round trip team travel are chargeable to the FY of the start of the TDY.

(3) *Combating Terrorism Fellowship Program.* The MTT may be programmed under Counterterrorism Fellowship Program only after receipt of Special Operations/Low Intensity Conflict and commanders of combatant commands approval.

(4) *Other programs.* The MTT may be programmed only after approval by commanders of combatant commands or Department of State (as appropriate).

d. Duration. The MTT and/or Mobile Education Team are authorized on a temporary duty basis for up to 179 days. Requirements for assistance in excess of 179 days are met by CONUS training of country personnel leading to an in-country capability or programming of U.S. ETSS.

4–8. Technical assistance field team

The TAFT deploy in PCS status under one of the security assistance authorities in 22 USC for the purpose of providing in-country technical or maintenance support to foreign personnel on specific equipment, technology, weapons, and supporting systems when MTT and ETSS are not appropriate for the purpose. The TAFT are Security Assistance services, but are not considered training and are not provided under IMET.

4–9. Technical assistance team

Technical assistance team (TAT) deploy in TDY status to place into operation, maintain, or repair equipment provided under one of the security assistance authorities in 22 USC TAT are Security Assistance services, but are not considered training and are not provided under IMET, except in the case of the installation of English language laboratories.

4–10. Survey teams

a. Requirements survey team. Requirements survey teams (RST) deploy to help the Security Cooperation Organization develop and define equipment, training and technical assistance requirements for the host nation.

b. Pre-deployment site survey. For a pre-deployment site survey, a Security Cooperation Education and Training team chief deploys alone or with other personnel as an advance party to ensure preparations for the main body are in place.

4–11. Combatant commander initiatives

Under the authority of 10 USC 166a, CJCS may provide funds to the combatant commanders to deploy personnel in a TDY status to foreign countries to provide military education and training (to include transportation, translation, and administrative expenses) to military and related civilian personnel of that country. These funds may also be utilized for force training, contingencies, selected operations, command and control, joint exercises (including activities of participating foreign countries), humanitarian and civil assistance, personnel expenses of defense personnel for bilateral or regional cooperation programs, and force protection.

4–12. Military-to-military contacts and comparable activities

Under the authority of 10 USC 168 the SECDEF may conduct military-to-military contacts and comparable activities that are designed to encourage a democratic orientation of defense establishments and military forces of other countries. The Secretary may provide funds to the combatant commanders to deploy DOD personnel in a TDY status as a Traveling Contact Team. These funds support Traveling Contract Team expenses including transportation, translation services, or administrative expenses. These funds may also be utilized for the activities of military liaison teams, exchanges of civilian or military personnel between DOD and defense ministries of foreign governments, exchanges of military personnel between units of the armed forces and units of foreign armed forces, seminars and conferences held primarily in a theater of operations, and distribution of publications primarily in a theater of operations. Except for the activities specifically authorized by this section, funds provided may not be used for the provision of any other defense articles or services, including training, to any foreign country.

4–13. Joint combined exchange training

Under the authority of 10 USC 2011 the Commander, Special Operations Command (SOC) may authorize special operations forces to deploy to a friendly foreign country to train armed forces and other security forces of that country as long as the primary purpose of the training is the training of the U.S. Special Operations Forces.

Section III
Programming Guidance Programming

4–14. Guidance

General programming guidance for Security Cooperation Education and Training teams varies with the type of program or authority under which the team is deployed. In general, however, there are some commonalities in teams that deploy under either 22 USC or 10 USC; requests should be included in the Combined Education and Training Program Plan and originate with the requesting country. The Security Cooperation Organization, combatant command and U.S. country team will review and vet the requests. Requests that are not identified as part of the Combined Education and Training Program Plan and submitted at the appropriate Security Cooperation Education and Training Working Group are considered out-of-cycle requests.

a. Teams programmed under FMS may be requested by the Security Cooperation Organization at any time and must be coordinated between all cognizant training organizations.

b. Teams programmed under IMET require DSCA waiver and must be included in the Combined Education and Training Program Plan and requested at the Security Cooperation Education and Training Working Group.

c. Teams programmed under Counterterrorism Fellowship Program require Special Operations/Low Intensity Conflict and commanders of combatant commands approval and must be included in the Combined Education and Training Program Plan and requested at the Security Cooperation Education and Training Working Group.

d. Teams in other programs should also be included in the Combined Education and Training Program Plan and presented at Security Cooperation Education and Training Working Group. However, often these types of requests are addressed in separate reviews tied directly to the development of the Theater Security Cooperation Strategy/Plan for a given geographic region. Security Cooperation Organization should make every effort to ensure full coordination of these types of requests regardless of the forum in which they are presented. Requests not presented at a Security Cooperation Education and Training Working Group or other appropriate meetings are considered out-of-cycle.

4–15. Extended training service specialist

The ETSS teams are normally programmed for a period of one year. Personnel selected for deployment on such teams typically do so on a PCS basis. Because of funding severability issues associated with the IMET, Counterterrorism Fellowship Program, or certain other security cooperation programs; the ETSS are not normally programmed under those programs. They are most often programmed under a FMS or FMF case. The case manager and the Security Cooperation Organization should assure that the case contains appropriate language to support such a deployment. All costs involved in furnishing the ETSS must be included in the LOA. These include such costs as dependent travel, movement of household goods, privately-owned vehicle (POV) (if authorized), and dependent schooling. The ETSS costs are estimated when first programmed.

4–16. Contract field services

The CFS costs depend on the value of a negotiated contract with the civilian firm involved and include such costs as salary, in-country maintenance, CONUS travel, and overhead. The contract cost will be reflected as unit cost in the country program; other costs are considered as TLA.

a. The CFS will be used only when needed to accomplish a military mission. However, it must be clearly shown that personnel with the required skill are not available from DOD resources. Also, the Service involved must determine that satisfactory provision of services by DOD personnel is not practicable.

b. Under the provision of a nonpersonal services contract, U.S. officers should have no supervisory control over contractor personnel.

c. The Security Cooperation Organization is responsible for advising the contractor of regulations and procedures for receipt, dispatch, storing, and safeguarding of military information, including classified defense information.

d. Contractors and their employees will not—

(1) Be placed in policy-making positions or in positions of command, supervision, administration, or control over DOD personnel or personnel of other contractors.

(2) Become part of the foreign government organization.

e. Subject to the provisions of applicable international agreements, CFS personnel performing under the provisions of this regulation are entitled to privileges and support equivalent to that furnished as GS–12 grade civilian, where available. When agreements between the United States and the foreign government do not expressly authorize the United States to accord these privileges to such personnel, they will be extended only with the consent of the foreign government.

f. Security clearance for employees of contractors performing field services will conform to the requirements of applicable DOD instructions or regulations. Other administrative requirements such as those involving certificates of performance, logistical support, travel, identification, privileges, and reports will conform to the appropriate provisions of the Service regulation, as incorporated within the contract for the services.

g. According to the terms of the contract, the contracting officer may require the contractor to remove from the job site any CFS employee who endangers persons or property or whose continued employment under the contract is inconsistent with the interests of the USG.

h. Travel and allowances for CFS personnel will be according to the appropriate provision of the Defense Acquisition Regulation (DAR) as incorporated within the contract for the services.

i. The CFS personnel are authorized leave for U.S. legal holidays as specified in MILDEP procurement procedures. All other leave and absence will be authorized at the discretion of the contractor.

4–17. Mobile education team/Mobile training team

a. General. The Mobile Education Team and MTT programming will include duration in weeks; number of team members; costs for overseas travel (round trip); in country travel; travel and living allowances; CONUS travel; baggage; and DOD civilian salaries. Per diem allowance costs during temporary duty travel outside CONUS are computed according to Joint Federal Travel Regulations (JFTR) rates for U.S. military personnel, and rates shown in the "Standard Regulations, Government civilians, Foreign Areas" (published by the DOS) for USG civilians. The MTT CONUS travel costs are programmed at an estimated rate to include commercial air transportation, baggage, and per diem. Only the Service International Affairs can approve excess baggage. Costs of team members traveling from overseas locations are computed using commercial air (tourist rate) transportation, per diem, and excess baggage. Additional travel costs should be based on the JFTR, JTR, and other applicable directives and regulations. When more than one Service is involved, a Joint MTT is programmed using the MASL line of the Service providing the most team members. If each Service provides an equal number of team members, the MTT is programmed using the MASL line of the Service counterpart to the requesting foreign country Service. All team member costs, including pre-deployment orientation or training costs are programmed as "unit costs" of the country program. Training aids (including parking, crating, handling and transportation) are programmed separately. Training aids for IMET funded MTT must be approved by DSCA (Programs Directorate).

b. Teams programmed under international military education training.

(1) The MTT are programmed by the Security Cooperation Organization in the FY program during which the team will be used. The teams are programmed on a man-week basis. An MTT cannot be funded under the 5th quarter concept since MTT funds cannot be extended from one FY into the next. Therefore, personnel on MTT duty must terminate their TDY and return to home station before 30 September unless action has been taken to reprogram the team in the new FY. Such reprogramming is subject to the 179-day restriction (see para 4–7d) and receipt of CRA or other budget authority in the new FY. Transportation costs for roundtrip team travel are chargeable to the FY at the start of the TDY. Initial programming of IMET MTT will be according to the SAMM. Once the formal MTT request is submitted according to Service instructions and the details of mission, concept, composition, duration, and source agency finalized, the IMETP will be adjusted to reflect the MTT cost estimate developed by the appropriate Service. The following factors will be included:

(a) CONUS travel and team orientation. Program per member to include CONUS airfare, per diem, and baggage.

(b) Transoceanic travel (round trip). Compute using current airfare rates.

(c) Travel and per diem allowances. Computed according to the JTR.

(d) In country travel.

(e) Team members. For civilians, the cost at base salary rate plus acceleration factor as prescribed by current DOD pricing instructions. No salary costs are included for military members.

(f) Fund-cite. U.S. regulations require that a U.S. person performing temporary duty be supported by an appropriated fund cite; therefore, all travel and per diem for IMET MTT members must be programmed and funded by IMET.

(2) Costs in paragraphs (a) through (e), above, are to be reflected as TLA in the country program. Civilian salaries will be shown under unit cost.

(3) Officers, enlisted personnel, and civilian members of the team will be shown in the country program on separate lines under the WCN alpha designator, as appropriate.

(4) MTT cannot be deployed under IMET until funds are available; therefore, lead times must be given careful consideration when requesting and programming MTT.

(5) For costing purposes, MTT are subject to IMET incremental pricing policy.

c. International military education training programming procedures The program may be followed for MTT funded by certain 10 USC or 22 USC authorities. These include teams funded under Regional Defense Counterterrorism Fellowship Program and Counter-Drug Training Support.

d. Teams programmed under an foreign military sales or foreign military financing case

(1) The MTT may be furnished under an LOA, either as a separate case or as part of an existing training case. MTT under FMS may span FY since these teams are not required to terminate at the end of the U.S. FY.

(2) Services develop cost data for MTT. The same cost elements as stated for IMET MTT are used, plus military pay and allowances with current acceleration factors for all military members for FMS teams.

(3) Requests for FMS MTT must be time-phased to allow for the following:

(a) Determination of price and availability.

(b) LOA preparation and processing.

(c) Submission to and acceptance by the country.

(d) Receipt of the initial deposit and issuance of obligation or expenditure authority.

(4) Funds for the MTT must be received in advance of MTT deployment. Teams cannot be deployed until country funds are available nor can team preparations requiring funds (for example, training aids and orientations) be initiated or accomplished.

(5) Light refreshments may be funded if providing such refreshments prevents disruption of the training agenda. Documentation must be provided to the DSCA IMET financial manager to show there is factually no convenient source for attendees to reasonably obtain refreshments during breaks. This documentation must be provided to the DSCA financial manager at least 30 days prior to the start of training.

4–18. Other security cooperation teams

Teams or personnel deployed under various authorities, such as, initiatives (combatant commander initiatives) (10 USC 166a), military-to-military contacts (10 USC 168), or JCET (10 USC 2011) are programmed as a part of the development of a combatant commander TSCP. Unlike those teams programmed under security assistance procedures (IMET/FMS/FMF), these deployments are typically tasked by the combatant commander directly to the Service Component involved. Funding is provided by the tasking combatant commander to the service component providing the team. Teams composed of SOF personnel require Special Operations Command (SOCOM) approval.

4–19. Requests for teams

The format in figure 4–1 will be used to request Mobile Education Team. Requesters will use the format in figure 4–2 to request MTT, TAT, ETSS, TAFT, pre-deployment site survey, RST, and CFS teams.

a. Foreign military sales/foreign military financing/international military education and training

(1) The Security Cooperation Organization should submit the request for MTT or ETSS/CFS teams during each annual Security Cooperation Education and Training Working Group or as soon thereafter as feasible. Specific training objectives and requirements will be stated in the team request. The data provided should be complete and detailed. This will enable furnishing Service to select and prepare the team properly for the mission. Teams included in a country-training program are not automatically called up. Specific action must be taken by the Security Cooperation Organization to formally request the team from the providing Service. Copies of this request must also be provided to the Combatant Commander and all interested activities and commands. Once a request is received, the Service will determine if deployment is feasible and supportable within current resources. If supportable, the Service will notify the Security Cooperation Organization. Short lead-times should be avoided when requesting teams.

(2) When requesting a team, the Security Cooperation Organization must ensure that the necessary equipment, instruction facilities, and technical publications are available before or with the arrival of the team. This action should be accomplished through requisition of the necessary equipment and publications in advance of team call-up. In-country training surveys to determine specific country training needs and to refine requirements are a normal part of team preparation.

(3) Necessary interpreter support will be the responsibility of the foreign country to provide. If interpreter support cannot be provided and funding source is IMET, then country must submit a waiver for DSCA approval. A waiver is not required when using IMET funding for E–IMET training.

(4) The Security Cooperation Organization will ensure foreign personnel to be trained meet the prerequisites and necessary to comprehend the technical level of presentation. The Security Cooperation Organization vets all personnel and units to be trained in accordance with current requirements.

(5) The Security Cooperation Organization programs in-country arrival date based on the availability of trainees, facilities, and equipment.

(6) The Security Cooperation Organization will request unprogrammed teams from the providing Service in sufficient time to permit that Service to determine supportability. Specific service timelines are found in Service specific sections of this chapter.

b. Regional Defense Counterterrorism Fellowship Program and Counter-Drug Training Support. Teams funded under these programs follow request procedures similar to the ones outlined for FMS/FMF/IMET teams; however, each requires additional vetting and approval before the request for this training is submitted to the providing Service. Security Cooperation Organization should allow sufficient additional time to permit this extra processing and approval.

c. Combatant commander initiatives, military-to-military contact, and Joint combined exchange training. Requests for these teams are initiated as a part of the development of a combatant commander TSCP. Approved teams are tasked directly to the supporting service component. Service components follow their prescribed internal procedures for filling these taskings.

Section IV
Quality of Life and Mission Sustainment Items

4–20. Definition

a. A QOL item is any article or Service that in the judgment of the Security Cooperation Organization chief and combatant command will have a positive effect on the living and work environment of a deployed team. Factors to be considered include the following:

(1) Availability of suitable entertainment.

(2) Climate/geography.

(3) Security.

(4) Language problems.

(5) Recreational facilities.

b. Quality of life items are procured for team rather than individual use. Quality of life items may include such things as the following (if approved/authorized by the combatant commander and deploying Service):

(1) Magazines (news and Service-related).

(2) Athletic gear (recreational).

(3) TVs/tapes/DVDs/VCRs/DVD players/CD players.

(4) Fishing tackle.

(5) Hunting equipment.

(6) Boats (canoes, rowboats, sailfish).

(7) Camping equipment.

(8) Scuba gear.

(9) Equipment repair.

c. Quality of life items are subject to the policy guidance for morale, welfare, and recreation publications. Items which are not considered appropriate for morale, welfare, and recreation funding will not qualify for FMS funding as QOL items.

4–21. Mission sustainment items

The following is a partial list of mission sustainment type items (not QOL items):

a. Dependent education.

b. Housing.

c. Medical support and medical evacuation (MEDEVAC).

d. Furniture.

e. Air conditioners (where required).

f. Housekeeping equipment.

g. Drivers.

h. Rations.

i. Security guards.

j. Electrical equipment (generators, transformers, and voltage regulators).

k. Physical conditioning equipment.

l. Environmental and morale leave.

m. Religious support.

4–22. Funding

a. The Security Cooperation Organization chief will use a data sheet to identify the QOL items recommended for funding.

b. A decision on funding will include the judgment of training management agencies and combatant commands.

c. Funding will be identified in the LOA under the team support line with a footnote.

d. IMET funds are not available for purchasing QOL items. Such items may be provided to IMET-funded teams from stock already available in country or by the parent Service from its supplies and resources.

e. Quality of life items may be purchased using resources from FMF-funded FMS cases with the express approval of the host country.

4–23. Fairness and uniform standards

a. The Security Cooperation Organization/combatant commander will determine what is fair and appropriate for team members.

(1) The combatant commander will assure fair and appropriate treatment of all teams within countries under the cognizance of the combatant commander. The level of support provided to a team member under an FMS case will not exceed that authorized for DOD personnel of equivalent grade in countries funded by U.S. appropriations.

(2) The Security Cooperation Organization will assure fair and appropriate treatment of all teams within a country.

b. The combatant commander will establish standards for treatment of team members.

4–24. Inventory control

a. The Security Cooperation Organization will ensure inventory control is according to the combatant command's procedures and guidance.

b. The combatant commander may require periodic physical inventory.

c. The LOA will include a statement, as appropriate, that QOL items will ultimately revert to the control of the host nation.

4–25. Roles

a. The combatant commander will—

(1) Establish a combatant command policy on fairness and equitability.

(2) Ensure compliance with the combatant command policy and also with the Service policy, to the extent possible.

(3) Establish combatant command policies and procedures on accountability.

b. The Security Cooperation Organization will—

(1) Review residential leases to ensure quarters are appropriate for rank and dependent status of team members and comply with DOD and DOS standards. The Security Cooperation Organization ensures each lease request is submitted to the Embassy Interagency Housing Board for approval prior to signature by the appropriate contracting officer. If

higher headquarters approval is required, ensure Embassy Interagency Housing Board reviews request before forwarding lease to the Service International Affairs, team management agency, the combatant commander, and/or the designated component command.

(2) Establish procedures to review all team TDY and approve requests for out-of-country travel.

(3) Review team request for purchase of QOL and/or MS items, and other items required to execute the team training and/or technical assistance mission. This includes healthcare items for the team members (see para 8–6). The Security Cooperation Organization provides Service International Affairs, team management agency, the combatant commander, and/or the designated Component Command with an itemized list of recommended QOL and MS articles to be included in the LOA. Security Cooperation Organization ensure the requested items are authorized in the LOA under which the team operates and that vendor discussions and actual purchases are made through a U.S. contracting office.

(4) Ensure team chief establishes supply and/or equipment accountability records that provide a complete audit trail from item acquisition to disposal. All nonexpendable, durable property costing $50.00 or more is to be recorded on a property record.

(5) Periodically review team property and inventory records for accuracy. Ensure continuous in-country accountability is maintained by conducting a physical inventory prior to team and/or team chief departure from country. As a minimum, physical inventories for PCS teams are conducted annually.

(6) Perform periodic reviews of team petty cash funds to ensure funds are adequately protected and cash management is in accordance with Embassy budget and fiscal office procedures.

(7) Assist the team chief to establish procedures with the Embassy for payroll support of any foreign Service employees hired to support the team.

(8) Assist the Service International Affairs, team management agency, the combatant commander, and/or the designated component command to identify country unique management and administrative duties associated with the team's deployment.

c. The team chief will—

(1) Assign duties to team members to ensure the team mission is accomplished within the prescribed timeframe.

(2) Submit requests and/or justification for QOL and/or MS items, and items required to execute the team mission to the Security Cooperation Organization prior to purchase.

(3) Establish and maintain supply and/or equipment accountability records for all QOL, MS, and mission essential property in accordance with Service directives and procedures. Provide Security Cooperation Organization with a copy of property records listing all non-expendable, durable equipment valued at $50.00 or more.

(4) Provide Security Cooperation Organization with access to team property for the purpose of conducting a physical inventory (at least annually for PCS teams and/or prior to team chief departure from country for TDY teams.)

(5) Identify problems that may impact team personnel and/or mission, and report these problems and recommended solutions to the Security Cooperation Organization, the Service International Affairs, team management agency, the combatant commander, and/or the designated component command, as appropriate.

(6) Send copies of receipts and vouchers to the Service International Affairs, team management agency, the combatant commander, and/or the designated component command, and hold copies on open actions until cleared through accounting and finance channels.

(7) Provide annual (for PCS teams) or end of tour (for TDY teams) progress report to the Service International Affairs, team management agency, the combatant command, and/or the designated component command, to include complete listing of personnel/units trained.

(8) Provide an after action report within 30 days of completion of the team's mission. See format at figure 4–3 for guidance.

After Action Report for Teams

After Action Reports should include, but are not limited to the following information:

a. Team Information (Team type designation, composition by name, grade, occupational specialty, and parent unit/location)

b. Relevant dates.
   (1)   Date departed home station.
   (2)   Dates and location of team assembly and orientation.
   (3)   Date of arrival in host country
   (4)   Date on which training/technical assistance started and ended
   (5)   Date of departure from host country
   (6)   Date of return to parent unit/organization

c. Mission.

d. Locations (Indicate the locations at which training/technical assistance was conducted.)

e. Number of Trainees. (Indicate the number of indigenous personnel trained by type. For example, maintenance, supply, instructor etc. indicate whether trainees were officer, enlisted or civilians. Use actual numbers of students rather than unit designations such as battalion, company etc.)

f. Installations. (Indicate schools, courses, or training installations/other facilities relating to the mission of the team)

g. Adequacy. (Indicate the adequacy of the in-country training installation and facilities relating to the mission of the team)

h. Materiel. (Indicate the type, quantity, condition, and state of maintenance of materiel on which the training or technical assistance was provided)

i. Interpreter Support. (Indicate the adequacy and effectiveness of interpreter support provided.)

j. Training conditions. (Provide a summary of training conditions as existed on arrival.)

k. Effectiveness. (Evaluation the effectiveness of training or technical assistance. Provide a summary of the success of the team effort to improve the effectiveness of the training program in the lost nation and qualification of host nation personnel to carry on.)

l. Problems. (Discuss problems encountered that affected the mission.)

m. Preparation (Indicate preparation for the mission, answering the following questions:
   (1) Did notification of the selection of the team provide adequate guidance on mission, type and level of training or assistance desired, training material and training aids required?
   (2) Were special or unusual problems anticipated?
   (3) Was the lead-time adequate for proper preparation for the mission?

n. Support. (Indicate the adequacy of the country team's support. Indicate any comments considered appropriate concerning accommodations, meals, medical facilities, transportation, and overall treatment)

Figure 4–3. Format for after actions report for teams

o. Conclusions. (Include conclusions and recommendations.) Provide the following:
    (1)   Necessity for the team as requested to accomplish the mission.
    (2)   Indicate if the mission was accomplished and how the team could have been more useful
    (3)   Indicate the follow-up actions the SAO might take
    (4)   Include essentials information to increase the effectiveness of future security cooperation teams

Figure 4–3. Format for after actions report for teams–Continued

Section V
Department of the Army

4–26. Programming security assistance teams under U.S. grant funded programs
a. Policy guidance for Army Security Assistance Teams (SAT) can be found in Army regulation (AR) 12–7.

b. The SATMO in coordination with SATFA will develop the SAT refined cost estimate.

c. The SATMO and the furnishing agency will determine the team composition necessary to achieve the team mission. SATMO will notify SATFA of any required program changes.

d. The Security Cooperation Organization may request training expertise, literature, and general information on training aids from the Commander, U.S. Army SATMO (AOJK–SA), Fort Bragg, NC 28310–5000.

4–27. Funding security assistance training under U.S. grant funded programs
a. The SATFA allocates funds to SATMO. SATMO will provide furnishing commands with coordination instruction and financial information for preparation of SAT orders.

b. The furnishing command will properly reimburse any civilian salaries to the correct account.

c. The SATMO will not deploy U.S. grant funded SAT before receipt of funding authorization from SATFA.

4–28. Programming security assistance training under foreign military sales
The SATMO will coordinate the development of cost data with SATFA.

4–29. Funding security assistance training under foreign military sales
The SATMO manages mission funds for FMS funded SAT and will not deploy SAT until receipt of FMS case funds from SATFA. SATMO issues fund cites/military interdepartmental purchase requests and TDY orders to furnishing commands/agencies as appropriate. Furnishing commands/agencies must provide copies of final settlement vouchers to SATMO as soon as possible after mission completion. Furnishing commands/agencies will forward all SAT related financial documents to: CDR, SATMO (AOJKSA–SASD), Fort Bragg, NC 28310–5000.

4–30. Security assistance team identification
The IMET and FMS SAT are identified as explained, below.

a. Include the following components in the SAT number:

(1) Type team (radio repair, personnel administration, general supply, and so forth).

(2) Designator (MTT, TAT, ETSS, TAFT, pre-deployment site survey, or RST).

(3) Two letter geopolitical (country) code as listed in the SAMM.

(4) For IMET, the four digit WCN. For FMS, the alphabetical FMS case designator.

(5) Four digits designating the FY in which the SAT is scheduled to deploy. (For IMET, an X following the FY indicates a SAT that has been added to the program).

b. The following are examples of MTT identification:

(1) For IMET: UH 1 Maint MTT–TH 0014–2000.

(2) For FMS: M113A1 Opns MTT–SR–OBQ–2000.

4–31. Temporary duty security assistance team request and authorized use

The TDY team request and Army decision process is depicted in AR 12–7, figure 4–1. The process starts with the country team receiving an letter of request or a country's request for a training team for an Army mission under an existing LOA. The country team will assist the country by preparing a detailed team request memorandum (TRM). The TRM format is provided at appendix D. The Security Cooperation Organization must send the TRM (see app D) for a TDY team in accordance with figure 4–1 through the combatant command to HQDA a minimum of 10 months before the date of deployment. The combatant command will validate and endorse TRM that do not meet the timeline in AR 12–7 and submit them with justification (operational requirements) to DASA DE&C for review and staffing to the Vice Chief of Staff, U.S. Army for decision. Copies will be provided to TRADOC/SATFA and SATMO.

 a. Before submitting the TRM, the Security Cooperation Organization may request assistance from SATMO concerning team composition, training concept, cost information, and general guidance on the availability of specific skills.

 b. The requirements must be written to achieve a specific objective during a specific timeframe.

 c. The requirements must be tied into the current combatant commander's TSCP or the country CETP to ensure specified objectives are achieved. Here are some examples of current commanders of combatant commands and Army strategic objectives:

 (1) Enhance partner capability to conduct internal stability operations.

 (2) Build partner capability to support commanders of combatant commands missions with a focus on regional interoperability and stabilization operations, peacekeeping operations, and humanitarian assistance.

 (3) Deter aggression and counter coercion, and defeat adversaries.

 (4) Develop capabilities of key allies and partners to dissuade potential adversaries.

 d. Requests for P&A must use the TRM format containing the planning information necessary to estimate costs and survey availability.

 e. The country team will then submit a detailed TRM through the commanders of combatant commands for validation. The TRM will clearly state the mission, training goals, end state of the mission, and the qualifications the team members should possess. The Security Cooperation Organization should also identify geographic or climatic conditions to be considered in selection of team members. The Security Cooperation Organization will include a SOW to be coordinated with SATMO as a part of the TRM. The commanders of combatant commands will coordinate with the ASCC to determine if the mission can be satisfied from internal theater assets. If so, the mission is executed intra-theater with no HQDA involvement required. If not, the commanders of combatant commands will forward the TRM to HQDA for decision. The Army action agency address is DASA DE&C, Suite 8200, (SAAL–NP), 1777 North Kent Street, Arlington, Virginia 22209.

 f. The DASA DE&C will coordinate with the DCS, G–1 and DCS, G–3/5/7 and make a decision on the TRM. If the TRM is disapproved, it will be sent back through the commanders of combatant commands to the country team with applicable justification. If the TRM is approved, DASA DE&C will draft an execution message to DCS, G–3/5/7, Operations Division Operations with a mission statement, metrics for measuring success, and a timeline for completion.

 g. The DCS, G–3/5/7 Operations Division Operations upon receiving the draft execution message from DASA DE&C will send a tasker to the USAR, NG, and TRADOC G–3/5/7 central tasking office to fill the request. Given an approved and implemented LOA, SATMO will execute the fill of the team and prepare them for deployment.

 h. The Security Cooperation Organization, in coordination with SATMO ensures that all necessary equipment, supplies, instructional facilities, and technical publications are on hand or available for the arrival of the team. Tools and ancillary equipment needed for the training or technical assistance must be on hand and available for the team use when the team arrives in country.

 i. The Security Cooperation Organization ensures that foreign personnel to be trained meet the prerequisites necessary to comprehend the technical level of presentation and that they are vetted for training.

 j. The Security Cooperation Organization programs the in-country arrival date and must consider the availability of trainees, facilities, and equipment.

 k. In accordance with 10 USC 167b, the Security Cooperation Organization will direct any requests for Army Special Operations Forces personnel to the theater SOC for validation, then to the theater combatant commander, who will forward the request to U.S. Special Operations Command (USSOCOM) for approval. Upon approval, USSOCOM will direct team sourcing. Approval to use IMET funds for SATs requires that the Combatant Commander forward a request for waiver to DSCA for consideration and approval before sending the TRM to HQDA. The waiver request should include a cost estimate for training aids and training materials. The Security Cooperation Organization can request P&A assistance from SATMO for the cost estimate for the IMET waiver.

4–32. The permanent change of station security assistance team request and authorized use

 a. The PCS team request and Army decision process is included in AR 12–7. The process starts with the country TRM.

b. Before submitting the TRM, the Security Cooperation Organization may request assistance from TRADOC concerning team composition, training concept, cost information, and general guidance on the availability of specific skills.

c. Need to add 15 months lead time for training and PCS teams into LOA.

d. The requirements must be written to achieve a specific objective during a specific timeframe.

e. The requirements must be tied into the current combatant commander's TSCP or the country CETP to ensure specified objectives are achieved. Here are some examples of current commanders of combatant commands and Army strategic objectives—

(1) Enhance partner capability to conduct internal stability operations.

(2) Build partner capability to support commanders of combatant commands missions with a focus on regional interoperability and stabilization operations, peacekeeping operations, and humanitarian assistance.

(3) Deter aggression and counter coercion, and defeat adversaries.

(4) Develop capabilities of key allies and partners to dissuade potential adversaries.

f. Requests for P&A must use the TRM format containing the planning information necessary to estimate costs and survey availability.

g. The country team will then submit a detailed TRM through the commanders of combatant commands for validation to HQDA for decision. The TRM will clearly state the mission, training goals, end state of the mission, and the qualifications the team members should possess. The Security Cooperation Organization should also identify geographic or climatic conditions to be considered in selection of team members. For contractor-staffed SAT, the Security Cooperation Organization will include, as part of the TRM, a SOW to be coordinated with TRADOC.

(1) The TRM will be submitted through the appropriate commanders of combatant commands staff to validate the requirements.

(2) Upon commanders of combatant commands validation of the TRM, it will be forwarded to HQDA for coordination and decision. The Army action agency address is DASA DE&C, Suite 8200, (SAAL–NP), 1777 North Kent Street, Arlington, Virginia 22209.

(3) The DASA DE&C will coordinate with the DCS, G–1 and DCS, G–3/5/7 and make a decision on the TRM. If the TRM is disapproved, it will be sent back through the commanders of combatant commands to the country team with applicable justification. If the TRM is approved, DASA DE&C will draft an execution message to DCS, G–3/5/7 Operations Division Operations with a mission statement, metrics for measuring success, and a timeline for completion.

(4) The DCS, G–3/5/7 Operations Division Operations upon receiving the draft execution message from DASA DE&C will send a tasker to the USAR, National Guard Bureau, and TRADOC G–3/5/7 central tasking office to fill the request. Given an approved and implemented LOA, TRADOC will execute the fill of the team and prepare them for deployment.

(5) The Security Cooperation Organization, in coordination with TRADOC ensures that all necessary equipment, supplies, instruction facilities, and technical publications are on hand or available for the arrival of the team. Tools and ancillary equipment needed for the training or technical assistance must be on-hand and available for the team use when the SAT team arrives in country.

(6) The Security Cooperation Organization ensures that foreign personnel to be trained meet the prerequisites necessary to comprehend the technical level of presentation and that they are vetted for training.

(7) The Security Cooperation Organization programs the in-country arrival date in accordance with AR 12–7 and must consider the availability of trainees, facilities, and equipment. The team chief, in coordination with SATMO and the Security Cooperation Organization, will meet reporting requirements in AR 12–7.

4–33. Extensions
Continuation of the duration of an Army non-contractor PCS SAT beyond 2 years requires HQDA approval. If a PCS team requires a continuation beyond 2 years, the Security Cooperation Organization will submit a team continuation request memorandum through the same process as the TRM for approval. To meet Army personnel management timelines, the team continuation request memorandum must be submitted by the end of the first year. No continuations will be granted without Human Resources Command approval.

4–34. Correspondence
All significant communications concerning SAT will include the Security Cooperation Organization, commanders of combatant commands, ASCC, SATFA, SATMO, furnishing agency, USASAC, and HQDA (DASA DE&C) as information or action addressees, as appropriate.

4–35. Country or area clearances
Since the SAT request initiates within the country and are approved by the commanders of combatant commands, HQDA (DASA DE&C), and OSD, the SAT is exempted from processing for theater or area clearance requirements

specified in AR 55–46. However, the provisions of DODD 4500.54E apply and SATMO will coordinate special actions for clearance specified therein.

4–36. Passports and visas
The requirements outlined in DOD 1000.21–R apply to SAT members. When establishing the desired arrival date for a SAT, the Security Cooperation Organization must consider the time required to process applications for passports and visas (approximately 6 weeks).

4–37. Temporary duty orders
The SATMO will issue funded SAT orders in accordance with AR 600–8–105. Furnishing commands will follow the instructions on these orders, such as, passport processing, immunizations, Soldier readiness, and so forth.

4–38. Team assembly
a. The CONUS teams will assemble under the team chief at a location SATMO designates. The SATMO will provide the Security Cooperation Organization the following information:
(1) Estimated time of departure from CONUS.
(2) Estimated time of arrival in the foreign country.
(3) Travel information.
b. Personnel deployed OCONUS under the Security Assistance Program as part of a security assistance team must attend the Security Assistance Training Team Orientation Course conducted at Fort Bragg, NC. The CDR, SATMO, may grant constructive credit for Security Assistance Training Team Orientation Course when the Security Cooperation Organization and CDR, SATMO agree that is not required. Should CDR, SATMO and host country team not agree, CDR, Security Assistance Training Management Organization will request constructive credit from HQDA (DASA DE&C).

4–39. Arrival or departure notice
The Security Cooperation Organization will notify Security Assistance Training Management Organization, SATFA, the furnishing agency, the commanders of combatant commands, and HQDA (DASA DE&C) of the arrival and departure date of the SAT or members of the team, using the team identification number.

4–40. Personnel evaluation reports
a. AR 623–3 (officers) and (enlisted) establish the requirement for personnel evaluations by grade.
b. In coordination with the Security Cooperation Organization, Security Assistance Training Management Organization will establish a rating scheme for PCS team members and for team members on TDY for more than 90 days.
c. Unless otherwise specified in MOU/MOA, CDR, Security Assistance Training Management Organization will be in the rating chain for all team chiefs.

4–41. After action report
a. Upon completion of an assignment and before departure, the chief of each SAT will prepare a report (see fig 4–3) on the effectiveness of the training presented and submit the original to the Security Cooperation Organization.
b. The Security Cooperation Organization will forward a copy of the SAT evaluation and the after action report through the commanders of combatant commands and the Service component to HQDA (DASA DE&C) with information copies to Security Assistance Training Management Organization, SATFA, USASAC, and to the chief of staff of each major subordinate command contributing to the composition of the team. On forwarding, the Security Cooperation Organization will endorse the report and address any problems or make recommendations that are within the Security Cooperation Organization purview. In the endorsement, the Security Cooperation Organization will also evaluate the team's overall effectiveness and performance.
c. HQDA (DASA (DE&C)) will take action, as required, upon receipt of the comments of the Security Cooperation Organization and commanders of combatant commands.

4–42. Flight physicals for U.S. Army security assistance team members
All aircrew personnel will complete a comprehensive annual flying duty medical examination (FDME) prior to departing home base. When aircrew are on duty at an OCONUS station with limited medical facilities, they will accomplish the FDME to the extent possible, and, in accordance with AR 40–501, paragraph 6–8*d*, attach a cover letter explaining facility limitations. They will accomplish a comprehensive FDME within 90 days of return to a station with adequate medical facilities. See AR 40–501, paragraph 6–8*d* for additional guidance.

Section VI
Department of the Navy (U.S. Navy, U.S. Marine Corps, and U.S. Coast Guard)

4–43. Mobile education teams

The Mobile Education Team are provided primarily under E–IMET programs in a seminar/educational forum in host countries taught by designated activities referred to as Mobile Education Team providers.

a. Programming procedures.

(1) The Naval Education and Training Security Assistance Field Activity is the Training Management Activity for all USN and Defense Institute for International Legal Studies Mobile Education Team, and USCG is responsible for all USCG Mobile Education Team. The Mobile Education Team should be programmed at the annual Combatant Command Security Cooperation Education and Training Working Group. Otherwise, a message should be submitted by the Security Cooperation Organization to the Naval Education and Training Security Assistance Field Activity or USCG Headquarters (G–CI) (as appropriate) no later than 120 days prior to the requested start date. The format for requesting a Mobile Education Team is provided in figure 4–2 in the general section of this chapter. DSCA, the combatant command, Navy IPO, and the Mobile Education Team provider should be copied on this correspondence.

(2) The Mobile Education Team providers and Security Cooperation Organization will be responsible for verifying programming entries on the Security Assistance Network Web. If there are discrepancies, the MILDEP should be notified immediately.

b. Security assistance officer responsibilities. The Security Cooperation Organization will ensure that the necessary technical support and instruction facilities are available and that participants in the Mobile Education Team meet the provider's requirements. The Security Cooperation Organization will provide logistical support, which includes the following:

(1) Determine Mobile Education Team location, that is, hotel or host country facility.

(2) Make reservations for lodging and arrange transportation (if applicable).

(3) Lecture room containing seats and tables for each class member, faculty, and visitors.

(4) Discussion rooms.

(5) Overhead projector, screen, power outlets, chalkboard/wetboard, transformers, extension cords, adapters, computer projector, and other requirements as indicated by the provider.

(6) Reproduction, clerical assistance.

(7) Interpreter support, if required.

(8) Ensure speakers (Ambassador, DCM, MOD, MOJ, and so forth) are arranged for opening/closing.

(9) Advise appropriate uniforms/civilian attire for receptions, and so forth.

(10) Country clearance and assistance in procuring lodging.

(11) Receive course materials from Mobile Education Team provider and ensure they are placed at the conference site the weekend prior to course start date.

(12) Provide list of attendees (name/rank/Service) to the Mobile Education Team provider and to Naval Education and Training Security Assistance Field Activity or USCG Headquarters (G–CI) (as appropriate) 2 weeks prior to Mobile Education Team.

(13) Advise Mobile Education Team provider of estimated in-country costs for authorized expenses in call-up message and more well defined estimate 90 days prior to Mobile Education Team.

(14) Brief Mobile Education Team personnel upon arrival in foreign country on the following topics:

(a) Training objectives.

(b) Political situations.

(c) Social customs.

(d) Guidelines for official and personal associations with foreign personnel.

(e) Currency control.

(f) Logistics support.

(g) Administrative support.

(h) Legal status in relation to the foreign country.

(15) Upon completion of the Mobile Education Team, the Security Cooperation Organization will notify the Naval Education and Training Security Assistance Field Activity or USCG International Affairs (G–CI) (as appropriate) via e-mail or message the arrival and subsequent departure date of the Mobile Education Team after completion.

c. Mobile Education Team provider actions. All significant communications concerning the Mobile Education Team especially information concerning dates, costs, participants and confirmed programming, will include the Security Cooperation Organization, the combatant command, the Mobile Education Team provider, and Naval Education and Training Security Assistance Field Activity, or USCG International Affairs (G–CI) (as appropriate). Once a Mobile Education Team is requested, the Mobile Education Team provider will communicate directly with the Security Cooperation Organization. The provider will send requirements to the host country no later than 15 days after receiving the request.

d. Mobile education team provider responsibilities.

(1) Confirm dates for the Mobile Education Team and provide cost estimates to the Naval Education and Training Security Assistance Field Activity or USCG International Affairs (G–CI) (as appropriate).

(2) Request country/area clearances.

(3) Coordinate instructors and class schedule.

(4) Conduct course.

e. Mobile education team chief actions. The team chief is authorized direct communication with the Security Cooperation Organization. While in the foreign country, the team chief will work closely with the Security Cooperation Organization to resolve problems. Problems that cannot be resolved at the local level will be reported to the Service Naval Education and Training Security Assistance Field Activity or USCG International Affairs (G–CI) (as appropriate). On completion of the team's mission and before departure from the foreign country, the team chief will orally brief the appropriate Security Cooperation Organization authorities on the effectiveness (for example, positive and/or negative comments) of the Mobile Education Team.

f. Reporting procedures.

(1) Monthly summary reports of planned Mobile Education Team whether programmed on the STL or not, will be provided by each Mobile Education Team provider to the Naval Education and Training Security Assistance Field Activity or USCG International Affairs (G–CI) (as appropriate) and will include the following information: country, start and end dates, phase, estimated cost (when available), MASL number, WCN, and location.

(2) After action reports should be provided upon completion of the Mobile Education Team; the Mobile Education Team provider will submit a report in the format provided in figure 4–3. This report should be prepared within 30 working days of mission completion. A copy of this report should be provided to DSCA, the combatant command, the Security Cooperation Organization/Embassy, Navy IPO, and Naval Education and Training Security Assistance Field Activity or USCG Headquarters (G–CI) (as appropriate). A list of attendees will be included.

g. Funding procedures. Final in-country cost estimate will be submitted to the Mobile Education Team provider by the Security Cooperation Organization no later than 90 days prior to the scheduled start of the Mobile Education Team. Final Mobile Education Team provider cost estimate will be submitted to the Naval Education and Training Security Assistance Field Activity or USCG International Affairs (G–CI) (as appropriate) and the Security Cooperation Organization no later than 60 days prior to the scheduled start of the Mobile Education Team. The Naval Education and Training Security Assistance Field Activity or USCG International Affairs (G–CI) (as appropriate) will provide a funding document to the Mobile Education Team provider 15 days after receipt of the cost and corresponding confirmation dates from the Mobile Education Team provider.

(1) *Authorized expenditures.*

(a) Airline costs.

(b) Per diem (meals & incidental expenses) and lodging.

(c) Course cost (includes curriculum development as well as Mobile Education Team delivery).

(d) Civilian/contractor labor.

(e) Guest speaker honorariums ($250 per day limit per speaker).

(f) Translation of material costs.

(g) Miscellaneous (printing costs, excess baggage, rental car, FEDEX/DHL costs).

(2) *In-country authorized expenditures.*

(a) Facility rental.

(b) Working lunch (in accordance with M&IE rates listed in the JTR).

(c) Morning and afternoon breaks.

(d) Interpreter support (minimum 2 simultaneous; add 2 more for discussion problems).

(e) Translation equipment.

(f) Duplication of materials.

(g) Projector/computer for overheads.

(h) Translation of materials (if not accomplished by Mobile Education Team provider).

(i) Air travel in accordance with the JTR.

(3) *Cancellation policy.* Navy IPO annual cancellation policy message addresses cancellation fees for Mobile Education Team. In general, a Mobile Education Team that has been programmed requires DSCA approval for cancellation and countries are liable for any charges incurred.

(4) *Medical Services.* If a team member requires routine or emergency health services and does not have ready access to the U.S. Embassy health unit or the Service required is not available at the health unit, the IMETP, or the FMS case (if it includes a medical line) will be responsible for—

(a) Cost of the treatment in-country.

(b) Cost of transportation to the nearest appropriate U.S. military treatment facility. The U.S. Embassy's regional

medical officer will make referral decisions. If there is not enough money in the FMS case or the IMETP to cover expenses, the FMS case or the IMETP will be amended to include these costs.

h. Regional Mobile Education Team. A regional Mobile Education Team is coordinated with the Mobile Education Team provider and programmed by Naval Education and Training Security Assistance Field Activity or Coast Guard International Affairs (G–CI) at the annual Security Cooperation Education and Training Working Group. Responsibilities are similar to other Mobile Education Team with the following differences:

(1) After receiving a reply from the Mobile Education Team provider acknowledging proposed Mobile Education Team and timeframe and/or programming in STL, either the Security Cooperation Organization or the combatant command will notify all countries in the region requesting participation. If the minimum class size (as coordinated by the Mobile Education Team provider and Security Cooperation Organization) is not met, the host country will be expected to provide additional students. Since tuition costs per student will be determined by dividing the total Mobile Education Team cost (for example, instructor travel, conference fees, and so forth) by the number of participants, class size should be determined NLT 30 days prior to course commencement.

(2) If a student is scheduled to attend a regional Mobile Education Team and has been included for purposes of course pricing, student cancellation charges will be 100 percent unless student's country can provide a substitute.

(3) Approved costs include travel, cost of lodging, meals and incidentals (in accordance with the JTR), and proportionate course cost. Charges will be made to the appropriate IMET program for students who participate from invited countries.

(4) Fund cite for travel will be provided by Naval Education and Training Security Assistance Field Activity to the Security Cooperation Organization in invited countries.

(5) The Security Cooperation Organization with students attending from other countries will—

(a) Provide names of vetted prospective students to the host Security Cooperation Organization, Mobile Education Team provider, and the Naval Education and Training Security Assistance Field Activity, or USCG International Affairs (GCI) (as appropriate) 2 weeks prior to the scheduled start of the Mobile Education Team.

(b) Coordinate payment of authorized living expenses with Security Cooperation Organization in host country. Advance payment to students prior to departure if requested by Security Cooperation Organization in host country.

(c) Issue ITOs and provide copies to all concerned.

(6) The Security Cooperation Organization in the host country will—

(a) Reserve lodging for visiting students as well as for the instructors teaching the course.

(b) Advise the Mobile Education Team provider concerning in-country expenses (to include lodging for participating students, working lunches, translator, and so forth).

(c) Coordinate with the Security Cooperation Organization from other countries regarding information on visas, flight itineraries, and transportation from the airport.

(d) Pay approved costs of lodging, meals, and incidentals in accordance with the JTR for the city where training is conducted (deduct meals that are provided by other sources) to each student from visiting countries from the fund cite issued by the Mobile Education Team provider. If unable to pay directly, coordinate with Security Cooperation Organization in participating countries to determine advance payment amounts.

(e) Provide a complete vetted roster of students to the Mobile Education Team provider, Naval Education and Training Security Assistance Field Activity, and the USCG International Affairs (G–CI) (if appropriate) one week prior to the scheduled start of the Mobile Education Team.

(f) Provide disbursement vouchers to the Mobile Education Team provider within 30 days of completion of the Mobile Education Team. Security Cooperation Organization in participating countries are authorized to issue travel advances in the amount recommended by the Security Cooperation Organization in host country or Mobile Education Team provider.

(g) If Mobile Education Team is funded by Counterterrorism Fellowship Program, provide Special Operations/Low Intensity Conflict via commanders of combatant commands a total cost estimate (Mobile Education Team provider cost, all in-country costs, and round-trip travel, lodging, meal and incidental costs for all participating students).

i. The CONUS E–IMET training in conjunction with a Mobile Education Team. Requirements for CONUS E–IMET training are submitted at the same time as the requirements for a survey/assessment. The CONUS training segment normally contains a mix of content and planning. Participants should be programmed using individual WCN and ITO. Participants should leave the CONUS planning segment with a clear idea of where the provider and the country will proceed with future training.

(1) The Security Cooperation Organization responsibilities are to—

(a) Request programming.

(b) Identify candidates and coordinate dates with E–IMET provider.

(c) Make airline reservations and assist with visas.

(d) Issue ITOs after receipt of authority from Naval Education and Training Security Assistance Field Activity.

(e) Provide students with standard briefing before attending training in the United States.

(f) Provide Mobile Education Team provider with arrival information.

(2) The training activity responsibilities are to—

(a) Schedule course dates with Security Cooperation Organization.

(b) Keep Naval Education and Training Security Assistance Field Activity or Military Service informed when communicating directly with Security Cooperation Organization.

(c) Coordinate instructors and class schedule.

(d) Make reservations for lodging and arrange transportation.

(e) After receipt of funding from Naval Education and Training Security Assistance Field Activity, pay expenses of delegates.

(f) Conduct course.

(3) Upon completion of course, submit an after action Report as shown in figure 4–3 within 30 days to DSCA, combatant command, Security Cooperation Organization/Embassy, Navy IPO, OSD, and the Naval Education and Training Security Assistance Field Activity or USCG International Affairs (G–CI), as appropriate.

(4) The Naval Education and Training Security Assistance Field Activity or Military Service: Program Mobile Education Team so that it can be seen in the Security Assistance Network Web.

(5) Naval Education and Training Security Assistance Field Activity—

(a) Provide ITO authority to Security Cooperation Organization.

(b) Enter financial data in STL/International Standardized Training Listing.

(c) Provide funding document to Mobile Education Team provider.

4–44. U.S. Navy teams

a. The Naval Education and Training Security Assistance Field Activity will act as the central reviewing authority for all U.S. Navy MTT requests. Upon receipt of the call-up for an MTT, Naval Education and Training Security Assistance Field Activity will issue the details necessary for team organization and deployment. This will include, but is not limited to, cost estimates, funding data, country background, general administrative instructions, logistics information, travel and transportation requirements and other information essential to the accomplishment of the team mission. An ETSS is processed similar to a MTT except that the length of time requires PCS. Billets must first be in place to support the team and the process to establish the billets and identify personnel requires a minimum of 18 to 24 months.

b. The Naval Education and Training Security Assistance Field Activity will coordinate with Navy commands to find team personnel, designate a furnishing activity, designate the team chief, in writing, and provide a letter of instruction for the team. The furnishing activity will normally be designated as the command responsible for team assembly. Naval Education and Training Security Assistance Field Activity will provide the necessary funding data or appropriate documentation to commands issuing temporary additional duty orders for MTT personnel.

c. The furnishing activity will prepare team orders according to existing Naval Military Personnel Command or BUPERS instructions using accounting data furnished by Naval Education and Training Security Assistance Field Activity. Country, area, or personnel clearance(s) required by the JTR will be submitted by the furnishing activity.

d. The Naval Education and Training Security Assistance Field Activity will specify required training prior to deployment and will specify where team or the team chief will travel to provide briefing and or debriefings. This could include Naval Education and Training Security Assistance Field Activity, Washington, DC commands or the combatant command.

e. The Security Cooperation Organization will notify the furnishing activity, combatant command and Naval Education and Training Security Assistance Field Activity by message of the arrival and departure of the team or team members. The Security Cooperation Organization will also prepare a report on team performance and mission accomplishment. This report can be an endorsement on the team chief's after action report, or prepared separately. The report should be mailed to Naval Education and Training Security Assistance Field Activity, copy to Navy IPO and the furnishing activity. For teams deployed over 90 days the Security Cooperation Organization or a military group officer senior to the team chief, will prepare a concurrent personnel evaluation concerning the team chief and forward it to the command officer of the furnishing activity.

f. Upon completion of an assignment, the team chief of each team will prepare an after action report as shown in figure 3–4 on the effectiveness of the training presented. This report should be prepared within 30 working days of mission completion and forwarded to Naval Education and Training Security Assistance Field Activity via the furnishing activity, copies to the Security Cooperation Organization and Navy IPO. For a team deployed over 90 days, the team chief will prepare a concurrent personnel evaluation on all team members and forward it to the commanding officer of the member's furnishing activity.

4–45. Ship transfer mobile training teams

The MTT associated with the transfer of a U.S. Navy ship to a foreign country by either sale, loan, or lease will be governed by the same general rules as listed in this chapter. Due to the differing nature in certain aspects; however, the following additional guidance is provided:

a. A ship transfer MTT is normally drawn from members of the crew of the U.S. Navy ship being transferred to take full advantage of the knowledge and expertise of these personnel with regard to the particular ship. The MTT will be under the administrative control of the type commander transferring the ship. This approach will be used in all cases where practicable. For ships being taken from the inactive fleet or from new construction, BUPERS will be tasked with selecting the required personnel. Every effort will be made to avoid depleting fleet personnel resources.

b. When an MTT is required to report to a location in a foreign country for embarkation aboard a foreign ship, extreme care will be exercised in the preparation of orders. Specifically, the MTT should be ordered to report to a U.S. activity such as an Security Cooperation Organization for onward routing to the ship. Members of the team may be housed in a foreign shipyard or ashore at a foreign naval activity while waiting to board the ship. The Security Cooperation Organization will incorporate this in the call-up message so that orders issued to the MTT may be comprehensive in nature.

c. In cases where an MTT reports in a foreign country for duty as a shipyard MTT, it is incumbent upon the Security Cooperation Organization to ensure that a workable system for the delivery of mail to the team is instituted.

d. The MTT members should be designated and assembled at a central location for shipboard MTT, whether embarkation is to be in the United States, in a foreign country, or at an overseas location. It is recommended that the MTT report to the appropriate fleet commander approximately 2 weeks prior to CONUS departure or boarding.

e. The MTT members should, where feasible, be volunteers. Experience has shown that non volunteer MTT members required to board a foreign ship, subsist in a foreign mess, live in non-U.S. Navy quarters, and accommodate themselves to foreign ship routine, frequently create problems for themselves, the team, the foreign navy, and the U.S. Navy.

f. Enlisted members of ship transfer MTT should be of a senior rate (chief petty officer or petty officer first class) if feasible.

g. The mission of the MTT is to assist the commanding officer in the training of the crew. An MTT should also be prepared to do the following:

(1) Supervise the maintenance or repair of equipment essential to the training mission.

(2) Participate in the Supply Overhaul Assistance Program.

(3) Schedule formal instruction.

(4) Ensure that work done by shore facilities is correct.

(5) Train the ship's company in the maintenance and operation of their equipment.

(6) Supervise and conduct team training.

(7) Act as a liaison between the ship, shore facilities, other ships, and activities as required for successful completion of the mission.

h. If a ship is being transferred from an inactive status, the MTT should comprise personnel from the same class of ship, so they will be familiar with the equipment on which they will be providing instruction. For example, ensure that engineering personnel are familiar with the propulsion plant on the ship being transferred (for example, 600-psi plant personnel should not be assigned to train on a ship with a 1200-psi plant).

i. If possible, at least two officers will be assigned to a shipboard MTT. One officer will be experienced in operations and one in engineering. Operations experience is necessary, as the ship will come under the control of different commands requiring an officer familiar with operation orders, movement orders, movement reports, and logistic requests. The major materiel problems encountered will usually be in engineering; therefore, an officer with engineering experience will be an extremely valuable asset.

4–46. Marine corps teams

The SC teams from the USMC are in high demand. Requests for USMC assistance come from a variety of sources that have different execution requirements, requiring differing policies and procedures.

a. The security cooperation teams requested by a regional combatant commander or country.

(1) The SC teams deploying under 10 USC (Armed Forces) Authorities. Many SC teams requested under a Title 10 authority follow the Joint Staff Joint Force Provider Request for Forces process. The USMC staffs and sources a team requested in this manner per the Joint Staff and Commander, U.S. Joint Forces Command tasking and applies CMC guidance. However, a commanders of combatant commands may direct its Marine Corps forces (MARFOR) to execute a SC team under a specific Title 10 program such as combatant commander initiatives, Traditional Commander's Activity (TCA) that might not be sourced via the Request for Forces process. In these cases, the procedure outlined in paragraph 4–46(b), below, applies as if the request originated from the regional MARFOR.

(2) The SC teams deploying under 22 USC authorities. Requests for teams that deploy under one of the applicable 22 USC authorities normally originate from the requesting country through the Security Cooperation Organization in that country. The Security Cooperation Organization forwards the request to Security Cooperation Education and Training Center following procedures outlined in paragraph 4–46c, below.

b. The security cooperation teams requested by a regional MARFOR.

(1) Regional MARFORs conduct many SC events in support of their commanders of combatant commands's TSCP under one of the Title 10 authorities. When such an event involves deploying a team that cannot be accomplished using assigned forces or through the Request for Forces process, the regional MARFOR submits a feasibility of support

message detailing the requirement to Marine Forces Command G–3/5/7 with an information copy to CMC P/PO/PL/ MP/IO and Security Cooperation Education and Training Center. If the SC event involves Marine Corps special operations command (MARSOC) assets the FOS message should include MARSOC and SOCOM as information addresses.

(2) Mission analysis and validation will be conducted by CMC POC/PLU and Security Cooperation Education and Training Center. Once validated, CMC POC commences coordination with Marine Forces Command and Security Cooperation Education and Training Center for sourcing feasibility. Mission analysis, validation, and sourcing for teams involving MARSOC assets will be coordinated with MARSOC and SOCOM.

c. General policy and procedure for requesting, staffing, and deploying Marine Corps security cooperation teams under Title 22 authorities. This section has been omitted pending the promulgation of revised policy and procedures for requesting, staffing, and deploying USMC security cooperation teams. Interim guidance for sourcing teams under Title 10 and Title 22 will be published by Marine Corps message. Formal guidance will be announced in a subsequent change to this publication as well as Marine Corps Order 5710.6B (USMC Security Cooperation.)

d. Reports.

(1) *Status reports.* USMC SC teams deploying for more than 30 days will normally be required to provide periodic status reports on their activities. Format and submission requirements will be provided to the team chief prior to deployment by the deploying activity/command.

(2) *Effectiveness reports.* Defense Security Cooperation Guidance requires each Service to evaluate the effectiveness of its SC events. In compliance with this guidance, an evaluation report is required for each USMC SC team regardless of the deploying authority. The format in figure 4–3 will be utilized as the basis of this evaluation for Marine Corps teams. The team chief is responsible for the preparation of this report. Item e (Number of Trainees) must accurately reflect the number of host nation personnel trained. If feasible, a roster indicating name, rank and unit of assignment of the trainees should be attached. At a minimum, the total number of trainees, broken down by category (that is, officer, enlisted, civilian) and their unit/organization of assignment must be provided. Item k (Effectiveness) should recap the Defense Security Cooperation Guidance objectives, as outlined in the original call up message, and evaluate the effectiveness of the team in meeting those objectives. A "hot wash" of this report should be provided to the Security Cooperation Organization, other appropriate members of the country team, or the supported command (if applicable) prior to the team's departure from country. The formal report will be submitted to CMC PLU, with copies to the supported commanders of combatant commands, the regional MARFOR, Security Cooperation Education and Training Center, and the Security Cooperation Organization/supported command not later than 30 days after the team's return to CONUS.

4–47. Coast Guard exportable maritime teams

a. The USCG mobile maritime teams provide training in all USCG mission areas and are tailored to the host nation's needs. USCG unique mission capabilities and techniques are focused on development of skills to meet the challenges of global maritime security. For example, USCG Military Law Enforcement training equips partner nation maritime services to respond to security threats associated with trafficking in persons, drugs, or weapons of mass destruction. Discussion with USCG International Affairs (G–CI) staff can align appropriate capabilities to global strategic objectives. The USCG can deliver a complete package of training to small groups, multi-agency audiences or several countries in a regional forum.

b. Training provided by a Mobile Education Team/MTT is conducted in English and is usually available in Spanish. When requested the USCG will coordinate with the host country to arrange for interpreters and the translation of course materials to conduct the training successfully. The USCG training is provided on an unclassified basis only.

c. Requests for USCG maritime training teams normally originate from the Security Cooperation Organization during the Security Cooperation Education and Training Working Group process. Training objectives, proposed date(s) and source of funding must be included in the request. Descriptions of course content are available in the USCG International Handbook. Course content can be tailored to meet a host nation's specific needs, based on skill levels, prior training, local conditions, or capabilities to meet specific maritime strategy objectives. Specific requirements not addressed in the International Handbook should be addressed with USCG International Affairs (G–CI) staff to determine feasibility and appropriate course delivery. The G–CI will evaluate the requirement, provide estimate of cost, specific support needs and possible date for completion.

d. Off cycle requests may be submitted at any time during the year directly to USCG International Affairs (G–CI) for consideration and possible inclusion in the annual training schedule. Since a schedule is nominally complete at the end of the Security Cooperation Education and Training Working Group cycle, Security Cooperation Organization are encouraged to forecast all team requirements during their respective SCETWGs.

e. Of special note is the source and receipt of funding. The process for each specific fund source varies as does the length of time required for student vetting and sponsoring agency approvals. Care must be given to incorporate these requirements into the planning process. Funds not received at least 30 days in advance of mission date could cause cancellation of the mission, as travel arrangements and country support requirements such as, translators cannot be accomplished prior to receipt of funding. Due to limitations posed by potential CRA on availability and release of funds, requests funded from multiyear sources (for example, FMF) should be programmed during the 1st quarter of a FY.

f. After review and coordination between the Security Cooperation Organization and G–CI staff to determine feasibility, availability of appropriate skill sets, and requested training dates, staff will compile the annual training schedule. Requests received after the schedule is complied will be filled as availability of teams allows.

g. The G–CI also sources all subject matter experts (SME) and combatant commander initiatives requests subject to available resources and based on alignment of strategic objectives.

h. A TAFT, TAT, Maritime Needs Assessment.

(1) A TAFT/TAT is a unique and economical method to provide ongoing assistance that may be used to develop regional maritime goals and objectives. As an example, USCG provided a TAFT funded by an FMS case to provide Service and assistance in the operation, maintenance and repair of equipment to specific Caribbean regional nations. This concept may be applicable in other developing maritime regions. As the process to coordinate funding, host nations needs, strategic objectives, phases and desired outcomes is complex, a request for a TAFT/TAT must be submitted directly to G–CI for implementation. Depending on the circumstances surrounding the creation of a team, the time frame necessary to stand up each TAFT/TAT may vary and be somewhat lengthy.

(2) Additionally, USCG receives many ambassador requests for long term assistance in the form of a maritime advisor for development of a new coast guard. In general, a maritime advisor would craft multiyear requirements based upon analysis of host nation training, personnel, material and missions. Initiation of a new training relationship with the USCG, creation of a new host nation maritime Service, or significant mission changes in existing missions may necessitate a maritime needs assessment. The assessment will yield a "road map" for the development of a new coast guard, develop specific mission capabilities or assist in the integration and development of communications between the various host nation agencies responsible for portions of coast guard-like functions.

(3) A TAFT/TAT both requires the establishment of a baseline in personnel, skills, equipment, facilities and assessment of legal authorities. To enable the gathering of relevant data, the USCG recommends Security Cooperation Organization schedule an MTT to do a maritime assessment. This team is composed of a variety of specific skills including training, legal and maritime security to determine requirements through observation and extensive discussions with U.S. Embassy and host nation maritime personnel. This assessment is the first step to identify capabilities, validate a need for a Maritime Advisor or determine other methods to meet host nation needs. The assessment will also make recommendations for follow on training requirements to be provided over a period of time. USCG International Affairs (G–CI) staff will work with Security Cooperation Organization to develop a strategic, phased and outcome based strategic plan to meet identified needs.

Section VII
Department of the Air Force

4–48. Air Force security assistance teams and mobile training teams

a. Air Force SAT will be deployed under the guidance of AFMAN 16–101 and this section.

b. A survey team should be programmed to deploy at least 120 days before the in-place date requested for a MTT unless otherwise justified by the Security Cooperation Organization. The purpose of the survey will be to assist the Security Cooperation Organization in defining the mission, duration, composition, and equipment or support requirements for the MTT, and to determine the country's ability to support the MTT. The follow-on team, will generally but not always, consist of survey team members. Security Cooperation Organization should consider survey team requirements during programming. Surveys under FMS cases should be determined during the negotiation phase between the purchasing country and the USAF.

c. When planning to introduce a weapon system into a country for the first time, survey teams may be provided to determine the overall country requirements. The SAF/International Affairs-sponsored teams are designated as systems planning teams. Responsibilities for this type of team are contained in AFMAN 16–101. The system planning team will normally include training representatives on all surveys.

d. The training representatives will determine the parameters for operational and logistics training needs of the country. The following country capabilities will be surveyed:

(1) Operations, maintenance, and supply concepts.

(2) Manpower and technical capabilities.

(3) Interface of specialty system with USAF Air Force Staff College (AFSC).

(4) Country training capabilities.

(5) Student English language capabilities, this prerequisite ECL for training conducted by SATs is the same as established for CONUS training. If IMS do not meet the prerequisite ECL, a plan to attain the ECL in country must be developed. Requests for waiver of the minimum ECL levels will require an increase in the SAT duration to accomplish the mission. The use of interpreters is not recommended as it degrades the quality of the training. Interpreters will not be used in conjunction with flying training or other training where safety is a prime concern.

(6) Requirements for peculiar equipment.

(7) Number of personnel to be trained in each specialty.

(8) Depot level training requirements.

(9) Familiarization and qualification requirements.

(10) Training milestone charts.

4–49. Mobile training team call-up

a. Team call-up must be requested independently from requesting price and availability, LOA acceptance, obtaining DSCA approval for IMET funding, or programming the requirement under the IMETP. The Security Cooperation Organization will initiate a request for call-up of an MTT at least 120 days before the desired in-place date, as follows:

(1) Send message to the Air Force Security Assistance Training Squadron RANDOLPH AFB TX// with an information copy to OSAF WASH DC//IAPX//, HQ AFMPC RANDOLPH AFB TX//DPMRPP4//, the Air Component Command and the unified command. If teams are from either DISAM, Defense Institute for Medical Operations, or DLIELC, those activities should be information addressees instead of AFMPC.

(2) Team members must be notified as early as possible to allow for preparation and mandatory pre-deployment training. Mandatory pre-deployment training includes area orientation and antiterrorism training. The call-up must include an MTT request if not previously provided. (See fig 4–1 for format and SAMM, fig C10.F1.)

b. The Security Cooperation Organization will provide necessary support; for example, transportation, office supplies, and housekeeping items not available from the local economy. Mobile training assistance will not be furnished if the necessary support is not available. Before deployment of personnel, the Security Cooperation Organization will notify the implementing command that the necessary support and equipment are available. If the Security Cooperation Organization is unable to make this determination, survey assistance should be requested. Under no circumstances should personnel arrive in a foreign country and be unable to perform the mission due to lack of advance support planning.

4–50. Field training detachments

The administration of the field training detachment (FTD) is described in AFI 36–2201.

a. Call-up of FTD to perform TDY as an MTT follows the same requirements and procedures for requesting and programming MTT.

b. Personnel provided as a part of an FTD are subject to the guidance outlined for MTT.

4–51. Ferry crews

USAF ferry crews are not considered to be MTT and do not provide transition or refresher training. If transition or refresher training is required after delivery of aircraft, the appropriate mobile training assistance must be requested, programmed, and approved.

4–52. Extensions

Any extension of the length of TDY for MTT members constitutes a deviation and must be submitted by the Security Cooperation Organization to the Air Force Security Assistance Training Squadron under current deviation procedures for IMET, or an amendment to an FMS case, when applicable. Parent organizations providing MTT personnel will not extend team personnel TDY without the specific approval of the Air Force Security Assistance Training Squadron.

4–53. Restrictions

The IMS on duty with USAF organizations will not be used as members of USAF MTT (for example CAO, foreign airmen, or personnel). Team members must be U.S. citizens. Security Cooperation Organization will not change nor will team members deviate from the team mission as outlined in the call-up without prior approval by the Air Force Security Assistance Training Squadron.

4–54. Substitutions

Commanders required to furnish MTT personnel are authorized to substitute U.S. Air Force airmen or officer's one grade higher or one grade lower than those requested if necessary to meet the other specified qualifications.

4–55. Team after action report

The senior member designated as the team chief of each MTT, CONUS or overseas, is required to submit the team after action report. The report will be prepared as outlined in figure 4–3. Evaluations are conducted as follows:

a. Initial report. Initial evaluations may be submitted via electronic message or letter to the Air Force Security Assistance Training Squadron, with information copies to the Security Cooperation Organization, SAF/International Affairs, DSCA, the unified command, air component command, and furnishing command.

b. Final report. The team chief will submit final report to the Security Cooperation Organization, with information copies to SAF/International Affairs, the Air Force Security Assistance Training Squadron, DSCA, unified command, air component command, and furnishing command upon completion of the team mission. The Security Cooperation

Organization will endorse the report and forward it to the Air Force Security Assistance Training Squadron, with copies to the same information addressees. Final report will normally be prepared before team chief departure from country. If this is not possible, the team chief will orally brief the Security Cooperation Organization on the team's effectiveness and will prepare the written report within 10 days of departure from country. When the period of TDY is less than 8 weeks, the initial and final reports may be combined and submitted upon completion of the mission.

c. Progress report. Progress reports are submitted immediately when difficulties arise that will have an impact on the successful completion of the mission or schedule. Progress reports may be submitted via electronic message to the agencies in paragraph (a), above.

4–56. Contractor field services/Air Force engineering and technical services/language training detachments

a. Contract field services.

(1) All CFS requirements under IMET sponsorship must be justified to and approved by DSCA before programming.

(2) Determination under the FAA, as amended (Section 635(h)), permits obligation of current FY IMET funds for CFS that extend into the succeeding FY.

(3) All requests for CFS will include a checklist for contractor training (see fig 4–3 for checklist).

(4) The Security Cooperation Organization will prepare and submit an effectiveness report for CFS upon completion of the mission according to AFMAN 16–101.

b. Air Force Engineering and Technical Services.

(1) Staffing and administration for Air Force Engineering and Technical Services will be as prescribed for ETSS (see fig 4–3 for format).

(2) The Air Force Engineering and Technical Services will be identified under the training MASL in an FMS case. Air Force Engineering and Technical Services not provided in conjunction with a system sale, will be assigned "T" case designator.

(3) The team chief will prepare and submit effectiveness reports according to AFI 16–103.

c. Language training detachment.

(1) Requests for this LTD will be forwarded from the Security Cooperation Organization in the same manner as requests for MTT. Each request should include the same information as that provided in requests for FTS (see fig 4–3).

(2) The Security Cooperation Organization must request call-up of LTD at least 120 days ahead of the projected in-place date.

(3) The LTD will prepare reports according to AFI 16–103.

4–57. Team preparation

Teams will normally be scheduled to attend area orientation and antiterrorism training course at the USAF Special Operations School (USAFSOS) before deployment. Arrangements for training will be made by the Air Force Security Assistance Training Squadron. Teams from DISAM and follow-on teams that can be briefed adequately by the furnishing unit or command will be exempt from attending USAFSOS if deploying to a low-threat country.

4–58. Disclosure review

a. Unclassified training. The training content must be reviewed for releasability before the team deploys. The furnishing MAJCOM will ensure that the review is accomplished.

b. Classified training Joint Security Cooperation Education and Training, chapter 8. This training applies.

4–59. Air Force security assistance training, extended training service specialist & long-term deployment budget call

Each year, ETSS teams, and LTD are required to provide the Air Force Security Assistance Training Squadron with their upcoming budget requirements. These reports are due to Air Force Security Assistance Training Squadron/FM and the Air Force Security Assistance Training Squadron/TOI (Teams Office) by the 1st week of September. To obtain electronic copies, complete the following steps:

a. The Air Force Security Assistance Training Squadron will make available electronic copies of the budget call forms at https://www.aetc.af.mil/afsat/afsat_fr.htm.

b. Select button "Budget Call."

c. Open and save to your computer.

d. Please do not try to save on the Air Force Security Assistance Training Squadron Web site.

e. These forms will be updated yearly, no later than 15 August.

Chapter 5
English Language Training (Policy, Planning, Programming, and Implementing English language training)

Section I
General

5–1. Requirements

a. Training in all U.S. military schools and installations is conducted in English, except for the military training conducted in Spanish at Fort Rucker, AL, and Fort Eustis, VA; the WHINSEC at Fort Benning, GA; the IAAFA at Lackland Base, TX; and the U.S. Naval Small Craft Instruction and Technical Training School (Naval Small Craft Instruction and Technical Training School) in Stennis, Mississippi. IMS usually attend classes with their U.S. counterparts. Therefore, the first prerequisite for IMS is the ability to understand, speak, read, and write the English language at a level of proficiency commensurate with that required by the course of training so they can participate in the training with their U.S. counterparts. This prerequisite cannot be overemphasized; any deficiency in this area will defeat or severely limit the primary purpose of the SCETP that IMS attain required skills and professional competence. All IMS selected for U.S. training must be carefully tested to determine that their English comprehension level (ECL) meets the minimum MILDEP standard before invitational travel orders (ITO) are issued and IMS are sent to U.S. training institutions. This requirement applies to all IMS except those from countries:

(1) Exempt from all ECL testing requirements as updated annually by a SECDEF/DSCA message.

(2) Granted a waiver by DSCA from in-country ECL testing requirements.

b. The IMS who meet the minimum requirements for entering courses that do not require Specialized English Training may be sent directly to the school/training activity. Others will be programmed for the required language training according to DLIELC Instruction 1025.7. IMS programmed for Specialized English Training only must have the minimum ECL required for entry into MILDEP courses before entering DLIELC. Those IMS entering DLIELC who have less than the required ECL will be entered into the general English phase of training and will not be entered into Specialized English Training until the required ECL is achieved. Some courses have a requirement for IMS to attain a specified comprehension/speaking rating in accordance with the Interagency language Roundtable Language Skill Level Descriptions (see figs 5–1 through 5–4). This ability is assessed through an OPI, which may be administered face-to-face or telephonically in-country. IMS must meet the OPI requirement before entering Specialized English Training and/or technical training.

INTERAGENCY LANGUAGE ROUNDTABLE
LANGUAGE SKILL LEVEL DESCRIPTIONS

SPEAKING

Preface

The following proficiency level descriptions characterize spoken language use. Each of the six "base levels" (coded 00 10, 20, 30, 40 AND 50) implies control of any previous "base levels" functions and accuracy. The "plus level" designation (coded 06, 16, 26, etc.) will be assigned when proficiency substantially exceeds one bases skill level and does not fully meet the criteria for the next "base level." The "plus level" descriptions are therefore supplementary to the "base level" descriptions.

A skill level is assigned to a person through an authorized language examination. Examiners assign a level on a variety of performance criteria exemplified in the descriptive statements. Therefore, the examples given here illustrate, but do not exhaustively describe, either the skills a person may possess or situations in which he/she may function effectively.

Statements describing accuracy refer to typical stages in the development of competence in the most commonly taught languages in formal training programs. In other languages, emerging competence parallels these characterizations, but often with different details.

Unless otherwise specified, the team "native speaker" refers to native speakers of a standard dialect.

"Well-educated," in the context of these proficiency descriptions, does not necessarily imply formal higher education. However, in cultures where formal higher education is common, the language-use abilities of persons who have had such education is considered the standard. That is, such a person meets contemporary expectations for the formal, careful style of this language, as well a range of less formal varieties of the language.

Speaking 0 (No Proficiency)

Unable to function in the spoken language. Oral production is limited to occasional isolated words. Has essentially no communicative ability.

Speaking 0+ (memorized Proficiency)

Able to satisfy immediate needs using rehearsed utterances. Shows little real autonomy of expression, flexibility, or spontaneity. Can ask questions or make statements with reasonable accuracy only with memorized utterances or formulae. Attempts creating speech as usually unsuccessful.

Examples: The individual's vocabulary is usually limited to areas of immediate survival needs. Most utterances are telegraphic, that is, functors (linking words, markers, and the like) are omitted, confused, or distorted. An individual can usually differentiate most significant sounds when produced in isolation, but when combines in words or groups of words, errors may be frequent. Even with repetition, communication is severely limited even with people used to dealing with foreigners. Stress, intonation, tone, etc. are usually quite faulty.

Speaking 1 (Elementary Proficiency)

Able to satisfy minimum courtesy requirements and maintain very simple face-to-face conversation on familiar topics. A native speaker must often use slowed speech, repetition, paraphrase, or a combination of these to be understood by this individual. Similarly, the native speaker must strain and employ real-worlds knowledge, to understand even simple statements/questions from this individual. This speaker has a functional, but limited proficiency. Misunderstandings are frequent, but the individual is able to ask for help and to verify

Figure 5–1. Interagency Language Roundtable Language Skill Level Descriptions - Speaking

comprehension of native speech in face-to-face interaction. The individual is unable to produce continuous discourse except with rehearsed material.

Examples: Structural accuracy is likely to be random or severely limited. Time concepts are vague. Vocabulary is inaccurate, and its range is very narrow. The individual often speaks with great difficulty. By repeating, such speakers can make themselves understood to native speakers who are in regular contact with foreigners but there is little precision in the information conveyed. Needs, experience or training may vary greatly from individual to individual; for example, speakers at this level may have encountered quite different vocabulary areas. However, the individual can typically satisfy predictable, simple, personal and accommodation needs; can generally meet courtesy, introduction and identification requirements; exchange greetings; elicit and provide, for example, predictable and skeletal biographical information. He/she might give information about business hours, explain routine procedures in a limited way, and state in a simple manner what actions will be taken. He/she is able to formulate some questions even in language with complicated question constructions. Almost every utterance may be characterized by structural errors and errors in basic grammatical relations. Vocabulary is extremely limited and characteristically does not include modifiers. Pronunciation, stress, and intonation are generally poor, often heavily influenced, by another language. Use structure and vocabulary is highly imprecise.

Speaking 1+ (Elementary Proficiency, Plus)

Can initiate and maintain predictable face-to-face conversations and satisfy limited social demands. He/she may, however, have little understanding of the social conventions of conversation. The interlocutor is generally required to strain and employ real-world knowledge to understand even some simple speech. The speaker at this level may hesitate and may have to change subjects due to lack of language resources. Range and control of the language are limited. Speech largely consists of a series of short, discrete utterances.

Examples: The individual is able to satisfy most travel and accommodations needs and a limited range of social demands beyond exchange of skeletal biographic information. Speaking ability may extend beyond immediate survival needs. Accuracy in basic grammatical relations is evident, although not consistent. May exhibit the more common forms of verb tenses, for example, but may make frequent errors in formation and selection. While some structures are established, errors occur in more complex patterns. The individual typically cannot sustain coherent structures in longer utterances or unfamiliar situations. Ability to describe and give precise information is limited. Person, space and time references are often used incorrectly. Pronunciation is understandable to native used to dealing with foreigners. Can combine most significant sounds with reasonable comprehensibility, but has difficulty in producing certain sounds in certain positions or in certain combinations. Speech will usually be labored. Frequently has to repeat utterances to be understood by the general public.

Speaking 2 (Limited Working Proficiency)

Able to satisfy routine social demands and limited work requirements. Can handle routine work-related interactions that are limited in scope. In more complex and sophisticated work-related tasks, language usage generally disturbs the native speaker. Can handle with confidence, but not with facility, most normal, high-frequency social conversational situations including extensive, but casual conversations about current events, as well as work, family, and autobiographical information. The individual can get the gist of most everyday conversations but has some difficulty understanding native speakers in situations that require specialized or sophisticated knowledge. The individual's utterances are minimally cohesive. Linguistic structure is usually not very elaborate and not thoroughly controlled; errors are frequent. Vocabulary use is appropriate for high-frequency utterances but unusual or imprecise elsewhere.

Figure 5–1. Interagency Language Roundtable Language Skill Level Descriptions - Speaking

Examples: While these interactions will vary widely from individual to individual, the individual can typically ask and answer predictable questions in the workplace and give straightforward instructions to subordinates. Additionally, the individual can participate in personal and accommodation-type interactions with elaboration and facility; that is, can give and understand complicated detailed and extensive directions and make non-routine changes in travel and accommodation arrangements. Simple structures and basic grammatical relations are typically controlled; however, there are areas of weakness. In the commonly taught languages, these may be simple markings such as plurals, articles, linking words, and negatives or more complex structures such as tense/aspect usage, case morphology, passive constructions, word order, and embedding.

Speaking 2+ (Limited Working Proficiency, Plus)

Able to satisfy most work requirements with language usage that is often, but not always, acceptable and effective. The individual shows considerable ability to communicate effectively on topics relating to particular interests and special fields of competence. Often shows a high degree of fluency and ease of speech, yet when under tension or pressure, the ability to use the language effectively may deteriorate. Comprehension of normal native speech is typically nearly complete. The individual may mission cultural and local references and may require a native speaker to adjust to his/her limitations in some ways. Native speakers often perceive the individual's speech to contain awkward or inaccurate phrasing of ideas, mistaken time, space, and person references, or to be in some way inappropriate, if not strictly incorrect.

Examples: Typically the individual can participate in most social, formal, and informal interactions; but limitations either in range of contexts, types of tasks, or level of accuracy hinder effectiveness. The individual may be ill at ease with the use of the language either in social interaction or in speaking at length in professional contexts. He/she is generally strong in either structural precision or vocabulary, but not in both. Weakness or unevenness in one of the foregoing, or in pronunciation, occasionally results in miscommunication. Normally controls, but cannot always easily produce general vocabulary. Discourse is often incohesive.

Speaking 3 (General Professional Proficiency)

Able to speak the language with sufficient structural accuracy and vocabulary to participate effectively in most formal and informal conversation on practical, social, and professional topics. Nevertheless, the individual's limitations generally restrict the professional contexts of language use to matters of shred knowledge and/or international convention. Discourse is cohesive. The individual uses the language acceptably, but with some noticeable imperfections; yet, errors virtually never interfere with understanding and rarely disturb the native speaker. The individual can effectively combine structure and vocabulary to convey his/her meaning accurately. The individual speaks readily and fills pause suitably. In face-to-face conversation with native speaking the standard dialect at a normal rate of speech, comprehension is quite complete. Although cultural references, proverbs, and the implications of nuances and idiom may not be fully understood, the individual can easily repair the conversation. Pronunciation may be obviously foreign. Individual sounds are accurate, but stress, intonation and pitch control may be faulty.

Examples: Can typically discuss particular interests and special fields of competence with reasonable ease. Can use the language as part of normal professional duties such as answering objections, clarifying points, justifying decisions, understanding the essence of challenges, stating and defending policy, conducting meetings delivering briefings or other extended and elaborate informative monologues. Can reliably elicit information and informed opinion from native speakers. Structural inaccuracy is rarely the major cause of misunderstanding. Use of structural devices is flexible and elaborate. Without searching for words or phrases, the individual uses the

Figure 5–1. Interagency Language Roundtable Language Skill Level Descriptions - Speaking–Continued

language clearly and relatively naturally to elaborate concepts freely and make ideas easily understandable to native speakers. Errors occur in low frequency and highly complex structure.

Speaking 3+ (General Professional Proficiency, Plus)

Is often able to use the language to satisfy professional needs in a wide range of sophisticated and demanding tasks

Examples: Despite obvious strengths, may exhibit some hesitancy, uncertainty, effort, or errors which limit the range of language-use tasks that can be reliably performed. Typically there is particular strength in fluency and one or more, but not all, of the following: breadth of lexicon, including low- and medium-frequency items, especially socio-linguistic/cultural references and nuances of close synonyms; structural precision, with sophisticated features that are readily, accurately, and appropriately controlled (such as complex modification and embedding in indo-European languages); discourse competence in a wide range of context and tasks, often matching a native speaker's strategic and organizational abilities and expectations. Occasional patterned errors occur in low frequency and high-complex structures.

Speaking 4 (Advanced Professional Proficiency)

Able to use the language fluently and accurately on all level normally pertinent to professional needs. The individual's language usage and ability to function as fully successful. Organizes discourse well, using appropriate rhetorical speech devices, native cultural references, and understanding. Language ability rarely hinders him/her in performing any task requiring language, yet the individual would seldom be perceived as a native. Speaks effortlessly and smoothly and is able to use the language with a high degree of effectiveness, reliability, and precision for all representational purposes within the range of personal and professional experience and scope of responsibilities. Can serve as an informal interpreter in a range of unpredictable circumstances. Can perform extensive, sophisticated language tasks, encompassing most matters of interest to well-educated native speakers, including tasks which do not bear directly on a professional specialty.

Examples: Can discuss in detail concepts which are fundamentally different from those of the target culture and make those concepts clear and accessible to the native speaker. Similarly the individual can understand the details and ramifications of concepts that are culturally or conceptually different from his/her own. Can set the tone of interpersonal official, semi-official, and non-professional verbal exchanges with a representative range of native speakers (in a range of varied audiences, purposes, tasks and settings). Can play an effective role among native speakers in such contexts as conferences, lectures, and debates on matters of disagreement. Can advocate a position at length, both formally and in chance encounters, using sophisticated verbal strategies. Understands and reliably produces shifts of both subject matter and tone. Can understand native speakers of the standard and other major dialects in essentially any face-to-face interaction.

Speaking 4+ (Advanced Professional Proficiency, Plus)

Speaking proficiency is regularly superior in all respects, usually equivalent to that of a well-educated, highly articulate native speaker. Language ability does not impede the performance of any language-use task. However, the individual would not necessarily be perceived as culturally native.

Examples: The individual organizes discourse will, employing functional rhetorical speech devices, native cultural references and understanding. Effectively applies a native speaker's social and circumstantial knowledge. However, cannot sustain that performance under all circumstances. While the individual has a wide range and control of structure, an occasional non-native slip may occur. The individual has a sophisticated control of vocabulary and phrasing that

Figure 5–1. Interagency Language Roundtable Language Skill Level Descriptions - Speaking–Continued

is rarely imprecise, yet there are occasional weaknesses in idioms, colloquialisms, pronunciation, cultural reference or there may be an occasional failure to interaction in totally native manner.

Speaking 5 (Functionally Native Proficiency)

Speaking proficiency is functional equivalent to that of a highly articulate well-educated native speaker and reflects the cultural standards of the country where the language is natively spoken. The individual uses the language with complete flexibility and intuition, so that speech on all levels is fully accepted by well-educated native speakers in all of its features, including breadth of vocabulary and idiom, colloquialisms, and pertinent cultural references. Pronunciation is typically consistent with that of well-educated native speakers of a non-stigmatized dialect.

Figure 5–1. Interagency Language Roundtable Language Skill Level Descriptions - Speaking–Continued

INTERAGENCY LANGUAGE ROUNDTABLE
LANGUAGE SKILL LEVEL DESCRIPTIONS

LISTENING

Preface

The following proficiency level descriptions characterize comprehension of the spoken language. Each of the six "base levels" (coded 00, 10, 20, 30, 40 and 50) implies control of any previous "base levels" functions and accuracy. The "plus level" designation (coded 06, 16, 26, etc) will be assigned when proficiency substantially exceeds one base skill level and does not fully meet the criteria for the next "base level." The "plus level" descriptions are therefore supplementary to the "base level" descriptions.

A skill level is assigned to a person through an authorized language examination. Examiners assign a level on a variety of performance criteria exemplified in the descriptive statements. Therefore, the examples given here illustrate, but do not exhaustively describe, either the skills a person may possess or situation in which he/she may function effectively.

Statements describing accuracy refer to typical stages in the development of competence in the most commonly taught language in formal training programs. In other languages, emerging competence parallels these characterizations, but often with different details.

Unless otherwise specified, the term "native listener" refers to native speakers and listeners of a standard dialect.

"Well-educated" in the context of these proficiency descriptions, does not necessarily imply formal higher education. However, in cultures where formal higher education is common, the language-use abilities of persons who have had such education are considered the standard. That is, such a person meets contemporary expectations for the formal, careful style of the language, as well as a range of less formal varieties of the language.

Listening 0 (Not Proficiency)

No practical understand of the spoken language. Understanding is limited to occasional isolated words with essentially no ability to comprehend communication.

Listening 0+ (Memorized Proficiency)

Sufficient comprehension to understand a number of memorized utterances in areas of immediate needs. Slight increase in utterance length understood but requires frequent long pauses between understood phrases and repeated requests on the listener's part for repetition. Understands with reasonable accuracy only when this involves short memorized utterances or formulae. Utterances understood are relatively short in length. Misunderstandings arise due to ignoring or inaccurately hearing sounds or word endings (both inflectional and non-inflectional) distorting the original meaning. Can understand

Figure 5–2. Interagency Language Roundtable Language Skill Level Descriptions - Listening

only with difficulty even such people as teachers who are used to speaking with non-native speakers. Can understand best those statements where context strongly supports the utterance's meaning. Gets some main ideas.

Listening 1 (Elementary Proficiency)

Sufficient comprehension to understand utterances about basic survival needs and minimum courtesy and travel requirements. In areas of immediate need or on very familiar topics, can understand simple questions and answers, simple statements and very simple face-to-face conversations in a standard dialect. These must often be delivered more clearly than normal at a rate slower than normal, with frequent repetitions or paraphrase (that is), by a native used to dealing with foreigners). Once learned, these sentences can be varied for similar level vocabulary and grammar and still be understood. In the majority of utterances, misunderstandings arise due to overlooked or misunderstood syntax and other grammatical clues. Comprehension vocabulary inadequate to understand anything but the most elementary needs. Strong interference from the candidate's native language occurs. Little precision in the information understood owing the tentative state of passive grammar and lack of vocabulary. Comprehension areas include basic needs such as: meals, lodging, transportation, time and simple directions (including both route instructions and orders from customs officials, policemen, etc.) Understands main ideas.

Listening 1+ (Elementary Proficiency, Plus)

Sufficient comprehension to understand short conversations about all survival needs and limited social demands. Developing flexibility evident in understanding into a range of circumstances beyond immediate survival needs. Shows spontaneity in understanding by speed, although consistency of understanding uneven. Limited vocabulary range necessitates repetition for understanding. Understands more common time forms and most question forms, some word order patterns, but miscommunication still occurs with more complex patterns. Cannot sustain understanding of coherent structures in longer utterances or in unfamiliar situations. Understanding of descriptions and the giving of precise information is limited. Aware of basic cohesive features, e.g., pronouns, verb inflections, but many are unreliably understood, especially if less immediate in reference. Understanding is largely limited to a series of short, discrete utterances. Still has to ask for utterances to be repeated. Some ability to understand facts.

Listening 2 (Limited Working Proficiency)

Sufficient comprehension to understand conversations routines social demands and limited job requirements. Able to understand face-to-face speech in a standard dialect, delivered at a normal rate with some repetition and rewording, by a native speaker not used to dealing with foreigners about everyday topics, common personal and family news, well-known current events, and routine office matters through descriptions and narration about current, past and future events; can follow essential points of

Figure 5–2. Interagency Language Roundtable Language Skill Level Descriptions - Listening–Continued

discussion or speech at an elementary level on topics in his/her special professional field. Only understands occasional words and phrases of statements made in unfavorable conditions, for example through loudspeakers outdoors. Understands factual content. native language causes less interference in listening comprehension. Abel to understand facts, i.e., the lines but not between or beyond the lines.

Listening 2+ (Limited Working Proficiency, Plus)

Sufficient comprehension to understand most routine social demands and most conversations on work requirements as well as some discussions on concrete topics related to particular interests and special fields of competence. Often shows remarkable ability and ease of understanding, but under tension or pressure may break down. Candidate may display weakness or deficiency due to inadequate vocabulary base or less than secure knowledge of grammar and syntax. Normally understands general vocabulary with some hesitant understanding of everyday vocabulary still evident. Can sometimes detect emotional overtones. Some ability to understand implications.

Listening 3 (General Professional Proficiency)

Able to understand the essentials of all speech in a standard dialect including technical discussions within a special field. Has effective understanding of face-to-face speech, delivered with normal clarity and speed in a standard dialect on general topics and areas of special interest; understands hypothesizing and supported opinions. Has broad enough vocabulary that rarely has to ask for paraphrasing or explanation. Can follow accurately the essentials of conversations between educated native speakers, reasonably clear telephone calls, radio broadcasts, news stories similar to wire service reports, oral reports, some oral technical reports and public addresses on non-technical subjects; can understand without difficulty all forms of standard speech concerning a special professional field. Does not understand native speakers if they speak very quickly or use some slang or dialect. Can often detect emotional overtones. Can understand implications.

Listening 3+ (General Professional Proficiency, Plus)

Comprehends most of the content and intent of a variety of forms and styles of speech pertinent to professional needs as well as general topics and social conversation. Ability to comprehend many sociolinguistic and cultural references. However, may miss some subtleties and nuances. Increase ability to comprehend unusually complex structures in lengthy utterances and to comprehend many distinctions in language tailored for different audiences. Increased ability to understand native speakers talking quickly, using nonstandard dialect or slang; however, comprehension not complete. Can discern some relationships among sophisticated listening materials in the context or broad experience. Can follow some unpredictable turns of thought readily in, for example, informal and formal speeches covering editorial conjectural and literary material in subject matter areas directed to the general listener.

Figure 5–2. Interagency Language Roundtable Language Skill Level Descriptions - Listening–Continued

Listening 4 (Advanced Professional Proficiency)

Abel to understand all forms and styles of speech pertinent to professional needs. Able to understand fully all speech with extensive and precise vocabulary, subtleties and nuances in all standard dialects on any subject relevant to professional needs with the range of his/her experience, including social conversations; all intelligible broadcasts and telephone calls;; and many kinds of technical discussions and discourse. Understands language specifically tailored (including persuasion, representation, counseling, and negotiating) to difference audiences. Able to understand the essentials of speech in some non-standard dialects. Has difficulty in understanding extreme dialect and slang; also in understanding speech in unfavorable conditions, for example through bad loudspeakers outdoors. Can discern relationships among sophisticated listening materials in the context of broad experience. Can follow unpredictable turns of thought readily in, for example, informal and formal speeches covering editorial, conjectural, and literary material in any subject matter directed to the general listener.

Listening 4+ (Advanced Professional Proficiency, Plus)

Increased ability to understand extremely difficult and abstract speech as well as ability to understand all forms and styles of speech pertinent to professional needs, including social conversations. Increased ability to comprehend native speakers using extreme non-standard dialects and slang, as well as to understand speech in unfavorable conditions. Strong sensitivity to sociolinguistic and cultural references. Accuracy is close to that of the well-educated native listener but still not equivalent.

Listening 5 (Functionally Native Proficiency)

Comprehension equivalent to that of the well-educated native listener. Able to understand fully all forms and styles of speech intelligible to the well-educated native listener, including a number of regional and illiterate dialects, highly colloquial speech and conversations and discourse distorted by marked interference from other noise. Able to understand how natives think as they create discourse. Able to understand extremely difficult and abstract speech.

Figure 5–2. Interagency Language Roundtable Language Skill Level Descriptions - Listening–Continued

INTERAGENCY LANGUAGE ROUNDTABLE
LANGUAGE SKILL LEVEL DESCRIPTIONS

READING

Preface

The following proficiency level descriptions characterize comprehension of the written language. Each of the six "base levels" (coded 00, 10, 20, 30, 40, and 50) implies control of any previous "base levels" functions and accuracy. The "plus level" designation (coded 06, 16, 26, etc.) will be assigned when proficiency substantially exceeds one bases skill level and does not fully meet the criteria for the next "base level." The "plus level" descriptions are therefore supplementary to the "base level" descriptions.

A skill level is assigned to a person through an authorized language examination. Examiners assign a level on a variety of performance criteria exemplified in the descriptive statements. Therefore, the examples given here illustrate, but do not exhaustively describe, either the skills a person may possess or situations in which he/she may function effectively.

Statements describing accuracy refer to typical stages in the development of competence in the most commonly taught languages in formal training programs. In other languages, emerging competence parallels these characterizations, but often with different details.

Unless otherwise specified, the team "native reader" refers to native readers of a standard dialect.

"Well-educated," in the context of these proficiency descriptions, does not necessarily imply formal higher education. However, in cultures where formal higher education is common, the language-use abilities of persons who have had such education is considered the standard. That is, such a person meets contemporary expectations for the formal, careful style of this language, as well a range of less formal varieties of the language.

In the following descriptions a standard set of text-types is associated with each level. The text-type is generally characterized in each descriptive statement.

The word "read" in the context of these proficiency descriptions, means that the person at a given skill level can thoroughly understand the communicative intent in the text-types described. In the usual case the reader could be expected to make a full representation, thorough summary, or translation of the text into English.

Other useful operations can be performed on written texts that do not require the ability to "read," as defined above. Examples of such tasks which people of a given skill level may reasonably be expected to perform are provided, when appropriate, in the descriptions.

Reading 0 (No Proficiency)

No practical ability to read the language. Consistently misunderstands or cannot comprehend at all.

Figure 5–3. Interagency Language Roundtable Language Skill Level Descriptions - Reading

Reading 0+ (Memorized Proficiency)

Can recognize all the letters in the printed version of an alphabetic system and high-frequency elements of a syllabary or a character system. Able to read some or all of the following: numbers. Isolated words and phrases, personal and place names, street signs, office and shop designations; the above often interpreted inaccurately. Unable to read connected prose.

Reading 1 (Elementary Proficiency)

Sufficient comprehension to read very simple connected written material in a formal equivalent to usual printing or typescript. Can read either representations of familiar formulaic verbal exchanges or simple language containing only the highest frequency structural patterns and vocabulary, including share international vocabulary items and cognates (when appropriate). Able to read and understand known language elements that have been recombined in new ways to achieve different meanings at a similar levels of simplicity. Texts may include simple narratives of routine behavior; highly predictable descriptions of people, places or things; and explanations of geography and government such as those simplified for tourists. Some misunderstandings possible on simple texts. Can get some main ideas and locate prominent items of professional significance in more complex texts. Can identify general subject matter in some authentic texts.

Reading 1+ (Elementary Proficiency, Plus)

Sufficient comprehension to understand simple discourse in printed form for informative social purposes. Can read material such as announcements of public events, simple prose containing biographical information or narration of events, and straightforward newspaper headlines. Can guess at unfamiliar vocabulary if highly contextualized, but with difficulty in unfamiliar contexts. Can get some main ideas and locate routine information of professional significance in more complex texts. Can follow essential points of discussion at an elementary level on topics in his/her special professional field.

In commonly taught languages, the individual may not control the structure well. For example, basic grammatical relations are often misinterpreted, and temporal reference may rely primarily on lexical items as time indicators. Has some difficulty with the cohesive factors in discourse, such as matching pronouns with referents. May have to read material several times for understanding.

Reading 2 (Limited Working Proficiency)

Sufficient comprehension to read simple, authentic written material in a form equivalent to usual printing or typescript on subjects within a familiar context. Able to read with some misunderstandings straightforward, familiar, factual material, but in general insufficiently experienced with the language to draw inferences directly from the

Figure 5–3. Interagency Language Roundtable Language Skill Level Descriptions - Reading–Continued

linguistic aspects of the text. Can locate and understand the main ideas and details in material written for the general reader. However, persons who have professional knowledge of a subject may be able to summarize or perform sorting and locating tasks with written texts that are will beyond their general proficiency level. The individual can read uncomplicated, but authentic prose on familiar subjects that are normally presented in a predictable sequence which aids the reader in understanding. Texts may include descriptions and narrations in contexts such as news items describing frequently occurring events, simple biographical information, social notices, formulaic business letters, and simple technical material written for the general reader. Generally, the prose that can be read by the individual is predominantly in straightforward/high-frequency sentence patters. The individual does not have a broad active vocabulary (this is which he/she recognized immediately on sight), but is able to use contextual and real-world cues to understand the text. Characteristically, however, the individual is quite slow in performing such a process. He/she is typically able to answer factual questions about authentic texts of the types described above.

Reading 2+ (Limited Working Proficiency, Plus)

Sufficient comprehension to understand most factual material in non-technical prose as well as some discussions on concrete topics related to special professional interests. Is markedly more proficient at reading materials on a familiar topic. Is able to separate the main ideas and details from lesser ones and uses that distinction to advance understanding. The individual is able to use linguistic context and real-world knowledge to make sensible guesses about unfamiliar material. Has a broad active reading vocabulary. The individual is able to get the gist of main and subsidiary ideas in texts which could only be read thoroughly by persons with much higher proficiencies. Weaknesses include slowness, uncertainty, inability to discern nuance and/or intentionally disguised meaning,

Reading 3 (General Professional Proficiency)

Able to read within a normal range of speed and with almost complete comprehension a variety of authentic prose material on unfamiliar subjects. Reading ability is not dependent on subject matter knowledge, although it is not expected that the individual can comprehend thoroughly subject matter which is highly dependent on cultural knowledge or which is outside his/her general experience and not accompanied by explanation. Text-types include news stories similar to wire service reports or international new items in major periodicals, routine correspondence, general reports, and technical material in his/her professional field; all of these may include hypothesis, argumentation, and supported opinions. Misreading rare. Almost always able to interpret material correctly, relate ideas, and "read between the lines, (that is understand the writers' implicit intents in texts of the above types). Can get the gist of more sophisticated texts, but may be unable to detect or understand subtlety and nuance. Rarely has to pause over or read general vocabulary. However, may experience some difficulty with unusually complex structure and low frequency idioms.

Figure 5–3. Interagency Language Roundtable Language Skill Level Descriptions - Reading–Continued

Reading 3+ (General Professional Proficiency, Plus)

Can comprehend a variety of styles and forms pertinent to professional needs. Rarely misinterprets such texts or rarely experiences difficulty relating ideas or making inferences. Able to comprehend many sociolinguistic and cultural references. However, many miss some nuances and subtleties. Able to comprehend a considerable range of intentionally complex structures, low frequency idioms, and uncommon connotative intentions; however, accuracy is not complete. The individual is typically able to read with facility, understand, and appreciate contemporary expository, technical, or literary texts which do not rely heavily on slang and unusual idioms.

Reading 4 (Advanced Professional Proficiency)

Able to read fluently and accurately all styles and forms of the language pertinent to professional needs. The individual's experience with the written language is extensive enough that he/she is able to relate inferences in the text to real-world knowledge and understand almost all sociolinguistic and cultural references. Able to "read beyond the lines" (that is, to understand the full ramifications of texts as they are situated in the wider cultural, political, or social environment). Able to read and understand the intent of writers' use of nuance and subtlety. The individual can discern relationships among sophisticated written materials in the context of broad experience. Cana follow unpredictable turns of thought readily in, for example, editorial, conjectural, and literary texts in any subject matter area directed to the general reader. Can read essentially all materials in his/her special field, including official and professional documents and correspondence. Recognizes all professionally relevant vocabulary known to the educated non-professional native, although may be some difficulty with slang. Can read reasonably legible handwriting without difficulty. Accuracy is often nearly that of a well-educated native reader.

Reading 4+ (Advanced Professional Proficiency, Plus)

Reading proficiency is functionally equivalent to that of the well-educated native reader. Can read extremely difficult and abstract prose; for example, general legal and technical as well as highly colloquial writings. Able to read literary texts, typically including contemporary avant-grade prose, poetry, and theatrical writing. Can read classical/archaic forms of literature with the same degree of facility as the well-educated, but non-specialist native. Reads and understands a wide variety of vocabulary and idioms, colloquialisms, slang, and pertinent cultural references. With varying degrees of difficulty, can read all kinds of handwritten documents. Accuracy of comprehension is equivalent to that of a well-educated native reader.

Figure 5–3. Interagency Language Roundtable Language Skill Level Descriptions - Reading–Continued

INTERAGENCY LANGUAGE ROUNDTABLE
LANGUAGE SKILL LEVEL DESCRIPTIONS

WRITING

Preface

The following proficiency level descriptions characterize written language use. Each of the six "base levels" (coded 00, 10, 20, 30, 40, and 50) implies control of any previous "base levels" functions and accuracy. The "plus level" designation (coded 06, 16, 26, etc.) will be assigned when proficiency substantially exceeds one bases skill level and does not fully meet the criteria for the next "base level." The "plus level" descriptions are therefore supplementary to the "base level" descriptions.

A skill level is assigned to a person through an authorized language examination. Examiners assign a level on a variety of performance criteria exemplified in the descriptive statements. Therefore, the examples given here illustrate, but do not exhaustively describe, either the skills a person may possess or situations in which he/she may function effectively.

Statements describing accuracy refer to typical stages in the development of competence in the most commonly taught languages in formal training programs. In other languages, emerging competence parallels these characterizations, but often with different details.

Unless otherwise specified, the team "native writer" refers to native writers of a standard dialect.

"Well-educated," in the context of these proficiency descriptions, does not necessarily imply formal higher education. However, in cultures where formal higher education is common, the language-use abilities of persons who have had such education is considered the standard. That is, such a person meets contemporary expectations for the formal, careful style of this language, as well a range of less formal varieties of the language.

Writing 0 (No Proficiency)

No functional writing ability.

Reading 0+ (Memorized Proficiency)

Writes using memorized material and set expressions. Can produce symbols in an alphabetic or syllabic writing system or 50 of the most common characters. Can write numbers and dates, own name nationality, address, etc., such as on a hotel registration form. Otherwise, ability to write is limited to simple lists of common items such as a few short sentences. Spelling and even representation of symbols (letters, syllables, and characters) may be incorrect.

Figure 5–4. Interagency Language Roundtable Language Skill Level Descriptions - Writing

Writing 1 (Elementary Proficiency)

Has sufficient control of the writing system to meet limited practical needs. Can create by writing statements and questions on topics very familiar to him/her within the scope of his/her very limited language experience. Writing vocabulary is inadequate to express anything but elementary needs; writes in simple sentences making continual errors in spelling, grammar, and punctuation but writing can be read and understood by a native reader used to dealing with foreigners attempting to write his/her language. Writing tends to be a loose collection of sentences (or fragments) on a given topic and provides little evidence of conscious organization. While topics which are "very familiar" and elementary needs vary considerably from individuals, any person at this level should be able to write simple phone messages, excuses, notes to service people and simple notes to friends. (800-1000 characters controlled.)

Writing 1+ (Elementary Proficiency, Plus)

Sufficient control of writing system to meet most survival needs and limited social demands. Can create sentences and short paragraphs related to most survival needs (food, lodging, transportation, immediate surroundings and situations) and limited social demands. Can express fairly accurate present and future time. Can produce some past verb forms but not always accurately or with correct usage. Can relate personal history, discuss topics such as daily life, preferences and very familiar material. Shows good control of elementary vocabulary and some control of basic syntactic patterns, but major errors still occur when expressing more complex thoughts. Dictionary usage may still yield incorrect vocabulary or forms although the individual can use a dictionary to advantage to express simple ideas. Generally cannot use basic pronouns, connectors, etc.,). Can take notes in some detail on familiar topics, and respond to personal questions using elementary vocabulary and common structures. Can write simple letters, summaries of biographical data and work experience with fair accuracy. Writing, tough faulty, is comprehensible to native speakers used to dealing with foreigners.

Writing 2 (Limited Working Proficiency)

Able to write routine social correspondence and prepare documentary materials required for most limited work requirements. Has writing vocabulary sufficient to express himself/herself simply with some circumlocutions. Can write simply about a very limited number of current events or daily situations. Still makes common errors in spelling and punctuation but show some control of the most common formats and punctuation conventions. Good control of morphology of language (in inflected languages) and of the most frequently used syntactic structures. Elementary constructions are usually handled quite accurately and writing is understandable to a native reader not used to reading the writing of foreigners. Uses a limited number of cohesive devices.

Figure 5–4. Interagency Language Roundtable Language Skill Level Descriptions - Writing–Continued

Writing 2+ (Limited Working Proficiency, Plus)

Shows ability to write with some precision and in some detail about most common topics. Can write about concrete topics relating to particular interests and special fields of competence. Often show surprising fluency and ease of expression But under time constraints and pressure language may be inaccurate and/or incomprehensible. Generally strong in either grammar or vocabulary, but not in both. Weaknesses or unevenness in one of the foregoing or in spelling result in occasional miscommunication. Areas of weakness range from simple constructions such as plurals, articles, prepositions and negatives to more complex structures such as tense usage, passive constructions, word order and relative clauses. Normally controls general vocabulary with some misuse of everyday vocabulary evident. Shows a limited ability to use circumlocutions. Uses dictionary to advantage to supply unknown words. Can take Fairly accurate notes on material presented orally and handle with fair accuracy most social correspondence. Writing is understandable to native speakers not used to dealing with foreigner's attempts to write the language, though style is still obviously foreign.

Writing 3 (General Professional Proficiency)

Able to use the language effectively in most formal and informal written exchanges on practical social and professional topics. Can write reports, summaries, and short library research papers on current events on particular areas of interest or on special fields with reasonable ease. Control of structure, spelling and general vocabulary is adequate to convey his/her message accurately but style may be obviously foreign. Errors virtually never interfere with comprehension and rarely disturb the native reader. Punctuation generally controlled. Employs a full range of structures. Control of grammar good with only sporadic errors in basic structures, occasional errors in the most complex frequent structures and somewhat more frequent errors in low-frequency complex structures. Consistent control of compound and complex sentences. Relationship of ideas is consistently clear.

Writing 3+ (General Professional Proficiency, Plus)

Able to write the language in a few prose styles pertinent to professional/educational needs. Not always able to tailor language to suit audience. Weaknesses may lie in poor control of low-frequency complex structures, vocabulary, or the ability to express subtleties and nuances. May be able to write on some topics pertinent to professional/educational needs. Organization may suffer due to lack of variety in organizational patterns or in variety of cohesive devices.

Writing 4 (Advanced Professional Proficiency)

Able to write the language precisely and accurately in a variety of prose styles pertinent to professional/educational needs. Errors of grammar are rare including those in low-frequency complex structures. Consistently able to tailor language to suit

Figure 5–4. Interagency Language Roundtable Language Skill Level Descriptions - Writing–Continued

audience and able to express subtleties and nuances. Expository prose is clearly, consistently and explicitly organized. The writer employs a variety of organizational patterns, use a wide variety of cohesive devices such as ellipsis and parallelisms, and subordinates in a variety of ways. Able to write on all topics normally pertinent to professional/educational needs and on social issues of a general nature. Writing adequate to express all his/her experiences.

Writing 4+ (Advanced Professional Proficiency, Plus)

Able to write the language precisely and accurately in a wide variety of prose styles pertinent to professional/educational needs. May have some ability to edit but not in the full range of styles. Has some flexibility within a style and show some evidence of a use of stylistic devices.

Writing 5 (Functionally Native Proficiency)

Has writing proficiency equal to that of a well-educated native. Without non-native errors of structure, spelling, style or vocabulary can wire and edit both formal and informal correspondence, official reports and documents, and professional/education articles including writing for special purposes which might include legal, technical, educational, literary and colloquial writing. In addition to being clear, explicit and informative, the writing and the ideas are also imaginative. The writer employs a very wide range of stylistic devices.

These descriptions were approved by the Interagency Language Roundtable, consisting of the following agencies:

Department of Defense	Federal Bureau of Investigation
Department of State	ACTION/Peace Corps
Central Intelligence Agency Development	Agency for International
National Security Agency	Office of Personnel Management
Department of the Interior	Immigration and Naturalization Service
National Institutes of Health	Department of Education
National Science Foundation	US Customs Service
Department of Agriculture	US Information Agency
Drug Enforcement Administration	Library of Congress

Figure 5–4. Interagency Language Roundtable Language Skill Level Descriptions - Writing–Continued

c. The DLIELC will report to the appropriate Military Service agency as soon as it is determined that an IMS will meet the language prerequisites for follow-on-training (FOT) in less time than scheduled. The Military Service agency in coordination with the FOT IMSO will determine if the IMS can be scheduled for earlier FOT or if the IMS should remain at DLIELC until the original scheduled departure date.

d. If an IMS with a language deficiency reaches a course of instruction, either as a graduate of DLIELC or as a direct entry from an in-country language training program, the IMS may be provided additional training at DLIELC on a one-time basis. Requests for this training, along with full details, will be forwarded to the appropriate MILDEP agency with an information copy to DLIELC. Upon completion of the additional English language training, the IMS will normally return to the same training installation to continue training.

e. The DLIELC will notify, via e-mail, Military Service and IMSO at follow-on training schools of IMS travel itinerary, TLA payments and potential language, academic and/or disciplinary problems.

5–2. Guidance and functions

a. Secretary of the Air Force. The Secretary of the Air Force is designated as Executive Agent for the Defense English Language Program. All requests for in-country ELTP, MTT and language training detachments (LTD), language instructor training and DLIELC curriculum materials and publications will be processed under AF SC programs. Requests for MTT and LTD will be forwarded according to paragraph 4–18.

b. Commandant of DLIELC. The Commandant of DLIELC, under USAF Air Education and Training Command, is directly responsible for technical control of English language training within CONUS for IMS and for the technical control of DOD-sponsored English language training in CONUS and overseas. The Commandant of DLIELC will—

(1) Command and operate the DLIELC at Lackland AFB, San Antonio, TX.

(2) Develop and distribute ECL tests; provide personnel to conduct OPI (when assessment of oral proficiency skills is required); establish English-testing policies and procedures; publish, and disseminate related testing directives to be used by all DOD agencies required to assess English proficiency and monitor nonresident English language testing programs.

(3) Develop, refine, approve and arrange for procurement of American Language Course audio/multimedia materials and other instructional aids.

(4) Deploy English language specialists overseas.

(5) Coordinate with the MILDEP on English language training requirements for the various courses attended by IMS.

(6) Provide English language instruction to IMS and offer basic and advanced English language instructor training and language program management courses.

(7) Evaluate and monitor all DOD-sponsored FMS, IMET, FMF, and related programs.

(8) Publish, maintain, and update DLIELC publications.

c. DLIELC publications.

(1) *DLIELC English Language Training Support for Security Cooperation Organizations.* This handbook provides detailed information pertaining to programming IMS for DLIELC training and programming services and materials in support of a foreign country's in-country ELTP.

(2) *DLIELC Catalog of Materials, Courses, and Support.* This catalog lists information and prices for American Language Course materials available for purchase through regular supply channels. Inquiries about ELT materials should be sent to Commandant, DLIELC/LEN, 2235 Andrews Ave, Lackland AFB, TX 78236–5259. The catalog is also available online at http://www.disam.dsca.mil/itm/.

(3) *DLIELC Instruction 1025.7, Planning and Programming Security Assistance English Language Training.* This regulation provides guidelines for planning and programming CONUS ELT, including Specialized English Training.

(4) *DLIELC Instruction 1025.15.* This regulation provides instructions for the Security Cooperation Organization and the ECL test control officer (TCO). It includes details on ECL testing kits, TCO appointments and procedures for ECL test administration.

(5) *DLIELC Manual 1025.5–M.* This pamphlet describes DLIELC training systems and presents guidance on administrative and academic features of intensive ELTP.

(6) *DLIELC Instruction 1025.9.* This regulation establishes guidelines for managing the OPI program and provides guidance to Security Cooperation Organization on OPI scheduling and administration procedures.

(7) *Handbook for the American Language Course Placement Test (ALCPT).* This pamphlet provides instructions for securing and administering ALCPT and interpreting test scores.

(8) *DLIELC curriculum materials and publications.*

(a) Materials provided under IMET Military Standard Requisitioning and Issue Procedure requisitions must be

processed through the Air Force Security Assistance Training Squadron/FMF, 315 J Street West, Randolph AFB, TX 78150–4354 with an information copy to DLIELC/LESL, 2235 Andrews Ave., Lackland AFB, TX 78236–5259.

(b) Requests under FMS will be forwarded using an FMS publication case to AFSAC/XMPP, 1822 Van Patton Drive, Wright-Patterson AFB, OH 45433–5337.

d. All Security Cooperation Organization (except those in countries exempt from all ECL testing requirements, as defined by the annual DSCA message) will—

(1) Encourage the teaching of English in foreign country military schools, particularly for prospective IMS.

(2) Assist the country in procuring English language course materials, laboratories, spare parts, portable tape recorders, and administrative requirements.

(3) Arrange for additional English language training, as necessary, to meet the highest ECL requirement of scheduled CONUS courses. This additional training should be conducted in country whenever possible.

(4) Appoint a U.S. member as TCO to supervise the administration of in-country ECL/OPI tests to ensure proper testing procedures and test security (except for countries granted a waiver by DSCA from in-country ECL/OPI testing requirements).

(5) Enter ECL and OPI information in the ITO (except for countries granted a waiver by DSCA from in-country ECL and/or OPI testing).

e. Commanders of training installations will appoint a TCO to supervise the administration of the CONUS course entry ECL test at the installation level (see DLIELC Instruction 1025.15). One copy of the ECL TCO Appointment letter will be sent to DLIELC/LEAT. The CONUS course entry ECL test will be administered to all direct-entry IMS scheduled for training in English except those granted an annual waiver by DSCA or those in special courses granted a onetime waiver of ECL test requirements by the MILDEP. The TCO will set up an OPI for IMS who are scheduled to attend a course with an OPI requirement and who do not have a comprehension/speaking rating less than 6 months old.

5–3. Technical control of in-country and CONUS English Language Training Program

Maintaining an effective English Language Training Program is predicated on technical control of the program by DLIELC.

a. Those LOA that include provisions for ELT must be coordinated with DLIELC before negotiation.

b. All security assistance sponsored CONUS ELT will be conducted by DLIELC unless unusual or extraordinary conditions exist that would warrant exceptional ELT arrangements under FMS training. No exceptions will be permitted for IMET-funded ELT. To request an exception for FMS-funded ELT, a written justification must be submitted by the military departments to the appropriate DSCA regional directorate prior to submission of LOA or LOA amendments to DSCA for countersignature. Waivers must be approved by DSCA. Justifications must include the following information:

(1) Written DLIELC comments and recommendations on the proposed exception.

(2) Explanation of the unusual or extraordinary conditions that would warrant training outside of DLIELC.

(3) Complete information on the ELT to be conducted to include location, description of training facilities, number of students, training objectives, duration of the overall ELTP, and estimated cost.

(4) A statement that DLIELC will coordinate and approve the ELT curriculum, teaching materials, and instructor qualification standards.

(5) A statement that DLIELC will monitor the ELT to ensure that DLIELC technical standards are being met and that DLIELC will certify the ELTP every 6 months.

(6) A statement that the LOA will contain an appropriate line item for DLIELC to monitor and provide quality control of the proposed ELTP.

c. If a DSCA waiver is granted, the waiver will strictly apply to the scope of the proposed ELT program justified in the exception request. No change to the LOA will be made to increase the student load or extend the duration of the ELT program without submitting a revised request to DSCA, to include information in paragraph *b,* above.

d. When the Director, DSCA, approves that ELT be provided by a commercial contract, DLIELC will provide technical advice and assistance during the contracting process.

e. When the Director, DSCA, approves that Specialized English Training be conducted in CONUS by U.S. agencies other than DLIELC, the following conditions must be met:

(1) The trainees have achieved the prerequisite ECL/OPI proficiency as prescribed by Military Service regulations for entry into technical training.

(2) Training is given in conjunction with equipment-specific, hands-on training or familiarization.

(3) Training is effective and economical to the USG and foreign government and meets the technical standards set by DLIELC.

f. Specialized English Training must be conducted at DLIELC. Exceptions to this policy must be granted by DSCA. If DSCA grants an exception, DLIELC must evaluate and certify the in-country Specialized English Training ELTP and also certify that in-country Specialized English Training ELTP graduates meet all standards prescribed by DLIELC.

Section II
Security Assistance Program Services and Training

5–4. Services
The purpose of the in-country ELTP is to produce English-language-qualified IMS to directly enter U.S. military, technical or professional courses conducted in English or to qualify IMS for entry into DLIELC for additional intensive general English, Specialized English Training or instructor development training. DLIELC furnishes the following in support of the in-country ELTP:

a. Field training services. The DLIELC provides English language technical services on a PCS or TDY basis as follows:

(1) The LTD provides English language services, such as instructional or managerial assistance to in-country ELTP, on a PCS basis.

(2) The MTT performs several functions:

(a) Surveys to evaluate in-country ELTP capabilities and needs.

(b) The same services as LTD on a temporary basis.

(c) Pre-deployment surveys prior to the deployment of DLIELC personnel.

b. Language training materials. Information on obtaining personnel assistance and language training materials (texts, tests, audio/multimedia materials, and so forth) is contained in the DLIELC handbook, *English Language Training Support for Security Cooperation Offices*, which is available on request from Commandant, DLIELC/LEN, 2235 Andrews Ave., Lackland AFB, TX 78236–5259. Direct communication with DLIELC is authorized for requesting this handbook and assistance.

c. Language laboratories. The DLIELC handbook provides information about various types of language laboratory systems, guidance on their appropriateness for different types of ELTP and the operational components of an ELTP which should be established before a language laboratory system is purchased. The DA is the cognizant MILDEP for language laboratory system procurement. The procurement, installation and follow-on logistical support of language laboratory systems furnished to foreign countries under SC is the responsibility of the Commander, U.S. Army Communications-Electronics Command (CECOM), Fort Monmouth, NJ 07703–5000. Commander, CECOM directs subordinate commands and contractors to perform procurement, installation and follow-on logistical support for language laboratory systems. Requests for language laboratory systems utilizing FMS funds will be submitted to the Commander, United States Army Security Assistance Command (USASAC), 5701 21st Street, Building 216, Fort Belvoir, VA 22060–5940. Requisitions for language laboratory systems utilizing IMET funds will be submitted to Commander, USASAC, 54 M Avenue, Suite 1, New Cumberland, PA 17070–5069. CECOM provides detailed guidance on the language laboratory acquisition process. Requests for laboratory installation teams, regardless of host country Service, will be programmed by Director, SATFA (ATTG–TRI–S) and Commander, CECOM (AM-SELLC–SA–CCA). These teams will be programmed as MTT.

5–5. General English language training
The DLIELC offers courses designed to develop the English language capability of IMS so they can attend DOD schools. The mission is to teach IMS to understand, speak, read, and write English for the wide spectrum of training provided by the Military Service. DLIELC has an established student-to-instructor ratio of 6 to 1 to ensure adequate time to practice the four language skills so students will meet their graduation goals. In addition, DLIELC assists training installations in resolving problems related to English language training.

5–6. Specialized English training
The 9-week Specialized English Training provides intensive practice in the functional English language skills and technical terminology identified by Military Service as essential for success in technical training courses and professional military education. Excerpts from actual training materials associated with military occupational skills (MOS) areas are used as realistic vehicles for IMS language practice and solidification of FOT language proficiency requirements as well as orientation to the organization and format of military training documents. Military Service have identified in the Training Military Articles and Service List those courses for which Specialized English Training is either required or advised by an "SR," "SO," or "SC" suffix to the ECL score, respectively (for example, ECL 80SR, ECL 85SO, ECL 70SA).

a. The "SR" designation is usually assigned to highly technical courses such as flying courses, medical courses or courses in which safety is paramount (for example, pilot training, diving salvage and Army biomedical equipment specialist).

b. The "SC" designation is assigned to those courses not qualifying under paragraph *a*, above, but having sufficiently high or peculiar technical requirements as to warrant Military Service advisement of Specialized English Training in CONUS (for example, sonar maintenance, field artillery officer and jet engine accident investigation).

c. The "SO" designation is assigned to those courses requiring English oral proficiency skills in addition to Specialized English Training (for example, flying courses or the Public Affairs Officer course at the Defense Information School).

5–7. Additional special language training

The DLIELC has developed language training to assist IMS in meeting language requirements for certain courses.

a. Advanced English Language Program. This 16-week advanced English language course is designed for students who need to improve their language skills, with an emphasis on speaking and writing. This course prepares students who have not yet met their ECL and OPI requirements for professional military education training courses, officer basic and advanced courses, and so forth.

b. Oral Proficiency Skills for Aviation. This course concentrates on language skills needed by students going to aviation-related training. The course enables students to improve pronunciation for successful radio communication, to improve comprehension skills under adverse conditions, to practice immediate oral responses, and to practice speaking while performing a complex motor task. This is a 25-week course, the last nine weeks being Specialized English Training.

c. Test of English as a Foreign Language Preparation and Academic Writing Course. The TOEFL is a prerequisite for entering the graduate programs at certain senior professional military education courses. This 16-week course develops the advanced English language skills necessary to compete successfully at university level and to improve a minimum entry TOEFL score of 173 on the computer-based test and 61 on the Internet-based test. The course emphasizes the development of academic writing skills for university-level students and includes completion of one major research paper and numerous other writing assignments.

5–8. Forfeiture charge

Guidelines in paragraph 6–3 (forfeiture charge) are amplified, as follows, for IMS at DLIELC:

a. Late cancellation/reschedule/no-show. Assess 50 percent of the tuition for the training line.

b. Late arrival. For training priced on a per-week basis, assess 50 percent of the tuition for the number of weeks late, up to a maximum of 50 percent of the scheduled training.

c. Attrition. Charge for the actual number of weeks completed, but not less than 50 percent of the training line.

d. Military Service. This Service will immediately advise the Air Force Security Assistance Training Squadron/FM, in writing, of any forfeiture to be applied for training under their sponsorship.

5–9. Minimum entry score and waiver policy

a. The DSCA has established a minimum score of 55 ECL for entry of IMET IMS into CONUS English language training at DLIELC. Exceptions will be granted only where clearly justified in support of major programs, and with DSCA approval on a case-by-case basis, within the capability of DLIELC. Based on an in-depth review of in-country ELTP, DSCA publishes annually a list of IMET countries granted a waiver from the 55 ECL requirements.

b. FMS IMS are not restricted to a minimum ECL score for entry into DLIELC.

c. Requests for waivers of ECL prerequisites for direct-entry training will be addressed to the Military Service.

5–10. Objective of English comprehension level scoring

a. The Security Cooperation Organization are responsible for ensuring that IMS meet the minimum ECL score prescribed for direct entry into each follow-on course of instruction or for entry into DLIELC. The highest ECL required within a sequence of training will be the governing factor. Security Cooperation Organization will enter the highest ECL required in block 10 of the ITO (except for IMS from countries exempt from all ECL testing requirements, as defined by the annual DSCA message). The ECL score achieved (including the form and date of the test taken) will also be entered in block 10 of the ITO for all IMS required to be tested in-country.

b. The Training Military Articles and Service List may indicate a minimum ECL requirement for each course listed. The word "minimum" as used here is significant because it indicates the lowest possible ECL the IMS should possess to enter training. It should not be interpreted as an optimum ECL.

Section III
Tests

5–11. Test types and formats

The DLIELC currently uses three tests to assess general English proficiency. The ECL test and the ALCPT both measure non-interactive listening and reading skills, while the OPI assesses interactive listening and speaking ability. These tests have been developed to determine whether the English proficiency level of IMS considered for assignment to CONUS or overseas schools/training installations is sufficient to enter training at DLIELC or for direct entry to

Military Service courses of instruction. ECL and OPI (if applicable) requirements for each course conducted in English are determined by the school, approved by the Military Service and published in the Training Military Articles and Service List.

a. The ECL tests and ALCPT are standardized multiple-choice tests of the IMS' ability to understand spoken and written English of the variety that would be encountered in a military training environment. The audio portion of the tests consists of recorded questions, statements and dialogs. The reading components contain discrete vocabulary and grammar items, as well as reading passages. ECL tests and ALCPT are designed and validated in the same manner, and they render equivalent scores on a scale of 1 to 100. The main difference between the two tests is the amount of control and oversight required by DLIELC. ECL tests are strictly controlled and are provided (at no cost) by DLIELC only to duly appointed TCO, who must be both U.S. citizens and U.S. Government personnel. ECL TCO Appointment, Memorandum for Record, can be faxed or mailed to DLIELC. (See DLIELC Instruction 1025.15.) The ALCPT can be purchased from DLIELC through normal SC procurement channels for use in OCONUS ELTP. (Special "U.S." versions of the ALCPT are provided to the U.S. Army at no cost for use in lieu of the ECL to fulfill testing requirements for certain Army programs, such as the inter-Service Physician Assistant Training Program. These forms are not sold OCONUS.)

(1) A computer-adaptive training version of the ECL is used on the DLIELC resident campus. Scores on the computer-adaptive training ECL are equivalent to scores on the paper-and-pencil test.

(2) New paper-and-pencil versions of the ECL and instructions for administering them are developed and distributed to nonresident test sites by DLIELC every year. However, shipment of new tests is not automatic. The TCO must submit a questionnaire indicating the test site's ECL test material needs and must be in compliance with all testing documentation requirements before new materials are shipped. (See DLIELC Instruction 1025.15.)

(3) The ECL test is used for final certification of IMS for SC-sponsored training. The ALCPT is prescribed for screening candidates for ECL test readiness and for all other in-country testing purposes. To preserve the validity and reliability of ALCPT the same measures for security and accountability should be applied to them as are taken with regard to ECL tests. Failure to comply with the guidelines in the ALCPT Handbook (for example, allowing the materials to fall into the hands of unauthorized parties, duplicating them, or using them in an unauthorized manner-such as for training or teaching purposes) can result in test compromise and sanctioning of future sales of ALCPT to the buyer.

b. The OPI is a test of a candidate's interactive listening comprehension and speaking ability, conducted under controlled conditions by two certified OPI raters provided by DLIELC. It is a standardized method of measuring actual performance and proficiency in language skills required to function in given life/job situations. During the 20–40-minute interview, OPI raters ascertain the examinee's highest level of listening comprehension and speaking abilities and rate them on an eleven-point scale (0 to 5, including plus levels) in accordance with the Interagency language Roundtable skill level descriptions. OPI can be conducted face-to-face or via telephone. TCO can schedule an in-country OPI for an IMS through DLIELC only after the IMS has achieved the required ECL score. (See DLIELC Instruction 1025.9.)

5–12. Test score validity and reliability

The OPI scores are valid for 6 months. IMS who fail to make the required score OCONUS will not be retested for 90 days, and they should be enrolled in an intensive ELTP that stresses oral communication during that time. In-country ECL test scores are valid up to 105 calendar days. When the date of testing is more than 105 days from the report date, the IMS will be retested with a different form of the ECL test before departure for CONUS. An individual who does not make the required score on the first exam must wait 30 days before taking another in-country ECL test (a different form). Waivers to required "wait" periods before retesting must be approved by DLIELC. The TCO will mail all in-country ECL answer sheets monthly by certified or other secure mail to DLIELC/LEAT 2230 Andrews Ave., Lackland AFB, TX 78236–5207.

a. One of the greatest concerns in language testing is the reliability of tests administered overseas. Some of the causes of lower test reliability are—

(1) Test compromise through physical loss of test materials, failure to maintain test security, or granting access to unauthorized personnel.

(2) Overexposure of test forms, due to excessive test administration (a result of poor scheduling and insufficient management oversight) or failure to rotate ECL test forms in an unpredictable manner.

(3) Substandard procedures for examinee identification, ineffective monitoring or failure to follow test administration procedures to the letter.

(4) Changes in test administration personnel and/or facilities.

(5) Testing candidates too frequently or when inappropriate.

(6) Errors in scoring or recording data.

b. To check test reliability and to ensure that IMS entered into training are English-language-qualified, the following testing procedures will be used at all training installations:

(1) Within 3 to 5 calendar days after IMS' arrival at the first training location and, if possible, before course entry,

the TCO will administer the CONUS course entry ECL test to all direct-entry IMS (except those from countries listed as exempt from all ECL testing in the annual DSCA message). Once a month, ECL test answer sheets will be mailed by certified or other secure mail to DLIELC/LEAT, 2230 Andrews Ave., Lackland AFB TX 78236–5207. Answer sheets will reflect the test site number, the name of the IMS, the country of origin, IMET worksheet control number (WCN), or FMS case designator and WCN, the sponsoring Service, the required ECL score and the actual ECL score. On a quarterly basis, DLIELC will upload a report of test results on the Security Assistance Network.

(2) The TCO will adhere to testing procedures defined in DLIELC Instruction 1025.15. Measures will be taken to ensure careful control over the administration of the ECL examinations and security of test materials to prevent possible compromise.

(3) If the IMS fails to achieve the prerequisite ECL at first testing, the IMSO will notify the appropriate MILDEP agency by telephone and schedule the IMS for another ECL test within the next 2 to 3 working days to confirm the score using an alternate ECL test form. If the score achieved on the second ECL test is less than the established prerequisite, the IMSO will immediately notify the appropriate MILDEP and DLIELC by telephone of the score achieved. MILDEP will determine required action and disposition of the IMS and notify all concerned. A second retest will not be administered unless permission is obtained from the MILDEP and DLIELC.

(4) English comprehension level testing of IMS is normally the responsibility of the IMSO. However, the Base Education Office TCO may be appointed the ECL TCO if local conditions require.

(5) A forfeiture charge of at least 50 percent will be imposed in all instances when direct-entry IMS fail to achieve the prerequisite ECL on the CONUS course entry ECL test and when failure results in rescheduling or cancellation of the direct-entry training due to a language deficiency. This forfeiture policy applies to all direct-entry IMS, including those from countries granted a waiver from in-country ECL testing.

Section IV
Department of the Army

5–13. Minimum entry score and waiver policy

a. Requests for waivers of the ECL requirement for direct entry into formal training except for medical training will be addressed to Director, SATFA. Requests for waivers for medical training will be addressed to Office of the Surgeon General, International Programs. Immediately upon being notified that an IMS has failed to achieve the required ECL, IMSO will notify the appropriate SATFA country program manager by telephone or e-mail. If the student fails the second test, IMSO will coordinate with the course director or equivalent to determine if the school recommends a waiver of the ECL requirement. IMSO will contact SATFA country program manager via e-mail and forward the school recommendation, including justification. Director, SATFA will determine, taking the school recommendation into account, which of the following will occur:

(1) The SATFA may grant a waiver and allow the IMS to enter or continue training as scheduled. In recommending a waiver, the IMSO should remember that the ECL for a particular course is the minimum required, not the optimum.

(2) Director, SATFA may determine that the IMS must be sent to DLIELC for English language training prior to enrolling in the course. This option depends on the ability of SATFA and the installation, along with concurrence of the home country, to reschedule the course to follow language training.

(3) Director, SATFA may determine that the IMS ECL is not sufficient to allow successful course completion, that training cannot be rescheduled, and that the IMS must be returned to their home country.

(4) Director, SATFA may, in conjunction with the IMSO, coordinate with DLIELC for a second re-test. If a student fails the second retest as stated in paragraphs (1), (2), or (3), above, will apply.

b. Students will meet the highest ECL required within a sequence of training. The only exception is when the Army Basic Instructor Course (ABIC) is the highest ECL requirement and is programmed as the last training line. In this case, the next highest ECL requirement within the training sequence will take precedence.

c. The IMS may be admitted to training after failing an initial ECL test if there is not sufficient time for a second test to be administered prior to the course starting.

5–14. Establishing English comprehension levels

Each installation is responsible for establishing the ECL requirement, subject to the approval of SATFA, for each course to which a Training Military Articles and Service List is assigned. The IMSO should monitor the progress of students with various ECL to make recommendations concerning the appropriate ECL for each course. The ECL, once established, may not be changed without the approval of Director, SATFA. The following factors should be considered when recommending new ECL to SATFA:

a. Determine the historical success/failure data for IMS at different ECL for the course in question.

b. Analyze changes that have taken place in the course in terms of both course content and methods of instruction. For example, determine if the reading grade level has changed, if it includes DL, if it has become faster-paced, and so forth.

c. Coordinate with the appropriate school personnel and SATFA P4 prior to sending a recommended ECL change to Director, SATFA.

5–15. English language refresher program
Depending on installation resources, an English Language Refresher Program may be available. This program is normally conducted in coordination with the on-post educational activity. Additionally, IMS should be encouraged to engage in available off-post programs offered in the local community. The ECL test will not be used for testing in refresher programs.

5–16. Required in-country English comprehension level testing
Students attending Army courses that encourage dependents are required to be ECL tested in country even if they are from countries which are exempt from in-country ECL testing.

Section V
Department of the Navy (U.S. Navy, U.S. Marine Corps, and U.S. Coast Guard)

5–17. English language training actions required
Navy IPO is responsible for the establishment of DON policy regarding ELT, to include authority to concur/non-concur with decision to "contract out" ELT and to ensure Services comply with DOD Regulation on ELT. In the execution of this policy for courses under their cognizance, Naval Education and Training Security Assistance Field Activity, CG, Security Cooperation Education and Training Center TECOM, and USCG International Affairs (G–CI), will—

a. Evaluate the English proficiency of IMS in the schools and installations under their cognizance and recommend to DLIELC measures for improvement, both for IMS who receive all language training in their own country and those who attend DLIELC.

b. Provided DLIELC with information on courses under their cognizance that require special language training.

c. Set ECL requirements for the courses under their cognizance.

d. Schedule ELT at DLIELC for students under their cognizance, as required.

e. Recommend to DLIELC changes in language curricula to enhance the English proficiency of IMS scheduled for specialized training.

f. Coordinate disposition of an IMS that does not possess an ECL adequate for scheduled training. Disposition may include scheduling of additional ELT at DLIELC or termination of training, as appropriate.

g. Ensure TCO appointment letters have been issued in accordance with DLIELC Instruction 1025.15.

5–18. Establishing the English comprehension level scores
The Command providing training to an IMS is responsible for establishing the course ECL requirement, subject to the approval Naval Education and Training Security Assistance Field Activity, CG, TECOM Security Cooperation Education and Training Center or USCG International Affairs (G–CI). The IMSO is responsible for reporting ECL requirements and monitoring IMS progress to make ECL recommendations to Naval Education and Training Security Assistance Field Activity, USMC Security Cooperation Education and Training Center or USCG G–CI.

5–19. Minimum English comprehension level
The ECL requirements vary and the Training Military Articles and Service List should be checked for the minimum ECL for each course.

a. Professional military education. Minimum ECL requirement for Naval Command College and Naval Staff College is 80. Minimum ECL requirement for Joint Forces Staff College is 85. Minimum ECL requirement for USMC Command and Staff College and Expeditionary Warfare School is 80 with Specialized English Training advised. A computer based TOEFL test score of 207 is required for entry into the Naval Postgraduate School graduate degree programs. (TOEFL test results are valid for 2 years from the test date.) A candidate with a TOEFL of 173 or greater is eligible to enter the TOEFL Preparatory Writing Course at DLIELC.

b. Flight training The minimum ECL score for flight training (including simulator training) is 85 plus an OPI plus 9 weeks of Specialized English Training is also required.

c. Hazardous duty training. The minimum ECL for swimming, diving, Basic Underwater Demolition/Seal and explosive ordnance disposal training is 85 plus 9 weeks of Specialized English Training is also required.

d. Medical. Medical officer training usually requires an 80 ECL with 9 weeks of Specialized English Training. An ECL of 70 with 9 weeks of Specialized English Training is normally required for medical technician training.

e. Observer and technical training Most OJT, observer and technical training require an ECL of 70. There are no specific requirements for ship transfer crews, but a qualified interpreter at a ratio of one interpreter to 10 crewmembers is recommended. Ship shakedown training is greatly enhanced if all or most of the crew understands English.

f. English Comprehension Language requirements. There are no specific ECL requirements for IMS who are trained by a deployed team, provided the numbers of interpreters as determined during the mission analysis or site survey are available.

5–20. Waivers of English comprehension level requirements for Department of the Navy courses

Requests for waivers of ECL requirements for DON training will be forwarded to Naval Education and Training Security Assistance Field Activity for Navy training, with information copy to Navy IPO (02CT), CG, Security Cooperation Education and Training Center MCCDC for Marine Corps training, and to USCG International Affairs (G-CI) for Coast Guard training. Naval Education and Training Security Assistance Field Activity, CG, Security Cooperation Education and Training Center MCCDC and USCG International Affairs (G-CI) will coordinate with the commands involved for determination. Requests for waivers will be considered on a case-by-case basis. The factors that determine if a waiver is appropriate include, but are not limited to the following:

 a. Method of presentation of the course, level of difficulty of material presented, experience level of the prospective IMS, presence of other IMS from the same country and previous U.S. training.

 b. No ECL waiver is required for Spanish speaking students attending Naval Small Craft Instruction and Technical Training School.

Section VI
Department of the Air Force

5–21. Continental United States English language training

 a. The IMS who are selected for flying training, air traffic controller, weapons controller, and other courses that require Specialized English Training and who meet minimum ECL prerequisites will proceed first to DLIELC, regardless of ECL. A minimum of 9 weeks for processing, physical examination, and additional language training is required. This requirement may be reduced or waived if the IMS meets all AF administrative and training prerequisites and has had recent, frequent contact with English-speaking personnel in their country.

 b. Request for waiver or reduction of the 9-week Specialized English Training course requirement will be forwarded to the Air Force Security Assistance Training Squadron. Requests will cite the appropriate AF medical and physiological training certification and circumstances of contact with English-speaking personnel.

 c. The AWC, Air Command and Staff College (ACSC), and the Secretary of State are each preceded by a mandatory International Officers School preparatory course at Maxwell AFB, Alabama. Direct entry into other Air University courses is commensurate with ECL and AF ETCA requirements.

5–22. Language training detachment manpower requirements packages

The Air Force Security Assistance Training Squadron will prepare the Manpower Requirements Package, Manpower Travel Data Sheet, obtain all associated costs, and prepare the LOA or amendment as required to comply with the letter of request. The Manpower Requirements Package and MTDS will be accomplished using the Security Assistance Manpower Requirements System (SAMRS).

Chapter 6
Financial Management

Section I
General

6–1. Purpose

The purpose of the chapter is to establish policies and procedures for financial management of funding provided to cover expenses associated with training international students under the SCETP.

6–2. Tuition pricing

The tuition price as shown in the Training Military Articles and Service List is a unit cost per IMS. The types of cost (direct, indirect, incremental, and attrition, Field Studies Program (formerly Informational Program), and mailing fee) applicable to the different tuition rates are identified in DOD 7000.14–R. Regardless of the funding source, the tuition price charged is the cost in effect at the time the student enters each course.

6–3. Forfeiture charge

 a. Training contracted/dedicated for international customers. Once a contract is let or a quota is confirmed, a forfeiture charge up to 100 percent will apply if the country fails to send a student to the training, unless the quota is filled by another international student. Dedicated/contract training includes courses which rely on contract support and/or courses that are designated for international students only.

(1) The MILDEP will identify those courses that are dedicated/contract training by message to the Security Cooperation Organization on an annual basis.

(2) If the contractor cancels or reschedules training no penalty will be assessed.

b. Training contracted for a single international customer Under USG direct contract, all costs incurred up to the point of contract cancellation shall be paid. This could include total charges or partial charges. Each element of cost will be reviewed and negotiated for a final settlement cost by appropriate USG contracts personnel and the contractor.

c. All other training. There will be a 50 percent charge for all confirmed training canceled or rescheduled with less than 60 days notification unless the quota is filled by another student. The charges will be applied to all confirmed training within the 60-day window. Additionally, a 50 percent forfeiture charge will be applied to all training that falls within and outside the 60-day window if the training is part of a sequential pipeline that a student would attend as part of a complete curriculum. MILDEP will specify training that is part of a sequential pipeline by message to Security Cooperation Organization on an annual basis. Any cancellation or rescheduling of training that was scheduled at the request of the country without the required lead time to cancel/reschedule similarly will incur a 50 percent charge.

d. Procedures. The date the request is received from the country by the Security Cooperation Organization or other duly appointed and recognized U.S. representative will constitute the official notification date. The Security Cooperation Organization must immediately comply with the cancellation procedure established by the MILDEP, indicating the date that formal cancellation was received from the country.

e. Forfeiture charges. These charges will not be applied when cancellation is the fault of the USG, such as deletion of classes or rescheduling, nor will it be applied when the cancellation is due to unavoidable circumstances within the country, such as national disasters or airline strikes. Ultimate assessment of the penalty is at the discretion of the Military Service.

f. The country should be provided training dates at least 90 days before the start date. Forfeiture charges will not be applied if country cancels or declines training and dates were provided less than 90 days in advance. However, if later training dates were provided at the request of country, the charges will be applied.

g. For training under IMET only. When IMET appropriations do not materialize at the program CPD levels and DSCA directs countries to reduce their program, they are allowed 60 days to make the required adjustments without penalty for course cancellations. The 60-day adjustment period begins with State Department notification of IMET levels. Waiver of penalty charges under this paragraph does not apply to contract/dedicated or sequential training or to normal program adjustments to accommodate new courses during the same timeframe.

h. Access charges. The following guidelines apply to assess charges after arrival of the IMS at the first CONUS or OCONUS training activity.

(1) When the direct-entry IMS fails to achieve the prerequisite ECL on the CONUS course entry ECL test resulting in rescheduling or cancellation of training, charges will apply according to paragraphs 6–3a through 6–3c. When IMS attending ELT at DLIELC fail to meet the language prerequisite of the follow-on course, the country will be charged for the language training received and for follow-on training according to paragraphs 6–3a through 6–3c.

(2) When the IMS is recalled by their country for official reasons or the IMS has disciplinary problems, illness, or disability incurred before departing country, forfeiture charges will be assessed for the current course or phase and for the follow-on course according to paragraphs 6–3a through 6–3c.

(3) When the IMS has an injury, illness incurred during training, or compassionate return, the country will be assessed forfeiture charges for all contract/dedicated/sequential pipeline training according to paragraph 6–3a through 6–3c. For all other training courses, assess forfeiture charges for the course started but not completed; do not assess forfeiture charges for the follow-on course.

Section II
International Military Education and Training

6–4. General

a. The DOS in consultation with the DOD will determine IMET dollar levels for each IMET country. The DOS will provide approved country allocation levels to the DSCA Directorate of Business Operations Comptroller (DSCA–DBO–CMP). DSCA manages and issues the IMET funds to the MILDEP, who allocates funds to each of the Service training activities to fund program execution. Actual annual IMET appropriations may be less than anticipated in the Congressional Budget Justification; therefore, country allocation levels may be lower that the Congressional Budget Justification country levels which were used previously for planning purposes. Consequently, training programs should be adjusted to reflect the allocation level. Finally, during the course of the year, the stated allocation levels may not change except as reallocated at the DSCA end-of-year IMET meeting held during the fourth quarter of the current FY. The reallocation is dependent upon the country's ability to utilize the funds.

b. IMET under Budget Project N10 commencing during the first quarter (Oct, Nov, and Dec) of the subsequent FY may be programmed and funded in the current FY's IMET program under the fifth-quarter concept. Project N10 includes CONUS and OCONUS formal courses, OBT, OJT, and familiarization training. If this method is desired, the IMS reporting for initial training during the first quarter of the subsequent FY will be programmed in the current fiscal year's IMET program. Training requirements programmed in the current year with an availability of fifth quarter must be re-priced as soon as FY course costs are known.

6–5. Funding

a. Upon receipt of IMET funding authority from DSCA, funds for international training are distributed by MILDEP.

b. The IMET funded MTT and Mobile Education Team must return to CONUS prior to end of the FY.

c. The IMET funds must be obligated before the close of each FY. This includes funds for training programmed under the fifth-quarter concept and for IMS who have follow-on training that will commence after the end of the current FY.

d. Country allocations are received through the DSAMS throughout the FY, and country programs are executed by the training activities within the limits of both funding and country allocation levels.

Section III
Foreign Military Sales Training

6–6. General

a. The FMS training is financed through payment in U.S. dollars.

b. The FMS training will be provided at no cost to the USG except as authorized by law. All costs, as specified in the AECA and DOD 7000.14–R, will be identified and included in tuition pricing.

c. The FMS training cannot commence until DFAS–DE has implemented the case. FMS CONUS training cannot begin until the MILDEP has authorized the Security Cooperation Organization to issue an ITO.

d. Except as specifically authorized by statute, the law requires that the U.S. recoup all expenses from a country under FMS. Training provided to a foreign country that results in identifiable expenses to the USG is fully reimbursable from the purchaser country. Unless identifiable expenses are authorized through independent statutory or other legal authority, they are considered to be under the SCETP and must be fully recouped.

e. Bilateral, combined, or multilateral exercises conducted to test and evaluate mutual capabilities do not require authorization or funding under the SCETP. In the absence of independent, statutory, or other legal authority, costs of foreign participation in such exercises will not be directly paid for or reimbursed from DOD funds. DOD funds will bear only the costs of U.S. Armed Forces participation in such exercises. The costs of any U.S. support provided to the participating countries or international organizations for training exercises for defense Service is pursuant to the AECA. The extension and receipt of services furnished as reciprocal international courtesies (10 USC 2350g), when authorized under the general provisions of the DOD annual Appropriations Act, may serve as authority for bearing certain costs of providing these services to foreign participants when such services are offered to U.S. Forces on a reciprocal basis.

f. In the absence of statutory and other legal authority to the contrary, visits of eligible IMS to U.S. units that are conducted for training purposes will be fully reimbursable through FMS procedures. Visits by IMS to U.S. units extended for periods beyond 3 working days at one location will be considered as training subject to reimbursement. Visits of three working days or less at one location will be considered as nontraining and administered as a self-invited visit.

6–7. Funding

The FMS Training will not commence until the purchasing country has deposited sufficient funds against the appropriate FMS case and has issued obligation authority. The use of MILDEP-appropriated funds for training under FMS is not permitted by law.

Section IV
Counter-Drug Training Support

6–8. General

Counter narcotics under Public Law 101–510, Section 1004 (reference by the National Defense Authorization Act for Fiscal Year 1991), is authorized to obtain defense articles and services via direct arrangements with the MILDEP or other DOD agencies. More information on Counter-Drug Training Support is available in the DOD 5105.38M, chapter 11, C11.3.

6–9. Funding

Under the Counter-Drug Training Support Program, Deputy Assistant Secretary of Defense-Counter-Narcotics (DASD–CN) issues authority to release funding to MILDEP.

Section V
International Narcotics Control and Law Enforcement

6–10. General
The International Narcotics Control and Law Enforcement has two strategic goals: minimize the impact of international crime on the United States; and reduce the entry of illegal drugs into the United States. More information on International Narcotics Control and Law Enforcement is available in the SAMM DOD 5105.38M, chapter 10, C10.7.9.

6–11. Funding
Under the International Narcotics Control and Law Enforcement Program, State Department issues each MILDEP a separate MOA for each FY and country as International Narcotics Control and Law Enforcement funding authorization.

Section VI
Regional Defense Combating Terrorism Fellowship Program

6–12. General
Programming and financial guidance on the Counterterrorism Fellowship Program is available in DOD 5105.38M, chapter 10 and Implementation of Guidance Message Numbers One and Two for the Regional Defense Counterterrorism Fellowship Program, DSCA Policy 04–40 and Counterterrorism Fellowship Program FY 05 Financial Severability Procedures Memorandum, DSCA Policy 05–02.

6–13. Funding
a. The DSCA contracts (DBC) division will be the primary point of contact for all financial accounting questions and issues related to the routine processing of Global Security Affairs approved STL including but not limited to quarterly funding releases.

b. All Mobile Education Team/MTT must be programmed in the FY program in which the training will be performed. Teams must deploy and return to CONUS by the last day of the FY (30 Sep).

c. To permit appropriate identification and obligation of funds by country, funding for the Counterterrorism Fellowship Program will be provided from DSCA–DBO to the MILDEPS via the Program Budget Accounting System. After MILDEP STL has been certified as accurate by Global Security Affairs, DSCA–DBO will issue all funding (to the nearest thousand) each quarter based on requirements for that quarter in the country's STL.

d. The MILDEP will not be permitted to authorize Counterterrorism Fellowship Program training funding authority until Global Security Affairs has provided final policy approval via the Counterterrorism Fellowship Program functions on the Security Assistance Network Web.

e. The DSCA–DBC division will conduct comptroller reviews of the program as required during the FY and notify Global Security Affairs/Counterterrorism Fellowship Program of findings and recommendations for improvement.

Section VII
Other Security Cooperation Education and Training Programs

6–14. Presidential drawdown authority (see Foreign Assistance Act, Section 506)
a. Drawdown authority authorizes the disposition of U.S. property or services to foreign countries, in support of unforeseen military emergencies, humanitarian efforts, peacekeeping needs, or counter-narcotics requirements. The signed Presidential Determination is the official authorizing document for execution of a drawdown. The DOD is not authorized to initiate provision of property or services until the Presidential Determination is signed. This approval is cited in message traffic tasking the drawdown. Each Presidential Determination is assigned to a control number that is also referenced in any message traffic, or other correspondence associated with the drawdown.

b. Each Presidential Determination cites a dollar ceiling for the drawdown. The DOD is not authorized to exceed the drawdown authority ceiling provided in the Presidential Determination. The total authority is divided among the supporting services, and then within each Service, as required. There is no budget authority associated with drawdowns.

6–15. Exchange Training
The FAA, Section 544 authorizes reciprocal PME exchanges. The President may provide the attendance of foreign military personnel at PME institutions in the United States (other than Service academies) without charge, if such attendance is part of an international agreement. These international agreements provide for the exchange of students on a one-for-one reciprocal basis each FY between the two military Services participating in the exchange. Each country is responsible for paying TLA for their own students. Institutions specifically included are the National Defense University, U.S. Military Service Command and Staff Colleges, Joint Forces Staff College, U.S. Military Service War Colleges, Naval Postgraduate School, and the Air Force Institute of Technology. MILSVCs are authorized to designate schools as PME institutions for security cooperation training. Requests for new PME exchanges should be

sent to DSCA (Regional Directorate) in coordination with DSCA (Policy, Plans, and Programs Directorate) so that an umbrella (DOD and/or MOD) level exchange agreement is negotiated and completed. Specific Service-level requests are sent to the Implementing Agency after the DOD-level agreement is in place.

Section VIII
Department of the Army

6–16. Recycle charge
Training requirements are considered to be confirmed when dates have been in the STL for a period of at least 30 days. When SATFA recommends a CONUS IMS be recycled or set back because of illness, injury, emergency leave, or academic failure, the training installation in conjunction with SATFA will determine the additional costs of the recycling/set back action to include any additional course costs. SATFA country program manager will advise Security Cooperation Organization of options complete with associated costs and with concurrence of Security Cooperation Organization to recycle/set back IMS, training will be programmed and costs assessed. SATFA will assist activities in assessing the appropriate reimbursement pertaining to cancellation or rescheduling.

6–17. International military education and training funding
a. The IMET funds for Army school training are distributed by SATFA, as DA implementing agent, to agencies from funds provided by DSCA.

b. To obtain reimbursement for IMET funded IMS, the training activity submits a SF 1080 (with copy of IMS ITO) through DFAS channels. This is required so that IMET funds will be collected as reimbursement to DA appropriations indicated in the approved course costs.

6–18. Foreign military sales funding
a. The FMS funds for Army school training are distributed by SATFA. The funding authority is in a specific amount for total training costs obligation authority and the portion attributable to operations and maintenance, Army (OMA) for station costs.

b. To obtain reimbursement for FMS funded IMS, training activities not on automatic bill submit a SF 1080 (with copy of IMS ITO) to DFAS–DE. To obtain reimbursement for FMS training activities on automatic bill, DFAS–DE creates SF 1080 through the automatic billing cycle 30 days after the student start date.

6–19. Section 1004 - Counter-drug training support funding
a. Section 1004 funds for Army school training are distributed by SATFA.

b. To obtain reimbursement for Counter-Drug Training Support, training activities not on automatic bill submit a SF 1080 (with copy of IMS ITO) to DFAS–DE. To obtain reimbursement for Counter-Drug Training Support, training activities that are on automatic bill, DFAS–DE creates SF 1080 through the automatic billing cycle 30 days after the student start date.

6–20. International narcotics control and law enforcement funding
a. The International Narcotics Control and Law Enforcement funds for Army School training are distributed by SATFA.

b. To obtain reimbursement for International Narcotics Control and Law Enforcement, training activities not on automatic bill submit a SF 1080 (with copy of IMS ITO) to DFAS–DE. To obtain reimbursement for International Narcotics Control and Law Enforcement, training activities that are on automatic bill, DFAS–DE creates SF 1080 through the automatic billing cycle thirty days after the student start date.

6–21. Regional Defense Combating Terrorism Fellowship Program funding
a. The Counterterrorism Fellowship Program funds for Army School training are distributed by SATFA.

b. To obtain reimbursement for Counterterrorism Fellowship Program, training activities not on automatic bill submit a SF 1080 (with copy of IMS ITO) to DFAS–DE. To obtain reimbursement for Counterterrorism Fellowship Program, training activities that are on automatic bill, DFAS–DE creates SF 1080 through the automatic billing cycle 30 days after the student start date.

6–22. Presidential drawdown authority funding
a. The President approves a drawdown through the execution of a signed Presidential Determination document. The Presidential Determination is the official authorizing document for execution of a drawdown. DOD is not authorized to initiate provision of property or services until the Presidential Determination is signed. This approval is cited in message traffic tasking the drawdown. Each Presidential Determination is assigned a control number that is also referenced in any message traffic, or other correspondence associated with the drawdown.

b. Each Presidential Determination cites a dollar ceiling for the drawdown. DOD is not authorized to exceed the drawdown authority ceiling provided in the Presidential Determination. The total authority is divided among the supporting services, and then within each Service, as required. There is no budget authority (no funds) associated with drawdowns. Simply put, it is a charitable donation. Activities receiving drawdown authority should not expect or anticipate reimbursement, and are required to "cash flow" requirements. TRADOC will attempt to reimburse supporting TRADOC schools/activities for costs incurred if year end funding is available.

6–23. Exchange training funding
No funds are executed for exchange training.

6–24. Section 1206 funding
a. Section 1206 funds for Army school training are distributed by SATFA.

b. To obtain reimbursement for 1206, training activities not on automatic bill submit a SF 1080 (with copy of IMS ITO) to DFAS–DE. To obtain reimbursement for 1206, training activities that are on automatic bill, DFAS–DE creates SF 1080 through the automatic billing cycle 30 days after the student start date.

Section IX
Department of the Navy (U.S. Navy, U.S. Marine Corps, and U.S. Coast Guard)

6–25. International military education and training funding
The Naval Education and Training Security Assistance Field Activity has program and financial oversight for all DON IMET programs, regardless of whether training is under USN, USMC, or USCG. The Security Cooperation Organization must provide the amount of the country's total IMET allocation to be allocated to the DON. If changes occur during the FY, the Security Cooperation Organization must request the amount of funds to be transferred between the three MILDEPs. As funds are received and quotas are confirmed, Naval Education and Training Security Assistance Field Activity will send messages throughout the FY, providing authority to issue the ITO for each individual IMS/WCN which is annotated as "Priority A." If TLA is authorized, this message will also provide the fund cite.

6–26. Foreign military sales funding
The Naval Education and Training Security Assistance Field Activity will have financial oversight for all FMS training cases regardless of whether training is under USN, USMC, or USCG. The Naval Education and Training Security Assistance Field Activity must be informed of all changes that may affect the scope of an FMS training case. When a new FMS training LOA is implemented, Naval Education and Training Security Assistance Field Activity will issue a message providing authority to issue ITO. This authority will continue throughout the scope of the case. If the FMS LOA includes funds for TLA, fund cites will be provided with this message. The fund cite will be included on each ITO throughout the scope of the FMS case.

6–27. Regional defense combating terrorism fellowship program funding
The Naval Education and Training Security Assistance Field Activity provides financial oversight and issues funds for all DON training under Regional Defense Counterterrorism Fellowship Program, regardless of whether courses are under USN, USMC, or USCG. Upon approval by commanders of combatant commands and Special Operations/Low Intensity Conflict, Naval Education and Training Security Assistance Field Activity, CG, Security Cooperation Education and Training Center MCCDC, and USCG International Affairs (G–CI) will program their respective training, request and confirm quotas (or Mobile Education Team/MTT dates). After candidate vetting has been approved by Special Operations/Low Intensity Conflict and funds have been authorized/provided by DSCA, Naval Education and Training Security Assistance Field Activity will issue a message providing authority to issue the ITO or authorize a Mobile Education Team/MTT and provide funds to the Mobile Education Team/MTT provider. If TLA is authorized, this message will provide the fund cite and other funding with information copy to Navy IPO.

6–28. Counter-narcotics program
Under the Counter-Narcotics program, DASD–CN issues authority to release funding to either Naval Education and Training Security Assistance Field Activity or USCG International Affairs (G–CI). Upon receipt of funding, a message will be issued providing authority to issue the ITO or authorize the Mobile Education Team/MTT and provide funds to the Mobile Education Team/MTT provider.

6–29. Export control/border security, Georgian border security and law enforcement and similar programs
The USCG International Affairs (G–CI) provides program support and issues funding authority for all USCG training under export control border and similar Department of State programs for which the USCG provides training under the provisions of 22 USC 2420(b)(3) and 22 USC 2420(b)(7). Upon acceptance and subsequent approval of training requests, USCG (G–CI) will program their respective training, request and confirm quotas (or Mobile Education Team/MTT dates). Funds will be provided via an Interagency Acquisition Agreement (IAA) to USCG (G–CI). As with all other funding sources, services cannot be provided until funding is received. Funding must be received at least 30 days

in advance of commencement of training. USCG-(G–CI) will provide via e-mail to the appropriate training center the funding authority to issue the ITO or authorize a Mobile Education Team/MTT and provide funds to the Mobile Education Team/MTT provider. If TLA is authorized, this message will provide the fund cite and other funding information as required. All requirements for scheduling, student administration, background and security checks and processing are exactly as outlined in chapters 4 and 10.

6–30. Forfeiture fee

a. Navy IPO is responsible for the establishment of DON policy regarding forfeiture charges. If a country cancels a confirmed quota in a DON course within 60 days of commencement, a 50 percent cancellation fee will normally be applied unless the quota is filled by another student. Navy IPO releases an annual message during the first quarter of the FY to provide a list of courses that will incur a 100 percent tuition fee if a country cancels after a contract is let or a quota is confirmed (unless a waiver is requested and approved). In addition to the courses listed in the message, there are other courses where a forfeiture charge will apply. In those cases, the customer will be informed up front, either when provided price and availability data, with a note in the LOA, or in correspondence dealing with scheduling. These courses generally fall into two categories:

(1) Training where a contract must be in place prior to student arrival. This is most likely to happen during ship transfers or aircraft sales where regular U.S. training is not available.

(2) Training that incurs up-front costs prior to actual commencement of training. Examples would be: changes to computer programs (such as, aviation training where computer software must be changed or modified in either the aircraft or the simulator or both) and up-front translation cost or tailoring of course material to meet a specific country requirement.

b. Many of the E–IMET Mobile Education Team and all MTT programmed through DON fall into category (1) above. Additional clarification on Mobile Education Team is provided as follows:

(1) A Mobile Education Team which is already programmed (whether funded or not) requires DSCA approval if the country via the Security Cooperation Organization requests cancellation. Programmed is defined as appearing in TMS or on the Security Assistance Network Web. The Security Cooperation Organization (versus the Mobile Education Team provider) should request DSCA approval via the regional combatant commander to cancel, info Navy IPO and Naval Education and Training Security Assistance Field Activity.

(2) If approval is granted by DSCA for cancellation of a Mobile Education Team the country canceling the Mobile Education Team pays 100 percent of the variable preparation costs that may have been incurred prior to the time of cancellation (that is, travel, per diem, honorariums, miscellaneous trip preparation costs, in-country site costs, and salary costs for preparation and conduct of the Mobile Education Team). The Mobile Education Team providers will detail such expenditures and notify Naval Education and Training Security Assistance Field Activity, who will review and charge to appropriate country's IMET account. Questions concerning appropriateness of charges should be forwarded via Naval Education and Training Security Assistance Field Activity to Navy IPO/DSCA.

c. The Mobile Education Team and MTT funded programmed under Regional Defense Counterterrorism Fellowship Program will be subject to the same requirements as stated in paragraph *b,* and will also require commanders of combatant commands and Special Operations/Low Intensity Conflict approval.

d. A forfeiture charge will not be applied when cancellation is due to the following:

(1) Decisions by the U.S. such as deletion or rescheduling of classes.

(2) Significant unavoidable circumstances affecting the armed forces within a country such as a national disaster.

(3) Personnel required to support the Global War on terrorism. Forfeiture charges will be programmed for applicable courses and will be designated by an "S" in the WCN suffix to indicate that a forfeiture charge was charged for the training line. The appropriate Military Service will make the final determination regarding the forfeiture charge.

Section X
Department of the Air Force

6–31. Financial management

a. The IMET. Generally, the cost of foreign training under IMET is initially financed by Air Force appropriated funds with subsequent reimbursement from IMET funds. Reimbursement includes indirect costs such as, tuition, training aids, publications, and proficiency flying hours. Direct costs reimbursable from IMET funds are as follows—

(1) Travel.

(2) Living allowances. (DOD 5105.38M, SAMM, chapter 10, table titled "Daily Supplemental Living Allowances for International Military Students Under Security Cooperation Programs."

(3) Certain medical and burial costs.

(4) The Field Studies Program activities.

(5) Extraordinary expenses.

(6) Travel and per diem of U.S. personnel in support of IMET.

b. The FMS. The FMS training is paid for by the recipient countries. Payment for FMS cases is generally on a cash-in-advance basis. Normally, the Air Force Security Assistance Training Squadron notifies DFAS of the costs of the country's quarterly training requirements. The DFAS–DE provides the purchasing country with a quarterly statement of charges for training. Training is considered "delivered" as of the date the IMS enters the course, or the date funds are released for an MTT.

c. Inter-America. Air Forces Academy.

(1) The fixed operating costs of IAAFA are financed by appropriated funds. Guest instructor costs are considered "fixed costs" when guest instructors are assigned to authorized USAF Unit Manning Document positions. Guest instructor positions will be reflected on Part 4 of the Unit Manning Document.

(2) Guest instructors will receive a living allowance, round trip transportation for guest instructor and dependents; 2,000 pounds household goods (HHG) allowance; furnishings for quarters according to Table of Allowance 414 (or increased HHG allowance); limit of $2,000 per year medical coverage per guest instructor Family.

(3) Administration and control of the guest instructor, USAF and parent country financial responsibilities, guest instructor benefits, and other pertinent information will be addressed in an attachment to the ITO for all guest instructors.

(4) Additions to IAAFA curriculum will be processed according to paragraph 3–77.

d. Military assistance other agency funded. The Military Assistance Other Agency Funded training is provided without charge to the recipient country with subsequent reimbursement to the Air Force by the sponsoring U.S. Agency. Reimbursement for training is accomplished by the Air Force Security Assistance Training Squadron/FM. All other costs are the responsibility of the sponsoring U.S. agency, the foreign student, or their Government. The USAF support to other U.S. Government agencies is authorized by the U.S. Economy Act.

6–32. Forfeiture charges and adjustments

To avoid forfeiture charges, training must be canceled at least 60 days prior to the course start date and 180 days for all flying training. Training dates are provided to the Security Cooperation Organization in the STL or by message. The training dates are considered acceptable unless the Security Cooperation Organization requests a change. If an IMS is eliminated before completing a course, tuition costs will be adjusted as follows:

a. Flying courses-prorated basis but not less than 50 percent.

b. Technical courses-prorated basis but not less than 50 percent.

c. Training cost on a per week basis-for the number of weeks training was received.

6–33. Transportation allowances

The IMET IMS are authorized transportation allowances as prescribed in their ITO. (See chaps 7 and 8.)

6–34. Living allowances

The IMET IMS are authorized living allowances as prescribed in their ITO. (See chaps 7 and 9.)

6–35. Subsistence

At training bases where messing facilities are available, the base food service officer will submit a certified invoice monthly (in triplicate) to the Air Force Security Assistance Training Squadron/FM through the IMSO for payment. This invoice will list the following data:

a. Names and nationalities of the IMS.

b. Number and type of meals furnished.

c. Total amount.

6–36. Housing security assistance training program and other cooperative programs personnel

a. For IMET enlisted personnel provided quarters, reimbursement for quarters is made as follows if these students are receiving a living allowance under IMET. The base billeting or housing officer must submit certified invoices monthly in three copies to the local Accounting and Finance Officer (AFO) through the IMSO for payment. Invoices must list names, nationalities, number of days that quarters were furnished, and total amount of charges. A copy of each student's ITO must be furnished with the invoice. The AFO prepares a SF 1034 (Public Voucher for Purchases and Services other than Personal) upon receipt of the IMSO verification for reimbursement to the base billeting or housing office. The accounting classification cited in the ITO is charged for these services.

b. Other IMET students and all FMS students assigned Government housing are required to pay the cost from personal funds.

c. The charge for Air Force unaccompanied personnel housing is the Service fee. Rates for family housing are provided in the DOD 7000.14–R and AFI 32–9003.

6–37. Budget and funding

Procedures for SCETP and other cooperative programs are contained in AFI 65–601 and DFAS–Denver 7010.3–R.

6–38. Costing

Course costing will be accomplished by the MAJCOM in accordance with SAF/Budget Management and Execution Security Assistance Division directives and resulting tuition prices forwarded to the Air Force Security Assistance Training Squadron/FM comptroller for incorporation into the Air Force Security Assistance Training Squadron database. The SCETP and other cooperative programs unit cost for each course or item is listed in the Training Military Articles and Service List. For those items marked "EST" (estimate), separate pricing will be used, as required.

6–39. Accounting and finance

Accounting, paying, collecting, and reporting will be as stated in accordance with applicable DFAS guidance on "Accounting and Obligations" and "Accounting for Commitments." IMS entitlement to expenses and eligibility such as travel, transportation, living allowances, subsistence, medical care, and burial will be as stated in chapters 8 and 9.

   a. All AFO or other offices that forward invoices to higher headquarters for payment will submit invoices on a controlled transmission basis.

   b. The AFO or other office will include in each applicable invoice package a preaddressed acknowledgment form letter that can be returned to the originating office. If acknowledgment is not received within 15 days after forwarding, the sending office will conduct a follow-up.

Chapter 7
Travel/Transportation, Quarters, Meals, and Living Allowance

The purpose of this chapter is to provide guidance for travel/transportation, quarters, and meals for an IMS, both when these expenses are funded by their country; and when travel and living allowances are included in the U.S. funded training program. U.S. funded training programs that normally include these funds (referred to as TLA) usually refer to training under the IMET, Counterterrorism Fellowship Program, and other USG-funded programs. In rare cases; however, TLA may also be included in FMS cases (when DSCA waiver is provided).

Section I
Travel and/or Transportation

7–1. Scheduling International Military Student travel

The IMS are discouraged from reporting to a training installation prior to the published report date because access may be denied based upon the installation security policy.

   a. When travel/transportation is funded by the country. All travel/transportation expenses incurred by IMS will be borne by either the IMS or their country. Although any desired mode of travel or carrier can be used for IMS when travel is funded directly by country, use of U.S. commercial carriers is encouraged. IMS will bear all expenses in connection with OCONUS travel by POV, if authorized on the IMS ITO. The Security Cooperation Organization will assist with scheduling as necessary. Every effort should be made to schedule transportation so that IMS arrive at training installations during normal working hours, Monday through Friday.

   b. When travel/transportation is funded by the USG training program..

   (1) The Security Cooperation Organization will arrange transportation for IMS to the United States according to ITO when overseas transportation is funded by the U.S. The Security Cooperation Organization will receive a line of accounting (fund cite) from the MILDEP, which will be annotated on the ITO. The Security Cooperation Organization will then arrange ticketing to the first CONUS training activity charged to the fund cite. Every effort should be made to schedule transportation so that IMS arrive at training installations during normal working hours, Monday through Friday.

   (2) Tariff regulations preclude honoring airline tickets issued more than 6 months in advance of travel completion. One-way tickets will be issued for all students for training that exceeds five weeks duration. For training with duration of five weeks or less, the Security Cooperation Organization is authorized to purchase round-trip transportation.

   (3) In-country travel from the IMS duty station to point of departure in country is not authorized at USG expense. In-country travel for a student to attend a Mobile Education Team/MTT within their own country is not authorized at USG expense.

7–2. Excess baggage

   a. When travel/transportation is funded by the country, the cost of transporting FMS IMS personal excess baggage is the responsibility of IMS or their country. If country has requested and DSCA has approved student travel under the LOA, student baggage allowances are limited to the baggage authorizations described below (see para 7–2*b*).

   b. When travel/transportation is included in the USG training program:

   (1) The baggage weight allowances described in paragraphs (3) through (7), below, are authorized for IMS when travel costs are charged to the U.S. funded program, and apply to both overseas travel and travel to U.S. training

installations. Baggage in excess of the amount authorized in this regulation will be at the expense of the IMS or their government.

(2) Excess baggage is authorized for IMS under certain conditions (length of training and type of course(s)). Excess baggage is that amount over the two bags generally allowed free of charge for OCONUS travel. Training duration indicated in paragraphs (3) through (6), below, will be determined using the report date for the first course and the projected graduation date for the last course.

(3) Two pieces of checked baggage, not to exceed 50 pounds each, are authorized for IMS receiving TLA when training is 12 weeks or less. (No excess baggage is authorized.)

(4) Three pieces of checked baggage, not to exceed 50 pounds each, are authorized for IMS receiving TLA when training is 13 through 23 weeks. (One piece of excess baggage is authorized.)

(5) Four pieces of checked baggage, not to exceed 50 pounds each, are authorized for IMS receiving TLA for 24 through 35 weeks. (Two pieces of excess baggage are authorized.)

(6) Five pieces of checked baggage, not to exceed 50 pounds each, are authorized for IMS receiving TLA for 36 weeks and longer. (Three pieces of excess baggage are authorized.)

(7) In addition to the allowance in paragraphs (3) through (6), above, one additional piece of baggage (Six pieces of checked baggage/four pieces of excess baggage, not to exceed 50 pounds each) is authorized for the following IMS receiving TLA for:

(a) Accompanied IMS attending the PME, graduate, and postgraduate programs listed in DOD 5105.38–M, table C10.T3, (see table 7–1).

(b) IMS attending flight training.

(8) If U.S. and foreign flag carrier airlines differ in free baggage allowance, or baggage is authorized over 100 pounds, transportation officers may issue a Miscellaneous Charge Order, or the equivalent to cover the difference, up to the free allowable amount of the U.S. flag carriers, and also any authorized excess baggage allowance. The IMSO may determine the cost of the authorized excess baggage and include it in the last living allowance payment, if a Miscellaneous Charge Order is not available. If neither a Miscellaneous Charge Order, nor advance payment of the authorized excess baggage is feasible, the IMS may file a travel reimbursement claim upon return to home country with the assistance of the Security Cooperation Organization.

(9) Baggage size, dimensions, and weight, will conform to carrier stipulations. Baggage must accompany the IMS. No change in baggage allowances will be made after students have departed country.

(a) If IMS baggage is unable to accompany the student on the flight due to airline imposed baggage embargos in country, IMSO is authorized to mail IMS baggage to the home address via the most economical rate available.

(b) The baggage being mailed back must be in accordance with applicable airline regulations and authorized number of bags and weight as authorized on the ITO.

(10) When any portion of the travel cost is paid by the foreign government the baggage allowance for that portion of the travel is without restriction if the cost of the excess weight is paid by the foreign government. However, for that portion of the travel paid from the program funds, each IMS is authorized baggage allowance not to exceed the limitations in paragraphs (1) through (7), above.

7–3. Disposition of unauthorized excess baggage when travel/transportation is funded by the U.S. Government Training Program

Disposition of unauthorized excess baggage will be made at the expense of the IMS or their Government. The following procedures apply for control of unauthorized excess baggage for IMS when travel is charged to the U.S. Funded Program.

a. The IMS will ensure that unauthorized excess baggage will be shipped at the IMS expense prior to the departure from the installation.

b. The IMS reporting to the port of departure with unauthorized excess baggage will be requested to forward the unauthorized excess baggage to their home country by commercial means at no expense to the USG. If the time element prohibits this, the unauthorized excess baggage will be taken into custody by the IMSO or the USG representative and the IMS will be given a receipt for the baggage. The IMS will sign a notification/release statement, acknowledging that their baggage is being held by the IMSO, and that if no disposition instructions are provided by the IMS or the foreign consulate within 30 days, the IMSO may then dispose of the baggage. The IMS will proceed on the scheduled flight or carrier.

c. After the carrier departs, the IMSO or the USG representative will hold the unauthorized excess baggage no longer than 30 days awaiting further instructions from the IMS or nearest foreign consulate. If no action is taken either by the IMS or the foreign consulate, the unauthorized excess baggage may be sold, donated, or destroyed, as appropriate, with documentation to record the transaction. If sold, the sale value should be forwarded to the Security Cooperation Organization for delivery to the IMS.

7–4. Arrival notification for all international military students regardless of funding source

a. After travel arrangements have been completed, the Security Cooperation Organization will send an advance arrival notice through the Security Assistance Network Security Cooperation Organization training Web, to the first training installation, with information copies to the Military Service as appropriate. This notice must arrive at the first training installation at least 15 days prior to IMS scheduled arrival or 30 days in advance if accompanied by dependents. If the IMS name or arrival information is not available, the Security Cooperation Organization will inform the IMSO at the first training installation and the appropriate Military Service by e-mail. Training activities including DLIELC will provide arrival notification to the next training location at least one week prior to completion of training.

b. The advance notice of IMS arrival will include the following information:

(1) Name, grade, Service, and sex.

(2) Travel itinerary with dates, airline flight numbers, and times of arrival in CONUS for first training location.

(3) ITO number, date, WCN, initial course, and report date.

(4) FMS case designator, IMET program year, or other USG-funded case designator.

c. Names, ages, and relationships of accompanying dependents if applicable. Changes that occur after transmittal of the advance arrival notice will be forwarded by e-mail to the addressees shown in the original arrival notice.

d. Security Cooperation Organization will advise IMS to contact the first training installation immediately after arrival in CONUS and provide information on the mode of onward travel and estimated time of arrival.

7–5. Continental United States travel

When an IMS is scheduled for consecutive training at different locations, the IMSO at each training installation should review the ITO to determine if the travel cost is funded by the IMS's own country, or a U.S. funded training program.

a. *When travel/transportation is funded by the country.* The IMSO should review the airline ticket(s) against the ITO for accuracy. If an airline ticket is incorrect, the IMSO will notify the Security Cooperation Organization or the Military Service for assistance. If the IMS has follow-on training at another location, the IMSO will inform the gaining installation of the arrival of the IMS by the most expeditious means. If the duration of the last training course is 2 weeks or less, the IMSO at the training installation prior to the last will coordinate with the last training installation to determine if training dates are firm and inform the Military Service and Security Cooperation Organization if dates have changed and a change in ticketing is required.

b. *When travel/transportation is funded by a USG training program.* Normally, the program includes all transportation costs, travel allowances, and all authorized expenses in connection with the official travel of IMS. However, certain countries defray all or part of these costs. The original ITO must stipulate the specific responsibility for funding of travel. When CONUS travel is authorized, the IMSO will make the necessary transportation arrangements and will inform the gaining installation of the arrival of the IMS by the most expeditious means. If the duration of the last training course is 2 weeks or less, the IMSO at the training installation prior to the last will coordinate with the last training installation to determine if training dates are firm or have the potential to change. If training dates are firm, the IMSO will make travel arrangements to the last training installation and return to homeland, taking into account leave authorized in the IMS ITO. This IMSO will also arrange for advance payment of living and travel allowance to the day of arrival in home country, except for periods of leave. The IMS ITO will be endorsed to indicate the student has received advanced living and travel allowances due through arrival in home country and issued a government transportation request (identify number) or provided funds for excess baggage if authorized in accordance with paragraph 7–3 of this regulation for return travel to home country. Travel by IMS in CONUS will be by the most direct routes between points specified in the travel orders. The mode of transportation used will be that which is most economical, subject to availability, and in the best interest of the USG. Distances will be determined by provisions in the JTR.

c. Transportation costs for an IMS returning to their home country on emergency leave are the responsibility of the IMS or their government, if the IMS is to return for continuation of training. Only one round trip between the home country and the United States is authorized.

d. When an IMS is permitted by their own Government to deviate from the most direct return route for visiting other countries, USG sponsorship will terminate at the point and time of such deviation. Further, should IMS elect to remain at a point en route to their home country beyond the time normally required to make travel connections, living allowance during that excess time is not authorized.

e. In no instance will U.S. funds be used to provide transportation for dependents of IMS. However, IMS attending courses identified in DOD 5105.38–M (SAMM), table C10.T3, (see table 7–1 "Additional Information" para (7)) of this regulation may be reimbursed for the cost of transportation to which they are entitled based on normal routing and mode to travel with their dependents. Normal routing and mode of transportation will be included in item 15 of the IMS ITO. U.S. flag carriers must be used wherever available. The IMS will be reimbursed for their own transportation costs at the first CONUS training installation in the amount it would have cost the USG. IMS will not be reimbursed for travel on foreign airlines if U.S. airlines service the same route.

Table 7–1
Daily supplemental living allowance for international military students under security cooperation programs

	Government or contracted Government quarters	Mess	Dependents encouraged	Dependents accompany student	Living allowance rate	Remarks
1	Yes	No	No		Actual cost of lodging (NTE) maximum lodging authorized in the JFTR + JFTR local meal rate + $11 special International Military Student incidentals	
2	No	No	No		Actual cost of lodging (NTE maximum lodging authorized in JFTR) + JFTR local meal rate + $11 special International Military Student incidentals	A statement of non-availability or equivalent must be issued to the International Military Student and filed with voucher. International Military Student must show proof of rental agreement or lodging receipt.
3	Yes	Yes	No		Actual cost of lodging (NTE maximum lodging authorized in JFTR) + JFTR Government meal rate + $11 special International Military Student incidentals	
4	Yes	One or two meals are available	No		Actual cost of lodging (NTE maximum lodging authorized in JFTR) + JFTR proportional meal rate + $11 special International Military Student incidentals	
5	Yes and free of charge	Yes and free of charge	No		$11 special International Military Student incidentals	
6	Yes and free of charge	Available aboard ship	No		Government meal rate + $11 special International Military Student incidentals	
7	Yes but International Military Student chooses to live off base/post				$0	
8	No		Yes	Yes	Actual cost of lodging (NTE maximum lodging authorized in JFTR) + JFTR local meal rate + $11 special International Military Student incidentals	Availability of quarters is based upon the availability of Government family housing. International Military Student must show proof of rental
						agreement and certify that dependents reside with International Military Student for at least 75 percent of the course duration.

Table 7–1
Daily supplemental living allowance for international military students under security cooperation programs—Continued

	Government or contracted Government quarters	Mess	Dependents encouraged	Dependents accompany student	Living allowance rate	Remarks
9	Yes	No	Yes		Actual cost of lodging (NTE maximum lodging authorized in JFTR) + JFTR local meal rate + $11 special International Military Student incidentals	
10	Yes	Yes	Yes	Yes	Actual cost of lodging (NTE maximum lodging authorized in JFTR) + JFTR local meal rate + $11 special International Military Student incidentals	Availability of quarters is based upon the availability of Government family housing.
11	Yes	One or two meals are available	Yes	Yes	Actual cost of lodging (NTE maximum lodging authorized in JFTR) + JFTR local meal rate + $11 special International Military Student incidentals	Availability of quarters is based upon the availability of Government family housing.
12	Bachelor Govt or Contracted Quarters are available but student chooses to reside off base/ post		No	Yes	$0	
13	N/A	N/A			Actual cost of lodging (NTE maximum lodging authorized in JFTR) + meals in accordance with JFTR + applicable OCONUS incidentals.	When a student from one country is attending a regional Mobile Education and Training (Mobile Education Team) course in another country.

Additional Information for Table C10.T3

(1) Quarters available means that USG quarters or contracted Government quarters were either furnished or made available. For International Military Student currently attending training in the U.S. that elected to reside off-base/post under the old 1999 TLA policy, the student is authorized to continue to receive TLA at 1999 TLA policy rates until their current line of training is completed and the student has returned home. However, if the student is scheduled for follow-on training at a different training location, the TLA rates in this table ($0) apply at the new training location.

(2) Mess available means three meals per day are available in a USG mess, whether or not actually consumed.

(3) When TLA is authorized, the travel allowance rate includes the day of departure from home country to the day of arrival at, and day of departure from, each training installation, and the day of arrival at home country. TLA rates, while the International Military Student is on travel status including unscheduled delays, are based on rates equal to those in the JFTR for U.S. personnel. In most cases, the student does not receive their first TLA payment until they have been in CONUS for 2 weeks; therefore, the Security Cooperation Organization is encouraged to advance student sufficient funds in U.S. dollars to meet all expenses while the student is enroute to include 2 weeks advance TLA. Any such advances shall be annotated in the special conditions block of the ITO to prevent duplicate payment of entitlements at CONUS training activities.

(4) When the International Military Student is scheduled to attend training for 5 weeks or less, the Security Cooperation Organization is authorized to purchase roundtrip transportation and to pay the student total authorized living allowance entitlements at the time of departure. Government Transportation Request number (government transportation request #) and amounts paid for transportation and living allowances are annotated in the special conditions block of the ITO to prevent duplicate payment of entitlements.

(5) If the duration of training at the last training installation is 2 weeks or less, and/or the last training installation has no means of paying the International Military Student, the IMSO at the next-to-last training installation arranges for advance payment of travel and living allowance for that period of time to the day of arrival at the next follow-on training installation or country. Except for periods of leave, the student ITO is endorsed in the Special Conditions Block to identify the period of time for which advanced living and travel allowances were made.

(6) If it is determined that an International Military Student who has departed the CONUS or overseas training activity was overpaid in CONUS or at the overseas activity, no attempt is made to collect the overpayment from the student. The Implementing Agency determines whether a funding adjustment via the Security Cooperation Training Program is necessary.

Table 7–1
Daily supplemental living allowance for international military students under security cooperation programs—Continued

Government or contracted Government quarters	Mess	Dependents encouraged	Dependents accompany student	Living allowance rate	Remarks

(7) The International Military Student is encouraged by the Department of Defense to bring dependents ONLY to the following courses: Air Command and Staff College Air War College Armed Forces Staff College Army War College Army Command and General Staff College at Fort Leavenworth and at the WHINSEC Graduate Programs at Naval Postgraduate School Graduate Programs at the Institute of Technology, The Inter-American Defense College National Defense University, Naval Command College, Naval Staff College Sergeants Major Academy Squadron Officer School, USMC, Command and Staff College, USMC Expeditionary Warfare School USMC School of Advanced Warfighting An International Military Student scheduled to attend any of the above courses may also bring dependents to prerequisite courses, follow-on courses, and authorized leave periods. Students are not encouraged to bring dependents to any other courses. The "with dependent" TLA rate is intended/authorized when the dependents reside with student for the majority (75 percent) of the course duration. The "with dependent" TLA rate is not intended/ authorized for students with dependents who come only for periodic visits.

(8) Accompanied students living off post/base attending courses where dependents are encouraged by the Department of Defense (see note (7), above) may draw a living allowance advance upon arrival in CONUS of an amount not to exceed 10 percent of their total maximum living allowance authorized at a particular location. The student living allowance drawn during the period of training is adjusted to ensure that the amount of the advance is fully recovered before the student completes training at that location.

(9) When an International Military Student is authorized the "with dependent" TLA rate and is subsequently hospitalized, the "with dependent" TLA rate will continue to be paid.

(10) TLA is not authorized for leave periods before or following completion/termination of training. Leave with living allowance may be granted during periods of class breaks, authorized holidays, and between consecutive courses.

(11) Guest instructors assigned to WHINSEC, IAAFA, or Naval Small Craft Instruction and Technical Training School are paid a living allowance based upon the installation's Government quarters or Government contracted quarter's rates by grade and a standard subsistence allowance regardless of rank. Guest instructors' allowances are paid out of the military Service's Operations and Maintenance account, not security assistance training programs.

(12) When an IMS is authorized TLA and is concurrently TDY, the IMS will be reimbursed for travel and per diem (lodging, subsistence, and incidentals) in accordance with the JFTR rate for the TDY location plus the TLA authorized at the training location.

7–6. Travel by privately-owned vehicle when travel and/or transportation is funded by a U.S. Government Program

a. Travel by POV within CONUS is normally permitted except when it would not be in the best interests of the USG or would result in late arrival for scheduled training. The Security Cooperation Organization must indicate on the ITO when travel by POV is authorized. The IMSO must ensure that the ITO indicates travel by POV is authorized.

b. When all or partial travel is performed by POV in CONUS under orders permitting this mode of travel, the IMS responsible for paying POV operating expenses is entitled to a monetary allowance in lieu of transportation. This monetary allowance will be paid at the currently authorized rate for official highway distance according to the JTR. Reimbursement will be limited to the official distance from the installation to the next training site or point of departure, not to exceed the economy class commercial airfare cost. Living allowance will be authorized for a period not to exceed constructive travel time by air. If IMS travels as a passenger in a POV, they are not entitled to mileage, but is entitled to per diem.

(1) No separate shipment of baggage at USG expense is authorized. IMS will bear cost of shipment of personal baggage not carried in the POV.

(2) Shipment of a POV cannot be charged to IMET or other USG-funded program.

(3) Shipment of household goods is not authorized at USG expense.

(4) Security Cooperation Organization will identify point of entry and point of departure on the ITO (or amendment) if IMS is authorized POV travel within the U.S.

c. Advance travel allowance is allowed when IMS are—

(1) Permitted to travel by POV between CONUS training facilities and departure point.

(2) Traveling to and from Central America when authorized travel by POV.

7–7. Arranging return transportation when travel/transportation is funded by a United States Government program

Approximately 2 weeks before the end of the IMS last course, arrangements for return transportation should be completed. The last training installation to which the IMS is assigned will make arrangements for return travel. IMSO at installations where dependents are encouraged to attend should make return arrangements early enough for IMS to secure transportation for Family members. When travel is paid under the USG program, the cost of the airfare will be charged to the fund cite indicated on the IMS ITO. The last training installation will notify the Security Cooperation

Organization by message of the IMS return itinerary in sufficient time before the IMS departs so that the Security Cooperation Organization can meet the student upon return to home country if desired.

Section II
Quarters and Meals

7–8. Quarters and meals

The IMS will be provided quarters and meals (messing/subsistence) in USG facilities when available. However, IMS are not guaranteed USG quarters. The commander of the U.S. installation or designated representatives will endorse ITO to indicate that USG quarters and messing were or were not made available. To be consistent and to avoid possible embarrassment, guidance applicable to U.S. personnel should be applied, insofar as possible, to IMS. When quarters are provided, they will be of a comparable standard to that provided U.S. personnel of comparable rank. The IMSO is responsible for making reservations for IMS quarters. When USG quarters are not available, the IMSO will make commercial lodging reservations if possible. If commercial lodging reservations cannot be made without a credit card to secure payment, the IMSO will not use their personal account. The IMSO must contact the Military Service or Security Cooperation Organization for further assistance.

   a. Quarters.

   (1) Quarters are defined as 'provided' if made available to officers and civilian IMS including periods of hospitalization. In all cases, Government quarters, which include USG controlled or privatized quarters, will be used where available. The fact that an IMS is accompanied by dependents has no bearing in determining the availability of quarters for the IMS.

   (2) IMS should not occupy military quarters before the report date for scheduled training at that installation or more than one week after termination of the last training course scheduled at an installation. IMS whose travel and or living allowance is paid by the U.S. funded program should be scheduled to depart the day following graduation; however, when a delay is caused by extenuating circumstances and MILDEP approval is granted, students may be paid a living allowance and remain in military quarters until departure. An IMS who elects to arrive earlier than their scheduled report date will not receive living allowance payments for the period prior to the report date.

   (3) Unaccompanied personnel housing (UPH) when available; is authorized for IMS on a scale to that authorized for U.S. personnel, according to MILDEP regulations.

   (4) Officer and civilian IMS occupying UPH will personally be required to pay custodial fees in the same amount charged and on the same payment schedule as U.S. counterparts.

   (5) Enlisted IMS occupying UPH may personally be required to pay custodial fees in the same amount charged and on the same payment schedule as their equivalent U.S. counterparts or as prescribed by installation commanders.

   (6) USG family housing is not guaranteed, and IMS are not generally encouraged to bring their families with them while training under the SCETP. The IMS will be responsible for payment of a monthly rental fee if occupying USG family housing. (See DOD 7000.14–R, volume 15.) If an IMS is ineligible for government quarters because they are accompanied by dependents while attending a course where dependents are NOT encouraged they will no longer be eligible to receive a living allowance (if previously authorized) and a statement of nonavailability will not be issued to an accompanied IMS when quarters are available for unaccompanied personnel.

   (7) When training within their own country, IMS will not be furnished quarters at USG expense.

   b. Meals.

   (1) The IMS will be required to pay the standard rate, including surcharge fees if applicable, at USG dining facilities.

   (2) Enlisted IMS receiving living allowances are authorized subsistence (meals) in kind without charge, according to food service management directives currently in force at some installations. Subsistence without charge to the IMS in USG dining facilities may be provided while the IMS is attached to training installations or duty stations, while in transit, and while either in CONUS or overseas training. When meal tickets are issued to enlisted and civilian equivalent IMS in a travel status, appropriate endorsement will be made on the ITO so that the value of the meal ticket may be deducted from amounts otherwise payable as living allowance. Enlisted IMS authorized and electing to subsist in a NCO mess will personally reimburse the mess for any cost in excess of the commuted ration value chargeable to the USG-funded training program.

   (3) Officer and civilian IMS will not be provided subsistence in kind, but will pay for meals taken in USG dining facilities at the food rates prescribed.

   (4) An effort should be made to satisfy special dietary requirements of IMS who are unable to eat certain foods due to religious reasons. However, additional pay and allowances will not be authorized just because the IMS does not like American food, or USG messing facilities are unable to provide proper food for a diet imposed by an IMS's religion. In countries where problems of this nature are anticipated, IMS will be briefed on the above policy before departing for CONUS. Additional living allowances will not be authorized for IMS on the basis of a medical officer recommendation. IMS must consider following three alternatives:

   (a) Adapting to the American diet.

(b) Providing food to their own liking at their own expense.

(c) Requesting disenrollment from training and return to the home country.

7–9. Messing

a. Temporary duty/temporary additional duty. When IMS are on a cross-country training flight or TDY/temporary additional duty in connection with a required course of training, IMS are eligible for TDY entitlements which will be included in the course tuition. When an IMS is authorized TLA and is concurrently TDY, the IMS will be reimbursed for travel and per diem (lodging, subsistence, and incidentals) in accordance with the JFTR rate for the TDY location plus the TLA authorized at the training location, which will be charged to the fund cite on the ITO.

b. Payment of USG-funded quarters and meals.

(1) A certification or endorsement provided by the installation commander or designated representative, indicating appropriate dates and availability of quarters and or subsistence, will accompany the original and two certified copies of the ITO in support of a claim for living allowance. The original, with appropriate endorsement by the disbursing officer indicating payment, will be returned to the IMS. The two certified copies will support the original and retained copies of the DD Form 1351 (Travel Voucher) and DD Form 1351–2 (Travel Voucher or Sub-voucher). All payments of living allowance will conform to the rates listed in DOD 5105.38–M, table C10.T3, (see table 7–1). Group payments of living allowances are authorized when all IMS are listed and identified by their ITO numbers on DD Form 1351 and DD Form 1351–2. Payment of living allowance due and unpaid at the port of departure may be made through Security Cooperation Organization disbursing channels in local currency at official rates of exchange.

(2) The IMSO will verify subsistence and housing invoices for—

(a) An IMS who was in a duty or authorized leave status during the time specified on the invoice for subsistence. The IMSO will insert on the invoice the WCN and, as proper, the project line and training number for each enlisted IMS. The IMSO will submit the invoice and a copy of the ITO to the finance and accounting officer for payment.

(b) An IMS who was furnished quarters. The IMSO will insert on the invoice the WCN and country, IMET program year, or applicable FMS case and or other SC program case designator for each enlisted IMS. The IMSO will submit the invoice and a copy of the ITO for processing.

c. Subsistence. Subsistence provided to IMS by USG messes will be reimbursed by SF 1080 USG charging the designated funded training program. It will be substantiated by a certification that rations were provided without reimbursement. Each certificate will cite the applicable country and ITO numbers. NCO messes will be reimbursed at the rate applicable to military personnel as a direct charge to USG-funded Training Program according to authorizing publications. Commissioned officers' closed messes subsisting IMS cadets will be reimbursed by local finance officers at the current rate.

d. IMS status changes. If an IMS changes from enlisted to officer status while undergoing training, the effective date of change of living allowance will be the date the IMS is promoted, as certified by the Security Cooperation Organization or official foreign representative of the IMS concerned. However, the date of the change in living allowance will not be before the date the IMS leaves enlisted quarters.

e. Students. Students whose governments require a record of payments received must be reminded to maintain vouchers for record since that information cannot be furnished at a later date.

Section III
Living Allowance

7–10. Requirements

a. When travel/transportation is funded by the country. The foreign government should ensure that IMS receive sufficient allowances to defray all living costs and personal expenses. These expenses are the responsibility of the IMS or the country purchasing the training. Living allowances for IMS will not be included in an FMS case unless approved by DSCA. When approval is granted to pay living allowance under an FMS case, it will be at the same rates authorized for IMET students.

b. When travel/transportation is funded by the USG training program. Certain programs include costs for IMS living allowances. Most IMET, Regional Defense Counterterrorism Fellowship Program, and Counter-Drug Training Support programs will include living allowances.

7–11. Funding guidance

a. Living allowance rates authorized for IMS when living allowance is funded by the USG program as shown in table 7–1. Where training is conducted under contract or at civilian institutions, it will be ascertained if USG quarters and messing facilities are not available.

b. Each ITO must be carefully scrutinized to determine what payments, if any, are authorized. The IMSO and finance officer will examine each ITO when the IMS reports and discuss the funding authorization with the IMS. This is done to ensure mutual understanding. Living allowance expenses will be charged to a fund cite/line of accounting provided on the ITO.

7–12. Restrictions

a. Living allowances are programmed only to defray costs of meals and personal necessity items while in training.

b. IMS who are authorized living allowances will be paid for periods of hospitalization while in a training status. Payment for the period of hospitalization will be substantiated by an endorsement on the ITO by the installation commander concerned.

c. Living allowance will be computed in accordance with the JTR as stated in DOD 5105.38–M, table C10.T3, (see table 7–1 in this regulation).

d. IMS from countries for which the USG pays transoceanic and CONUS travel are entitled to living allowances in a travel status to include the day of departure from the home country through the day of arrival at the first training location and to include the day of departure from the last training location until the day of arrival in the home country. This excludes periods of leave authorized by the IMS government following termination of training. In no case will living allowances be paid for travel within the IMS's own country.

e. The IMS whose governments pay only for transoceanic travel costs are entitled to living allowances to include the day of departure from the U.S. entry port en-route to the training location, through the day of arrival at the training location and includes the day of arrival at the U.S. departure point.

f. Living allowances are authorized for periods between courses and between schools when such periods are included in the overall training schedule. Appropriate living allowances will be programmed to cover the entire period of training.

g. Leave with living allowances may be granted IMS within CONUS as specified below.

(1) During authorized holidays.

(2) During periods between consecutive courses. It is not the intent of this provision that leave be given or used indiscriminately to occupy the IMS during periods between courses of instruction.

(3) During periods of delay while awaiting transportation to the home country.

h. The installation commander or the designated representative will make every attempt to collect an overpayment of living allowance prior to the IMS departure from that installation. Failure to collect overpayment will be reported to the Military Service. Underpayment will be resolved by the Security Cooperation Organization in local currency.

i. When official travel is performed at personal expense, living allowances at the prescribed travel status rate are authorized for a period not to exceed the authorized travel time for mode of transportation most advantageous to the USG.

j. DD Form 652 (Uniformed Services Meal Ticket), although authorized, is not normally issued to USG-funded Training Program IMS while in a travel status. When tickets are issued, living allowances are payable at the rate prescribed in the JTR for "travel status and USG mess available."

k. When travel has been completed to the first training installation, IMS will be paid living allowances covering periods of unscheduled delay that occurred before their arrival at the port of embarkation in the United States or in overseas commands.

(1) A delay of 10 hours or more will be substantiated by a statement from a port, air, or other transportation terminal official and be attached to the IMS ITO.

(2) When USG quarters and meals are not available at a military installation for periods of delay en route, the commanding officer or designated representative will give the IMS a written statement to that effect. The statement will indicate the dates those quarters and meals (by number) were not available. If the delay en route is at other than a military installation, the IMS written statement as to the non-availability of USG quarters and meals will substantiate the voucher.

(3) Care must be taken to clearly define periods of leave or delay en route and, upon completion of training, to ensure proper payment of living and travel allowances.

l. Living allowances are not authorized for the following:

(1) Periods of unauthorized absence (UA) from duty.

(2) Excess travel time when proceeding by other than USG transportation not authorized by the administrative authority of the Military Service concerned.

(3) Periods of delay not connected with training, except for hospitalization or outpatient care.

(4) IMS whose country assumes the payment of all living allowances.

(5) Periods of travel from country duty station to country port or vice versa.

(6) A period of leave authorized by IMS government following the termination of all training courses.

m. IMS may choose to rent cars from commercial sources at their own expense. Cost of rental vehicles will not be charged to the U.S. Funded Training Program.

7–13. Advance

The IMS initial living allowance payment may be delayed until they have been in CONUS for 2 weeks; therefore, the Security Cooperation Organization is encouraged to advance the IMS sufficient funds in U.S. dollars to meet all expenses while the student is en-route, to include 2 weeks advance living allowance. Any such advances will be annotated in the special conditions block of the ITO to prevent duplicate payment of entitlements at CONUS training activities.

Section IV
Department of the Army

7–14. Baggage allowance

a. Miscellaneous charge order. The most efficient way to pay for excess baggage is to use a Miscellaneous Charge Order. The IMSO provides the size and weight of each bag several days in advance of travel to the ticket office; any excess bags must be authorized on the ITO. The ticket office issues a paper Miscellaneous Charge Order voucher along with the student's ticket (paper or e-ticket). The fund cite on the ITO pays for the Miscellaneous Charge Order. Department of the Army has agreed to the use of the Miscellaneous Charge Order for IMS provided it does not adversely impact the central billing account process.

b. Excess baggage. Another method is for the student to pay for the excess baggage and obtain reimbursement for that amount either prior to departure from CONUS training site or after arrival in home country. The former requires payment several weeks in advance of travel.

7–15. Retainable instructional material

a. The SATFA will reimburse the cost of shipping retainable instructional material (RIM) from Army installations through course tuition.

b. The Army courses in table 7–2 are considered to be in the senior PME category. The IMS attending these courses are authorized a RIM weight allowance of up to 200 pounds per course.

c. Costs for the shipment of RIM are not applicable to DL training/courses.

d. The IMS attending all formal courses of instruction not specifically covered in table 7–2 are authorized a RIM weight allowance of up to 50 pounds per course.

e. Some Army schools provide compact discs (CDs) containing reference material used in courses to students enrolled in certain courses, making RIM weight negligible.

f. If school officials determine that IMS require publications not retained by U.S. students, the cost of the publications must be specifically identified on the TRADOC ATRM–159 or on the appropriate document for non-TRADOC schools so that they will be included in course costs.

Table 7–2
Army courses in the senior PME category authorized 200 pounds of RIM

MASL ID	Course title
B171200	Sergeants Major Academy
B171765	Advanced Operational Studies Fellowship
B171768	Intermediate Level Education
B171425	Command and General Staff - Spanish
B171798	Combating Terrorism Fellows Program
B171800	Army War College
B171801	National Defense University International Fellows Program
B171806	Industrial College of the Armed Forces International Fellows Program

7–16. Quarters

a. The IMS will be considered as neither TDY nor PCS for purposes of assignment of UPH.

(1) So far as possible, IMS will be housed in UPH permanent party quarters (see AR 420–1; priority V). IMS will not be charged rent but will be responsible for payment of the same custodial (maid service) charges as U.S. personnel occupying UPH permanent party quarters. IMS will receive custodial (maid service), if available.

(2) With approval of the installation commander, IMS may elect assignment to UPH transient quarters (VOQ/VEQ).

IMS will be responsible for payment of custodial (maid service) charges at the established rate. When occupying UPH transient quarters, IMS will be authorized 'space confirmed' reservations.

(3) For IMS with dependents refer to paragraph 10–60.

b. DFAS–IN 37–1 contains specific guidelines and steps for developing and calculating monthly rental charges for Government family housing provided to IMS.

7–17. Subsistence
Payment for meals, per AR 30–22, taken in U.S. Army dining facilities will be according to food rates as prescribed by the Office of the Secretary of Defense (OSD, Comptroller). New rates are developed annually and are posted and effective 1 October each year.

Section V
Department of the Navy (U.S. Navy, U.S. Marine Corps, and U.S. Coast Guard)

7–18. Round trip tickets when travel/transportation is funded by a U.S. funded training Program
Round trip tickets are discouraged for IMS overseas travel unless training duration is 5 weeks or less due to difficulties in making changes to tickets issued OCONUS. If there is significant cost savings however, the Security Cooperation Organization may request a waiver to purchase a round trip ticket for training durations over 5 weeks. The waiver request must be sent to Naval Education and Training Security Assistance Field Activity, with information copy to the Service providing the training, for all IMS training in all DON courses. The Security Cooperation Organization can authorize the purchase of a round-trip ticket for IMS attending training at a commercial site.

7–19. Quarters when living allowance is funded by a United States funded program.
a. Officer IMS lodging costs will be included in the living allowance. Officers will be responsible for payment of lodging costs directly.

b. Enlisted IMS (E–8 and below) occupying base quarters are generally not required to pay fees. Bills for services should be forwarded the Naval Education and Training Security Assistance Field Activity for payment for all DON IMS. When enlisted IMS are billeted in a transient or public private venture facility on base that requires direct payment, the cost of the lodging may be included in the living allowance.

7–20. Travel and living allowance payments - Coast Guard
The USCG IMS TLA payment process is managed by USCG, G–CI Resource Management. Disbursements are processed from a central location. Requests for payment should be submitted for processing through USCG training center Yorktown Resource Management. An IMS initial payment request must be accompanied by a funds request form and a copy of the ITO. Resource Management validates the student entitlement and funding authorization. Payment of TLA is made through a convenience check to the IMS.

Section VI
Department of the Air Force

7–21. Air Force travel information for international military student officers
The IMSO will send required travel information by the Security Assistance Network Web.

7–22. Tickets
a. The Randolph AFB commercial travel office will send tickets to the IMSO by an overnight parcel delivery service or certified mail. For short-notice reservations or ticketing, the Randolph AFB commercial travel office will confirm the reservations by phone, followed by the hard-copy backup to the requesting agency. A prepared ticket advice will be generated by the carrier at the departure airport. The carrier will issue a ticket against the prepared ticket advice to the traveler on demand (with positive identification; for example, passport).

(1) Tickets issued by the Randolph AFB commercial travel office (only) that are not used will be returned to that office with three copies of the international student's ITO. Partially used tickets will be returned to the Randolph AFB commercial travel office who will process a refund. Notify the Air Force Security Assistance Training Squadron/FM of any returned tickets that are sent to Randolph AFB commercial travel office for refunds.

(2) The IMSO is responsible for receipt or verification of tickets until delivered to the IMS.

(3) Change of departure date on an issued ticket may be made by the local commercial travel office if time does not permit changes by the Randolph AFB commercial travel office.

(4) In case of an emergency, each Randolph AFB commercial travel office confirmation will include a toll-free number should the student encounter any difficulty regarding their reservations or tickets.

(5) If travel arrangements are required for an IMS with fewer than four hours lead time, the IMSO may use the local commercial travel office for obtaining the necessary tickets or reservations.

(6) IMS transoceanic travel by Air Mobility Command is arranged according to applicable Air Force policies using the USG (common user) tariff rate.

b. Ticketing requests for Maxwell AFB IMS students may be processed locally through the Maxwell AFB official travel office using JFTR guidance for ticketing for official travel.

7–23. Air Force International Military Education and Training travel payment

Control methods for travel payment for IMS will be as outlined in DFAS guidance on Procedures for Travel Accounting Operations. DD Form 1588 (Record of Travel Payment) will be forwarded to each AFO at the new training location. When final payment is made to the IMS at the final training location, the AFO will forward DD Form 1588 to the Air Force Security Assistance Training Squadron/FM, 315 J Street West, Randolph AFB, TX 78150–4302, for final auditing and file.

7–24. Air Force retainable instructional materials

The USAF PME courses for which the shipment of up to 200 pounds of RIM is authorized are the Air War College, Air Command and Staff College Course, USAF Test Pilot School, and AFIT graduate programs. IMS attending language instructor courses at DLIELC are authorized the shipment of 100 pounds of RIM. For all other formal CONUS training courses, up to 50 pounds of RIM for each course is authorized.

7–25. Billeting service charges

a. Officer IMS under FMS or IMET are required to personally defray the billeting service charge.

b. Enlisted IMS under FMS or IMET will not normally be subject to service charges when occupying USAF quarters for durations of 20 or more consecutive weeks. Enlisted IMS occupying USAF quarters for fewer than 20 weeks are subject to a service charge.

(1) Enlisted IMS with ITO authorizing them an IMET living allowance will not be required to personally defray these charges. Base billeting offices will submit invoices to their servicing DFAS office.

(2) The IMET enlisted IMS who are not authorized an IMET living allowance and all FMS enlisted IMS will personally defray the billeting service charge.

7–26. Supplemental payment

Claims for supplemental payment after a student has returned to the home country should be filed with the Security Cooperation Organization and a copy forwarded to the Air Force Security Assistance Training Squadron/FM.

7–27. Family housing

On-base family housing is seldom available. When available, it will be according to AFI 32–6001.

7–28. Reimbursement for temporary duty to international military students

a. Reimbursement of quarters cost in connection with TDY must be made from assigned training base funds since these costs are calculated in the tuition rate.

b. All IMS receiving a living allowance under IMET and attending AF professional or military education courses identified in table 7–1, note 4, will continue to receive the accompanied rate while TDY. The IMS will also receive the per diem rates for the location(s) to which they are TDY as part of their course of study without forfeiture of their basic TLA. The SAMM, table C10.T3, (see table 7–1) and Defense Security Cooperation Agency policy letters provide additional information concerning travel and living allowance issues.

7–29. Subsistence

Billing will be as prescribed in chapter 6.

7–30. International military student paydays

The IMS entitled to receive supplemental living allowances under IMET or an FMS case will normally be paid on the 1st day of the month. Travel and living allowances will be in accordance with JFTR where the individual is attending training.

Chapter 8
Medical Requirements and Healthcare

Section I
General

8–1. Purpose
The purpose of this chapter is to delineate the medical requirements, entitlements, and reporting procedures for IMSs and their authorized dependent(s). This chapter covers the required examinations, eligibility, benefits and reimbursements for healthcare, hospitalization, and other medical topics. For the purposes of this regulation, the term healthcare refers to both medical and dental care.

8–2. Responsibilities
a. The Security Cooperation Officer (Security Cooperation Organization) will ensure—

(1) Each IMS has completed a medical and dental examination by a medical authority (see para 8–3c) within 3 months prior to departure from home country for training before issuing an ITO.

(2) Each dependent authorized on the ITO has completed a medical examination by a medical authority within three months prior to departure from home country before issuing an ITO or amendment. See paragraph 8–4, Pregnancy Policy, and paragraph 8–7a, Healthcare coverage.

(3) All examinations are completed on DD Form 2807–1 (Medical History and DD Form 2808, Report of Medical Examination). These forms and instructions for completing them are located within Health Affairs under Functional Areas on the DISAM International Training Management Web site at http://www.disam.dsca.mil/itm. The forms and associated laboratory results will be recorded in English using U.S. measurements. Also refer to paragraph 8–5 and the MILDEP sections in this chapter for additional course specific medical examination requirements.

(4) The IMS and dependents authorized to accompany or join the IMS are briefed on their responsibilities to maintain healthcare coverage. If the IMS is financially responsible for coverage, the Security Cooperation Organization will verify that the IMS has adequate health insurance prior to the issuance of an ITO.

(5) Item 12 of the ITO specifies the correct source for IMS and/or dependent healthcare coverage/reimbursement. See paragraph 8–6.

(6) A sealed medical packet is developed that includes the following items. The IMS will hand carry this packet to be delivered to the healthcare provider at the training installation, and will deliver a second copy in English of the medical insurance policy to the IMSO.

(a) DD Form 2807–1, Medical History.

(b) DD Form 2808, Report of Medical Examination.

(c) Radiology report of the chest x-ray (for those age 15 and older).

(d) Human immunodeficiency virus (HIV) laboratory results (for those age 15 and older).

(e) Pregnancy laboratory results (female IMS only).

(f) Dental panorex (only if required in the course prerequisites).

(g) Other tests as required.

(h) Health insurance policy (if applicable; must be in English).

(i) Medical waiver approval (if applicable).

b. International Military Student Office (IMSO) will review the ITO for the required healthcare statements and the medical packet for completeness. Discrepancies will be reported to the MILDEP Country Program Manager and the Security Cooperation Organization. The IMSO will forward the packet on to the local medical authority for storage and the creation of an outpatient medical record.

8–3. Medical requirements
a. The IMS selected by their country for training are presumed to be in good physical and mental health, as well as being free from communicable diseases (see table 8–4). If it is discovered that an IMS cannot qualify for training by reason of physical or mental condition and, in the opinion of medical authorities, will require treatment before entering training, the IMS will be returned to the home country immediately, or as soon thereafter as their condition will permit travel.

b. Medical examinations are required for the IMS and each dependent listed on the ITO.

c. Examination forms DD Form 2807–1 and DD Form 2808 combined serve as the official record and fulfill the examination requirements of the Security Cooperation Education and Training Program (SCETP). These forms serve as a single medical document certifying that the participant is free from communicable diseases and is medically qualified for training or accompany the IMS. A DD Form 2808, block 81 will be signed by a physician, by a dentist in block 83 and by a foreign military representative in block 84. The foreign military representative is validating that the exam was conducted in accordance with DSCA and Military Service requirements. The examination will include any laboratory test that is deemed necessary for the examining physician to reach a conclusion about the presence of any abnormalities, diseases, disabilities, or disqualifiers. Laboratory investigation for the diseases listed at table 8–4 are not mandatory unless clinically indicated. The IMS (not dependents) from DSCA approved "fast track" countries may use their national forms.

(1) *Medical examinations.*

(a) Serological tests for HIV and Acquired Deficiency Syndrome (AIDS) are required for the IMS and each dependant listed on the ITO. Dependants under the age of 15 will not be tested unless there is a medical reason to suspect such infection. IMS with serologic evidence of HIV/AIDS are not necessarily ineligible for training. Country may request a waiver for HIV/AIDS positive IMS and/or dependants from the MILDEP sponsoring the training. If the MILDEP determines that the IMS is healthy enough to participate in training, that dependants are healthy, and that neither present a threat to anyone else, the waiver may be approved.

(b) Immunizations for each IMS will maintain current immunizations as prescribed by the World Health Organization and the Public Health Service. (See table 8–1.) Authorized dependents are required to maintain those immunizations recommended by the World Health Organization and Public Health Service. Results will be recorded on DD Form 2808, Item #73.

(c) Chest x-ray for tuberculosis (TB) is a chest x-ray is required for the IMS and each authorized dependent 15 years of age or over. Dependents under the age of 15 are not required to have a chest x-ray for TB; however, if the dependent has evidence of contact with a person with TB, a tuberculin skin test will be performed and if positive, an x-ray will be performed. If the initial chest x-ray shows any abnormalities, further evaluation will be performed via a sputum smear test. If an individual needs to travel to the United States for training more than once in a 12 month period and the chest x-ray prior to the initial training period is documented to be negative for active disease, a repeat chest x-ray is not required unless the individual has symptoms or a clinical examination is suspicious for a pulmonary (lung) problem. The same applies to the dependents with initial negative chest x-rays who accompany this student more than once in a 12 month period. Results will be recorded on DD Form 2808, Item #73 and a copy of the laboratory results will be attached.

Table 8–1
Immunizations

Required immunizations for IMS	
Disease	**Remarks**
Measles, Mumps, Rubella	
Polio	
Diphtheria, Pertussis, Tetanus (DPT)	If immunization is given in U.S. then recommend; Tetanus, diphtheria, and Pertussis (Tdap)
Varicella (Chickenpox)	
Influenza B	If vaccinated for Influenza within U.S., recommend using term "Influenza."
Hepatitis A & B	If attending medical training
Yellow fever	If traveling from or through an infected area

b. Recommended immunizations for dependents	
Disease	**Remarks**
Measles, Mumps, Rubella	
Polio	
Diphtheria, Pertussis, Tetanus	If immunization is given in U.S. then recommend; Tetanus, diphtheria, and Pertussis (Tdap)
Varicella (Chickenpox)	
Influenza B	If vaccinated for Influenza within U.S., recommend using term "Influenza."
Pneumococcal	Ages 0–18

Table 8–1
Immunizations—Continued

Yellow fever	Ages 19 and above if traveling from or through an infected area

Notes:
[1] The Security Cooperation Organization will contact the school IMSO for local and state primary and secondary school immunizations for dependents. These will vary from locale to locale. For immunization updates or questions, refer to: www.cdc.gov/nip or call 1–800–232–2522.

(d) Female IMS will undergo a pregnancy examination. Results will be recorded on DD Form 2808 Item #73 and a copy of the laboratory results will be attached. In order to participate in training, pregnant IMS are required to submit a waiver request. See paragraphs 8–4 and 8–13.

(2) *Dental examinations.* Each IMS will have a complete dental examination to ensure that the IMS does not require treatment during training for caries (cavities), an infection or an oral disease. IMS who require an aviation/flight examination will also undergo a dental panorex. If countries are not capable of performing a panorex, the panorex will be performed at country expense at the first U.S. installation attended. The panorex will be included in the IMS medical packet and hand carried to each training location. Results will be recorded on DD Form 2808 Item #43. Dental examinations are not required for dependents.

(3) The physician and dentist who sign the examination forms are verifying that the IMS is medically qualified to attend training and is free from any communicable diseases of public significance. The IMS diagnosed with a communicable disease(s) listed on table 8–4, communicable diseases, will not be issued an ITO. Dependents diagnosed with a communicable disease(s) listed on table 8–4 will not be listed on the ITO.

(4) If an IMS is certified capable of successfully undergoing instruction even though medical or dental conditions capable of impacting training exist (for example, diabetes, cardiac condition, metabolic disorder, prosthetics), those conditions will be noted on DD Form 2808, Item #77 and a statement will be included in Item #78 and ITO Item #15 that those medical conditions may have an impact on training if not properly controlled or monitored.

d. When U.S. education/training of IMS takes place in a third country, the IMS must meet all of the medical screening requirements of the third country.

Note. A third country is defined as a country other than the CONUS or the IMS home country.

e. When training is to take place in home country; the medical screening per this chapter is not required. Security Cooperation Organization should make sure the country understands that the IMS must meet the medical prerequisites for the training.

f. When the individual is in the United States for a noneducation/training purpose and the non-education/training purpose remains the main reason that person is in the United States, medical screening is not required prior to attendance at security cooperation education/training programs in the United States.

g. When the individual is in the United States. for noneducation/training purpose and the purpose changes such that the primary reason that person is now in the United States is to attend security cooperation education/training the regular medical screening requirements and statements on the ITO will apply.

8–4. Pregnancy Policy

Dependents known to be pregnant will not be placed on the ITO or approved for travel unless/until the IMS shows proof of medical coverage including pre/post natal care, delivery, and postpartum care for the dependent and care for the newborn, a medical line is included in a FMS case, or the foreign government pays all expenses connected with childbirth. In the latter case, the ITO remarks section will include the address to which the bills will be sent for payment. If the IMS cannot or does not secure medical coverage for pregnancy prior to departure, IMS will proceed to the United States unaccompanied. Dependents may proceed to the United States with an amended ITO after proper medical coverage is obtained. Also see paragraph 8–6*a* healthcare coverage for dependents.

8–5. Course related medical requirements

The MILDEPs have identified courses that require additional or extensive medical/dental examinations. Such courses are aviation, airborne, ranger, special forces, diving, explosive ordnance disposal, mountain warfare, reconnaissance, and swimming. These courses are identified in the Training Military Articles and Services List. The Security Cooperation Organization must carefully review the course requirements to determine if there are special medical and dental requirements associated with attending the course. The Security Cooperation Organization must notify the examiner of the additional examination requirements. If IMS home country is not able to perform the required course examination requirements, the common examination listed in paragraph 8–3 will be performed to allow the IMS to proceed to a U.S. training location. The Security Cooperation Organization will contact the first U.S. base training location to coordinate further medical examinations set by the course. If the IMS is required to have an examination in CONUS, the cost of the examination and transportation will be borne by the foreign government. See Health Affairs link under functional areas at http://www/disam.dsca.mil/itm/.

8–6. Medical eligibility

a. The IMS and authorized dependents, except parents and parent-in-laws, under the SCETP are eligible to receive healthcare in DOD facilities for the length of the training posted on the ITO.

(1) The IMS and dependents from a country under the North Atlantic Treaty Organization (NATO) and or Partnership for Peace (PFP) that have a status of forces agreement (SOFA) on file with the U.S. Government have the same access to healthcare as U.S. military personnel and dependents.

(2) The IMS and dependents from non-NATO/PFP SOFA countries have access to healthcare facilities on a space available basis.

(3) The IMS and dependents covered by a Reciprocal Healthcare Agreement have the same access and priority to healthcare in DOD facilities as U.S. military personnel and dependents. See paragraph 8–6*d*(3).

(4) Exchange IMS and dependents are eligible for access to healthcare facilities subject to any existing exchange agreements. Reimbursement for healthcare will be made if required by the exchange agreement, laws, and regulations of the United States.

(5) Paramilitary and civilian IMS and their authorized dependents are eligible for emergency care only.

(6) The Security Cooperation Organization will inquire with the appropriate MILDEP regarding healthcare for IMS in training at civilian or contractor locations.

b. When IMS and/or authorized dependent reports to any medical facility for treatment, they must have in their possession their ITO, a photo identification and if applicable, their health insurance card or policy. A parental identification card will be used for children under the age of 10. Dependents listed on the ITO are the only dependents authorized to have access and receive care in DOD healthcare facilities.

c. Tri-Service Medical Care (TRICARE) is a DOD, regionally managed healthcare program for U.S. only active duty and retired members of the uniformed services and their Families. The IMS and dependents are not enrolled in the TRICARE healthcare plan. However, NATO/PFP SOFA countries participate in the TRICARE Standard program for dependent outpatient healthcare only. Those TRICARE Standard dependents will have the same deductible and co-pay as U.S. dependents when outpatient care is provided at civilian facilities.

d. Medical treatment for the various SCETP is funded as follows, (ITO, Item #12):

(1) The USG-funded programs, such as, the IMET Program, Regional Defense Combating Terrorism Fellowship Program, International Narcotics Control and Law Enforcement Program, Counter-Drug Training Support Program and others will pay for the IMS healthcare but not for dependent(s) healthcare. Dependents are required to maintain medical coverage either through the foreign government or health insurance. USG-funded programs will not provide medical coverage when training occurs in the IMS home country or a third country. See paragraph 8–4.

(2) FMS.

(a) FMS cases may have a medical line that is designated to fund medical care for the student. In some cases the country authorizes and funds dependent healthcare coverage, as well.

(b) The foreign government may elect to directly pay the IMS and/or dependent medical bills. The ITO, Items #12 and #15 will state where the bills are to be sent to for payment.

(c) When the IMS is responsible for payment, they must have health insurance that meets DSCA standards.

(3) Reciprocal Healthcare Agreements.

(a) Reciprocal Healthcare Agreement are individual agreements between the U.S. DOD and the defense organization of another country which offers comparable reciprocal healthcare to certain military, and in some instances, their dependents from that country in U.S. based DOD facilities only, at no cost. These agreements will vary by country and each one has an expiration date. Security Cooperation Organization will validate the training duration with the Reciprocal Healthcare Agreement expiration date prior to issuing an ITO using this coverage. The U.S. authority for Reciprocal Healthcare Agreement is the U.S. Assistant Secretary of Defense for Health Affairs.

(b) Reciprocal Healthcare Agreement has precedence over all other U.S. government-funded programs when treated in a U.S. based DOD facility.

(c) Reciprocal Health Care Agreement is not applicable for treatment at civilian facilities. Many military installations do not have full-Service military treatment facilities. The Security Cooperation Organization should check with IMSO concerning availability of medical care at the installation.

(d) Reciprocal Health Care Agreement do not cover civilian and para-military students nor their dependents.

(e) The IMS and accompanying dependent(s) who rely on a Reciprocal Healthcare Agreement for healthcare coverage must also have healthcare coverage from the foreign government or health insurance per paragraph 8–7 to cover care that may be received from civilian healthcare providers when DOD services are not available.

(4) Aviation Leadership Program students are provided medical coverage by the U.S. Air Force.

8–7. Healthcare coverage

a. Every IMS and accompanying dependent is required to have and maintain coverage for healthcare for the duration of their travel and training. Failure to maintain coverage may result in the IMS removal from training and return to home country. Coverage can be provided by the U.S. Government-funded program, FMS Case, foreign government, Reciprocal Healthcare Agreement as noted in paragraph 8–5*d*(3); health insurance or a combinations of these.

b. Dependents are not authorized to accompany or join IMS in the U.S. unless the foreign government ensures medical coverage for the dependents is provided during the IMS training through the FMS case medical line, directly through the Foreign Government, NATO/PFP SOFA, through health insurance, a DOD Reciprocal Healthcare Agreement, if applicable, or a combination of these programs. If there is a lapse in medical coverage or a situation arises where coverage does not include the disease, illness, pregnancy or treatment, or the IMS fails to pay a co-pay/deductible, the medical bills are the responsibility of the foreign government and will be forwarded to the foreign government address listed on the ITO section 12, 15 or the Defense Attaché in the United States for payment. The IMS will be removed from training and the IMS and dependents returned home if at any time the foreign government fails to provide coverage or payment within 30 calendar days of notification by the MILDEP. If medical coverage is not obtained for dependents prior to departure of the IMS for CONUS, dependents will not be authorized to accompany the IMS. Dependents may be authorized to join IMS in CONUS after the required coverage is obtained and the ITO amended.

c. When the IMS is financially responsible for their authorized dependent healthcare costs, adequate health insurance is required and must be demonstrated to the Security Cooperation Organization prior to issuance of an ITO or listing of dependents on the ITO. Minimum acceptable insurance coverage is described in detail in the current DSCA medical coverage policy message. Health insurance must remain in effect for the duration of the IMS and dependents stay in the U.S. under security cooperation sponsorship.

d. When medical coverage is provided by health insurance, a copy of the policy in English will be provided to the Security Cooperation Organization, IMSO, and the servicing medical treatment facility. If the insurance company is not U.S. based, the policy must have international benefits that cover care in the U.S. The lack of medical coverage for IMS or dependent(s) (if applicable) revealed at any time during their stay in the U.S. will result in IMS or the foreign government being responsible for the payment of incurred medical bills, removal of the IMS from training and the IMS and or dependent(s) return to home country.

e. All IMS participating in U.S. training in a third country are required to have insurance as their sole means of medical coverage. Insurance coverage must be applicable to and must meet the requirements of the third country. See paragraphs 8–3*d* and *e.*

f. The IMS and or dependents who plan to visit other countries while attending education and training under sponsorship of Security Assistance or Security Cooperation must also obtain healthcare coverage and meet the insurance requirements, if applicable, of the countries they plan to visit.

8–8. Security assistance teams

a. If a U.S. team member requires routine or emergency healthcare, and does not have ready access to the U.S. Embassy health unit or the required medical service is not available, a referral decision will be made by the U.S. Embassy's regional medical officer in concert with the responsible U.S. MILDEP.

b. The cost of treatment in a host nation medical facility will be borne by the foreign government.

c. The cost of transportation to the nearest U.S. military treatment facility with the appropriate Service will be borne by the foreign government.

d. Medical and transportation costs will be charged to country FMS case or USG-funded Program. If there is not enough money in the FMS case or USG-funded Program to cover expenses, the FMS case or USG-funded Program will be amended to include these costs.

e. Team members who are U.S. contractors are responsible for their own healthcare, including routine health services and emergency medical evacuation, under provisions of the contract.

8–9. Hospitalization and disposition

a. When an IMS or dependent requires hospitalization, the training installation will notify the Military Service and local agencies in the chain of command, as appropriate. The notification will include all pertinent information concerning the IMS or dependent's condition as well as prognosis (see para 8–10). The Military Service will notify DSCA, the Security Cooperation Organization, the commanders of combatant commands and other agencies in the chain of command as appropriate. The IMSO will notify the Military Service when the patient status changes or when, in the opinion of U.S. medical authorities, the hospitalization or disability could prevent the successful competition of training. The School Commandant or IMSO will notify the Military Service by message and request disposition instructions.

b. When the IMS is scheduled for additional training at another installation, the IMSO at that installation will also be notified if follow on training is terminated.

c. When an IMS dependent hospitalization impacts on the IMS's training, has political implications, or will result in excessive medical charges, the school commandant, IMSO or designated representative will send a message to the Military Service and appropriate agencies in the chain of command.

d. For Service specific requirements, see sections II, III, or IV.

8–10. Medical reports and health records

a. The Health Insurance Portability and Accountability Act of 1996 institutes business practices to protect the use and disclosure of protected health information. The medical facility ensures the Health Insurance Portability and Accountability Act compliance prior to the release of information to the military chain of command. The individual's right to privacy of medical information will be adhered to. The military chain of command will use the below format when reporting medical information.

b. When reporting a serious medical situation or hospitalization, use the WCN in lieu of patient names. If the patient is a dependent, use the WCN and the dependent # from the ITO block 12b; for example, WCN 5004–2 with "2" being the second dependent listed in block 12b. For Service specific requirements, see sections II, III, or IV.

c. Each IMS or dependent who receives care at a medical facility is entitled to a personal copy of their inpatient and outpatient medical records. Outpatient records will be provided to the IMS/dependent during their routine out-processing. Inpatient records can be obtained upon the patient's written request.

8–11. Subsistence while hospitalized

All patients are charged for hospital rations when hospitalized as an inpatient. Reimbursements are made as follows:

a. Cost of subsistence for IMS with meal cards will be sent to the MILDEP for reimbursement.

b. IMS without meal cards will pay locally at the medical facility.

c. Dependents will pay locally at the medical facility.

8–12. Emergency healthcare

a. Emergency healthcare is defined as care that saves life, eyesight, and limbs. A dental emergency is a situation where dental treatment is required for relief of painful or acute conditions. Dentists are authorized to include in the concept of a dental emergency, care that is required to keep the student progressing in their studies. Medical/dental care that can wait until the following normal work day is not emergency care.

b. Healthcare required during a Field Studies Program trip, when more than 40 miles from a DOD medical facility, will be considered an emergency. See paragraph 8–16.

c. Procedures—

(1) The IMS or dependent shall report to the nearest emergency room, military or civilian, when emergency care is required. If emergency medical services are required, the IMS will notify the IMSO as soon as practicable. The IMS will provide a copy of their ITO, a copy of their ID card and insurance, if applicable, to the emergency room for billing purposes. All care provided must be recorded as an "Emergency" for billing purposes.

(2) When emergency care is received from a civilian healthcare facility the IMSO will—

(a) Notify the nearest DOD medical facility Medical Services Account Office (MSCO) of the IMS/dependent visit to a civilian emergency facility. If care is provided during an Field Studies Program trip, the IMSO will notify the installation MSCO at the conclusion of the trip.

(b) In situations where the medical bills are paid by the USG or a medical line on a FMS case, IMSO will obtain three copies of the bill(s) for treatment and services including a statement signed by the doctor that states: "I certify that the above services are necessary in treatment of the above named individual, that services were as stated, and that charges are not in excess of those customarily made in this vicinity." If care is provided during an Field Studies Program trip, the IMSO will also provide a statement including the fact that treatment occurred during an Field Studies Program trip.

(c) Forward the bill(s), the civilian medical statement, and three copies of the IMS' ITO to the appropriate MILDEP agency for payment. See paragraph 8–16 for details.

(d) When the ITO states the IMS is financially responsible for healthcare, the IMS will either pay the bill, or in the case of insurance, will pay the deductible and any co-payment. The medical facility will collect the IMS insurance information and directly bill the insurance firm for the balance due

(e) When the ITO states the foreign government will pay for healthcare, the civilian medical facility will directly bill the foreign government point of contact listed on the ITO.

(f) The local DOD medical facility MSCO will assist and process reimbursements. The MSCO will forward these forms to the appropriate MILDEP for disbursement.

(g) For Service specific requirements, see section II, II, or IV.

8–13. Waivers

a. The IMS may have medical conditions that do not prohibit their training. Also, while requirements dictate that the IMS must be free of communicable diseases and in good health an individual may have a communicable disease that is no longer a risk to the general populace. In such instances, a medical waiver may be warranted/requested. However, the communicable diseases listed in table 8–4 will not be waived. Requests for medical waivers will be submitted through the commanders of combatant commands to the MILDEP Training Policy Officer(s) and will contain the information listed below. Everyone will take the necessary precautions to protect the patient's identity. The request will be submitted as a standard memorandum and will include—

(1) Country.

(2) WCN and IMET FY or FMS case number (if the waiver is for an accompanying dependent, state WCN xxxx dependent and relationship, that is, xxx, dependent, spouse).

(3) Scheduled Training Military Articles and Service List and report date.

(4) Medical condition and copies of the appropriate laboratory results.

b. Medical waivers will not be approved for pregnant IMS under a USG Grant Program unless the foreign government submits a signed statement with the waiver request agreeing that the foreign government will pay for pre/postnatal care, delivery and postpartum care for the IMS and care for the newborn. Medical waivers will not be approved for pregnant IMS under any other program unless IMS has medical coverage for pre/postnatal care, delivery and postpartum care and care for the newborn.

c. The MILDEP Training Policy Officer(s) will coordinate the waiver request with the MILDEP/Military Service. IMS will not depart home station until a decision is rendered by the MILDEP Training Policy Officer.

d. If a waiver is granted, Security Cooperation Organization will enter the following information on the ITO, Item #15: Medical waiver for (name) approved on mm-dd-yyyy. Do not list the nature of the waiver.

8–14. Constraints

a. Under no circumstances will the SCETP be utilized for the sole purpose of obtaining medical care for IMS or dependents. Pre-existing conditions will be considered on a case-by-case basis.

b. Elective medical, surgical, or dental care is that type of care desired or requested by the individual or recommended by the physician or dentist which, in the opinion of professional authority, can be performed at another time or place without jeopardizing the health or well-being of the patient. The overall policy regarding pre-existing conditions, elective and definitive healthcare is that moderation should prevail, except for bona fide emergency situations. Security Cooperation Organization personnel will not imply to an IMS that U.S. DOD medical facilities will be available for elective care.

c. Prosthetic devices, such as eye glasses, hearing aids or orthopedic footwear, are not authorized for issue to non-NATO/PFP SOFA IMS or to any dependents. Eyeglasses may be furnished to non-NATO IMS when necessary for the IMS to perform their assigned duties but only when eyeglasses are not available through civilian/commercial sources.

d. When an IMSO is notified that an IMS or their dependents have a communicable disease, no travel arrangements will be made until they are cleared or received a waiver by the medical authority. Circumstances will be reported to the Military Service. For Service specific requirements, see sections II, III, or IV.

8–15. Medical screening, urinalysis, blood screening, and mandatory drug testing programs in CONUS

a. Medical screening. Except as noted below, medically certified IMS are exempt from medical examinations or Implementing Agency screening programs before beginning training at U.S. training installations. Students may be tested medically as follows:

(1) At and by any U.S. training installations when the associated physical examination is an established prerequisite for admission for training that involves exceptional physical activity or safety.

(2) At and by a U.S. training installation on an exceptional basis pending development of particular testing capability, that does not exist in country. In this instance, country will pay for the cost of testing.

(3) Physical examination in conjunction with sick call, emergency treatment or hospitalization in order to diagnose or treat a student's ailment.

b. Mandatory urinalysis, blood screening, and mandatory drug testing. The IMS are excluded from any mandatory Military Service urinalysis and blood screening programs other than for selected training that involves exceptional physical activity, aviation training, or safety and for which the associated physical examination is a prerequisite of the course. Any indication or evidence of alcohol or drug abuse or a debilitating or communicable disease will be reported to the IMSO and Military Service. IMS may be tested under the following circumstances:

(1) During a command-directed probable cause search or seizure when there is reason to believe the urine to be collected contains evidence of illegal drug use.

(2) When consent has been provided voluntarily by IMS as part of a consent search conducted or self-referral to substance abuse counseling.

(3) Following any safety mishap under the regulations of the Military Service involved, a specimen may be collected from any individual directly or indirectly involved. Samples so collected may be used for inclusion as independently collected evidence in a safety mishap investigation or other investigations. Specimens will be treated in accordance with DODI 6055.7 and applicable Military Service regulations.

(4) During a command-directed examination of an IMS to determine IMS competence for training or need for counseling, rehabilitation, or other medical treatment when the commander has reason to question IMS behavior (for example, aberrant, bizarre or uncharacteristic behavior, unauthorized absences, violations of safety regulations, and breaches of discipline).

c. HIV/AIDS. The IMS country authority will be notified immediately through CONFIDENTIAL U.S. Military Service channels of an IMS who is diagnosed as antibody positive following a physical examination or as a result of the IMS treatment or hospitalization. In order to protect the confidentiality of the individual, only the country code, WCN, and the foreign identification number will be used. Report shall be made when confirmed by the Western Blot Test. The CONFIDENTIAL message should also contain the results of the medical evaluation for fitness for continued training.

(1) An IMS who manifests evidence of progressive clinical illness or immunological deficiency will be immediately released from training and returned to home country.

(2) An IMS who is antibody positive but manifests no evidence of progressive clinical illness or immunological deficiency (physical and laboratory assessment, demonstration of ability to respond to immunizations, and ability to mount a protective immune response to immunizations or exposure to naturally occurring pathogens) subject to the approval of the IMS military authority will continue in training or be rescheduled. The following conditions will be included as part of the notification to the IMS country referred to in paragraph 8–9, medical reports.

(a) Each IMS will accept counseling; will agree to follow standard preventive medicine requirements designed to reduce the risks of disease transmission to other persons; and will agree not to donate blood. IMS members that do not agree to follow preventive medicine requirements will be returned to their home country.

(b) The IMS will receive a comprehensive clinical and immunological evaluation at least annually.

(c) Noncompliance with the above will be cause for the termination of training and return of the IMS to their home country. The cost of return travel of the student will be at the expense of the IMS USG-funded Country Program or their government. The Country Program will be charged a proportionate share of the training completed by the IMS but not less than 50 percent of the course cost.

(d) While it may not be necessary to limit the activities of IMS who do not have evidence of progressive disease, the school may consult with the appropriate base, post, or station medical authority to determine if training and related activities should be limited in order to protect the IMS health and safety as well as that of others. If such limitations result in failure to meet the requisites for successful completion of training, the IMS will be terminated from training and returned home at the expense of the USG-funded Program or the foreign government. The country will also be charged a proportionate share of the training completed by the IMS as outlined in the paragraph, above.

(3) The IMS who voluntarily request HIV screening will be tested, provided that the student's government approves and agrees to assume the cost of such testing. The IMS must also agree to accept the possible consequences to include:

(a) Counseling on the risks of disease transmission, methods of prevention, and IMS agreement not to donate blood.

(b) A comprehensive clinical immunological evaluation at least annually.

(c) Possible return to the home country.

8–16. Reimbursements

a. Regardless of where or by whom care is rendered, military or civilian, those facilities will be reimbursed in accordance with DOD and MILDEP regulations (see item #12 and or #15 on the ITO). The exceptions are for care rendered under a Reciprocal Health Care Agreement, or outpatient care provided to NATO/PFP SOFA IMS and authorized dependents in DOD medical facilities.

b. The IMS who are responsible for their dependents' healthcare per the ITO are required to maintain health insurance. The IMS and/or dependent(s) are required to pay any deductibles and co-payments. The medical facility (DOD or civilian) will directly file for reimbursement with the insurance company.

c. In situations where the medical bills are paid by the USG or charged to the medical line of the FMS case, the servicing medical facility will send the bills to the appropriate MILDEP on DD Form 7 (Report of Treatment Furnished, Pay Patients, Hospitalization Furnished (Part A)) or DD Form 7A (Report of Treatment Furnished, Pay Patients, Outpatient Treatment Furnished (Part B)).

d. Civilian facilities will contact the local DOD medical facility MSCO or the MILDEP for verification of billing instructions for non-insurance claims. DOD facilities will process civilian reimbursements in accordance with Military Service procedures. See sections II. III. and IV. IMSOs are required to provide their local DOD billing contact information to the civilian provider.

e. For Service specific requirements, see sections II, III, or IV.

8–17. Air evacuation

a. Aeromdical evacuation is authorized for IMS in accordance with DODI 6000.11 when necessary. Reimbursement rates for patient movement include both the cost of transportation and the cost of en-route medical care. The full daily hospitalization rate is charged for each day patients are in the Aeromedical Evacuation System. The cost of transportation and enroute medical care will be borne by the foreign government. Applicable patient movement reimbursement policies and third party billing procedures and guidance for collections in accordance with 32 CFR Part 220 (reference (m)).

b. The SCOs will be contacted if IMS requires air evacuation to their home country. SCOs will notify the appropriate foreign government representative(s).

Section II
Department of the Army

8–18. References
Additional references for the Department of the Army are listed in appendix A.

8–19. Filing for healthcare reimbursement
Reimbursements for medical costs will be processed to the Army MILDEP: Commander, U.S. Army Medical Command (MCRM–F), 2050 Worth Road, Suite 9, Fort Sam Houston, TX 78254–6000, telephone (210) 221–7860. Refer to the ITO, Item #12. DD Forms 7 and or 7A will be used for DOD reimbursements and SF 1034 for civilian reimbursements.

8–20. Medical reports
Per paragraph 8–9, medical reports will be forwarded to SATFA country program manager.

8–21. Unique examination requirements
a. U.S. Army aviation examinations. International military pilots and IMS attending U.S. Army flight training are required to meet the appropriate U.S. Army Aviation Class medical standards per AR 40–501, chapter 4–1c. IMS from NATO/PFP nations will adhere to standardized agreement (STANAG) 3526 (see para (1)). IMS from non-NATO/PFP nations will adhere to policy and procedures outlined below (see para (2)).

(1) In accordance with NATO/PFP STANAG 3526 edition 6, NATO and PFP IMS members will conduct their normal flight physical examination using their military's qualified flight surgeons. Parent nations are responsible for standards of primary selection, permanent medical disqualification, and determination of temporary flying disabilities exceeding 30 days.

(a) The U.S. Army will accept the medical category and qualification for flying status, including the expiration date. Parent nations will provide a medical statement in English describing the IMS's medical fitness for flying duties, and forward the latest flight physical report with pertinent medical information and other pertinent documentation helpful in case of post-mishap identification purposes (fingerprints, dental records, and so forth) to the U.S. Army Aero-medical Activity (USAAMA) (MCXY–AER), Building 301, Fort Rucker, AL, USA 36362.

(b) Upon reporting to the U.S. Army training facility, the local flight surgeon will review the IMS's medical information, insure there has been no change in medical status, and issue a DA Form 4186 (Medical Recommendation of Flying Duty), using the expiration date assigned by the parent nation, for medical clearance for local flying duties.

(c) In cases where the expiration date for flying status occurs during training, periodic flight, physical examinations will be conducted in accordance with U.S. Army policies and procedures, and entered in the Aeromedical Electronic Resource Online. A copy of the flight physical report will be forwarded to the appropriate aeromedical authority of the Parent Nation for review and determination of fitness to fly.

(d) If a medical issue is discovered or occurs prior to completion of training, any provider may temporarily ground the IMS until resolution using U.S. Army policies and procedures. Only a U.S. DOD Flight Surgeon may return the IMS to flying status. If the grounding condition is of more than 30 days or potentially permanently disqualifying, the case will be referred to the parent nation for action in accordance with its regulations. The parent nation is responsible for the costs per established agreements.

(2) If the IMS is not from a NATO/PFP nation, and not subject to STANAG 3526, the IMS will need to meet U.S. Army standards with submission and approval through the USAAMA (MCXY–AER), Building 301, Fort Rucker, AL, USA 36362.

(a) If available, a U.S. Army aviation medical examination will be performed by a qualified U.S. DOD flight surgeon before the IMS departs from their home station; the cost of the examination and transportation will be borne by the foreign government. A flight student must meet Class 1 standards. A rated aviator must meet Class 2 standards.

(b) If a U.S. DOD flight surgeon is not available, a U.S. Army aviation medical examination may be performed by a parent nation flight surgeon and submitted to the USAAMA for review. A flight student must meet Class 1 standards. A rated aviator must meet Class 2 standards.

(c) Flight physical examinations should be documented in English on DD Forms 2807–1 and 2808 in accordance with U.S. Army flight standards. The flight physical examination will be given as soon as possible to prevent cancellation of training because of physical non-qualification. References and forms are available at https://aamaweb. usaama.rucker.amedd.army.mil/.

(d) Host nation waivers for medically disqualifying conditions will be reviewed by the U.S. Army Aviation School and the USAAMA.

(e) Upon the IMS's arrival at the U.S. Army training location, a U.S. DOD flight surgeon will review Aeromedical Electronic Resource Online and all examinations/applicable waivers prior to completing a DA Form 4186 and prior to the IMS participation in actual aerial flight.

(f) If a new disqualifying defect is discovered upon arrival to the U.S. Army training location, the IMS will undergo the necessary evaluations for requesting the new medical waiver/exception to policy through the appropriate U.S. Army Aviation Waiver Authority. The parent nation is responsible for the costs per established agreements. The medical examination/aeromedical summary will be referred from the DOD flight surgeon to the Director, USAAA (MCXY–AER), Building 301, Fort Rucker, AL 36362–5377, for advice, recommendation for waiver/exception to policy approval. Waiver approval authority for IMS will be in accordance with AR 40–501, chapter 6–20*a*, Commander, Human Resource Command (TAPC–PLA), 200 Stovall Street, Hoffman Building, Room 3N25, Alexandria, VA 22332–0413. Temporary up-slips (DA Form 4186) may be given pending receipt of the waiver per the aeromedical policy letters. For further questions or requests status please contact the Chief, Flight Physical Review and Disposition, by phone (334–255–7430/7575, DSN 558 or e-mail: flight_physical_review_and_disposition@usaama.amedd.army.mil.

b. Cardiovascular screening.

(1) All IMS age 40 and older and required to participate in mandatory physical fitness training and testing will undergo a cardiovascular screening (CVS) as a component of their predeparture examination. The CVS consists of a fasting blood sugar test; a fasting lipid profile, including total cholesterol, low density lipoprotein, high density lipoprotein, and triglycerides; and an electrocardiogram with results posted on DD Form 2808 Item #73 and attach a copy of the laboratory results. A smoking history, if applicable, will be recorded on DD Form 2807–1, section 30.

(2) If countries do not have the capability of performing a CVS during the predeparture examination, the CVS will be performed at country expense at the school location requiring mandatory physical fitness participation.

(3) The school(s) requiring PT participation and testing will forward the IMS medical packet to the local medical authority for review. The IMS may take part in physical training, to include diagnostic physical fitness tests, unless profiled or contra-indications to exercise exist. The IMS will not take part in a physical fitness test for record until cleared by the local U.S. medical authorities.

c. Certain courses, such as flight, special operations, airborne, and ranger have medical requirements in addition to those in the routine examination required for all IMS. The Security Cooperation Organization should check the course requirements in Training Management System to determine what is needed to attend each course.

Section III
Department of the Navy (United States Navy, United States Marine Corps, and the United States Coast Guard)

8–22. References
Additional references for the Department of the Navy are listed in appendix A.

8–23. Ship transfers and foreign vessel overhaul
If IMS of foreign naval ships being overhauled use messing and berthing facilities at U.S. Navy activities ashore, the local U.S. Navy authority concerned will ensure that such IMS are medically screened. IMS of foreign ships undergoing overhaul who receive training at USN activities during the overhaul period will also be medically screened. The activity accomplishing the medical examinations will endorse the ITO to the effect that a physical examination was conducted in accordance with this regulation. Reimbursement for the medical examination will be in accordance with the ITO.

8–24. High risk training
a. Aviation training. The Security Cooperation Organization must ensure that the required medical examination, medical records and laboratory test accompany the IMS in the sealed medical packet. USN aviation program physical standards are determined by USN in coordination with the parent nation. Some medical conditions may exist that are within the country's physical standards, yet may or may not be waived under the USN standards. The USN retains authority to determine permanent medical disqualification from USN aviation programs. The USN in coordination with the country is responsible for determination of temporary flying disabilities exceeding 30 days. Periodic examinations will be conducted according to USN procedures.

(1) *Undergraduate flight training.* All undergraduate flight training begins at the Naval Aviation Schools Command, Pensacola, FL, where all aviation students must pass an additional rigorous medical examination performed by USN designated medical officers at the Naval Operational Medical Institute. Cost of this examination and any treatment required to meet course medical prerequisites will be paid by the country. IMS must be prepared to pass a physical readiness test and a swim test in accordance with standards as outlined in the Navy International Training Catalog.

(2) *Graduate flight training.* The Security Cooperation Organization must ensure the required medical examination,

medical records, laboratory test and country Flight Physical, in English, are included in the sealed medical packet. The local U.S. Medical Treatment Facility flight surgeon shall prepare Aeromedical Clearance Form NAVMED 6410/2 (Clearance Novice (Aeromedical)) based on the statement of medical fitness for flying duties issued by the foreign country and any additional medical examinations required to meet USN physical standards. Pre-existing conditions waived by the country will be accepted unless the condition represents a risk to safety of flight. If there is progression of the IMS existing medical condition, USN medical standards apply regarding fitness to perform flight duty and remain in effect when in the United States.

(3) *New medical conditions.* If a new medical condition arises (for example, illness or injury), the military flight surgeon providing routine care will determine the IMS fitness to fly based on USN aviation medical regulations and procedures. Conditions with potential waiver implications shall be handled in accordance with paragraph 8–26, below.

(a) Temporary flying disabilities likely to exceed 30 days and conditions likely to lead to permanent aeromedical disqualification should be referred to the country via the command of record, Chief of Naval Air Training and Naval Education and Training Security Assistance Field Activity.

(b) The IMS who develop new medical problems and are determined not to be within established USN aviation standards that can be waived, may request a waiver of physical standards. Waivers will be routed via the command of record, Chief of Naval Air Training and Naval Education and Training Security Assistance Field Activity.

(c) The IMS that develop new medical problems that are determined not to be within established USN aviation standards, when waivers are not granted, will have this condition reported, by the attending flight surgeon. This notification shall be routed via the command of record, Chief of Naval Air Training and Naval Education and Training Security Assistance Field Activity.

(d) Medical conditions that develop or are discovered that are within the USN physical standards but may pose a risk to safety of flight will be referred to Chief of Naval Air Training and Naval Education and Training Security Assistance Field Activity for resolution or disposition.

(4) *Medical delays.* The IMS who experience significant medical delays shall be managed in accordance with existing Naval Training Command (NATRACOM) directives regarding medical surveillance of any student who experiences medical delay.

(5) *Anthropometrics.* IMS shall receive anthropometric codes prior to aerial training to ensure anthropometric compatibility in accordance with Naval Air Instruction 3710.9C for all planned phases of flight training to be conducted.

(6) *Conflicting directives.* For IMS for which specific MOAs exist between the United States and home country that conflict with this directive, the MOA shall take precedence.

b. Basic underwater demolition seal training. The basic underwater demolition seal course is the most physiologically challenging course offered in the maritime environment and has the highest attrition rate. All candidates must have a Diver/Bud/S Medical Screening Questionnaire prepared and signed by a competent medical authority in advance of training and included in the sealed medical packet. Copy of the questionnaire can be found at http://www.disam. dsca.mil/itm/. If additional medical examination/test is required the cost will be paid by the country.

c. Diver training. All candidates must have a Diver/Bud/S Medical Screening Questionnaire prepared and signed by a competent medical authority in advance of training and included in the sealed medical packet. Copy of the questionnaire can be found at http://www.disam.dsca.mil/itm/. If additional medical examination/test is required the cost will be paid by the country.

d. Explosive ordinance disposal training. Medical examination requirements can be found at http://www.disam.dsca. mil/itm/functional/hlth_affairs. IMS must have this medical examination prior to reporting for training. A copy of the examination and all required medical/laboratory test will be included in the sealed medical packet. If additional medical examination/test is required the cost will be paid by the country.

e. Mountain warfare training (high altitude). Medical examinations for the courses at the Marine Corps Mountain Warfare Training Center must include additional medical screenings when indicated in the course descriptions in the Marine Corps Desktop Guide for sickle cell traits and the enzyme deficiency G6PD. These medical screenings must be completed prior to arriving at the Mountain Warfare Training Center.

f. Reconnaissance training. Students must have normal color and visual acuity, and be medically qualified and free of any cold, upper respiratory, ear, nose, or skin disorders, or any other disorders that would preclude participation in prolonged salt water training.

g. Examination availability. If the country does not have the capability to perform the required medical examinations for high risk training, the Security Cooperation Organization must arrange to have the IMS examined at the closest U.S. medical facility. Cost of transportation and examination will be borne by the country.

8–25. Hospitalization/serious medical incident notification procedures

a. Notification of hospitalization/serious medical incident for Navy IMS and dependents will be sent to Naval Education and Training Security Assistance Field Activity with information copies to Navy IPO, BUMED, DSCA, the Combatant Command, the Security Cooperation Organization and others, as appropriate.

b. Notification of hospitalization/serious medical incident for USMC IMS and dependents will be sent to Security

Cooperation Education and Training Center, in accordance with current Marine Corps Serious Incident Report (SIR) procedures, with information copies to Navy IPO, BUMED, Naval Education and Training Security Assistance Field Activity, DSCA, the Combatant Command, the Security Cooperation Organization and others as appropriate.

c. Notification of hospitalization/serious medical incident for USCG IMS and dependents will be sent to G–CI. Upon receipt, G–CI will disseminate to Navy IPO, DSCA, DOS, the Combatant Command, the Security Cooperation Organization and others, as appropriate.

8–26. Waiver request
Navy IPO is the waiver approval authority. Requests for medical waivers will be sent to Navy IPO Training Policy Officer with a copy to the appropriate Military Service. Navy IPO will coordinate with BUMED and Military Service prior to granting or disapproving a waiver request. Requests for medical waivers for the USCG will be coordinated on a case-by-case basis by USCG International Affairs (G–CI). Requests for medical waivers for USMC will be coordinated on a case-by-case basis with Security Cooperation Education and Training Center.

8–27. Reimbursement procedures
a. USG-funded IMS and FMS IMS and dependents whose care/medical examination is charged to the FMS Case.

(1) Request for reimbursement for care/medical examination received in DOD medical activities will be sent to Commanding Officer (Code N–8), Naval Education and Training Security Assistance Field Activity, 250 Dallas Street, Suite B, Pensacola, FL 32508–5269. Invoices will be accompanied by a complete ITO. IMSO who have an IMS in USCG training programs who receives care from a USCG medical facility must coordinate with their respective location to ensure that medical billings are sent to USCG International Affairs (G–CI) for processing. Billings must contain student name, country, WCN, date of treatment, and Medical Expense and Performance Reporting System code and total cost.

(2) Request for reimbursement for care/medical examination received in Civilian medical activities will be sent through the IMS to Commanding Officer (Code N–8), Naval Education and Training Security Assistance Field Activity, 250 Dallas Street, Suite B, Pensacola, FL 32508–5269. The bill with completed NAVMED Form 2161 (Referral for Civilian Care), will be accompanied by a complete ITO. For IMS in USCG training programs, invoices should be sent to USCG International Affairs (G–CI). A copy of the civilian healthcare invoice, a statement of non-availability and a copy of the ITO must be forwarded to USCG International Affairs (G–CI). The IMSO will describe the circumstances on the NAVMED Form 2161 when the civilian care is required during an Field Studies Program event.

b. When healthcare (for either IMS or dependent) is the responsibility of the foreign government; care/medical examination received in DOD and civilian medical facilities, bills will be sent directly to the cognizant Embassy in Washington DC. The IMSO will provide the healthcare provider with a copy of the IMS ITO and address of the appropriate embassy if it does not appear on the ITO.

c. When healthcare (for either IMS or dependent) is covered by health insurance, DOD and civilian medical facilities will bill the insurance company directly.

Section IV
Department of the Air Force

8–28. References (http://www.e-publishing.af.mil)
Additional references for the Department of the Air Force are listed in appendix A.

8–29. Billing procedures
Billing procedures are identified in the individual's ITO, item #12. If the ITO states payment is to be made under the FMS case, then send the bill to the Military Service sponsoring the individual. For the Air Force, the address is Air Force Security Assistance Training Squadron/FM 315 J Street West, Randolph AFB, TX 78150–4302, in accordance with AFH 41–114.

8–30. Medical reports
Medical reports per paragraph 8–7 and 8–8 will be forwarded to the Air Force Security Assistance Training Squadron country program manager at the Air Force Security Assistance Training Squadron/FM 315 J Street West, Randolph AFB, TX 78150–4302, and info copy SAF/International Affairs, 1740 AF Pentagon, Washington, DC 20330–1740. Include the individuals name, grade, service number, home country, diagnosis, prognosis, expected time, and type of disposition, and recommendation on whether return to home country is indicated. If "MINIMIZE" restrictions are in place, send the message priority and note "MINIMIZE CONSIDERED." If the patient is subsequently transferred to their home country, provide a complete set of medical records and ensure the patient's personal effects accompany the individual. Movement is requested by Air Force Security Assistance Training Squadron, not by the Medical Treatment Facility through GPMRC, in accordance with AFH 41–114.

8–31. Physical standard requirements

a. Physical standards of all international students attending Air Force training programs must be in accordance with AFI 48–123.

b. Any student who fails to meet medical standards will be managed in an individual basis by HQ AETC/SG and HQ AETC/International Affairs, who will in turn, coordinate with AF/SG, SAF/International Affairs, as appropriate.

8–32. Unique examination requirements

a. Air Force aviation medical examinations—

(1) IMS who are scheduled for flight training in U.S. Air Force Service schools are required to meet USAF Flight Class I, International Affairs, or II medical standards. (See AFI 48–123 V3, chap 1 and Attachment 4. Also see AFI 48–123 V3, chap 5.)

(2) IMS who have received a current, valid aviator rating in the armed forces of their respective countries will be considered the same as USAF aviators and will be required to pass a Flying Class II medical examination and posses an oral panorex. The Security Cooperation Organization will issue the necessary travel order and fund cite.

b. The predeparture examination should be performed as early as possible to prevent cancellation of training because of physical non-qualification. The examining officer will determine the individual's physical qualification for the flying course. Requests for a waiver will be sent to the HQ AETC/SGP, HQ AETC/SGPS 63 Main Circle, Ste 3 Randolph AFB, TX 78150–4549, DSN 487–3900, Comm (210) 652–3900. (See AFI 48–123 V3, chap 5.)

c. Examination records, DD Form 2807–1 and DD Form 2808 and an oral panorex will be hand carried by the IMS and will accompany the individual throughout aviation training.

d. IMS undergoing physical reexamination in the United States prior to beginning flight training will be required to meet Flying Class II medical standards for flying (See AFI 48–123 V3, chap 1 and attachment 4).

Table 8–2
International military student medical benefits and eligibility

Benefit	Eligibility					
	NATO/PFP SOFA USG-funded programs	NATO/PFP SOFA FMS & PME	NON NATO USG-funded programs	NON NATO FMS & PME	Paramilitary & civilian USG-funded programs	Paramilitary & civilian FMS & PME
Outpatient, direct care	YES See note 1	YES See note 1	YES	YES	NO	NO
Outpatient, emergency	YES See note 1	YES See note 1	YES	YES	YES	YES
Inpatient, direct care	YES	YES	YES	YES	NO	NO
Inpatient, emergency	YES	YES	YES	YES	YES	YES
Immunizations	YES See note 1	YES See note 1	YES	YES	NO	NO
Dental care	YES See note 1	YES See note 1	Emergency only	Emergency only	Emergency only	Emergency only
CHAMPUS TRICARE	NO	NO	NO	NO	NO	NO
Supplemental care	Diagnostic test only	Diagnostic test only	Diagnostic tests only	Diagnostic tests only	NO	NO
Prosthetic devices	YES	YES	NO	NO	NO	NO
Aeromedical evacuation	YES	YES	YES	YES	NO	NO
Reimbursement rate	IMET Rate	Full Reimbursable Rate	IMET Rate	Full Reimbursable Rate	IMET Rate	Full Reimbursable Rate

Notes:

[1] Reimbursement is not required in accordance with the NATO PFP SOFA agreement.

[2] If the country has a Reciprocal Health Care Agreement, the agreement takes precedence in DOD facilities.

[3] Supplemental care purchased/provided by nongovernmental healthcare.

[4] Providers/facilities.

Table 8–3
Authorized dependents medical benefits and eligibility

Benefit	Eligibility		
	NATO/PFP SOFA	NON NATO	Paramilitary and civilian
Outpatient, direct care	YES See note 1	YES	NO
Outpatient, emergency	YES See note 1	YES	YES
Inpatient, direct care	YES	YES	NO
Inpatient, emergency	YES	YES	YES
Immunizations	YES See note 1	YES	NO
Dental Care	Emergency only	Emergency only	Emergency only
Civilian Health and Medical Program of the Uniformed Services/TRICARE Standard	Outpatient care only	NO	NO
Supplemental care	Diagnostic test only	NO	NO
Prosthetic devices	NO	NO	NO
Aeromedical evacuation	YES	YES	NO
Reimbursement rate	Full Reimbursable Rate	Full Reimbursable Rate	Full Reimbursable Rate

Notes:

[1] Reimbursement is not required in accordance with the NATO PFP SOFA agreement.

[2] If the country has Reciprocal Health Care Agreement, the agreement takes precedence in DOD facilities.

[3] Supplemental Care purchased/provided by nongovernmental healthcare.

[4] Providers/facilities.

Table 8–4
Communicable diseases of public significance

The presence of the following diseases makes the individual ineligible to enter the U.S. or obtain a Visa. Waivers will not be granted.

Chancroid
Cholera or suspected cholera
Gonnorhea
Granuloma Inguinal
Hansen's Disease (leprosy), Infectious
HIV Infection
Lymphogranuloma Venereum
Plague
Severe Acute Respiratory Syndrome
Suspected viral hemorrhagic fevers (Lassa, Marburg, Ebola, Congo-Crimean, other not yet isolated or named)
Suspected smallpox
Syphilis, Infectious state
Tuberculosis, infectious state
Yellow Fever

Chapter 9
Invitational Travel Orders

Section I
Preparation and Use

9–1. Purpose
The purpose of this chapter is to provide procedures for the preparation and use of the ITO for IMS trained under security cooperation and other programs administered by the security cooperation community.

9–2. Basic document
An ITO must be issued for every IMS being administered under the security cooperation program and the responsibility for doing this is the singular responsibility of the overseas security assistance office (Security Cooperation Organization). This includes students funded under all of the programs listed in the Joint Security Cooperation Education and Training, paragraph 3–6. The ITO provides recognition of the military status of the IMS and is the controlling document for authorized training terms, conditions, and privileges. The ITO is also the basic document used for accounting purposes. In addition, it provides guidance to the appropriate agencies to determine which support is payable. The Security Cooperation Organization will issue a separately numbered ITO for each IMS: multiple students will not be entered on a single ITO.

9–3. Format
a. The Security Cooperation Organization training manager will prepare each ITO separately using the Training Management System. The letter format ITO that is generated by Training Management System is the only authorized document that will be used for IMS provided training under the provisions of this regulation. The previously used DD Form 2285 (Invitational Travel Order (ITO) for International Military Students (IMS)) is no longer authorized to enter an IMS into training, as there is no provision for the required reporting and tracking of the IMS. The Training Management System generated ITO will not be altered or shortened from that published by use of the Training Management System.

b. A complete explanation of the informational content of the ITO is provided in figure 9–1 of this chapter. Instructions for preparation of an ITO are also provided with user instructions of the Training Management System. Examples of the Training Management System generated ITO are provided in figures 9–2 through 9–5 of this chapter.

c. For training at WHINSEC, IAAFA, Naval Small Craft Instruction and Technical Training School, and other Spanish speaking schools, Security Cooperation Organization training managers may attach a Spanish language translation to the Training Management System published ITO.

Following is the specific paragraph content of the Invitational Travel Order:

Invitational Travel Order (ITO) for International Military Student (IMS)

Note: If the ITO is prepared from data different from that provided by the DSAMS system (data downloaded from the SAN), the following statement will be entered following the above heading, "Note: This ITO was prepared from data different from that provided by the DSAMS system."

1. ITO Number. The ITO number is automatically generated by the Training Management System and uniquely identifies each and every Invitational Travel Order.
    a. Rescinded ITO. If the original ITO is rescinded (as a result of a different IMS being authorized in Item 6 of the ITO), the replacement ITO will carry a "-A, -B, etc." suffix that will distinguish it from the original ITO.
    b. Office Tracking Number. If desired, an SAO defined tracking number can be entered just after the ITO number (in a hidden data field), to assist in office record keeping. This record number will then print out at the bottom of each page with the TMS generation notice and the ITO page number.

2. Country/International Organization. Country name or name of international organization that the IMS comes from. In addition, all ITO for IMS from NATO countries will be identified in this ITO Item with the words "NATO member" following the Country name.

3. Date. The date of the ITO is automatically generated by TMS and is entered when the SAO training manager publishes (generates) the ITO. All dates in the ITO will be entered by TMS in the format, 10-Jan-05.

Note: The ITO Number, Country/International Organization, and Date of the ITO will automatically be entered at the top of each ITO page. The words "TMS Generated Invitational Travel Order" will likewise be entered at the bottom of each ITO page.

ITO Issuance:
    The U.S. Government hereby issues this ITO for the IMS herein named to attend the course(s) of instruction herein   listed, subject to the terms and conditions contained herein, and as may be amended by competent authority. This ITO is the only document that will be used and is valid only for the IMS entering U.S. training under the Foreign Assistance Act of 1961 and the Arms Export Control Act (as amended) or other security cooperation managed program (Reference SAMM Paragraph C10.7).
    Definitions of acronyms and abbreviations contained in this document, and instructions for ITO preparation are provided in the Joint Security Cooperation Education and Training (JSCET) Regulation (NAVIPO Inst XX/AR 12-15/AFI 16-105).
    This computer generated, letter format ITO is authorized in accordance with the Security Assistance Management Manual (SAMM), DoD 5105.38-M, Paragraph C10.10 and JSCET Regulation, Paragraph 9-3.

4. Issuing Security Assistance Organization (SAO).
    a. Name of Organization. SAO organizational name.
    b. Mailing Address. SAO U.S. postal system mailing address.
    c. E-mail Address. The E-mail address of the primary SAO POC for management of the training program.

5. Program Type. Reference SAMM Paragraph C10.7. Enter only the applicable item.
    IMET Program and the IMET case identifier: BN-B-06I
    FMS Case and the FMS case identifier: BN-B-TAQ
    Other Program Type and the case identifier of any other funding program: Counter Terrorism Fellowship Program (CTFP)—BN-B-B06, International Narcotics Control and Law Enforcement (INCLE)—BN-B-INL, Counter-Drug Training Support (CDTS)—BN-B-POT, Aviation Leadership Program (ALP)—BN-D-ALP, FAA Drawdown Authority—BN-B-506, etc.

6. IMS Information.
    a. Name [Surname (all CAPS), First, Middle]. Student's name.
    b. Sex - Male or Female.
    c. Country Service Rank. The actual Country rank.
    d. U.S. Equivalent Rank/Pay Grade. Corresponding U.S. pay grade and Officer/Enlisted, etc.

Figure 9–1. Invitational travel order

e. Country Service. The military service to which the student belongs.
f. Country Service Number. The student's Country service number.
g. Date of Birth. Student's date of birth.
h. Place of Birth. City or province/district and Country of birth.
i. Passport Number. IMS current passport number or NATO Identification Number.
j. Country of Citizenship. IMS current country of citizenship.
k. Visa Number. IMS visa control number.
l. Visa Type. IMS visa type.

7. Invitation. The Secretary of (Applicable U.S. MILDEP)_____ invites the IMS listed in Item 6 of this Order, to proceed on or about (Report Date)_____ from (Debarkation point)_____ to (Training Location)_____ for the purpose of commencing training listed in Item 8 of this Order.

8. Authorized Training. Separate paragraph for each authorized course with the following: content:
a. WCN. Worksheet control number for training line and the WCN authorization code.
b. Training Line Action ID. This code is intended for MILSVC use only, it informs the DSAMS system if the SAO entries are based on other than data provided via the DSAMS system.
c. MASL ID. MASL identification number.
d. Course Title. MILDEP short title for the course.
e. Military Service Course Number. The military service's course number.
f. Training Activity or School. Name of the training activity or school.
g. Training Location. Actual location of the training activity.
h. Report Date. Date by which the student is to arrive for training.
i. End Date. The expected date of course completion.

9. Funding. Only used when IMET or other specific authority for funding living allowance and /or travel has been received. Enter only the applicable item.
a. Fund Cite. Up to five fund cites entered for Army implemented training. Air Force fund cite is followed by a Not to Exceed dollar amount (NTE: $X)
b. Navy Fund Cite and Standard Document Number. Up to five Navy Standard Document Numbers entered when Navy implemented training.
c. RTS Travel Order Number. Reserve Travel System (RTS) entered for Air Force implemented training.

10. Language Prerequisites. Enter only the applicable items.
a. Highest Required ECL. Highest required ECL of courses IMS will attend.
b. IMS Completed In-country English Language Testing as follows:
(1) Exam Number. DLIELC assigned ECL test number, Oral Proficiency Interview, or TOEFL test number.
(2) Date Completed. Date of test.
(3) Test Score. Score of above test.
c. Waiver of In-country English Language Testing by authority of. Referenced document that exempts student from in-country testing (annual test exemption message).
d. IMS is Exempt from all English Language Testing by authority of. Referenced document that exempts country from all English language testing (annual test exemption message).

11. Security and Student Screening. Enter a. and applicable b. or c. item.
a. In accordance with JSCET Paragraph 10-38, screening has been accomplished by Country and U.S. Embassy personnel for IMS listed in Item 6 of this Order. This entry must appear on all ITO, or IMS may not be sent to U.S. for training.
b. U.S. security requirements have been complied with. All training will be conducted on an unclassified basis.
c. U.S. security requirements have been complied with. The home government has granted the IMS a security clearance. This of itself does not permit the disclosure of classified U.S. information. Such disclosure must be specifically authorized by an official delegated authority and U.S. foreign disclosure regulations or directives.
(1) The highest U.S. classification level required for scheduled training is _____.
(2) The U.S. equivalent classification level of the security classification granted by the home government is _____.

Figure 9-1. Invitational travel order-Continued

12. Conditions.
    a. Dependents (are/are not)_____ authorized by U.S. authority to accompany or join the IMS while in training. Dependents are not authorized to be transported or subsisted at U.S. Government expense. Only the following authorized dependents will be issued the U.S. DOD/Uniformed Services Identification and Privilege Card.

Accompanying Dependents:
Name   Relationship   Date of Birth   Passport No.   Visa No. and Type

    b. Medical Services. Enter only the applicable items.
        (1) International Military Student.
        (a) IMS under IMET.
        1. NATO/PFP SOFA IMS. Charges for DOD inpatient care and civilian healthcare in the U.S. are chargeable to the IMETP and will be forwarded to the appropriate MILDEP for processing.
        2. NON NATO IMS. Charges for outpatient and inpatient care, immunizations, and medical examinations are chargeable to the IMETP and will be forwarded to the appropriate MILDEP for processing.
        3. RHCA. Healthcare in DOD facilities is provided under the Reciprocal Healthcare Agreement. Reimbursement for DOD services provided is not required. Healthcare not covered by the RHCA is chargeable to the IMETP and will be forwarded to the appropriate MILDEP for processing.
        (b) IMS under FMS.
        1. FMS Case for NATO/PFP SOFA IMS. Charges for inpatient care in the U.S. are chargeable to the FMS Case and will be forwarded to the appropriate MILDEP for processing.
        2. FMS Case for NON NATO IMS. Charges for outpatient and inpatient care, immunizations, and medical examinations are chargeable to the FMS Case and will be forwarded to the appropriate MILDEP for processing.
        3. Health Insurance for NATO/PFP SOFA IMS. IMS has acquired qualifying health insurance for inpatient care covering the entire period he/she will be present in the U.S. for scheduled training. Health insurance information:
            a. [Policy Number]
            b. [Insurance Company]
            c. [Insurance Company Address]
            d. [Insurance Company Telephone Number]
        4. Health Insurance for Non NATO IMS. IMS has acquired qualifying health insurance for outpatient and inpatient care, immunizations, and medical examinations covering the entire period he/she will be present in the U.S. for scheduled training. Health insurance information:
            a. [Policy Number]
            b. [Insurance Company]
            c. [Insurance Company Address]
            d. [Insurance Company Telephone Number]
        5. Foreign Government pays for NATO/PFP SOFA IMS.
            a. IMS is required to first pay the charges for DOD inpatient care and civilian healthcare, then obtain reimbursement from his/her country. In case the individual has returned to his country or is not capable of paying for healthcare cost, the bill incurred should be sent to the following for payment: [Billing Address]
            b. DOD inpatient care and civilian healthcare bills should be sent to the following for payment: [Billing Address]
        6. Foreign Government pays for Non NATO IMS.
            a. IMS is required to first pay the charges for outpatient and inpatient care, immunizations, and medical examinations and obtain reimbursement from his/her country. In case the individual has returned to his country or is not capable of paying for healthcare cost, the bill incurred should be sent to the following for payment: [Billing Address]
            b. Outpatient and inpatient care, immunizations, and medical examination healthcare bills should be sent to the following for payment: [Billing Address]
        7. RHCA.
            a. Healthcare in DOD facilities is provided under the Reciprocal Healthcare Agreement. Reimbursement for DOD services provided is not required. Healthcare not covered by the RHCA will be paid by the Foreign Government. Bills will be sent to the following for payment: [Billing Address]

Figure 9–1. Invitational travel order–Continued

b. Healthcare in DOD facilities is provided under the Reciprocal Healthcare Agreement. Reimbursement for DOD services provided is not required. IMS has acquired qualifying health Insurance to cover healthcare not covered by the RHCA for the entire period he/she will be present in the U.S. for scheduled training. Health insurance information:

    (1) [Policy Number]
    (2) [Insurance Company]
    (3) [Insurance Company Address]
    (4) [Insurance Company Telephone Number]

(c) IMS under Other Grant Programs. For the various other grant training programs (CTFP, INL, Counter Drug, 506 Draw Down, etc.), this paragraph applies to all. The TMS program will automatically insert the correct funding program when preparing the Invitational Travel Order. The user merely makes the applicable selection from the following (CTFP is used as the example program):

1. NATO/PFP SOFA IMS. Charges for DOD inpatient care is at the IMET rate. Charges for DOD inpatient care and all civilian healthcare in the U.S. are chargeable to the CTFP and will be forwarded to the appropriate MILDEP for processing.

2. NON NATO IMS. Charges for outpatient and inpatient care, immunizations, and medical examinations are chargeable to the CTFP at the IMET rate and will be forwarded to the appropriate MILDEP for processing.

3. RHCA. Healthcare in DOD facilities is provided under the Reciprocal Healthcare Agreement. Reimbursement for DOD services provided is not required. Healthcare not covered by the RHCA is chargeable to the CTFP and will be forwarded to the appropriate MILDEP for processing.

(d) Medical Examinations. To be entered automatically on all ITO.

1. Medical examination, to include HIV Test, was completed on (medical screening date) _____. Program requirements have been complied with.

2. The IMS listed on this ITO is presently in the United States for reasons other than the SCETP. The training being conducted under this ITO is incidental to the primary purpose of this person's stay in the United States. Accordingly, further medical screening is not required.

(2) Dependents.

(a) NATO/PFP SOFA Authorized Accompanying Dependents.

1. Health Insurance. Charges for inpatient care will be collected from dependents health insurance. At the time the IMS ITO was annotated to authorize accompanying family members, IMS provided proof of qualifying health Insurance to the training office. The IMS has been made fully aware that a "lack" of health insurance coverage for accompanying family members, revealed at anytime during training, could result in the student's removal from scheduled training and return to country. Health insurance information:

    a. [Policy Number]
    b. [Insurance Company]
    c. [Insurance Company Address]
    d. [Insurance Company Telephone Number]

2. Foreign Government. Charges for inpatient care will be collected from the Foreign Government.

a. IMS is required to first pay the charges for healthcare and obtain reimbursement from his/her country. In case the individual has returned to his country or is not capable of paying for healthcare cost, the bill incurred should be sent to the following for payment: [Billing Address]

b. Healthcare bills should be sent to the following for payment: [Billing Address]

3. FMS Case. Charges for inpatient care are chargeable to the FMS Case and will be forwarded to the appropriate MILDEP for processing.

4. RHCA. Healthcare in DOD facilities is provided under the Reciprocal Healthcare Agreement. Reimbursement for DOD services provided is not required.

a. Healthcare not covered by the RHCA will be paid by the Foreign Government. Bills will be sent to the following for payment: [Billing Address]

b. IMS has acquired Qualifying Health Insurance to cover healthcare not covered by the RHCA for the entire period he/she will be present in the U.S. for scheduled training. Health insurance information:

    (1) [Policy Number]
    (2) [Insurance Company]
    (3) [Insurance Company Address]
    (4) [Insurance Company Telephone Number]

(b) Non NATO Authorized Accompanying Dependents.

1. Health Insurance. Charges for outpatient and inpatient care will be collected from dependents health insurance. At the time the IMS ITO was annotated to authorize accompanying family members, IMS provided proof of

Figure 9–1. Invitational travel order–Continued

qualifying health Insurance to the training office. The IMS has been made fully aware that a "lack" of health insurance coverage for accompanying family members, revealed at anytime during training, could result in the student's removal from scheduled training and return to country. Health insurance information:

    a. [Policy Number]
    b. [Insurance Company]
    c. [Insurance Company Address]
    d. [Insurance Company Telephone Number]

  2. Foreign Government. Charges for outpatient and inpatient care will be collected from the Foreign Government.

    a. IMS is required to first pay the charges for healthcare and obtain reimbursement from his/her country. In case the individual has returned to his country or is not capable of paying for healthcare cost, the bill incurred should be sent to the following for payment: [Billing Address]

    b. Healthcare bills should be sent to the following for payment: [Billing Address]

  3. FMS Case. Charges for outpatient and inpatient care are chargeable to the FMS Case at the FMS rate and will be forwarded to the appropriate MILDEP for processing.

  4. RHCA. Healthcare in DOD facilities is provided under the Reciprocal Healthcare Agreement. Reimbursement for DOD services provided is not required.

    a. Healthcare not covered by the RHCA will be paid by the Foreign Government. Bills will be sent to the following for payment: [Billing Address]

    b. IMS has acquired Qualifying Health Insurance to cover healthcare not covered by the RHCA for the entire period he/she will be present in the U.S. for scheduled training. Health insurance information:

      (1) [Policy Number]
      (2) [Insurance Company]
      (3) [Insurance Company Address]
      (4) [Insurance Company Telephone Number]

    c. Participation in Hazardous Duty. Enter only the applicable item.

      (1) IMS is authorized to participate in hazardous duty training.

      (2) IMS is parachute qualified and authorized to participate in jumps from U.S. aircraft.

      (3) Qualified IMS are authorized to participate in flights as air crew members. The Government of (home Country)_____ certifies that IMS is physically, professionally, and administratively qualified to participate in flights in his country's military aircraft as (flight crew position)_____. IMS meets medical clearance requirement as specified by the appropriate U.S. MILDEP flight qualification records accompanying the IMS.

    d. Physical Fitness Training. Participation in physical fitness training (is/is not)_____ required. Check TMS MASL Course Description, International Notes and Prerequisites for prerequisite physical fitness requirements.

    e. Leave. Enter only the applicable entries.

      (1) Upon completion of training, IMS is not authorized leave, and will proceed immediately as directed to home country.

      (2) Upon completion of training, IMS is authorized (number)_____ days leave at no cost to the U.S. government. Upon completion of leave, IMS will proceed immediately to home country or as directed by competent authority.

    f. Living Allowances. Enter only the applicable item.

      (1) Living allowance is responsibility of the foreign government.

      (2) Living allowance is authorized during period covered by this order, from day of departure from, to day of return arrival in home country, excluding period covered by leave, in accordance with SAMM Table C10.T3, and is chargeable to the fund cite in Item 9 of this Order.

      (3) Living allowance is authorized from day of departure from, to day of return arrival in (Country other than Home Country)_____, excluding periods covered by leave, in accordance with SAMM Table C10.T3, and is chargeable to the fund cite in Item 9 of this Order.

      (4) Living allowance is authorized from day of departure from the CONUS entry port to day of return arrival at the CONUS departure point, excluding periods covered by leave, in accordance with SAMM Table C10.T3, and is chargeable to the fund cite in Item 9 of this Order.

      (5) Living allowance is authorized while in training status only, in accordance with SAMM, Table C10.T3, and is chargeable to the fund cite in Item 9 of this Order.

      (6) See Item 15, "Special Conditions/Remarks".

Figure 9–1. Invitational travel order–Continued

g. Travel. Enter only the applicable item.
 (1) Travel is responsibility of the foreign government.
 (2) Travel covered by this order, overseas and CONUS, is chargeable to the fund cite in Item 9 of this Order.
 (3) Travel to and return from (Country other than Home Country)_____ is the responsibility of the foreign government. Travel from (Country other than Home Country)_____ to CONUS and return is chargeable to the fund cite in Item 9 of this Order.
 (4) Travel to CONUS and return is responsibility of the foreign government. Travel within CONUS is chargeable to the fund cite in Item 9 of this order.
 (5) IMS has been issued one way ticket to (Training Location)_____. Cost of OCONUS travel chargeable to fund cite in Item 9 of this Order, is ($)_____; Government transportation request (GTR NO.) is_____. Last training installation will arrange return transportation to home country.
 (6) See Item 15, "Special Conditions/Remarks".
 h. Travel by POV. IMS (is/is not)_____ authorized to travel by POV.
 i. Baggage. Enter only the applicable item.
 (1) No baggage will be transported at U.S. government expense.

Note: Baggage allowances outlined below are total allowances: excess baggage being that amount between the baggage permitted by the transportation carrier and that stipulated below. Baggage sizes and dimensions will conform to carrier stipulations. These allowances apply for that portion of travel whose costs are paid from U.S. funds (See Paragraph 12.g above) and cost of authorized excess baggage is chargeable to the fund cite in Item 9 of this Order.
 (2) Training less than 12 weeks in total duration: IMS authorized 2 pieces, not to exceed 50 pounds (22.6 kilograms) each.
 (3) Training is 12 to 23 weeks in total duration: IMS authorized 3 pieces not to exceed 50 pounds (22.6 kilograms) each. (One piece of excess baggage is authorized.)
 (4) Training is 24 to 35 weeks in total duration: IMS authorized 4 pieces not to exceed 50 pounds (22.6 kilograms) each. (Two pieces of excess baggage are authorized.)
 (5) Training 36 weeks or more in total duration: IMS authorized 5 pieces, not to exceed 50 pounds (22.6 kilograms) each. (Three pieces of excess baggage are authorized.)
 (6) In addition to above allowances, IMS attending the Professional Military Education, graduate, and postgraduate programs listed in SAMM Table C10.T3--Note (7), with authorized accompanying dependents (Item 12 this Order) or IMS attending flight training are authorized one additional piece of baggage (six pieces of checked baggage/four pieces of excess baggage).

13. Terms. All of following will be entered in each ITO.
 a. Prior to departure from home country, the IMS and dependents listed herein are required to be medically examined and found physically acceptable in accordance with the health provisions of the Immigration and Nationality Act (8 USC 1182(A)(1)-(7); Public Health Service, Department of Health and Human Services, 42 CFR Part 34, Medical Examination of Aliens, and 42 CFR Part 71, Foreign Quarantine; applicable U.S. MILDEP regulations; and other U.S. laws or DOD directives and regulations which may be enacted from time to time.
 b. The home country will ensure that the IMS has sufficient funds in United States dollar instruments to meet all expenses while in route to, and for the first 30 days of training pending receipt of applicable pay and allowances by the IMS.
 c. IMS will be responsible for custodial fees and personal debts incurred by self or family members. IMS unable to meet these financial obligations may be withdrawn from training and returned to home country.
 d. The IMS will bring adequate uniforms and work clothing for field duty or technical work. U.S. fatigue uniforms and foot wear will be purchased by the IMS in the event that the country work uniforms are inadequate. When flying training is involved, required special flight clothing and individual equipment will accompany the IMS, or provisions will be made by the home country or the IMS to obtain the use of all necessary equipment prior to start of training. The IMS will also possess adequate civilian clothing for off-duty wear.
 e. The Government of the United States is responsible for IMS travel which is part of the training program and for which costs are part of the course tuition.
 f. The IMS will comply with all applicable U.S. Military Service regulations.

Figure 9–1. Invitational travel order–Continued

g. The United States may cancel training and return to country IMS who violate U.S. law or Military Service regulation or who are found otherwise unsatisfactory. The IMS government will be alerted to such action in accordance with U.S. MILDEP regulations.

h. The Government of the United States disclaims any liability or financial responsibility for injuries received by the IMS listed herein while in transit to and from the training installation, while under going training or while in leave status, and any liability or financial responsibility for personal injury claims or property damage claims resulting from the IMS action.

i. The IMS will participate in flights of U.S. military aircraft as required for scheduled course(s) or as specified in U.S. MILDEP regulations.

j. The acceptance of this order by the host country constitutes agreement that an IMET funded student will be utilized, upon return to the host country, in the skills for which he was trained for a period of time sufficient to warrant the expense to the U.S. Government, in accordance with the SAMM, Chapter 10.

14. Implementing Authority.
    a. MILDEP Authorization No. Number provided via MILDEP automated system.
    b. Date. Date of MILDEP authorization.

15. Special Conditions / Remarks. SAO training manager may enter any additional clarifying information that pertains to IMS and the specific country. In addition, TMS program will enter regulatory direction, such as required medical statements.

16. Distribution. Required distribution from the MILDEP unique sections of Chapter 9.

17. ITO Authorization.
    a. Signature of U.S. Authority Authenticating Orders.
    b. Title.

Figure 9–1. Invitational travel order–Continued

Parameters for this sample ITO: IMET funded travel and living allowance, accompanying dependents authorized, dependents healthcare funded by medical insurance.

INVITATIONAL TRAVEL ORDER (ITO) FOR INTERNATIONAL MILITARY STUDENT

1. ITO Number: BN05B11005   2. Country/International Organization: BANDARIA
3. Date: 02-May-05

   The U.S. Government hereby issues this ITO for the IMS herein named to attend the course(s) of instruction herein   listed, subject to the terms and conditions contained herein, and as may be amended by competent authority. This ITO is the only document that will be used and is valid only for the IMS entering U.S. training under the Foreign Assistance Act of 1961 and the Arms Export Control Act (as amended) or other security cooperation managed program (Reference SAMM Paragraph C10.7).
   Definitions of acronyms and abbreviations contained in this document, and instructions for ITO preparation are provided in the Joint Security Cooperation Education and Training (JSCET) Regulation (SECNAVINST 4950.4A/AR 12-15/AFI 16-105).
   This computer generated, letter format ITO is authorized in accordance with the Security Assistance Management Manual (SAMM), DoD 5105.38-M, Paragraph C10.10 and JSCET Regulation, Paragraph 9-3.

4. Issuing Security Assistance Organization (SAO):
       a. Name of Organization: Office of Defense Cooperation (ODC)
       b. Mailing Address: Unit 4095-PSC 80
                                 APO AE 09765-1005
       c. E-mail Address: jsmith@san.osd.mil

5. Program Type: IMET 05

6. IMS Information:
       a. Name: VULKE, Hadin
       b. Sex: Male
       c. Country Service Rank.: Commandante
       d. U.S. Equivalent Rank/Pay grade: OFF-O4
       e. Country Service: Army
       f. Country Service No: OF100096
       g. Date of Birth: 10-Jan-58
       h. Place of Birth: Harare, BANDARIA
       i. Passport No: BL3829567
       j. Citizenship: Bandaria
       k. Visa No: 20012060350002
       l. Visa Type: A2

7. Invitation: The Secretary of the Department of the Army invites the IMS listed in Item 6 of this Order, to proceed on or about 25-May-05 from BANDARIA to FT LEE VA 23801-1705 for the purpose of commencing training listed in Item 8 of this Order.

8. Authorized Training: No additional training to that specified in this order will be provided.
       a. WCN: 1005A   MASL: B159000   TITLE: INTERNATIONAL OFF LOG PREP
       Military Service Course No: ALMC-IL   School: USA LOGISTICS MANAGEMENT
       COLLEGE   Location: FT LEE VA 23801-1705   Report Date: 25-May-05
       End Date: 11-Jun-05
       b. WCN: 1005B   MASL: B171545   TITLE: COMBINED LOG CPT CAREER
       Military Service Course No: 8-10-C22-LO School: USA LOGISTICS
       MANAGEMENT   COLLEGE   Location: FT LEE VA 23801-1705
       Report Date: 12-Jun-05   End Date: 02-Aug-05
       c. WCN: 1005C   MASL: B171360   TITLE: COMBINED LOG CCC-QM
       Military Service Course No: 8-10-C22-LO   School: US ARMY QM CNT &
       SCHOOL   Location: FT LEE VA 23801-1509   Report Date: 04-Aug-05
       End Date: 10-Sep-05
       d. WCN: 1005D   MASL: B171546   TITLE: COMBINED LOG CPT CAREER
       Military Service Course No: 8-10-C22-LO School: USA LOGISTICS MANAGEMENT
       COLLEGE   Location: FT LEE VA 23801-1705   Report Date: 12-Sep-05
       End Date: 28-Oct-05

Figure 9–2. Sample Training Management System generated ITO for IMET-funded training

9. Funding: Army Fund Cite 4563-45UY-36300226 564 000 346ER 4567

10. Language Prerequisites:
    a. Highest Required ECL: 75SA
    b.   IMS completed the in-country English language testing as follows:
        Exam No: 361   Date Completed: 01-Apr-05   Score: 77

11. Security and Student Screening:
    a. In accordance with JSCET Paragraph 10-38, screening has been accomplished by Country and U.S. Embassy personnel for IMS listed in Item 6 of this Order.
    b. U.S. security requirements have been complied with. The home government has granted the IMS a security clearance. This of itself does not permit the disclosure of classified U.S. information. Such disclosure must be specifically authorized by an official delegated authority and U.S. foreign disclosure regulations or directives.
       (1) The highest U.S. classification level required for scheduled training is Secret.
       (2) The U.S. equivalent classification level of the security classification granted by the home government is Secret.

12. Conditions:
    a. Dependents: Dependents are authorized by U.S. authority to accompany the IMS or join the IMS while in training. Dependents are not authorized to be transported or subsisted at U.S. Government expense. Only the following authorized dependents will be issued the U.S. DOD/Uniformed Services Identification and Privilege Card.
        Accompanying Dependents:

Name	Relation	DOB	Passport No.	Visa No. and Type	
Ms. Marta VULKE	Wife	01-Feb-60	YC8253036	20012060350003	A2
Fatima VULKE	Daughter	14-Jan-93	XC4859319	20012060350004	A2

    b. Medical Services:
       IMS: Charges for outpatient and inpatient care, immunizations, and medical examinations are chargeable to the IMETP and will be forwarded to the appropriate MILDEP for processing.
       Dependents: Charges for outpatient and inpatient care will be collected from dependents health insurance. At the time the IMS ITO was annotated to authorize accompanying family members, IMS provided proof of qualifying health insurance to the training office. The IMS has been made fully aware that a "lack" of health insurance coverage for accompanying family members, revealed at anytime during training, could result in the student's removal from scheduled training and return to country. Health insurance information:
          Policy No: WW 1289075
          International Health Insurance Worldwide
          B.P. 3032
          Geneva Switzerland 20569-2654
          Tel No: 011-52-2-365-9870
          Singular Conditions: See item 15, "Special Conditions."
    c. Participation in Hazardous Duty: IMS is authorized to participate in hazardous duty training.
    d. Physical Fitness Training: Participation in physical fitness training is required.
    e. Leave: Upon completion of training, IMS is authorized 15 days leave at no cost to the U.S. Government. Upon completion of leave, IMS will proceed immediately to home country or as directed by competent authority.
    f. Living Allowance: Living allowance is authorized during the period covered by this order, from the day of departure from, to the day of return arrival in home country, excluding period covered by leave, in accordance with SAMM Table C10.T3, and is chargeable to the fund cite in Item 9 of this Order.
    g. Travel: Travel covered by this order, overseas and CONUS, is chargeable to the fund cite in Item 9 of this Order.
    h. Travel by POV: IMS is authorized to travel by POV.
    i. Baggage: Baggage allowances outlined below are total allowances; excess being the difference between the baggage permitted by the transportation carrier and that stipulated below. Baggage sizes and dimensions will conform to carrier stipulations. These allowances apply for that portion of travel whose costs are paid from U.S. funds (see Item 12.g) and cost of authorized excess baggage is chargeable to the fund cite in Item 9 of this Order. Training less than 22 weeks in total duration: IMS authorized 3 pieces, not to exceed 50 pounds (22.6 kilograms) each.

Figure 9–2. Sample Training Management System generated ITO for IMET-funded training–Continued

13. Terms:
   a. Prior to departure from home country, the IMS and dependents listed herein are required to be medically examined and found physically acceptable in accordance with the health provisions of the Immigration and Nationality Act (8 USC 1182(A)(1)-(7); Public Health Service, department of Health and Human Services, 42 CFR Part 34, Medical Examination of Aliens, and 42 CFR Part 71, Foreign Quarantine; applicable U.S. MILDEP regulations; and other U.S. laws or DOD directives and regulations which may be enacted from time to time.
   b. The home country will ensure that the IMS has sufficient funds in United States dollar instruments to meet all expenses while in route to, and for the first 30 days of training pending receipt of applicable pay and allowances by the IMS.
   c. IMS will be responsible for custodial fees and personal debts incurred by self or family members. IMS unable to meet these financial obligations may be withdrawn from training and returned to home country.
   d. The IMS will bring adequate uniforms and work clothing for field duty or technical work. U.S. fatigue uniforms and foot wear will be purchased by the IMS in the event that the country work uniforms are inadequate. when flying training is involved, required special flight clothing and individual equipment will accompany the IMS, or provisions will be made by the home country or the IMS to obtain the use of all necessary equipment prior to start of training. The IMS will also possess adequate civilian clothing for off-duty wear.
   e. The Government of the United States is responsible for IMS travel which is part of the training program and for which costs are part of the course tuition.
   f. The IMS will comply with all applicable U.S. Military Service regulations.
   g. The United States may cancel training and return to country IMS who violate U.S. law or Military Service regulation or who are found otherwise unsatisfactory. The IMS government will be alerted to such action in accordance with U.S. MILDEP regulations.
   h. The Government of the United States disclaims any liability or financial responsibility for injuries received by the IMS listed herein while in transit to and from the training installation, while under going training or while in leave status, and any liability or financial responsibility for personal injury claims or property damage claims resulting from the IMS action.
   i. The IMS will participate in flights of U.S. military aircraft as required for scheduled course(s) or as specified in U.S. MILDEP regulations.
   j. The acceptance of this order by the host country constitutes agreement that an IMET funded student will be utilized, upon return to the host country, in the skills for which he was trained for a period of time sufficient to warrant the expense to the U.S. Government, in accordance with the SAMM, Chapter 10.

14. Implementing Authority:
      MILDEP Authorization No: 2105   Date: 25-Apr-05

15. Special Conditions/Remarks:
   a. IMS must report 3 days in advance of normal report date due to limited transportation availability.
   b. The Defense Attache', Embassy of Bandaria, Washington DC has administrative control over all personnel of the Armed Forces of Bandaria.
   c. Leave in excess of 15 days from graduation date is not authorized and training activity is not authorized to change specification in Item 12.e of this Order.
   d. Upon return from training, IMS will report to ODC-Bandaria when notified, for debriefing, processing of travel voucher, and issuance of instructional materials.
      MEDICAL EXAM: Medical examination, to include HIV Test, was completed on 05-Apr-05. Program requirements have been complied with.

      MEDICAL COVERAGE: At the time the ITO was annotated to authorize accompanying family members, said IMS provided proof of qualifying medical insurance to the SAO Training Office. The IMS has been made fully aware that a "lack" of medical insurance coverage for accompanying family members, revealed at any time during CONUS training could result in the IMS removal from scheduled CONUS training and return to country.

Figure 9-2. Sample Training Management System generated ITO for IMET-funded training—Continued

16. Distribution:
       5 - International Student
       2 - SATFA
       1 - Health Services Command
       1 - Bandarian Embassy
       1 - Training Activity IMSO   USA LOGISTICS MANAGEMENT COLLEGE
                                           FT LEE VA 23801-1705
                                           US ARMY QM CTR & SCHOOL
                                           FT LEE VA 23801-1509

17. ITO Authorization:
   a. Signature of U.S. Authority Authenticating Orders: John C. Smith, MAJOR US
Army
    b. Title: Training Officer

Figure 9–2. Sample Training Management System generated ITO for IMET-funded training–Continued

Parameters for this sample Amendment: IMS has been promoted to Lieutenant Colonel – O5.

                                                                        17-Aug-05
TO: MAJ VULKE, Hadin, WCN 1005, Country Service No. OF100096
FROM: Office of Defense Cooperation (ODC)
        Bandaria

SUBJECT: Invitational Travel Order - BN05B11005, Amendment Number 1, BANDARIA

   1. Subject order is amended to read as follows:
        Section: 06.c. Country Service Rank:
        Amend to Read As: Lieutenant Colonel, O-5

                                     John C. Smith, MAJOR US Army
                                     Training Officer

Distribution:
5 - International Student
2 - SATFA
1 - Health Services Command
1 - Bandarian Embassy
1 - Training Activity IMSO   USA LOGISTICS MANAGEMENT COLLEGE
                                    FT LEE VA 23801-1705
                                    US ARMY QM CNT & SCHOOL
                                    FT LEE VA 23801-1509

Figure 9–3. Sample Training Management System generated amendment for ITO

Parameters for this endorsement: IMS has been paid IMET living allowance from date of departure from home country through 11 Jun 05.

12-Jun-05

FROM: International Military Student Office (IMSO)
       Attn: LMC/ISD
       US Army Logistics Management College
       Ft Lee VA 23978

SUBJECT: Invitational Travel Order - BN05B11005, BANDARIA, 2 May 05

1. Following individual has been paid authorized IMET living allowance from 23 May 05 (date of departure from Bandaria) through 11 Jun 05: Major Hadin VULKE, OF100096, Bandaria.

2. Funding program: IMET, 2005, Army, WCN 1005.

Mr. Joseph Ready
International Military Student Officer
Ft Lee VA 23801-1705

Distribution:
5 - International Student
2 - SATFA
1 - Health Services Command
1 - Bandarian Embassy
1 - Training Activity IMSO

USA LOGISTICS MANAGEMENT COLLEGE
FT LEE VA 23801-1705
US ARMY QM CNT & SCHOOL
FT LEE VA 23801-1509

Figure 9–4. Sample endorsement for ITO

Parameters for this ITO: Country funds travel and living allowance, accompanying dependents not authorized, IMS healthcare funded by FMS case.

INVITATIONAL TRAVEL ORDER (ITO) FOR INTERNATIONAL MILITARY STUDENT

1. ITO Number: BNTOCBF1005   2. Country/International Organization: BANDARIA
3. Date: 02-May-05

   The U.S. Government hereby issues this ITO for the IMS herein named to attend the course(s) of instruction herein listed, subject to the terms and conditions contained herein, and as may be amended by competent authority. This ITO is the only document that will be used and is valid only for the IMS entering U.S. training under the Foreign Assistance Act of 1961 and the Arms Export Control Act (as amended) or other security cooperation managed program (Reference SAMM Paragraph C10.7).
   Definitions of acronyms and abbreviations contained in this document, and instructions for ITO preparation are provided in the Joint Security Cooperation Education and Training (JSCET) Regulation (SECNAVINST 4950.4A/AR 12-15/AFI 16-105).
   This computer generated, letter format ITO is authorized in accordance with the Security Assistance Management Manual (SAMM), DoD 5105.38-M, Paragraph C10.10 and JSCET Regulation, Paragraph 9-3.

4. Issuing Security Assistance Organization (SAO):
   a. Name of Organization: Office of Defense Cooperation (ODC)
   b. Mailing Address: Unit 4095-PSC 80
                             APO AE 09765-1005
   c. E-mail Address: jsmith@san.osd.mil

5. Program Type: FMS BN-B-TOC

6. IMS Information:
        a. Name: VULKE, Hadin
        b. Sex: Male
        c. Country Service Rank.: Commandante
        d. U.S. Equivalent Rank/Pay grade: OFF-O4
        e. Country Service: Army
        f. Country Service No: OF100096
        g. Date of Birth: 10-Jan-58
        h. Place of Birth: Harare, BANDARIA
        i. Passport No: BL3829567
        j. Citizenship: Bandaria
        k. Visa No: 20012060350002
        l. Visa Type: A2

7. Invitation: The Secretary of the Department of the Army invites the IMS listed in Item 6 of this Order, to proceed on or about 25-May-05 from BANDARIA to FT LEE VA 23801-1705 for the purpose of commencing training listed in Item 8 of this Order.

8. Authorized Training: No additional training to that specified in this order will be provided.
        a. WCN: 1005A   MASL: B159000   TITLE: INTERNATIONAL OFF LOG PREP
        Military Service Course No: ALMC-IL   School: USA LOGISTICS MANAGEMENT
        COLLEGE   Location: FT LEE VA 23801-1705   Report Date: 25-May-05
        End Date: 11-Jun-05
        b. WCN: 1005B   MASL: B171545   TITLE: COMBINED LOG CPT CAREER
        Military Service Course No: 8-10-C22-LO School: USA LOGISTICS MANAGEMENT
        COLLEGE   Location: FT LEE VA 23801-1705   Report Date: 12-Jun-05
        End Date: 02-Aug-05
        c. WCN: 1005C   MASL: B171360   TITLE: COMBINED LOG CCC-QM
        Military Service Course No: 8-10-C22-LO   School: US ARMY QM CNT &
        SCHOOL   Location: FT LEE VA 23801-1509   Report Date: 04-Aug-05
        End Date: 10-Sep-05
        d. WCN: 1005D   MASL: B171546   TITLE: COMBINED LOG CPT CAREER
        Military Service Course No: 8-10-C22-LO School: USA LOGISTICS MANAGEMENT
        COLLEGE   Location: FT LEE VA 23801-1705   Report Date: 12-Sep-05
        End Date: 28-Oct-05

Figure 9–5. Sample Training Management System Generated ITO for FMS-funded Training

9. Funding: Not Applicable

10. Language Prerequisites:
    a. Highest Required ECL: 75SA
    b. IMS completed the in-country English language testing as follows:
       Exam No: 361   Date Completed: 01-Apr-05   Score: 77

11. Security and Student Screening:
 a. In accordance with JSCET Paragraph 10-38, screening has been accomplished by Country and U.S. Embassy personnel for IMS listed in Item 6 of this Order.
 b. U.S. security requirements have been complied with. The home government has granted the IMS a security clearance. This of itself does not permit the disclosure of classified U.S. information. Such disclosure must be specifically authorized by an official delegated authority and U.S. foreign disclosure regulations or directives.
     (1) The highest U.S. classification level required for scheduled training is Secret.
     (2) The U.S. equivalent classification level of the security classification granted by the home government is Secret.

12. Conditions:
 a. Dependents: Not Applicable
 b. Medical Services:
    IMS: Charges for outpatient and inpatient care, immunizations, and medical examinations are chargeable to the FMS Case and will be forwarded to the appropriate MILDEP for processing.
    Dependents: Not Applicable
    Singular Conditions: See item 15, "Special Conditions."
 c. Participation in Hazardous Duty: IMS is authorized to participate in hazadous duty training.
 d. Physical Fitness Training: Participation in physical fitness training is required.
 e. Leave: Upon completion of training, IMS is authorized 15 days leave at no cost to the U.S. Government. Upon completion of leave, IMS will proceed immediately to home country or as directed by competent authority.
 f. Living Allowance: Not Applicable
 g. Travel: Not Applicable
 h. Travel by POV: IMS is authorized to travel by POV.
 i. Baggage: Not Applicable

13. Terms:
 a. Prior to departure from home country, the IMS and dependents listed herein are required to be medically examined and found physically acceptable in accordance with the health provisions of the Immigration and Nationality Act (8 USC 1182(A)(1)-(7); Public Health Service, department of Health and Human Services, 42 CFR Part 34, Medical Examination of Aliens, and 42 CFR Part 71, Foreign Quarantine; applicable U.S. MILDEP regulations; and other U.S. laws or DOD directives and regulations which may be enacted from time to time.
 b. The home country will ensure that the IMS has sufficient funds in United States dollar instruments to meet all expenses while in route to, and for the first 30 days of training pending receipt of applicable pay and allowances by the IMS.
 c. IMS will be responsible for custodial fees and personal debts incurred by self or family members. IMS unable to meet these financial obligations may be withdrawn from training and returned to home country.
 d. The IMS will bring adequate uniforms and work clothing for field duty or technical work. U.S. fatigue uniforms and foot wear will be purchased by the IMS in the event that the country work uniforms are inadequate. When flying training is involved, required special flight clothing and individual equipment will accompany the IMS, or provisions will be made by the home country or the IMS to obtain the use of all necessary equipment prior to start of training. The IMS will also possess adequate civilian clothing for off-duty wear.
 e. The Government of the United States is responsible for IMS travel which is part of the training program and for which costs are part of the course tuition.
 f. The IMS will comply with all applicable U.S. Military Service regulations.
 g. The United States may cancel training and return to country IMS who violate U.S. law or Military Service regulation or who are found otherwise unsatisfactory. The IMS government will be alerted to such action in accordance with U.S. MILDEP regulations.
 h. The Government of the United States disclaims any liability or financial responsibility for injuries received by the IMS listed herein while in transit

Figure 9–5. Sample Training Management System Generated ITO for FMS-funded Training–Continued

to and from the training installation, while under going training or while in leave status, and any liability or financial responsibility for personal injury claims or property damage claims resulting from the IMS action.

i. The IMS will participate in flights of U.S. military aircraft as required for scheduled course(s) or as specified in U.S. MILDEP regulations.

j. The acceptance of this order by the host country constitutes agreement that an IMET funded student will be utilized, upon return to the host country, in the skills for which he was trained for a period of time sufficient to warrant the expense to the U.S. Government, in accordance with the SAMM, Chapter 10.

14. Implementing Authority:
 MILDEP Authorization No: 2106   Date: 25-Apr-05

15. Special Conditions/Remarks:
 a. IMS must report 3 days in advance of normal report date due to limited transportation availability.
 b. The Defense Attache', Embassy of Bandaria, Washington DC has administrative control over all personnel of the Armed Forces of Bandaria.
 c. Leave in excess of 15 days from graduation date is not authorized and training activity is not authorized to change specification in Item 12.e of this Order.
 d. Upon return from training, IMS will report to ODC-Bandaria when notified, for debriefing, processing of travel voucher, and issuance of instructional materials.
 MEDICAL EXAM: Medical examination, to include HIV Test, was completed on 05-Apr-05. Program requirements have been complied with.

16. Distribution:
    5 - International Student
    2 - SATFA
    1 - Health Services Command
    1 - Bandarian Embassy
    1 - Training Activity IMSO   USA LOGISTICS MANAGEMENT COLLEGE
                                        FT LEE VA 23801-1705
                                        US ARMY QM CTR & SCHOOL
                                        FT LEE VA 23801-1509

17. ITO Authorization:
 a. Signature of U.S. Authority Authenticating Orders: John C. Smith, MAJOR US Army
 b. Title: Training Officer

Figure 9–5. Sample Training Management System Generated ITO for FMS-funded Training–Continued

Amendment parameters: IMS has been granted permission to have dependent wife join him while in training.

1-Jul-05

TO: MAJ VULKE, Hadin, WCN 1005, Country Service No. OF100096
FROM: Office of Defense Cooperation (ODC)
      Bandaria

SUBJECT: Invitational Travel Order - BNTOCBF1005, Amendment Number 1, BANDARIA

1. Subject order is amended to read as follows:
   Section: <u>12.a. Dependents:</u>
   Amend to Read As: Dependents are authorized by U.S. authority to join the IMS while in training. Dependents are not authorized to be transported or subsisted at U.S. Government expense. Only the following authorized dependents will be issued the U.S. DOD/Uniformed Services Identification and Privilege Card.
      Accompanying Dependents:
      Name-- MS. Marta VULKE
      Relation-- wife
      Date of Birth-- 1 Feb 60
      Passport No-- YC8253036
      Visa No. and Type--20012060350003   A2

   Section: <u>12.b. Medical Services: Dependents:</u>
   Amend to Read As: Health Insurance. At the time the IMS ITO was annotated to authorize accompanying family members, IMS provided proof of Qualifying Health Insurance to the Training Office. The IMS has been made fully aware that a "lack" of Health Insurance coverage for accompanying family members, revealed at anytime during training, could result in the student's removal from scheduled training and return to country. Health insurance information:
      Policy No: WW 1289075
      International Health Insurance worldwide
      B.P. 3032
      Geneva Switzerland 205659-2654
      Tel No: 011-52-2-365-9870

John C. Smith, MAJOR US Army
Training Officer

Distribution:
5 - International Student
2 - SATFA
1 - Health Services Command
1 - Bandarian Embassy
1 - Training Activity IMSO

USA LOGISTICS MANAGEMENT COLLEGE
FT LEE VA 23801-1705
US ARMY QM CNT & SCHOOL
FT LEE VA 23801-1509

Figure 9–6. Sample Training Management System Generated Amendment for ITO in figure 9–5

9–4. Original invitational travel order and copies

a. A signed original of the ITO will be considered by the training installation as final authorization for admission of the IMS named therein to the courses listed in paragraph 8 of the ITO. If an IMS arrives at a training installation without a signed original, the training installation will notify its MILDEP international training agency and will not enter the IMS into training until approval is received. It is emphasized that each IMS must have in their possession the original ITO, bearing an original signature and not a facsimile. Certain U.S. commands and activities will not disburse funds on a document bearing non-original signature.

b. If determined that the original ITO of the IMS was lost, a copy of the ITO may be certified as an original by adding in paragraph 15 of the ITO the following certification: "I certify that my original ITO was lost and that if the original is located later, no further claims will be submitted on the basis of recurrent copy of orders. If the original is located, it will be returned by direct mail to the appropriate Service." This certification must be signed by the IMS with their name and rank listed in full.

9–5. Distribution

a. The IMS scheduled for training will report with the original ITO and the following copies in their possession:

(1) IMS reporting to DLIELC as first training installation–15 copies.

(2) Direct entry IMS–5 copies.

b. The ITO distribution is automated through use of the IMSO training web on the Security Assistance Network. The Military Service sections of this chapter provide any other required distribution. The ITO will be prepared and distribution made at least 2 weeks (4 weeks if accompanied) before the IMS scheduled arrival at the first training installation.

c. In the event that an IMSO office does not exist at a training activity or installation and, therefore, is not using the automated IMSO training Web, the ITO may be distributed via e-mail attachment or conventional mail to the training activity.

d. If copies of the ITO are not available 2 weeks before the first training report date, the first training installation will query the Security Cooperation Organization concerned on the status of the student and the ITO.

e. Distribution, by activity, will be listed in item 16 of the ITO. A local distribution formula (such as "DIST A") will not be used.

9–6. Amendments

When an ITO has been published using the Training Management System, any subsequent change to the ITO must be done by publishing an amendment to the ITO. The ITO and ITO amendment data is then uploaded to the Security Assistance Network from the Training Management System.

a. All ITO amendments will be prepared separately by the Security Cooperation Organization training manager using the Training Management System. Thus, using the Training Management System, all amendments will be identified and linked to the original ITO. Amendments will no longer be published by the IMSO at the training activity.

b. For routine administrative issues, the IMSO may contact the Security Cooperation Organization directly and request that an ITO be amended. The Military Service country program manager should be provided an information copy.

c. The Military Service country program manager must direct the Security Cooperation Organization to amend the ITO whenever there is a cost impact on the training program, such as a change in training duration. Upon receipt of conclusive written evidence of the promotion of an IMS while in training, the Military Service training agency must contact the Security Cooperation Organization to amend the ITO to reflect the IMS change in rank. Conclusive evidence is defined as notification from the Security Cooperation Organization, the IMS attaché in Washington, DC, or the CLO. Evidence may also be received from a staff maintained by a foreign government in the United States for administering training in CONUS.

d. An ITO amendment will not be used to replace a specific student on a previously issued ITO. The Military Service training agency will rescind the original ITO by directing the preparation of an ITO amendment that rescinds the ITO. And the Military Service will then direct preparation of a completely new ITO with a different ITO number for the new student who is to attend the training.

e. Examples of Training Management System generated ITO amendments are provided in figures 9–3 and 9–6.

9–7. Endorsements

a. An endorsement is a written record of actions that have been accomplished for or to an IMS. ITO is to be endorsed upon the issuance of transportation requests and meal tickets. They will also be endorsed upon payment of a living allowance (from and to dates), change of training installation, and issuance and return of the U.S. DOD/ Uniformed Services Identification and Privilege Card. Certificates or endorsements indicating that Government quarters and subsistence were or were not available will be provided and affixed by appropriate commanding officers, designated representatives, or the IMSO. Appropriate authorities at each training installation will endorse the original of the ITO showing dates and times of arrival and departure and the mode of transportation.

(1) An ITO endorsement will be prepared separately by the IMSO using the Security Assistance Network IMSO training Web. Headings will contain as a minimum the following data:

(a) Name of organization and official address of publishing activity.

(b) Original ITO number and date.

(c) Rank/grade and name (surname (all capitals), first, middle) of IMS.

(d) Country.

(2) Program type and WCN.

(a) For IMET IMS, indicate IMET FY and WCN.

(b) For FMS IMS, indicate FMS case identifier and WCN.

(c) For other program types, enter the case identifier.

b. All ITO endorsements will be signed by an authorized representative with the same distribution as that in paragraph 16 of the ITO. IMSO will provide IMS with 5 copies of the endorsement. Distribution via e-mail attachment is authorized.

c. Example of IMSO training web generated ITO endorsement is provided in figure 9–4.

9–8. Authorized training
Schools and training activities are only authorized to provide the training that is listed in paragraph 8 of the ITO. Additional training can only be provided by the training activity upon receipt from an Security Cooperation Organization of a properly authorized ITO amendment. Only through this process can the training installation be sure that the training has been authorized by the Military Service, has been funded, and that disclosure authority has been issued.

9–9. Security and screening of student
a. Screening of the student's background by the country and U.S. Embassy personnel in accordance with the SAMM, paragraph C10.3.4 and Joint Security Cooperation Education and Training, paragraph 10–38 must be accomplished before the ITO can be published or officially distributed.

b. Compliance with security requirements will be indicated by the statement of training classification in accordance with Joint Security Cooperation Education and Training paragraph 10–8 in item 11 of the ITO. The ITO document itself will not be classified on the basis of these statements.

c. U.S. training installations will not train the IMS until the above security requirements are met. If the appropriate classification is not entered in paragraph 11 of the ITO, the training installation will contact the Military Service country program manager for compliance. The statement of country security clearance as stated in the ITO only specifies the level of security clearance of the IMS as granted by their government.

9–10. Appropriation citation
a. An IMET funded ITO will cite the appropriation to which travel, living allowance, and other authorized expenses are chargeable if appropriate. These fund cites are the responsibility of the appropriate Military Service and are provided as a data element to the Training Management System. If for any reason the appropriation citation is not provided as a data element, it is important that the manual entry be accurately cited in paragraph 9 of the ITO. If DSCA has authorized funding of travel and or living allowances from an Foreign Military Financing Program funded FMS case, include fund cite provided by the Service in paragraph 9 of the ITO. Likewise for all other grant assistance programs where funding of travel and or living allowances is authorized, the fund cite provided by the Military Service will be entered in paragraph 9 of the ITO.

b. An ITO for cash funded FMS cases, does not contain fund cites, as all expenses are the responsibility of the purchasing country. However, if an FMS case is funded by U.S. grant funds (such as Foreign Military Financing Program funds) there will be an appropriation citation on the ITO and the travel and living allowance, and other authorized expenses will be funded by that fund citation.

9–11. Dependents
Dependents (as defined in Joint Security Cooperation Education and Training, para 10–9.b.(12)) accompanying or joining the IMS must be authorized in the ITO to be eligible for privileges: for example, identification (ID) cards, exchange and commissary privileges, and medical services. If dependents are authorized, their names, relationships, dates of birth, passport numbers and visa type and number will be listed in paragraph 1–2a of the ITO.

9–12. Medical care
Medical care to international military students and their authorized dependents is not free, rather it is provided on a reimbursable basis. The only exceptions to this are outpatient care for NATO/PFP SOFA countries and healthcare authorized under a reciprocal healthcare agreement. Only ITO authorized medical care can be provided to the IMS and authorized dependents. All medical activity patient administrators/treasurer offices must be provided a copy of the ITO to insure that appropriate billing is accomplished in accordance with ITO content.

Section II
Department of the Army

9–13. General
a. Foreign military sales. On receipt of a signed LOA, obligation authority from DFAS–DE, and letter of instruction from USASAC, SATFA will provide the Security Cooperation Organization authority to release the ITO for FMS IMS.

b. International Military Education and Training. As funds are received from DSCA, SATFA will issue authorization for the ITO. Request for authorization prior to receipt of fund cite message will be addressed to SATFA country program manager.

9–14. Distribution

a. The ITO for IMS under U.S. Army sponsorship for CONUS training will be distributed electronically to individuals/organizations as shown, below.

(1) Each IMS.

(2) SATFA country program manager.

(3) Commanders of CONUS MSCs other than TRADOC (that is, FORSCOM) conducting the training, as appropriate.

(4) IMSO at each U.S. Army Service school, installation, and/or Army managed DOD entity at which the IMS will be training.

(5) Commander, U.S. Army Medical Command.

(6) Government of country concerned and its Washington Embassy.

(7) Other addressees - as considered appropriate by the issuing authority.

(8) For distinguished visitor orientation tour and OT only, NDU Operations.

(9) For AWC, ILE, and USASMA only, add DASA (DE&C) (SAAL–NP).

b. In addition to appropriate distribution, the Security Cooperation Organization will be provided a copy of all endorsements prepared by other agencies.

Section III
Department of the Navy (U.S. Navy, U.S. Marine Corps, and U.S. Coast Guard)

9–15. Invitational travel orders authority

a. Foreign military sales training. On receipt of appropriate funding authority, Naval Education and Training Security Assistance Field Activity will provide the Security Cooperation Organization with authority to publish ITO for USN, USMC, and USCG IMS. When a new FMS training LOA is implemented, Naval Education and Training Security Assistance Field Activity will issue a message providing authority to issue ITO. This authority will continue throughout the scope of the case. If the FMS LOA includes funds for TLA, a fund cite to be included on the ITO will be provided with this message. This fund cite will be included on all ITO throughout the scope of the FMS case. Naval Education and Training Security Assistance Field Activity will authorize all amendments to ITO for USN sponsored training. CG, Security Cooperation Education and Training Center MCCDC will authorize all amendments to ITO for USMC sponsored training, and USCG International Affairs (G–CI) will authorize all amendments to ITO and for USCG sponsored training. Security Cooperation Organization are responsible for preparing the amendments to the ITO.

b. International Military Education and Training funding. Naval Education and Training Security Assistance Field Activity has financial oversight for all DON IMET programs, regardless of whether training is under USN, USMC, or USCG. On receipt of appropriate funding authority, Naval Education and Training Security Assistance Field Activity will send messages throughout the FY, providing authority to issue the ITO for each individual IMS/WCN which is annotated as "Priority A." If TLA is authorized, this message will also provide the fund cite to be included on the ITO. Naval Education and Training Security Assistance Field Activity will authorize all amendments to ITO for USN sponsored training. CG, Security Cooperation Education and Training Center MCCDC will authorize all amendments to ITO for USMC sponsored training, and USCG International Affairs (G–CI) will authorize all amendments to ITO for USCG sponsored training. The Security Cooperation Organization is responsible for preparing all amendments to the ITO.

c. Regional Defense Regional Defense Combating Terrorism Fellowship Program funding. Naval Education and Training Security Assistance Field Activity provides financial support for all DON training under Regional Defense CTFP, regardless of whether courses are under USN, USMC, or USCG. After candidate vetting has been approved by Special Operations/Low Intensity Conflict and funds have been authorized/provided by DSCA, Naval Education and Training Security Assistance Field Activity will issue a message providing authority to issue the ITO or authorize a Mobile Education Team/MTT and provide funds to the Mobile Education Team/MTT provider. If TLA is authorized, this message will provide the fund cite and other funding information as required to be included on the ITO. Naval Education and Training Security Assistance Field Activity will authorize all amendments to ITO for USN sponsored training. CG, Security Cooperation Education and Training Center MCCDC will authorize all amendments to ITO for USMC sponsored training, and USCG International Affairs (G–CI) will authorize all amendments to ITO and for USCG sponsored training. The Security Cooperation Organization is responsible for preparing all amendments to the ITO.

d. Counter-Narcotics Program. Under the Counter-Narcotics program, DASD–CN issues authority to release funding to either Naval Education and Training Security Assistance Field Activity or USCG G–CI. Upon receipt of funding, a message will be issued providing authority to issue the ITO or authorize the Mobile Education Team/MTT and provide funds to the Mobile Education Team/MTT provider. Naval Education and Training Security Assistance Field Activity will authorize all amendments to ITO for USN sponsored training. USCG International Affairs (G–CI) will authorize all amendments to ITO and for USCG sponsored training. The Security Cooperation Organization is responsible for preparing all amendments to the ITO.

9–16. Distribution

The distribution list of an ITO and amendments should be tailored to the training listed therein and include the IMS, Naval Education and Training Security Assistance Field Activity, commanders of combatant commands, CG, Security Cooperation Education and Training Center MCCDC for IMS if attending any USMC courses, USCG International Affairs (G–CI) if IMS is attending any USCG courses, appropriate SYSCOM if IMS is attending SYSCOM training, CFFC if IMS is attending Commander, Fleet Forces Command training, COMPACFLT if IMS is attending any Commander, Pacific Fleet training, BUMED if IMS is attending any Bureau of Medicine training, DLIELC if IMS is attending English language training and the IMSO at each of the training sites.

Section IV
Invitational Travel Orders (Department of the Air Force)

9–17. General

On receipt of appropriate funding authority, the Air Force Security Assistance Training Squadron will provide the Security Cooperation Organization with authority to publish ITO. Security Cooperation Organization will not use the STL programming document as the basis to publish ITO.

9–18. Invitational travel orders amendments

The ITO amendments to reflect changes should be accomplished as soon as data becomes known and sent via e-mail attachment to the Air Force Security Assistance Training Squadron/FM, Randolph AFB, TX 78150–5001, to facilitate recording of obligations and financial payments against the ITO.

9–19. Distribution

The ITO for IMS under U.S. Air Force sponsorship will be distributed as shown in table 9–1.

Table 9–1
Air Force distribution guide for invitational travel order

Recipient	CONUS and overseas training	Number of copies
Air Force Security Assistance Training Squadron/ FM (Note 1)		1
Air Force Security Assistance Training Squadron/ Regional Division (Note 1)		1
BASE IMSO		1
IMS (see para 9–5a)		
Country Liaison Officer, if assigned		1
Country Air Attach, Washington, DC		1

Notes:
[1] The Air Force Security Assistance Training Squadron distribution may be mailed under one cover but should be assembled in sets plainly marked for the respective activities.

Chapter 10
International Military Student Administration

Section I
General

10–1. Scope

This chapter outlines procedures for administering IMS under the SCETP. Unless otherwise indicated herein, IMS administration policies and procedures apply to all IMS participating in the SCETP.

10–2. Responsibilities to international military student

In fulfilling the responsibility of the United States to IMS undergoing education and training, all personnel will afford IMS traditional American courtesies. Responsibilities to IMS include not only the obligation to teach a particular skill, but also the fostering of friendly relations by a genuine display of hospitality, interest in their welfare, and personal assistance. Beyond this, a basic rule requires that the IMS be treated, so far as possible, like their U.S. counterparts.

10–3. Unauthorized commitments

Only Military Service representatives engaged in the administration and training of IMS will make any training commitments to individual IMS or foreign country representatives. Further, no agreements will be entered into with regard to curricula, types of training, or length of stay of IMS in the United States. Doubtful situations will be referred to the appropriate Military Service for resolution.

10–4. Channels of communication, international military student officer Web, and correspondence

a. Direct communication between training installations and Security Cooperation Organization is authorized only on routine administrative matters concerning IMS such as ITO, biographical data, and travel arrangements.

b. All matters originating at the training installation that involve policy determinations or program changes will be directed to the implementing Military Service through the chain of command. Any prior commitment for training made to IMS must be in accordance with the policies and procedures contained in this regulation. For all cross-Service and Joint training programs, the Military Service providing the training will communicate through and coordinate with the sponsoring Military Service prior to taking any action to change the training program or to remove the IMS from training. An exception is where safety is an issue. In this case, the IMS will be eliminated from training and the sponsoring Military Service notified.

c. The subject line in message traffic or correspondence should be comprehensive so action officers throughout the Military Service can readily identify the subject and resolve the problem as quickly and smoothly as possible. When communicating about an IMS, the subject line will contain, as a minimum, the IMS name, country, case, WCN, and FY.

d. The combatant command and Security Cooperation Organization will be provided information copies of communication between the Military Service and training installation regarding controversial IMS matters.

Section II
Responsibilities

10–5. Security cooperation officer

a. See paragraph 2–11 for a comprehensive description of the Security Cooperation Organization duties and responsibilities.

b. In regard to international education and training, the Security Cooperation Organization responsibilities include——

(1) Make recommendations concerning Security Cooperation Education and Training for their host country and assist in the development of these programs.

(2) Assist in the selection of IMS and ensure that they meet security, medical, English language, technical qualifications, and course prerequisites, as required.

(3) Ensure IMS are briefed prior to departure from their home country.

(4) Prepare necessary administrative documents and provide appropriate records to the initial training installation.

(5) Obtain feedback from returning IMS concerning the education or training received.

(6) Administer approved programs in country, including Security Cooperation Education and Training Teams.

(7) Prepare ITO and all amendments.

10–6. International military student officer

Each commander or delegated authority will appoint in writing a U.S. military or civilian IMSO during any period the installation is engaged in training (classroom, and equipment, such as simulators) IMS with ITO.

a. Selection. It is extremely important that IMS are received and treated with the proper consideration. Therefore, the commander must exercise care in selecting the IMSO. The IMSO must be tactful and mature, possess a pleasant personality, and have the ability to associate with and understand IMS. The name, office, telephone number, and e-mail address of IMSO will be reported to the Military Service. Changes will be furnished as they occur. Appointment of an overseas IMSO is at the discretion of the overseas command.

b. Functions. In addition to the overall administration of IMS, the IMSO will—

(1) *Keep IMSO Training Web information up to date.* The IMSO Training Web on the Security Assistance Network provides for the entry of IMSO office point of contact information and detailed training location information. This information is entered only by the IMSO (not by the Military Service) and must be kept current by the IMSO. In addition, IMSO can enter specific international notes and prerequisites that pertain to specific courses of instruction at

their training activity. Again, this information is entered by the IMSO and is thus tailored to a need to provide specific information for the international community on their courses.

(2) *Brief IMS.* As a complement to the in-country predeparture briefing, IMSO will also brief IMS as soon as possible after the IMS arrive at the training installation. This briefing will cover items contained in section IV and other information pertaining to the local installation and surrounding community.

(3) *Implement procedures to avoid the indebtedness of IMS to the USG or a nonappropriated fund.* See paragraph 10–31.

(4) *Maintain IMS records.* The IMSO will accurately maintain a complete personnel and training record on each IMS. The IMS will not hand-carry these records or review their contents. The personnel and training record will be established at the first U.S. military training installation. Information such as, but not limited to, that listed below will be filed in chronological sequence of action in the record.

(a) Copy of ITO, amendments, and endorsements.

(b) Application for ID cards for IMS, and for their authorized accompanying dependents; copies of passport, visa, and U.S. Citizenship and Immigration Services (USCIS) Form I–94.

(c) Maintain a copy of the IMS Academic Report.

(d) Record of courses attended.

(e) Any correspondence relating to indebtedness, traffic violations, civil law violations and charges, and similar incidents or actions regardless of action taken. Such collection of documents should indicate the result of each action if available.

(f) Record of individual counseling given the IMS.

(g) Record of DOD Field Studies Program activities in which IMS either participated or were given the opportunity to participate.

(h) Any other documents that would furnish data beneficial to IMSO at subsequent training locations.

(5) *Transmit IMS records.*

(a) The IMSO will forward original IMS personnel and training records to the gaining installation as soon as possible (not later than 10 days) after IMS complete training. Training records will be retained in accordance with Military Service regulations.

(b) Classified notebooks, workbooks, and similar documents developed by IMS will be forwarded to their home service, through the Security Cooperation Organization, using appropriate disclosure release procedures. (See para 10–41.)

(c) Individual flight records may be hand-carried between training installations by IMS or mailed to the gaining installation. The last installation will forward these records to the Security Cooperation Organization after IMS complete training.

(d) Unclassified medical records may be hand-carried between training installations by IMS or mailed to the gaining installation. See paragraph 8–9c.

(6) *Check IMS installation clearance and checkout procedures.* IMSO will ensure that proper installation clearance and checkout processing procedures are followed.

(7) *Plan and conduct Field Studies Program for assigned IMS.* See chapter 11.

c. The IMSO Training and Liaison visits.

(1) The IMSO will attend the DISAM SAM–TO course using quotas allocated by the respective MILDEP. DISAM controls and issues the fund-cite for travel and per diem for attendance at this course.

(2) The MILDEPs will hold conferences/workshops for IMSO and other U.S. persons charged with the training, administration, and orientation of IMS every 18 months or as required. Attendance at conferences of U.S. personnel charged with the training, administration, and orientation of IMS may be charged to the Field Studies Program funds.

(3) The IMSO are encouraged to visit other installations to exchange ideas and information. The cost of travel and per diem for these visits is normally chargeable to administrative funds. IMSO are encouraged to occasionally visit their Military Service Security Cooperation Field Activity and other training activities, as funds will allow, for exchanging ideas and information.

d. Controversial matters. The IMSO will immediately initiate action through Military Service chain of command where unique or controversial situations exist that may be detrimental to IMS successful completion of training.

10–7. Country liaison officer

The Military Service may request that a CLO be certified to a command in the United States to assist with administrative details for IMS from the CLO country. When a CLO is not assigned for a particular country, the country's senior IMS located at the training installation may be used in this capacity.

a. The controlling command will designate the location within the command where the CLO will perform their duties. Assignment at overseas installations will be at the discretion of the appropriate commander.

b. Installation commanders requiring the assistance of a CLO may contact the appropriate command that has a CLO assigned and coordinate visits of CLO to other installations with the commanders concerned. The commander of the installation to be visited will be informed of the following:

(1) Purpose of the CLO visit.

(2) Mode of transportation.

(3) Arrival time.

(4) Names of individuals to be contacted.

c. The CLO may be authorized to travel by POV between training facilities.

d. The CLO, programmed in the USG-funded programs and assigned to administer IMS, are eligible to receive travel and living allowances as authorized by the ITO.

e. The CLO will not be assigned duties that will interfere with their responsibilities to the SCETP. Specifically, CLO will:

(1) Be the contact between the IMSO and the IMS they represent.

(2) Ensure that IMS adhere to appropriate regulations.

(3) Assist in correcting problems associated with dress, personal appearance, grooming standards, and IMS indebtedness.

(4) Be responsible for whatever action is necessary in connection with breaches of discipline involving IMS.

(5) Assist in routine inspections of IMS and quarters.

(6) Act as nonvoting members of a faculty or administrative board as required. Commanders will advise CLO of the time and place of meetings. CLO will inform the commander whether they plan to attend. Requests for CLO participation as nonvoting members of boards will be forwarded to the controlling command.

(7) Assist in administrative details regarding the disposition of graduates and IMS.

(8) Advise the IMSO of any customs and traditions that should be recognized.

(9) Make routine administrative reports as required by their government.

(10) Pay IMS any allowances received from the home country if so directed by their government.

(11) Assist in the orientation of IMS.

(12) The CLO will not be entered into formal training without prior Military Service approval.

(13) The CLO will be handled in the same manner as IMS for medical and dental care. (See chap 8.)

(14) The CLO are subject to the same security restrictions and regulations as those governing IMS.

Section III
Predeparture

10–8. International military student screening, passports, visas, and Department of Defense foreign visit system

a. The Security Cooperation Organization will develop a student-screening checklist which will include the records identified in this paragraph 10–38*a*, and making adjustments to accommodate regional guidance. The Security Cooperation Organization should inform the host country of the required checks. When a country formally submits a student name, this constitutes certification that the required host country-conducted checks have been completed. U.S. Embassy personnel, including the human rights officer, regional security officer, Drug Enforcement Agency, consular section, and other offices as appropriate then thoroughly screen each student candidate. The checklist will include the items below and when completed, the checklist will be included with other documents related to each country nominee and maintained for 10 years. The Security Cooperation Organization can issue the ITO only after the checklist is complete with no disqualifying results.

(1) In-country U.S. officials will screen IMS for records of human rights abuses, drug trafficking, corruption, criminal conduct, or other activities inconsistent with U.S. policy goals. If an individual's reputable character cannot be validated, the individual will not be approved for training.

(2) In-country U.S. officials will perform a security screening of each student prior to issuance of the ITO regardless of the level of classification of the training. The level of security clearance will be shown in item 11 of the ITO by selecting either statement (a) or statement (b) as shown below:

(a) "U.S. security screening has been accomplished. All training will be conducted on an unclassified basis."

(b) "U.S. security requirements have been complied with. The home government has granted the IMS a security clearance. This in and of itself does not permit the disclosure of classified U.S. information. Such disclosure must be specifically authorized by an official delegated authority and U.S. foreign disclosure regulations or directives."

(c) The level of the security classification granted by the home government will be indicated in block 11 (1) of the ITO and the U.S. equivalent classification level will be shown in block 11(2) of the ITO.

b. The foreign government is responsible for issuing necessary passports and for requesting visas for travel to the United States. Passports and visas of IMS and their dependents must be valid for the entire duration of the IMS training period. Security Cooperation Organization will ensure that IMS and dependents have appropriate visas by visually inspecting copies of each for currency and correctness. Candidates who fail to meet the medical requirements of chapter 8 are ineligible to receive a visa or to enter the U.S.

c. The U.S. visa is the authority to travel to the United States during the valid period; it has no relation to the period of stay in the United States. The USCIS will issue Form I–94 to the IMS when they enter the United States. The USCIS Inspector will write a date or "D/S" (duration of status) on the Form I–94. This date, in conjunction with the ITO, forms the documentation that governs the IMS status in the United States. The IMSO at the first training location should verify that the IMS Form I–94 has enough time to complete the training or is marked "D/S." The IMSO should initiate action to extend the date on the Form I–94 if there is insufficient time to complete the planned training.

(1) Visas for the United States are obtained through procedures prescribed by the Department of State. Dependents of NATO Armed Forces personnel are entitled to "NATO–2" visas. Civilian IMS from NATO countries and their dependents are entitled to "NATO–6" visas. IMS from other than NATO countries and their dependents are authorized and will be issued "A–2" visas in most cases. "B" visas are not appropriate for IMS or their dependents.

(2) Visas should contain multiple entry provisions.

(3) Group visas for IMS traveling together should not be obtained. This practice causes complications when the group is divided or when IMS return independently.

(4) The IMS training in CONUS are responsible for finding out from their embassies whether they need in-transit visas while enroute to their home country. When visas are required, IMS should forward their passports and documentation to their embassies early enough to be processed and returned before graduating from the last phase of training.

d. The SECDEF policy requires that all foreign personnel visiting a DOD component shall be screened for terrorist and criminal associations prior to their arrival in the United States, and that their arrival and departure from their assigned duty stations are documented. This documentation is accomplished in the DOD's Foreign Visits System (FVS), a database that captures key information about international personnel and their itinerary as they travel to U.S. military facilities. For IMS under the sponsorship of a SCETP, the data is transferred to the FVS from the Security Assistance Network Training Web after the Security Cooperation Organization enters student information from the ITO. As IMS carry out their training and the Security Assistance Network Training Web is updated by the IMSO, the training status and location of the IMS will be updated in the FVS.

10–9. In-country predeparture briefing

a. In-country predeparture briefing-general.

(1) *Predeparture briefing.* Proper preparation of IMS for U.S. training can create a favorable attitude toward achieving the objectives for which they are being trained. Therefore, a thorough predeparture briefing is essential for each IMS selected for U.S. training.

(2) *Oral predeparture briefing.* Each Security Cooperation Organization will ensure that IMS selected for training at DOD installations receives a thorough oral predeparture briefing. The DISAM CD–ROM predeparture briefing standardizes the information provided to IMS, and covers all topics required in this paragraph. The Security Cooperation Organization should utilize the DISAM predeparture briefing as part of their departure procedures, and supplement with specific training location information listed on the Training Management System and Security Assistance Network Web, as well as their locally prepared information. The predeparture briefing is available in Spanish for IMS enroute to Spanish-speaking schools.

b. In-country predeparture briefing content. The Security Cooperation Organization will ensure that all areas of concern to the IMS and their authorized dependents when authorized on the ITO are covered in the predeparture briefing. Also, each IMS and orientation tour participant will be given an explanation of the Field Studies Program and its objectives before departing for the United States. (See chap 11 for information on the Field Studies Program and its objectives.) The briefing will include the following:

(1) *The Military Service training organization overview.* Give IMS a brief description of the organizational structure of the Military Service to which they will be assigned for training. Emphasize the commands, schools, and geographic locations where IMS will receive training.

(2) *Passports, visas, and DOD FVS.* Inform IMS of their personal responsibility to obtain any required in-transit visas and other passport documentation from their embassies before leaving the last U.S. training installation. Inform IMS that it is important to retain the USCIS Form I–94, which is the authority to enter the United States.

(3) *Travel.* Advise IMS that transportation, when provided at USG expense, is by the mode and routing most advantageous to the USG and that special routing will not be made for individual benefit. The Security Cooperation Organization will explain travel arrangements in detail. IMET IMS must obtain statements verifying any delays at transportation terminals.

(a) Make IMS aware of the different means of transportation that may be required to travel to their training assignments. For example, when traveling by train or air, some inter-Service transportation may be required, such as, taxis or limousines. IMS must use the most direct route and should ask for the cost before departing. Receipts for such services must be retained by the IMS to present to the finance officer making any living allowance or transportation payments.

(b) The IMS entering the United States must present their passports and ITO to the immigration authorities to receive an entry permit. Passport and ITO must be kept on the person at all times while traveling.

(c) Health, immigration, and customs officials are located at the point of entry. For a health inspection, the individual must show the International Certificate of Immunization. Immigration officials will stamp the passport or ITO and issue an entry permit; the customs inspector will require a customs declaration. In this regard, each individual will bring items for personal use only. Merchandise for resale or for gifts is subject to a duty tax.

(4) *Baggage.* Thoroughly explain the baggage policy to each IMS. (See chap 7.) No exception to this policy will be made.

(a) Excess baggage is the weight over that permitted by the carrier and should not exceed the total authorized. See paragraph 7–2b for further information.

(b) The IMS may bring into the United States, duty-free only items required for personal use by themselves or their Families. On their return home, no duties are imposed on necessary personal belongings taken out of the United States. These items, however, may be subject to home-country duties.

(c) Discourage IMS from bringing firearms with them to CONUS. However, when IMS choose to bring ammunition, handguns, shotguns, or rifles for sporting purposes, they will be advised that they are subject to federal, state and local laws and regulations. Compliance is without exception; failure to comply can result in confiscation of firearms by authorities or possible administrative or judicial action.

(d) Checked baggage should not be locked, since it will be subject to inspection. Also, items of value should not be packed in checked baggage.

(e) Advise IMS to mark each item of baggage with the address of their first training installation. Additionally, one copy of the IMS ITO should be placed in each piece of baggage to help locate the owner if the baggage is lost, misrouted, or misplaced.

(5) *Reporting to the training installation.* Advise IMS of the following:

(a) An IMS training at a military installation will usually be met by a representative of the installation at the local airport, rail, or bus station when advance notice of the arrival has been received. If the IMS are not met, they should call the training installation IMSO or duty officer for assistance.

(b) Since IMS reporting to a civilian installation may sometimes not be met, they should be briefed on what action to take in that event. IMS should be provided telephone number of the gaining IMSO or installation POC.

(c) The IMS should be briefed to contact the gaining IMSO if they encounter unexpected travel delays, and provide IMSO with new arrival time and flight numbers if possible.

(6) *Information about the first training installation.* The Security Cooperation Organization should review the Security Assistance Network Web for current information regarding the first training installation, course of instruction, and points of contact. Significant information should be provided to the IMS. In particular, the IMS should be informed that the IMSO will be of great assistance to them. If problems or complaints arise, the IMS should bring them to the IMSO's attention.

(7) *Country liaison officer.* Explain the role of the CLO, a foreign officer in the United States, who will supervise and administer the IMS from their country. See paragraph 10–7. Some of the CLO responsibilities are as follows:

(a) Monitor the IMS adherence to regulations.

(b) Advise the training installation commander of national customs and habits.

(c) Help IMS become acquainted with the installation and the training program.

(d) To take disciplinary action and make disposition of IMS as authorized by their country.

(8) *Clothing.* Advise IMS of the general climatic conditions within the geographic areas where they will be receiving training. Actual clothing requirements will vary depending on the assigned training area; changes in training locations may change the clothing needs of the individual. Clothing requirements for various courses can generally be found on the Security Assistance Network IMSO Web, either as general information for a particular location, or in the course specific section. Advise IMS that they may use DOD clothing sales stores at U.S. military installations. All U.S. insignia must be removed before wearing U.S. military clothing.

(a) The recommended minimum for military clothing is as follows:

1. Two complete winter uniforms and four complete summer uniforms.

2. One raincoat.

3. One winter topcoat or jacket (if appropriate).

4. Two work uniforms (as appropriate).

5. One pair of work shoes (if appropriate).

6. Other necessary items such as dress shoes, socks, underwear, caps, and military insignia.

(b) The requirement for special clothing and equipment for IMS is significant for some courses. This is especially true regarding flying training. The Security Cooperation Organization must determine these requirements well in advance and advise the prospective IMS.

(c) Explain the custom in the United States of military personnel wearing uniforms only during duty hours, although uniforms may be worn at any time.

(d) The IMS should also pack appropriate civilian clothing, including casual clothes for free time, travel, and leave. They should also pack a business suit for official functions, as appropriate.

(9) *Money.* Explain the American monetary system to IMS. This may require considerable explanation depending on the country and the IMS' familiarity with the American monetary system. Make a comparison between expected prices on general commodities and the cost relationship between those items in the IMS' country and the same items in the United States. Also, discuss the following points with the IMS:

(a) The IMS should have in their possession upon entry into the United States sufficient funds to cover expenses for a minimum of 30 days. Point out that banking facilities and travelers checks may be conveniently used during the stay in the United States. Explain the travelers check, personal checking account custom, and credit card use followed by most U.S. personnel. Large amounts of cash should not be carried by the IMS.

(b) All IMS will be concerned with payment procedures; how they will be paid, when they will be paid, how much will be paid them, and whether per diem will be authorized. Security Cooperation Organization should ensure that IMS understand when and how they will be paid during the course of their education or training in the United States. Most countries pay their IMS an allowance in addition to their regular pay; some pay less than the normal allowance. Most IMET IMS will receive a USG living allowance, which is intended to supplement their normal pay and allowances.

(c) When required, IMS will obtain certificates of nonavailability of USG quarters and messing facilities from the training installation. Inform IMS that certificates of non-availability will not be issued if the IMS is accompanied by authorized or unauthorized dependents to a course that does not encourage dependents.

(d) The IMS will keep a complete record of all travel, including dates of arrival and departure at various locations and modes of transportation used. This information is the basis for travel and living allowance payments.

(e) The IMET IMS should always retain copies of vouchers that must be provided to U.S. finance offices making payments against their orders. This is especially true for tour participants for whom no intermediate orders are published to indicate the date they were last paid living allowances. Unless the participants can furnish the last paid voucher to the next finance officer, they will have difficulty in receiving their living allowances. IMS whose governments require a record of payments received must maintain vouchers for that record since training installations cannot furnish the information at a later date.

(10) *Privately-owned vehicle.* When IMS buy POV in the United States, make them aware of ownership responsibilities. As a condition to registration, IMS must purchase public liability and property damage insurance in the amount required by the IMS country or the amount required by U.S. State, or local law, or the training installation, whichever is higher. There are varying requirements among various states. Insurance costs vary, depending upon area and company; however, the IMS should be prepared to pay a substantial amount per year for insurance. The IMS may be required to obtain a U.S. driver's license under state laws. The IMS planning to drive in the United States should bring their international driver's license. An international driver's license will generally facilitate obtaining insurance and installation decals. Although some states will accept a valid driver's license from a foreign country, military installations may require either an international driver's license or a valid U.S. State license in order to drive on the installation. An outline of traffic laws is usually available at the installation security and law enforcement office.

(11) *Standards of conduct.* Advise IMS that they will be required to conduct themselves in a manner that will bring credit to themselves and their country. Standards prescribed for counterpart DOD personnel also apply to IMS. This includes duty hours, off-limit establishments, travel distance limitations, military courtesy, financial responsibility, military bearing, appearance, and hair grooming. IMS are required to abide by U.S. sexual harassment laws and policy. See paragraph 10–46. IMS will maintain these standards; failure to do so or committing an act that would bring discredit to themselves or to their country could result in disenrollment and immediate return to the home country.

(12) *Dependents.*

(a) Definitions of dependents and their eligibilities are governed by Title 10 USC 1072; DODI 1000.1, DODI 1341. 2, and DODD 1441.1. This Joint Security Cooperation Education and Training regulation is subordinate to these statutes, DOD Regulations and Directives, but for the purpose of this regulation, ITO authorized dependents are defined as follows:

1. Some countries may allow legally recognized, nontraditional marriage customs (by U.S. standards), which may include multiple spouses. In the case of multiple spouses, the IMS will have to decide which one or their spouses will be the one spouse authorized on the ITO to be eligible for an ID card and other benefits.

2. Unmarried children or wards under the age of 21, including legitimate, adopted, stepchild, illegitimate child of member, or illegitimate child of spouse. A ward is defined as a person whose care and physical custody has been entrusted to the sponsor by a legal decree or other instrument that a court of law or placement agency. The Security Cooperation Organization will validate the status of wards prior to authorizing the ward as a dependent on ITO.

3. An unmarried child or ward, age 21 years and over, if either a or b apply—

a. The child or ward is enrolled in a full-time course of study at an institution of higher learning and is dependent on the IMS for over one-half of their support.

b. The child or ward is over 21 years of age and is incapable of self-support because of mental or physical incapacity that occurred while a dependent of the IMS before the age of 21.

c. The child or ward is over 21 years old and incapable of self-support because of a mental or physical incapacity that occurred while a dependent of the IMS before the age of 21.

d. Dependent children or wards defined in this paragraph are not eligible for benefits unless they are full time students and are dependent on the IMS for over one-half of their support. In this circumstance, benefits are extended until the child reaches the age of 23.

4. An IMS father, mother, father-in-law, mother-in-law, stepparent, or parent by adoption or ward, if the IMS provides for over 50 percent of their support.

5. Siblings, other extended family members, maids, au pairs, and other family support personnel are NOT authorized dependents on the ITO and will not be eligible for ID cards or other benefits.

(b) Except for expressly designated courses or training, encourage IMS not to have their dependents accompany or join them during their training period outside their country. The IMS are responsible for the conduct and expenses, and financial obligation of their dependents.

1. Except for those courses specifically identified by the Military Service, the administration of IMS is geared to IMS without dependents. IMS with dependents are invariably confronted with problems that interfere with their training and their timely movement between the station and the port. Training programs, movement schedules, and reporting dates will not be altered to meet the special requirements of IMS with dependents.

2. An IMS unaccompanied by a spouse but accompanied by dependent children are responsible for developing and maintaining a dependent care plan for their dependents. The following instructions and forms can provide guidance in developing such plans:

a. DA Form 5305 (Family Care Plan); DA Form 5304 (Family Care Plan Counseling Checklist).

b. Chief of Naval Operations instruction (OPNAVINST) 1740.4B; NAVPERS 1740/7 (S/N 0106- LF–985–2900).

c. AFI 36–2908; AF Form 357 (Family Care Certification).

3. U.S. government family housing is normally not available and is not guaranteed to IMS with dependents, and additional living allowances for dependents, whether authorized or unauthorized, are not provided. Civilian housing is generally distant, expensive, and difficult to obtain. However, Military Service have identified certain schools where Family members are encouraged to accompany the IMS during their course of education or training. See SAMM, table C10.T3, note 7 for the list of schools, and specific details regarding living allowances.

4. For training at sites where dependents are encouraged, make IMS aware that only unaccompanied housing will be authorized unless dependents accompany the IMS for 75 percent of the training at the course location.

(13) *Military status.* Advise IMS that they will be treated in the same manner as their U.S. Military Service counterparts of equivalent grade. No training program will be arranged to treat the many IMS in exactly the manner to which they are accustomed. IMS are accorded the same privileges and, therefore, assume the same responsibilities as U.S. personnel. Although IMS are not subject to U.S. military law, they do remain under the criminal and civil jurisdiction of U.S. Federal and State laws. They also remain under the jurisdiction of the military authorities from their own countries.

(14) *Military, social, and athletic privileges.* Ensure that IMS understand that clubs for officers, noncommissioned officers, enlisted personnel, and civilians on most training installations are supported by the members and not by DOD funding. On some training installations, IMS are authorized membership without charge, while at others a small monthly payment is required. Clubs generally provide dining rooms, bars, cocktail lounges, game rooms, reading and television lounges, snack bars, and swimming pools. Most training facilities also have areas where IMS can play golf, basketball, football, soccer, volleyball, and softball. Roller skating rinks, gymnasiums, tennis courts, and libraries are generally available. Movies are normally shown nightly for a nominal price at theaters located on the training installation.

(15) *Medical care in the United States is expensive.* Ensure the IMS is aware of and in compliance with the requirements for medical coverage outlined in chapter 8.

(16) *Military courtesy.* IMS are required to observe universally recognized military courtesies.

(17) *Student and instructor relationship.* Advise IMS that an instructor in a Military Service facility is responsible for maintaining control of a training situation at all times, even if an enlisted instructor is teaching senior personnel or officers. The rules of conduct apply equally to all IMS; any breach of etiquette or protocol will be brought to the attention of the appropriate IMSO, and if necessary, the Security Cooperation Organization and country military authorities.

(18) *Cultural differences.* Make the IMS aware of customs and beliefs that are markedly different from those of the U.S. to avoid embarrassing situations. Also, mention the behavior pattern of Americans, their spirit of independence, and their freedom of action in matters such as, religion and politics.

(19) *Quarters.* Advise IMS that they must follow the billeting procedures and policies of each school or training installation throughout the course of their education or training. This includes maintaining a clean, healthy, and safe living environment.

(20) *Smoking.* Advise IMS that there are significant restrictions and limitations on smoking, both on military installations and throughout American society. This includes smoking restrictions in schools, government quarters,

office areas, restaurants, shopping areas, and public transportation. IMS and their dependents are expected to abide by these restrictions and limitations.

(21) *Military meals.* Advise IMS that military dining halls usually are not equipped to accommodate special requests for national dishes. However, attempts are made to accommodate religious dietary habits at installations with large numbers of IMS. There will be no increase in living allowances if IMS refuse, for any reason, to eat food served in military dining halls. Dependents are generally not authorized to eat in military dining facilities.

(22) *Invitational travel order.* Explain in detail the use of the ITO for identification, itinerary, payment, medical services, baggage limitations, and authorization of dependents. This is necessary since many IMS have little or no knowledge of the importance and use of their ITO. Special emphasis should be given to Block 13, Terms. Also, stress the need to retain the original ITO and sufficient copies, explaining that the ITO is the controlling document for the training and administration of the IMS. The IMS will be authorized only the training and privileges stated in the ITO and any amendments.

(23) *Requests for changes to training.* Inform IMS of the training they are scheduled to receive. Also advise them that they are not to contact representatives of the training installation to arrange unprogrammed training. Any requests for changes to training, as contained in item 8 of the ITO, must be processed through Military Service channels.

(24) *Leave policy and delay enroute.* Ensure that IMS understand the policies and regulations concerning leave and delay enroute. Cover the following points:

(a) IMET living allowances are not authorized during a delay enroute.

(b) Authority for a delay enroute must be included in the ITO.

(c) For tour participants, a delay enroute may be authorized only from the last point in their itinerary to the CONUS point of departure.

(d) Policies concerning stopover in other countries enroute to the home country should be carefully explained.

(e) Delay enroute will automatically be terminated upon arrival at the first training installation. (IMS with approved delay enroute sometimes report early to the training installation, wanting to receive accrued living allowances, store their baggage, and continue their delay enroute. Training installations are not staffed to administer such Services.)

(25) *Military records.* Advise IMS that when they move between training installations that their military records are kept by various offices. For that reason, they will be asked to execute in- and out-processing forms when they report to or depart from training installations. All records will be transferred by the training installation except for medical records, which the IMS hand-carries. Training installations are authorized to transfer medical records with other documents if deemed advisable for processing or administrative purposes.

(26) *Postal facilities.* Advise the IMS to contact the nearest post office on postal rates or postal problems. The IMS should inform their Families and friends that certain articles (for example, meat and food products) are prohibited from being imported into the United States and that any package containing such items must be returned at the senders expense. A list of prohibited or restricted items will be prepared both in English and in the local language.

(27) *Tax-free merchandise.* Emphasize that purchases of tax-free merchandise will not be abused, especially as they pertain to alcoholic beverages that may be purchased for personal use.

(28) *Off-duty employment.* Indicate that IMS and their alien family members are not permitted to engage in employment.

(29) *Religious services.* Explain to IMS that religious services for most faiths are available at training installations or in the local community. IMS should NOT expect release from training or other duties for routine religious activities.

(30) *Course entry English Comprehension Level testing.* All direct-entry IMS (except from countries exempt from all ECL testing requirements) will be administered the CONUS course entry ECL test within 3 to 5 calendar days after the IMS arrival at the first training location. This also includes IMS from those countries granted a waiver from in-country screening ECL testing.

(31) *Instructional material.* Advise IMS that personal items and household goods will not be packed or shipped as instructional material.

10–10. International military student arrival arrangements

a. The Security Cooperation Organization will provide the following information via the Training Management System and the Security Assistance Network IMSO Web to the receiving installation at least two weeks prior to arrival date if unaccompanied and 30 days prior if accompanied to ensure proper reception of the IMS (see para 7–5 for further information):

(1) Estimated time of arrival.

(2) Mode of travel.

(3) Flight number.

(4) Number of dependents and age of children accompanying the IMS.

(5) Other pertinent travel information.

b. The IMSO will coordinate IMS arrivals and departures within their area of responsibility. Generally, IMS will be met at the airport by an escort from the training installations. The following points should be stressed:

(1) An atmosphere of welcome, courtesy, efficiency, patience, and consideration is essential.

(2) Care and formality will be used in dealing with IMS, who are often sensitive in matters of propriety and rank. Whenever possible, personnel of equal grade should greet new arrivals, particularly general and flag ranks. Applicable protocol procedures will be followed.

(3) Information and instructions will be given in easily understood English, avoiding the use of slang or idioms.

(4) If arriving after normal work hours, the escort should ensure that the IMS knows where they should report for in-processing the following morning.

(5) Prior arrangements should be made to meet religious or national dietary requirements (for example, list of local restaurants including type and price of food served).

(6) General information should be available on items of local interest such as special events, bus schedules, taxi rates, hotels, and local community organizations established to assist IMS.

(7) Assistance to dependents should be provided, as appropriate.

c. Commanders of training installations, designated representatives, or IMSO are responsible for reporting the failure of an IMS to arrive as scheduled. This report will be sent to the Military Service and, if appropriate, to the losing activity, with an information copy to the appropriate Security Cooperation Organization within 48 hours after scheduled arrival.

10–11. Biographical data

a. Unless otherwise specified in MILDEP sections of this chapter, the Security Cooperation Organization will furnish biographical data for each officer IMS not later than 15 days before the IMS reporting date. If at all possible, the biographical data for senior PME schools is to be provided 60 days prior to the reporting date.

b. The biographical data is entered by the Security Cooperation Organization using the Training Management System International Military Student Information function, and is then uploaded to the Security Assistance Network.

c. Distribution of the biographical information is automatic to all training activities via the Security Assistance Network IMSO Web system and is available to all Military Service within the DSAMS Training System.

Section IV
International Military Student Arrival

10–12. Reporting to training installation

a. The IMS will comply with the reporting date as shown in Item 8 on the ITO. The reporting date at the first training installation is usually 3 to 5 business days prior to the commencement of training. Reporting earlier or later than the stated reporting date can cause administrative and academic problems. This could result in IMS being denied admission to training.

b. If IMS arrive in the United States early for purposes of tourism, personal business, or for other reasons not related to Security Cooperation Education and Training, they will be considered as being under the cognizance of their Washington-based attaché or other appropriate U.S. based foreign national representative. A statement to this effect should be placed in their ITO. During this pre-reporting period, IMS will not be under DOD sponsorship. In cases where the Security Cooperation Organization is aware of such circumstances, competent authority should be appraised as early as possible before the IMS arrival in the United States.

10–13. Training installation briefing

The IMSO will brief IMS as soon as possible after IMS arrival at the training installation. The IMSO will ensure that all elements of concern to the IMS are covered in the briefing with special attention to chapters 10 and 11 of this regulation. The briefing will include the following:

a. The IMSO-duties and functions.

b. Policy and regulations-privileges; restrictions; conduct, appearance, and grooming; medical and dental care; identification cards, and financial responsibility.

c. Legal status-applicability of federal and state laws; indebtedness; shoplifting; purchase of duty-free, tax-exempt liquor and the penalties for abuse; passports and visas.

d. Training program-ITO governing document; unprogrammed training; officers in enlisted courses; elimination from training for cause; meeting schedules and appointments; English language testing; clothing and equipment; release and shipment of instructional material.

e. Full studies program objectives and activities.

f. Conduct and personal appearance-grooming standards; cleanliness; morale problems; military discipline and courtesies.

g. Sexual harassment, fraternization, or conduct as defined in DOD policy (see para 10–45).

h. Student and instructor relationship-male; female; officer; enlisted; civilian; minority instructors.

i. Travel-arrangements; accommodations; baggage allowance; delays enroute; travel schedules.

j. Privately-owned vehicle-purchase; registration; insurance; operation; travel; laws.

k. Living allowances-authorized amount; payment schedule.

l. Dependents-authorization; housing; cost of living; access to medical care, charges, payment procedures and health insurance.

m. An IMS unaccompanied by a spouse but accompanied by dependent children are responsible for developing and maintaining a dependent care plan for their dependents. The following instructions and forms can provide guidance in developing such plans:

(1) DA Form 5305; DA Form 5304.

(2) OPNAVINST 1740.4B; NAVPERS 1740/7 (S/N 0106–LF–985–2900).

(3) AFI 36–2908; AF Form 357.

n. Currency-monetary exchange; banking.

o. Mail - postal facilities; official and personal mail.

p. USG quarters-occupancy; duration, housekeeping; custodial fees.

q. Firearms - purchase; possession; transportation.

r. Employment - restriction against IMS and alien Family members being employed during their stay in the United States.

s. Identify theft - IMS should be cautioned not to divulge personal information to anyone who does not have an official, legitimate reason for having the information.

10–14. Legal status and claims

a. Jurisdiction.

(1) Military and civilian IMS and their dependents, while in the United States, are subject to the jurisdiction of the U.S. courts, both state and federal. This is true unless they are exempted by treaty, or other specific authority, or have diplomatic immunity.

(2) Questions on the jurisdictional status of IMS or their dependents should be referred to the servicing judge advocate.

b. Diplomatic status. IMS usually do not have diplomatic immunity; however, those who believe themselves entitled to diplomatic immunity or other special status should have their claimed status verified. The IMSO should contact the Military Service for determination of IMS status. As a general rule, a sponsor's diplomatic immunity extends to their dependents as well.

c. Authority over international military student. The IMS are not subject to the UCMJ. Generally, no authority exists under which U.S. military authorities may place IMS in military confinement. Under the federal statutes, however, Australian military authorities in the United States may request the assistance of U.S. military authorities to apprehend and confine members of Australian forces in the United States. U.S. civil authorities, State or federal, may also apprehend and confine IMS for breaches of State or federal law. Except for authorization by treaty or agreement (such as NATO SOFA), or by statute, Executive Order, or Presidential Proclamation (such as in the case of Australia), foreign military attaches or commanders stationed in this country have no authority to arrest, detain, or confine members of their forces within the United States; nor can they empower U.S. military authorities to arrest, detain, or confine members of their forces. When warranted by urgent circumstances, the installation commander may authorize temporary restraint to prevent bodily harm to the IMS or to other persons, pending arrival of civilian authorities. Such IMS may not be returned to their home country without written approval of the appropriate Military Service.

d. Claims against international military student. For information concerning claims arising in the United States from the activities of IMS from countries that have ratified the NATO SOFA, see MILDEP regulations and the provisions of NATO agreements. For information concerning claims that arise incident to the activities of IMS in overseas areas, see pertinent command claims directives. If an inquiry is made concerning a claim involving non-NATO personnel, the claimant should be advised to seek redress from the IMS or their Government. IMS training in the United States have no special status to equate them to members of the U.S. Armed Forces for the purpose of filing claims in accordance with 10 USC 2731–2738. If otherwise a proper party claimant under U.S. law, an IMS may, subject to the commander's discretion, present an appropriate claim for relief.

e. Living allowance claims involving deceased USG-funded international military student. An appointed U.S. officer will determine the amount of living allowance or other payments due to the deceased member. To get this information, the U.S. officer will check with the last finance and accounting office serving the deceased member. The officer should ascertain from the Security Cooperation Organization the name of the deceased's next of kin to whom check payment is to be made. Checks will be forwarded to the Security Cooperation Organization for disposition.

f. Reports. The IMSO will refer legal questions concerning IMS to the local military legal office. An incident involving IMS that might lead to or has led to the exercise of criminal jurisdiction by state or federal authorities should be reported immediately according to appropriate Military Service regulations.

10–15. Alien registration

The IMS in CONUS on valid ITOs are not required to register as alien residents of the United States. These IMS are exempt from the provisions pertaining to registration, fingerprinting, and reporting of address as outlined in 8 USC 1302. The above statement does not apply if a student's status changes, and the student is no longer pursuing the training prescribed in the ITO. Dependents of IMS will register according to immigration determination.

10–16. Family members

See paragraph 10–9b(12) for definitions of authorized Family members.

a. The IMS attending PME programs identified in the SAMM, table 10.2 are encouraged to bring their dependents with them for the duration of their education. The IMS attending these schools will be responsible for the cost of housing, food, and health insurance (if applicable) for their dependents while in the United States.

b. The IMS attending all other schools and courses will not be encouraged to bring their dependents to the U.S. during their training periods. The presence of their dependents will not in any manner alter their (IMS) duty status or availability for training. If IMS insist on bringing dependents at their own expense, they will be directed to acquire suitable housing before the family arrives. Housing on and around most military installations may be expensive, scarce, or unavailable. Furthermore, IMS should understand that the TLA they receive is to defray the cost of USG quarters and meals. They will, in most cases, not be entitled to TLA if they occupy civilian housing (see para 7–8a(6)).

c. Travel and living allowance of dependents cannot be funded by the U.S. Government. Scheduled reporting dates will not be altered merely to accommodate IMS travel with dependents. The use of USG-owned vehicles in the reception and departure of bona fide dependents of IMS is authorized, subject to local vehicle availability.

d. Exchange, commissary, and medical privileges for dependents are limited to those IMS dependents authorized in the ITO. Responsibility for payment of medical care expenses will be clearly indicated on the ITO by selecting the appropriate block in figure 9–1, item 12b(2). When dependents accompany or join IMS without authorization on the ITO, the dependents are not authorized commissary or exchange privileges nor medical care at DOD medical facilities. These privileges cannot be extended without an amendment to the ITO by the Security Cooperation Organization.

e. When necessary, IMS will finalize and implement dependent care plans before commencement of training.

10–17. Identification cards

a. Identification (ID) cards, DD Form 1173 (United States Uniformed Services Identification and Privilege Card (Dependent)) will be furnished to IMS and civilian students undergoing DOD Security Cooperation Education and Training, and to each authorized, accompanying dependent by the first training installation, according to Military Service regulations. DD Form 2765 (DOD/Uniformed Services Identification and Privilege Card) (see DODI 1000.13, AR 600–8–14, BUPERSINST 1750.10, and AFI 36–3026(I)) has been replaced by the Common Access Card for students.

b. The IMS foreign identification number will be indicated on the card. An endorsement to the individual's ITO will indicate that an ID card has been issued and will include the number of the IMS card. The ID card expiration date will be the date that out processing is expected to be completed at the last training site.

c. ID cards will be issued to the one spouse and other dependents authorized to accompany the IMS. (See para 10–9b(12)) ID cards will be surrendered by IMS and their dependents during out-processing at the last training installation. Cards will be disposed of according to DOD instructions. An endorsement will be made on the sponsor's ITO that the cards have been returned. IMS may use their ITO if identification is required while on leave.

d. Foreign active duty or retired personnel and their dependents that meet the situations below are not eligible for medical or dental care, commissary, theater, exchange or similar privileges.

(1) Those living in the U.S. at their own convenience or the convenience of their government.

(2) Those present in the U.S. in connection with the purchase of U.S. defense articles or services or for collecting information relating to FMS programs.

10–18. Mail

a. The IMSO is authorized to send correspondence in support of the SCETP by registered or certified mail.

b. Personnel at CONUS training installations will not address mail directly to an IMS in country through APO facilities. Material should be addressed to the Security Cooperation Organization with instructions for delivery to the IMS.

c. The IMS may use military postal facilities for the purchase of stamps and the receipt and dispatch of mail.

10–19. Public affairs

a. General. Public affairs activities will be conducted under the appropriate MILDEP provisions. Data on the number of IMS, by nationality, who are training at any given time, may be released. A general description of the training being conducted may also be released. All requests received from the civilian media for the interviews or for photographs of IMS undergoing training will be referred through channels to the Office of the Assistant Secretary of Defense (Public Affairs) (OASD (PA)), 1400 Defense Pentagon, Washington DC 20301–1400, for evaluation before making any commitment.

(1) If OASD (PA) grants approval, all IMS involved will be given an opportunity to contact their embassy or a

senior advisor from their country before they participate. The OASD (PA) specifies that IMS are not required to contact their embassy or seek counsel unless they choose. In many cases, IMS will feel there is no need to avail themselves of that opportunity.

(2) The IMS should be aware that representatives of news organizations, including film crews, have access to areas normally open to the public, and that IMS could be photographed or be in contact with the media in those areas without prior knowledge.

(3) The release of hometown-type stories and pictures of IMS and visitors are governed by separate MILDEP instructions. Installation commanders, their designated representatives, or IMSO will dispatch hometown-type releases directly to the Security Cooperation Organization. Releases require coordination by the Security Cooperation Organization with ambassadors or public affairs officers of the U.S. International Communication Agency. Hometown-type news releases and photographs of IMS undergoing training should stress the following:

(a) Stories of graduations and honor graduates.

(b) Highlighted training activities and individual achievements of IMS.

(c) Action photographs showing IMS training with equipment that they are likely to use when they return to their home countries. Off-duty photographs should emphasize activities that support the DOD Field Studies Program for IMS. Examples of such activities are visits to state legislative offices, public works, educational institutions, industrial plants, and historical sites.

b. Constraints.

(1) When routine queries on IMS are received from federal government agencies it is permissible to provide them routine STL information for the current FY. If the requesting agency desires additional information they must request through the Military Service.

(2) No cumulative figures will be released except through the Military Service Public Affairs Office.

(3) No news releases will be made when in violation of applicable agreements between the USG and the foreign government.

(4) No press coverage will be initiated for orientation tour participants without their prior consent.

Section V
Military Matters

10–20. Warrant officers, midshipmen, and cadets
The U.S. equivalent warrant officers, midshipmen, and cadets will be considered officers unless otherwise indicated on the IMS ITO, and are eligible to be accommodated in officers quarters while in training at DOD installations.

10–21. Clothing, uniforms, and equipment
The Security Cooperation Organization should familiarize themselves with courses requiring special clothing and equipment.

a. Organizational clothing and equipment. Organizational clothing and equipment required by IMS for a prescribed training course are authorized for issue. Maintenance costs of equipment, replacement costs of clothing, and issue expenses are normally included in course costs. Issue to IMS will be as authorized for officers and enlisted personnel of the Military Service. Lost, damaged, or destroyed property will be accounted for, to include cash collection from IMS, if determined appropriate.

b. Individual clothing and equipment. Individual clothing and equipment required for prescribed training courses will be made available to IMS as required. Issue expenses are normally included in the course costs. Issued individual clothing and equipment will be collected from IMS on completion of their training at each installation. Items that cannot be returned for hygienic or aesthetic reasons may be retained by the IMS. However, retention of other items by IMS will vary with Military Service policy.

c. Clothing purchases. Installation commanders may extend to IMS the privilege of purchasing nondistinctive clothing for cash from Military Service clothing stores. Nondistinctive clothing will be sold in reasonable amounts to comply with the requirements of the individual concerned. Distinctive items of the Military Service uniform other than those authorized by Service regulations will not be sold.

d. Wearing of United States uniforms. IMS may wear the basic U.S. uniform if the country concerned does not provide a uniform suitable for climatic conditions in the United States. The U.S. buttons, insignia, and distinguishing marks must be removed and replaced by the distinguishing marks of the country concerned. Authorized uniforms may be purchased by the country or by individual IMS.

10–22. Laundry
Laundry service may be available to IMS on a cash basis. Collections will be made by the local laundry officer at the rates charged U.S. military personnel.

10–23. Grooming standards

a. The determination of appearance and grooming standards is a U.S. Military Service requirement. IMS are expected to comply with Military Service regulations. It is a mandatory responsibility of the Security Cooperation Organization to brief each IMS prior to departure for U.S. training.

b. To ensure operational efficiency and safety, IMS undergoing U.S. military training must comply with the host U.S. Military Service regulations pertaining to that training.

c. Noncompliance with Military Service regulations may subject the IMS to disciplinary action. Situations that cannot be resolved at training installation level will be referred to the Military Service.

10–24. Name tags

The wearing of a name tag by the IMS while in training is of significant assistance to all personnel connected with the training. Name tags provide easy identification and ensure proper treatment of IMS. Name tags will indicate the equivalent U.S. grade or rank, name, and country of the individual. U.S. equivalent rank may also be issued/purchased and worn next to the name tag.

Section VI
Academic Matters

10–25. Officer and enlisted courses

a. Officer and warrant officer IMS are permitted to attend enlisted courses. These IMS will be thoroughly briefed before departing that they are to attend enlisted courses. They will be informed that their officer status does not entitle them to special treatment or academic privileges while attending these courses. These IMS will be given officer privileges when not participating in training.

b. Enlisted IMS are not authorized to attend officer courses.

10–26. Physical training

All IMS will be encouraged to participate in physical training. IMS are required to participate in physical training when successful course completion depends on physical condition (for example, ranger and airborne training), or when physical training is a part of the program of instruction and is considered necessary for leadership development. See MILDEP specific sections for additional information.

10–27. Graduation, diplomas, certificates of attendance, and awards

a. Upon successful completion of a formal course of instruction, each IMS will be issued a certificate or diploma. Diplomas issued IMS will be identical to diplomas issued to U.S. students.

b. Diplomas for graduation from U.S. formal courses of instruction will be given to IMS only when they have met the established training standards. It is not the intent of this policy that only numerical grades be used in determining whether the IMS has achieved the standards set for U.S. military personnel. The determining factor is whether IMS can accomplish satisfactorily the objectives for which they were trained. This determination will be influenced by aptitude, application, practical effort, and demonstrated understanding, as well as by numerical grades. Classified hours of instruction not available to IMS will not be considered in this determination.

c. In most cases, certificates of attendance in U.S. formal courses of instruction will be given IMS when they do not meet the minimum established training standard but have attended the complete course and have been diligent and sincere in their training efforts. The reasons for issuance of a certificate of attendance should be fully explained in the IMS academic report.

d. For pay purposes, some foreign governments require their embassies to report the actual training period of IMS in the United States. When embassy officials request such information concerning an IMS—

(1) The IMSO should include the actual training dates in the ITO final endorsement.

(2) The IMS will be provided a certificate of study confirming the dates of training.

e. Special awards for superior academic achievement, such as school plaques, may be awarded to outstanding IMS as determined appropriate by the installation commander. Commanders have the authority to establish and authenticate these awards and are encouraged to do so. Other acts of recognition might include special commendation letters, signed appropriately by the installation commander or school commandant, and special remarks on the IMS academic report. Annual cost of special awards is properly chargeable to the Field Studies Program.

f. The military attaché of the country may be invited to the award or graduation ceremony; however, the invitation must state that an approved official visit request is required.

g. Copies of letters of appreciation, recognition of exceptional performance, and similar documents will be included in the IMS personnel and training record. Additionally, the IMSO should note if the IMS was a Distinguished Graduate in the Remarks section of the Completion/Departure Report in the Security Assistance Network IMSO Web.

h. The presentation of departure mementos (such as coins, school emblems, and other commemorative items) is authorized under the following conditions:

(1) Each item should be of a permanent nature, with the exception of photographs. Ball caps and T-shirts are not considered to be of a permanent nature.

(2) Presentation is limited to one item per IMS at each training installation at a cost not to exceed a limit set forth by each Military Service. Annual cost of departure mementos is properly chargeable to the Field Studies Program. Exceptions must be approved by the appropriate Military Service.

10–28. Academic reports

a. The academic report is the major source of information available to the Security Cooperation Organization and the foreign government to assess the overall IMS selection program and the individual IMS academic accomplishment. In addition, countries often use it for promotion and assignment considerations.

b. An DD Form 2496 (International Student Academic Report) must be prepared for each IMS as they complete a course of instruction. A sample of a completed DD Form 2496 is provided in figure 10–1, and instructions for completing the DD Form 2496 are provided in figure 10–2. Once completed and signed, the International Student Academic Report will be scanned and uploaded to the IMSO Web by the IMSO. This will streamline the overall reporting process, eliminate the need to mail a hard copy, and will make the report available to all those who are authorized to receive it.

c. The written comments in DD Form 2496, blocks 15 and 16 are very important, and they should be provided for every IMS at the conclusion of a course. Faculty members and IMSO should ensure that these comments are included in the DSAMS final DD Form 2496. Comments from one academic report should not be duplicated on another report. Reports that do not meet the above criteria may be returned by the Security Cooperation Organization to the preparing installation for revision as appropriate with info to appropriate Military Service.

d. Occasions may arise when an IMS cannot complete a course because of injury, illness, or personal hardship. When such an event occurs and is confirmed, the IMS should be disenrolled, and the circumstances surrounding the disenrollment should be documented in the Academic Report. If completed and signed, the IMS may be provided a copy of the Academic Report upon departure from the training site.

e. The IMS numerical grades or class standing will not be released by training installations except as listed below. Other exceptions must be authorized by the appropriate Military Service.

(1) An individual IMS may be provided their grade and class standing. The academic report can be used as a guide for counseling the IMS.

(2) Training installations may release class standing of IMS who are first in class standing.

f. For special classes of IMS from a single country, and at the discretion of the training installation concerned, an academic report may be given on the class as a whole rather than on each IMS. A separate report will be submitted on IMS who do not complete the course.

g. Requests for IMS academic records and reports or information relating to them, from an activity or organization outside the Security Cooperation Education and Training framework, will be referred to the appropriate Military Service.

INTERNATIONAL STUDENT ACADEMIC REPORT

(For International Military Students attending CONUS schools.)
(See AR 12-15, AFJI 16-105, and SECNAVINST 4950.4 for forms completion instructions.)

1. FORWARDING ADDRESS *(Subsequent training, if applicable, or country SAO)*	2. FROM *(Training installation preparing form)*
American Embassy Bandara Department of State Washington, DC 20521-5260	International Military Student Office A Company, TSB 10000 Hampton Parkway Fort Jackson, SC 29207-7025

3. STUDENT NAME *(Last, First, Middle Initial)*	4. GRADE/RANK	5. COUNTRY	6. FMS CASE OR IMET FY AND WCN
1LT Doe, John	02/1LT	Bandara	IMET 09 WCN: 9999

7. COURSE TITLE	8. COURSE ID NO.	9. COURSE MASL	10. DURATION OF COURSE	
Adjutant General Captains Career Course	7-12-C22	B171590	a. FROM *(YYMMDD)* 20091022	b. TO *(YYMMDD)* 20100328

11. DID STUDENT COMPLETE COURSE? *(X one)*	12. STUDENT WAS AWARDED: *(X one)*	13. ENGLISH COMPREHENSION LEVEL *(Enter test score)*	

X YES
   NO *(Explain in Item 15)*
	X a. DIPLOMA/CERTIFICATE OF COMPLETION
	   b. CERTIFICATE OF ATTENDANCE
	   c. OTHER *(Explain in Item 15)*
		a. IN-COUNTRY TEST 98	b. CONUS TEST 99

14. STUDENT'S ACADEMIC EVALUATION

a. RATINGS SCALE *(Enter in Items 14.b. and 14.c.)*	b. LANGUAGE PROFICIENCY		c. PERFORMANCE IN CLASS	
			ITEM	RATING
1 EXCEPTIONAL	(1) COMPREHENSION	1	(1) ATTITUDE AND MOTIVATION	1
2 EXCELLENT	(2) SPEAKING	1	(2) ATTENDANCE AND PUNCTUALITY	1
3 VERY SATISFACTORY			(3) ABILITY TO GRASP INSTRUCTION	1
4 SATISFACTORY	(3) READING	1	(4) PERFORMANCE IN PRACTICAL EXERCISES	1
5 UNSATISFACTORY *(Explain in Item 15)*			(5) PARTICIPATION IN CLASS ACTIVITIES	1
6 NOT OBSERVED *(Explain in Item 15)*	(4) WRITING	1	(6) POTENTIAL AS INSTRUCTOR *(If applicable)*	1

15. REMARKS ON ACADEMIC PERFORMANCE, AWARDS, AND OTHER INFORMATION *(Use back if more space is required)*

1LT Doe is a motivated and dedicated officer who performed exceptionally well during the Adjutant General Captains Career Course. 1LT Doe's exceptionally high grade point average earned him a spot on the Commandant's List as well as receiving the Diplomatic Medal, which is presented to the international officer who distinguished himself through consistent superior academic performance. He demonstrated complete understanding of the Human Resources (HR) core competencies of casualty operations, personnel accounting and strength reporting, replacement management and postal operations in addition to other essential HR support functions. 1LT Doe has an excellent grasp of how to interface with other staff sections toward unit mission accomplishment as evidenced by the great insight he provided to all during the Combined Arms Exercise. He performed superbly in a variety of leadership positions such as a trainer in a multi-echelon field training exercise that included NCOs and Soldiers in the Task Force S-1. 1LT Doe's level of professionalism, maturity, and dedication to excelling at all skills and knowledge presented during training reflect highly on himself and his role as an ambassador of the Armed Forces of Bandara. He set the standard for all to emulate!

16. REMARKS ON STUDENT'S PARTICIPATION IN EXTRACURRICULAR AND COMMUNITY AFFAIRS *(On and off training installation)* *(Use back if more space is required)*

1LT Doe was an enthusiastic participant in all of the Field Studies Program (FSP) activities offered by the International Military Student Office. He participated in tours to Charleston, South Carolina, Savannah, Georgia and Washington, DC. During these FSP activities, 1LT Doe was exposed to a wide range of topics ranging from the events that led to the opening battle of the American Civil War, to the vital role that international commerce has played in the economic development of the local region over the past 270 years, to the structure and function of the U.S. government and its commitment to human rights. 1LT Doe prepared and presented a detailed briefing on his country and its culture for the officers and the senior NCOs of the Training Support Battalion, for the local elementary school International Celebration Day and for the local Rotary Club members. His outstanding presentations greatly enhanced the intercultural understanding of all program participants. He was always willing to share his culture and forge international friendships with everyone he met!

17. EVALUATOR

a. NAME *(Last, First, Middle Initial)*	b. GRADE	c. SIGNATURE
Henry, Patrick I.	Major	

18. INTERNATIONAL MILITARY STUDENT OFFICER

a. NAME *(Last, First, Middle Initial)*	b. GRADE	c. SIGNATURE
Revere, Paul S.	GS12	

DD FORM 2496, FEB 96   PREVIOUS EDITION IS OBSOLETE.   Reset   Adobe Professional 7.0

Figure 10–1. Sample of DD 2496 International Student Academic Report, page 1

General Instructions for DD Form 2496 Completion

Complete this form for all scheduled training, except for language, flight, observer and preparatory training/programs where different written evaluation is appropriate.

ITEM 1 - Refer to the student's Invitational Travel Order (ITO) to obtain the mailing address of the country Security Cooperation Officer (SCO). Enter the proper address. If subsequent training is scheduled, send electronic copy of student's completed DD Form 2496 to gaining installation.

ITEM 2 – Enter the training activity/organization mailing address.

ITEMS 3 – 9 – Refer to the student's ITO and subsequent amendments or endorsements, if applicable, for this information.

ITEM 10 -

    a.   FROM: Enter the course start date.

    b.   TO: Enter the date the student graduates or disenrolls from class. If the student completed training on a date other than what is programmed on ITO, or was disenrolled prior to course completion, explain circumstances in Item 15.

ITEM 11 – Self explanatory.

ITEM 12 – Self explanatory.

ITEM 13 – This item is to be completed by the first CONUS training activity at which the student is scheduled. Refer to student's ITO for in-country ECL test score. Mark N/A (not applicable) if in-country testing is not required per Defense Security Cooperation Agency annual ECL and OPI Country Exemption Lists. Enter the CONUS ECL test score achieved. If the ECL test is administered more than once, enter the most recent test score.

ITEM 14.a. – Rating Scale Explanation. Use the following scale to rate the elements of the student performance in items 14.b. and 14.c.

Figure 10-2 Genl Inst For Completing DD Form 2496

    a.   EXCEPTIONAL – Student is one of the best; honor student; very proficient in skills and knowledge for which trained; highly motivated; high potential for more advanced training and assignments to positions of increased responsibility; English fluency of natives; takes part fully in class activities.

    b.   EXCELLENT – Student completed course with considerable ease; full proficiency in skills and knowledge for which trained; considerable potential for advanced training and selected assignments of increased responsibility; considerable English fluency; responds when called upon; volunteers frequently.

    c.   VERY SATISFACTORY – Student may have experienced occasional difficulty in course completion; considered proficient in skills and knowledge for which trained; can be expected to achieve full proficiency with more experience or training; motivated enough to exceed course requirements; exhibits potential for selected advanced training; assignment to positions of great responsibility depends on local appraisal based on increased proficiency attained with experience; English fluency just enough to meet course requirements; responds when called upon; volunteers occasionally.

Figure 10–2. General instructions for DD Form 2496 completion

d. SATISFACTORY – Student performance is adequate, meeting only minimum course standards; experienced difficulty in completing course; minimal proficiency; requires job experience under close supervision to achieve desired proficiency, potential for more training and assignment to positions of greater responsibility depends on increased proficiency attained with experience; English fluency weak and a contributing factor to academic understanding; responds only when called upon.

e. UNSATISFACTORY – Student performs below desired standards; unable to meet minimum course standards; not recommended for more advanced training; very limited class participation; insufficient language proficiency.

ITEM 14.b – Enter the student's English language proficiency using the rating scale provided in

ITEM 14.a. above.

ITEM 14.c. – Enter the student's performance in class using the rating scale provided in Item 14.a. above.

ITEM 15 – Remarks on Academic Performance, Awards, and Other Information. Use this block to provide explanation for items 10, 11, 12 and 14. Also use to state student's overall performance, special abilities, and awards received. Do not use letter or numerical grades. Awards should be explained, e.g., "Distinguished Graduate Award" for graduating at the top of a class for international students or for graduating in the top percentage of a combined US/international class. List any additional training the student may have completed through the installation learning center or in the civilian community.

ITEM 16 – Remarks on Student's Participation in Extra-curricular and Community Affairs. Provide a general statement of the student's involvement in Field Studies Program (FSP) and other extra-curricular activities. Do not simply list FSP trips or activities in which the student participated.

ITEM 17 – Evaluator. The senior instructor, or course director, should evaluate the student and sign the academic report. The evaluator should be of equal or higher rank/grade to the IMS if possible.

ITEM 18 – International Military Student Officer. All academic reports for officer IMS should have at least one signature by a US officer of equal or higher rank to the IMS. If the senior instructor or course director does not meet this rank criteria, the IMSO (or other officer in the IMSO chain of command) of equal or higher rank to the student should sign the report.

Figure 10–2. General instructions for DD Form 2496 completion–Continued

10–29. Reporting of international military student academic problems

a. Timely reports on academic deficiencies should be addressed to the appropriate Military Service. Often these deficiencies can be corrected by the foreign representative or by programming other training. The objective is to train the IMS at the least expense to the United States or country concerned.

b. The IMS who fail to meet the training standards set for U.S. personnel may be dismissed from the school. When it is apparent that an IMS should be withdrawn from training, the appropriate Military Service will be advised immediately of the full particulars of the case. This will include recommendations on suitability for other training or disposition of the IMS. The IMS will not be relieved for cause without authority from the responsible Military Service. Pending receipt of this authority, suspension is authorized at the discretion of the installation commander. Disposition instructions are provided in each Service specific section of this chapter.

10–30. Commissary and exchange privileges

a. Commissary, exchange, and other privileges ordinarily available to U.S. military personnel in CONUS will be extended to IMS of equivalent rank and their authorized accompanying dependents.

b. Privileges extended to IMS in overseas areas will be according to applicable international agreements. When there is no agreement between the USG and host government authorizing the USG to grant these privileges, they may be granted nonetheless to IMS unless the host country objects.

10–31. Indebtedness

a. The following procedures are to be implemented by the IMSO to avoid IMS indebtedness to the USG or a non-appropriated fund, such as billeting fees or medical charges:

(1) Make arrangements with the installation billeting office, and other facilities as deemed appropriate, to ensure the IMSO is immediately notified of delinquent IMS accounts.

(2) Discuss procedures for payment of billeting fees or laundry during IMS inprocessing to ensure the IMS is aware of how and when payments are to be made.

(3) Include a check with the billeting office, as part of the IMS out-processing, to ensure their account has been paid.

(4) When an IMS is responsible for payment of medical charges for themselves or their authorized dependents, discuss procedures for payment during IMS inprocessing to ensure the IMS is aware of how and when these payments are required.

b. Upon notification of IMS indebtedness, meet with the IMS, CLO, or senior representative at the training activity to determine the reason for the indebtedness.

(1) If the reason for indebtedness is beyond the IMS control, notify the appropriate Military Service immediately.

(2) When it appears that a medical condition for the IMS or authorized dependents will result in extensive medical charges, counsel the IMS regarding responsibility for payment. If it appears the IMS will not be able to make the required payment, notify the appropriate Military Service for disposition instructions. Include the diagnosis, prognosis and estimated cost of medical care.

(3) If the indebtedness is determined to be within the IMS control, take the following actions:

(a) Counsel the IMS. Taking into consideration the amount of debt and the financial support received by the IMS, set up a payment plan to ensure past and future payment requirements are satisfied.

(b) If the IMS does not agree to the arrangement or does not adhere to a payment plan, refer the matter of indebtedness to the training installation commander, designated representative, or training school commandant.

(c) Notify the appropriate Military Service through the chain of command if the problem is not resolved after counseling by the training installation commander.

(d) Diploma will not be issued until IMS has paid all outstanding bills.

(e) If the IMS departs the training activity before resolving the indebtedness problem, and is scheduled for FDT, notify the IMSO at the gaining activity. Notify the sponsoring Military Service through the chain of command if the IMS is to return to their home country. In the latter event, the Military Service will notify the IMS embassy or the Security Cooperation Organization.

10–32. Off-duty employment

The IMS or their alien dependents are not permitted to hold employment during their stay in the United States. The U.S. Embassy or Security Assistance personnel should explain this to students at predeparture briefings. Security Cooperation Organization should ensure passports with A–2 Visas or related documents concerning students and their alien dependents are NOT annotated with "Employment Authorized."

10–33. Public benefits

a. In general IMS and their family members are ineligible for federal public benefits and state and local public benefits with the following exceptions:

(1) Medical care and services that are necessary for the treatment of an emergency medical condition and are not related to an organ transplant procedure, if the alien involved otherwise meets the eligibility requirements for medical assistance under the approved State Medicaid Plan.

(2) Short-term, non-cash, in-kind emergency disaster relief.

(3) Public health assistance for immunizations with respect to immunizable diseases and for testing and treatment of symptoms of communicable disease whether or not such symptoms are caused by a communicable disease.

(4) Programs, services, or assistance, which deliver in-kind services at community level, including through public or private nonprofit agencies and do not condition the provision of assistance, the amount of assistance provided, or the

cost of assistance provided on the individual recipient's income or resources and are necessary for the protection of life or safety.

b. Medicaid plans vary from state to state. IMSO must check with local authorities on medicaid criteria for their state. In reporting income for qualification IMSO must ensure that the IMS includes salary received from home country and living allowance.

10–34. Purchase and possession of firearms

The IMS who desire to bring personal firearms or ammunition into the United States or to purchase such items must comply with federal, state, and local laws and regulations, including training installation regulations, governing the possession, use, and transportation of firearms. IMSO should check with the installation Staff Judge Advocate to determine current laws and regulations governing firearms prior to briefing IMS.

10–35. Purchase and use of privately-owned vehicles

a. The IMS who want to purchase a POV will be advised to consult the IMSO before signing any purchase contract.

b. Purchase of power-driven vehicles by orientation tour participants will be deferred until completion of the tour.

c. The IMS must comply with training installation and state regulations for the registration and operation of such vehicles. IMS will be required to purchase and maintain public liability and property damage insurance. This insurance will be in the amount required by law in the state in which the vehicle is registered, or in the amount required by the military installation on which the vehicle is registered, whichever is higher. IMS are encouraged to consult U.S. authorities for additional insurance information.

d. The IMSO must maintain close coordination with training installation authorities to ensure that vehicle registration is issued only to IMS who meet all requirements for owning and operating a power-driven vehicle.

e. The IMS and/or dependents from countries that are parties to NATO/PFP SOFA, Article IV, or to other international agreements may be entitled to use the civilian or military driver's license issued by their own countries. IMS should be encouraged to bring their valid international driver's license. A translated copy in English of the driver's license should be provided to the IMSO.

10–36. Purchase of duty-free and tax-exempt articles and liquor

a. In general, members of the armed forces of any foreign country on duty in the United States are authorized to have certain articles entered duty-free and tax-free. This is true if the articles are for the member's personal use or the use of any member of their immediate family. (See 19 USC 1202 and section 8, part 2, items 820.40 and 822.20, Revised Tariff Schedule.)

b. Unless prohibited by state or local laws, alcoholic beverages may be introduced under the authority in paragraph 10–36*a*, above. Amounts cannot exceed one case per month for persons entitled to this privilege. The servicing judge advocate will be consulted on state and local laws on the introduction, possession, and use of alcoholic beverages.

c. All IMS will be given a complete orientation on the foregoing personal exemptions. It will be explained that this privilege is extended solely for the convenience of IMS. It will also be explained that abuse of the privilege by the sale, gift, or trade of duty-free and tax-free articles to U.S. personnel is unlawful and can result in withdrawal of the privilege, administrative penalties, and disciplinary action against all concerned.

Section VIII
Leave, Holidays, and Temporary Duty

10–37. Leave and holidays

a. Leave during training.

(1) An IMS may request leave for short periods to travel in CONUS. This leave may take place between certain courses or phases of instruction (such as non-applicable phases or classified phases of instruction). The IMS request for leave may be jointly approved by the commander and CLO or by the Military Service with the concurrence of the country representative by telephone. Continuation of IMET living allowance is authorized during these periods.

(2) Leave or leave extensions are granted to USG-funded IMS only when authorized in the original ITO or if the Security Cooperation Organization amends the ITO via the Security Assistance Network Web. The written communication must be completed no later than 15 days prior to completion of scheduled training.

(3) Except for emergency leave, leave granted IMS will not interfere with, nor prolong, the period of training.

(4) Holiday leave is covered in paragraph 10–37*f*, below.

b. Leave between training periods. Between consecutive courses, the commander of a training installation or their designated representatives may authorize leave, with living allowance, not to exceed 7 days. It is not the intent of this provision that leave be given or used indiscriminately to occupy the IMS during the period between courses of instruction.

c. Emergency leave. Requests for emergency leave will be submitted electronically directly to the Security Cooperation Organization concerned, with copies to the appropriate Military Service, cognizant Combatant Command, and others as appropriate. Requests will reflect the IMS present course of instruction, graduation date, and scheduled additional training and information necessary to substantiate the request. The student or the student's government must pay the round trip transportation cost to return home on emergency leave if the student is to return to the United States to continue training.

d. Leave outside the continental United States.

(1) The IMS wishing to travel outside the United States in excess of 72 hours must obtain prior approval from their home country leave-approval authority. The U.S. officials are not authorized to approve leave in any country other than the United States.

(2) The IMS are responsible for making their own travel arrangements including visa, travel, accommodations and re-entry requirements. IMS must also comply with all immigration regulations, and meet any other requirements that may be imposed on travel to the country desired.

(3) USG-funded living allowances are authorized during international leave periods, in order for the IMS to maintain their quarters at the training site.

e. Leave at the completion of training.

(1) The IMS are not authorized to receive USG-funded living allowance during periods of leave authorized by student's government following completion of training courses.

(2) The IMS are authorized to receive up to a maximum of 7 days USG-funded living allowance following completion of training, provided that the IMS departure is delayed through no fault of their own.

(3) Leave at an IMS request between the last training installation and the point of CONUS departure is not authorized. The foreign country may authorize leave in the U.S. between the last training installation and the point of CONUS departure for IMS upon completion of training before returning to home country. Leave should be approved before the IMS departs from their home country and authority included in the IMS ITO. Requests for leave or leave extension upon completion of scheduled training, will not be granted unless the Security Cooperation Organization has amended the ITO by written communication with school(s)/training installations not later than 15 days prior to the completion of scheduled training. No USG-funded living allowance will be paid for such leave.

(4) Homeward travel for USG-funded IMS leaving the United States will be the most direct route using U.S. flag carriers. When an IMS is permitted by their government to deviate from the most direct route to visit other countries, USG-funded sponsorship will be suspended during such deviation. Further, if a USG-funded IMS elects to remain at a point enroute to their country beyond the time normally required to make travel connections, funding of allowances during that excess time is not authorized. The ITO will be endorsed by the training installation to indicate the foregoing provisos, as appropriate.

f. Holidays.

(1) Installation commanders or their designated representative are authorized to grant nonchargeable holiday leave, and USG-funded IMS are authorized living allowance during—

(a) Authorized holidays observed by the U.S. MILDEP.

(b) Major national and religious holidays of the IMS country not to exceed 1 academic day for each holiday authorized. IMS are authorized not more than 2 of their country's religious or national holidays in one calendar year. Academic progress will be the deciding factor in each case. The MILDEP will advise training installations of the holidays to be observed.

(c) The Christmas holiday period when activities at training installations have been curtailed.

(2) If additional training is scheduled at another installation immediately following the Christmas holiday period, the losing installation will be responsible for IMS during the holiday period.

10–38. Temporary duty

Orders authorizing TDY may be published for IMS participating—

a. As team members in an organized Military Service sports activity away from the IMS training installation. Permissive orders at no expense to the USG may be issued.

b. In programmed trips that are a scheduled part of the formal course curriculum. All identifiable costs, including TDY required by the course curriculum, are included in the tuition cost. Trips as part of a regular curriculum will not affect the IMS USG-funded living allowance.

Section IX
Security

10–39. International military student security clearance

In-country U.S. officials will perform a security screening of each student prior to issuance of the ITO regardless of the level of classification of the training. The level of security clearance will be shown in item 11 of the ITO by selecting either statement (a) or statement (b) as shown below—

a. "U.S. security screening has been accomplished. All training will be conducted on an unclassified basis."

b. "U.S. security requirements have been complied with. The home government has granted the IMS a security clearance. This in and of itself does not permit the disclosure of classified U.S. information. Such disclosure must be specifically authorized by an official delegated authority and U.S. foreign disclosure regulations or directives." The level of the security classification granted by the home government will be indicated in block 11 (1) of the ITO and the U.S. equivalent classification level will be shown in block 11(2) of the ITO.

10–40. Disclosure of classified military information and controlled unclassified information

Personnel involved with SCETP must be familiar with MILDEP and DOD policies concerning the disclosure of classified military information (CMI) and controlled unclassified information (CUI) to IMS. CUI is unclassified information to which access or distribution limitations have been applied in accordance with national laws, policies, and regulations of the originating country. All official information not cleared for public release must be reviewed and subsequently approved for release to a foreign government or organization.

a. The CMI and CUI will only be disclosed or released to IMS according to MILDEP regulations and only on a need-to-know basis.

b. Training that involves the disclosure of classified information must be reviewed and approved by the appropriate U.S. disclosure authority before the training can be programmed. The release of classified information to a country that is not currently eligible for access will be denied.

c. The T–MASL identifies those formal courses that require a security clearance for attendance; however, this designation does not mean that all countries can attend the course. Only those countries that have been specifically authorized can be programmed for these courses; individual IMS attendance depends on specific Military Service authorization.

d. Instruction on a weapon system or equipment the country does not have or has not shown a firm intent to acquire is not authorized.

e. Courses may cover more than one weapon system. If so, IMS will be retained in class for instruction only on those weapon systems that their country has in its inventory or has shown a firm intent to acquire.

f. Disclosure of communications security information will be according to MILDEP regulations and NSA approval.

g. Access to NATO classified information may be provided to IMS from NATO nations upon receipt of access certifications by the respective training installations as prescribed by treaty regulations and properly cleared by HQ, NATO. Each certification should show the highest level of NATO access granted to the IMS. Granting of this access will allow NATO IMS to receive NATO classified information and briefings available during the course.

10–41. Restricted courses

Many courses are not available to IMS due to security limitations or due to the orientation of course content to U.S. standards. MILDEP maintain the T–MASL as a current listing of courses that may be available to IMS. The availability of any known course not included in the T–MASL can be requested from the Military Service on a case-by-case basis.

10–42. Release of instructional related material

Release of instructional related material to IMS is authorized as outlined below. Other than as stated in paragraphs *a*, *b*, or *c*, below, training installations are not authorized to release U.S. military documents directly to foreign requesters.

a. Unclassified material. Commanders of training installations may authorize the release of unclassified student notes and locally prepared training materials to IMS at the conclusion of training. These may be included in RIM.

b. Controlled unclassified materiel. Controlled unclassified material within the parameters of the MILDEP disclosure authorization. IMS participating in training may be issued CUI publications and training material during the training. IMS must be briefed that all CUI provided to them must remain under their control at all times; that it may not be copied, reproduced, or distributed to anyone else, and that all controlled unclassified material must be returned to the school at the conclusion of the training course. Publications may then be shipped to the appropriate Security Cooperation Organization in accordance with appropriate release procedures.

c. Classified materiel. Classified material within the parameters of the MILDEP disclosure authorization. IMS participating in classified training may be issued classified publications used as texts and schematics during the training. All notes, including those written in the student's language, and other classified publications will be collected at the end of the training and shipped to the appropriate Security Cooperation Organization in accordance with appropriate release procedures.

Section X
Special Circumstances

10–43. Marriage

An IMS desiring to marry while undergoing training will comply with local U.S. laws and will be encouraged to comply with the instructions of their government. The IMSO will furnish pertinent information directly to the Military Service concerned, with information copies to the Security Cooperation Organization, on each IMS who plans marriage or who is married while in training. IMSO will refer all questions regarding ITO, dependent authorizations, medical coverage, and authorized privileges to the Security Cooperation Organization and Military Service.

10–44. Political asylum

Requests by IMS for political asylum in the United States, or for temporary refuge, must be treated with urgent and careful attention to the procedures, established by DODD 2000.11, and implementing instructions of the MILDEP. (See AR 550–1, SECNAVINST 5710.22, and AFI 51–704.) The IMSO should advise the IMS that Security Cooperation sponsorship, to include enrollment in training and all associated applicable living allowances terminates once the IMS applies for political asylum.

10–45. Disciplinary action

a. Within prescribed limitations concerning access to and security of classified or protected USG information, IMS will be treated in the same manner as DOD personnel. In this regard, IMS will be subject to pertinent laws of the United States concerning the safeguarding of military and other Government information affecting the national defense. IMS will also be expected to comply with U.S. MILDEP administrative regulations governing access to and security of such information.

b. Any IMS involved in serious breaches of military discipline or incident within civilian jurisdiction may be temporarily suspended from training by local military authorities pending resolution. As more details become available following the initial report, they will be reported through the chain of command, along with recommendations. Incidents such as those below may not appear serious at first, but may develop into situations with international implications.

(1) Confrontations between IMS and local authorities.

(2) IMS involved in civil disturbances.

(3) Hostile acts between IMS of different nationalities.

c. The principles in paragraphs (1) through (5), below, will be observed by U.S. personnel exercising control over IMS. These instructions will not conflict with action that Federal, State, or local authorities may elect to take with respect to acts committed in violation of civil law or authority.

(1) When an IMS is involved in a situation requiring immediate action to prevent bodily injury or any breach of the peace on or off a military installation, the military authorities will take steps within their legal competence to restore order. Where the offense committed by an IMS does not involve the necessity of restoring order, the military authorities may, depending on the seriousness of the offense, detain the IMS for the protection and safety of the installation. When confinement is appropriate, the IMS will be promptly delivered to civilian authorities unless military confinement is authorized by competent military authority. When a breach of the peace involving civil law occurs off a military installation, appropriate action will be taken to inform civilian authorities.

(2) The punishment of IMS in connection with military offenses committed by them will be the responsibility of the foreign military Service of which the IMS are members.

(3) In disciplinary cases, U.S. installation commanders may conduct an investigation and forward it through channels to determine whether the conduct of the IMS warrants a recommendation that they be returned to the home country. This action should be coordinated with the appropriate CLO if assigned. Concurrence of the CLO is desirable but not mandatory and should be addressed in the implementing correspondence or message traffic. The Military Service will be advised of the recommended action, together with a recommendation for substitute training or disposition. The Security Cooperation Organization, Combatant Command, and foreign representative will be included as information addressees, as appropriate.

(4) Military authorities will follow the same procedures with respect to breaches of the peace or other incidents involving IMS dependents as they would in the case of dependents of U.S. military personnel. However, installation commanders will investigate serious incidents involving IMS dependents to determine whether circumstances warrant a recommendation, through channels, that the IMS sponsor and dependents be returned to their home country. In all cases where dependents are involved in breaches of the peace or other incidents involving either civil or military authorities, the cognizant installation commander will have the IMS informed that—

(a) They are administratively accountable for the conduct of all dependents.

(b) Misconduct may be cause for a recommendation that the IMS and their Family members be returned to the home country.

(5) Breaches of discipline in overseas areas will be reported as directed by the overseas commander.

10–46. Sexual harassment laws and policy and fraternization

a. The IMS should be briefed on U.S. sexual harassment laws and policy and fraternization policies, both by the Security Cooperation Organization prior to departure from their home nation, and by the IMSO upon arrival at the first training installation. Confirmation of this briefing should be included in appropriate briefing checklists.

b. Sexual harassment is a form of sex discrimination that involves unwelcome sexual advances, requests for sexual favors and other verbal or physical conduct of a sexual nature when—

(1) Submission to such conduct is made either explicitly or implicitly a term or condition of a person's job, pay or career; or

(2) Submission to, or rejection of, such conduct by a person is used as a basis for career or employment decisions affecting that person; or

(3) Such conduct has the purpose or effect of unreasonably interfering with an individual's work performance or creates an intimidating, hostile or offensive working environment.

c. It is the policy of the DOD that any person in a supervisory or command position who uses or condones any form of sexual behavior to control, influence, or affect the career, pay, or job of a military member or civilian employee is engaging in sexual harassment.

d. Any military member or civilian employee who makes deliberate or repeated unwelcome verbal comments, gestures or physical contact of a sexual nature in the workplace is also engaging in sexual harassment.

e. Fraternization involves an improper superior-subordinate relationship which detracts from the authority of the superior and thereby adversely effects good order and discipline. Fraternization is gender neutral. It does not have to involve intimate relationships between members of the opposite sex. Fraternization can be between officers, between officers and enlisted Service members, and between enlisted Service members. For purposes of this regulation, fraternization can also be between members of a foreign military force/forces, and between foreign military members and U.S. forces.

f. Fraternization should not be confused with normal unit/team building functions or normal social interaction between people, such as, community functions, religious activities, unit social functions, and athletic events. Also, fraternization does not include routine, limited business transactions such as, landlord/tenant relationships, or one-time transactions like the sale of a vehicle, or home.

g. The following are examples of prohibited fraternizing activities:

(1) Dating.

(2) Cohabitation - except in situations of operational necessity.

(3) Intimate/sexual relationships.

(4) Gambling.

(5) Loaning/borrowing money.

(6) Business partnerships - Service members of different ranks cannot go into business together.

(7) Commercial solicitation - if a higher ranking Service member operates or is affiliated with a private company, they cannot solicit business for that company from a lower ranking Service member.

h. Sexual harassment and fraternization policy also apply to IMS who receive education or training at a U.S. military training installation or through a contractor employed by the U.S. Armed Forces to carry out international education and training. Any IMS who engages in conduct that could be considered sexual harassment or fraternization will be subject to appropriate administrative action and/or disenrollment.

10–47. Unauthorized absence

a. When an IMS is absent from scheduled activities for more than 24 hours without proper authorization, the IMS will be considered in an UA status. IMSO will carefully check before making a determination of UA to ensure that the IMS is not absent because of misunderstanding the schedule, sick in quarters, or for other plausible reasons.

b. When it has been determined that an IMS is UA, the IMSO will immediately—

(1) Notify appropriate school/installation personnel, ICE (both the local office and the national office at alrccu@dhs. gov) and the appropriate Military Service country program manager, including the following information:

(a) IMS name and country.

(b) Effective date and time of absence

(c) Date of birth.

(d) Place of birth.

(e) Last known location.

(f) Case identification number/WCN.

(g) Type of training and any previous and/or programmed follow-on training.

(h) Known travel circumstances (flight arrangements, layovers).

(i) Information pertaining to events that may have contributed to IMS absence.

(j) Known variations in name spelling.

(k) Known relatives in the United States.

(l) Information on U.S. driver's license (if any), including number, issuing state, and expiration date.

(2) Notify the issuing DOD ID card office to ensure ID card is cancelled.

(3) Notify the local DFAS facility/local finance officer to post UA information to the IMS DD Form 1588 to preclude unauthorized payments.

(4) Notify appropriate installation facilities to ensure no unauthorized services are provided.

(5) Ensure the proper progress message (absent without leave–TG) is entered in the Security Assistance Network.

(6) Hold personal effects of UA IMS for 7 days; then forward to the nearest foreign country representative or dispose of in the same manner as prescribed for deceased IMS (see para 10–48). Cost of shipping personal effects is the responsibility of the foreign government.

(7) If a UA IMS voluntarily returns to U.S. military control or is known to be detained by local authorities, notify the personnel indicated in paragraph 10–47b(1), and await disposition instructions. The ITO fund cite for an IMET IMS may be used for required transportation of the IMS to their proper station and for living allowances until disposition instructions have been made.

c. The Military Service will—

(1) Forward IMSO-provided information to the relevant Security Cooperation Organization, Commanders of Combatant Commands, and DSCA.

(2) Notify the appropriate military criminal investigative organization.

(3) Provide disposition instructions received from DSCA to the IMSO for any UA IMS who voluntarily returns to a DOD installation.

d. The Security Cooperation Organization will—

(1) Amend the student's ITO to cancel all training, all authorizations including dependants and terminate DOD sponsorship.

(2) Notify the consular section of the U.S. embassy that issued the student's visa.

(3) Notify the Ministry of Defense in the student's country.

e. Personal effects of the IMS will be held for 30 days. Personal effects will then be forwarded to the nearest foreign country representative or disposed of in the same manner as prescribed for deceased IMS (see para 10–48*j*).

10–48. Casualty report, death, and disposition of remains

a. If an IMS under SCETP sponsorship dies, the activity at which death occurs will immediately notify the appropriate Military Service.

b. The Military Service will notify DSCA, the foreign attaché, public affairs office, and others, as appropriate.

c. The activity will furnish a casualty report according to MILDEP regulations. The following additional information will be included in the remarks section of the casualty report:

(1) The IMS ITO number and date, WCN, and country.

(2) Request for instructions for disposition of remains.

(3) Request for permission to perform autopsy if required.

(4) Identification and location of next of kin if available.

d. Funeral or memorial services will not be conducted for IMS until instructions concerning the disposition of the remains have been received from the appropriate Military Service. The Military Service will obtain special instructions on the disposition of remains from the IMS government.

e. The training installation will coordinate the preparation and transportation of the remains of IMS according to authorized disposition instructions. If a local funeral home is utilized to assist in the arrangements for preparation and transportation of the remains, the IMSO at the current training installation (or last training installation if the IMS was on leave when the death occurred) should coordinate payment of the funeral home expenses. Under IMET, the appropriate MILDEP financial office should ensure funds are issued to the training installation financial office. Under FMS, the home country government should provide the funds. In all cases, IMSO should refer to the Health Affairs Handbook, chapter 6 for specific guidance.

f. If an escort is desired, the official representative of the country concerned may designate a staff member or an IMS to accompany the remains. U.S. personnel are not authorized for escort assignment.

(1) Per diem and travel costs of the escort accompanying the remains of an USG-funded IMS within the U.S. are chargeable to USG funds.

(2) Travel and transportation expenses for escorts accompanying the remains of an FMS IMS will be borne by the foreign government concerned.

g. The IMET fund cite in the IMS ITO will be used to defray preparation expenses and costs for transportation of the remains to the home country. Overseas return transportation costs will be paid from IMET funds only for deceased IMS from countries for which travel costs are defrayed from IMET funds. For transportation to a country which defrays all or part of the IMS travel costs, the country concerned must arrange and pay for that portion, either through the CLO or the official foreign government representative.

h. Expenses involved in the death of FMS IMS are the responsibility of the foreign government; however, the activity concerned will offer all assistance possible. If the assistance of the installation mortuary officer is desired by the foreign government, that officer will, without charge and as a matter of courtesy, negotiate with a civilian mortuary on behalf of the foreign government for the preparation of the remains for burial or shipment. All related charges are the responsibility of the foreign government. Arrangements for other U.S. agency-sponsored IMS will be handled by the sponsoring agency.

i. Expenses involved in the death of dependents of IMS are the responsibility of the IMS or the foreign government, and will be handled in the same manner as stated in paragraph *h*, above.

j. The activity concerned will appoint an individual to officially handle the deceased IMS affairs; for example, obtaining final IMET allowances due, settling valid debts, disposing of an automobile, and inventorying personal effects. Unless otherwise directed, personal effects of deceased IMS will be forwarded with the inventory list to the appropriate Security Cooperation Organization for release to the next of kin.

k. An investigative report of death as a result of accident or homicide will be forwarded to the Military Service. The report can be in letter format. It should—

(1) Address all circumstances surrounding the IMS death.

(2) Contain copies of all necessary supporting documents; for example, accident report, medical reports, and death certificate.

10–49. Reporting of international military student special circumstances

a. Timely reports on academic deficiencies should be addressed to the appropriate Military Service. Often these deficiencies can be corrected by the foreign representative or by programming other training. The objective is to train the IMS at the least expense to the U.S. or country concerned.

b. An IMS who fails to meet the minimum training standards set for U.S. personnel may be disenrolled and returned to home country. When it is apparent that an IMS should be withdrawn from training, the appropriate Military Service will be advised immediately of the full particulars of the case. This will include recommendations on suitability for other training or disposition of the IMS. The IMS will not be relieved for cause without authority from the responsible Military Service. Pending receipt of this authority, suspension is authorized at the discretion of the installation commander or school commandant. The Military Service will advise the Security Cooperation Organization, Combatant Command concerned, and the appropriate foreign representative in Washington, DC, when authority has been given to terminate an IMS.

c. The following incidents involving IMS will be reported initially to the Military Service by phone. Before making recommendations on disposition of IMS, priority message summarizing the incident will be sent to the Military Service, Combatant Command, and Security Cooperation Organization.

(1) Hospitalization. Include date of hospitalization, diagnosis, prognosis, and probable date of release. Reports on Family members are not required unless illness, injury, or condition affects IMS training or has political implications or will result in extensive medical charges, which are beyond the IMS ability to pay. See paragraph 8–8 for further information.

(2) Requirement to reschedule training due to academic deficiency.

(3) Accident reports involving IMS or their Family members.

(4) Emergency leave or other significant items affecting IMS welfare.

(5) UA status.

(6) Any event involving an IMS that may have international implications. This will include any complaint by an IMS, or behavioral attitude indicated or reported, revealing the IMS dissatisfaction with their environment or social acceptance.

d. Following initial notification, the Military Service will be kept informed. Written reports will be provided when appropriate.

e. When IMS attending training at OCONUS installations fail to meet standards, they will be released and returned to their home country upon authority of the overseas commander. The Security Cooperation Organization will be fully advised of all details in the case.

Section XI
International Military Student Departure

10–50. Departure to the next training installation

The IMSO will inform the appropriate gaining activity of the departure and itinerary of all IMS. This notification will include information about the IMS in paragraphs (a) through (g), below. If the gaining activity is not identified on the ITO, the sponsoring Military Service must be contacted for this information.

a. Name, grade, country, and Service.

b. Date and hour of departure and scheduled arrival.

c. Name of carrier.

d. Flight or train number.

e. Information that the IMS is traveling by POV.

f. Ensure that each departing IMS has the original ITO with all amendments and, if applicable, a copy of the last pay voucher.

g. Advance TLA payments and TLA payment history (if any).

10–51. Departure from final training installation

a. Military Service specific checklists should be utilized in the process of coordinating the departure of an IMS from their final training installations. These Service specific checklists may be supplemented by locally prepared checklists.

b. At a minimum, the following items should be covered during the departure of an IMS from the final training installation. The corresponding sections and paragraphs in this regulation should be reviewed to ensure all essential issues are addressed.

(1) Administrative—

(a) Student ITO reviewed - all amendments and endorsements signed.

(b) Collect/destroy ID card(s) collected and destroyed.

(c) Training records complete, forwarded, as required.

(d) Classified material disposition confirmed.

(e) Medical records/health insurance matters reviewed/confirmed.

(f) Security Cooperation Organization notified of IMS return to home country.

(2) Financial—

(a) Final pay/allowance confirmed.

(b) Outstanding debts resolved.

(c) Final billeting payments complete.

(3) Travel—

(a) Flight Reservations confirmed.

(b) Request port calls for IMS returning to their home country according to MILDEP regulations.

(c) Baggage complies with USG limitations.

(d) Shipment of personal goods arranged.

(e) The RIM packed separately.

(f) Leave enroute confirmed.

10–52. Retainable instructional materials

The RIM will consist only of unclassified books, pamphlets, maps, charts, or other course material issued to and retained by the IMS and their U.S. classmates. It also includes official Field Studies Program materials. It will not include articles procured by the IMS for personal use and not directly related to the course of instruction. A shipment weight allowance is authorized for each IMS for their RIM. The cost of shipment of RIM is included in the tuition rates for all formal courses based on standard rates set by DOD 7000.14–R, volume 15.

a. Materials will be packaged and labeled at the training installation and shipped via fourth-class mail to the country Security Cooperation Organization for delivery to the student, or to the official address for classified material. A copy of the student's ITO will be placed inside the box. Use of the Army and Air Force Post Office or Fleet Post Office address of the sponsoring Security Cooperation Organization is authorized. Boxes must be addressed to the Security Cooperation Organization (student's name must not be entered on address label) and include (on the side of the package) the WCN and Program Year for IMET students and the WCN and FMS case for FMS students.

b. Personal items and household goods will not be packed or shipped as RIM; cost of packing and shipping these items will be borne by the IMS. The IMS is also not permitted to ship these items with RIM by paying for excess charges over the authorized weight.

c. An endorsement to the ITO will cite the weight shipped. The following RIM weight allowances will apply:

(1) Up to 200 pounds for each course the Military Service consider to be in the PME category (see MILDEP sections in this chap.)

(2) Up to 50 pounds for all other courses. IMS wishing to send RIM via international mail or over the total authorized weight allowance will do so at their own expense.

10–53. In-country debriefings

The Security Cooperation Organization should debrief IMS upon their return to the home country to determine their impressions of the United States, the quality of training received, and suggestions for improvements that should be made for subsequent IMS. Noteworthy data will be forwarded to the appropriate Military Service, with an information copy to the combatant command.

10–54. Follow-up on graduates

School commandants are encouraged to maintain contact with graduates of career and similar top-level courses after the IMS return to their home country. Such contact may include the following:

a. Letters from the commander, along with the annual school newsletter or similar school publications, and informal correspondence among classmates.

b. Professional publications subscriptions for IMS enrolled in CONUS staff and career courses. Each subscription must be appropriate to the course taken by the IMS and will be initiated before the IMS leaves the United States. The subscription will be for a maximum of 1 year and can be funded under the Field Studies Program.

Section II
Department of the Army

10–55. International military student officer

a. Staffing.

(1) Staffing levels and grades for the IMSO are predicated on the annual international military student through put as well as established quantitative and qualitative manpower requirements based on the performance of regular, repetitive and non-repetitive tasks within an IMSO. It's normally stated as a mathematical equation relating required IMSO man-hours to execute the mission to the number of IMS that come on an annual basis. This system referenced is called the Manpower Staffing Standard System. It is periodically reviewed via studies to ensure continued validity. An expression of the number of personnel required to run the IMSO is developed through the Manpower Staffing Standard System process and is incorporated into a TDA, which lists the number of personnel, job series, and appropriate grades. IMSO will be staffed according to the results of the Manpower Staffing Standard System process and resultant TDA. If a dramatic fluctuation in the student throughput occurs, it may be necessary to either add or remove personnel from the IMSO.

(2) Notify SATFA P4 as soon as a determination is made to adjust IMSO staffing levels so specific guidance can be obtained on proper procedure, possible alternatives, and to ensure funds will be both approved by Director, SATFA, and made available through course tuition costs to pay for an increase, if appropriate, in personnel costs.

(3) Should government transportation, including IMSO leased vehicle, not be available to support and execute the IMSO mission to include the Field Studies Program, IMSO personnel are authorized to use their POV for the mission and be compensated for doing so. An official designation letter must be prepared allowing named IMSO individual to use their POV for administrative and support functions, to include for the Field Studies Program. Mileage only compensation at current JTFR rates is permissible. Copy of designation letters and all payment vouchers with substantiating documentation is to be kept on file in accordance with AR 25–400–2.

b. Training.

(1) Training and orientation opportunities for the IMSO, their staff and chain of command include paragraphs (a) through (e), below.

(a) A one week course, the Security Assistance Management-Training Officer (SAM–TO) Course, conducted at DISAM at Wright-Patterson AFB, OH. Quotas for this course are allocated by SATFA P4.

(b) An orientation visit to SATFA will be coordinated and scheduled by SATFA P4 shortly after assignment as an IMSO Chief.

(c) Conferences and regional reviews/workshops conducted on an as needed basis by SATFA for IMSO personnel and immediate chain of command.

(d) Liaison visits to other installations to exchange ideas and information will be coordinated with SATFA P4.

(e) The Cross Cultural Communication Course and regional orientation courses conducted at Hurlburt Field, FA.

(2) Except for the SAM–TO course, the costs of these orientations, visits, and conferences should be charged to IMSO administrative funds captured in the course tuition costs. If such funds are not available, costs for these activities may be charged to Field Studies Program funds.

c. Responsibilities. (see para 10–6). The name, office, and telephone number of assigned IMSO personnel will be reported semiannually to SATFA P4. Changes will be furnished as they occur. IMSO responsibilities fall into three primary categories, which are not mutually exclusive—

(1) *IMSO administrative and support functions.* These are clearly delineated throughout chapter 10 of this regulation. Army IMSO have the following specific responsibilities: Keep the IMSO Training Web information up to date. The Security Assistance Network IMSO Web provides for the entry of IMSO point of contact information, detailed training location information, and any other international only information. This information is entered by the IMSO (not by SATFA) and must be kept current by the IMSO. In addition, IMSO can enter specific international notes and prerequisites that pertain to specific courses of instruction at their training activity. Again, this information is entered by the IMSO and is thus tailored to a need to provide specific information for the international community on their courses. SATFA pulls scope and prerequisites from the Army Training Resource and Requirements System. The IMSO should periodically check this information to ensure it is current. The IMSO will prepare STL report for servicing resources management personnel to assist their efforts to accurately project earnings from course tuition rates. Execute an orientation program for IMS and include the training installation briefing as outlined in paragraph 10–13.

(2) *IMSO training functions.* These include—

(a) Briefing IMS on general U.S. Army training procedures, to include the U.S. Army honor code, small group

instruction, computer based training, practical exercises, field training exercises, physical training requirements, interacting with NCOs, female and civilian instructors, use of training schedules, and other topics which will assist IMS in fitting into their courses.

(b) Monitoring academic progress of IMS throughout their stay at the installation. This requires constant coordination with instructional departments and early intervention for IMS that may experience academic difficulties. IMSO will notify appropriate SATFA country program manager if student is experiencing continuing academic difficulty or is in danger of failing.

(c) Coordinating with appropriate agency personnel to execute distributed learning (DL) courses in residence for IMS.

(d) Ensuring that U.S. students in courses with IMS are briefed on the SC Program.

(e) Ensuring that instructors are briefed on the SC Program and on interacting with IMS.

(f) Implementing an academic or in-class sponsor program, including briefing both IMS and academic or in-class sponsors on their responsibilities and on the SC Program.

(3) *IMSO Field Studies Program.* These are detailed in chapter 11 of this regulation.

10–56. Channels of communication and correspondence

a. When an IMSO communicates directly with Security Cooperation Organization on routine administrative matters concerning IMS, information copies will be sent to the SATFA country program manager, and other training commands as appropriate. Initial reports of a disciplinary nature should not include Security Cooperation Organization as information addressee. IMSO will immediately initiate action through Director, SATFA chain of command when unique or controversial situations arise that might be detrimental to the IMS successful completion of training. SATFA country program manager will provide information copies to the combatant commands and Security Cooperation Organization on controversial IMS matters.

b. Foreign attaches and liaison offices in the Washington, DC area are authorized to communicate with schools/training activities only on routine administrative matters. Other issues regarding IMS, training, and so forth will be coordinated with SATFA. Schools receiving unauthorized telephone or written communication will notify SATFA country program manager.

c. Foreign officers such as TRADOC Foreign Liaison Officers (FLO) and exchange instructors have no official role in the SCETP. They may communicate informally with IMS from their countries, but do not have roles in issues pertaining to the training of IMS.

10–57. Arrival and departure arrangements

The following actions are taken by the IMSO:

a. Student arrival information. Obtain student arrival information from the Security Assistance Network IMSO Web. The Security Assistance Network IMSO Web system should be routinely screened to determine reporting/arrival data available for each scheduled IMS. If arrival information is not available 15 days before a student's report date the IMSO should communicate by message directly with the appropriate Security Cooperation Organization. The IMSO should notify the appropriate SATFA country program manager if a particular country is habitually late with student arrival information. If the IMS does not arrive as scheduled, the IMSO should contact the appropriate SATFA country program manager as soon as feasible.

b. IMS arrival. As soon as projected IMS arrival has been determined by information provided by the Security Cooperation Organization in Training Management System and the Security Assistance Network Training Web, the IMSO will communicate advance information packets by either hard copy or electronic media such as on a CD or a Web site URL to the Security Cooperation Organization of each country for dissemination to IMS. The information should be sent as early as possible, but NLT 60 days before student's projected arrival. Content should include information that is interesting and useful to a student traveling to the United States for the first time. Items that should be included are: general information about the installation; maps of the local area; estimates of living costs; types of clothing required; housing facilities and availability; information concerning family members; amount of American currency required for the initial period; a general address for forwarding mail to the United States; and reporting instructions. Be sure to include instructions to the Security Cooperation Organization on procedures to be followed regarding timely notification of the IMS travel itinerary. Also, include instructions to IMS on reporting in the event they are not met at the arrival point. In addition, a special text containing the terminology, along with applicable acronyms, peculiar to the course should be included to help the IMS prepare for training. This text provides most IMS their first insight into U.S. military training and is an indispensable part of their orientation.

c. Initiate student file. The IMSO will initiate a student file for each IMS. The student file will include arrival notice, ITO, biographical information and any other pertinent IMS information or correspondence that will transpire during training. The ITO contains personal information that potentially may be used in identity theft and should be protected and covered with a DA Label 87 Form (For Official Use Only Sheet). The ITO or forms with sensitive personal IMS information including their foreign identification number will be shredded versus discarded in a waste receptacle. The final CONUS training installation IMSO will retain the student file in the current files area until no longer needed for conducting business, but not longer than 6 years, then destroy in accordance with the record retention schedule as stated in AR 25–400–2.

d. Student arrival at installation. The IMSO or designee should take IMS to the temporary lodging facility, give them welcome packets, and advise them when they will be picked up to begin in-processing. If possible, IMS should be given time to rest and obtain basic subsistence for the first few hours on the installation. IMSO staff will provide information in the student welcome packets such as, items of local interest, such as, special events, bus schedules, taxi rates, hotels, and local community organizations established to assist IMS. If IMS have religious or national dietary requirements, the person meeting them should provide them with a list of local restaurants that meet these requirements. If the sponsor is available, they can be of great assistance during this time.

e. IMSO at initial training installation. This installation will review passports and visas upon arrival of IMS and authorized Family members, if applicable. Visas other than A–2, conflict of names with ITO and other discrepancies will be immediately reported through the SATFA country program manager to Security Cooperation Organization for resolution. IMSO will encourage IMS to contact their embassies at least 60 days prior to departure to determine any transit visa requirements or country travel restrictions.

f. Billeting arrangements. The IMS should be housed in the same quarters as U.S. students, rather than in separate quarters or language groups. If IMS from several countries are at the same training location and U.S. personnel cannot be billeted with them, the students should be quartered in heterogeneous groupings. If possible, IMS should occupy unaccompanied personnel housing equivalent to that for U.S. personnel of the equivalent rank. If students are to stay in the temporary lodging facility, the IMSO should notify the billeting office prior to the students arrival.

g. Sponsors. The IMSO should provide sponsors with student arrival dates, country notes/culture-grams, and background information on the student if available. If possible, the IMSO should arrange for the sponsor to meet with the IMS during the in-processing period, particularly if the student is accompanied by family members.

h. Departure. Advise the IMS to report to the IMSO in sufficient time before departure to ensure that arrangements for transportation to the airport, final pay, tickets and baggage are complete. Ensure that the driver/escort personnel are aware of all requirements and that any special transportation/vehicle needs are addressed in advance. IMSO personnel escorting IMS to the airport are to remain with the IMS through the entire check-in process. Once the IMS has checked their baggage and received their boarding pass, the IMSO escort is free to depart the airport.

i. Shipment of retainable instructional material. The IMSO assists students in packing, labeling, and shipping RIM, and ensures that no personal effects are packed with the instructional materials when they inspect the contents of the mailing box. Students who wish to send instructional materials over the authorized weight allowance must do so at their own expense.

(1) Refer to student's ITO to make sure that the correct address is included on the mail label. Failure to refer to the ITO is the main cause of misrouted RIM.

(2) Each RIM container will be clearly marked in the lower left-hand corner of the label showing IMS ITO number, WCN, and FMS case, if applicable. Do not include IMS name on either the outside of the box or on the mailing label.

(3) Place a copy of the IMS ITO inside of each package of RIM.

j. Other requirements. The IMSO will ensure that the IMS has returned any issued equipment, and that the IMS ID card and meal card, if applicable, have been turned in. The ID card will be turned in and disposed of at the last training site.

10–58. Biographical data

Submission of biographical data for enlisted personnel attending the U.S. Army Sergeants Major Academy (USASMA) shall be done by the Security Cooperation Organization using the Training Management System IMS information function which is then uploaded to the Security Assistance Network at least 60 days prior to student arrival.

10–59. Legal status and claims

a. See AR 27–20 for information about the jurisdiction of service courts regarding treatment specific to members of the Australian forces in the United States.

b. The servicing judge advocate will contact HQDA (DAJA–IA), Washington, DC 20310–2214, for information about the diplomatic or other status of the IMS concerned.

c. See AR 27–20 for information about claims arising in the United States due to the activities of IMS from countries that have ratified the NATO SOFA..

d. See AR 27–20, chapter 11, for the status of IMS in training. Also see AR 27–20 chapters 3 and 4, for proper party claimant status. See AR 27–20, chapter 3, for baggage claims.

e. Any incident that may lead to the exercise of some form of jurisdiction by local authorities should be reported immediately to Director, SATFA and the appropriate SATFA country program manager.

10–60. Family members

For in-depth information on Family members, refer to paragraph 10–16 and table 7–1 in this regulation. It should be noted that just because a dependent is "authorized" on an ITO does not mean that they are "encouraged." The allowances for each are not the same. For clarification of "encouraged" Family members, please refer to the SAMM, table C10.T3.

a. Should the commander of the training installation determine that the length and nature of the course and the availability of housing and other amenities support the presence of Family members, they may forward a request for approval for a specific course to Director, SATFA. If the request is approved, exceptions will apply to all IMS for the approved course.

b. When IMS choose not to live in available government provided quarters, whether accompanied by Family members or not, all living allowances will be forfeited. A statement of non-availability will not be issued to IMS with Family members when government quarters for unaccompanied students are available. The exception to this is if Family members are "encouraged" as stated above.

c. Scheduled reporting or departure dates and routing will not be altered merely to accommodate IMS travel with Family members. The use of government owned vehicles in the reception and departure of bona fide Family members of IMS, as listed on the ITO, is authorized, subject to local vehicle availability.

d. The Security Cooperation Organization will notify training installations one month before the arrival of IMS accompanied by Family members. Names and ages of authorized Family members will be annotated in the ITO to facilitate administrative/logistical coordination. Failure to give adequate notice may cause embarrassing situations as to initial reception and the availability of quarters and sponsors.

10–61. Commissary and exchange privileges
Commissary and post exchange privileges will be extended to IMS and their authorized accompanying Family members.

10–62. Clothing, uniforms, and equipment
a. Organizational clothing and equipment. Lost, damaged, or destroyed property will be accounted for according to AR 735–5.

b. Individual flying equipment. Flying equipment issued to an IMS at the initial aviation training facility may be retained throughout the IMS CONUS pilot training. This equipment will be turned in at the issuing facility.

c. Clothing purchases. The sale of distinctive uniforms or items of uniforms listed in AR 670–1 is prohibited unless specifically authorized by the installation commander.

(1) Installation commanders may extend to IMS the privilege of purchasing non-distinctive clothing from the clothing sales store. IMSO should tell IMS about the policy at their installation. When an IMS reports for training, the IMSO should check personal items of equipment and clothing to ensure they are adequate for the prescribed training course. Before commencement of training, the IMSO is required to conduct an inventory of these items, noting any shortages and immediately make provisions for purchase from an on-post source if available. Unless otherwise specified in the course information included in the IMSO Web, the following minimum clothing allowance must be considered before the IMS is sent to CONUS for training:

(a) Two complete winter uniforms and four complete summer uniforms.

(b) One raincoat.

(c) One winter topcoat or jacket (if appropriate).

(d) Two work uniforms battle dress uniform (if appropriate).

(e) One pair of work shoes (safety shoes/combat boots) (if appropriate).

(f) Other necessary items such as dress shoes, socks, gloves, underwear, caps, and military insignia.

(2) The use of tuition cost to fund the purchase of personal items of clothing for IMS is not authorized. Exceptions to this policy must be approved by SATFA. IMS without sufficient clothing/uniforms or funds sufficient to purchase these items to meet climatic conditions at the training site are subject to return to country.

(3) Unresolved problems should be brought to the attention of the appropriate SATFA country program manager at the earliest possible time.

10–63. Rank insignia
To help identify IMS equivalent U.S. rank, IMS are authorized to wear the equivalent U.S. rank insignia directly below their name tags. The cost of IMS U.S. rank insignia is properly chargeable to the IMSO administrative funds earned through course tuition rates.

10–64. Grooming standards
The IMS will maintain acceptable standards of appearance, conduct, health and hygiene so as not to affect the discipline or morale of U.S. personnel or negatively impact ability to successfully complete training. Strict adherence to AR 670–1 will be required in courses in which safety is an issue. IMSO will include applicable grooming standards within IMS requirements for courses in the IMSO Web.

10–65. Disclosure of classified military information and controlled unclassified information

a. The CMI and CUI will only be released to IMS according to AR 380–10.

b. Disclosure of CMI and CUI to IMS will be addressed on a case-by-case basis according to AR 380–10. A DCS, G–2/DCS, G–3/5/7 clearance will be obtained for each request for training that includes CMI/CUI, unless a prior blanket clearance has been granted. All appropriate clearances will be obtained before offering the training to the requesting country.

10–66. Graduation, diplomas, certificates of attendance, and awards/badges

a. In general, IMS should complete the same requirements and meet the same standards as U.S. students to be awarded a diploma in a U.S. Army course. Exceptions other than for classified instruction will be justified. IMS will complete all other course requirements, including field training exercises and blocks of instruction that appear to pertain only to U.S. students. Schools may substitute appropriate training for blocks of instruction unavailable to IMS. Standards are not compromised by allowing IMS additional time to complete written exams, or by allowing them to have translating aids/dictionaries. Flexibility and common sense should prevail when considering course requirements and standards.

(1) The IMS will participate in the class graduation ceremony. It is highly encouraged that country flags for graduating IMS be displayed at the graduation ceremony if the U.S. Flag is displayed.

(2) Any school wishing to grant additional special IMS recognition is encouraged to do so. It is important to remember that IMS attending military schools face academic challenges far greater than U.S. students, for they must overcome barriers such as language and cultural differences while maintaining academic competitiveness. Theirs is a special accomplishment, and should be recognized as such.

b. If an IMS is eligible for early graduation, the IMSO will notify the appropriate SATFA country program manager. Actions should not be taken to return student back to country early until approval is obtained in writing from the country program manager. IMS completion report in the IMSO Web should reflect actual dates of training.

c. Should a student fail their course of instruction, notify appropriate country program manager. They will in turn notify Security Cooperation Organization of such. Country may elect, with course manager's approval, to let student remain in course for a certificate of attendance. A certificate of attendance is a locally developed certificate which attests to the fact that the student attended the training but is not eligible for a graduation diploma. Completion report in the IMSO Web should reflect that the student did not graduate from the course but received, if applicable, a certificate of attendance instead.

d. Special badge qualifications normally given graduates of certain courses will be awarded to IMS upon successful completion and graduation from the attended course. These special badge qualifications such as jump wings, aviator wings, and aviation crewmember wings are permissible for IMS to wear on their uniforms, and are authorized by special orders. Completion report in the IMSO Web should reflect the authorization for the student to wear the badge.

10–67. Physical training

Except for mandatory requirements listed in paragraph 10–26, all other IMS will be encouraged to participate in MILDEP physical training programs and tests. Local commanders may require participation in formations and physical training to the best of an individual's ability. However, in some instances, passing the U.S. Army Physical Fitness Test (APFT) is a requirement for attendance and/or graduation.

10–68. Serious incident reporting

The IMSO will comply with established school/installation notification procedures in the event of a serious incident involving an IMS or IMS Family member. Incidents include but are not limited to DUI, incarceration, theft, security violations, serious illness, or injury, hospitalization, and any incident that could cause removal of student from course/training. IMSO will report immediately via e-mail to the respective SATFA country program manager with info copies to the respective branch chief and the Regional Operations Division Chief.

a. Very serious incidents involving felony crime, life threatening injury or death will be immediately reported to the Director, SATFA via telephone with e-mail follow up to the Director and the Regional Operations Division Chief (dual hatted as the SATFA Deputy).

b. If the incident occurs during off-duty hours, contact the SATFA Duty Officer (follow the contact protocol listed on the SATFA Web site under "Contact Information.")

c. In the event of a conflict concerning notification procedures, IMSO will follow established school policy. IMSO will document incidents in the Security Assistance Network IMSO Web by selecting the appropriate progress message and completing details.

10–69. Disciplinary actions

See paragraph 10–45 for general information. In the absence of standard agreements with countries involved in SC training, IMS cannot be disciplined according to the UCMJ. Disenrollment should be considered as the last disciplinary option available in the case of an IMS who has demonstrated a refusal to conform to the rules and regulations at the command where training takes place. The following should be used as a guideline when disciplinary action(s) is required:

a. Warning.

(1) Disenrollment of an IMS indicates that the mission of training contracted for under the Security Cooperation Training Program has not been accomplished. Experience has shown that contact with IMS by officials of their own government can resolve most disciplinary problems. In many cases such contacts can also have a positive influence on academic problems, especially where the cause may be the IMS attitude in pursuing the course of instruction. Notify appropriate SATFA country program manager as early as possible.

(2) When an IMS indicates nonconformity to established standards of behavior or has failed to achieve required academic progress, the IMSO will formally counsel the IMS concerning these shortcomings. The IMS will be advised of the exact nature of the behavior or performance that has failed to meet established or required standards. The IMS will be advised that an official warning is being provided and that change is required to avoid placement on probation (the last stage before disenrollment). The IMS will be advised of the exact nature of the change required, and of the time period the IMS is being given to make the required change.

(3) The IMSO will make an official record of the counseling session and enter it into the IMS training record. The IMS will be informed that if the required changes in either behavior or academic performance are made within the time period specified, the official record of the counseling session will be removed from the IMS training record upon successful completion of the current course of instruction.

b. Probation.

(1) When an IMS fails to make the changes in either behavior or academic performance required as a result of being formally placed on warning status, or when an IMS indicates serious nonconformity to established standards of behavior, the IMS will officially be placed on probation.

(2) If the IMS is placed on probation, the IMSO will formally counsel the IMS. The IMS will be advised of the exact nature of the behavior or performance that has failed to meet established or required standards and as a result the IMS is officially being placed on probation. The IMS must change to avoid recommendation for disenrollment. Inform IMS that their Washington, DC based attaché or government official will be notified of this action. The details will be recorded in an official letter to the IMS from the IMSO during the official counseling session. A copy of this letter will be placed in the IMS training record and will remain in the record.

c. Disenrollment. When an IMS fails to make changes in either behavior or academic performance required as a result of being formally placed on probation, or when an IMS exhibits behavior prejudicial to good order and discipline, the commandant of the training activity or the commanding officer of the installation, or both, as appropriate, are authorized to recommend disenrollment. This recommendation will be forwarded to SATFA country program manager, P4, and Director, SATFA.

10–70. Casualty report, death and disposition of remains

See paragraph 10–48 for general information.

a. If an IMS under DA sponsorship dies, the U.S. Army activity at which the death occurs will immediately notify appropriate SATFA country program manager, branch chief and Director, SATFA. Notification information can be found on the SATFA Web site under "Contact Information." If the death occurs during off duty hours, follow contact protocol listed in the aforementioned section labeled "Contact Information." SATFA will notify the appropriate foreign attaché at HQ, TRADOC and HQDA (DASA (DE&C)). The initial report will include as much information as possible on the Fatal Accident Notification and Interim Report. In addition to the initial report and the operations reporting required, a follow-up interim report must be submitted to HQ, TRADOC via Director, SATFA, within 72 hours. The interim follow-up report will address any additional information obtained since the initial notification.

b. The training activity or installation will furnish a casualty report according to AR 600–8–1; SATFA (AT-TG–TRI–SR) will be included as an action addressee. HQDA (DASA (DE&C)), the combatant commands, and the Security Cooperation Organization will be included as information addressees to the casualty report.

c. The senior mission commander will convene a Fatality Review Board and conduct a fatality after action review within 14 days of the incident. A copy of the final review report of an accidental death or homicide will be forwarded to the Director, SATFA.

10–71. School crests

The IMS will be presented with a special crest with an accompanying locally developed authorization certificate. The crest will consist of the distinctive insignia for each school superimposed on a background identical for all schools. The gold-colored metal background consists of a star with rays surmounted by a wreath of leaves encircled by a wavy continuous scroll with the words: U.S. ARMY SCHOOLS. The time of issue for the crest and accompanying certificate will be determined by the school commandant. Exceptions to the standard school crest are authorized for CGSC and AWC.

10–72. Academic reports

Academic reports should accurately reflect IMS achievement and performance. DD Form 2496 (International Student Academic Report) must be prepared for IMS upon completion of each course of instruction (except preparatory courses). If the school commandant determines the same academic and grading standard can be applied to follow-on courses in a series, one academic report will be prepared for that series of training. (See fig 10–1 for a sample of the completed form and fig 10–2 for instructions.) If an IMS has follow-on training at another installation, a copy of the academic report for the previous training will be forwarded to the next installation IMSO for information and guidance.

a. Signed academic reports on IMS will be scanned and uploaded to the Security Assistance Network IMSO Web student information page within 60 days after graduation.

(1) The Security Cooperation Organization will download the academic report from the Security Assistance Network Web. The Security Cooperation Organization will release academic reports to foreign governments as appropriate, taking into consideration the possible political or military implications of the academic report.

(2) The foreign government may choose to have the academic reports for FMS IMS delivered to the country's embassy in Washington, DC. In such cases, the foreign government must forward an official request through the Security Cooperation Organization to SATFA.

(3) The IMSO may provide a copy of the academic report to the IMS if it is complete and signed at time of departure.

b. The distribution list will not be shown on DD Form 2496.

10–73. Public affairs

a. Public affairs activities will be conducted under the provisions of AR 360–1.

b. Requests for IMS interviews or other IMS-related public affairs activities will be referred to the installation Public Affairs Officer, who will coordinate with OASD Public Affairs. Security concerns may preclude IMS from certain countries from participating in media events.

c. Hometown-type release of stories and pictures of IMS and visitors are governed by a separate message issued annually by the Adjutant General (TAG).

d. Inquiries regarding IMS via the Freedom of Information Act shall be dealt with in accordance with AR 25–55. Director, SATFA should be notified immediately of any official Freedom of Information Act requests regarding IMS and concurrence to release information obtained prior to doing so.

e. Routine requests for IMS information from other Federal Government agencies may be received and it is permissible to provide the requestor with routine STL information for the current FY. If the requestor desires additional information IMSO must first notify Director, SATFA and receive the Director's concurrence to release the additional information.

10–74. Visits (see para 12–3 for foreign personnel not enrolled in a training program)

The IMSO will refer visit requests to the installation protocol office.

10–75. Release of maps

Release of official maps is restricted and will be in accordance with AR 115–11.

Section III
Department of the Navy (U.S. Navy, U.S. Marine Corps and U.S. Coast Guard) (Student Administration)

10–76. International military student officer

a. The IMSO will be appointed for a minimum of 2 years, when possible, and will receive the necessary training to perform this important function. Training of Navy command IMSO will be coordinated by Naval Education and Training Security Assistance Field Activity, training of Marine Corps IMSO will be coordinated by USMC/CG, SECTC MCCDC, and training of Coast Guard IMSO will be coordinated by USCG International Affairs (G–CI).

b. The IMSO name, office, and telephone number (both commercial and defense switched network (DSN), must be reported to Naval Education and Training Security Assistance Field Activity for Navy, USMC/CG, SECTC MCCDC for Marine Corps training activities, and USCG International Affairs (G–CI) for Coast Guard training activities.

c. The IMSO will be responsible for the administration of IMS while assigned to the training activity.

d. The IMSO will maintain biographical records on IMS. The IMSO must report infractions, incidents of a serious nature, or serious medical conditions or emergencies involving either IMS or their Family members. The initial report will be by telephone followed immediately by a priority message. For Navy- sponsored IMS, reports will be made to Navy IPO via the chain of command and Naval Education and Training Security Assistance Field Activity. For Marine Corps-sponsored IMS, reports will be made to USMC/CG, SECTC MCCDC via the chain of command, with information copies to Navy IPO and Naval Education and Training Security Assistance Field Activity. For Coast

Guard-sponsored IMS, reports will be made to USCG International Affairs (G–CI) via the chain of command, with information copies to Navy IPO and Naval Education and Training Security Assistance Field Activity.

e. The IMSO will be the commanding officer's principal advisor for the Field Studies Program.

10–77. Correspondence procedures

a. The Security Cooperation Organization should consult cognizant Commanders of Combatant Commands directives for specific details on their correspondence routing requirements.

(1) For Navy or predominantly Navy-sponsored training, Security Cooperation Organization should address correspondence to Naval Education and Training Security Assistance Field Activity with information copies to Navy IPO, the Commanders of Combatant Commands, and other addressees, as appropriate.

(2) For Marine Corps or predominantly Marine Corps- sponsored training, Security Cooperation Organization should address correspondence to CG SECTC MCCDC with information copies to Navy IPO, the unified commander, Naval Education and Training Security Assistance Field Activity, and other addressees, as appropriate.

(3) For Coast Guard or predominantly Coast Guard-sponsored training, Security Cooperation Organization should address correspondence to USCG International Affairs (G–CI) with information copies to Navy IPO, Naval Education and Training Security Assistance Field Activity, the Combatant Commanders, and other addressees as appropriate.

b. Training activities should address correspondence to Naval Education and Training Security Assistance Field Activity for Navy or predominantly Navy-sponsored training, to CG SECTC MCCDC for Marine Corps or predominantly Marine Corps-sponsored training, and to USCG International Affairs (GCI) for Coast Guard sponsored training. In each instance, information copies should be sent to Navy IPO, Naval Education and Training Security Assistance Field Activity, the Security Cooperation Organization, and other addressees, as appropriate.

c. Direct correspondence for routine matters relating to IMS administration is authorized between Security Cooperation Organization and training activities and between training activities. Training activities may also forward command generated information packages to Security Cooperation Organization for forwarding to prospective students.

d. The "Subject" line of all correspondence relating to DON SC training should contain as a minimum five critical elements - FY of training discussed, type of program (IMET or FMS), country concerned, WCN, and (for FMS training) FMS case designator. Additionally, a short narrative description of the contents and the T–MASL number (if applicable) may also be included.

e. When the subject line of record correspondence is not suited to the system outlined in d above, care should be taken to ensure that the subject is clearly identified.

10–78. Family members

a. Although IMS are generally discouraged from bringing their Family members to CONUS while attending courses, they are encouraged to bring their Family members while attending the following:

(1) Joint Forces Staff College.

(2) Naval Command College.

(3) Naval Staff College.

(4) Marine Corps Command and Staff College.

(5) Marine Corps Expeditionary Warfare School.

(6) Marine Corps School of Advanced Warfighting.

(7) Long-term resident postgraduate courses at NPS

b. The Security Cooperation Organization will notify training installations 1 month before the arrival of IMS accompanied by dependents. Failure to give such notification may cause embarrassing situations during initial reception and in the availability of quarters and sponsors.

c. The IMS reporting to the Naval Postgraduate School, Monterey, CA; Naval War College, Newport, RI; and Marine Corps Command and Staff College, Expeditionary Warfare School, and School of Advanced Warfighting, Quantico VA, will be advised that Family members should obtain A–2 visas instead of B–1 or B–2 visas, as the latter require renewals and fees.

10–79. Student control number assignment procedures

Most IMS undergoing training in the United States will receive a foreign identification number, in accordance with BUPERSINST 1750.10. In exceptional circumstances when a foreign identification number cannot be issued, the IMS will receive a student control number. The student control number is issued by Naval Education and Training Security Assistance Field Activity.

10–80. Public affairs and information

Current policy regarding public affairs and information for the U.S. Navy and U.S. Marine Corps are contained in SECNAVINST 5720.44B.

10–81. Visits

Procedures for the approval of visits by representatives of foreign governments or international organizations to DON commands, activities, or facilities, are outlined in SECNAVINST 5510.34A. IMS desiring to visit a DON command, activity, or facility for a purpose not related to their SCETP, must submit a request to Navy IPO for such a visit, through normal country visit request channels.

10–82. Shipyard training

Before any commitment is made to perform training in United States shipyards or repair facilities, permission must be obtained from the Commander, Naval Sea Systems Command (NAVSEASYSCOM). Facilities involved in naval nuclear propulsion will provide training only after approval has been given and then only rarely. When it is imperative that an IMS receive training in a shipyard engaged in work on nuclear-powered vessels, the following applies:

a. The requester must provide complete justification for the proposal to train in such a facility. This justification will address the following items:

(1) Specific need for such training.

(2) Reasons why the training cannot be provided elsewhere.

b. Procedures for obtaining approval are outlined in the SECNAVINST 5510.34A.

c. A full-time escort will be required if training is permitted. The requester must address provisions for reimbursement of appropriate charges incurred.

10–83. Distributive/distance learning

The Navy has transformed many legacy systems and business processes through the implementation of the ILE to enable access to a growing number of DL courses for sailors and marines that are delivered through a variety of formats that includes the Internet, the Intranet, CD–ROM, and DVD, as well as, automated electronic classrooms (AEC). Naval Education and Training Security Assistance Field Activity will monitor the training delivery method (TDM), or the methodology the Navy uses to provide training to ensure T–MASL notes are updated and reflect the most current course delivery method to facilitate IMS selection and preparation for the classroom environment. The training location may be at the traditional training location, or at a Distance Learning Center, but will be reflected in the T–MASL.

a. The IMET IMS may attend DL courses in CONUS, but require DSCA waiver for OCONUS delivery. FMS IMS may attend courses in CONUS or OCONUS. DL courses delivered OCONUS will have a "P4" MASL per DSCA guidance.

b. Procedures for DL course attendance generally mirrors processes for all other courses, with the following exceptions.

(1) Prerequisites. All prerequisites, whether for DL or traditional classroom courses, will apply.

(a) ECL. The IMS must meet the established ECL for all DL courses. In fact, English reading comprehension is vital to successful completion of DL courses.

(b) Basic computer skills. IMS must be proficient in basic computer and internet navigation skills, including keyboard and mouse familiarization, start menu, minimize/maximize/close buttons, copy/cut and paste text, save and/or save as, print command, web browser navigation. Management Information Systems (PDET002) is a prerequisite for all DL courses unless IMS has a requisite level of proficiency.

(2) Minimum computer requirements for OCONUS courses.

• An IBM-compatible PC which runs Windows 95/98/ME with 64 Mb RAM, or which runs Windows 2000/NT with 128Mb RAM.
• An internet connection of at least 56 Kb.
• Internet Explorer 4.0 or later.
• A 256-color monitor capable of a resolution of 800 x 600.
• A current version of apple QuickTime and Adobe Acrobat Reader.

(3) *Distance learning registration.* The Navy designated POC will establish IMS access to authorized course(s) after proper ITO authorization to ensure standardized and consistent procedures are followed in the establishment of learning accounts for the IMS. The IMSO at the traditional training site or at the Distance Learning Center will request IMS access by submitting IMS full name, foreign identification number, and date of birth to the Navy designated POC who will then proceed with the registration process.

(4) *Student administration.* If course is locally managed by a facilitator or instructor, all student administration functions will be performed at the training location. If course is delivered at a Distance Learning Center, the designated POC will be responsible for the student administration functions. In all cases, IMS information must be communicated to the country program manager at Naval Education and Training Security Assistance Field Activity, CG SECTC MCCDC or USCG International Affairs (G–CI). The DL student administrative functions include the following tasks in the Learning Management System:

(a) Finding and moving learner from a waitlist to a roster.

(b) Assigning a "job" (content).

(c) Assigning a seat if tracking seats.

(d) Creating transcripts for any labs/tests that are not CBT.

(e) Creating and/or editing transcripts for CBT under special circumstances.

(f) Verifying all content, labs, and tests required for curriculum completion are completed, and transcripts are in the system.

(g) Removing the seat assignment and job from learner.

(h) Dropping the learner from a roster and creating a roster transcript that indicates the number of days the learner was on the roster going through training.

(5) A cancellation penalty will be applied if course is cancelled after establishment of the IMS learning account.

c. See the Marine Corps Desktop Guide for current information on requirements for the Marine Corps Distance Education Programs.

10–84. Contractor training

NAVYIPOINST 4950.1 of 6 April 2004 provides policy guidance for DON and Coast Guard organizations through which contractors provide training to IMS under the security assistance training program (SATP). This includes training provided by contractors in USG facilities by USG and contract instructors, and contractor training provided in non-USG facilities by non-USG personnel.

a. ITO shall be issued for each IMS attending contractor-provided training.

b. When the training is provided by a contractor in non-USG facilities, the contract SOW must include requirements to provide students the same basic student management and life support afforded international students attending training on a USG installation, to include payment of TLA (when applicable); travel arrangements; lodging; dining facilities; daily transportation between IMS quarters, training facility and dining facility; student reporting; medical support; general administration; and Field Studies Program if training is 4 weeks or longer. The cost of these administrative services will be included in the cost of the contract.

10–85. On the job training

a. The OJT is usually follow-on technical training devoted to practical application of skills and knowledge gained during a formal course of study. This training is planned in advance as part of the country's training program.

(1) The Security Cooperation Organization should provide a summary of the general goals and objectives of the OJT, and ensure that OJT is included as a training line on the IMS ITO.

(2) The Naval Education and Training Security Assistance Field Activity/CG SECTC MCCDC/G–CI will confirm the specific goals and objectives of the OJT, determine the location, dates and costs for the OJT, and will ensure that sufficient funds are available to conduct the training.

b. When there is no IMSO at the OJT site, an IMSO will be designated by the Military Service to coordinate the IMS administrative requirements, including—

(1) Pay living allowance, if authorized (based upon berthing/messing availability).

(2) Brief IMS on OJT program.

(3) Request transportation/airline ticket.

(4) Coordinate excess baggage (as required).

(5) Provide student arrival/departure information to OJT unit/site.

(6) Coordinate with the OJT command for the IMS travel.

c. The OJT command will—

(1) Meet student at airport or upon arrival at OJT unit/site.

(2) Verify ITO (retain copy).

(3) Arrange/ensure follow on transportation has been completed (may be arranged in advance by the IMSO).

(4) Brief student on OJT program/schedule and expectations.

(5) Conduct OJT.

(6) If the OJT includes a Field Studies Program event:

(a) Request from Naval Education and Training Security Assistance Field Activity/Security Cooperation Education and Training Center/G–CI to conduct Field Studies Program activities.

(b) Provide report of Field Studies Program activity conducted to the Receiving Training Command or the Security Cooperation Organization, as appropriate.

(7) At the end of the OJT:

(a) Complete and present appropriate OJT completion certificate to the IMS.

(b) Have student complete an IMS OJT evaluation form.

(c) Complete an IMS academic report (DD Form 2496) to document the IMS performance during the OJT. Forward

the IMS OJT evaluation and the DD Form 2496 to the IMSO at the Receiving Training Command or the Security Cooperation Organization as appropriate.

(d) Mail RIM to the IMS home country via the Security Cooperation Organization office or embassy.

(e) If the OJT is the last line of training, collect the IMS ID card and destroy.

(f) Deliver IMS to the departure airport.

10–86. Department of the Navy foreign disclosure policy

a. SECNAVINST 5510.34A provides DON policy with regard to the disclosure of CMI and CUI to foreign nationals by DON personnel. This directive also assigns responsibilities within DON with respect to the control of foreign visitors, liaison officers, exchange personnel, cooperative program personnel, and other foreign nationals or their representatives who may have contact with the DON.

b. SECNAVINST 5510.34A, paragraph 7.1(2) of is particularly important for DON training activities, and is restated here: DON activities responsible for the development of training materials, particularly computer-based training, shall develop the material keeping in mind that the training may be provided to foreign nationals. In those instances where there is a reasonable expectation of foreign participation in the training, to the greatest extent possible, the training should be designed in a modular fashion or in a fashion that may easily be tailored or sanitized.

c. Security and political screening of IMS will be accomplished by the appropriate activity before issuing any ITO authorizing DON Security Cooperation Training. If there is any concern that an IMS might be a security risk, full particulars will be forwarded to Navy IPO, USMC/CG, SECTC MCCDC, or USCG International Affairs (G–CI) as appropriate. USCG International Affairs (G–CI) coordinates disclosure through Navy IPO following all procedures as outlined below.

10–87. Classified training

The IMS are permitted to participate in classified training if disclosure has been authorized by Navy IPO, Commandant USMC, or by a commander delegated authority in the SECNAVINST 5510.34. Under no circumstances will classified training be provided without a disclosure authorization.

a. Proposals for enrollment of IMS in formal classified courses conducted by the U.S. Navy must be submitted to Naval Education and Training Security Assistance Field Activity for coordination. Proposals for enrollment of IMS in formal classified courses conducted by the U.S. Marine Corps must be submitted to USMC/CG, SECTC MCCDC for coordination. Naval Education and Training Security Assistance Field Activity or USMC/SECTC will coordinate with Navy IPO as required. Disclosure authorization will be provided to the appropriate commands upon notification that the training is definitely scheduled. Proposals for unclassified training involving U.S. submarine-related information will also be forwarded to Navy IPO for approval.

b. When the annual Security Cooperation Education and Training Working Group requirements are submitted, the information listed below should be forwarded to Naval Education and Training Security Assistance Field Activity (for U.S. Navy training) or USMC/CG, SECTC MCCDC (for U.S. Marine Corps training) for advance planning coordination. Naval Education and Training Security Assistance Field Activity and USMC/CG, SECTC MCCDC will coordinate with Navy IPO, as required.

(1) Training commands at which classified training is desired.

(2) The T–MASL identification number, course identification number, and course title.

(3) Countries scheduled to attend.

(4) Classification of course.

(5) Class convening data.

c. Approval for programming classified training will not constitute a disclosure authorization. A minimum of 45 working days is required for disclosure processing. Upon completion of the processing, the appropriate commands will be given the necessary disclosure authorization. USMC/CG, SECTC MCCDC or other commands delegated this authority will advise Navy IPO by record correspondence of all disclosure authorizations granted.

d. Training installations are required by SECNAVINST 5510.34A to submit an up-to-date list of classified information and materials used both in regular DON courses in which IMS can be enrolled and in courses specifically designed for IMS. These listings of classified information and materials are submitted to Naval Education and Training Security Assistance Field Activity (for Navy courses) or USMC/CG, SECTC MCCDC (for Marine Corps courses). Naval Education and Training Security Assistance Field Activity or USMC/CG, SECTC MCCDC will coordinate with Navy IPO as required. When course content changes from the previous submission, training installations will submit to Navy IPO (info Naval Education and Training Security Assistance Field Activity for Navy courses or USMC/CG, SECTC MCCDC for Marine Corps courses) a revised listing of classified information and materials proposed for use in the course. Naval Education and Training Security Assistance Field Activity and USMC/CG, SECTC MCCDC will coordinate with Navy IPO as required. In this submission, an asterisk should be used to identify new information or materials. A listing of classified information and materials to be used in classified courses subsequently proposed for the training of IMS will be provided to Navy IPO (info Naval Education and Training Security Assistance Field Activity for Navy courses or USMC/CG, SECTC MCCDC for Marine Corps courses) at least 45 working days before the start date of the proposed training. Again, Naval Education and Training Security Assistance Field Activity and USMC/CG, SECTC MCCDC will coordinate with Navy IPO as required. All listings of classified information and materials used in classified courses will be in the format outlined in the SECNAVINST 5510.34A by 15 March annually. Advise Naval Education and Training Security Assistance Field Activity or USMC/CG SECTC MCCDC as to the latest listings of classified information and materials used in classified courses remain valid. If they are not, a new listing of classified information and materials must be submitted for each course where there is a change. Naval Education and Training Security Assistance Field Activity and USMC/CG, SECTC MCCDC will coordinate with Navy IPO as required.

e. In the case of classified OJT, disclosure authorization by Navy IPO (or USMC/CG, SECTC MCCDC or another command acting under a disclosure delegation set forth in SECNAVINST 5510.34A) cannot be granted until Navy IPO (or the appropriate command) has been informed of the classified content of the training by the activity conducting the training. This applies whether OJT was arranged through the annual training program or by other means. A minimum of 45 working days must be allowed for processing the disclosure authorization.

10–88. Release of course catalogs
SECNAVINST 5510.34A requires requests for the release of course catalogs to be relayed to Naval Education and Training Security Assistance Field Activity for Navy courses or USMC/CG, SECTC MCCDC for Marine Corps courses. Training installations are not authorized to issue course catalogs direct to foreign requesters unless approved by Navy IPO or USMC/CG, SECTC MCCDC, as appropriate.

10–89. Release of international military student training notes
a. Only student notes and locally prepared course materials can be provided by DON training activities to the pertinent Security Cooperation Organization with appropriate release forms. Other classified publications used during instruction of the classified course such as texts and schematics must be requested by the foreign government through normal channels in accordance with SECNAVINST 5510.34A.

b. Before shipping classified student notes and locally prepared course materials, the training activity will ensure these materials are reviewed and bear the appropriate U.S. security classification markings. Student notes and course materials that cannot be reviewed because they are written in a foreign language should be marked with the highest classification of information disclosed during the course. All classified materials will be conspicuously marked by stamp or other means, to indicate- highest classification of included material, date of review, name, and rank of reviewing official, name of cognizant activity and course of training involved. The "Third Country" marking required by SECNAVINST 5510.34A will also be applied to the cover of each classified document. After the appropriate markings are applied, the material will be forwarded to the Security Cooperation Organization for transmittal to the foreign government. (If the authorized address in the Standard Navy Distribution List is other than the Security Cooperation Organization, passing instructions should be included.) In the case of ship's crew training, classified student notes and locally prepared material may be delivered directly to the ship if it is accessible.

c. Classified material that contains communications security information must be forwarded via Commander, Naval Security Group Command (COMNAVSECGRU) to the Security Cooperation Organization for transmittal.

10–90. Incident reporting
a. Infractions or incidents of a serious nature, or serious medical conditions or emergencies, involving either IMS or their Family members will be reported immediately. The initial report will be by telephone followed immediately by a priority message. For Navy-sponsored IMS, reports will be made to Navy IPO via the chain of command and Naval Education and Training Security Assistance Field Activity. For Marine Corps-sponsored IMS, reports will be made to Security Cooperation Education and Training Center with information copies to CMC, Navy IPO and Naval Education and Training Security Assistance Field Activity. For Coast Guard-sponsored IMS, reports will be made to USCG International Affairs (G–CI) with information copies to Navy IPO. Due to the sensitive nature of such reports, distribution will be limited to only these organizations or activities. Refer to paragraph 10–48 for further instructions.

b. The following will be immediately reported as outlined in paragraphs *a,* above:

(1) Serious breaches of discipline.

(2) Matters involving civil authorities.

(3) Incidents considered having politico-military implications.

(4) Situations considered outside the purview of local commands or installations.

(5) Death.

10–91. Unauthorized absence
When an IMS is on UA for more than 24 hours, notify Naval Education and Training Security Assistance Field Activity (for Navy training) or USMC/CG, SECTC MCCDC (for Marine Corps training), or USCG International Affairs (G–CI) (for Coast Guard training.) See paragraph 10–47 for more information.

10–92. Decedent affairs

a. For United States Navy and United States Marine Corps.

(1) When a USG-funded IMS under DON sponsorship dies while undergoing training with U.S. forces or while traveling in relation to the training, the repatriation of remains is the responsibility of the DON. Refer to Descendent Affairs Manual (NAVMEDCOMINST 5360.1) for guidance. Detailed instructions on actions to be taken with respect to the remains will be provided by Navy Mortuary Affairs (Medical Support Office), Great Lakes, IL after coordination with Navy IPO (for USN sponsored IMS) or USMC/CG, SECTC MCCDC (for USMC sponsored IMS).

(2) Statements of expenses for services in connection with the disposition of a deceased IMS under a USG-funded program will be submitted to Navy Mortuary Affairs for certification. The statements will then be forwarded to Naval Education and Training Security Assistance Field Activity for addition of the appropriate accounting data before submitting for payment. Statements for services in connection with the disposition of remains of a FMS IMS in a training status will be submitted to Navy Mortuary Affairs for certification and forwarded to the appropriate embassy for payment.

b. For USCG. Contact USCG International Affairs (G–CI) for guidance.

10–93. Disenrollment

a. In the absence of standard agreements with countries involved in SC training, IMS cannot be disciplined according to the UCMJ. Disenrollment is the only disciplinary option available in the case of an IMS who has demonstrated an inability to conform to the rules and regulations at the command where training takes place. Disenrollment is also the only option available in the case of an IMS who cannot succeed academically.

b. Authority to disenroll IMS will be executed by the Deputy Director, Navy IPO for Navy sponsored IMS. Authority to disenroll IMS will be executed by the Commanding General, Training and Education Command (CG, TECOM) for Marine Corps sponsored IMS.

c. Disenrollment of an IMS indicates that the mission of training contracted for under an IMET or FMS training program has not been accomplished. Therefore, disenrollment must be viewed as the last resort. Experience has shown that contact with IMS by officials of their own government can resolve most disciplinary problems. In many cases such contacts can also have a positive influence on academic problems, especially where the cause may be the IMS attitude in pursuing the course of instruction. To effect this contact, disciplinary and academic problems must be brought to the attention of SC training points of contact within the chain of command and either Naval Education and Training Security Assistance Field Activity, or USMC/CG, SECTC MCCDC, as appropriate, should be contacted as early as possible.

d. To facilitate the proper documentation, reporting, and resolution of academic and disciplinary problems, the following system will be implemented by all DON activities providing SC training to IMS:

(1) *Warning.*

(a) When an IMS indicates nonconformity to established standards of behavior or has failed to achieve required academic progress, the IMSO will formally counsel the IMS concerning these shortcomings. The IMS will be advised of the exact nature of the behavior or performance that has failed to meet established or required standards. The IMS will be advised that an official warning is being provided and that change is required to avoid the IMS placement on probation (the last stage before disenrollment). The IMS will be advised of the exact nature of the change required, and of the time period the IMS is being given to make the required change.

(b) The IMSO will make an official record of the counseling session and enter it into the IMS training record. The IMS will be informed that if the required changes in either behavior or academic performance are made within the time period specified, the official record of the counseling session will be removed from the IMS training record upon the IMS successful completion of the current course of instruction.

(2) *Probation.*

(a) When an IMS fails to make the changes in either behavior or academic performance required as a result of being formally placed on warning status, or when an IMS exhibits serious nonconformity to established standards of behavior or conduct creating a safety risk, the IMS will officially be placed on probation.

(b) If an IMS is placed on probation, the commanding officer will formally counsel the IMS. The IMS will be advised of the exact nature of the behavior or performance that has failed to meet established or required standards, that the IMS is officially being placed on probation, that the IMS must change to avoid recommendation for disenrollment, of the exact nature of the change required, of the time period in which the change must occur, and that the IMS Washington, DC, based attaché or other government official will be notified of this action. These details will be recorded in an official letter to the IMS from the commanding officer that will be provided to the IMS during the official counseling session. A copy of this letter will be placed in the IMS training record and will remain in that record until the IMS successfully completes all CONUS based training. If the IMS conduct or academic progress so warrants, the IMSO at the last activity or installation providing training to the IMS will remove this letter from the training record prior to forwarding the training record to the Security Cooperation Organization.

(c) Navy IPO, USMC/CG, SECTC MCCDC, or USCG International Affairs (G–CI) as appropriate, will notify the Washington, DC, based representative of the IMS government.

(3) Disenrollment.

(a) When an IMS fails to make the changes in either behavior or academic performance required as a result of being formally placed on probation, or when an IMS exhibits behavior prejudicial to good order and discipline or conduct creating a safety risk, the Commanding Officer of the training activity is authorized to recommend disenrollment. This recommendation will be made through the chain of command to Navy IPO (info CNO (N52)) for Navy sponsored IMS, to USMC/CG, SECTC MCCDC for Marine Corps-sponsored IMS. Information copies of any correspondence relating to disenrollment will be provided Naval Education and Training Security Assistance Field Activity. The initial report will be by telephone followed immediately by a priority message. The report will include appropriate recommendations. Copies of all record correspondence relating to disenrollment will become a permanent part of the IMS training record and will be forwarded to the Security Cooperation Organization after the IMS return to homeland.

(b) Navy IPO and USMC/CG, SECTC MCCDCG, as appropriate, will notify the Washington, DC based representative of the IMS Government.

(c) Naval Education and Training Security Assistance Field Activity and USMC/CG, SECTC MCCDC will provide disposition instructions to the training activity involved. Copies will be provided to Navy IPO, CNO (N52), the combatant command, the Security Cooperation Organization, and the Washington, DC based representative of the IMS Government.

10–94. Political asylum

a. Procedures to be followed when political asylum is requested are implemented within the DON by SEC-NAVINST 5710.22A. The U.S. Navy point of contact for implementation of these policies is the Deputy Chief of Naval Operations Information Plans (Strategy and Policy Division) The U.S. Marine Corps point of contact for implementation of these policies is the Operational Law Branch (JAO), Marine Corps Judge Advocate General Division, Headquarters, U.S. Marine Corps.

b. Distribution of messages concerning this subject should be strictly limited to protect the confidentiality of the IMS. In no case shall a training activity include in-country addresses. Message should be addressed as follows:

(1) Navy activities should address reports to CNO (N514G), info Navy IPO, Naval Education and Training Security Assistance Field Activity and the chain of command.

(2) Marine Corps activities should address reports to USMC/CG, SECTC MCCDC and CMC (JAO), info Navy IPO, Naval Education and Training Security Assistance Field Activity and the chain of command.

(3) Further dissemination of information will be determined at the SECNAV, CNO, or CMC levels.

(4) The USCG policy for political asylum is outlined in COMDTINST M 16247.1D. Notifications for IMS attending training at USCG training activities should be addressed through USCG International Affairs (G–CI) with info copy through the chain of command. G–CI will provide further notification and coordination, as required.

10–95. Termination of training and security cooperation education and training program records disposition

a. The Navy IMSO Guide provides guidance on actions required by the IMSO when CONUS training is terminated by graduation/completion, at the request of the IMS government, as a result of illness, as a result of disenrollment, or for any other reason.

b. Naval Education and Training Security Assistance Field Activity, as FMS Training Case and U.S.-funded Program Administrator, is responsible for the disposition of all SCETP records dealing with individual IMS and individual country training programs; USMC/CG, SECTC MCCDC has similar responsibilities for Marine Corps SCETP records. This includes, but is not limited to, ITO, status reports, correspondence, and messages. If Naval Education and Training Security Assistance Field Activity is an info addressee on any such correspondence, activities may destroy their copy when no longer needed. If Naval Education and Training Security Assistance Field Activity is not in receipt, the report should be forwarded to Naval Education and Training Security Assistance Field Activity for determination and further disposition on a case-by-case basis. Reports dealing with the IMS academic evaluation should be included in the individual IMS training jacket that is eventually forwarded to the Security Cooperation Organization, who in turn keeps a permanent copy. Training activities may destroy their copy of evaluation records as directed in SECNAVINST 5212.5C, section SSIC 4950. For all other SCETP-related correspondence or reports apply pertinent subject matter instructions from SECNAVINST 5212.5C.

Section IV
Department of the Air Force

10–96. International military student administration

A report of IMS failing to arrive as scheduled will be submitted by the gaining IMSO to the last training installation with information copies to the Air Force Security Assistance Training Squadron, 315 J Street West, Randolph AFB, TX 78150–4300, SAF/International Affairs, 1080 Air Force Pentagon, Washington, DC 20330–1080, and the appropriate Security Cooperation Organization within 48 hours after scheduled arrival.

10–97. U.S. Air Force standards

The Security Cooperation Organization must make sure that each IMS is briefed on USAF grooming standards in AFI 36–2903.

 a. IMS will normally be required to comply with the provisions of AFI 36–2903. Training installation commanders will expect IMS to maintain acceptable standards of appearance, conduct, health, and hygiene so as not to affect the discipline or morale of U.S. personnel.

 b. International students enrolled in flying training courses or in other training where operational or ground safety requirements require strict adherence to AFI 36–2903 standards must maintain those standards or face disenrollment as no waiver will be granted.

 c. When religious precepts or national laws preclude compliance, a substantiated request for waiver to AFI 36–2903 standards will be forwarded by the Security Cooperation Organization to the Air Force Security Assistance Training Squadron and will include a copy of the country's proposed grooming standards. These requests will be evaluated on a case-by-case basis; approved exemptions will be recorded and maintained by the Air Force Security Assistance Training Squadron. The Air Force Security Assistance Training Squadron will be responsible for updating and advising CONUS IMSO of approved exemptions. Waivers do not apply to flying training courses or to courses where operational or ground safety is a consideration.

 d. The physical standards prescribed by Air Force regulations should be enforced only when deviation from the standard would present an operational or safety hazard or would prevent successful completion of the course.

10–98. Responsibilities of country liaison officers

 a. Air Force training units requiring a CLO to assist the USAF with IMS administration must forward a request to the Air Force Security Assistance Training Squadron for review, approval, and further staffing with SAF/International Affairs. The request will contain the following information.

 (1) Proposed position description of the CLO to include the USAF supervisor.

 (2) Justification for the position.

 (3) The USAF installation and location of the extended visit authorization (only one location may be specified.)

 (4) Other USAF or contractor facilities to be included in the position for recurring visits and justification.

 (5) Disclosure considerations, to include—

 (a) Highest level of security classification required for the position.

 (b) Methods of information disclosure.

 (c) Descriptions of military information disclosures that will be necessary including the categories of disclosure in accordance with AFI 16–201.

 (d) Security arrangements (that is, badging, escort requirements, and so forth).

 b. After SAF/IAPD approval of the CLO position description, the Air Force Security Assistance Training Squadron will forward the proposal to country. Upon country approval and identification of the officer to be assigned as CLO, the Air Force Security Assistance Training Squadron will process a request for an Extended Visit Authorization to SAF/International Affairs. Once approved, the training unit will—

 (1) Maintain a current copy of the Extended Visit Authorization.

 (2) Insure that specific restrictions included in the Extended Visit Authorization are complied with.

 (3) Insure that the local FDO, MAJCOM/FDO, and SAF/IAPD are informed of the CLO supervisor, physical location, or other proposed changes to the extended visit authorization.

 (4) Revalidate the CLO position NLT 60 days prior to the expiration date of the extended visit authorization.

 c. MAJCOM/FDO and local FDO which have CLO under their control will—

 (1) Insure that the USAF supervisor is adequately briefed on their responsibilities.

 (2) Insure that the CLO work environment is separated to the extent necessary to preclude uncontrolled access to files, materials, and discussions not authorized for release.

 (3) Complete the extended visit authorization paperwork required for the CLO position.

 d. While assigned to USAF installations, CLO will comply with all USAF, MAJCOM, and local installation rules and regulations.

 e. The use of unclassified information systems (DSN, USAF mail/distribution system, FAX machines, and so forth) will be at the discretion of the USAF supervisor in coordination with the local FDO. When using USG information systems, the CLO will—

 (1) Identify themselves in conversation or writing as CLO.

 (2) Use country specific stationery (use of official USAF letterhead stationary is not authorized).

 f. Other policy issues and CLO duties are delineated in paragraph 10–8.

10–99. Designation and duties of international military student officers

 a. The installation commander or designated installation HQ directorate will designate, in writing, an individual as IMSO to serve as the primary focal point for IMS matters and will forward the name, grade, organization, and telephone number to Air Force Security Assistance Training Squadron, Randolph AFB, TX 78150–4302. Individuals designated as IMSO should be people-oriented, possess tact, and be of an appropriate grade or rank to enable them to deal effectively with the projected IMS. If projected IMS loads do not justify a dedicated position for the IMSO function, it may be combined with other functions. However, IMSO duties will receive top priority in event of conflict. The IMSO may be either military and/or civilian. IMSOs will be appointed for a minimum of 2 years, when possible, and will receive the necessary training to perform this important function. Contact Air Force Security Assistance Training Squadron to schedule orientation and DISAM to schedule training. IMSO will attend the USAF IMSO conference hosted by Air Force Security Assistance Training Squadron every 18 months. Installations should program funds for IMSO to attend cross-cultural communications training at the USAFSOS. Contact USAFSOS/EDRC, Alison Building, 357 Tully Street, Hurlburt Field, FL, 32544–5800 for quotas.

b. IMSO will initiate action through Air Force Security Assistance Training Squadron to resolve problems related to grooming standards and religious principles that deviate from AFI 36–2903.

c. The IMSO will maintain the IMS personnel and training record, using the four-part AF Form 10 (Unit Personnel Record Group (Folder)). A complete personnel and training record file will be maintained on each IMS except for those participating in OT. Specific record maintenance, transmittal, and disposition instructions are contained in other U.S. Air Force sections. IMS records will be organized as follows:

(1) *Section 1.*

(a) DD Form 1172 (Application for Uniformed Services Identification Card Defense Enrollment Eligibility System (DEERS) Enrollment).

(b) ITO (two copies).

(2) *Section 2.*

(a) Student training records.

(b) Qualification/observation/familiarization training request.

(c) AF Form 797.

(d) IMS academic report.

(e) Certificates or awards.

(f) Notification of faculty board actions.

(g) Holdover actions, advancements, withdrawals.

(3) *Section 3.*

(a) Incident reports with final results.

(b) Complete history of individual counseling.

(c) Miscellaneous correspondence (for example, hospitalization, arrival, in/out processing checklists).

(4) *Section 4.* AF Form 1217 (Information Program (IP Data Card).

d. Specific Air Force records will be maintained (in accordance with AFMAN 33–363) by the IMSO; that is, flight and personnel records for technical school IMS. IMS will hand carry their flight records between training locations.

e. The Security Cooperation Organization is responsible for the initial preparation of biographic data. In cases where the biographic data records are not received from the Security Cooperation Organization, base IMSO are authorized direct communication with the Security Cooperation Organization to obtain the data required to complete this record. An information copy will be sent to Air Force Security Assistance Training Squadron.

f. The IMS academic report (DD Form 2496 or AF Form 475 (Educational/Training Report)) will be used to record instructor comments on the IMS' strengths, weaknesses, idiosyncrasies, and attitude. Comments should be made during the course of instruction as well as after completion. Instructions for completion of DD Form 2496 and AF Form 475 are contained in figure 10–2.

g. The IMSO will transmit IMS training records to the gaining base or activity as soon as practicable (not later than 10 days) after IMS graduation date. Failure to fulfill this requirement will be explained through channels to Air Force Security Assistance Training Squadron, 315 J Street West, Randolph AFB, TX 78150–4302.

(1) The IMSO will collect all appropriate documents and forward the complete personnel and training record file to the gaining installation. Every effort will be made to ensure that the file contains the final grade sheet for the course. However, the file will not be held pending receipt of the final grades. An appropriate notation that the IMS did complete the course and that the final grade sheet is forthcoming will suffice.

(2) The final CONUS training installation IMSO will personally review the contents of this file. After review, the IMSO will forward the records not later than 60 days after the IMS graduation to the appropriate Security Cooperation Organization.

(a) Release of information in the training record to foreign country personnel will be at the discretion of the Security Cooperation Organization.

(b) Records should be screened carefully to ensure that information of a sensitive nature is removed.

(3) Personnel and training record files maintained on IMS training outside CONUS will be transmitted as directed by the component command.

(4) Privileged medical records and classified training records will be forwarded to the appropriate Security Cooperation Organization for review and disposition.

h. Classified notebooks, workbooks, and similar documents developed by IMS attending formal training in the United States will be transmitted to the home Service of the IMS through the Security Cooperation Organization; AF Form 349 (Receipt for Document Released to Accredited Representative of Foreign Nations) will be obtained for this purpose.

i. The Air Force Security Assistance Training Squadron is authorized to issue the appropriate SATP and other cooperative programs fund citations when justified for the purposes listed in paragraph 10–7c(1) and (2). This includes attendance at the special IMSO course conducted by DISAM, when invitations have been extended through appropriate command channels.

j. The IMSO will use AF Form 623 or an outline of the familiarization or qualification training provided to an IMS (to include the type of equipment used) when applicable. The IMSO will—

(1) Brief the project officer or NCO on the use of appropriate training and evaluation records.

(2) Be familiar with all familiarization and qualification training being conducted on the installation as well as the classification of that training.

(3) Brief each IMS undergoing familiarization or qualification training and their supervisor to ensure that all understand the method of training. The IMS must realize that they will receive only the training described on the training detail sheet (see fig 4–2). Therefore, careful preparation of the detail sheet by the Security Cooperation Organization is critical to avoid any misunderstanding.

(4) Ensure that the training detail sheet and associated documents are included in the IMS personnel and training record file upon completion of training. This file will be forwarded to the next training location or to the Security Cooperation Organization via the Security Assistance Network Web.

k. For familiarization or qualification training, the training activity will—

(1) Prepare necessary training records or documents.

(2) Brief IMS on organizational policies, procedures, and responsibilities related to their environment.

(3) Perform an initial evaluation of IMS and brief them on the training objectives within the first full duty day after in processing.

(4) Evaluate and monitor the effectiveness of the training program and ensure the IMS meets the training objectives listed on the forms. Ensure that all training is properly documented and the classification is stated and clearance obtained prior to providing training.

(5) Ensure that the installation IMSO is informed on the IMS progress.

(6) Notify the installation IMSO of any interruption of or deviation from the scheduled training.

(7) Coordinate training problems with the appropriate agency.

(8) Forward all training records to the installation IMSO upon completion of training.

(9) Ensure IMS receive AF Form 1256 (Certification of Training).

l. When it has been determined that an IMS is absent without leave, the installation IMSO will advise Air Force Security Assistance Training Squadron within 24 hours by message. See paragraph 10–47 for details.

m. When the IMSO determines that a request for political asylum has been made, the IMSO will immediately comply with AFI 51–704.

n. The IMSO should be advised of intended CONUS Faculty Board Action at least ten days in advance of board proceedings. The IMSO should advise Air Force Security Assistance Training Squadron/CC by telephone of intended board action as soon as the requirement for faculty board action is known; Air Force Security Assistance Training Squadron will then inform the country air attaché or embassy and invite those representatives to attend the faculty board if they wish to attend. In the notification to Air Force Security Assistance Training Squadron, faculty board action for flying students should contain the type of aircraft flown and the number of hours flown. Board proceedings will be processed as expeditiously as possible. Immediately upon receipt of the approved proceedings, the IMSO will forward the original to Air Force Security Assistance Training Squadron for appropriate action. After processing at Air Force Security Assistance Training Squadron, the faculty board proceedings will be forwarded to the Security Cooperation Organization.

(1) If the IMS is eliminated, the specific cause must be cited. English language per se will not be cited as the specific cause of elimination; however, if it was a contributing factor, this will be noted in board proceedings. The eliminated IMS will not receive further training without approval from the Security Cooperation Organization or the country concerned.

(2) If the faculty board determines that a flying training student displays a lack of aptitude or dangerous tendencies that cannot be safely corrected, the IMS will be eliminated regardless of the number of hours flown.

(3) The IMSO will inform the Air Force Security Assistance Training Squadron country program manager immediately, and the country program manager will notify the Air Force Security Assistance Training Squadron/CC.

o. In the event of base evacuation or natural disaster, IMSO will adhere to the installation commander's established emergency evacuation plan. Evacuation procedures must address transportation, lodging and medical provisions for

IMS. Entitlements for international students depend on the direction given by the installation and its evacuation plan. Students entitled to TLA would be covered the same as USG members while enroute and during safe haven.

10–100. Clothing and equipment

The Security Cooperation Organization must determine special clothing and equipment requirements, which are generally listed in AF Education and Training Course Announcements. The AF Education and Training Course Announcements describes the special clothing and equipment provided for undergraduate pilot training and undergraduate navigator training (UNT). The AF Education and Training Course Announcements also contains a detailed listing of the items IMS will receive, all of which are for retention whether the IMS completes the course or not. Lost, damaged, or destroyed special clothing or individual equipment will be accounted for as stated in AFMAN 23–110. Every attempt will be made to have the IMS use personal funds to purchase clothing or equipment not included in the tuition rate. When the IMSO verifies that the IMS does not have funds and the items are required to accomplish the training, the IMSO will immediately notify Air Force Security Assistance Training Squadron and obtain a signed statement from the student that the individual does not have funds to defray the cost of the items. This statement will be submitted to Air Force Security Assistance Training Squadron, along with the SF 1080 billing, student's ITO, and a receipt indicating charges.

   a. For FMS IMS, a "Services" WCN, T–MASL D365005 (clothing and equipment), will be established in the applicable FMS case (if one does not already exist), and the billing will be processed. The purchasing government will be advised of the charges and items of clothing or equipment, when charges are known. These charges will be charged to the applicable FMS case.

   b. For IMET IMS, Air Force Security Assistance Training Squadron will process the billing against available IMET funds, taking action to increase the IMET funding by adjusting the IMET tuition rate for the specific WCN. IMS whose Service uniforms are not suitable for CONUS climates are permitted to purchase USAF uniforms and clothing (without distinctive buttons or insignia) on a cash-only basis from Air Force clothing sales stores. Items authorized for purchase are listed in AFMAN 23–110. When uniforms are to be purchased in the United States, Security Cooperation Organization will ensure that IMS have sufficient funds in their possession for such purchases.

10–101. Deceased international military students

Funeral services will not be conducted until appropriate instructions concerning the disposition of the remains have been received from HQ, USAF (AFI 34–242). As stated in AFI 34–501 and other applicable mortuary affairs publications, services, and supplies will be acquired from a funeral home holding a contract for care of remains, if a contract is in effect in the area in which the death occurs. If a contract is not in effect, necessary services and supplies will be acquired through negotiation. Funeral director invoices for services and supplies will be submitted to Air Force Security Assistance Training Squadron/FM, Randolph AFB, TX 78150–4302. Requirements for foreign flags suitable for covering a casket should be established under applicable Air Force instructions. Flags should be procured through supply channels. Accounts for deceased SATP and other cooperative programs IMS will be submitted to the local accounting and finance officer for processing according to AFR 177–103 as follows:

   a. The original plus four copies of the appropriate series of DD Form 1351 computed to show the amounts due the deceased and certified by the personnel officer.

   b. Three copies of the current ITO, attached to the applicable DD Form 1351 series.

   c. AF Form 1122 (Personal Property and Personal Effects Inventory) to accompany the effects as listed in AFI 34–501. Articles that cannot be shipped (for example, automobiles) will be disposed of as directed, in writing, by the appropriate country representative.

10–102. Family members

Students will not be encouraged to bring their Family members with them or to have their Family members join them later. Exceptions to this policy are approved for CLO and for IMS attending the Air War College, Air Command and Staff College, the Squadron Officers School, and the AFIT graduate programs, provided the IMS is financially able to defray the cost of housing, food, and medical care for Family members in the U.S. This exception is valid for any programmed prerequisite and follow-on training for these IMS. Authorized Family members (reference or listed in para 10–9b(12)) must be reflected in the IMS ITO and must have required medical healthcare insurance coverage listed in Joint Security Cooperation Education and Training chapter 8. On-base housing for IMS with Family members is not guaranteed and normally not available.

10–103. Channels of communication for reporting IMS issues/incidents

   a. The IMS issues/incidents include any situation identified in chapter 10 (for example, academic, faculty board, political asylum, disciplinary, misconduct, medical and so forth) or any situation that may result in delayed graduation or possible disenrollment of high profile students or any students from high interest training (for example, flight training, PME). The goal of prompt initial and follow-on reporting is to ensure training decisions impacting and IMS are properly coordinated/decided in an international affairs context before final implementation (for example, disenrollment).

b. USAF training activities report IMS issues/incidents to Air Force Security Assistance Training Squadron via e–mail or message traffic (telephone courtesy calls are also encouraged).

(1) Reports of issues/incidents include a brief summary of the issue/incident, any involvement by law enforcement authorities, status of training activity resolution action and the appropriate commander's recommendation concerning the IMS (when recommendation is available). In accordance with paragraph 10–4b, training installation decisions concerning safety are implemented immediately.

Note. Reports are prepared with the assistance of the servicing staff judge advocate when appropriate, and in all situations where criminal conduct appears to have occurred.

(2) Reports are updated as necessary to ensure current IMS status is known and appropriate decisions concerning IMS are properly coordinated.

(3) Reports can be made by the applicable training activity Commander directly to the Air Force Security Assistance Training Squadron/CC or by the IMSO to the applicable Air Force Security Assistance Training Squadron Country Manager (who informs the Air Force Security Assistance Training Squadron chain-of-command).

c. The Air Force Security Assistance Training Squadron promptly takes any required notification actions within HQ AETC and notifies the applicable SAF/International Affairs regional division (Division Chief and/or Country Director) via e-mail with a courtesy copy to SAF/IAPX (telephone courtesy calls are also encouraged). Air Force Security Assistance Training Squadron/CC proposed/recommended actions are always forwarded in addition to the issue/incident summary.

d. SAF/International Affairs regional divisions—

(1) Report issues/incidents with serious or apparently serious international implications via the chain-of-command to SAF/International Affairs for awareness or guidance as deemed appropriate.

(2) Ensure SAF/IAPX is kept aware of communication on the IMS issue/incident (IAPX will advise on policy issues).

(3) Ensure SAF/GCI is notified and updated on issues/incidents with any legal impact, to include any issue where the local staff judge advocate office has, or should have been consulted. Paragraph 10–14c clarifies U.S. military authority relevant to IMS issues/incidents.

(4) Provide guidance or take action on notifying the appropriate Commanders of Combatant Commands and Security Cooperation Organization. All actions required in paragraph 10–4d will be taken.

(5) Provide guidance or take action on notifying the foreign Service counterpart (for example, CLO, Attaché). The Air Force Security Assistance Training Squadron normally makes notification to CLOs and SCOs. SAF/International Affairs regional divisions make notification to Attachés.

e. Air Force Security Assistance Training Squadron, SAF/International Affairs regional divisions, and USAF training activities (and any other offices considered appropriate) continue to communicate unit the IMS issue/incident is resolved with a final decision/action.

f. The USAF training commander's decision concerning an IMS is followed unless changed by proper chain-of-command authority; however, in accordance with situations outlined paragraph 10–14. IMS are not returned to their home country without proper approval (communicated via SAF/International Affairs channels).

10–104. Disposition of international military students

The Air Force Security Assistance Training Squadron will be advised of pending faculty boards by message or AF Form 1761. If an IMS is considered permanently disqualified for flying duty, a report of medical examination will be prepared as indicated in AFI 48–123, and forwarded through the Command Surgeon for review by HQ, USAF/SGPA, 170 Luke Avenue, Boiling AFB, Washington DC 20332–5113, to determine final disposition. For IMS, attending familiarization or qualification training the training installation will request disposition instructions from Air Force Security Assistance Training Squadron by message.

10–105. Flying in United States Air Force aircraft

Item #12c(3) of the original ITO issued by the Security Cooperation Organization will indicate when IMS government certifies that they are physically, professionally, and administratively qualified to fly in aircraft from their home country air force as pilots or other applicable crew members. If flying hours for flying are not available, IMS should be advised to obtain a waiver of proficiency flying requirements from their home country air force covering the duration of their training. When IMS who are authorized to participate as aircrew members report for duty or training at AF installations, they must have a transcript of their flying records or certification outlining qualifications, aeronautical rating, and flying time (conventional or jet). In addition, IMS must complete all USAF requirements such as physical and written examinations and flight proficiency checks before assuming flying duties. Space-available travel in military aircraft during leave is not authorized. Consistent with the provisions of DOD 4515.13R, Government use of administrative support airlift may be authorized for IMS as indicated in paragraphs (1) and (2), below. IMS may fly as passengers on USAF passenger carrying aircraft when space is available. However, aircraft used for this purpose must be flying in support of assigned command mission requirements.

a. From the port to the first training installation, between training installations, and from final training installations to port of embarkation.

b. When an IMS is in official TDY status as part of a scheduled training course or is performing duties as a CLO, including organized Field Studies Program activities. IMS may be authorized to participate as crew members as prescribed by AFI 11–401. DODI 7230.08 is the governing publication for demonstration flights requiring an FMS case.

10–106. Graduation

Upon successful completion of a formal course of instruction, each IMS will be issued a suitably embellished certificate or diploma (AF Form 1256 or similar document), provided all outstanding debts to USG activities are paid. IMS to be graduated with distinction will be reported to the appropriate Security Cooperation Organization by message with the information given in paragraphs *a* through *e*, below. An information copy will be sent to Air Force Security Assistance Training Squadron, and the unified command.

a. Name, grade, and country.

b. Course of instruction.

c. Date of graduation.

d. Type of award.

e. Brief citation that indicates the size and composition of the class and the IMS accomplishment.

10–107. Laundry service

Laundry service is authorized for IMS at rates charged USAF officers and airmen as stated in AFR 34–901.

10–108. Name tags and rank insignia

Name tags will be issued by the first training installation. This will assist U.S. military personnel in affording the appropriate military protocol to IMS. USAF rank insignia may also be issued to IMS.

10–109. Quarters

Generally, IMS are considered to be in a TDY status if the length of training is less than 20 weeks; however, all IMS assigned to DLIELC, Lackland AFB, TX, are considered to be in a TDY status regardless of course length. IMS in TDY status are provided separate accommodations from those in PCS status. The provisions of AFI 32–6005 apply to unaccompanied students occupying unaccompanied personnel housing. All SATP and other cooperative programs IMS who occupy USAF VOQ or visiting airmen quarters facilities must personally pay the applicable service charge with the exception of those enlisted personnel authorized a living allowance under IMET. The IMS in PCS status also may be required to pay service fees. Rates vary by location, depending on the services provided. Reimbursement for quarters assigned to enlisted personnel authorized a living allowance under IMET will be according to paragraph 5–19*a*. Questions regarding these procedures should be forwarded through channels to HQ USAF/SV, 1770 Air Force Pentagon, Washington, DC 20330–1770.

a. Family housing. Officers in the United States as security assistance CLO or assigned to Air University Military Personnel Exchange positions, who are accompanied or joined by their authorized Family members may be assigned family housing when available according to DOD 4165.63–M.

b. Other international military student. Other than those listed in the paragraph above, IMS accompanied by their Family members may, at the discretion of the installation commander, be assigned family housing when it is excess to the needs of assigned base personnel.

c. Airmen. Quarters will be assigned to SATP and other cooperative programs airmen IMS while in training in CONUS in the same manner as for counterparts in the MILDEP who are not authorized Family-type quarters. When bachelor airmen housing is not available, other appropriate SATP and other cooperative programs allowances will be provided by the base commander under existing directives.

10–110. Temporary duty

a. Temporary duty authorization. Orders that authorize TDY may be published for taking part in the following:

(1) As a team member in an organized Air Force sports activity. Permissive orders (at no expense to IMET, FMS, or the Air Force) may be issued.

(2) In programmed trips within CONUS that are a scheduled part of the formal course curriculum. Students taking these trips are considered to be in TDY status. The CLO may be placed on TDY in an official capacity using the fund citation in their original ITO.

b. Temporary duty approval for international students.

(1) The base IMSO may approve TDY as outlined in paragraph *a*, above.

(2) The Air Force Security Assistance Training Squadron approves and monitors all the CLO TDY and special requests for TDY within CONUS that are not included in paragraph *a*, above.

c. Reimbursement for temporary to foreign military sales international military student. FMS IMS on a cross-country training flight or TDY in connection with a required course of training are reimbursed only for payment of quarters (in accordance with AFI 34–246) and actual cost of transportation if applicable; for example, mileage if POC is authorized.

10–111. Unauthorized absence

When an IMS is absent without leave in excess of 24 hours, the absence will be reported to local U.S. immigration authorities; SAF/International Affairs and Air Force Security Assistance Training Squadron will be advised. See paragraph 10–47 for details.

10–112. Disclosure considerations

Disclosure of USAF classified and unclassified information to a foreign government, organization, or representatives must be made under the guidelines of NDP. Paragraph 10–76 addresses AFI 16–201 as it pertains to the SATP and other cooperative programs. Each MAJCOM or training location (if applicable) has an FDO who is responsible for assuring compliance with AFI 16–201. Implementing Commands will work with their (MAJCOM) FDO in disclosure considerations. U.S. security screening of SATP and other cooperative programs IMS must be accomplished before they depart from their home country according to AFI 16–201 and AFI 31–401. Installation IMSO will assure compliance with AFI 31–401 and AFI 16–201. Unless specifically authorized, in writing, foreign country programs are not releasable to third-country parties. Classified notebooks, workbooks, and similar documents developed by IMS while attending training in the United States will be transmitted to the home service of the IMS through the Security Cooperation Organization; AF Form 349 will be obtained for this purpose.

10–113. Medical and dental care

a. Eligibility for healthcare in medical treatment facilities is outlined in AFI 41–115. While the basic entitlement for medical care is the same for SATP and other cooperative programs active duty as for U.S. active duty, there are differences that are detailed in AFI 41–115.

b. There is a charge for in-patient care for SATP and other cooperative programs IMS unless they are included under a reciprocal healthcare agreement between the U.S. and the individual's country. The AFI 41–115 details the charges.

c. Under all cases, AFI 41–115 takes precedence if there is a conflict between that regulation and this publication. Conflicting guidance should be identified to SAF/IAPX.

d. The USAF facilities will be fully reimbursed for all medical services provided to students sponsored by another USG agency. These students are normally provided a sickness and accident insurance policy by the sponsoring U.S. agency to defray all medical expenses. When the student is not covered by insurance, reimbursement will be made locally by the student or bills will be forwarded to Air Force Security Assistance Training Squadron for reimbursement from the sponsoring agency.

e. In the rare instance when elective medical care is considered necessary, the complete facts of the case will be transmitted by message to HQ, USAF WASH DC //SGPC// for approval. The message will include the following information:

(1) Name, grade, and country of origin.

(2) Diagnosis.

(3) Type of elective medical care.

(4) Prognosis.

f. Reimbursement procedures are as follows:

(1) Procedures for IMS who receive outpatient or inpatient medical services at USAF facilities will be billed as directed in the IMS ITO. Services to be billed under IMET or an FMS case will be made by the servicing medical facility to Air Force Security Assistance Training Squadron on DD Form 7 (Part A) or DD Form 7A (Part B). Air Force Security Assistance Training Squadron will make appropriate disbursement.

(2) Officers will reimburse USAF medical facilities for subsistence furnished. Subsistence charged for airmen is authorized as a direct payment to the hospital and may be included in the invoice for medical care.

(3) Expenses for IMET medical care in other than U.S. Air Force hospitals are charged directly to IMET funds.

10–114. Hospitalization or casualties

a. When a CONUS IMS is hospitalized, the details will be reported immediately by message to Air Force Security Assistance Training Squadron/CC and the Security Cooperation Organization concerned. Progress reports will be made in a timely manner and include a final report indicating the date the IMS returned to duty.

b. Casualty messages concerning IMS who die, who are seriously injured, or who are missing will be administered and transmitted by the base personal affairs office (DPMAP) according to AFI 36–3002. Casualty messages will be addressed to HQ USAF WASH DC//CVAI//, with information copies to OSAF WASH DC//IAPX//; Air Force Security Assistance Training Squadron RANDOLPH AFB, TX//CC//; HQ AFMPC RANDOLPH AFB,// PMCC//; the Security Cooperation Organization that published the original ITO; and other commands as required.

c. The "circumstance letter" for deceased or missing IMS will be mailed to the Headquarters, U.S. Air Force, Office of the Vice Chief of Staff, International Affairs Division (HQ USAF/CVAI), 1670 Air Force Pentagon, Washington, DC 20330–1670, in lieu of the addressees indicated in AFI 36–3002.

d. The AFI 36–3002 will be used as a guide in reporting casualties occurring in overseas training installations. Action and information addressees will be as directed by the applicable component commander.

10–115. Air evacuation

a. An IMS is authorized aeromedical evacuation when necessary as prescribed in DOD 4515.13R. The full daily hospitalization rate prescribed in AFI 41–305 is charged for each day they are in the Aeromedical Evacuation System. Additionally, the aeromedical evacuation transportation rate is charged for evacuation to or from the IMS home country. This rate is 3 times the non-USG fare, and one additional fare for a nonmedical management system accompanying the patient, or 3 times the commercial first class fare plus one dollar, where no USG rate exists. Ambulatory patients will be charged the non-USG single seat fare, plus one additional fare for any accompanying nonmedical management system or the first class commercial fare where appropriate.

b. Hospital commanders in the United States with IMET IMS requiring air evacuation to their home country should request Commander, 375th AW, 101 Heritage Drive, Suite 208, Scott AFB, IL 62225–5000, to make travel arrangements. Submit requests for travel through Air Force Security Assistance Training Squadron/CC, 315 J Street West, Randolph AFB, TX 78150–4302 with information copies to SAF/IAPX, 1080 Air Force Pentagon, Washington, DC 20330–1080 and HQ, USAF/SGMR, 170 Luke Avenue, Bolling AFB, DC 20332–5113. Requests will identify the IMS by name, the training project under which the IMS was being trained, and will include the following additional data:

(1) Diagnosis.

(2) Prognosis.

(3) Class of patient.

(4) Date patient will be available for travel.

(5) Funding information.

c. Air evacuation from overseas training installations for IMET IMS will be accomplished as indicated in instructions by the respective component commanders.

10–116. Holidays

In addition to the holidays observed by the USAF, IMS may be authorized not more than 2 days per year to observe their country's national or religious holidays. The authorized holidays are derived from the Combined Education and Training Program Plan or directly from the Security Cooperation Organization in the American Embassies overseas. Holidays occurring on Saturday will be observed on Friday. Those occurring on Sunday will be observed on Monday. Training organizations/educational institutions will determine whether IMS will be excused based on individual's academic progress/standing. The IMS in training with US personnel will not routinely be excused from class for prayer.

10–117. International military student officer handbook

The Air Force Security Assistance Training Squadron and SAF/IAPX will publish expanded guidance for IMSO in the Air Force IMSO Handbook. The IMSO will comply with the provisions of this handbook. Contact Air Force Security Assistance Training Squadron or SAF/IAPX, 1080 Air Force Pentagon, Washington DC 20330–1080 for clarification if the information in the handbook differs from that contained in this publication.

10–118. Security assistance training program and other cooperative programs disclosure guidance

a. Security cooperation officer guidance.

(1) Classified and unclassified training courses for international use listed in the T–MASL must be staffed by the implementing command for releasability and availability through its FDO; releasability or availability must not be assumed by the Security Cooperation Organization. Releasability is initially staffed within the guidelines of NDP and AFI 16–201. If training is not releasable within these guidelines or if it requires an NDP exception, the training cannot be provided to IMS without further justification.

(2) If the Security Cooperation Organization believes the training is justified, the Security Cooperation Organization will forward a request to Air Force Security Assistance Training Squadron. This request must include, as a minimum, the information in paragraphs (a) through (c), below. Exceptions to the NDP require approximately 120 days for processing after receipt of the request.

(a) Course title, number, classification level, and T–MASL (if assigned).

(b) Demonstration of the country's needs for training and how the requested course will satisfy these needs.

(c) Benefits to the United States if training is provided.

(3) The Security Cooperation Organization will ensure that a security screening is accomplished on IMS selected for unclassified training. The Security Cooperation Organization will verify that IMS selected for classified courses have security clearances equivalent to the U.S. level required for the course. The Security Cooperation Organization will

check the T–MASL for the required security clearance and will ensure that the appropriate statement and security level for classified training is checked on the IMS ITO.

b. Implementing command guidance.

(1) The IC will ensure (through the MAJCOM FDO) that the training to be provided to IMS has been determined to be releasable by the appropriate disclosure authority. Classified training will not be programmed nor will dates be provided before determination of releasability.

(2) The IC FDO may authorize disclosure if delegated by SAF/IAPD. To reflect current policy, unclassified courses should be staffed at the MAJCOM level. If not within the MAJCOM delegated authority, a disclosure request will be staffed with and determined by SAF/IAPD. When staffing disclosure requests to SAF/IAPD, the request for disclosure will have a suspense date of not later than 70 days before the course start date and will allow an additional 60 days for SAF/IAPD processing. It will also include the following:

(a) Course title, number, and T–MASL if applicable.

(b) Country or countries for which a determination of releasability is required.

(c) Course syllabus, outline, and other documents that outline subject areas, classification levels in each area, training aids and equipment used during the instruction, and locations at which training will be conducted or visited as part of the instruction. Additional information will be requested if required by SAF/IAPD.

(3) The IC will advise Air Force Security Assistance Training Squadron if training is not releasable.

(4) The IC will ensure that courses developed for international students are developed according to the guidance below. (Courses, for this purpose, include qualification and observer training and training provided by security assistance training teams.)

(a) Courses will include only the instruction required to meet the objective of the training. Instruction, student handouts, and visits to other U.S. Air Force installations that are valuable in broadening the students knowledge but not necessary to meet the course objective will not be provided.

(b) Retainable instructional materials authorized to be shipped to the students will be kept to a minimum and, as much as possible, will be devoid of references to other U.S. Air Force publications.

(c) Equipment used in the course will be of a common nature and not part of a sophisticated weapon system, unless the course is specifically weapon-system related. The course curriculum developers will advise the IC if, during the course update, modification, or development, the guidelines in paragraph (4), above, cannot be adhered to.

(5) The IC will advise Air Force Security Assistance Training Squadron and IMSO of the required U.S. equivalent security clearance. Air Force Security Assistance Training Squadron will advise the Security Cooperation Organization of the required U.S. equivalent security clearance when authority to publish the ITO is provided.

(6) The IC will ensure that RIM is cleared as part of the course releasability determination.

c. IMSO or international military student guidance.

(1) The IMSO will review the IMS ITO to ensure that the ITO reflects the security clearance required for classified courses. Proper accomplishment of the ITO and/or required amendments remains the primary responsibility of the Security Cooperation Organization.

(2) The IMSO will ensure that the guidance in paragraph *b*(4), above, is provided to instructors of IMS. Further, the IMSO will inform the instructors that additional training will not be recommended directly to the IMS but, rather, to the IMSO, who will then forward the recommendation to the IC.

Chapter 11
U.S. Field Studies Program for International Military and Civilian Students and Military Sponsored Visitors

This chapter describes the policy, goal, objective, responsibilities, planning and development, implementation strategies and methods, funding and constraints of the Field Studies Program, formerly known as the International Program.

Section I
Policies, Goal, and Objective

11–1. Field studies program policy

a. Each IMS attending military and selected contractor training in the United States, or participating in an orientation tour arranged under SCETP sponsorship will be given the opportunity to participate in the Field Studies Program according to DODI 5410.17. The Field Studies Program is an integral part of the total training program, and is second in importance only to the military objectives for which the IMS is in training. Participation in Field Studies Program activities other than those that are integral parts of the course program of instruction is voluntary but highly encouraged.

(1) The provisions of this chapter also apply to IMS undergoing training at U.S. training installations overseas as appropriate to the surrounding environment.

(2) The provisions of this chapter do not apply to foreign personnel visiting at the personal invitation of the Chief of Staff, U.S. Army; self-invited visits; or other programs not managed in accordance with the security assistance training process.

b. The specific Field Studies Program objective to provide IMS with an awareness and understanding of the American democratic way of life has been derived from the laws authorizing the programs that make up the Security Assistance Training Program: the Foreign Assistance Act of 1961 as amended, and the Arms Export Control Act, as amended.

c. The Field Studies Program implementation funds will be included in course tuition rates. Funds will cover transportation, meals, lodging, admissions, tours and associated fees and service charges in accordance with current versions of DOD 5105.38–M and DOD 7000.14–R Volume 15.

d. Public Law 108–7, Foreign Operations, Export Financing and Related Programs Appropriations Act, imposes constraints on the Field Studies Program. Funds supporting the Field Studies Program shall not be expended to pay for alcoholic beverages or for activities that are substantially recreational, including but not limited to entrance fees at sporting events, theatrical and musical productions and amusement/theme parks.

11–2. Field studies program goal and specific objective

The goal of the Field Studies Program is to ensure that international students return to their homelands with an understanding of the responsibilities of governments, militaries, and citizens to protect, preserve, and respect the rights of every individual. The Field Studies Program will be developed and implemented with the specific objective of promoting an understanding of U.S. society, institutions, and ideals and the way in which these elements reflect U.S. commitment to basic principles of internationally recognized human rights. To achieve this objective, the Field Studies Program will provide students and visitors with an understanding of the following facets of American life, within the limits of time and availability:

a. Human rights. U.S. commitment to basic principles of internationally recognized human rights as reflected in United Nations General Assembly Resolution 217 A (III), "Universal Declaration of Human Rights," and The Constitution of the United States of America. This aspect of American life shall be emphasized in conjunction with all subsequent Field Studies Program topics.

b. Diversity & American Life. How the United States fosters political, economic, and social pluralism; the geographic, religious, and social diversity of American life; progress in applying American ideals to ethnic minorities and women, including how they address gender-based violence. How American Families live and work in cities, towns and rural areas; how Americans function in communities, worship, work together in organizations, participate in and support cultural and historical events; the role of volunteerism in American life.

c. U.S. Government Institutions. U.S. institutions of democratic governance, including electoral and legislative processes and civilian control of the military, and the institution and improvement of public administration at the national, intergovernmental, state and local levels.

d. Political processes. American democracy and political reform, including opening the political process to all members of society, the practice of free elections, freedom of association, and the influence of various governmental and non-governmental organizations that promote democracy, the rule of law, transparence, and accountability in the political process.

e. The Judicial System. The U.S. establishment of the rule of law and an effective judicial system, the role of the military justice system and its procedures, and the laws and institutions for addressing extremist violence and taking effective action to prosecute those who are alleged to have committed crimes.

f. The Free Market System. The success of the U.S. economy due to land and tax system reform, encouragement of private enterprise and individual initiative, creation of favorable investment climates, curbing corruption where it exists, and spurring balanced trade; the independent roles of labor and management in negotiating pay, working hours and conditions, and other benefits associated with employment; the factors underlying industry and agricultural production, and how environmental protection has altered each; and the role of environmental protection.

g. Education. The purpose and range of educational institutions, the value of an educated and responsible citizenry, and the educational opportunities available to all citizens.

h. Health and Human Services. The U.S. institutions that provide quality healthcare and voluntary Family planning services, housing, and other services, and the policies that are components of a social safety net, particularly for infants, children, and people with disabilities.

i. Media. The role of a free press and other communications media in American life; how diversity of media ensures people of all races, creeds and political persuasions can be heard (for example, editorials, letters to the editor) and ensures diverse, pluralistic culture.

j. International Peace & Security. How the United States accomplishes effective and mutually beneficial relations and increased understanding with foreign countries in furtherance of the goals of international peace and security.

k. Law of War. The part of international law that regulates the conduct of armed hostilities, often called the "law of armed conflict." For the purposes of this facet, the law of war encompasses all international law for the conduct of hostilities binding on the United States or its individual citizens, including treaties and international agreements to which the United States is a part, and applicably customary international law.

Section II
Field Studies Program Responsibilities

11–3. Defense Security Cooperation Agency
a. The DSCA directs and supervises the Field Studies Program, including program funding.

b. The DSCA publishes Field Studies Program implementing instructions in DOD 5105.38–M.

11–4. Under Secretary of Defense
The Under Secretary of Defense (Comptroller) establishes pricing policy for the Field Studies Program in DOD 7000. 14–R, Volume 15, chapter 7.

11–5. Military services
a. The Military Services will establish, administer, operate, and review the Field Studies Program at their respective installations based upon guidance in DODI 5410.17 and DOD 5105.38–M.

b. Each Military Service will designate an Field Studies Program manager/Field Studies Program point of contact.

c. The Military Service will ensure that each installation commander or school commandant involved in training international students implements the Field Studies Program in accordance with the references cited in paragraph 11–1, above. Military Service will also ensure adequate personnel support for the Field Studies Program, generally through an IMSO.

11–6. Combatant commanders
Combatant Command staff will ensure that Security Cooperation Organization are educated on the Field Studies Program objective and goal and that all IMS are briefed on the Field Studies Program prior to their departure for training.

Section III
Field Studies Program Planning Considerations

11–7. Place of field studies program in the Security Cooperation Education and Training Program
One of the objectives of the SCETP is to promote better understanding of the United States, its people, political systems, institutions, values, and way of life. Consequently, it is critical that IMS be exposed to non-military aspects of life in the United States in addition to their military training.

11–8. Types of field studies program events
The Field Studies Program activities and events must be both interesting and educational in order to meet the objective of the program and to get maximum participation from IMS. The Field Studies Program Handbook provides many examples of possible Field Studies Program events along with information packets, sample student information and evaluation forms for both escorts and students. Local conditions will have a major impact on planning an Field Studies Program.

a. Local events can be conducted at the military installation or in the surrounding civilian community. These could include—

(1) A guest speaker, film and discussion, or a roundtable discussion on a topic in the news. These events should generally prepare students for an upcoming trip.

(2) A day trip to a local city council meeting, court, business, school, or other public institution.

(3) A social event such as a picnic planned in conjunction with a local civic group, providing IMS the opportunity to get to know people in the local civilian community.

b. Overnight events can be conducted within in the surrounding area. These trips could include:

(1) A trip to the state capitol, including meetings with and or briefings by elected or appointed officials.

(2) A trip to a university, farm, business or historical site including tours, meetings, and/or speakers.

c. A Washington, DC field trip is authorized for IMS in selected courses designated by the Military Service. A maximum of 4 days plus travel time is authorized for the trip.

(1) The purpose of this trip is to provide opportunities for IMS to achieve a deeper understanding and appreciation of the U.S. Federal Government and how governmental institutions affect U.S. citizens and people and nations throughout the world. It is important that, before arrival in Washington, DC, IMS be familiar with local and state government in the area of the military installation where they are undergoing training.

(2) Training installations are responsible for arranging roundtrip transportation to meet the approved trip schedule and for preparing IMS for their experience in Washington, DC.

(3) U.S. personnel designated as escorts will be knowledgeable about the SCETP in general and the Field Studies Program in particular. They will also have a general knowledge about how the U.S. government functions and be prepared to make maximum use of the Washington, DC field trip to attain the Field Studies Program objective. Escorts will brief IMS on each day's itinerary, describing the significance of the places to be visited. Escorts will emphasize that IMS will follow the full planned itinerary, with exceptions only in case of illness or other emergency.

d. Sponsorship programs are important in assisting IMS in getting to know American people and how they live. Sponsorship programs, both military and civilian, are voluntary and labor-intensive, but their value cannot be overestimated. IMSO will exercise care in selecting sponsors who have a genuine interest in helping international students and their Families to understand the American people. Sponsors will not use their positions to enhance their personal or commercial businesses, enterprises or interests.

(1) Military sponsors are normally U.S. classmates of IMS who volunteer to assist the IMS in understanding unfamiliar terms, and so forth. Often sponsors and IMS become good friends and associate both inside and outside the classroom.

(2) Civilian sponsors generally come from the local community. They invite the IMS into their homes and may take them on family trips, to sporting events, and so forth. Chambers of Commerce and other civic groups may welcome IMS to civilian communities, and members may become sponsors. Civilian organizations established for welcoming foreign visitors to the United States exist near most training installations, and can play an important role in the sponsor program.

e. Events such as receptions, luncheons, and so forth, will encourage the mingling of IMS and U.S. personnel, military, civilian or both. These special events, like the other events in the program, should support the goals and objectives of the Field Studies Program.

11–9. Travel and transportation

a. The USG or USG-contracted transportation will be used to the fullest extent possible for economy. IMSO are authorized to arrange for transportation and other support required for the Field Studies Program through installation support activities.

b. Commercial transportation is authorized if USG transportation is unavailable or inadequate.

c. The Field Studies Program funds are authorized for use as a gratuity for the driver of a USG-contracted or commercial means of transportation. Gratuity amount shall not exceed normal percentage rate for such.

d. The Field Studies Program trips will be limited to a MILDEP-determined radius in miles from the training installation. See paragraph 11–24 for Army, paragraph 11–35a(b) for Navy, paragraph 11–36g for Marine Corps, and paragraph 11–49 for Air Force for MILDEP limitations. Exceptions are the Washington, DC field trip for selected students and Field Studies Program trips planned in conjunction with academic trips. In the latter situation the MILDEP-determined radius begins at the temporary duty location. Additional limited exceptions must be authorized by the appropriate Military Service Field Studies Program Manager.

e. Excess baggage is not authorized on Field Studies Program trips.

11–10. Family members in the field studies program

When considered appropriate, Family members may accompany their sponsors on Field Studies Program trips at no additional cost to the USG. An exception is for minor costs, when individual collection from Family members for their share is impracticable; for example, parking fees or tolls.

Section IV
Developing the Field Studies Program Plan

11–11. Developing the annual field studies program plan

a. Annual Field Studies Program plan requirement. Each training installation/activity IMSO or designated POC will prepare an annual Field Studies Program plan which will be sent to the responsible Military Service Field Studies Program Manager for approval in advance of implementation. Planning details including suspense dates are provided in the Service specific sections of this chapter.

b. Identifying conditions. In order to plan effectively, IMSO must first determine the conditions that prevail at their installations, including funds required. The following should be considered in developing an annual Field Studies Program plan:

(1) The target audiences for the Field Studies Program events: grade/rank, countries/regions of origin, type of military training, and so forth. Some events that are appropriate for senior officers are not appropriate for junior enlisted personnel.

(2) The length of time students will be at the installation, along with periods of maximum student load to facilitate timing of significant Field Studies Program events.

(3) When the training schedule can accommodate Field Studies Program events (during duty hours, only on weekends or after duty hours, and so on). In courses consisting only of IMS, Field Studies Program events can

sometimes be made part of the course of instruction. Maximum use should be made of time that becomes available when IMS are excluded from classified portions of courses.

(4) Installations whose education/training programs are primarily academic in nature may find it appropriate to include lectures and seminars on Field Studies Program topics in their courses of study. In all instances where seminars, lectures, or film showings are scheduled, the atmosphere should be informal. Questions and open discussion periods should be encouraged.

c. *Identifying available resources.* The IMSO should become familiar with elected and appointed officials in the local city or county government(s) in the local civilian community. Local civic groups, organizations, agencies, businesses, and historical attractions should be contacted for potential program support and as possible sponsor sources. Local primary and secondary schools as well as colleges and universities can be very helpful in planning Field Studies Program events. Local events in which IMS mix with U.S. citizens should make up the foundation of the Field Studies Program. It is important for IMS to become familiar with state as well as local governments, and so the IMSO should also be familiar with elected and appointed officials at the state level. In addition, attractions in the general vicinity that focus on Field Studies Program topics should be investigated (for example, civil rights museums/tours, presidential libraries, Revolutionary and Civil War battlefields, Native American reservations).

d. *Using the building block approach.* The IMSO is responsible for preparing IMS for Field Studies Program events in order to achieve the maximum benefit. IMS should always be briefed in advance of an event so that they understand the purpose of the event and have sufficient information to profit from the event. For example, a trip to a local elementary school should be preceded by a guest speaker, film, or the IMSO describing the American educational system. Events should be followed by a discussion period with a frank and open exchange of ideas. Both escorts and students should complete event evaluation sheets, which can be used to determine the value of the event for future students.

e. *Establishing priorities.* All Field Studies Program events should include human rights aspects, and these should be discussed with IMS prior to the event. The words "human rights" do not have to be used with IMS, but the right itself, such as the right to freedom of peaceful assembly and association, should be identified prior to the event, such as observing a political rally, a march endorsing or opposing a government action. Field Studies Program events should provide IMS with out-of-the classroom, practical experiences that reinforce the Field Studies Program goal. Top priority events are those that have clear human rights aspects, demonstrate American values and diversity in a democratic society, and focus on such topics as the Constitution and Bill of Rights; local, State and Federal Government institutions; judicial systems; civilian and military relationships and the U.S. political process. The IMSO, with the assistance of the Military Service Field Studies Program Manager, should develop an Field Studies Program plan that ensures that every IMS has the opportunity to participate in the Field Studies Program.

f. *Scheduling events.* Scheduling requires careful coordination with training departments and tracking of students to determine IMS availability. The IMSO should determine the desirability of conducting Field Studies Program events for students in selected classes as opposed to opening every event to every IMS. Planning quality events is of the utmost importance.

11–12. Field studies program event escorts

a. In most cases the IMSO will serve as the primary DOD escort for IMS participating in an Field Studies Program event. The IMSO is responsible for carefully preparing any additional escorts for their duties.

(1) DOD escorts must be knowledgeable about the SCETP in general and the Field Studies Program in particular. In addition, escorts should clearly understand and be able to articulate the objective(s) of the event in which they are participating.

(2) DOD escorts should have sufficient information to be able to answer some IMS questions, and to be able to carry on a conversation on the topic at hand. They should have a basic knowledge of U.S. Government and history, particularly the Constitution, and of internationally recognized human rights.

(3) DOD escorts should be accustomed to working with IMS.

b. The recommended number of DOD escorts for Field Studies Program trips will be one escort for every ten IMS. If for any reason an IMS becomes incapacitated during an extended Field Studies Program trip, a DOD escort will be designated to stay with the IMS and make the necessary change in travel arrangements for both of them to return to home station. IMSO will immediately notify the appropriate MILDEP should this occur.

11–13. Planning and conducting individual field studies program events

Individual events must be carefully planned. The IMSO is the key figure in the planning, and is assisted as appropriate by additional personnel both within the IMSO and outside the office. The Field Studies Program Handbook contains information packets with sample event information sheets along with sample student and escort evaluation sheets. In general, the "learning by seeing and experiencing" process should be followed. Local trips and other events at which knowledgeable military and civilian experts receive IMS and make presentations or conduct discussions in their particular areas can be valuable. Those who address IMS should be familiar with the goal of the Field Studies Program, the specific purpose of the visit, and the English language comprehension level of the IMS. This requires advance coordination by IMSO personnel.

a. The IMSO or escort will be knowledgeable, although not necessarily expert, about all aspects of the planned event. Logistical requirements must be arranged in advance so that the event will proceed smoothly.

b. The IMSO or escort will brief IMS on the event, to include the learning objective(s), in advance. Any written material provided to IMS should be carefully prepared and reviewed to ensure it is clear, concise, and designed to enhance IMS experience.

c. Escorts will engage IMS in conversation as appropriate during the event to ensure IMS questions are answered and that objectives of the event are met.

d. Escorts will conduct an after action review with students following the event in order to summarize the event and to reemphasize the objectives, then provide students with Field Studies Program event evaluation sheets.

e. Escorts will complete an escort assessment sheet.

f. The IMSO will review event evaluation and escort assessment sheets and use the resulting information to determine events that should be retained, revised, or eliminated from the annual Field Studies Program.

Section V
Field Studies Program Funding

11–14. Source of funding
Funds for the Field Studies Program are derived from course tuition costs.

11–15. Funding field studies program activities
The following are general funding-related guidelines for Field Studies Program activities:

a. The IMS participating in Field Studies Program field trip are considered to be in a duty status. Therefore, appropriate orders will be published for IMS participating in Field Studies Program activities in excess of 10 hours.

b. The IMET and other IMS authorized living allowances paid by the USG will continue to receive the living allowance during Field Studies Program activities, regardless of length.

c. The Field Studies Program funds generally are used for field trip, admissions, and other activities that accomplish one or more Field Studies Program facets. However, Field Studies Program funds may also be used to support certain activities on the training installation that accomplish specific Field Studies Program objectives provided the activities are approved by the appropriate Military Service Field Studies Program Manager.

d. The Field Studies Program overnight trips must be approved by the appropriate Military Service Field Studies Program Manager.

e. The Field Studies Program field trips, including the Washington, DC field trip, will be conducted on an all-expense-paid basis.

(1) An escort may be appointed as a class A paying agent/cashier to permit advance withdrawal of Field Studies Program funds to defray trip costs.

(2) Authorized expenses include transportation, lodging, meals, gratuities for meals and transportation, admissions and related fees, and brochures, pamphlets, and maps used as handouts. Personal expenses of the IMS, such as laundry, phone calls, and room service, are the responsibility of the IMS.

f. Funding is authorized for guests at Field Studies Program functions such as luncheons, dinners, and receptions that are planned to facilitate IMS and U.S. personnel meeting and engaging in conversation. The ratio for guests to students is 3 to 1. Exceptions must be authorized by the appropriate Military Service Field Studies Program Manager in advance.

11–16. Funding constraints
a. Funds supporting the Field Studies Program will not be expended to pay for alcoholic beverages or for activities that are substantially recreational, including but not limited to entrance fees at sporting events, theatrical and musical productions and amusement/theme parks.

b. The Field Studies Program funds will not be used to support purely academic objectives, such as trips that are an integral part of the course curriculum for U.S. students. IMS expenses for such trips will be included in the course tuition apart from Field Studies Program.

c. The Field Studies Program funds will not be used to defray transportation expenses for trips with academic and entertainment rather than Field Studies Program objectives. However, Field Studies Program funds may be used for Field Studies Program events conducted in conjunction with academic trips.

11–17. Use of field studies program funds
Funds are authorized by respective Military Service for implementation of the Field Studies Program. Control of expenditures under this category is the responsibility of the Military Service and is addressed in the MILDEP sections.

a. The IMSO may be authorized to be reimbursed for legitimate out-of-pocket expenses incurred as a direct result of

Field Studies Program activities. Reimbursement will be made from Field Studies Program funds available to the training installation based on itemized expenditures as approved by the installation commander.

(1) Examples of legitimate out-of-pocket expenses are POV mileage to and from transportation centers to transport IMS when official vehicles are not available, associated tolls, and parking fees.

(2) The IMSO will itemize out-of-pocket expenses directly related to official Field Studies Program duties. The itemized list supports the SF 1164 (Claim for Reimbursement for Expenditures on Official Business) and will show the proper fund citation. This document will be submitted through the IMSO commander to the appropriate finance and accounting office for reimbursement. Reimbursement will be made from Field Studies Program funds available to the training installation.

b. Advance of funds for Field Studies Program activities may be authorized.

(1) When an advance of funds is required, the training installation authorized to incur obligations for Field Studies Program purposes will perform the following actions:

(a) Designate and authorize a DOD individual to incur and pay for expenses.

(b) Indicate the number of officer, enlisted, and civilian international students and the maximum amount to be expended.

(c) Authorize the appropriate finance officer to advance the required amount of funds.

(2) When billing is made directly by an agency, club, or organization in connection with the Field Studies Program, an invoice or receipt will be provided. The appropriate accounting data will be entered on SF 1034 and processed by the appropriate finance officer.

c. The designated class A paying agent/cashier will arrange payment of expenses. The IMSO will brief the IMS prior to the event to ensure a clear understanding of the expenses that will be paid, or reimbursed by, the escort. Emergency expenditures must be accounted for with full justification.

d. Alcoholic beverages, if served at Field Studies Program events, must be at no cost to the Field Studies Program

e. Escort expenses should be included in the estimated cost of Field Studies Program field trip, since they are required to participate in all aspects of the event. Escorts will receive single room accommodations. All related authorized expenses will be paid from Field Studies Program funds.

f. Escorts will receive Field Studies Program meal allowances in accordance with the JFTR rate for the location of the Field Studies Program activity when meals are not provided.

11–18. Extraordinary expenses

a. The EE are those expenses incident to representational activities for IMS. Representational activities include, and EE funds help defray the costs of, commanding officer's receptions, civilian-or military-sponsored banquets, faculty-student luncheons, graduations, and other similar activities on a military installation that bridge cultural differences and enhance the relationship between the training installation and the local community.

b. Requests for funds for EE activities will be submitted to the MILDEP under established procedures.

c. Budget Project N60 funds are included in the IMET non-regional program to help defray the anticipated cost of EE for IMET IMS with the exception of alcoholic beverages. The expenditure of N60 funds for IMS not sponsored under the IMET is not authorized. However, joint activities are cost-effective and will be conducted with FMS-funded IMS. In that case, N60 funds and Field Studies Program funds will be prorated on the basis of the respective number of IMET and FMS IMS. In determining the amount of N60 funds to be used for representational activities, the following guidelines pertain:

(1) The basic allowance is $1.00 for each officer and $.50 for each enlisted IMS per course week.

(2) N60 funds may also be used to finance the cost of certain contingency expenditures when they are within the legislative constraints contained in the FAA. Disbursement of funds under these circumstances is authorized only after approval of DSCA.

(3) N60 requirements will be included in the annual Field Studies Program funding requirements determined by the MILDEP. Expenditure of these funds will be authorized by an allotment issued by the MILDEP.

d. Extraordinary expenses activities for FMS IMS are funded from Field Studies Program funds.

e. Units making operational visits to the United States (foreign ships, aircraft squadrons and similar units) are not under either the FAA or AECA; hence, they do not qualify for EE funds.

Section VI
Other Field Studies Program Considerations

11–19. Field Studies Program support mementos

The Field Studies Program support mementos may be presented to sponsors, guest speakers, and other individuals/ institutions that support the Field Studies Program at a cost not to exceed a limit set forth by each Military Service. Annual cost of Field Studies Program support mementos is properly chargeable to the Field Studies Program. Coins and plaques are examples of appropriate Field Studies Program support mementos. The FSP support mementos are not intended for IMS. Departure mementos for IMS are referenced in paragraph 10–27. Request for exception will be forwarded to each MILDEP on a case-by-case basis.

11–20. Reporting requirements

a. Training installations will maintain records of completed Field Studies Program activities so they can respond readily to requests for information.

b. Specific Field Studies Program reporting requirements are set forth in the MILDEP sections.

Section VII
Department of the Army

11–21. Purpose

This section prescribes Army policies, responsibilities and procedures for the conduct of the Field Studies Program both at the school/training activity level and the Washington DC field trip for IMS in selected courses. It applies to all Army agencies conducting training for IMS under the SCETP to include those students training under reciprocal agreements.

11–22. Minimum requirements

In order to assist the IMSO in developing an effective Field Studies Program, the following minimum requirements and priorities are established. They are based upon the objectives of the program and the length of time students are at the installation/training activity location. Table 11–1 recognizes that duration of IMS training varies greatly between schools/training activities. In addition, students at the same school attend courses of varying lengths, and arrive and depart at different times. These priorities were developed to provide structure while maintaining flexibility. This table should not be construed as a building block approach. It is not necessary or desirable to complete all Priority B events before conducting a Priority C event.

Table 11–1
Minimum requirements

Letter Priority Order A. Diversity & American Life B. U.S. Government Institution or Political Processes or Judicial System C. The Free Market System or Education D. Health & Human Services or Media E. International Peace & Security or Law of War	
Student Availability	Minimum Field Studies Program Event Requirement
Less than 4 weeks	None required; include if feasible
4 to 7 weeks	Priority A event
8 to 11 weeks	Priority A event and Priority B event
12 to 15 weeks	Priority A event and Priority B event and Priority C event
16 to 19 weeks	Priority A event and Priority B event and Priority C event and Priority D event
*20 weeks and over	Priority A event and Priority B event and Priority C event and Priority D event and Priority E event
*For each additional 4 weeks, add another event, preferably focusing on a facet not previously covered	

11–23. Responsibilities

Table 11–2 identifies U.S. Army organizations and their responsibilities for various aspects of the Field Studies Program.

Table 11–2
Responsibilities

Organization	Responsibilities
DASA (DE&C)	Policy and resource oversight for the conduct of the Army Field Studies Program.
DCS, G–2 foreign liaison officer (FLO)	DA Schools Washington, DC field trip. Prepare detailed itinerary in conjunction with SAFTA. Make logistical and student/escort life support arrangements including accommodations, meals, in and around travel. Receive, reconcile for accuracy, and process for payment designated bills for lodging, meals, transportation, and miscellaneous authorized expenses. Submit final FLO approved itemized costs to SATFA (ATFA–P4) within 10 days of trip completion. Coordinate Pentagon, Congressional luncheon, and Arlington National Cemetery wreath laying events complete with appropriate briefings, tours, and photos. Arrange official receptions to include host designation, invitation process/guest list maintenance.
DCS, G–3/5/7	Provide for Pentagon event desk officer participation.
HQDA Congressional Liaison	Assist with congressional functions/requirements.
TRADOC	Implementing agent for the U.S. Army Security Cooperation Education and Training Program.
Director, SATFA	Provide installation/training activity level Field Studies Program oversight. Responsible for policy guidance, administration and execution of the installation/training activity Field Studies Program. Review Field Studies Program plans/execution reports for compliance with stated objectives. Approve funding/ensure adequate earnings in course costs for approved Field Studies Program plans. Conduct Washington, DC field trip Develop annual schedule designating participating schools/classes. Develop costs for each field trip/ensure adequate earnings in course costs. Task participating schools for a qualified field trip director and escort officer(s). Train as required. Provide guidance for individual school itinerary development. Coordinate with DCS, G–2 (Intelligence) on itinerary development, provide IMS/escort(s) logistical and life support information. Provide fund cites to field trip director/IMSO for TDY expenses and to DCS, G–2 (Intelligence). Receive reimbursement vouchers and initiate obligation adjustments, as required. Ensure completion of AAR by field trip director with copies furnished to SATFA (ATFA–P4). Conduct annual review of the Washington, DC field trip with DCS, G–2 (Intelligence), making appropriate adjustments.

11–24. Factors for an effective field studies program

An effective Field Studies Program will enhance IMS experiences at U.S. Army schools/training activities and ensure that IMS return to their home countries with a better understanding of Americans and the American way of life. Subsequent paragraphs provide guidelines for effective planning and execution of the Field Studies Program. IMSO should always be aware of individual IMS life support issues, academic progress, personal associations and experiences outside the classroom, which might affect IMS participation in and reaction to the Field Studies Program.

a. The IMSO should make every effort to ensure IMS are properly received within the military and civilian communities to bridge the geographic, economic, social, and cultural differences that naturally exist. IMS should be shielded from potential affronts and indignities.

(1) The use of FSP funds to purchase coffee, tea and other nonalcoholic beverages for the IMS lounge for use by the IMS is authorized.

(2) Field Studies Program funds will be used solely for Field Studies Program events, not to support command or other non-Field Studies Program events.

b. An effective Field Studies Program requires adequate resources in terms of both personnel and funds. The Manpower Staffing Standard System (see para 10–53a) delineates the number of personnel required for student support. TRADOC schools and other training activities with three or more IMSO staff under this standard will have a dedicated Field Studies Program Manager and, for larger programs, a sponsor coordinator and/or assistant Field Studies Program Manager. The IMSO is ultimately responsible for the Field Studies Program, and should work closely with the Field Studies Program Manager and others to plan and execute an effective program.

c. The Field Studies Program should include opportunities for IMS to have personal contact with American people, civilian as well as military, through a sponsorship program or by other means. IMSO should ensure such opportunities by setting up a civilian sponsor program. This involves identifying people who are interested in inviting IMS into their homes and including them in Family and community activities, matching them with IMS, giving them information and or training on the SCETP and working with people from other cultures, and recognizing them for their contributions. A successful sponsor program is a critical component of a well-rounded, effective Field Studies Program.

d. The Chief, IMSO, IMSO staff, and trained escorts should engage students in dialogue about Field Studies Program facets both within and outside the formal Field Studies Program. IMS are naturally curious about how Americans live and what Americans think about current affairs. Informal conversation is a good way to learn what IMS think about America.

(1) All escorts must be USG employees and should be accustomed to working with IMS.

(2) Escorts must understand the goals and objectives of the SCETP, and be particularly well-informed about the significance of the Field Studies Program, its goal, and the duties described in paragraph 11–13. In addition, escorts should clearly understand and be able to articulate the objective(s) of the event(s) in which they are participating.

(3) Escorts should have sufficient information to be able to answer some IMS questions, and to be able to carry on a conversation on the topic at hand. They should have a basic knowledge of U.S. Government and history, particularly the Constitution, and of internationally recognized human rights.

(4) For the Washington, DC field trip, the SATFA Field Studies Program Manager will designate experienced IMSO as trip directors. The recommended number of U.S. escorts for the Washington, DC field trip will be one escort for every 15 IMS. Since it is important to involve school leadership in the Washington, DC field trip when possible a separate designation of senior escort has been developed. Senior escorts should be familiar with the local Field Studies Program at their school, and interact with both escorts and students on the trip. Contact the SATFA Field Studies Program Manager if you have a candidate and particular trip in mind.

e. Family members are encouraged to participate in Field Studies Program events at no charge to the IMS when local guests with Family members are invited. Family members may participate in selected additional Field Studies Program events at no cost to the USG. Spouses who accompany IMS on the Washington, DC field trip are authorized to take part in selected official scheduled events on a space available basis. Spouses may attend the official evening reception hosted by the U.S. Army. An IMSO should not collect nor deposit money for Family members participating in Field Studies Program events. Efforts must be undertaken as not to commingle funds. Students must personally pay for their Family members on these trips. Costs for dependent participation must be provided in advance of the event.

f. SATFA will carefully review plans for school-conducted trips that involve extensive travel and costs in view of the Field Studies Program objectives to be achieved. Trips will normally be limited to a 250 mile radius from the training installation; requests for exceptions to the 250 mile radius must be submitted to SATFA. Requests must include complete justification consisting of Field Studies Program objectives to be met by the proposed trip, evaluation of closer alternative activities, projected costs and the impact if the exception is not granted.

11–25. Examples of field studies program events

Paragraph 11–2 lists the facets of American life to be used in developing an Field Studies Program. Listed below are typical events which might appropriately be scheduled for IMS to acquaint them with these aspects of American life, and which fit into the framework of the minimum coverage for the Field Studies Program. The IMSO should use this as a guide, programming actual visits after consideration of local assets, conditions, and other means that could be employed to meet the same objectives, including guest speakers.

a. Human rights. This topic is to be emphasized in all Field Studies Program events. Specific human rights-related events include museums and monuments such as the Holocaust Museum, Andersonville Prison, and institutions that focus on civil rights.

b. Diversity & American Life. The Sponsorship Program provides many opportunities within this topic. Other possibilities include—

(1) Exposing IMS to ethnic, religious and other minority groups in order to give the students an idea of the challenges and opportunities for these groups.

(2) Local community organizations offer many opportunities for IMS observation and participation. For example, some IMS have volunteered with Habitat for Humanity.

(3) The IMS should be invited to participate in typically American celebrations such as Halloween, Thanksgiving, Martin Luther King Day, and other special emphasis programs, preferably with an American sponsor.

(4) Students should be given a balanced picture of religion in America, to include the vast array of religious institutions which exist as a result of the First Amendment to the U.S. Constitution. The IMS should be offered an opportunity to visit houses of worship of various religious denominations.

(5) Trips to local, state and national parks, and national monuments demonstrate the care Americans have taken to preserve and commemorate our history and preserve the natural environment.

c. U.S. Government institutions. The IMSO must become familiar with elected and appointed officials at all governmental levels in order to plan events around this topic.

(1) *Local government.* The IMSO should introduce IMS to agencies and principal personnel of local government at the city, township or county level at the earliest opportunity. Students may be formally presented to local officials and provided a certificate of honorary citizenship. One purpose of such an introduction is to make the point that local government officials are locally elected and responsible, within broad limits, to local people rather than to the central authorities. IMS should also meet appointed officials and learn how elected and appointed personnel work together.

(2) *State government.* The IMS should be taken to the state capital to be presented to the Governor and/or other

officials, and to have an opportunity to observe selected operations of the state government. One purpose of this visit, like those outlined above, is to stress the autonomy of state governments and the independence of governors and state legislatures. Where possible, the state Supreme Court should also be included in such visits.

(3) *Federal Government.* The IMS should meet the member of Congress from the district where the training site is located, and become familiar with the basics of the American form of government. This is especially important for those students who will participate in the DC field trip.

d. Political processes. The IMS should gain a basic understanding of the electoral process in the United States. They should be able to observe candidates campaigning for office and the voting process.

(1) An understanding of the "grass roots" character of the American political party organization is best gained by bringing IMS in touch with representatives of the political parties in order to give them some idea of the problems of local party organizations, the means by which candidates are chosen, the use of publicity and other means to gain support, and the relationships between local and national party organizations.

(2) The IMSO should arrange for IMS to talk with leaders of opposition parties, preferably office holders rather than party workers. Such a visit should be designed to show students the nature of the "loyal" opposition in this country, that its leaders perform official duties and have official status and that the parties in power and opposition are in fact more united than divided on most of the basic problems facing American society.

e. The Judicial System. Arrangements should be made for visits to jails and detention centers and our municipal, state and federal courts, as well as meetings with officials of these facilities, who should describe the functions and responsibilities of these institutions and the rights of prisoners and defendants under our judicial system.

f. The Free Market System. The following types of trips are designed to suggest the scope and diversity of American business enterprise:

(1) Visits to industrial enterprises should be designed to give IMS an idea of the range of different kinds of industrial enterprises in the American economy, including dams and hydroelectric facilities, local affiliates of large national corporations, and smaller, locally-owned industries. Company officials should be encouraged to discuss decision-making procedures in the fields of product research and development, production scheduling, marketing, and cost controls, and the character and effect of governmental controls over operations.

(2) Visits to banks, Savings and Loan Associations, Federal Housing Administration offices, and agricultural cooperative credit facilities emphasize the range and ease of credit facilities available to the average American.

(3) Visits to local brokerage houses and discussions with stockbrokers emphasize the principles on which American financial investment is based and the procedures through which it is undertaken.

(4) Visits to large transportation centers for rail, air, water, truck or pipeline give IMS an opportunity to discuss the problems of management, maintenance, scheduling, and interconnection with transport officials.

(5) In addition to putting interested IMS in touch with local union officials, tours to regional and national headquarters will serve the useful purpose of emphasizing the scope of such organizations, the objectives of their leadership, and their political and financial independence. In addition, students should be introduced to plant union officials during visits to industrial plants.

(6) The IMSO should arrange tours to farms to show IMS American agriculture. It may be advisable to match the interests and regional background of students with certain specialized types of farming operations in the vicinity. Marketing procedures, facilities, farm loans, and the type of aid farmers receive from federal, State and other agricultural services in combating pests and diseases, controlling breeding stock should be emphasized.

(7) Trips to agricultural experiment stations will permit IMS to view development of new and hybrid plants, animal and fish stock, experiments in controlling local soil conditions, pests and diseases, and so forth. Emphasis should be placed on the financing of the station and the means it uses to make information available to farmers.

g. Education.

(1) Visits to nearby schools and colleges should show IMS the general availability of education, school laboratories and research facilities, extension course programs, agricultural experimental stations and cultural activities such as symphony performances, drama workshops, and so forth. College and university area study and exchange programs will be of special interest to IMS. These visits should emphasize the role of U.S. schools and universities - to teach and learn, not to function as political instruments - and to show the diversity of our educational institutions, including privately endowed colleges, state or city colleges, land grant universities, junior colleges, and church-affiliated institutions.

(2) Arrangements should be made for IMS to speak to classes at local elementary and secondary schools, answer student questions, meet with administrators and faculty, eat lunch in the cafeteria, and observe and participate in other school-related events.

h. Health and Human Services.

(1) The IMSO should arrange visits to publicly supported housing, assisted living facilities, and/or housing supported by religious, or other organizations in order to demonstrate the way in which the elderly and less fortunate are cared for in American society.

(2) Visits to a Red Cross or other disaster relief facility would be of value in demonstrating how Americans contribute time and money to mitigate the effects of disasters.

(3) Visits to public health agencies such as, clinics, welfare agencies, national and state employment services and the local Social Security Office will give the students an overall picture of the social service facilities available in the United States.

i. Media. Visits to media offices should be arranged in order to emphasize how a free press works and the ways in which editors, publishers, and owners define their responsibilities to the public. While radio and TV stations and the printing plants of newspapers are interesting from a technical point of view, discussions with media management and news-gathering personnel are critical to understanding freedom of the press. A discussion of the various points of view expressed in letters to the editor of the local newspaper could be useful.

j. International Peace and Security. The IMS training at installations near Mexico or Canada can be taken to border control checkpoints and meet with officials involved in immigration issues. Meetings with local officials and citizens involved in Sister City Programs with foreign cities can be instructive, as can meetings with groups involved in the peace movement. Visits to Model United Nations events at local schools can be helpful, as can guest speakers from nearby universities.

k. Law of War. The IMSO can arrange for the IMS to participate in discussion with judges, lawyers, and scholars with expertise in the Law of War, Geneva Conventions and their Additional Protocols, and other International Treaties.

11–26. Planning

Planning begins mid-FY prior to the execution year when school schedules are complete and IMS input for the year has been entered into Army Training Resource and Requirement System. Table 11–3 lays out the timeframe and IMSO actions required to develop the Annual Field Studies Program Plan. Table 11–4 lays out the Washington DC field trip planning schedule.

Table 11–3
Annual Field Studies Program planning

Date	Planning action	Description
Jun - Jul	Event review	Review each event conducted during the previous FY for compliance with Field Studies Program objectives and priorities; review escort and IMS assessments for each activity and determine if event is effective enough to repeat.
Jun-Jul	Calendar search	Check calendars from all sources including the installation, school and city to avoid conflicts and ensure key individuals are available for applicable activities.
Jun-Jul	IMS Input for FY	Compile IMS input for each course for the next FY from Security Assistance Network Web to determine when IMS will be arriving and departing.
Jun-Jul	Event contact review	Contact sponsoring personnel at proposed event locations to ensure their continued participation.
Jun-Jul	Cost review	Review previous expenses for each activity (cost per participant and cost per IMS); research current costs for meals, lodging, transportation (military and commercial) and miscellaneous expenses; determine projected Field Studies Program funds for next FY given current rate.
Jul	Develop the plan	Determine dates and number of times each event should be conducted in accordance with Field Studies Program priorities; determine funds required to support plan; compare with projected Field Studies Program funds for the next FY.
NLT 1 Aug	Submit the plan and enter in the Security Assistance Network Web	Update IMSO Annual Field Studies Program Plan for the next FY (enter event templates and pending event reports in Security Assistance Network Web) and submit to SATFA with justification for additional funding if required.
NLT 1 Sep	Submit end of year financial report	Compile financial data from previous FY and submit to SATFA. The report should include all Field Studies Program expenditures (to include non-event related expenses such as mementos and any Field Studies Program-funded TDY). Events conducted at no cost should be listed as well. Estimate expenditures for any events during September.

Table 11-3
Annual Field Studies Program planning—Continued

Date	Planning action	Description
15 Sep	Adjust plan	Make necessary adjustments to plan based on Director, SATFA review.
NLT 30 Sep	Adjust Security Assistance Network Web Plan	Adjust all upcoming Field Studies Program event templates and pending events into Security Assistance Network Web with estimated expenditures and participation.

Table 11-4
Washington, DC field trip planning

Date	Planning action	Description
Jan	Establish senior PME school DC field trip dates	Coordinate with senior PME schools for recommended dates for DC field trip (SATFA)
Feb	Reserve dates for total number of field trip	Coordinate with hotel; reserve field trip dates for the following year (SATFA/FLO)
Mar	Reserve dates for field trip events	Coordinate with agencies supporting the field trip for event reservations (FLO)
Apr	School coordination	Coordinate dates with schools (SATFA)
May	Draft schedule development	Develop draft schedule including dates, schools, and projected IMS numbers (SATFA)
Jun-Jul	School schedule review	Coordinate draft schedule with schools (SATFA)
Aug	final schedule publication	Publish final schedule (SATFA)
Sep	Guest list review	Review guest list to be used for the field trip reception; update as necessary (SATFA/FLO)
15 Oct	Incorporation of field trip costs in course costs	Project costs for field trip and enter appropriate costs for each school into course (SATFA)
Trip - 30 Days Trip - 30 Days Trip - 30 Days Trip + 5 Days Trip + 10 Days	School participation notification Field trip itinerary notification Funds distribution After action review Itemized costs	Notify SATFA and FLO 30 days prior to each scheduled field trip: flight arrival and departure information; IMS names, countries, and rooming assignments; escort names; any special requirements (School IMSO). Notify participating schools and SATFA of final field trip itinerary (FLO). Provide funds to FLO and participating schools for necessary expenses (SATFA). Compile all escort and IMS feedback and submit final report to SATFA (Trip director). Submit final itemized costs to SATFA (FLO).

11-27. Field studies program event execution

Table 11-5 identifies each of the actions IMSO will take in order to execute an individual Field Studies Program event.

Table 11–5
Field Studies Program event execution

Not all enumerated items apply to each type of Field Studies Program event
1. Notify command of the event
2. Develop strawman itinerary
3. Select knowledgeable escorts
4. Train new escorts
5. Coordinate each individual activity on the itinerary to include admission, tour guides
6. Coordinate guest speakers
7. Coordinate all IMS life support items for the event to include hotels, transportation and meals
8. Develop event flyer for IMS including topics to be covered
9. Require IMS/guests to RSVP for attendance
10. Double check all previously coordinated actions for completion
11. Pre-brief IMS at least 5 days prior to the event
12. Distribute itinerary to IMS
13. Conduct event
14. Distribute escort and IMS event assessment sheets
15. Collect and review assessment sheets
16. Prepare/submit Field Studies Program event report to SATFA via Security Assistance Network Web NLT 10 days after event completion

11–28. Reporting

a. The IMSO will prepare and submit a report to SATFA for all Field Studies Program events conducted NLT 10 days after completion utilizing the Field Studies Program Events tool on the Security Assistance Network Web. The report will include the cost of transportation, meals, lodging and miscellaneous expenses. The report will also include an official by-name list of IMS at all events and the number of attendees to include IMS, escorts, guests, and sponsors.

b. The IMSO will locally file the following information in separate event folders (not all inclusive).

(1) Written information packet and related handouts.

(2) Itinerary.

(3) Documentation and justification of guests invited to all events.

(4) An overall escort and IMS assessment will be included for each event. Guest speaker effectiveness will be addressed. A recommendation on repeating or deleting the event will also be included.

(5) Detailed receipts for all Field Studies Program expenditures.

11–29. Source of Field Studies Program funding

As a result of the annual planning process as described in paragraph 11–26, a final cost has been calculated by the IMSO to administer the execution year Field Studies Program. SATFA Field Studies Program Manager will review proposed Field Studies Program submitted by the IMSO for the execution year to determine its compliance with the stated objectives/guidelines of the program. Once the SATFA Field Studies Program Manager approves the proposed Field Studies Program plan, the SATFA Field Studies Program Manager will present the plan to Director, SATFA for final approval. Upon Director, SATFA approval the required monies will be incorporated into the training activity's course costs. The Field Studies Program funds are actually earned when IMS enter their scheduled training. Field Studies Program funds are identified on course costs sheets sent annually to the IMSO and servicing resource management office and are generated via funding documents into the local training installation/activity OMA account. At the end of each FY, funds earned but not used for students continuing to the next FY should be obligated by use of a miscellaneous obligation document (MOD). The funds on the MOD are immediately available at the beginning of the next FY for Field Studies Program use and should be used prior to any new funds received.

11–30. Use of Field Studies Program funds

a. The IMSO is charged with the responsibility of executing the approved Field Studies Program for IMS and has been provided funds to do so through earnings generated in course costs. It is imperative that the IMSO have oversight of the projected Field Studies Program earnings/budget for the FY. The tool to accomplish this is the monthly funds status report they will receive from their servicing resource management office. Field Studies Program earnings and expenses should be captured in separate account processing codes from other Security Assistance earnings and expenses. The IMSO is also charged with making adjustments to the annual Field Studies Program based on the available funds balance as it changes with IMS additions/deletions throughout the year. Care should be taken not to spend more than the projected earnings for the Field Studies Program for the FY. Prior coordination with servicing resource management and contracting personnel is recommended to choose the best vehicle for payment of services rendered and goods procured. To assist in the execution of the Field Studies Program the following options are available:

(1) *Class A Agent.* The IMSO or escort officers for Field Studies Program events may be appointed as Class A agents. The Class A agent will receive an advance of Field Studies Program funds to cover the estimated cost of Field Studies Program activities. Upon completion of the Field Studies Program activities, the Class A agent will reconcile with the finance and accounting office for settlement. A copy of the settlement document must be retained in the IMSO files.

(2) *Government purchase card.* The government purchase card (GPC) will be used for the Field Studies Program when possible to pay for administrative program costs and actual event execution costs. IMSO will coordinate with the local contracting officer for the issue of the credit card. IMSO will reconcile monthly GPC statements to ascertain all charges are legitimate and properly charged to the Field Studies Program. A copy of reconciled statements must be retained in the IMSO files.

(3) *Unit travel cards.* Unit travel cards will be issued to IMSO by local officials to defray cost of transportation, lodging and meals for large groups participating in an Field Studies Program event. IMSO will reconcile monthly unit travel card statements to ascertain all charges are legitimate and properly charged to the Field Studies Program. A copy of reconciled statements must be retained in the IMSO files.

(4) *Single room accommodations.* These accommodations are authorized only for IMS equivalent to O–7 and above. All other IMS will be assigned double room accommodations. IMS below the O–7 equivalent rank who want a single room will pay the difference in cost.

(5) *Contract.* A contract is another option available for use when paying for Field Studies Program events, to include guest speakers and trips. Once the services/goods contracted for have been received, then the receiving report, SF 1449 (Solicitation/Contract/Order for Commercial Items), is signed by the IMSO. A copy of the signed receiving report must be retained in the IMSO files.

b. Payments for meals for IMS while participating in an Field Studies Program event should not exceed published per diem meal costs as specified by the JTR. Exceptions must be approved in advance by the SATFA Field Studies Program manager.

c. Funds, to include cash, will not be given directly to IMS, but will be used by the escort(s) to meet expenses connected with the Field Studies Program.

11–31. Funding of Security Assistance Training Field Activity-managed Washington, DC field trip

The SATFA Field Studies Program Manager will develop costs for each Washington, DC field trip to be conducted in the following FY. The costs developed will be based on historical cost data with consideration given to inflation and other pertinent factors such as increased transportation and lodging costs. A projected budget will be developed taking all factors into consideration. A Washington, DC Field Trip cost is customized, and included in the course costs for eligible courses, for each school (such as captains career courses). The costs for the Washington, DC Field Trip are identified separately from the regular Field Studies Program funds on the course costs sheets. SATFA ultimately retains and manages the funds for the Washington, DC Field Trip and issues fund cites to pay for appropriate charges to the program.

a. Proper expenses for the Washington, DC field trip include IMS roundtrip transportation from the school and expenses in the local Washington, DC area, that is, lodging accommodations, guide service, official receptions, luncheons, and dinners. Escort officer(s) expenses are also proper expenses chargeable to the field trip.

b. The field trip director's installation will prepare travel orders using the fund cite issued by SATFA. The field trip director will defray their expenses using the fund cite in the TDY orders.

c. The SATFA Field Studies Program Manager will determine the appropriate method for payment of field trip expenses in the Washington, DC area. SATFA will serve as ordering officer when necessary.

d. The SATFA allocates the extraordinary expenses (see para 11–18) issued to HQDA in accordance with DFAS 37–100 to help defray Washington, DC field trip expenses.

Section VIII
Department of the Navy (United States Navy, United States Marine Corps) (Field Studies Program)

11–32. Responsibilities for funding the Field Studies Program

a. All Navy and Marine Corps commands will implement a comprehensive and integrated Field Studies Program based upon the general guidance set forth in sections 11–1 through 11–20 of the Security Cooperation Education and Training Center and this section. Commanding officers will ensure maximum effectiveness of the Field Studies Program within their command or activity.

b. The Navy IPO (IPO–04) will supervise, administer, and authorize the expenditure of Field Studies Program funds within the DON. USN major claimants will implement and manage Field Studies Program for their respective commands and activities. Security Cooperation Education and Training Center will centrally supervise, manage, and authorize the expenditure of Field Studies Program for USMC commands and activities.

11–33. Designation of international military student officer
Each command directly concerned with IMS will designate at least one individual to serve as IMSO. The IMSO will act as the commanding officer's principal advisor for the Field Studies Program.

11–34. Source of funding
The Field Studies Program funds are obtained from weekly course cost assessments and are part of the overall course tuition courses. Since Navy IPO centrally manages the Field Studies Program funds, all assessments should be credited to the Navy IPO's line of accounting.

11–35. Submission of annual data requirements
a. During the fourth quarter of each FY, Navy IPO will provide guidance to all activities regarding data required to justify the next FY's Field Studies Program. The Field Studies Program budget submissions will include the following information at a minimum:

(1) An estimate of the number of IMS to be trained during the next reporting period (BY) and actual number of IMS that were trained in the current and prior years.

(2) An estimate of the total number of IMS weeks of training during the next training cycle (BY) and actual number of IMS training weeks for the current and prior years.

(3) Types of students: number of IMET and FMS; grades/ranks of students for the BY and actual data for the current and prior years.

(4) Detailed Field Studies Program plan for the BY, listing the estimated dates, events, and detailed cost data. Each Field Studies Program event should be tied to achieving one or more of the specific objectives of the Field Studies Program.

(5) Quarterly funding phasing plan.

(6) Detailed justification for waiver requests for trips exceeding the 300 mile radius limitation.

b. Marine Corps commands and activities will submit their annual requirements to Security Cooperation Education and Training Center MCCDC for consolidation and forwarding to Navy IPO (IPO–04). At a minimum, the submission will include the information outlined in paragraph a. above.

11–36. Funding field studies program events
a. Advance of funds for Field Studies Program activities is authorized by DOD 7000.14–R, Volume 5. Upon approval of the activity annual budget submission, Navy IPO will provide funding to the activity via the NAVCOMPT Form 2275 (Order for Work and Services). Funding will be provided at the beginning of the FY and quarterly, based on the activity's approved funding plan and available funds.

b. Payments for meals while participating in local Field Studies Program events should not exceed $15 per IMS for lunch/breakfast/picnics or $25 per IMS for dinners/receptions/graduations.

c. The total cost of mementos should not exceed $25 per IMS. They should be of a permanent nature. (Ball caps and t-shirts are not considered to be of a permanent nature). Funding for mementos for guest speakers/community leaders/sponsors should be identified separately in the annual budget submission to Navy IPO.

d. The Field Studies Program tours, funds permitting, are conducted on an all-expense paid basis. Group meals while participating in overnight trips should not exceed the local per diem rate as set by the JTR. The IMSO may decide; however, to require participants to pay for some meals if limited funding would otherwise preclude proceeding with the tour.

e. Funds supporting the Field Studies Program will not be expended to pay for alcoholic beverages or for activities that are substantially recreational, including but not limited to entrance fees at sporting events, theatrical and musical productions, and amusement/theme parks.

f. Given limited Field Studies Program funds, events such as picnics, receptions, and dinners, although allowed if meeting Field Studies Program objective(s), should be not be a substantial cost component of the overall Field Studies Program. In addition, the number of guests should be in reasonable proportion to the number of IMS.

g. Marine Corps commands and activities will obtain funding for Field Studies Program events from Security Cooperation Education and Training Center. Funds available for Marine Corps FSPs will be based on an allocation from Navy IPO. Activities with an Field Studies Program will request funds on an as-required basis. Security Cooperation Education and Training Center will review each request and authorize funding for each Field Studies Program event. Detailed justification for Field Studies Program trips that exceed the 300 mile radius limitation must be included in Security Cooperation Education and Training Center's annual budget submission to Navy IPO. All of the preceding funding limitations are applicable to Marine Corps commands.

h. Single room accommodations are authorized only for IMS equivalent to O–7 and above. All other IMS will be assigned double room accommodations. IMS below the O–7 equivalent rank who want a single room will pay the difference in cost.

11–37. Disbursing funds
Disbursement of funds authorized by Navy IPO for Field Studies Program activities will be made by a designated Class A agent/cashier, according to DOD 7000.14–R, volume 5. The IMSOs at local commands may be authorized to draw advance funds by the commanding officer according to DOD 7000.14–R, volume. 5.

a. The designated individual will submit a claim using SF 1164 to the authorizing officer for approval according to DOD 7000.14–R, Volume 5. Each claim will be supported by accounting instructions specified in the NAVCOMPT Form 2275 document provided by Navy IPO authorizing the expenditure of these funds.

b. A copy of the liquidated SF 1164 indicating final cost of Field Studies Program event must be submitted to the Field Studies Program activity providing the funds. Marine Corps Commands and activities will submit liquidation documents to the Security Cooperation Education and Training Center MCCDC.

c. Field Studies Program activities must return unobligated funds to Navy IPO in a timely manner (no later than 90 days after the end of the FY). The reversion of funds will be accomplished via an amendment to the NAVCOMPT Form 2275 or via a final 2193.

Section IX
The U.S. Coast Guard (Field Studies Program)

11–38. Responsibilities for the Field Studies Program
a. All USCG activities directly concerned with IMS will devise comprehensive and integrated Field Studies Program based upon the general guidance set forth in paragraphs 11–1 through 11–21 and this section.

b. The USCG International Affairs (G–CI) will fund, implement and manage Field Studies Program for IMS attending Coast Guard training.

11–39. Designation of international military student officer
Each command directly concerned with IMS will designate at least one officer to serve as IMSO. The IMSO will act as the commanding officer's principal advisor for the Field Studies Program.

11–40. Source of funding
The Field Studies Program funds are obtained from a weekly course cost assessment set each year. The USCG has selected the course/percentage method as the approach best suited to its purpose. This methodology does not apply to OJT. Although OJT courses do not generate Field Studies Program funds, IMS involved in OJT courses are eligible to use activity Field Studies Program funds. Activities providing OJT may obtain appropriate funds through submission of an USCG Field Studies Program request form.

11–41. Submission of annual requirements
a. By 31 July each FY, activities with an annual requirement of more than $10K must provide USCG International Affairs (G–CI) via the appropriate chain of command, a detailed line item estimate per trip of Field Studies Program funds required during the next FY. Training activities must carefully review and weigh plans for trips that involve extensive travel and costs against the Field Studies Program objectives to be achieved. The budget request must be formatted by event (that is, East Coast Field Studies Program trip), and include narratives, which are brief descriptions of the events highlighting the Field Studies Program topics and anticipated travel dates, cost estimates, and identify number of escorts and students, per diem rates, transportation costs, special event costs, meal, and other incidental costs. Budget estimates exceeding 5 percent of prior year submission should provide a narrative to explain significant increases (for example, new course included, increase in students, anticipated increase in bus costs, and so forth).

b. Training facilities with an estimated annual Field Studies Program budget less than $10K, will request authorization and funding by submitting an Field Studies Program Activity Request Form not less than 15 working days prior to the event date. Completed forms should be forwarded to the USCG International Affairs (G–CI) via fax or electronically.

11–42. Funding field studies program events
Detailed justification for Field Studies Program trips that exceed the mileage limitations outlined in paragraph 11–10 of this instruction must be submitted with each Field Studies Program funds request. Waiver requests are to be submitted at least 30 days prior to Field Studies Program event and must include—

a. Number of IMS (include country of origin and rank for each IMS) participating in event.

b. Total round trip Field Studies Program distance.

c. The specific Field Studies Program objectives that the trip will accomplish.

d. A statement of why Field Studies Program objectives cannot be accomplished by local area trips must be included with the waiver request.

e. Single room accommodations are authorized only for IMS equivalent to O–7 and above. All other IMS will be assigned double room accommodations. IMS below the O–7 equivalent grade who want a single room will pay the difference in cost.

Section X
Department of the Air Force (Field Studies Program)

11–43. Management of the Field Studies Program

a. The SAF/IAPX is responsible for Field Studies Program policies and procedures. Air Force Security Assistance Training Squadron implements and manages the program.

b. The MAJCOM have overall management responsibilities to ensure maximum effectiveness of the program at bases within the command. Each commander will designate an OPR to control and manage the Field Studies Program within the command. Staff visits and communication among bases, OPR, and Air Force Security Assistance Training Squadron, are encouraged to realize the greatest benefit of the Field Studies Program.

c. CONUS base commanders will implement the Field Studies Program at each base where IMS are trained. Base commanders overseas will carry out the FSP at bases where IMS are trained to the extent that local conditions permit. Commanders are encouraged to make maximum use of one-on-one interchange and associations between IMS and members of the staff, local military, and U.S. citizens to promote dialogues on the FSP objectives, especially where organized U.S. sponsored activities are limited.

d. The SAF/IAPX encourages the planning of events in the civilian community.

11–44. Funding field studies program activities

Funds for conducting the Field Studies Program for IMET students are approved by the U.S. Congress and are paid as part of the tuition rate for IMS.

a. During each quarter of each FY, each installation programmed to receive IMS will submit their Field Studies Program activities 60 days prior to the beginning of each quarter, that is, 1 November, 1 February, 1 May, and 1 August. Plans will cover a 90-day period and will be submitted quarterly to the Air Force Security Assistance Training Squadron Field Studies Program Manager, 315 J Street West, Randolph AFB, TX 78150–4302. All USAF training installations will submit their Field Studies Program activities based on the general guidance set forth in paragraphs 11–1 through 11–20 and this section.

b. In addition to local activities, the plan should include special activities and extended trips (Washington DC tours or visits to large metropolitan areas) that are planned when specific objectives cannot be accomplished in the local area.

c. Requests for legitimate out-of-pocket expenses, as outlined in paragraph 11–10*a*, must be submitted quarterly to Air Force Security Assistance Training Squadron not to exceed $50 per quarter. Expenses may then be processed against the obligation authority for out-of pocket expenses.

d. Payments for meals while participating in local Field Studies Program events will not exceed $15 per IMS for lunch/breakfast/picnics or $25 per IMS for dinners/receptions/graduations. Exceptions will be handled on a case-by-case basis.

11–45. Field Studies Program participation

a. An Field Studies Program may be conducted for FMS students attending contractor training implemented by Air Force Security Assistance Training Squadron as line manager provided—

(1) The training is being conducted within the general area of an USAF base with an IMSO.

(2) The Field Studies Program does not adversely impact the student's training.

(3) The estimated cost factor of the Field Studies Program is included in the estimated training cost and reimbursed under the FMS case.

b. If the above conditions can be met, the contractor should provide for the release of the students for the Field Studies Program.

c. Family members are not authorized on academic trips. Family members may accompany the IMS when the Field Studies Program trip is not part of the scheduled training curriculum.

11–46. Data card

AF Form 1217 (Field Studies Program Data Card) or electronic database that identifies each IMS will be used to record students participation in Field Studies Program activities. AF Form 1217 may be temporarily stored in a card file to permit easy access by the IMSO while the IMS is in training. However, AF Form 1217 must be transferred to the IMS training records before they are forwarded to the next training installation or to the country Security Cooperation Organization.

11–47. Plaques and mementos
The cost of special awards, plaques, and mementos in connection with Field Studies Program activities may be chargeable to Field Studies Program funds. The amount is not to exceed $25.

11–48. Quarterly report
The IMSO will have participating IMS evaluate each Field Studies Program event just prior to completion. Four groups of 25 IMS or less, each IMS will complete an evaluation. For larger groups, a sampling may be taken. The IMSO will also assess each Field Studies Program event. Use the formats provided in the DOD Field Studies Program Handbook. A sampling of IMS evaluations and the IMSO assessment for each activity will be forwarded to Air Force Security Assistance Training Squadron/Field Studies Program Office, 315 J Street West, Randolph AFB, TX, 78150–4302. IMSO will submit a recap of all Field Studies Program events, provided at cost or no cost, and N60-funded activities NLT 15 days following the end of the fiscal quarter.

11–49. Use of field studies program funds
Requests for the use of Field Studies Program funds for activities for items and activities that do not clearly relate to the Field Studies Program objectives, must be forwarded for a case-by-case decision to SAF/IAPX through Air Force Security Assistance Training Squadron. The request must contain sufficient details and justification on which to make a decision. The Field Studies Program trips will be limited to a 300 mile radius from the base unless an exception is granted by SAF/IAPX. Single room accommodations are authorized only for IMS equivalent to O–7 and above. All other IMS will be assigned double room accommodations. IMS below the O–6 equivalent rank who want a single room will pay the difference in cost.

11–50. International military student officer workshop
The Air Force Security Assistance Training Squadron will budget for and host an IMSO workshop. Air Force IMSO workshops will be conducted approximately every 18 months. Proposed agenda items will be forwarded to SAF/IAPX for review prior to publication.

11–51. Implementing Washington, DC, tours
a. All IMS attending Professional Military Education, language instructor training, and officers with CONUS course durations, totaling 20 weeks or more will be afforded the opportunity to participate in the Washington Field Studies Program tour. At least 90 days notice is required by SAF/IAPX to plan the applicable Air Staff Officers', Country Directors', and Air Attachés reception. Bases must coordinate with Air Force Security Assistance Training Squadron/ Field Studies Program Office for approval of the proposed tour dates with the estimated cost for the DC tour. After arrival in Washington, DC, group itineraries will not be changed without the approval of Air Force Security Assistance Training Squadron/Field Studies Program Office.

b. After coordination, funding requests describing the tour and the estimated costs for conducting the tour will be forwarded to Air Force Security Assistance Training Squadron/Field Studies Program Office as stated below.

(1) Proposed dates and tour itinerary.

(2) Number of IMS by country.

(3) Estimated commercial transportation costs and hotel accommodations, venue admission costs, and meals.

(4) Number of DOD escorts.

c. Air Force Security Assistance Training Squadron/Field Studies Program Office will forward fund approval at least 20 days before the tour date. Direct contact between the base and SAF/IAPX is authorized after tour approval for planning and programming activities to achieve Field Studies Program objectives. Upon completion of the tour, the DOD escort will submit a report of the tour to Air Force Security Assistance Training Squadron/Field Studies Program Office, 315 J Street West, Randolph AFB TX 78150–4354.

11–52. Accountability
The IMSO disposes of receipts for expenditure of funds according to Air Force instructions. Copies of SF 1034 approval for expenditures, total expenditure reports, and individual receipts will be filed together with a monthly folder.

a. Military and civilian agencies providing services for Field Studies Program activities are required to indicate the appropriate breakout of costs such as room rates, meal charges, venue admission costs, hotel accommodations, transportation, and other individual services. However, receipts for individual services are neither required nor desired (except when payment is made directly to the IMS in lieu of payment by the DOD escort officer for meals). DOD escort officers or IMSO will complete SF 1034 and include copies of all receipts for finance agencies to account for expenses. An administrative certificate or statement on the SF 1034 that the services were performed in connection with the authorized activity will be prepared.

b. The IMSO will advise Air Force Security Assistance Training Squadron/Field Studies Program Office of the total amount of funds expended within 30 workdays after completing the tour.

c. Base IMSO are encouraged to contact other IMSO within the same area so they are aware of other activities of interest to IMS at their location.

d. The Field Studies Program funds will not be obligated or expended to pay for food outside the military installation unless associated with a Field Studies Program trip where students do not stay at or have the opportunity to dine upon a military installation.

Chapter 12
Orientation Tours

Section I
General

12–1. Objectives
a. OT are provided under the Security Cooperation Education and Training Program (SCETP) to selected foreign officers and government civilians of new or transitioning countries for familiarizing them with U.S. military doctrine, techniques, procedures, facilities, equipment, organization, management practices, and operations and civil-military theories and practices.

b. OT may be one of the first SCETP for a new or transitioning country, whose government structure is undergoing a transition as a result of the end of a civil war, or military rule. These leaders often need quick and time-sensitive ways to learn how to better manage their country's defense resources, or how to interact within their new civil-military defense structure, or how to better train their newly-designed Armed Forces. OT provide this opportunity. These tours are conducted as short-term orientations as opposed to long-term formal courses.

c. OT are usually limited to countries with lesser developed relations with the United States, but in recent years, transitioning countries not new to security assistance have conducted tours to deepen their knowledge of democracy, peacekeeping, military modernization and interoperability, and counterterrorism. These tours are conducted as short-term orientations as opposed to long-term formal courses.

d. In addition to the military and expanded civil-military objectives to be achieved through OT, it is intended that they serve to enhance mutual understanding, cooperation, and friendship between U.S. forces and participating nations.

12–2. Types of orientation tours
The two types of OT-sponsored by DOD under the SCETP are as follows:

a. Distinguished visitors orientation tour. A distinguished visitor orientation tour is conducted only for high-level or senior foreign military officers and government civilians (below the equivalent U.S. position of Chief of Staff, Chief of Naval Operations, or Commandant of the Coast Guard or the Marine Corps) holding positions of major importance or selected for such positions. A distinguished visitor orientation tour normally is of flag or general rank and civilian equivalent. A distinguished visitor orientation tour is conducted for a period not to exceed 14 calendar days plus overseas travel time and distinguished visitor orientation tour is limited to not more than seven participants per tour. For waiver exceptions to increase the number of participants the Security Cooperation Organization must get approval from DSCA. Courtesies and honors should be afforded a distinguished visitor orientation tour according to the participant's rank and position. Such honors and other appropriate activities (such as receptions, dinners, or luncheons) should be modest. Personal aides are not authorized to accompany flag or general officers.

b. Orientation tour. An OT is conducted for selected foreign officers and government civilians who are destined for responsible positions in their country's military and or parliamentary establishment. These officers and civilians do not presently qualify for DVOTs. An OT is conducted for a period not to exceed 14 calendar days plus overseas travel time and is limited to not less than three but no more than seven participants per tour. An OT is provided on a modest basis with minimum official entertainment.

12–3. Other visits
a. Chief of Staff or head of Service visits. Visits by the heads of foreign military Services, or officers designated to occupy such positions, are arranged through diplomatic channels under the auspices of the head of the U.S. sponsoring Military Service. These visits are not implemented under security assistance sponsorship or procedures.

b. Self-invited visits. Self-invited visits are requested by the foreign country through diplomatic channels and all expenses are the responsibility of the foreign country. Security Cooperation Organization will coordinate requests for self-invited visits with the appropriate U.S. country team.

12–4. Programming and implementation
a. OT will be programmed in the FY IMET or FMS programs in the same way as other training at the annual

Security Cooperation Education and Training Working Group hosted by the Combatant Commands. (See fig 12–1 for programming information for orientation tours.)

b. All OT under IMET sponsorship must be approved by DSCA before implementation. Itinerary, justification, and adequate supporting rationale should be forwarded by the Security Cooperation Organization along with the ambassador's statement attesting to the importance of providing such training.

c. Unless otherwise directed, NDU will schedule, cost, coordinate and plan OT, which can be single Service or Joint-oriented in nature and scope. NDU will charge the country program an OT coordination fee (or manpower fee). See section III for final guidance.

d. Requests for unprogrammed orientation tours will be considered only by exception, on a case-by-case basis. Requests will be sent through the Combatant Command to the NDU no less than 120 days before the requested tour start date.

e. OT are not "off-the-shelf" programs, OT are hand-tailored, intensive training programs that are developed to meet the defense and civil-military needs of a new or transitioned country. Each is tailored to country requirements and U.S. objectives. One itinerary is provided for each tour, regardless of the number, grade, or assignment of tour participants.

12–5. Restrictions and limitations

a. Tours will have training/education as the primary focus.

b. Tours will not be programmed or implemented in conjunction with other sequential training.

c. Tours will be conducted on an unclassified basis.

d. Tour participants should have a minimum ECL of 70, if not an interpreter will accompany the team.

e. Tours to the U.S. Service academies will not be arranged during examination and graduation periods (normally 1 May to 1 June).

f. The tour program will not be used to support visits that have materiel acquisition as an objective.

g. Tours funded under IMET will not be used to promote foreign military sales.

h. Persons who have taken part in training in the United States will be scheduled for an orientation tour under IMET only when fully justified by the Security Cooperation Organization. The combat commander, DSCA, and the Military Service must also approve such actions.

i. The foreign country may program only (1) OT per year subject to the Military Service or NDU capability to implement the tour.

12–6. Biographical data

Biographical data on each tour participant will be provided in accordance with paragraph 10–11. Biography data will be sent to the Military Service at least 60 days before the scheduled arrival of the participants in CONUS.

12–7. Invitational travel orders

Each orientation tour participant requires an Invitational Travel Order (ITO). ITO will be sent to Military Service in accordance with chapter 9.

12–8. Pre-departure briefing

a. Foreign officers selected to participate in OT will be thoroughly briefed by Security Cooperation Organization personnel before departure to the United States.

b. The following items should be given special emphasis during the in-country predeparture briefing:

(1) *Itinerary.* No changes will be made to the final itinerary established for the orientation tour and all orientation tour participants will travel together for the duration of the tour.

(2) *Clothing.* Military uniforms are required; however, participants should bring some seasonal casual clothes and at least one civilian suit.

(3) *Family members.* Family members are not authorized to accompany orientation tour participants.

(4) *Medical services.* Only emergency medical services will be provided. See chapter 8 for eligibility requirements.

(5) *Leave.* If authorized, leave can be taken only upon conclusion of the orientation tour. Appropriate leave authorization will be included in the ITO.

(6) *Privately-owned vehicle.* Purchase of a POV by orientation tour participants will be deferred until completion of the tour.

(7) *Orientation tour authorized expenditures.* Inform orientation tour participants about the charges the program will cover and incidental charges they will have to cover with their own personal funds.

(8) *Events.* Gift exchanges, office calls with U.S. officials, receptions, and distinguished visitor orientation tour representational events.

(9) *Economy coach air.* Tour participants will generally fly CONUS at the economy government rate.

12–9. Baggage

a. Each IMET orientation tour participant is authorized two pieces of baggage not to exceed the weight limit for U.S. domestic air travel. For that portion of the travel funded under IMET, baggage will accompany the individual. This authorization will be included in the ITO. The tour participant will pay the cost for excess baggage or weight. Additional allowance for instruction material is authorized.

b. Because of baggage handling problems, the baggage limitations applicable to IMET participants in paragraph *a*, above should be adhered to by FMS participants.

12–10. Field Studies Program activities

Field Studies Program requirements are discussed in chapter 11. As part of the SCETP, every effort must be made to include some areas of the FSP programs in the orientation tour to expose tour participants to cultural, social, economic and historical aspects of America. The SAMM, paragraph C10, 11.5. Extraordinary Expenses, offers additional guidance.

12–11. United States escorts

a. The Security Cooperation Organization will normally furnish U.S. escorts from their office resources. If available, escorts fluent in the language of the tour participants will be furnished. The escort will accompany the tour group from the time of departure from OCONUS to arrival in CONUS, until the group departs for the group's home country, except during authorized leave periods.

b. The Security Cooperation Organization representatives should not be used as escort officers for IMET-sponsored OT. However, in exceptional cases and with prior approval of DSCA, a Security Cooperation Organization representative may serve as an escort officer. This is justified when special qualifications, workload, unusual rapport with key host country personnel, and associated projects or contacts may be useful. The Security Cooperation Organization representative selected as an escort officer is under the complete jurisdiction of the implementing agency (NDU) and remains with the tour at all times until the tour participants return to host country. Temporary duty (TDY) travel and per diem costs for the escort officer for the duration of the tour are chargeable to IMET funds, and are programmed as a separate line in the country program. U.S. personnel other than bona fide escort officers designated or agreed to by NDU for tour implementation are not authorized to accompany tour groups. The dollar value of escort officer expenses is programmed in the TLA data field.

c. U.S. personnel assigned within the foreign country may act as escorts if recommended by the Security Cooperation Organization, Combatant Command and approved by DSCA and NDU.

d. If the Security Cooperation Organization cannot provide escort officers and/or interpreters, Military Service will provide and budget costs to the tour.

e. The escort will use billeting accommodations at the same location (hotel, motel, or bachelor officer quarters) as provided to the tour participants.

f. The use of foreign country personnel as escorts is not authorized. They can serve as interpreters, if qualified, but must accompany the U.S. escort officer.

g. If interpreters are required, but cannot be provided by the Security Cooperation Organization, Military Service must provide by other sources and ensure they are qualified, budgeted for, cleared, and properly briefed of their tour responsibilities.

h. The U.S. escort may be appointed as class A agent/cashier for disbursing funds to defray the cost of Field Studies Program activities. Installations hosting official functions, chargeable to the Field Studies Program, should ensure that appropriate charges are presented to the U.S. escort before the tour leaves the installation.

Section II
Programming

12–12. Orientation tours

a. OT are programmed as separate WCN and all tour participants will be programmed as separate WCN (tour participants) entries.

b. The cost of the tour line is included in the travel and living allowance (TLA) column and includes the following:

(1) Round trip transportation to the CONUS port (if IMET or CTFP pays overseas transportation). When U.S. funds are used, U.S. carriers will be used at the lowest cost. For IMET waivers refer to figure 12–2. Orientation tours funded under FMS cases will not include overseas transportation unless a waiver has been provided by DSCA.

(2) The costing factor determined by NDU or the Military Service to cover the costs of CONUS travel, quarters, meals, and Field Studies Program. OT-funded under FMS cases may include all; a portion; or none of these costs as directed by the country.

(3) The U.S. escort may be programmed for the duration of the tour plus one additional week to allow for the Military Service briefing, travel to the port of tour arrival, and travel from the port of tour departure.

(4) Tour and U.S. escort must be programmed in the current FY program.

(5) Installations that host official functions can be reimbursed through the distinguished visitor orientation tour implementing agency.

(6) Tour participants are responsible for personal expenses and must have sufficient funds to defray their costs.

c. A meal and incidental allowance is payable to IMET OT participants in accordance to the JTR. OT participants should be given an advance payment for meals and incidentals by the US Embassy in country. In extraordinary circumstances this payment may be made by the OT implementing agency. Upon return to the home country and completion of the TDY voucher, OT participants will be reimbursed the remaining 20 percent meal and incidental allowance.

d. Installations can request EE funds. The amount of expenditure per installation visited will be as determined by the NDU or the Military Service.

e. The escort officer may be appointed as class A agent/cashier for disbursing funds to defray the cost of participants' and International Program activities.

f. When possible, OT participants should be assigned double room accommodations within JTR lodging allowance, if funded by the IMETP.

g. The tour and the U.S. escort must be programmed in the current FY program.

h. Installations that host official functions, chargeable to security assistance funds, should ensure appropriate charges are presented to the escort officer before the tour leaves the installation.

i. Tour participants are responsible for personal expenses and must have sufficient funds to defray their costs.

12–13. Distinguished visitor orientation tour

a. A meal and incidental allowance is payable to IMET distinguished visitor orientation tour participants in accordance to the JTR. Distinguished visitor orientation tour participants should be given an advance payment for meals and incidentals by the U.S. Embassy in country. In extraordinary circumstance this payment may be made by the distinguished visitor orientation tour implementing agency. Upon return to the home country and completion of the TDY voucher, distinguished visitor orientation tour participants will be reimbursed the remaining 20 percent meal and incidental allowance.

b. Installations can request EE funds. The amount of expenditure per installation visited will be as determined by the NDU or the Military Service.

c. When the use of commercial quarters is required, distinguished visitor orientation tour should be provided with single room accommodations.

12–14. Procedures for requesting orientation tours

a. Requests for OT visits in the United States must be submitted via the Combatant Commander to DSCA, the Military Service and NDU at least 120 days before the desired departure date from the country. An IMET waiver and tour objective worksheet whether IMET-, FMS- or RDCTP-funded must be completed by the Security Cooperation Organization and submitted to DSCA for approval and NDU coordination respectively. The objectives worksheet should include the following information:

(1) General scope of interest of tour participants.

(2) Suggested itinerary with specific areas of interest at the activities recommended to visit.

(3) Recommended International Program activities.

(4) Number of participants and the name and rank of the senior officer.

b. Upon receipt of the information in, NDU will contact the proposed installations immediately as to the feasibility of hosting the requested OT visit and will submit a detailed itinerary within 10 days. At the same time, the Security Cooperation Organization is required to forward the following information so that it will arrive no later than 45 days before commencement of the visit:

(1) ITO of participants.

(2) List of participants in order of precedence, including rank as U.S. rank equivalent) and billet currently held or anticipated.

(3) Biographical data on plain bond paper for all participants. These must be in English. An original and two copies are required, each with a photograph affixed.

(4) Roommate assignments when applicable.

(5) Name and rank of the designated Class A agent/cashier if the Security Cooperation Organization is supplying escorts.

c. Based on the information received from the Security Cooperation Organization and from the commands to be visited, NDU will prepare a final itinerary approximately 30 days prior to execution of the scheduled tour.

Section III
Department of the Army (National Defense University)

12–15. Letter of offer and acceptance pricing

a. To ensure proper pricing of FMS OT and to ensure that costs incurred are borne by the purchasing country, the following cost guidance will be applied in preparing the letter of offer and acceptance (LOA):

(1) *U.S. escort.* The cost estimated for pay and allowances should be computed using the standard composite rate plus a 20-percent acceleration factor. Per diem should be computed according to the JTR for the duration of the tour plus 1 week. All transportation costs should be included.

(2) *Project officers.* Local project officer and staff charges should be computed for each installation visited to cover and estimated 1man-week of preparation for and participation in activities connected with the tour.

(3) *CONUS transportation for tour participants.* Costs for all CONUS travel will be based on current commercial, USG-purchased coach fares unless otherwise specifically requested by the country involved.

(4) *Field Studies Program.* A standard cost per week of $150 per OT participant and $250 per distinguished visitor (DV) tour participant may be included to pay for International Program activities and official host functions at the installations visited. These funds will not be used for any other purpose.

b. Local asset use charge.

(1) One through four $200.

(2) Over four $250.

c. FMS OT will be conduced on a cash-in-advance basis; no other terms are authorized. Funds stipulated in the LOA will be deposited with DFAS not less than 90 days in advance. If funds are not available, a U.S. escort cannot be appointed nor can CONUS travel arrangement be made.

d. Each orientation tour will be covered by a separate sales case unless the foreign country desired to fund from an existing FMS training case.

12–16. Responsibilities for orientation tours

a. The NDU will—

(1) Act as implementing agent and primary Army and Joint Point of Contact for interface with DSCA PGM/flight training exchanges.

(2) Coordinate with Security Cooperation Organization on available tour dates.

(3) Develop, coordinate, cost, plan and execute tour itineraries

(4) Coordinate with Director, SATFA, to ensure funds are transferred to support the tour.

(5) Transfer fund cite to appropriate agencies, that is, airlines, interpreter support, and contractor in support of the tour.

(6) Prepare class A agent orders for escort officer.

(7) Close expense account with escort officer following completion of the tour.

b. Director, SATFA, will—

(1) Program OT under appropriate U.S. government funded program or FMS program.

(2) Ensure that appropriate fund cites are forwarded to NDU and Security Cooperation Organization in ample time to meet administrative requirements.

c. Military Service and Joint commands will—

(1) Assist NDU, SATFA, and commanders of combatant commands in conducting OT.

(2) Provide NDU and SATFA with a detailed itinerary for tour participants at least 30 days prior to participant arrival in CONUS.

d. Security Cooperation Organization will—

(1) Ensure general scope and objectives of the visit are submitted to NDU NLT 120 days prior to the visit.

(2) Provide specific areas of interest and suggested installations to visit to NDU NLT 90 days prior to the visit.

(3) Provide number and names of participants to NDU NLT 90 days prior to the visit and in the proper rank order, annotating the senior participant/head of delegation, including U.S. rank equivalent.

(4) Obtain OCONUS transportation using the ITO fund cite unless circumstances preclude obtaining tickets locally. In that case, Security Cooperation Organization will coordinate with NDU who will make the travel arrangements and have prepaid, round trip tickets issued directly at the originating flight.

12–17. Other visits

a. Chief of Staff, Army visits. AR 37–47 covers visits of foreign personnel who hold positions equal to the CSA.

b. Self-invited visits. AR 380–10 covers self-invited visits to CONUS Army installations.

12–18. Biographical data

Biographical data or professional curriculum vitae will be submitted by the Security Cooperation Organization to NDU who will ensure they are distributed to installations participating in the orientation tour.

12–19. Invitational travel orders

The ITOs for OT will be distributed as prescribed in paragraph 9–5.

12–20. Travel

Information on the mode of travel to and from CONUS, including the confirmed flight schedules and ports for arrival in and departure from the United States, will be furnished by Security Cooperation Organization message at least 30 days before the arrival date to the following

 a. NDU.

 b. Each OCONUS headquarters through which the tour participants are routed.

 c. Appropriate commanders of combatant commands.

12–21. Tour reports

Within 10 days after the completion of each tour, a tour report will be prepared by the escort officer and sent to NDU distinguished visitor orientation tour, with an information copy to—

 a. Security Cooperation Organization.

 b. Appropriate commanders of combatant commands and Army component command.

 c. HQDA (DASA (DE&C)), 102 Army Pentagon, Washington DC 20310–0102.

 d. Director, SATFA.

12–22. International military education and training orientation tour funding

The following guidelines in funding and reimbursing programmed tour costs will be used:

 a. Funds for tour participants are distributed from the country program allocation through IMET funding channels. SATFA will provide fund cite to NDU for tour execution and to Security Cooperation Organization for inclusion in ITO and roundtrip OCONUS ticket purchase.

 b. The escort officer's travel and per diem funds (generic code N7B) are allocated to SATFA. SATFA will furnish the fund cite to Security Cooperation Organization and/or NDU for the preparation of TDY orders.

 c. The escort officer will be appointed as class A agent/cashier for disbursing funds.

12–23. Foreign military sales orientation tour funding

The following guidelines in funding and reimbursing programmed tour costs will be used:

 a. The SATFA will furnish a fund cite to Security Cooperation Organization or NDU for travel and per diem of escort officer, NDU for CONUS travel of tour participants, and Field Studies Program monies. The OMA funds will be reimbursed from the FMS case. The escort officer will be appointed by NDU as class A agent/cashier.

 b. Upon completion of the tour, SATFA will submit SF 1080 for reimbursement of OMA funds, MPA for escort officer and local project officers.

Section IV
Orientation Tours (Department of the Navy (U.S. Navy, U.S. Marine Corps, and U.S. Coast Guard)

12–24. Procedures for requesting orientation tours

The National Defense University is available to program, coordinate, cost and plan OT or distinguished visitor orientation tour for USN and USMC activities and should be submitted to them unless directed otherwise by Naval Education and Training Security Assistance Field Activity or CG, Security Cooperation Education and Training Center MCCDC. Requests for OT visits to predominately USCG activities will be submitted to USCG International Affairs (GCI).

12–25. Limitations

Visits to the U.S. Naval Academy and other military and civilian colleges will not be scheduled during examination or graduation week. Visits to DON installations whose activities are classified must be fully justified and are subject to the provisions of the SECNAVINST 5510.34A.

12–26. Restrictions

Heads of foreign services and officers scheduled to occupy those positions in the near future normally will not participate in IMET-sponsored OT visits. Visits of this nature are handled by CNO (or CMC) and occur only at the personal invitation of the CNO or CMC respectively, reference SECNAVINST 5720.44A, SECNAVINST 7042.14A, and OPNAVINST 5710.27B.

12–27. Publicity
Current policy regarding public affairs and information is contained in SECNAVINST 5720.44B DON Public Affairs Policy and Regulations. Requests by the civilian media will be referred through channels to the Office of the Assistant Secretary of Defense (Pubic Affairs). See chapter 10, paragraph 10–19 of this publication for further information

Section V
Orientation Tours (Department of the Air Force)

12–28. General
The NDU is available to program, coordinate, cost and plan OT or distinguished visitor orientation tour for the USAF and unless otherwise directed, requests may be submitted to them. Should the USAF choose to program the OT or distinguished visitor orientation tour, the following applies:

a. All tours and visits under IMET sponsorship must be approved by DSCA before implementation. Proposed itinerary and justification should be forwarded by the Security Cooperation Organization to DSCA, Washington DC 20301–2800, with information copies to SAF/IAPX/IAPD,1080 Air Force Pentagon, Washington DC 20330–1080, and Air Force Security Assistance Training Squadron, 315 J Street West, Randolph AFB, TX 78150–4302, as soon as the requirement is known.

b. OT and DV are available to FMS countries on a fully reimbursable basis to the U.S. Air Force. Itinerary approval is required. Security Cooperation Organization will plan OT to be funded by an existing blanket order training case at least 120 days in advance to permit adequate CONUS planning. If an LOA must be written for the tour, the request and the proposed itinerary to Air Force Security Assistance Training Squadron, 315 J Street West, Randolph AFB, TX 78150–4302, not later than 180 days in advance of the proposed start date. During the negotiation phase of an OT, Security Cooperation Organization will specify any unusual tour requirements. Consistent with the OT information provided by the Security Cooperation Organization, Air Force Security Assistance Training Squadron will review the itinerary to ensure that reasonable time is allowed for travel between locations.

c. The ITO for DV and OT will be prepared by the Security Cooperation Organization when authorization to publish the orders has been provided by Air Force Security Assistance Training Squadron. Authority to publish ITO for OT will be provided by Air Force Security Assistance Training Squadron.

d. When travel in CONUS is to be via commercial air, ITO must reach Air Force Security Assistance Training Squadron at least 30 days before the arrival date of the visitors at the CONUS port of debarkation to ensure sufficient time to make travel reservations. Air Force Security Assistance Training Squadron will be informed of the mode of travel and estimated time of arrival of the visitors at least 20 days before the arrival date at the CONUS port of debarkation.

12–29. Orientation tour implementation
a. The Air Force Security Assistance Training Squadron implements, funds, and monitors OT.

b. The Air Force Security Assistance Training Squadron designates the MAJCOM to sponsor the tour based on tour objectives and the proposed itinerary. When more than one MAJCOM is involved, the command with greatest participation and interest is the sponsor.

c. The sponsoring agency reviews the proposed itinerary and recommends changes to assure accomplishment of tour objectives, submits a recommended itinerary to Air Force Security Assistance Training Squadron for approval, appoints an escort officer, and identifies a point of contact at each location in the approved itinerary.

d. The Security Cooperation Organization will provide Air Force Security Assistance Training Squadron with biographic data on OT participants at least 60 days before their arrival in CONUS.

12–30. Escort officer functions
a. A U.S. Air Force escort officer will be provided for all tours. The escort officer will be included as part of the tour requirement in the country's IMET or FMS program.

(1) The escort officer will be briefed on the specific duties and responsibilities regarding funding and the Field Studies Program. (See chap 11, sec II.) In addition, the escort officer's TDY orders will include two additional days after completion of the OT to prepare an after-action report and settle finances.

(2) The escort officer will be responsible for submitting SF 1034 covering the authorized expenditures.

(3) Travel and per diem of the escort officer will be funded from IMET N70 funds or charged to the applicable FMS case.

b. The escort officer will be designated as the paying agent.

12–31. Completion of orientation tours

The Security Cooperation Organization will debrief OT participants upon return to their home country. A summary of this debriefing will be submitted to Air Force Security Assistance Training Squadron, 315 J Street West, Randolph AFB, TX 78150–4302. An information copy will be sent to SAF/IAPX, 1080 Air Force Pentagon, Washington, DC 20330–1080, DSCA, Washington, DC 20301–2800 and the unified command.

12–32. Distinguished visitor implementation

The Air Force Security Assistance Training Squadron implements DV tours as follows:

a. The proposed itinerary for the DV will be submitted by the Security Cooperation Organization to arrive at Air Force Security Assistance Training Squadron at least 120 days before the projected start date. An information copy will be provided to the unified command, the appropriate SAF/International Affairs regional division, and SAF/IAPX. The itinerary will list specific items of interest for briefing or discussion at HQ USAF and at each installation to be visited.

b. Air Force Security Assistance Training Squadron will forward the approved schedule to the Security Cooperation Organization. In no case will firm commitments be made or orders published before receipt of approval from Air Force Security Assistance Training Squadron.

c. The Security Cooperation Organization will inform Air Force Security Assistance Training Squadron (with information copies to the unified command, the appropriate SAF/International Affairs regional division, SAF/IAPX, and Air Force Security Assistance Training Squadron) of the country Air Force's acceptance of the proposed dates and schedule or recommended changes as soon as possible. Biographical data on the team member will be provided at least 60 days in advance of the tour start date.

d. Activities that host a tour will provide color photographic coverage of the visit. Each unit should provide the escort officer with no fewer than two rolls of 36 exposure (ASA 100) film or digital camera and memory chip prior to departure. Emphasis of photographic coverage should be on the professional aspect of the visit (such as tour demonstrations, equipment, and briefings) and limited coverage of social events. The film will be processed at Randolph AFB, TX; Air Force Security Assistance Training Squadron will prepare and forward an album to the Security Cooperation Organization for presentation to the officer.

Chapter 13
Exchange Training

Section I
General

13–1. Exchange of professional military education

a. Authorization. The PME exchanges are authorized by Section 544 (Exchange Training) of the FAA of 1961, chapter 5, part II. Section 544 authorizes the President to provide for the attendance of foreign military personnel at PME institutions in the United States (other than Service academies) without charge, if such attendance is part of an international agreement (see fig 3–4), to be negotiated, that provides for the exchange of students on a one-for-one, reciprocal basis each FY between the two military Services participating in the exchange. Each country is responsible for paying their own students' TLA. Definitions applicable to PME exchanges are included in figure 13–1.

b. Professional military education institutions. For purposes of PME exchanges, PME institutions will include, but not be limited to the following US Service Schools and comparable foreign schools:

(1) U.S. Army War College.

(2) U.S. Army Command and General Staff College.

(3) USAF Air War College.

(4) USAF Air Command and Staff College.

(5) USAF Institute of Technology.

(6) U.S. Naval Command College.

(7) U.S. Naval Staff College.

(8) U.S. Naval Postgraduate School.

(9) USMC Command and Staff College.

(10) NDU.

(a) NDU International Fellows Program.

(b) Joint Forces Staff College.

c. Quota allocations. The PME exchanges will be made according to existing guidelines for quota allocations in schools listed above.

d. Time constraints. The PME exchanges must commence within the same U.S. FY.

e. Cost constraints.

(1) Tuition costs shall not be charged to the parent country/Service or to PME exchange students. All costs associated with instruction, instructional materials, tutorials, projects, study visits, and field exercises undertaken by the PME Exchange Student as part of the approved course program will be considered as tuition costs. Other costs associated with training, such as student's meals, custodial fees for quarters, medical care, and transportation, are not included in tuition costs.

(2) The IMET, MAP, and FMS cash or credit funds will not be used for student support costs (for example, transportation, housing, or living allowances) incurred in PME exchanges nor will any charges be made against FMS cases.

f. Reciprocity. All reciprocal agreements will be made in expectation of fulfillment on the part of both sponsoring and parent countries.

g. Selection criteria.

(1) The selection of PME exchange students will be on a highly selective basis from among qualified personnel of the Parent Service. The Parent Service will be solely responsible for the selection of its PME exchange students based on the criteria that students should meet the school's prerequisites and have the school-required level of language comprehension.

(2) The Host Service will be authorized to discharge PME exchange students from the PME Exchange Program who do not meet the above criteria. This decision is within the sole discretion of the Host Service.

h. Leave. PME exchange students may be granted leave according to their entitlements under the regulations of the Parent Service, provided such is approved by the Parent Service and coordinated with the proper authorities of the Host Service. PME exchange students may observe the holiday schedules of both Parent and Host Services according to Host Service regulations. (See para 10–37a.)

i. Intention to participate. Each Service will notify the other, 6 months prior to the effective school reporting date, of their intention to participate in the PME Exchange Program and will forward the name(s) of the PME Exchange student (s) who will be participating three months prior to report date.

j. Financial responsibilities.

(1) The Parent Party or Service and the PME exchange personnel, as appropriate, are responsible, during the period of the exchange, for the following:

(a) Basic pay and cash allowances due PME exchange students.

(b) All permanent change of station costs including per diem and other travel allowances and transportation (Including leave travel) and storage costs.

(c) All temporary duty costs including per diem and other travel allowances and transportation, when such temporary duty is directed by the Parent Party.

(d) Compensation for loss of, or damage to, the uniform or other personal equipment of PME exchange students.

(e) Cost of movement of Family members and household effects of PME exchange students as authorized by the Parent Party.

(f) Cost of housing and mess for PME exchange students and their Family members.

(g) Cost of preparation and shipment of remains and funeral expenses in event of death of PME exchange students or their Family members.

(h) Expenditures in connection with any special duty performed on behalf of the Parent Party.

(i) Expenses incurred in the interest of Family members permitted to accompany or join PME exchange students.

(j) Medical and dental charges for treatment of PME exchange students or their Family members that require reimbursement under the laws or regulations of the Host Party's country.

(k) Cost of language training.

1. All expenses in connection with the return of PME exchange students who have been discharged from this Exchange Program and their accompanying Family members.

2. The Host Party is responsible during the exchange period for all temporary duty costs, including per diem and other travel allowances and transportation, when temporary duty is directed by the Host Party.

3. The Parent Party or Service and PME exchange students, as appropriate, will be liable for all other services and expenses for PME exchange students, including any that are unconnected with the duties of the exchange.

4. U.S. IMET, FMF, and FMS cash or credit funds cannot be used to meet the financial responsibilities of the Parent Party or Service.

(2) The obligations of each Party under the PME Exchange shall be subject to the authorization and availability of funds. Prior to implementing any exchange, all Parties and Services will ensure that adequate funds are available.

k. Security.

(1) The PME exchange students must comply at all times with security laws, regulations and procedures of the Government of the Host Party (see chap 10, sec IX). Any violation of security procedures by PME exchange students during their assignment will be reported to the Parent Service for appropriate action. PME exchange students

committing willful violations of security procedures during their assignments will be removed from the Exchange Program with a view toward administrative or disciplinary action by the Parent Party.

(2) The Host Service and the Parent Service will ensure that assigned PME exchange students are fully cognizant of applicable laws and regulations concerning the protection of proprietary information (such as copyrights), classified information and controlled unclassified information to which access might be gained under this Exchange Program, both during and after completion of training.

(3) All classified information made available to PME exchange students will be considered as classified information furnished to their Parent Party, and will be subject to all provisions and safeguards provided for under the General Security of Military Information Agreement (GSOMIA) in force between the United States of America and the country participating in the PME Exchange.

l. Administration and control.

(1) For all purposes except academic matters, PME exchange students will be administered and controlled as prescribed by the Parent Services. The organizations responsible for administrative supervision of specific PME exchange students will be specified in the applicable appendices.

(2) With respect to academic matters, PME Exchange Students (U.S. and foreign) will be under the administrative supervision of the school commandant or equivalent. For all purposes except academic matters, PME exchange students will be administered and controlled as prescribed by the Parent Service.

m. Identification. The PME exchange students and their accompanying Family members will be required to possess valid identification cards according to the regulations of the Parent Service. PME exchange students and their accompanying Family members will also be issued identification cards by the Host Service for the duration of the exchange. (See para 10–17.)

n. Respect for sponsoring country law. The PME exchange students and their Family members will be required to respect the law of the Host Party and abstain from any activity inconsistent with the spirit of the exchange and from any political activity in the Host Party.

o. Entry and exit. The PME exchange students and their accompanying Family members will possess appropriate documentation issued by the Parent Party and required by the country of the Host Party for entry into and exit from that country. (See para 10–8.)

p. Weapons. See paragraph 10–33.

(1) PME exchange students will not be permitted to import or carry personal weapons in the country of the Host Party except when authorized by the Host Party authorities and registered according to applicable laws.

(2) Weapons issued to PME exchange students for military purposes by the Parent Service will be introduced into the country of the Host Party only if authorized by the Parent Service and according to the laws of the Host Party.

q. Discipline. See paragraph 10–44.

(1) The PME exchange students will comply with the regulations, orders, instructions, and customs of the Host Service insofar as they are appropriate and applicable under the circumstances and consistent with the laws and regulations of the Parent Party.

(2) The PME exchange students who commit an offense against the military laws and regulations of either the Parent or Host Service may be withdrawn from the PME exchange program with a view toward further administrative or disciplinary action by the Parent Service. Disciplinary action will not be taken by the Host Service against PME exchange students. The withdrawal of PME exchange students from the program will not affect the right of civil authorities of the Host Party or its political subdivisions to exercise criminal jurisdiction over such personnel. Authorities of the Host Service will convey, on behalf of the Parent Service, any request for waiver of the right of such authorities to exercise jurisdiction over PME exchange students. Further, authorities of the Host Service will maintain close coordination with civil authorities of the Host Party or its political subdivisions in such matters and will urge, upon request of the Parent Service/Party that sympathetic consideration be given to waiver requests where the Parent Service/Party indicates the waiver to be of particular importance. The foregoing is without prejudice to the provisions of an applicable status of forces agreement.

(3) Consistent with paragraphs (1) and (2), above, PME exchange students should extend normal military courtesy to military personnel of the Host Service who are superior in rank to them.

(4) To the extent authorized by its laws and regulations, the Host Service will cooperate in the application of administrative or disciplinary action by the Parent Service against offending PME exchange students.

r. Use of facilities.

(1) The PME exchange students and their authorized accompanying Family members in the United States are entitled to the same use of administrative, logistical, and commissary facilities that are accorded to other security assistance-sponsored PME students.

(2) U.S. PME exchange students and their Family members will be entitled to the same use of administrative, logistical, and commissary facilities as other U.S. military personnel and their Family members stationed in the country of the Host Party or attached to the U.S. diplomatic mission.

s. Uniform. The PME exchange students are required to comply with the dress and grooming (see para 10–23) regulations of the Parent Service. The order of dress for any occasion will be that which most nearly conforms to the order for the particular unit of the Host Service to which Exchange Students are attached. Customs of the Host Service will be observed with respect to the wearing of civilian clothes.

t. Quarters and messing. The Host Service may provide, if available, quarters and messing for PME exchange students according to its own regulations. PME exchange students or their Parent Service are responsible for paying charges made by the Host Service for quarters and messing, when provided, and for any attendant services provided by the Host Service. If the Host Service is unable to provide quarters, the PME Exchange Student or the Parent Service will be responsible for arranging and financing private accommodations.

u. Medical and dental services.

(1) Any medical and dental care that may be provided to PME exchange students and their authorized accompanying Family members at Host Party medical facilities will be subject to the laws and regulations of the government of the Host Party, including reimbursement when required by such laws and regulations.

(2) The Parent Service is responsible for ensuring that PME exchange students and their authorized accompanying Family members are in good medical and dental health prior to commencing the exchange program.

v. Reports and evaluations.

(1) Reports that PME exchange students may be required to make by their Parent Service or which they wish to make concerning their exchange training will be submitted according to Parent Service regulations.

(2) Individual evaluation reports will be prepared and submitted according to Host Party regulations and procedures. (See para 10–28.)

w. Privileges and exemptions. The SOFA with NATO and other countries, which pertain to the rights and privileges of military personnel while in the country of the Host Party, will apply to PME Exchange Students and their Family members. In the event of conflict, SOFA takes precedence over PME Exchange Agreements. For non-NATO countries without SOFA, the following applies:

(1) To the extent authorized by the laws and regulations of the Host Party, the following privileges will be available to PME exchange students and their authorized accompanying Family members:

(a) Exemption from any tax by the government of the Host Party upon income received from the Parent Party.

(b) Exemption from any customs, import duty, or similar tax upon articles brought into the country of the Host Party in connection with their official, personal, or Family use, including their baggage, household effects, and private motor vehicles.

(c) Privileges at military commissaries, exchanges, theaters, and clubs on the same basis as equivalent personnel of the Host Party.

(2) PME exchange students will be eligible for any other privilege provided by a status of forces agreement or granted by the government of the Host Party under its laws and regulations.

x. Decorations, awards, or insignia. Decorations, awards, or insignia bestowed on PME exchange students by the Host Service will be made according to the regulations of the Host Service. The awards will not be accepted by PME exchange students without the prior approval of the Parent Service.

y. Claims.

(1) For SOFA countries, the following applies:

(a) Claims against either Party or its personnel will be dealt with according to the terms of Article VIII of the Status of Forces agreement.

(b) The PME Exchange Students and those Family members accompanying them must obtain motor vehicle liability insurance coverage according to applicable laws and regulations of the government of the Host Party, or its political subdivision, where they are located. In case of claims involving the use of private motor vehicles, the first recourse will be against such insurance.

(2) The following applies to non-SOFA countries.

(a) The Parties waive all their claims, other than contractual claims, against each other, and against the military members and civilian employees of each other's Department or Ministry of Defense, for damage, loss or destruction of property owned or used by its respective Department or Ministry of Defense, if such damage, loss or destruction: (one) was caused by a military member or a civilian employee in the performance of official duties; or (two) arose from the use of any vehicle, vessel, or aircraft owned by the other Party and used by its Department or Ministry of Defense, provided that the vehicle, vessel, or aircraft causing the damage, loss or destruction was being used for official purposes, or that the damage, loss or destruction was caused to the property being so used.

(b) The Parties will waive all their claims against each other and against the military members and civilian employees of each other's Department or Ministry of Defense for injury or death suffered by any military member or civilian employee of their Department or Ministry of Defense while such member or employee as engaged in the performance of official duties.

(c) Claims, other than contractual claims, for damage, loss, injury, or death, not covered by the waivers contained in paragraphs 1 and 2 of this Article, arising out of an act or omission by the military member or civilian employees of its Department or Ministry of Defense, or out of an act or omission for which the Parent Party is legally responsible, will be presented to the Parent Party for consideration under its applicable laws and regulations.

(d) PME exchange students and their accompanying Family members will obtain motor vehicle liability insurance coverage according to applicable laws and regulations of the government of the Host Party, or its political subdivision, where they are located. In case of claims involving the use of private motor vehicles, the first recourse will be against the insurance.

z. Requests. Requests for new PME exchanges will be sent to DSCA (Regional Directorate in coordination with DSCA (Programs Directorate) so that an umbrella PME Exchange MOA (DOD and/or MOD) is negotiated and completed in accordance with figure 13–1. Specific Service-level requests are sent to the Implementing Agency after the DOD-level agreement is in place. Exchanges at specific schools will be identified in an appendix to the PME Exchange MOA in accordance with figure 13–2. After signature by both countries participating in the exchange, DSCA will forward copies of the PME Exchange MOA to the Department of State, (L/T), Washington, DC 20520; DOD/ General Counsel, 1600 Defense Pentagon, Washington, DC 20301–1600, MILDEP for PME Exchange MOAs. The Military Service will forward a copy to their General Counsel and Judge Advocate General, and other internal organizations. Appendices to the MOA will be signed by the U.S. military Service participating in the exchange.

aa. Invitational travel order. All PME exchange students attending CONUS schools will do so under the authority of an ITO. The PME exchange status will be noted in blocks 5 and 13. (See chap 9.)

13–2. Unit exchanges

a. Authorization. Unit exchanges are authorized by the addition to the AECA of chapter 2C and section 30A (Exchange of Training and Related Support). Under Section 30A, the President may provide training and related support to military and civilian defense personnel of a friendly foreign country or international organization. Such training and related support will be provided by a Secretary of a MILDEP and may include the provision of transportation, food services, health services, logistics, and the use of facilities and equipment. Unit exchanges may be arranged only as part of an international agreement to be negotiated as defined in DODD 5530.3. (Also see figs 3–5 and 3–6.) Under the agreement, the recipient foreign country will provide, on a reciprocal basis, comparable training and related support. Prior to entering into any agreement, the initiating authority will seek the recommendations of the regional unified commander in whose area of responsibility the foreign nation is located. Generally, the Secretary of a MILDEP or designee is the approving authority for the exchange of units. Exchange programs of significant political and military importance or operationally sensitive exchanges will be approved by the Under Secretary of Defense (Policy) (USD (P)).

b. Types of units. For purposes of this legislation, a unit eligible for exchange is defined as substantially all the individuals from an established unit necessary to accomplish the intent of the exchange. Legislation does not authorize exchanges of individuals or other ad hoc units.

c. Time constraints. Reciprocal exchanges must take place within 12 months of each other.

d. Cost constraints. If a foreign country or international organization receives training and support and does not initiate comparable training and support to U.S. units within 12 months, the foreign country or international organization must reimburse the U.S. for the full cost of training and support provided by the U.S. IMET, FMF, and FMS cash or credit funds may not be utilized for reimbursement or to meet the expenses of an exchange unit. However, DOD funds or authorities may be used to support these exchanges.

e. Reporting. By 1 January each year the Military Service will provide the Director, Washington Headquarters Services, with a report of unit exchanges conducted during the preceding U.S. FY with information copy to DSCA. Report Control Symbol DD–DA&M (A) 1789 is assigned to this report. The report will include the following information for each exchange, by country:

(1) The number of exchanges.

(2) The date by which each reciprocal exchange is required or the date on which it was supplied.

(3) The subject or purpose.

(4) The number of persons included.

(5) The estimated full costs of the training and related support provided by the United States to the country.

(6) The estimated value of the training and related support provided to the United States to that country.

(7) Action taken to recover the cost of any exchanges that were not reciprocated during that FY, if applicable. (Costs of those exchanges not completed by the end of the FY will be estimated and actual costs provided as available.)

f. Reciprocity. All reciprocal agreements will be made in expectation of fulfillment on the part of both sponsoring and parent countries. Reciprocity, in the context of the statutory authority for this unit exchange program, involves the mutual exchange of comparable rather than exactly similar training and related support. Determination of comparable worth is not required to be accomplished solely by using the dollar equivalent of the training and related support received. However, the results of valuation must document that the U.S. military department or established joint organization has received value comparable to that provided during the exchange.

g. Assignment and utilization.

(1) The assignment of exchange units will be for facilitating small unit operations.

(2) Exchange unit personnel may receive short programs of military instruction when such instruction is part of the

normal orientation, familiarization, and checkout or safety process for Host Service personnel reporting to a particular duty station. Instruction provided to exchange unit personnel by the Host Service will be strictly limited to short programs designed for the purposes stated above.

(3) In no case may Exchange Students be assigned to a position that would require exercise of command over personnel of the Host Service.

(4) Unless otherwise authorized by authorities of the Parent State, Exchange Students will not participate in combat operations. This applies to all hostilities, including civil-military actions within the Sponsoring State in which its armed forces are called upon to assist in restoring law and order. In any case where involvement in hostilities or civil-military actions becomes imminent, military duties of Exchange Students will be terminated until further instructions are received from authorities of the Parent State.

(5) Exchange units will be assigned duties by the Host Service that is agreeable to the Parent Service. These duties will conform to the range of qualifications held by exchange unit personnel, but the exchange unit must always be prepared to function fully as a member of the unit or activity to which assigned.

h. Selection criteria and discharge.

(1) The selection of exchange units will be on a highly selective basis from among military units of the Parent Service. The Parent Service will be solely responsible in the selection of its exchange units based on the following criteria:

(a) Unit personnel must be well versed in current practices and doctrine of their Service or branch and be particularly qualified to participate in the unit exchange.

(b) Unit personnel must possess the required skill and training qualifications.

(c) Unit personnel should hold the grade authorized for the position that they occupy.

(2) The requirements, qualifications, and experience of the exchange units must meet the standards of the Host Service. The determination and decision on unit performance is within the sole discretion of the Host Service. The Parent State or Service will be responsible for all expenses in connection with the return of exchange unit personnel.

i. Tour length and number exchanged.

(1) The normal tour of duty for exchange units, exclusive of travel time between countries, will be as specified in an appendix to the MOA. Exceptions to and or adjustments of any tour will be based on mutual agreement.

(2) One unit from the U.S. military department or established joint organization and one unit from the military department or established joint organization will take part in the exchange. Exchange units will be assigned to units or positions as described in an appendix to the MOA. Expansion of the exchange program and cancellation, postponement, or substitution of a specific exchange will be as mutually agreed between the Host Service and the Parent Service.

j. Administration and control. Unit exchange students will be administered and controlled as prescribed by the Parent Service.

(1) Headquarters, Department of the Army (HQDA) will designate an individual who will serve as the Chief, HQDA Unit Exchange Program. DA units on exchange with the foreign unit will be under administrative supervision of the Chief, HQDA Unit Exchange Program as designated by HQDA.

(2) International exchange units on duty with exchange units in the United States will be under the administrative control of the appropriate military attaché of their country.

k. Identification. Unit exchange personnel will be in possession of valid identification cards and identification discs (tags) according to the regulations of the Parent State and the requirements of the laws and regulations of the Host Service and Sponsoring State and, if applicable, those of the third country on whose territory the exchange takes place.

l. Respect for local law. Unit exchange personnel will respect the law of the State on whose territory the exchange takes place and abstain from any activity inconsistent with the spirit of the exchange and, in particular, from any political activity in that State.

m. Entry and exit. Unit exchange personnel will be in possession of appropriate documentation issued by the Parent State and required by authorities of the State on whose territory the exchange takes place for entry into and exit from that State.

n. Weapons.

(1) Exchange unit personnel will not carry personal weapons into the State on whose territory the exchange takes place except if authorized by the Parent Service and when authorized by Sponsoring State authorities and registered according to applicable law.

(2) Military weapons issued to exchange unit personnel by the Parent Service will be introduced into the State on whose territory the exchange takes place only if authorized by the Parent Service and competent authorities of the State on whose territory the exchange takes place.

o. Discipline.

(1) Exchange unit personnel will comply with the lawful regulations, orders, instructions, and customs of the Host Service insofar as they are appropriate and applicable under the circumstances and consistent with laws and regulations of the Parent State.

(2) Exchange unit personnel who commit an offense against the military laws and regulations of either the Parent or Host Service may be separated from the exchange program with a view toward further administrative or disciplinary action by the Parent Service. Disciplinary action will not be taken by the Host Service against exchange unit personnel. The separation of exchange unit personnel from the program will not affect the right of civil authorities of the Sponsoring State or its political subdivisions to exercise criminal jurisdiction over such personnel. Authorities of the Host Service will convey, on behalf of the Parent Service, any request for waiver of the right of such authorities to exercise jurisdiction. Further, authorities of the Host Service will maintain close coordination with civil authorities of the Host State or its political subdivisions in such matters and will urge, upon request of the Parent Service that sympathetic consideration be given to waiver requests where the Parent Service or State indicates such waiver to be of particular importance. The foregoing will be without prejudice to the provisions of an applicable status of forces agreement.

(3) Exchange unit personnel will not exercise disciplinary powers over military personnel of the Host Service.

(4) Consistent with paragraphs 1 and 2 above, exchange unit personnel are subject to the lawful commands of military personnel of the Host Service who are senior in rank to them.

(5) To the extent authorized by its laws and regulations, the Host Service will cooperate in the application of administrative or disciplinary action by the Parent Service against offending exchange unit personnel.

p. Security. Exchange Students must comply at all times with security regulations of the Host Service or State. Assignment, duties, and the handling of classified information will be subject to the security and disclosure policies of the States and Services concerned and applicable international agreements.

q. Use of facilities. Use of facilities of the Host Service by Exchange Students for their military specialty proficiency will be granted according to the policies and directives of the Host Service and any agreements or arrangements with the State on whose territory the exchange takes place.

r. Uniform. Exchange Students will comply with the dress regulations of the Parent Service. The order of dress for any occasion is to be that which most nearly conforms to the order for the particular unit of the Host Service to which the exchange unit is assigned. Customs of the Host Service will be observed with respect to the wearing of civilian clothes.

s. Leave and passes. Exchange Students may be granted leave and passes according to their entitlements under the regulations of the Parent Service, provided such is coordinated with the proper authorities of the Host Service. Exchange Students may observe the holiday schedules of both the Parent and Host Service.

t. Medical and dental services.

(1) Exchange students will be granted access to military medical and dental services of the Sponsoring State to the same extent that the Host Service provides such services to its own military personnel. Reimbursement of the Host Service for medical and dental services provided to Exchange students may be required unless otherwise specified in the appendix to the MOA pursuant to Article XVIII.

(2) It is the responsibility of the Parent Service to ensure that Exchange Students are medically and dentally fit prior to commencing the exchange program.

u. Financial responsibilities. The following financial responsibilities apply to the exchange program:

(1) The Parent State or Service and Exchange Students, as appropriate, are responsible during the period of the exchange for the following costs:

(a) Basic pay and cash allowances due Exchange Students.

(b) Per Diem and other travel allowances associated with the movement of exchange units and their personnel to and from the Sponsoring State.

(c) Compensation for loss of or damage to the uniform or other personal equipment of Exchange Students.

(d) The cost of preparation and shipment of remains and funeral expenses in the event of death of Exchange Students.

(e) Expenditures in connection with any special duty performed on behalf of the Parent State.

(f) Expenses incurred in the interest of Family members permitted to accompany or join Exchange Students.

(g) Except for instruction of a brief duration provided according to paragraph g(2), above, the costs of any training, services, or requirements not listed in any appendix to the MOA.

(2) The Sponsoring State or Service is responsible for the cost of providing the training and related services specifically identified in any appendix to the MOA, subject to the reciprocity and reimbursement provisions of paragraph v below.

v. Reciprocal provision of training and related support.

(1) The parties may agree, on the basis of reciprocity, for the provision by the Sponsoring State or Service of training and related support as listed in paragraphs "t" and "u," above. An agreement for the reciprocal provision of training and related support, if executed, will be incorporated in the MOA and will appear as an appendix thereto.

(2) Regardless of whether an appendix to provide the training and related support as listed in paragraphs t and u, above, is agreed to or not, units will be exchanged within 12 months in order that a balance of costs involved in

sending and receiving units is maintained or so that reimbursement for the full costs of the training and related support provided can be accomplished.

(3) To the extent that one party (to which training and related support specified in an appendix to the MOA is provided) does not initiate comparable training and related support to the other party within 12 months, the party provided such training and related support shall reimburse the providing party for the full costs of such training and support.

w. Claims.

(1) Third party claims arising out of the activities of Exchange Students or exchange units may be submitted to the Parent Service for settlement consistent with its authority under the laws and regulations of the Parent State. Nevertheless, Exchange Students will be required to obtain civil liability insurance for their private motor vehicles according to applicable Sponsoring State's laws and regulations, and first recourse will be had against any such insurance in the case of claims involving motor vehicles.

(2) Neither Service will make any claim against the other for loss or damage to its property caused by military personnel of the other Services in the execution of duties during the course of any exchange.

(3) Neither Service will make any claim against the other for injury or death suffered by any member of its armed Services while engaged in the performance of official duty during the course of any exchange.

(4) Neither the Host Service nor the Sponsoring State will be responsible for loss of or damage to personal property of Exchange Students.

(5) The foregoing is without prejudice to the provision of an applicable status of forces agreement between the sponsoring and Parent States and, if applicable, to agreements or arrangements with the third country on whose territory the exchange takes place.

x. Reports and evaluations. Reports that exchange units may be required to make by their own Service or that they wish to make concerning their exchange duties will be submitted as follows.

(1) U.S. military department exchange units will forward their reports according to appropriate departmental guidance.

(2) International exchange units and Exchange Students will forward their reports according to Parent Service instructions.

y. Privileges and exemptions. To the extent authorized by the laws and regulations of the State on whose territory the exchange takes place and by an applicable status of forces agreement, the following privileges will be available to exchange units and Exchange Students:

(1) Exemption from any tax by the Sponsoring State upon income received from the Parent State.

(2) Exemption from customs, import duty, or similar taxes upon articles brought into the Sponsoring State in connection with official or personal use, including baggage and household effects.

(3) To the extent authorized by Sponsoring State laws and regulations, purchasing and patronage privileges at military commissaries, exchanges, theaters, and clubs of the Host Service on the same basis as equivalent personnel of the Host Service.

(4) Any other privilege provided by an applicable status of forces agreement or granted by the State on whose territory the exchange takes place under its laws and regulations

z. Decorations, awards, or insignia. Decorations, awards, or insignia of military qualifications bestowed on exchange units or PME exchange students by the Host Service will be made according to the regulations of the Host Service. These decorations, awards, or insignia will not be accepted by the unit or personnel concerned without the prior approval of the Parent Service.

aa. Requests. Requests for unit exchanges must be forwarded to the appropriate Military Service with an information copy to DSCA. The request will contain a justification for the exchange; desired dates; identification of the type and size of unit to be exchanged; a statement of the availability of funds required to support the exchange; a summary of the training to be conducted; an estimate of cost, to include (as a minimum) transportation, housing, mess, logistics, medical, and dental costs; identification of the country with which the exchange is proposed; if the exchange is proposed with a unit stationed outside the territory of its Parent State, details concerning the coordination accomplished with the State(s) in whose territory the exchange will take place; and details concerning the legal status of personnel under a status of forces agreement or other arrangement, or a statement that no such arrangement currently exists.

ab. Rights and liabilities. The standard Memorandum of Agreement (MOA) for use when the proposed exchange will take place on the respective territories of the two signatories is found at figure 13–3. It contains a definitive statement of rights and responsibilities since the exchange involves only the two countries that are signatories of the MOA. However, if the proposed exchange is to take place with a unit stationed outside the territory of its Parent State, the standard MOA to be used is found at figure 13–4. Of necessity, rights and responsibilities are qualified since they are subject to the decisions of the government of the State in whose territory part or all of the exchange will take place. It is imperative that U.S. personnel recognize the peculiarities created by such an exchange, particularly with regard to claims and discipline.

13–3. Exchange of flight training

a. Authorization. Flight training exchanges is authorized by Section 544 (Exchange training) of the FAA of 1961, chapter 5, part II. Section 544 authorized the President to provide for the attendance of foreign military and civilian defense personnel at flight training schools and programs (including test pilot schools) in the United States, without charge, if such attendance is pursuant to an agreement providing for the exchange of students on a one-for-one basis each FY between those U.S. flight training schools and programs and comparable flight training schools and programs of foreign countries. The flight training to be exchanged must be of comparable type and scope.

b. International agreement. The approved international agreement for flight training exchanges is provided at figure 13–5. Deviations are not authorized unless approved by DSCA/General Counsel and the Director, International Security Programs, with the concurrence of DSCA and the MILDEP. The MOA will be staffed according to procedures established for PME Exchange MOA.

c. Training performance objectives and standards. Training will be conducted using the performance objectives and standards of the Host Service. Exceptions to successful completion of Host Service standards may be considered on a case-by-case basis.

d. Tuition costs. All costs associated with instruction, instructional materials, special clothing, or equipment, tutorials, projects, study visits, and field exercises undertaken by the field training exchanges Student as part of the approved course syllabi are considered as tuition costs. Other costs associated with training, such as Student's meals, custodial fees for quarters, medical care, and transportation, are not included in tuition costs.

e. Student selection/discharge criteria.

(1) The selection of flight training exchanges students will be on a highly selective basis from among qualified personnel of the Parent Service. The Parent Service will be solely responsible for the selection of its flight training exchanges students based on the criteria that students should—

(a) Be well versed in the practices and doctrines of their own service;

(b) Meet the basic criteria, including aviation physiology, established by the Host Service for the applicable training through a combination of training, experience, and ability.

(c) Meet the language prerequisites established by the Host Service for the applicable training;

(d) Possess a security clearance to the level required for the applicable training.

(2) Each Service will notify the other 12 months prior to the effective reporting date of their intention to participate in the flight training exchanges and will forward the name(s) and other requested information on flight training exchanges Student(s) who will be participating as required by the Host Service.

(3) The Host Service/Party will be authorized to discharge flight training exchange Students from the Exchange Program who do not meet the above criteria, fail to meet the established training standards, or cannot safely complete the program. This decision is within the sole discretion of the Host Service/Party. The flight training exchanges students who do not meet the Host Service/Party performance standards will be treated the same as Host Service/Party students. Such flight training exchanges students will be entitled to any hearing or board afforded to host service students. The Host Service will notify the Parent Service of the names of flight training exchanges students who are not meeting the Host Service performance standards. A Parent Service representative may attend, as an observer, any hearings or boards held with respect to exchange personnel eliminated from training by the Host Service.

f. Leave. The flight training exchange Students may be granted leave according to their entitlements under the regulations of the Parent Service, provided such is approved by the Parent Service and the proper authorities of the Host Service. The flight training exchange Students may observe the holiday schedules of both Parent and Host Services according to Host Service regulations.

g. Special clothing/equipment. The Host Service may issue special clothing or equipment required for the flight training on the same basis conditions as to its own students. Any rank or other insignia worn will, to the extent possible, conform to Parent Service Standards.

h. Casualty reports. In the event of injuries to, or death of, flight training exchange students, the Host Service will submit casualty reports through the appropriate channels to the Parent Service. Any reports and investigations conducted by the Host Service concerning a casualty will be made available to the Parent Service. The Parent Service may conduct a separate investigation/inquiry.

i. Aircraft accident investigation procedures. In the absence of a standardization agreement between the participating countries for aircraft accident investigation procedures, Host Service aircraft accident investigation procedures will be followed.

j. Flight training exchange requests. Requests for flight training exchanges must be forwarded to the appropriate MILDEP with an information copy to DSCA. The request will contain a justification for the exchange; desired timeframe or dates; identification of the type of training and the number of students to be exchanged; security classification of training; an estimate of cost per student of training to be exchanged; frequency of proposed exchange (for example, on a one-time basis or for a 5-year period); student prerequisites; and other relevant information. MILDEP will include the Department of State on correspondence relating to proposed flight training exchanges.

k. Discharge/elimination of flight training exchange students. Once an flight training exchange Student commences training, the obligation of the Host Party/Service are met regardless of whether the flight training exchange Student successfully completes the program or is discharged under the provisions of Article IV, paragraph 2, Article VI, paragraph 2, or Article XII, paragraph 2 of the flight training exchange MOA.

l. Other provisions. The provisions of paragraph 13–1*j* through 13–1*ac* for PME Exchanges also apply to flight training exchanges.

Section II
Department of the Army

13–4. Professional military education exchanges

a. Quotas. All PME exchanges will be arranged within existing quotas or invitations at CGSC and AWC. No additional quotas will be created to accommodate a PME exchange.

b. Programming. SATFA (ATFA–R) will carry PME exchange students on the STL.

c. ITO. The Security Cooperation Organization will issue an ITO for PME exchange students after authorization by DASA (DE&C). The Security Cooperation Organization will note PME exchange status in blocks 5 and 13 of the ITO.

d. Requests.

(1) The Security Cooperation Organization will submit country request for a PME exchange following country acceptance of a seat at CGSC or AWC to DASA (DE&C) and DAMO–SSF by message. The corresponding country invitation will accompany the request for PME exchange.

(2) DAMO–SSF will coordinate the participation of U.S. Army exchange students at foreign PME institutions.

(3) Upon DA approval of the PME exchange, DASA (DE&C) will negotiate a MOA with country embassy personnel in Washington, DC, using the format provided at figure 13–1 if an MOA is not already in place.

(4) After the MOA is signed, DASA (DE&C) will notify SATFA, and the Security Cooperation Organization of final authority to implement the PME exchange. DASA (DE&C) will then authorize the Security Cooperation Organization to issue an ITO for the PME exchange.

AGREEMENT BETWEEN

THE DEPARTMENT OF DEFENSE

OF

THE UNITED STATES OF AMERICA

AND

THE MINISTRY OF DEFENSE

OF

(COUNTRY)

REGARDING THE EXCHANGE

OF

PROFESSIONAL MILITARY EDUCATION (PME)

Figure 13–1. Memorandum of agreement between the United States Department of Defense and the Ministry of Defense of (Country) Regarding the Exchange of Professional Military Education

PREAMBLE

The Department of Defense of the United States of America ("DOD") and the Ministry of Defense of *(Country)* ("MOD"), hereinafter referred to as "the Parties," have agreed to establish a Professional Military Education (PME) Exchange Program, which is designed to strengthen bonds of friendship and understanding between the countries and their respective Military Service.

ARTICLE I
DEFINITION OF TERMS

1. Professional Military Education (PME). Training provided by senior Service schools and staff colleges. For the purposes of this Agreement, this involves the following United States senior Service schools and staff colleges: U.S. Army War College,; U.S. Army Command and General Staff College; USAF Air War College; USAF Air Command and Staff College; USAF Institute of Technology; U.S. Naval Command College; U.S. Naval Staff College; U.S. Naval Postgraduate School; U.S. Marine Corps Command and Staff College; National Defense University (National Defense University International Fellows Program and the Joint Forces Staff College). On the part of *(Country),* this involves the following senior Service schools and command and staff colleges: *(Service schools).*

2. PME Exchange Students. Any individual on active duty with the Parent Service who is attending school in the host country pursuant to this Exchange Program.

3. Parent Service. The military Service to which the PME Exchange Students belong.

4. Host Service. The military Service whose school the PME Exchange Student is attending pursuant to this Exchange Program.

5. Parent Party. The Defense Department or Ministry of Defense (DOD/MOD) to which the Parent Service belongs.

6. Host Party. The Defense Department or Ministry of Defense (DOD/MOD) to which the Host Service belongs.

7. Dependent. A person present in the country of the Host Party with the consent of the Parent Service and Host Service who is the spouse, minor child, or other relative who depends for support upon and is supported by a PME Exchange Student.

8. Reciprocal PME Exchange. PME of comparable value for the institutions outlined in paragraph 1 above commencing within the same United States fiscal year by means of a reciprocal one-for-one exchange of students between the Parties.

9. Tuition Costs. All costs associated with instruction, instructional materials, tutorials, projects, study visits, and field exercises undertaken by the PME Exchange Student as part of the approved course program. Other costs associated with training such as Student's meals, custodial fees for quarters, medical care, and transportation, are not included in tuition costs.

Figure 13–1. Memorandum of agreement between the United States Department of Defense and the Ministry of Defense of (Country) Regarding the Exchange of Professional Military Education–Continued

ARTICLE II
PURPOSE AND SCOPE

This Agreement establishes the terms and conditions by which the Parties agree to establish a PME Exchange Program to provide for a reciprocal exchange of PME of comparable value between the two Parties. This Agreement sets forth the general terms and conditions by which the training experience, professional knowledge, and doctrine of both Parties are shared for maximum mutual benefit to the extent permissible under existing policies, laws, and regulations of the United States of America and (Country). The PME Exchange Program shall be a one-for-one reciprocal exchange of fully qualified students, of equivalent qualifications.

ARTICLE 111
SPECIAL PROVISIONS

1. When an invitation to provide PME of comparable value has been offered and accepted by each of the Services concerned, a reciprocal PME Exchange Program may then be conducted.

2. This Agreement does not constitute a commitment on the part of either Party to provide an annual quota(s) to the schools specified in Article I, paragraph 1, above, or their counterparts. An invitation to attend any school shall be at the discretion of the Host Service in accordance with the established policies of the Host Party. The offer of an invitation shall be conditioned upon a reciprocal invitation in accordance with paragraph 1 of this Article.

3. The details of each reciprocal PME Exchange(s) for a particular Service shall be set forth in an appendix to this Agreement, which shall be considered a part of this Agreement.

ARTICLE IV
SELECTION OF STUDENTS

1. The selection of PME Exchange Students shall be on a highly selective basis from among qualified personnel of the Parent Service. The Parent Service shall be solely responsible for the selection of its PME Exchange Students based on the criteria that students should:
    a. Meet the school's prerequisites.
    b. Have the level of language comprehension that is required by the school.

2. Consistent with the nomination process, the Host Service/Party shall be authorized to discharge PME Exchange Students from this Exchange Program who do not meet the above criteria. This decision is within the sole discretion of the Host Service/Party.

ARTICLE V
FINANCIAL ARRANGEMENTS

1. The tuition costs for PME training shall not be charged to the Parent Party/Service or to PME Exchange Students. The Parent Party/Service and PME Exchange Students, as appropriate, shall be responsible, during the period of the exchange, for the costs listed below:
    a. Basic pay and cash allowances for the PME Exchange Students.
    b. All permanent change of station costs including per diem and other travel allowances and transportation (including leave travel) and storage costs.
    c. All temporary duty costs, including per diem and other travel allowances and transportation, when such temporary duty is directed by the Parent Party.
    d. Compensation for loss of, or damage to, the uniform or other personal equipment of PME Exchange Students.
    e. Cost of movement of dependents and household effects of PME Exchange Students as authorized by the Parent Party.
    f. Cost of housing and mess for PME Exchange Students and their dependents.

Figure 13–1. Memorandum of agreement between the United States Department of Defense and the Ministry of Defense of (Country) Regarding the Exchange of Professional Military Education–Continued

g. Cost of preparation and shipment of remains and funeral expenses in the event of death of PME Exchange Students or their dependents.

h. Expenditures in connection with any special duty performed on behalf of the Parent Party.

i. Expenses incurred in the interest of dependents permitted to accompany or join PME Exchange Students.

j. Medical and dental charges for treatment of PME Exchange Students or their dependents that require reimbursement under the laws or regulations of the Host Party's country.

k. Cost of language training.

l. All expenses in connection with the return of PME Exchange Students who have been discharged from this Exchange Program and their accompanying dependents.

2. The Host Party shall be responsible during the exchange period for all temporary duty costs, including per diem and other travel allowances and transportation, when such temporary duty is directed by the Host Party.

3. The Parent Party/Service or PME Exchange Students, as appropriate, shall be liable for all other services and expenses for PME Exchange Students, including any which are unconnected with the duties of the exchange.

4. U.S. International Military Education and Training (IMET) program funds, Foreign Military Financing (FMF) funds, or Foreign Military Sales (FMS) cash funds shall not be used to meet financial responsibilities of the Parent Party/Service that are part of the PME Exchange.

5. The obligations of each Party under this Agreement shall be subject to the authorization and availability of funds for such purposes. Prior to implementing any exchange, all Parties/Services shall ensure that adequate funds are available.

ARTICLE VI
SECURITY

1. PME Exchange Students shall at all times be required to comply with the security laws, regulations and procedures of the government of the Host Party. Any violation of security procedures by PME Exchange Students during their assignments shall be reported to the Parent Service for appropriate action. PME Exchange Students committing willful violations of security procedures during their assignments shall be removed from the Exchange Program with a view toward administrative or disciplinary action by the Parent Party.

2. The Host Service and the Parent Service shall ensure that assigned PME Exchange Students are fully cognizant of applicable laws and regulations concerning the protection of proprietary information (such as copyrights) and controlled unclassified information to which access might be gained under this Exchange Program, both during and after completion of training.

3. PME Exchange Students shall not have access to classified information under this Agreement. In the event such access is required in the future, this Article shall be amended to describe security requirements prior to the granting of access.

ARTICLE VII
ADMINISTRATION AND CONTROL

1. For all purposes except academic matters, PME Exchange Students shall be administered and controlled as prescribed by the Parent Services. The organizations responsible for administrative supervision of specific PME Exchange Students shall be specified in the applicable appendices.

2. With respect to academic matters, PME Exchange Students shall be under the administrative supervision of the school commandant or equivalent.

Figure 13–1. Memorandum of agreement between the United States Department of Defense and the Ministry of Defense of (Country) Regarding the Exchange of Professional Military Education–Continued

ARTICLE VIII
IDENTIFICATION

PME Exchange Students and their accompanying dependents shall possess valid identification cards issued in accordance with the regulations of the Parent Service. PME Exchange Students and their accompanying dependents shall also be issued identification cards by the Host Service for the duration of the exchange. The Host Service identification cards shall be used only to gain access to facilities for services, such as medical care or commissary use, that are authorized pursuant to this Agreement.

ARTICLE IX
RESPECT FOR HOST PARTY LAW

Subject to the terms of this Agreement, PME Exchange Students and their accompanying dependents shall be required to respect the law of the government of the Host Party and abstain from any activity inconsistent with the spirit of this Agreement and from any political activity in the country of the Host Party.

ARTICLE X
ENTRY AND EXIT

PME Exchange Students and their accompanying dependents shall possess appropriate documentation issued by the Parent Party and required by the country of the Host Party for entry into and exit from that country.

ARTICLE XI
WEAPONS

1. PME Exchange Students shall not be permitted to import or carry personal weapons in the country of the Host Party except when authorized by Host Party authorities and the weapons are registered in accordance with applicable laws.

2. Weapons issued to PME Exchange Students for military purposes by the Parent Service shall be introduced into the country of the Host Party only if authorized by the Parent Service and in accordance with the laws of the government of the Host Party.

ARTICLE XII
DISCIPLINE

1. PME Exchange Students shall be required to comply with the regulations, orders, instructions, and customs of the Host Service insofar as they are appropriate and applicable under the circumstances and consistent with the laws and regulations of the government of the Parent Party.

2. PME Exchange Students who commit an offense against the military laws and regulations of either the Parent or Host Service may be withdrawn from the PME Exchange Program with a view toward further administrative or disciplinary action by the Parent Service. Disciplinary action shall not be taken by the Host Service against the PME Exchange Students. The withdrawal of the PME Exchange Student from the program shall not affect the right of civil authorities of the government of the Host Party or its political subdivisions to exercise criminal jurisdiction over such personnel. Authorities of the Host Service shall convey, on behalf of the Parent Service, any requests for waiver of the right of such civil authorities to exercise jurisdiction over such personnel. Further, authorities of the Host Service shall maintain close coordination with civil authorities of the government of the Host Party or its political subdivisions in such matters and shall urge, upon request of the Parent Service that sympathetic consideration be given to waiver requests where the Parent Service/Party indicates such waiver to be of particular importance. The foregoing is without prejudice to the provisions of an applicable status of forces agreement or any other applicable international agreements.

Figure 13–1. Memorandum of agreement between the United States Department of Defense and the Ministry of Defense of (Country) Regarding the Exchange of Professional Military Education–Continued

3. Consistent with paragraphs 1 and 2 of this article, PME Exchange Students should extend normal military courtesy to military personnel of the Host Service who are superior in rank to them.

4. To the extent authorized by its laws and regulations, the Host Service shall cooperate in the application of administrative or disciplinary action by the Parent Service against the offending PME Exchange Student.

ARTICLE XIII
USE OF FACILITIES

1. *(Country)* PME Exchange Students and their authorized accompanying dependents in the United States shall be entitled to the same use of administrative, logistical, and commissary facilities as are accorded to other security assistance sponsored PME Students.

2. U.S. PME Exchange Students and their dependents shall be entitled to the same use of administrative, logistical, and commissary facilities as other U.S. military personnel and their dependents stationed in the country of the Host Party or attached to the U.S. diplomatic mission.

ARTICLE XIV
UNIFORM

PME Exchange Students shall be required to comply with the dress and grooming regulations of the Parent Service. The order of dress for any occasion shall be that which most nearly conforms to the order of the particular unit of the Host Service to which they are attached. Customs of the Host Service shall be observed with respect to wearing of civilian clothes.

ARTICLE XV
LEAVE

PME Exchange Students may be granted leave according to their entitlements under the regulations of the Parent Service, provided such leave is approved by the Parent Service and coordinated with the proper authorities of the Host Service. PME Exchange Students may observe the holiday schedules of both the Parent and the Host Services in accordance with Host Service regulations.

ARTICLE XVI
QUARTERS AND MESSING

The Host Service may provide, if available, quarters and messing for PME Exchange Students in accordance with its own regulations. PME Exchange Students or their Parent Service shall be responsible for paying charges made by the Host Service for quarters and messing when provided, and for any attendant services provided by the Host Service. In the event that the Host Service is unable to provide quarters, the PME Exchange Student or the Parent Service shall be responsible for arranging and financing private accommodations.

ARTICLE XVII
MEDICAL AND DENTAL SERVICES

1. Any medical and dental care that may be provided to PME Exchange Students and their accompanying dependents at Host Party medical facilities shall be subject to the laws and regulations of the government of the Host Party, including reimbursement when required by such laws and regulations.

2. The Parent Service shall ensure that PME Exchange Students and their accompanying dependents are in good medical and dental health prior to commencing the exchange program.

Figure 13–1. Memorandum of agreement between the United States Department of Defense and the Ministry of Defense of (Country) Regarding the Exchange of Professional Military Education–Continued

ARTICLE XVIII
REPORTS AND EVALUATIONS

1. Reports which PME Exchange Students may be required to make by their Parent Service or which they wish to make concerning their exchange training shall be submitted in accordance with Parent Service regulations.

2. Individual evaluation reports shall be prepared and submitted in accordance with Host Party regulations and procedures.

ARTICLE XIX
PRIVILEGES AND EXEMPTIONS

Alternative A
(Note: For agreements with Parties who are NATO members or other countries with which there are SOFAS use this Alternative.)

The U.S. *(Country)* Status of Forces Agreement *(or NATO SOFA, as applicable)*, dated *(date)*, pertaining to rights and privileges of military personnel while in the country of the Host Party shall apply to PME Exchange Students aid their dependents, and in the event of conflict, shall take precedence over this Agreement.

Alternative B
(Note: Use this Alternative for agreements with non-NATO countries without SOFAs)

1. To the extent authorized by the laws and regulations of the government of the Host Party, the following privileges shall be available to PME Exchange Students and their accompanying dependents:
   a. Exemption from any tax of the government of the Host Party on income received from the Parent Party.
   b. Exemption from any customs, import duty, or similar tax on articles brought into the country of the Host Party in connection with their official, personal, or family use, including their baggage, household effects, and private motor vehicles.
   c. Privileges at military commissaries, exchanges, theaters, and official, personal, or family use, including their baggage, household effects, and private motor vehicle clubs on the same basis as equivalent personnel of the Host Party.

2. PME Exchange Students shall be eligible for any other privilege granted by the government of the Host Party under its laws and regulations or by bilateral agreements between the two governments.

ARTICLE XX
DISCHARGE OF FTE STUDENTS

Once an FTE Student commences training, the obligations of the Host Party/Service are met regardless of whether the FTE Student successfully completes the program or is discharged under the provisions of Article IV, paragraph 3, Article VI, paragraph 2, or Article XII, paragraph 2.

ARTICLE XXI
DECORATIONS, AWARDS, OR INSIGNIA

Decorations, awards, or insignia bestowed on PME Exchange Students by the Host Service shall be made in accordance with the regulations of the Host Service. These awards shall not be accepted by PME Exchange Students without the prior approval of the Parent Service.

Figure 13–1. Memorandum of agreement between the United States Department of Defense and the Ministry of Defense of (Country) Regarding the Exchange of Professional Military Education–Continued

ARTICLE XXII
NOTIFICATION

Pursuant to Service-to-Service appendices to this Agreement, each Service shall notify the other, six months prior to the effective school reporting date, of their intention to participate in this PME Exchange Program and forward the name(s) of the PME Exchange Students) who will be participating three months prior to report date.

ARTICLE XXIII
CLAIMS

Alternative A
(Note: For agreements with Parties who are NATO members or other countries with which there are SOFAs use this Alternative.)

1. Claims against either Party or its personnel shall be dealt with in accordance with the terms of Article VIII of the NATO Status of Forces Agreement *(NATO SOFA or other SOFA as applicable)* dated *19* June 1951.

2. PME Exchange Students and those dependents accompanying them shall obtain motor vehicle liability insurance coverage in accordance with applicable laws and regulations of the government of the Host Party, or its political subdivision, where they are located. In case of claims involving the use of private motor vehicles, the first recourse shall be against such insurance.

Alternative B
(Note: Use this Alternative for agreements with non-NATO countries without SOFAS.)

1. The Parties waive all their claims, other than contractual claims, against each other, and against the military members and civilian employees of each other's Department or Ministry of Defense, for damage, loss or destruction of property owned or used by its respective Department or Ministry of Defense, if such damage, loss or destruction:

    a. was caused by a military member or a civilian employee in the performance of official duties, or
    b. arose from the use of any vehicle, vessel or aircraft owned by the other Party and used by its Department or Ministry of Defense, provided that the vehicle, vessel or aircraft causing the damage, loss or destruction was being used for official purposes, or that the damage, loss or destruction was caused to the property being so used.

2. The Parties shall waive all their claims against each other and against the military members and civilian employees of each other's Department or Ministry of Defense for injury or death suffered by any military member or civilian employee of their Department or Ministry of Defense while such member or employee was engaged in the performance of official duties.

3. Claims, other than contractual claims, for damage, loss, injury, or death, not covered by the waivers contained in paragraphs 1 and 2 of this Article, arising out of an act or omission by the military members or civilian employees of its Department or Ministry of Defense, or out of an act or omission for which the Parent Party is legally responsible, shall be presented to the Parent Party for consideration under its applicable laws and regulations.

4. PME Exchange Students and those dependents accompanying them, shall obtain motor vehicle liability insurance coverage in accordance with applicable laws and regulations of the government of the Host Party, or its political subdivision, where they are located. In case of claims involving the use of private motor vehicles, the first recourse shall be against such insurance.

Figure 13–1. Memorandum of agreement between the United States Department of Defense and the Ministry of Defense of (Country) Regarding the Exchange of Professional Military Education–Continued

ARTICLE XXIV
SETTLEMENT OF DISPUTES

Disputes arising under or relating to this Agreement shall be resolved only by consultation between the Parties and shall not be referred to an individual, a national or international tribunal or to any other forum for settlement.

ARTICLE XXV
ENTRY INTO FORCE, AMENDMENT, DURATION, AND TERMINATION

1. All activities of the Parties under this Agreement shall be carried out in accordance with the national laws and regulation of the Parties subject to the terms of this Agreement.

2. In the event of a conflict between an Article of this Agreement and any Appendix to this Agreement, the Article shall control.

3. Except as otherwise provided, this Agreement may be amended by the mutual written consent of the Parties.

4. This agreement may be terminated by mutual written consent of the Parties or by either Party upon 180 days' written notification to the other Party of its intention to do so. Such notice shall be the subject of immediate consultation by the Parties to ensure termination on the most economical and equitable terms.

5. The respective rights and responsibilities of the Parties regarding Article XXII (Claims) shall continue notwithstanding termination or expiration of this Agreement.

6. This Agreement, which consists of the Preamble, twenty-four (24) Articles and one (1) or more Appendices, shall enter into force upon signature by both Parties and shall remain in force for ten (10) years. It may be extended by written agreement of the Parties.

IN WITNESS WHEREOF, the undersigned, being duly authorized by their governments, have signed this Agreement.

**FOR THE DEPARTMENT OF
DEFENSE OF THE UNITED STATES
OF AMERICA**

**FOR THE MINISTRY OF
DEFENSE OF** *(Country)*

_____
(SIGNATURE)

_____
(SIGNATURE)

_____
(TYPED NAME)

_____
(TYPED NAME)

_____
(RANK/TITLE)

_____
(RANK/TITLE)

_____
(DATE)

_____
(DATE)

_____
DONE AT (PLACE)

_____
DONE AT (PLACE)

Figure 13–1. Memorandum of agreement between the United States Department of Defense and the Ministry of Defense of (Country) Regarding the Exchange of Professional Military Education–Continued

13–5. Unit exchanges

a. Objectives. The objectives of unit exchange training are as follows:

(1) Provide training incentives for units and individuals.

(2) Assist in improving relations and mutual understanding between the United States and the country with which the exchange is conducted.

(3) Provide a sharing of expertise between the participating units.

(4) Validate, test, exercise, and or complement interoperability capabilities.

(5) Provide recruitment and retention incentives.

(6) Foreign participants in unit training exchanges are to be permitted access only to UNCLASSIFIED information, except as may be specifically authorized according to AR 380–10 or approved by DCS G–2 on a case-by-case basis.

b. Policy.

(1) Authority to approve proposed exchanges with allied and friendly military Services is reserved at HQDA. Once approved, MSCs are authorized to formally negotiate with the allied or friendly military Service involved.

(2) The exchange of units, when conducted in the context of mission training, is encouraged. Such exchanges provide for interesting and challenging formal or informal training, orientation, observation, or familiarization and can serve as an incentive for units and individuals to broaden their professionalism as part of their normal training programs. Further, the fostering and developing of professional relationships between units of the U.S. Army and allied or friendly armies is critical to the success of combined operations.

(3) The exchange of units will be conducted as an adjunct to mission training and will be approved only after the U.S. units involved have demonstrated training proficiency to the degree necessary to accomplish stated mission objectives. The proficiency of a unit can be determined from the result of a recently completed U.S. Army Training and Evaluation Program evaluation or by the commander who administered the evaluation.

(4) Aggregate units will not be eligible for exchange training.

(5) The clothing and equipment furnished to accompany the guest unit will be limited to the minimum individual requirement.

(6) Personnel participating in exchange programs will be briefed on the provisions of AR 381–12.

(7) Personnel will be briefed concerning customs inspections according to DOD 5030.49–R.

(8) Foreign participants in unit training exchanges are to be permitted access only to UNCLASSIFIED information, except as may be specifically authorized according to AR 380–10 or approved by DCS G–2 on a case-by-case basis.

(9) Personnel who will depart CONUS must be qualified according to AR 612–2.

c. Responsibilities.

(1) DCS G–3/5/7 will serve as the HQDA proponent for unit exchange training. DAMO–TR will receive, review, coordinate, and process proposed unit exchanges. Exchanges of significant political and military importance or operationally sensitive unit exchanges will be received, reviewed, coordinated, and processed by DAMO–ODSO.

(2) MSCs will manage unit exchanges according to the provisions of this regulation.

d. Approving authority.

(1) Generally, the Chief of Staff, U.S. Army, is the approving authority for the exchange of units. Exchange programs of significant political and military importance will be approved by the Assistant Secretary of Defense for International Security Affairs.

(2) Requests for recurring exchange programs will require one-time approval rather than approval for each exchange. However, periodic reviews (at least once a year) of unit exchange programs will be made jointly by HQDA and MSCs to ensure compliance with current procedures and directives.

e. Procedures.

(1) Proposals for exchanges will be submitted through the appropriate MSCs to HQDA (DAMO–TR), Washington, DC 20310–0450, for Chief of Staff approval. Information copies will be provided to DSCA, 1111 Jefferson Davis Highway, Arlington, Virginia 22202–4306 and HQDA (DAMI), Washington, DC 20310–1040. Consolidated requests reflecting a proposed annual program are welcome. The request will contain—

(a) Identification of the country with which the exchange is proposed.

(b) Identification of the type and size of unit to be exchanged.

(c) Desired dates.

(d) Justification for the exchange.

(e) A summary of the training to be conducted.

(f) An estimate of cost, to include (as a minimum) transportation, housing, mess, logistics, medical, and dental costs.

(g) A statement of the availability of funds required to support the exchange.

(h) Details concerning the coordination accomplished with the State(s) in whose territory the exchange takes place, if the exchange is proposed with a unit stationed outside the territory of its parent state.

(i) Details concerning legal status of personnel under a status of forces agreement or other arrangement, if any exist.

(2) Prior to submitting to Chief of Staff, U.S. Army, for approval, the MSCs sponsoring the exchange will solicit the comments of the country team (ambassador), through the Army attaché or senior U.S. military representative on each specific exchange proposal.

(3) After Chief of Staff approval, HQDA (DAMO–TR) will authorize the MSCs to negotiate directly with the allied military Service to coordinate and resolve details of the exchange. The DCS, G–1, if necessary, after coordination with the Office of Foreign Military Rights Affairs, Office of the Assistant Secretary of Defense for International Security Affairs, will provide guidance to the major Army commander concerning arrangements at the diplomatic level for the status of personnel involved.

(4) When a request is approved, the MSCs is responsible for execution of the exchange memorandum of agreement, using the format provided at either figures 13–2 or 13–3, for accomplishing the reporting requirements set forth in AR 550–51 and for submitting the request for the movement directive.

(5) Units will submit after-action reports to appropriate MSCs within 120 days after completion of an exchange.

(6) By 15 November each year, MSCs will submit a report to HQDA (DAMO–TR) on the specific unit exchange activities conducted during the preceding FY. The report will include the following:

(a) Estimated full costs of the training and related support provided to allied and friendly military services.

(b) Estimated value of the training provided to the United States by that country.

(c) Action taken during FY to recover the cost of any exchanges that were not reciprocated, if applicable.

f. Funding responsibilities.

(1) The parent State or Service will be responsible for pay and allowances for unit members. All other costs related to the reciprocal provision of training and related support will be borne by the participating State or Service that incurs them. If an allied or friendly nation is unable to provide training or related support of comparable worth within 1 year, MSCs will initiate administrative action to collect cash reimbursement. IMET and FMS cash or Foreign Military Financing Program (repayable/nonrepayable) credit funds may not be used for reimbursement or to meet the expenses of an exchange unit. For exchanges with Latin American military forces, funding may be available from Latin American Cooperation Funds.

(2) Exchanges involving Active Army units will be funded from OMA Program 2, General Purpose Forces Funds, within the context of normal mission training. Movement of TOE equipment will be funded from Program 7, Second Destination Transportation Funds, according to appropriate fiscal regulations. Exchanges will not be funded separately. Exchanges sponsored by MSCs will be funded by that command, whereas those exchanges directed by HQDA will be funded by HQDA.

(3) RC units participating under this regulation will be funded by the Chief, National Guard Bureau or Chief, Army Reserve, from their respective appropriations.

Section III
Exchange Training (Department of the Navy (U.S. Navy, U.S. Marine Corps, and U.S. Coast Guard)

13–6. United States Navy exchanges

a. Professional military education exchanges.

(1) *General.* The PME will be used as an additional method to enable foreign naval officers and USN officers to participate in mutually beneficial professional naval education. Requests for new PME exchanges should be sent to DSCA (Regional Directorate) in coordination with DSCA (Programs Directorate) so that an umbrella (DOD and/or MOD) level exchange agreement is negotiated and completed. Specific Service-level requests are sent to the U.S. Navy after the DOD-level agreement is in place, PME exchanges offer countries with comparable PME institutions another means, other than IMET or FMS, to send a student to the Naval War College (Naval Command College/Naval Staff College, Joint Forces Staff College and the NPS.

(2) *Responsibilities.* PME exchanges require close coordination and participation among CNO, Navy IPO, Naval War College, Joint Forces Staff College, NPS, Navy Judge Advocate General, Naval Education and Training Security Assistance Field Activity, and the Security Cooperation Organization in country to implement an effective program.

(a) CNO (N3/N5), in coordination with the Naval War College, will develop, coordinate, and issue under CNO's signature, invitations for foreign nominations to the Naval Command College/Naval Staff College. The N3/N5 and Naval War College will also determine priorities for countries on the visiting list for invitations to these programs.

(b) When a country accepts an invitation and also desires it to be a PME exchange, the following applies. If an existing DOD and/or MOD level exchange agreement is in place, the Security Cooperation Organization will submit the country's request for a PME exchange to CNO, Navy IPO, and Naval Education and Training Security Assistance Field Activity. The message will also include the approximate time frame in which the foreign war college invitation will be tendered to the U.S. Navy. If a U.S. Navy officer has never attended the country's Navy PME institution, or has not attended within the last 5 years, the Security Cooperation Organization will provide curriculum content information

to Bureau of Navy Personnel (Pers-60), with an information copy to Navy IPO, so professional institutional comparability can be ascertained. Upon confirmation of comparability, Navy IPO, in coordination with CNO (N3/N5) and Navy Judge Advocate General, will direct Naval Education and Training Security Assistance Field Activity to prepare a Service Appendix to the Memorandum of Agreement (MOA) using the format provided at figure 13–1. CNO (N3/N5) will coordinate the Appendix with the country embassy personnel in Washington, DC, and is authorized to sign the Appendix for CNO by direction, Navy IPO will inform Naval Education and Training Security Assistance Field Activity and the Security Cooperation Organization of the signed Appendix. Upon that notification, Naval Education and Training Security Assistance Field Activity will program the change to reflect PME exchange status with a zero financial obligation. Naval Education and Training Security Assistance Field Activity will also authorize the Security Cooperation Organization to issue an ITO indicating the exchange status in item 5 and 15 of the ITO.

(c) Bureau of Naval Personnel will coordinate and direct the participation of the U.S. Navy exchange students at foreign PME institutions.

(d) Naval Education and Training Security Assistance Field Activity will submit an annual report of the U.S. Navy PME exchanges via Navy IPO to DSCA with a copy to CNO (N3/N5) and Bureau of Naval Personnel (Pers-60). This report will be submitted not later than 1 January of each year.

b. Unit exchanges.

(1) *General.* Unit exchanges are appropriate when they offer a clear advantage to the U.S. Navy. Advantages range from improved relations and mutual understanding between the United States and the foreign country, through the sharing of expertise, to enhancing combined evolutions and interoperability.

(2) *Policy.* The authority to approve unit exchanges with foreign countries is reserved to the CNO. The procedures to be followed and the coordination required will be determined for each proposed unit exchange based on its own merits.

(3) *Requests.* Unit exchanges will be requested from CNO (N3/N5) with a copy to Navy IPO and Naval Education and Training Security Assistance Field Activity via the chain of command. As a minimum, the request will identify and describe the participating units in the proposed exchange, outline the objectives of the exchange, describe the benefits of the exchange to the U.S. Navy, and specify disclosure of classified information issues involved in the exchange.

13–7. U.S. Marine Corps professional military education exchanges

a. Any country desiring a Professional Military Education (PME) exchange with the U.S. Marine Corps will submit a request in writing or by message to CG, Security Cooperation Education and Training Center MCCDC after country acceptance of an invitation to nominate one officer to attend Marine Corps Command and Staff College.

b. The CG, Security Cooperation Education and Training Center MCCDC will review the request and, if the request is approved, will negotiate an international agreement with the appropriate embassy personnel in Washington, DC. The standard memorandum (see fig 13–1) will serve as the basis for these negotiations.

c. Proposed changes to the standard memorandum will receive legal review prior to signature.

d. The U.S. Marine Corps signature will take place at Headquarters, Marine Corps. Either the Commandant of the Assistant Commandant of the Marine Corps will sign the negotiated memorandum for the Marine Corps on behalf of the Secretary of the Navy.

e. The office of record for these agreements will be CG, Security Cooperation Education and Training Center MCCDC.

f. After an agreement has been negotiated and signed, be CG, Security Cooperation Education and Training Center MCCDC will send a message authorizing the appropriate Security Cooperation Organization to issue an ITO to the IMS nominated to attend Command and Staff College. The Security Cooperation Organization will note PME exchange status in blocks 5 and 13 of the ITO.

g. The PME exchange will be given its own price code equal to zero. The CG, Security Cooperation Education and Training Center MCCDC will enter the PME exchange student into the DON SATP database with this price, thus allowing PME exchange students to be tracked.

h. For reporting purposes, a pseudo case designator will be used for each country, which will keep exchange students separate and also show execution agency. The CG, Security Cooperation Education and Training Center MCCDC will prepare a yearly report and submit it to DSCA not later than 1 January of each year. The report will include, by country, the number of exchanges, the subject or purpose of each, the number of individuals included, and the incremental tuition cost of comparable value.

i. The PME exchanges will be made within existing quotas at U.S. Marine Corps Command and Staff College. No additional quotas will be created to accommodate PME exchanges. No PME exchange is possible if a USMC student is not available for exchange or if a comparable foreign PME institution does not exist. Final determination of comparability will be the responsibility of be CG, Security Cooperation Education and Training Center MCCDC and not the country concerned.

13–8. Requests for a United States Coast Guard unit exchange

Requests for a USCG unit exchange should be forwarded to USCG Headquarters International Affairs (G–CI) for determination of feasibility and coordination procedures. The USCG exchanges are developed as outlined in COMDINST 5710.3–International Agreements. This instruction outlines the required coordination process between the USCG and the Department of State to develop a unit exchange Memorandum of Agreement. Each request for an exchange should contain (at a minimum)—

a. Justification for the exchange.

b. Tour of duty, proposed dates, and proposed duration.

c. Identification of the type and size of unit to be exchanged.

d. A summary of the type of training to be conducted.

e. Outline of administrative and support services.

13–9. Reporting requirements for international agreements

Under the provisions of Title 1 USC 112b, all Federal Government agencies entering into international agreements on behalf of the United States must transmit to the Department of State a copy of that agreement no later than 20 days after it is signed. Within DON, the SECNAVINST 5710.25 requires that five certified copies of any DON negotiated and concluded international agreement be forwarded directly to the Office of the Judge Advocate General within 10 days after an agreement is concluded. The Judge Advocate General then takes action to comply with the reporting requirements. For all international agreements negotiated and concluded by the U.S. Navy, five certified copies will be forwarded to the Office of the Judge Advocate General as outlined above. For all international agreements negotiated and concluded by the U.S. Marine Corps, five certified copies (along with background file information) will be forwarded to the Marine Corps Judge Advocate Division (Operational Law Branch), Headquarters, Marine Corps, for forwarding to the Navy Judge Advocate General as required above. USCG procedures for proposing, preparing, negotiating, and concluding international agreements are outlined in COMDINST 5710.3—International Agreements.

SERVICE APPENDIX TO THE

AGREEMENT BETWEEN

THE DEPARTMENT OF DEFENSE

OF

THE UNITED STATES OF AMERICA

AND

THE MINISTRY OF DEFENSE

OF

(COUNTRY)

REGARDING THE EXCHANGE

OF

PROFESSIONAL MILITARY EDUCATION (PME)

Figure 13–2. Memorandum of agreement between DOD & MIN of Defense Service appendix

**Service Appendix (Number) to the Agreement between
The Department of Defense of The United States of America
and
The Ministry of Defense of (Country)
on the Exchange of Professional Military Education (PME)
Between
The United States (Service)
and the
(Country Military Service)**

Pursuant to the terms and conditions of the Agreement on the Exchange of Professional Military Education (PME) between the U. S. Department of Defense and the (country) Ministry of Defense, signed (date), the (U.S. military service) and the (country military service) hereby establish the details of the exchange, which shall upon execution by both parties of this Appendix become a part of the aforementioned Agreement.

SCHOOLS AND NUMBER OF STUDENTS INVOLVED:

1. In the United States: (school), (number) students.
2. In (country): (school), (number) students.
3. Year: (Fiscal Year).
4. Organization responsible for administrative supervision of PME Exchange Students:
      a. U.S. (military service) PME Exchange Student in (country): (Organization responsible for administrative supervision).
      b. (Country military service) PME Exchange Student in the U.S.: (Organization responsible for administrative supervision).

For the United States (Military Service)   For the (Country Military Service):

(SIGNATURE)	(SIGNATURE)
(TYPED NAME)	(TYPED NAME)
(RANK/TITLE)	(RANK/TITLE)
(DATE)	(DATE)
DONE AT (PLACE)	DONE AT (PLACE)

Figure 13–2. Memorandum of agreement between DOD & MIN of Defense Service appendix–Continued

MEMORANDUM OF AGREEMENT

ON THE EXCHANGE OF UNITS

BETWEEN

THE UNITED STATES (MILITARY DEPARTMENT)

AND

THE ((COUNTRY) MILITARY DEPARTMENT)

Figure 13–3. Memorandum of agreement on the Exchange of Units between the United States (Military Department) and the (Country) Military Department)

MEMORANDUM OF AGREEMENT
ON THE EXCHANGE OF UNITS
BETWEEN THE U.S. (MILITARY DEPARTMENT)
AND THE (COUNTRY MILITARY DEPARTMENT)

ARTICLE I: GENERAL

The United States (military department) and the (country military department) hereby formally establish a unit exchange program for the purpose of providing a system for an active relationship between the two Services. This memorandum of agreement (MOA) sets forth the general terms and conditions that govern the two Services and by which the experience, professional knowledge, and doctrine of both Services are shared for maximum mutual benefit to the extent permissible under existing policies, laws, and regulations of the United States of America and (country). The exchange program operates under the concept of a reciprocal exchange of fully qualified units, of equivalent composition and qualifications, and is designed to strengthen bonds of friendship and understanding between the two Services.

ARTICLE II: DEFINITIONS

For the purpose of this MOA the following definitions apply:

1. Exchange personnel. Any individual on active duty with the exchange unit, of the Parent Service who is present in the territory of the Sponsoring State pursuant to this exchange program.

2. Exchange unit. Any unit on active duty with the Parent Service which is present in the territory of the Sponsoring State pursuant to this exchange program.

3. Parent Service. The military Service to which the exchange unit belongs.

4. Sponsoring Service. The military Service to which the exchange unit is attached pursuant to this exchange program.

5. Parent State. The State to which the Sponsoring Service belongs.

6. Sponsoring State. The State to which the Sponsoring Service belongs.

7. Unit exchange. The exchange of units rather than individuals

ARTICLE III: ASSIGNMENT AND UTILIZATION

1. The assignment of exchange units will be for the purpose of facilitating unit operations.

2. Exchange personnel may receive short programs of military instruction when such instruction is part of the normal orientation, familiarization, and checkout or safety process for Sponsoring Service personnel reporting to a particular duty station. Instruction provided to exchange personnel by the Sponsoring Service will be strictly limited to short programs designed for the purposes stated above.

3. In no case may exchange personnel be assigned to a position that would require exercise of command over personnel of the Sponsoring Service.

4. Unless otherwise authorized by authorities of the Parent State, exchange personnel will not participate in combat operations. This applies to all hostilities, including civil-military actions within the Sponsoring State in which its armed forces are called upon to assist in restoring law and order. In any case, where involvement in hostilities or civil-military actions becomes imminent, military duties of exchange personnel will be terminated until further instructions are received from authorities of the Parent State.

Figure 13–3. Memorandum of agreement on the Exchange of Units between the United States (Military Department) and the (Country) Military Department)–Continued

5. Exchange units will be assigned duties by the Sponsoring Service which are agreeable to the parent Service. These duties will conform to the range of qualifications held by exchange unit personnel, but the exchange unit must always be prepared to function fully as a member of the unit or activity to which assigned.

ARTICLE IV: SELECTION CRITERIA AND DISCHARGE

1. The selection of exchange units shall be on a highly selective basis from among military units of the Parent Service. The Parent Service shall be solely responsible in the selection of its exchange units based on the following criteria:

      a. They must be well versed in the current practices and doctrine of their service or branch thereof and be particularly qualified through experience to participate in the unit exchange.
      b. They must possess required skill and mining qualifications.
      c. Unit personnel should hold the grade authorized for the positions they occupy.

2. The requirements, qualifications, and experience of the exchange units must meet the standards of the Sponsoring Service. The determination and decision on unit performance is within the sole discretion of the Sponsoring service. The Parent State or Service will be responsible for all expenses in connection with the return of exchange unit personnel under this article.

ARTICLE V: TOUR LENGTH AND NUMBER EXCHANGED

1. The normal tour of duty for exchange units, exclusive of travel time between countries, will be as specified in an appendix to the MOA. Exceptions to and/or adjustments of any tour will be based on mutual agreement.

2. One unit from the U.S.(military department) and one unit from the (country military department) will take part in the exchange. Exchange units will be assigned to units or positions as described in an appendix to this MOA. Expansion of the exchange program and cancellation, postponement, or substitution of a specific exchange will be as mutually agreed between the Sponsoring Service and the Parent Service.

ARTICLE VI: ADMINISTRATION AND CONTROL

Exchange personnel will be administered and controlled as prescribed by the Parent Service:

1. (Name) will serve as the chief, U.S.(military department) exchange program, (country). U.S. (military department) exchange personnel in units on exchange with the (military department) will be under the administrative supervision of the Chief, U.S. (military department) exchange program (country).

2. (Military department) exchange personnel on duty with exchange units in the United States will be under the administrative control of the (military department) attache.

ARTICLE VII: IDENTIFICATION

Exchange personnel will be in possession of valid identification cards and identification discs (tags) in accordance with the regulations of the Parent State and meeting the requirements of the laws and regulations of the Sponsoring Service and Sponsoring State.

ARTICLE VIII: RESPECT FOR LOCAL LAW

Exchange personnel will respect the law of the Sponsoring State and abstain from any activity inconsistent with the spirit of this MOA and, in particular, from any political activity in the Sponsoring State.

Figure 13–3. Memorandum of agreement on the Exchange of Units between the United States (Military Department) and the (Country) Military Department–Continued

ARTICLE IX: ENTRY AND EXIT

Exchange personnel shall be in possession of appropriate documentation issued by the Parent State and required by authorities of the Sponsoring State for entry into and exit from the Sponsoring State.

ARTICLE X: WEAPONS

1. Exchange personnel will not carry personal weapons into the sponsoring State except when authorized by Sponsoring State authorities and registered in accordance with applicable law.

2. Military weapons issued to exchange personnel by the parent Service will be introduced into the Sponsoring State only if authorized by the Parent Service and competent Sponsoring State authorities.

ARTICLE XI: DISCIPLINE

1. Exchange personnel will comply with the lawful regulations, orders, instructions, and customs of the Sponsoring Service insofar as they are appropriate and applicable under the circumstances and consistent with laws and regulations of the Parent State.

2. Exchange personnel who commit an offense against the military laws and regulations of either the parent or Sponsoring Service may be separated from the exchange program with a view toward further administrative or disciplinary action by the Parent Service. Disciplinary action will not be taken by the Sponsoring Service against exchange personnel. The separation of exchange personnel from the program will not affect the right of civil authorities of the sponsoring State or its political subdivisions to exercise criminal jurisdiction over such personnel. Authorities of the sponsoring Service will convey,' on behalf of the Parent Service, any request for waiver of the right of such authorities to exercise jurisdiction. Further, authorities of the Sponsoring Service will maintain close coordination with civil authorities of the Sponsoring State or its political subdivisions in such matters and will urge, upon request of the Parent Service, that sympathetic consideration be given to waiver requests where the Parent Service/State indicates such waiver to be of particular importance. The foregoing is without prejudice to the provisions of an applicable status of forces agreement.

3. Exchange personnel will not exercise disciplinary powers over military personnel of the Sponsoring Service.

4. Consistent with paragraphs 1 and 2 of this article, exchange personnel are subject to the lawful commands of military personnel f the Sponsoring Service who are senior in rank to them.

5. To the extent authorized by its laws and regulations, the Sponsoring Service will cooperate in the application of administrative or disciplinary action by the Parent Service against offending exchange personnel.

ARTICLE XII: SECURITY

Exchange personnel must comply at all times with security regulations of the Sponsoring Service or State. Assignment, duties, and the handling of classified information will be subject to the security and disclosure policies of both States and Services concerned and any applicable international agreements.

ARTICLE XIII: USE OF FACILITIES

Use of facilities of the Sponsoring Service by exchange personnel for their military specialty proficiency will be granted in accordance with the policies and directives of the Sponsoring Service.

Figure 13–3. Memorandum of agreement on the Exchange of Units between the United States (Military Department) and the (Country) Military Department)–Continued

ARTICLE XIV: UNIFORM

Exchange personnel will comply with the dress regulations of the Parent Service and the order of dress for any occasion is to be that which most nearly conforms to the order for the particular unit of the Sponsoring Service to which their exchange unit is assigned. Customs of the Sponsoring Service will be observed with respect to wearing of civilian clothes.

ARTICLE XV: LEAVE AND PASSES

Exchange personnel may be granted leave and passes according to their entitlements under the regulations of the Parent Service, provided such is coordinated with the proper authorities of the Sponsoring Service. Exchange personnel may observe the holiday schedules of both Parent and Sponsoring Services.

ARTICLE XVI: MEDICAL AND DENTAL SERVICES

1. PME exchange personnel and their accompanying dependents will be granted access to military medical and dental services to the extent authorized by its governing laws and regulations. The provision of such care may be subject to reimbursement. Reimbursement of the Sponsoring Service for medical and dental services provided to exchange personnel may be required unless otherwise specified in the appendix to this MOA pursuant to Article XVIII.

2. It is the responsibility of the Parent Service to ensure that exchange personnel are medically and dentally fit prior to commencing the exchange program.

ARTICLE XVII: FINANCIAL RESPONSIBILITIES

The following financial responsibilities apply to the exchange program:

1. The Parent State or Service and exchange personnel, as appropriate, are responsible during the period of the exchange for the following costs:
    a Basic pay and cash allowances due exchange personnel.
    b. Per diem and other travel allowances associated with the movement of exchange units and their personnel to and from the Sponsoring State.
    c. Compensation for loss of, or damage to, the uniform or other personal equipment of exchange personnel.
    d. Cost of preparation and shipment of remains and funeral expenses in the event of death of exchange personnel.
    e. Expenditures in connection with any special duty performed on behalf of the Parent State.
    f. Expenses incurred in the interest of dependents permitted to accompany or join exchange personnel.
    g. Except for instruction of a brief duration provided in accordance with the provisions of paragraph 2, Article 111, of this MOA, the costs of any training, services, or requirements not listed in the appendix to this MOA pursuant to Article XVIII.

2. The Sponsoring State or Service is responsible for the cost of providing the training and related services specifically identified in the appendix, pursuant to Article XVIII, subject to the reciprocity and reimbursement provisions of that article.

ARTICLE XVIII:
RECIPROCAL PROVISION OF TRAINING AND RELATED SUPPORT

1. The parties. may agree, on the basis of reciprocity, for the provision by the Sponsoring State or Service of training and related support as listed in Articles XVI and XVII. An agreement for the reciprocal provision of training and related support, if executed, will be incorporated in this MOA and will appear as an appendix hereto.

Figure 13–3. Memorandum of agreement on the Exchange of Units between the United States (Military Department) and the (Country) Military Department)–Continued

2. Regardless of whether an appendix to provide the training and related support as listed in Articles XVI and XVII is agreed to or not, units will be exchanged within 12 months in order that a balance of costs involved in sending and receiving units is maintained or so that reimbursement for the full costs of the training and related support provided can be accomplished.

3. To the extent that one party to which training and related support specified in the appendix is provided under this MOA does not initiate comparable training and related support for the other party within 12 months, the party provided such training and related support shall reimburse the providing party for the full costs of such training and support.

4. IMET, and FMS cash or credit funds may not be utilized for reimbursement or to meet the expenses of an exchange unit.

ARTICLE XIX: CLAIMS

1. Third party claims arising out of activities of exchange personnel or exchange units may be submitted to the Parent Service for settlement consistent with its authority under the laws and regulations of the Parent State. Notwithstanding the foregoing, exchange personnel will be required to obtain civil liability insurance for their private motor vehicles in accordance with applicable host State laws and regulations, and first recourse shall be had against any such insurance in the case of claims involving motor vehicles.

2. Neither State shall make any claim against the other for loss or damage to its property caused by military personnel of the other State in the execution of their duties during the come of any exchange.

3. Neither State shall make any claim against the other for injury or death suffered by any member of its armed services while engaged in the performance of official duty during the course of any exchange.

4. Neither the Sponsoring Service nor the Sponsoring State shall be responsible for loss or damage of personal property of exchange personnel.

5. The foregoing is without prejudice to the provisions of an applicable status of forces agreement.

ARTICLE XX: REPORTS AND EVALUATIONS

1. Reports which exchange units may be required to make by their own Service or which they wish to make concerning their exchange duties will be submitted as follows
    a. U.S.(military department) exchange units will forward their reports in accordance with appropriate departmental guidance.
    b. Foreign exchange units and exchange personnel will forward their reports in accordance with Parent Service instructions.

ARTICLE XXI: PRIVILEGES. AND EXEMPTIONS

To the extent authorized by the laws and regulations of the Sponsoring State, and in any event to the extent provided in an applicable status of forces agreement, the following privileges will be available to exchange units and exchange personnel.

1. Exemption from any tax by the Sponsoring State upon income received from the Parent Sate.

2. Exemption from any customs, import duty, or similar tax upon articles brought into the Sponsoring State in connection with their official or personal use, including their baggage and household effects.

3. Purchasing and patronage privileges at military commissaries, exchanges, theaters, and clubs on the same basis as equivalent personnel of the Sponsoring Service.

Figure 13–3. Memorandum of agreement on the Exchange of Units between the United States (Military Department) and the (Country) Military Department–Continued

4. Any other privilege provided by an applicable status of forces agreement or granted by the Sponsoring State under its laws and regulations

ARTICLE XXII: AWARDS OR INSIGNIA

Awards or insignia of military qualifications bestowed upon exchange units or exchange personnel by the Sponsoring Service shall be made in accordance with the regulations of the Sponsoring Service. These awards or insignia shall not be accepted by the unit or personnel concerned without the prior approval of the Parent Service.

ARTICLE XXIII:
APPLICATION OF STATUS OF FORCES AGREEMENTS

The provisions of any agreement of general application between the Sponsoring and Parent States now or hereinafter in effect regarding the status of Parent State military personnel present in the Sponsoring State shall apply to exchange personnel and exchange units present in the Sponsoring State, provided that in the event of conflict between the provisions of such other agreement and articles XVII, XVIII, or XXIV of this MOA, such articles of this MOA shall prevail.

ARTICLE XXIV: DURATION

This agreement shall enter into force upon signature and shall remain in force for ten years. It may be terminated by either signatory upon written notice to the other signatory at least 60 days prior to the effective school reporting date.

IN WITNESS WHEREOF, the undersigned, being duly authorized by their governments, have signed this Agreement.

For the United States (Military Service)   **For the (Country Military Service):**

_____   _____
(SIGNATURE)   (SIGNATURE)

_____   _____
(TYPED NAME)   (TYPED NAME)

_____   _____
(RANK/TITLE)   (RANK/TITLE)

_____   _____
(DATE)   (DATE)

_____   _____
DONE AT (PLACE)   DONE AT (PLACE)

Figure 13–3. Memorandum of agreement on the Exchange of Units between the United States (Military Department) and the (Country) Military Department)–Continued

MEMORANDUM OF AGREEMENT

ON THE BILATERAL EXCHANGE OF UNITS

BETWEEN

THEUNITED STATES (MILITARY DEPARTMENT)

AND

THE ((COUNTRY) MILITARY DEPARTMENT)

Figure 13–4. Memorandum of agreement on the Bilateral Exchange of Units between the United States (Military Department) and the ((Country Name) Military Department)

MEMORANDUM OF AGREEMENT
ON THE BILATERAL EXCHANGE
OF UNITS
BETWEEN THE U.S. (MILITARY DEPARTMENT)
AND THE (COUNTRY MILITARY DEPARTMENT)

ARTICLE I: GENERAL

The United States (military department) and the (country military department) hereby formally establish a unit exchange program for the purpose of providing a system for an active relationship between the two Services. This memorandum of agreement (MOA) sets forth the general terms and conditions that govern the two Services and by which the experience, professional knowledge, and doctrine of both Services are shared for maximum mutual benefit to the extent permissible under existing policies, laws, and regulations of the United States of America and (country). The exchange program operates under the concept of a reciprocal exchange of fully qualified units, of equivalent composition and qualifications, and is designed to strengthen bonds of friendship and understanding between the two Services. Subject to the approval of the government of (country), exchange units of the (military department) may be assigned to duty with units of the U.S. (military department) in the territory of (third country).

ARTICLE II: DEFINITIONS

For the purpose of this MOA the following definitions apply:

1. Exchange personnel. Any individual on active duty with the exchange unit of the Parent Service who is present in the territory of the Sponsoring State pursuant to this exchange program.

2. Exchange unit. Any unit on active duty with the Parent Service which is present in the territory of the Sponsoring State pursuant to this exchange program.

3. Parent Service. The military Service to which the exchange unit belongs.

4. Sponsoring Service. The military Service to which the exchange unit is attached pursuant to this exchange program.

5. Parent State. The State to which the Sponsoring Service belongs.

6. Sponsoring State. The State to which the Sponsoring Service belongs.

7. Host State. The State in the territory of which the exchange unit is attached for duty under the provisions of this MOA.

8. Unit exchange. The exchange of units rather than individuals.

ARTICLE III: ASSIGNMENT AND UTILIZATION

1. The assignment of exchange units will be for the purpose of facilitating unit operations.

2. Exchange personnel may receive short programs of military instruction when such instruction is part of the normal orientation, familiarization, and checkout or safety process for Sponsoring Service personnel reporting to a particular duty station. Instruction provided to exchange personnel by the Sponsoring Service will be strictly limited to short programs designed for the purposes stated above.

3. In no case may exchange personnel be assigned to a position that would require exercise of command over personnel of the Sponsoring Service.

Figure 13–4. Memorandum of agreement on the Bilateral Exchange of Units between the United States (Military Department) and the ((Country Name) Military Department)–Continued

4. Unless otherwise authorized by authorities of the Parent State, exchange personnel will not participate in combat operations. This applies to all hostilities, including civil-military actions within the Sponsoring State in which its armed forces are called upon to assist in restoring law and order. In any case, where involvement in hostilities or civil-military actions becomes imminent, military duties of exchange personnel will be terminated until further instructions are received from authorities of the Parent State.

5. Exchange units will be assigned duties by the Sponsoring Service which are agreeable to the Parent Service. These duties will conform to the range of qualifications held by exchange unit personnel, but the exchange unit must always be prepared to function fully as a member of the unit or activity to which assigned.

ARTICLE IV: SELECTION CRITERIA AND DISCHARGE

1. The selection of exchange units shall be on a highly selective basis from among military units of the Parent Service. The Parent Service shall be solely responsible in the selection of its exchange units based on the following criteria:
    a. They must be well-versed in the current practices and doctrine of their Service or branch thereof and be particularly qualified through experience to participate in the unit exchange.
    b. They must possess required skill and training qualifications.
    c. Unit personnel should hold the grade authorized for the positions they occupy.

2. The requirements, qualifications, and experience of the exchange units must meet the standards of the Sponsoring Service. The determination and decision on unit performance is within the sole discretion of the Sponsoring Service. The Parent State or Service will be responsible for all expenses in connection with the return of exchange unit personnel under this article.

ARTICLE V: TOUR LENGTH AND NUMBER EXCHANGED

1. The normal tour of duty for exchange units, exclusive of travel time between countries, will be as specified in an appendix to the MOA. Exceptions to and/or adjustments of any tour will be based on mutual agreement.

2. One unit from the U.S. (military department) and one unit from the (country military department) will take part in the exchange. Exchange units will be assigned to units or positions as described in an appendix to this MOA. Expansion of the exchange program and cancellation, postponement, or substitution of a specific exchange will be as mutually agreed between the Sponsoring Service and the Parent Service.

ARTICLE VI: ADMINISTRATION AND CONTROL

Exchange personnel will be administered and controlled as prescribed by the Parent Service:

1. (Name) will serve as the chief, U.S. (military department) exchange program, (country). U.S. (military department) exchange personnel in units on exchange with the (military department) will be under the administrative supervision of the Chief, U.S. (military department) exchange program (country).

2. (Military department) exchange personnel on duty with exchange units in the United States will be under the administrative control of the (military department) attache.

ARTICLE VII: IDENTIFICATION

Exchange personnel will be in possession of valid identification cards and identification discs (tags) in accordance with the regulations of the Parent State and meeting the requirements of the laws and regulations of the Sponsoring Service and Sponsoring State.

Figure 13–4. Memorandum of agreement on the Bilateral Exchange of Units between the United States (Military Department) and the ((Country Name) Military Department)–Continued

ARTICLE VIII: RESPECT FOR LOCAL LAW

Exchange personnel will respect the law of the Sponsoring State and abstain from any activity inconsistent with the spirit of this MOA and, in particular, from any political activity in the Sponsoring State.

ARTICLE IX: ENTRY AND EXIT

Exchange personnel shall be in possession of appropriate documentation issued by the Parent State and required by authorities of the Sponsoring State for entry into and exit from the Sponsoring State.

ARTICLE X: WEAPONS

1. Exchange personnel will not carry personal weapons into the Sponsoring State except when authorized by Sponsoring State authorities and registered in accordance with applicable law.

2. Military weapons issued to exchange personnel by the Parent Service will be introduced into the Sponsoring State only if authorized by the Parent Service and competent Sponsoring State authorities.

ARTICLE XI: DISCIPLINE

1. Exchange personnel will comply with the lawful regulations, orders, instructions, and customs of the Sponsoring Service insofar as they are appropriate and applicable under the circumstances and consistent with laws and regulations of the Parent State.

2. Exchange personnel who commit an offense against the military laws and regulations of either the Parent or Sponsoring Service may be separated from the exchange program with a view toward further administrative or disciplinary action by the Parent Service. Disciplinary action will not be taken by the Sponsoring Service against exchange personnel. The separation of exchange personnel from the program will not affect the right of civil authorities of the Sponsoring State or its political subdivisions to exercise criminal jurisdiction over such personnel. Authorities of the Sponsoring Service will convey, on behalf of the Parent Service, any request for waiver of the right of such authorities to exercise jurisdiction. Further, authorities of the Sponsoring Service will maintain close coordination with civil authorities of the Sponsoring State or its political subdivisions in such matters and will urge, upon request of the Parent Service, that sympathetic consideration be given to waiver requests where the Parent Service/State indicates such waiver to be of particular importance. The foregoing is without prejudice to the provisions of an applicable status of forces agreement.

3. Exchange personnel will not exercise disciplinary powers over military personnel of the Sponsoring Service.

4. Consistent with paragraphs 1 and 2 of this article, exchange personnel are subject to the lawful commands of military personnel of the Sponsoring Service who are senior in rank to them.

5. To the extent authorized by its laws and regulations, the Sponsoring Service will cooperate in the application of administrative or disciplinary action by the Parent Service against offending exchange personnel.

ARTICLE XII: SECURITY

Exchange personnel must comply at all times with security regulations of the Sponsoring Service or State. Assignment, duties, and the handling of classified information will be subject to the security and disclosure policies of both States and Services concerned and any applicable international agreements.

Figure 13–4. Memorandum of agreement on the Bilateral Exchange of Units between the United States (Military Department) and the ((Country Name) Military Department)–Continued

ARTICLE XIII: IJSE OF FACILITIES

Use of facilities of the Sponsoring Service by exchange personnel for their military specialty proficiency will be granted in accordance with the policies and directives of the Sponsoring Service.

ARTICLE XIV: UNIFORM

Exchange personnel will comply with the dress regulations of the Parent Service and the order of dress for any occasion is to be that which most nearly conforms to the order for the particular unit of the Sponsoring Service to which their exchange unit is assigned. Customs of the Sponsoring Service will be observed with respect to wearing of civilian clothes.

ARTICLE XV: LEAVE AND PASSES

Exchange personnel may be granted leave and passes according to their entitlements under the regulations of the Parent Service, provided such is coordinated with the proper authorities of the Sponsoring Service. Exchange personnel may observe the holiday schedules of both Parent and Sponsoring Services.

ARTICLE XVI: MEDICAL AND DENTAL SERVICES

1. PME exchange personnel and their accompanying dependents will be granted access to military medical and dental Services to the extent authorized by its governing laws and regulations. The provision of such care may be subject to reimbursement. Reimbursement of the Sponsoring Service for medical and dental Services provided to exchange personnel may be required unless otherwise specified in the appendix to this MOA pursuant to Article XVIII.

2. It is the responsibility of the Parent Service to ensure that exchange personnel are medically and dentally fit prior to commencing the exchange program.

ARTICLE XVII: FINANCIAL RESPONSIBILITIES

The following financial responsibilities apply to the exchange program:

1. The Parent State or Service and exchange personnel, as appropriate, are responsible during the period of the exchange for the following costs:

    a. Basic pay and cash allowances due exchange personnel.

    b. Per diem and other travel allowances associated with the movement of exchange units and their personnel to and from the Sponsoring State.

    c. Compensation for loss of, or damage to, the uniform or other personal equipment of exchange personnel.

    d. Cost of preparation and shipment of remains and funeral expenses in the event of death of exchange personnel.

    e. Expenditures in connection with any special duty performed on behalf of the Parent State

    f. Expenses incurred in the interest of dependents permitted to accompany or join exchange personnel.

    g. Except for instruction of a brief duration provided in accordance with the provisions of paragraph 2, Article 111, of this MOA, the costs of any training, Services, or requirements not listed in the appendix to this MOA pursuant to Article XVIII.

2. The Sponsoring State or Service is responsible for the cost of providing the training and related Services specifically identified in the appendix, pursuant to Article XVIII, subject to the reciprocity and reimbursement provisions of that article.

Figure 13–4. Memorandum of agreement on the Bilateral Exchange of Units between the United States (Military Department) and the ((Country Name) Military Department)–Continued

ARTICLE XVIII:
RECIPROCAL PROVISION OF TRAINING AND RELATED SUPPORT

1. The parties may agree, on the basis of reciprocity, for the provision by the Sponsoring State or Service of training and related support as listed in Articles XVI and XVII. An agreement for the reciprocal provision of training and related support, if executed, will be incorporated in this MOA and will appear as an appendix hereto.

2. Regardless of whether an appendix to provide the training and related support as listed in Articles XVI and XVII is agreed to or not, units will be exchanged within 12 months in order that a balance of costs involved in sending and receiving units is maintained or so that reimbursement for the full costs of the training and related support provided can be accomplished.

3. To the extent that one party to which training and related support specified in the appendix is provided under this MOA does not initiate comparable training and related support for the other party within 12 months, the party provided such training and related support shall reimburse the providing party for the full costs of such training and support.

4. IMET, and FMS cash or credit funds may not be utilized for reimbursement or to meet the expenses of an exchange unit.

ARTICLE XIX: CLAIMS

1. Third party claims arising out of activities of exchange personnel or exchange units may be submitted to the Parent Service for settlement consistent with its authority under the laws and regulations of the Parent State. Notwithstanding the foregoing, exchange personnel will be required to obtain civil liability insurance for their private motor vehicles in accordance with applicable host State laws and regulations, and first recourse shall be had against any such insurance in the case of claims involving motor vehicles.

2. Neither State shall make any claim against the other or loss or damage to its property caused by military personnel of the other State in the execution of their duties during the course of any exchange.

3. Neither State shall make any claim against the other for injury or death suffered by any member of its armed Services while engaged in the performance of official duty during the course of any exchange.

4. Neither the Sponsoring Service nor the Sponsoring State shall be responsible for loss or damage of personal property of exchange personnel.

5. The foregoing is without prejudice to the provisions of an applicable status of forces agreement.

ARTICLE XX: REPORTS AND EVALUATIONS

1. Reports which exchange units may be required to make by their own Service or which they wish to make concerning their exchange duties will be submitted as follows:

      a. U.S. (military department) exchange units will forward their reports in accordance with appropriate departmental guidance.
      b. Foreign exchange units and exchange personnel will forward their reports in accordance with Parent Service instructions.

ARTICLE XYI: PRIVILEGES AND EXEMPTIONS

To the extent authorized by the laws and regulations of the Sponsoring State, and in any event to the extent provided in an applicable status of forces agreement, the following privileges will be available to exchange units and exchange personnel.

Figure 13–4. Memorandum of agreement on the Bilateral Exchange of Units between the United States (Military Department) and the ((Country Name) Military Department)–Continued

1. Exemption from any tax by the Sponsoring State upon income received from the Parent State.

2. Exemption from any customs, import duty, or similar tax upon articles brought into the Sponsoring State in connection with their official or personal use, including their baggage and household effects.

3. Purchasing and patronage privileges at military commissaries, exchanges, theaters, and clubs on the same basis as equivalent personnel of the Sponsoring Service.

4. Any other privilege provided by an applicable status of forces agreement or granted by the Sponsoring State under its laws aid regulations.

ARTICLE XXII: AWARDS OR INSIGNIA

Awards or insignia of military qualifications bestowed upon exchange units or exchange personnel by the Sponsoring Service shall be made in accordance with the regulations of the Sponsoring Service. These awards or insignia shall not be accepted by the unit or personnel concerned without the prior approval of the Parent Service.

ARTICLE XXIII APPLICATION OF STATUS OF FORCES AGREEMENTS

The provisions of any agreement of general application between the Sponsoring and Parent States now or hereinafter in effect regarding the status of Parent State military personnel present in the Sponsoring State shall apply to exchange personnel and exchange units present in the Sponsoring State, provided that in the event of conflict between the provisions of such other agreement and articles XVII, XVIII, or XXIV of this MOA, such articles of this MOA shall prevail.

ARTICLE XXIV: DURATION

This MOA is effective when signed by both Services and will be reviewed annually. It may be terminated by either Service upon written notice to the other Service at least 90 days prior to the effective date of such termination.

IN WITNESS WHEREOF, the undersigned, being duly authorized by their governments, have signed this Agreement.

For the United States (Military Service)

_____
(SIGNATURE)

_____
(TYPED NAME)

_____
(RANK/TITLE)

_____
(DATE)

_____
DONE AT (PLACE)

For the (Country Military Service):

_____
(SIGNATURE)

_____
(TYPED NAME)

_____
(RANK/TITLE)

_____
(DATE)

_____
DONE AT (PLACE)

Figure 13–4. Memorandum of agreement on the Bilateral Exchange of Units between the United States (Military Department) and the ((Country Name) Military Department)–Continued

AGREEMENT BETWEEN

THE DEPARTMENT OF DEFENSE

OF

THE UNITED STATES OF AMERICA

AND

THE MINISTRY OF DEFENSE

OF

(COUNTRY NAME)

REGARDING THE EXCHANGE

OF

FLIGHT TRAINING

Figure 13–5. Memorandum of agreement between the Department of Defense of the United States of America and the Ministry of Defense of (Country Name) regarding the Exchange of Flight Training

**AGREEMENT BETWEEN
THE DEPARTMENT OF DEFENSE
O F
THE UNITED STATES OF AMERICA
AND
THE MINISTRY OF DEFENSE
OF
(COUNTRY NAME)
REGARDING THE EXCHANGE
OF
FLIGHT TRAINING
PREAMBLE**

The Department of Defense of the United States of America (US) and the Ministry of Defense of (Country Name), hereinafter referred to as "the Parties," have agreed to establish a Flight Training Exchange Program, which is designed to strengthen bonds of friendship and understanding between the countries and further interoperability between their respective Military Services.

ARTICLE I
DEFINITION OF TERMS

1. Flight Training Exchange (FTE). Flight training of comparable type and scope provided in Service schools and other training locations. For the purposes of this Agreement, this involves undergraduate, instructor pilot, advanced, continuation, flight test and other flight training.

2. Flight Training Exchange (FTE) Student. Any individual on active duty with the Parent Service who is attending training in the host country pursuant to this Exchange Program.

3. Parent Service. The military Service to which the FTE Student belongs.

4. Host Service. The military Service whose training program the FTE Student is attending pursuant to this FTE Program.

5. Parent Party. The Defense Department or Ministry of Defense (DOD/MOD) to which the Parent service belongs.

6. Host Party. The Defense Department or Ministry of Defense (DOD/MOD) to which the Host Service belongs.

7. Dependent. A person present in the country of the Host Party with the consent of the Parent Service and Host Service who is the spouse, minor child, or other relative who depends for support upon and is supported by a FTE Student.

8. Reciprocal FTE. Flight training exchange as defined in paragraph 1 above commencing within the same United States fiscal year by means of a reciprocal one-for-one exchange of students between the Parties.

9. Tuition costs. All costs associated with training, training materials, special clothing or equipment, visits, and field exercises undertaken by the FTE Student as part of the approved course program. Other costs associated with training, such as student's meals, custodial fees for quarters, medical care, and transportation, are not included in tuition costs.

Figure 13–5. Memorandum of agreement between the Department of Defense of the United States of America and the Ministry of Defense of (Country Name) regarding the Exchange of Flight Training–Continued

ARTICLE II
PURPOSE AND SCOPE

This Agreement establishes the terms and conditions by which the Parties agree to establish a flight training exchange program for maximum mutual benefit to the extent permissible under existing policies, laws, and regulations of the United States of America and (country). The FTE Program shall be a one-for-one reciprocal exchange of students.

ARTICLE III
SPECIAL PROVISIONS

1. When a proposal to exchange flight training has been offered and accepted by each of the Services concerned, a reciprocal FTE Program may then be conducted.

2. Training will be conducted using the performance objectives and standards of the Host Service. Exceptions to successful completion of Host Service standards may be considered on a case-by-case basis.

3. This Agreement does not constitute a commitment on the part of either Party to provide an annual quota(s) for the training specified in Article 1, paragraph 1, above.

4. The details of each reciprocal FTE for a particular Service shall be set forth in an appendix to this Agreement and shall be considered a part of this Agreement.

ARTICLE IV
SELECTION OF STUDENTS

1. The selection of FTE Students shall be on a highly selective basis from among qualified personnel of the Parent Service. The Parent Service shall be solely responsible for the selection of its FTE Students based on the criteria that students should:

    a. Be well versed in the practices and doctrines of their own service.
    b. Meet the basic criteria, including aviation physiology, established by the Host Service for the applicable training through a combination of training, experience, and ability.
    c. Meet the language prerequisites established by the Host Service for the applicable training.
    d. Possess a security clearance to the level required for the applicable training

2. Consistent with the nomination process, the Host Service/Party shall be authorized to discharge FTE Students from this Exchange Program who do not meet the above criteria or who cannot safely complete the program. This decision shall be within the sole discretion of the Host Service/Party.

ARTICLE V
FINANCIAL ARRANGEMENTS

1. The tuition costs for FTE shall not be charged to the Parent Party/Service or to FTE Students. The Parent Party/Service and FTE Students, as appropriate, shall be responsible, during the period of the exchange, for the costs listed below:

    a. Basic pay and cash allowances due FTE Students.
    b. All permanent change of station costs including per diem and other travel allowances and transportation (including leave travel) and storage costs.
    c. All temporary duty costs, including per diem and other travel allowances and transportation, when such temporary duty is directed by the Parent Party.
    d. Compensation for loss of, or damage to, the uniform or other personal equipment of FTE Students.
    e. Cost of movement of dependents and household effects of FTE Students as authorized by the Parent Party.

Figure 13–5. Agreement Between The Department of Defense Of The United States Of America And The Ministry Of Defense Of (Country Name) Regarding The Exchange Of Flight Training–Continued

f. Cost of quarters and mess for FTE Students and their dependents.

g. Cost of preparation and shipment of remains and funeral expenses in the event of death of FTE Students or their dependents.

h. Expenditures in connection with any special duty performed on behalf of the Parent Party.

i. Expenses incurred in the interest of dependents permitted to accompany or join FTE Students,

j. Medical and dental charges for treatment of FTE Students or their dependents that require reimbursement under the laws or regulations of the Host Party's country.

k. Cost of language training.

1. All expenses in connection with the return of FTE Students who have been discharged from this Exchange Program and their accompanying dependents.

2. The Host Party shall be responsible during the exchange period for all temporary duty costs, including per diem and other travel allowances and transportation, when such temporary duty is directed by the Host Party.

3. The Parent Party/Service and FTE Students, as appropriate, shall be liable for all other services and expenses for FTE Students, including any which are unconnected with the requirements of the exchange.

4. U.S. International Military Education and Training (IMET) program funds, Foreign Military Financing (FMF) funds, or Foreign Military Sales (FMS) cash funds shall not be used to meet financial responsibilities of the Parent Party/Service that are part of the FTE Program.

5. The obligations of each Party under this Agreement shall be subject to the authorization and availability of funds for such purposes. Prior to implementing any exchange, all Parties/Services shall ensure that adequate funds are available.

ARTICLE VI
SECURITY

1. During the selection process, the Host Service shall inform the Parent Service of the level of security clearance required, if any, for participation in the FTE Program. The Parent Service shall provide documentation on the security clearances for FTE Students to the organization designated by the Host Service.

2. FTE Students shall at all times be required to comply with the security laws, regulations and procedures of the government of the Host Party. Any violation of security procedures by FTE Students during their assignments shall be reported to the Parent Service for appropriate action. FTE Students committing willful violations of security procedures during their assignments shall be removed from the Exchange Program with a view toward administrative or disciplinary action by the Parent Party.

3. The Host Service and the Parent Service shall ensure that assigned FTE Students are fully cognizant of applicable laws and regulations concerning the protection of proprietary information (such as copyrights), classified information and controlled unclassified information to which access might be gained under this Exchange Program, both during and after completion of training.

4. All classified information made available to FTE Students shall be considered as classified information furnished to their Parent Party, and shall be subject to all provisions and safeguards provided for under the General Security of Military Information Agreement (GSOMIA) (may also be referred to as a General Security Agreement (GSA) or General Security of Information Agreement (GSOIA) in' force between the United States of America and (Country Name).

Figure 13–5. Agreement Between The Department of Defense Of The United States Of America And The Ministry Of Defense Of (Country Name) Regarding The Exchange Of Flight Training–Continued

ARTICLE VII
ADMINISTRATION AND CONTROL

1. For all purposes except academic matters, FTE Students shall be administered and controlled as prescribed by the Parent Services. The organizations responsible for administrative supervision of specific FTE Students shall be specified in the applicable appendices.

2. With respect to academic matters, FTE Students shall be under the administrative supervision of the training unit commanding officer.

ARTICLE VIII IDENTIFICATION

FTE Students and their accompanying dependents shall be required to possess valid identification cards in accordance with the regulations of the Parent Service. FTE Students and their accompanying dependents shall also be issued identification cards by the Host Service for the duration of the exchange.

ARTICLE IX
RESPECT FOR HOST PARTY LAW

Subject to the terms of this Agreement, FTE Students and their accompanying dependents shall be required to respect the law of the government of the Host Party and abstain from any activity inconsistent with the spirit of this Agreement and from any political activity in the country of the Host Party.

ARTICLE X
ENTRY AND EXIT

FTE Students and their accompanying dependents shall possess appropriate documentation issued by the Parent Patty and required by the county of the Host Party for entry into and exit from that country.

ARTICLE XI
WEAPONS

1. FTE Students shall not be permitted to import or carry personal weapons in the country of the Host Party except when authorized by Host Party authorities and registered in accordance with applicable laws.

2. Weapons issued to FTE Students for military purposes by the Parent Service shall be introduced into the country of the Host Patty only if authorized by the Parent Service and in accordance with the laws of the government of the Host Party.

ARTICLE XII DISCIPLINE

1. FTE Students shall be required to comply with the regulations, orders, instructions, and customs of the Host Service insofar as they are appropriate and applicable under the circumstances and consistent with the laws and regulations of the government of the Parent Party.

2. FIE Students who commit an of false against the military laws and regulations of either the Parent or Host Service may be withdrawn from the FTE Program with a view toward further administrative or disciplinary action by the Parent Service. Disciplinary action shall not be taken by the Host Service against the FTE Students. The withdrawal of the FTE Student from the program shall not affect the right of civil authorities of the government of the Host Party or its political subdivisions to exercise criminal jurisdiction over such personnel. Authorities of the Host Service shall convey, on behalf of the Parent Service, any requests for waiver of the right of such authorities to exercise jurisdiction over such personnel. Further, authorities of the Host Service shall maintain close coordination with civil authorities of the government of the Host Party or its political subdivisions in such matters and shall urge, upon request of the Parent Service, that sympathetic consideration be given to waiver requests where the Parent Service/Party

Figure 13–5. Memorandum of agreement between the Department of Defense of the United States of America and the Ministry of Defense of (Country Name) regarding the Exchange of Flight Training–Continued

indicates such waiver to be of particular importance. The foregoing is without prejudice to the provisions of an applicable status of forces agreement.

3. Consistent with paragraphs 1 and 2 of this article, FTE Students should extend normal military courtesy to military personnel of the Host Service who are superior in rank to them.

4. To the extent authorized by its laws and regulations, the Host Service shall cooperate in the application of administrative or disciplinary action by the Parent Service against the offending. FTE Student.

ARTICLE XIII
USE OF FACILITIES

1. (Country) FTE Students and their authorized accompanying dependents in the United States shall be entitled to the same use of administrative, logistical, and commissary facilities as are accorded to other security assistance sponsored students.

2. U.S. FTE Students and their dependents shall be entitled to the same use of administrative, logistical, and commissary facilities as other U.S. military personnel and their dependents stationed in the country of the Host Party or attached to the U.S. diplomatic mission.

ARTICLE XIV
UNIFORM

1. FTE Students shall be required to comply with the dress and grooming regulations of the Parent Service. The order of dress for any occasion shall be that which most nearly conforms to the order of the particular unit of the Host Service to which they are attached. Customs of the Host Service shall be observed with respect to wearing of civilian clothes.

2. The Host Service may issue the FTE Student special clothing or equipment required for flight training on the same basis as to its own students. The rank or other insignia worn on such clothing or equipment shall, to the extent possible conform to Parent Service standards.

ARTICLE XV
LEAVE

FTE Students may be granted leave according to their entitlements under the regulations of the Parent Service, provided such is approved by the Parent Service and the proper authorities of the Host Service. FTE Students may observe the holiday schedules of both Parent and Host Services in accordance with Host Service regulations.

ARTICLE XVI
QUARTERS AND MESSING

The Host Service may provide, if available, quarters and messing for FTE Students in accordance with its own regulations. FTE Students or their Parent Service shall be responsible for paying charges made by the Host Service for quarters and messing, when provided, and for any attendant services provided by the Host Service. In the event that the Host Service is unable to provide quarters, the FTE Student or the Parent Service shall be responsible for arranging and financing private accommodations.

ARTICLE XVII
MEDICAL AND DENTAL SERVICES

1. Any medical and dental care that may be provided to FTE Students and their accompanying dependents at Host Party medical facilities shall be subject to the laws and regulations of the government of the Host Party, including reimbursement when required by such laws and regulations.

Figure 13–5. Memorandum of agreement between the Department of Defense of the United States of America and the Ministry Of Defense of (Country Name) regarding the Exchange of Flight Training–Continued

2. The Parent Service shall be responsible for ensuring that FTE Students and their accompanying dependents are in good medical and dental health prior to commencing the exchange program.

3. FTE Students will carry their medical and dental records by hand to their respective training units.

ARTICLE XVIII
REPORTS, EVALUATIONS, AND INVESTIGATIONS

1. Reports which FTE Students may be required to make by their Parent Service or which they wish to make concerning their exchange training shall be submitted in accordance with Parent Service regulations.

2. Individual evaluation reports shall be prepared and submitted in accordance with Host Service regulations and procedures.

3. In the event of injuries to, or death of, FTE Students, the Host Service shall submit casualty reports through established channels to the Parent Service. Any reports and investigations conducted by the Host Service concerning a casualty shall be made available to the Parent Service. The Parent Service may conduct a separate investigation.

4. In absence of a Standardization Agreement (STANAG) on aircraft mishap investigation procedures between the Parties, Host Service aircraft accident investigation procedures shall be used. The Parent Party/Service shall cooperate in any aircraft mishap analysis investigation.

ARTICLE XIX
PRIVILEGES AND EXEMPTIONS

Alternative A
(NOTE: For agreements with Parties who are NATO members or other countries with which there are SOFAS use this Alternative.)

The U.S.-(Country) Status of Forces Agreement (or NATO SOFA as applicable), dated (date), pertaining to rights and privileges of military personnel while in the country of the Host Party shall apply to FTE Students and their dependents, and in the event of conflict, shall take precedence over this Agreement.

Alternative B
(NOTE: Use this Alternative for agreements with non-NATO countries without SOFAS.)

1. To the extent authorized by the laws and regulations of the government of the Host Party, the following privileges shall be available to FTE Students and their accompanying dependents:

 a. Exemption from any tax of the government of the Host Party on income received from the Parent Party.
 b. Exemption from any customs, import duty, or similar tax on articles brought into the country of the Host Party in connection with their official, personal, or family use, including their baggage, household effects, and private motor vehicles.
 c. Privileges at military commissaries, exchanges, theaters, and clubs on the same basis as equivalent personnel of the Host Party.

2. FTE Students shall be eligible for any other privilege granted by the government of the Host Party under its laws and regulations or by bilateral agreements between the two governments.

Figure 13–5. Memorandum of agreement between the Department of Defense of the United States of America and the Ministry of Defense of (Country Name) regarding the Exchange of Flight Training—Continued

ARTICLE XX
DISCHARGE OF FTE STUDENTS

Once an FTE Student commences training, the obligations of the Host Party Service are met regardless of whether the FTE Student successfully completes the program or is discharged under the provisions of Article IV, paragraph 2, Article VI, paragraph 2, or Article XII, paragraph 2.

ARTICLE XXI
DECORATIONS, AWARDS, OR INSIGNIA

Decorations, awards, or insignia bestowed on FTE Students by the Host Service shall be made in accordance with-the regulations of the Host Service. These awards shall not be accepted by FTE Students without the prior approval of the Parent Service.

ARTICLE XXII NOTIFICATION

Pursuant to Service-to-Service appendices to this Agreement, each Service shall notify the other, twelve months prior to the effective school reporting date, of their intention to participate in this Exchange Program and forward the name(s) and other pertinent data for the Exchange Student(s) who will be participating as required by the Host Service.

ARTICLE XXIII
CLAIMS

Alternative A
(NOTE: For agreements with Parties who are NATO members or other countries with which there are SOFAS use this Alternative.)

1. Claims against either Party or its personnel shall be dealt with in accordance with the terms of Article VIII of the NATO Status of Forces Agreement (NATO SOFA or other SOFA as applicable) dated 19 June 1951.

2. FTE Students and those dependents accompanying them shall obtain motor vehicle liability insurance coverage in accordance with applicable laws and regulations of the government of the Host Party, or its political subdivision, where they are located. In case of claims involving the use of private motor vehicles, the first recourse shall be again such insurance.

Alternative B
(NOTE: Use this Alternative for agreements with non-NATO countries without SOFAS.)

1. The Parties waive all their claims, other than contractual claims against each other, and against the military members and civilian employees of each other's Department or Ministry of Defense, for damage, loss or destruction of property owned or used by its respective Department or Ministry of Defense, if such damage, loss or destruction:
    a. was caused by a military member or a civilian employee in the performance of official duties or
    b. arose from the use of any vehicle, vessel or aircraft owned by the other Party and used by its Department or Ministry of Defense, provided that the vehicle, vessel, or aircraft causing the damage, loss or destruction was being used for official purposes, or that the damage, loss, or destruction was caused to the property so used.

2. The Parties shall waive all their claims against each other and against the military members and civilian employees of each other's Department or Ministry of Defense for injury or death suffered by any military member or civilian employee of their Department or Ministry of Defense while such member or employee was engaged in the performance of official duties.

Figure 13–5. Memorandum of agreement between the Department of Defense of the United States of America and the Ministry of Defense of (Country Name) regarding the Exchange of Flight Training–Continued

3. Claims, other than contractual claims, for damage, loss, injury, or death, not covered by the waivers contained in paragraphs 1 and 2 of this Article, arising out of an act or omission by the military members or civilian employees of its Department or Ministry of Defense, or out of an act or omission for which the Parent Party is legally responsible, shall be presented to the Parent Party for consideration under its applicable laws and regulations.

4. FTE Students and those dependents accompanying them shall obtain motor vehicle liability insurance coverage in accordance with applicable laws and regulations of the government of the Host Party, or its political subdivision, where they are located. In case of claims involving the use of private motor vehicles, the first recourse shall be against such insurance.

ARTICLE XXIV
SETTLEMENT OF DISPUTES

Disputes arising under or relating to this Agreement shall be resolved only by consultation between the Parties and shall not be referred to an individual, a national or international tribunal, or to any other forum for settlement.

ARTICLE XXV
ENTRY INTO FORCE, AMENDMENT, DURATION, AND TERMINATION

1. All activities of the Parties under this Agreement shall be carried out in accordance with the national laws and regulation of the Parties.

2. In the event of a conflict between an Article of this Agreement and any Appendix to this Agreement, the Article shall control.

3. Except as otherwise provided, this Agreement may be amended by the mutual written consent of the Parties.

4. This Agreement may be terminated by mutual written consent of the Parties, or by either Party, upon 180 days written notification to the other Party of its intention to do so. Such notice shall be the subject of immediate consultation by the Parties to ensure termination on the most economical and equitable terms.

5. The respective rights and responsibilities of the Parties regarding Article VI (Security) and Article XXIII (Claims) shall continue notwithstanding termination or expiration of this Agreement.

6. This Agreement which consists of the Preamble, twenty-five (25) Articles and one (1) or more Appendices, shall enter into force upon signature by both Parties and shall remain in force for ten (10) years. It may be extended by written agreement of the Parties.

IN WITNESS WHEREOF, the undersigned, being duly authorized by their governments, have signed this Agreement.

For the United States (Military Service)   **For the (Country Military Service):**

_____   _____
(SIGNATURE)   (SIGNATURE)

_____   _____
(TYPED NAME)   (TYPED NAME)

_____   _____
(RANK/TITLE)   (RANK/TITLE)

Figure 13–5. Memorandum of agreement between the Department of Defense of the United States of America and the Ministry of Defense of (Country Name) regarding the Exchange of Flight Training—Continued

(DATE)	(DATE)
DONE AT (PLACE)	DONE AT (PLACE)

Figure 13–5. Memorandum of agreement between the Department of Defense of the United States of America and the Ministry of Defense of (Country Name) regarding the Exchange of Flight Training–Continued

Section IV
Department of the Air Force (Unit Exchanges)

13–10. Flight training exchanges

a. The USAF units proposing a flight training exchange will forward their request to the appropriate SAF/ International Affairs regional division, 1080 Air Force Pentagon, Washington, DC 20330–1080, with an informative copy to SAF/IAPX, the functional air staff organization, The Air Force Security Assistance Training (Air Force Security Assistance Training Squadron) Squadron, 315 J Street West, Randolph AFB, TX 78150–4302, DSCA/LPP, Washington, DC 20301–2800, the Air Component Command, and the Department of State, Washington, DC 20520. International units proposing an flight training exchange will forward their request through command channels to the Security Cooperation Organization in country. The Security Cooperation Organization will forward the proposal to the appropriate SAF/International Affairs geographic division, with information copies as identified above. The proposal will be forwarded a minimum of 12 months from the desired start date and will provide the information required by paragraph **"Exchange of Flight Training."** USAF units will also confirm that funds are available to support the proposed exchange.

b. The SAF/International Affairs Country Director will staff the feasibility and releasability of the flight training exchange and, if feasible, will prepare and staff an MOA according to figure 13–4, and paragraph **"Exchange of Flight Training."** Upon completion of staffing within the USAF, the country director will forward to DSCA for staffing within OSD.

c. Upon signature by both parties, the SAF/International Affairs country director will forward the original signed copy to DOD/ General Counsel, 1600 Defense, Pentagon, Washington, DC 20301–1600. Additional copies will be provided to SAF/GCI, 1740 Air Force Pentagon, Washington, DC 20330–1740, AF/JAO, 1420 Air Force Pentagon, Washington, DC 20330–1420, OSD (ISA–FRMA), Washington, DC 20301–2400; and the U.S. Department of State (L/ T), Washington, DC 20520. The country director will also forward an International Program Directive with a copy of the MOA and appropriate Service appendices to the Air Force Security Assistance Training (Air Force Security Assistance Training Squadron) Squadron, 315 J Street West, Randolph AFB, TX 78150–4302.

d. Field Studies Program flight training exchange students are eligible to participate in Field Studies Program activities available for international students under other security assistance training programs. The base IMSO will include and separately identify flight training exchange student requirements in the quarterly Field Studies Program plan. The USAF unit hosting the flight training exchange student will reimburse the Field Studies Program account for costs associated with flight training exchange student's participation.

e. Air Force Security Assistance Training Squadron will provide the Security Cooperation Organization authority to issue an ITO for flight training exchange students upon receipt of a copy of the agreement signed by both parties from the SAF/International Affairs country director. A pseudo FMS case designator will be assigned to the flight training exchange and flight training exchanges will be included in the International Standardized Training Listing along with other security assistance training.

f. The USAF flight training exchange officer administration and the unified command air component or AF element is responsible for the administration and support of the USAF flight training exchange officer. Similar to procedures for USAF PME Exchange Personnel, certain duties may be delegated to the U.S. Defense Attaché Office or Security Cooperation Organization in country.

13–11. Professional military education exchanges

a. General. Quotas for the ACSC and Air War College (AWC) will be allocated within the number available for foreign students under the SATP and other cooperative programs. Air Force policy and guidance for this program is the same for students under FMS and IMET sponsorship unless otherwise stated in the international agreement and this chapter. The signature on a PME exchange agreement does not imply the availability of a quota or a commitment to provide a quota. ACSC and AWC quotas are by invitation only. However, once a quota in the ACSC or AWC has been allocated, a country or international organization may wish to explore the student's sponsorship under the PME exchange program. The PME Exchange Program should not be confused with the Military Personnel Exchange Program as delineated in AFI 16–107.

   b. Scope. For foreign officers, International Officer School (IOS) is an integral part of both the USAF AWC and ACSC. All foreign officers participating in the PME exchange program must attend.

   c. Processing a request for a PME exchange.

   (1) If a country desires to pursue a PME Exchange Program, the Security Cooperation Organization should forward the request to the appropriate SAF/International Affairs Regional Division with an information copy to SAF/IAPX, AF/A1DL, DSCA/PGM/flight training exchange and the Department of State. MILDEPs will include the Department of State on correspondence relating to proposed PME Exchanges. The Security Cooperation Organization and/or DATT will be required to obtain from the international PME schoolhouse a copy of the syllabus, written in English, for Air University to evaluate for equivalency. When notified of a countries desire to participate in a PME exchange, the Security Cooperation Organization and/or DATT should also provide detailed information regarding any unique country requirements (that is, personal security, housing availability/non-availability, vehicles, Embassy support, anything that should be included in the decisionmaking of this proposed exchange.) Language requirements should be identified, length of PME training and any other data pertinent to this proposed exchange. Upon review of the syllabus, Air University will provide SAF/IAPX and AF/A1DL with the results of the review. The SAF/IAPX will forward to the regional country director who will provide to the Security Cooperation Organization/DATT in country.

   (2) If the foreign PME program is comparable to the desired USAF program (in accordance with AFI 36–3201), the SAF/International Affairs country director will confirm the availability of a quota in the comparable USAF PME program through SAF/IAPX, manpower authorization through AF/A1DLE, and availability of qualified USAF personnel through AFPC. If an exchange is feasible, the country director will prepare an "umbrella" PME Exchange MOA (see fig 13–1), if necessary, or an appendix identifying the specific Service schools involved. The proposal for the PME Exchange will be approved by AF/CC; SAF/International Affairs will sign appendices for exchanges involving USAF PME schools. See figure 13–1 for additional details on staffing the PME Exchange MOA. After signature by country, the Security Cooperation Organization will forward the original copy of the MOA to DSCA. The original copy of the Service appendix will be forwarded to the country director.

   (3) The SAF/International Affairs country director will forward the original copy of the appendix to DOD/General Counsel, 1600 Defense Pentagon, Washington, DC 20301–1600. Additional copies will be provided to SAF/IAPX; SAF/GCI, 1740 Air Force Pentagon, Washington, DC 20330–1740; OSD (ISA–FRMA), Washington, DC 20301–2400; and the U.S. Department of State (L/T), Washington, DC 20520. The country director will also forward an International Program Directive with a copy of the international agreement and applicable Service appendices to Air Force Security Assistance Training Squadron, 315 J Street West, Randolph AFB, TX 78150–4302.

   d. Lead-time required.

   (1) For foreign countries conducting PME programs in the English language, a minimum lead time of 1 year is required to program USAF manpower requirements, identify a USAF officer to attend the foreign PME school, and reserve a USAF PME quota for the foreign officer.

   (2) For foreign countries conducting PME programs in a foreign language, requests should be forwarded as soon as identified. Due to limited numbers of qualified USAF officers with foreign language proficiency and the lead time required to train an officer to the required level of fluency, as much as 2 years' lead time may be required. However, a PME exchange agreement may be effected if the intent to participate in a specified year is confirmed.

   e. Commitment. The Security Cooperation Organization will make no commitment as to participation by the USAF in a PME exchange program. Lack of qualified U.S. candidates with foreign language proficiency and limited USAF requirements for foreign PME schools may preclude USAF participation in an exchange program. Conclusion of a PME exchange agreement is not a commitment to provide USAF quotas on an annual basis.

   f. Identification number. Exchange agreements will be assigned a six-position pseudo-case identifier, which will be reflected in the upper-right-hand corner of each page of the agreement. The first two positions will reflect the country code, as contained in, DOD 5105.38M, appendix D. The third position will reflect a "D" to identify the Air Force as the U.S. implementing agency. The last three positions will reflect an alphabetical identifier starting with the letter "I" (for example, XX–D–IAA, XX–D–IAB). This identification number will be used in all requests for quotas and correspondence concerning the PME exchange program.

   g. Field trips. The USAF will be responsible for the basic cost of transportation and per diem when temporary duty is required under the PME program curriculum. Air University will budget for these costs in connection with field trip for PME exchange students.

   h. Field Studies Program. PME exchange students are eligible to participate in the Field Studies Program activities available to foreign students under the SATP and other cooperative programs. The base IMSO will include and separately identify PME exchange students' requirements in the quarterly Field Studies Program plan. Air University will budget and utilize operation and maintenance funds for PME exchange students Field Studies Program activities.

i. Administration. The PME exchange program will be administered according to the same policy and procedures as IMET and FMS training programs.

j. Invitational travel orders. Air Force Security Assistance Training Squadron will provide the Security Cooperation Organization authority to issue an ITO for the PME exchange students upon receipt of a copy of the agreement signed by both parties from the SAF/International Affairs country director. The international agreement number will be reflected in item 5e of the ITO in lieu of the FMS case. Check blocks 2 or 3 for items 12b(1)(c) or (d), and 12b(2)(a) or (b) to address payment for medical services provided exchange program personnel. Check block 1, items 12f, 12g, and 12i to address living allowances, travel, and baggage. Item 15 should contain the following note: "The individual identified in item 6 of this order is under the sponsorship of the PME Exchange Program. All references in this document to FMS and IMS will be construed to be references to the PME Exchange Program and or PME Exchange Personnel." Complete all other items of the ITO in the same manner as for FMS students.

k. USAF PME exchange officer administration. The unified command air component is responsible for the administration and support of the USAF PME exchange officer. Some of these responsibilities may be delegated to the U.S. Defense Attaché Office or Security Assistance Organization in country if necessary to insure PME officer support is adequate. Administrative responsibilities include, but are not limited to the following:

(1) Assign a sponsor for the USAF officer selected for a foreign PME school.

(2) Liaison with the foreign school, AFPC, SAF/International Affairs, AFDW, and other organizations involved in the PME Exchange Program.

(3) Providing budgetary information to AF/A1PT and AFDW on an annual basis for support of the USAF officer assigned to a foreign PME school, including tuition and temporary duty costs, if appropriate. AF/A1PT will include these expenses in the PME budget.

(4) Forward a request for fund cite to AFDW/FMB and use this fund cite when preparing payment vouchers to reimburse tuition costs to the PME institution, and fund travel and per diem to the USAF PME exchange offer, where appropriate. When requesting the fund cite, the responsible organization will identify the purpose and the estimate for the anticipated payments.

(5) Maintaining the geographically separated personnel and medical records for the USAF officer assigned to a foreign PME school.

(6) Prepare and transmit the training report for the USAF officer upon completion of the foreign PME school.

13–12. Unit exchanges

a. Exchanges under this legislation will apply only to units identified in USAF Unit Manning Document.

b. The purpose of the unit exchange program is to—

(1) Improve interoperability between the USAF and the military forces with which the exchange is conducted.

(2) Validate, test, exercise, and or complement interoperability capabilities.

(3) Provide opportunities for informal mission training, orientation, observation, or familiarization of USAF and foreign participants.

(4) Provide a sharing of experience between the participating units.

(5) Assist in improving relations and mutual understanding between the United States and the country or international organization with which the exchange is conducted.

c. Unit exchanges are authorized on a TDY basis, which will include travel time.

d. USAF and foreign PME exchange students must be fully qualified for participation in the exchange. Upgrade training is not authorized under this program.

e. Unit exchange training will normally be conducted in the English language.

f. Requests will be submitted as follows:

(1) The MAJCOM or organization proposing an exchange will first contact the appropriate SAF/International Affairs regional division to determine the appropriateness of an exchange with the desired country. If SAF/International Affairs considers the exchange appropriate from a politico-military standpoint, a formal proposal will be submitted as outlined below.

(2) The MAJCOM or organization sponsoring the exchange will submit the unit exchange proposal to the appropriate SAF/International Affairs regional division, 1080 Air Force Pentagon, Washington, DC 20330–1080, with information copies to SAF/IAPX; HQ USAFA5XX, 1480 Air Force Pentagon, Washington, DC 20330–1480; DSCA/LPP, Washington, DC 20301–2800; the air component; and the unified command. Air Force Reserve units and Air National Guard (ANG) units will forward their proposed unit exchanges to the SAF/International Affairs regional division through HQ USAF/RE, 1150 Air Force Pentagon, Washington, DC 20330–1150, or ANG/CS, 2500 Army Pentagon, Washington, DC 20310–2500. Consolidated requests reflecting a proposed annual program are welcome. The request will contain—

(a) Identification of the country with which the exchange is proposed.

(b) Desired dates and time frame.

(c) Identification of the type and size of unit to be exchanged.

(d) A statement of the availability of the funds required to support the exchange.

(e) A summary of the training to be conducted.

(f) An estimate of the cost of training and related support, such as housing, mess, logistics, medical, or dental costs, to be covered under the exchange.

(g) Justification for the exchange, including security considerations and classification of any possible information exchange.

(3) Before submitting the formal proposal for approval, the MAJCOM sponsoring the exchange will solicit comments or concurrence of the country team through the Security Cooperation Organization and the appropriate unified command, on each specific exchange proposal.

(4) International partner requests for unit exchanges will be forwarded by the Security Cooperation Organization to the appropriate SAF/International Affairs regional Division. SCOs will ensure requests contain (at a minimum) the following:

(a) Justification for the exchange.

(b) Proposed dates and proposed duration.

(c) Identification of the type and size of unit to be exchanged.

(d) A summary of the type of training/activities to be conducted.

(e) Outline of administrative and support services.

(5) Requests for programs of recurring exchanges will require 1-time approval rather than approval for each exchange, unless the classification changes. However, periodic reviews (at least once a year) of unit exchange programs will be made jointly by SAF/International Affairs regional divisions and the MAJCOM to insure compliance with current procedures and directives.

g. The SAF/International Affairs country director will coordinate a HQ USAF response to the request with appropriate Air Staff (for example, AF/A30–AT, AF/A5XX) and SECAF (for example, SAF/IAPX/IAPD/GCI) offices (at a minimum). If approved, the SAF/International Affairs country director will forward the approved request to the appropriate MAJCOM for further action.

h. After SAF/International Affairs approval, the MAJCOM is authorized direct coordination with the international partner service to propose and resolve details of the exchange. The MAJCOM is then responsible for execution of the exchange using the format provided at figure 13–3. No deviation in wording or change to the Memorandum of Agreement is authorized without prior approval of the SAF/International Affairs country director, SAF/IAPX and SAF/GCI. After signature by both parties, the MAJCOM will forward a copies of the signed agreement to the SAF/International Affairs regional division and as well as the SAF/International Affairs Security Assistance Policy and International Education and Training Division (SAF/IAPX), 1080 Air Force Pentagon, Washington, DC 20330–1080. The SAF/International Affairs Country Director will forward copies of the agreement within the Air Staff and SECAF, as necessary.

i. Units will submit an evaluation of the exchange to their MAJCOM within 60 days after return from country. Information copies will be forwarded to the SAF/International Affairs regional division, SAF/IAPX, HQ USAF/A5XX, the air component command, and unified command. The evaluation will be prepared by the unit chief or senior member.

j. Not later than 1 November of each year, the SAF/International Affairs regional divisions, HQ USAF/RE, and HQ ANG will provide SAF/IAPX a report of unit exchanges conducted during the preceding U.S. FY according to "PME Exchanges, Processing a request for a PME exchange" for units under their area of responsibility. This office will consolidate inputs and provide a report to the Director, Washington Headquarters Services, and /MI.

k. Exchanges involving active Air Force units will be funded from the applicable MAJCOM Major Force Program according to AFI 65–601V1. MAJCOM sponsoring unit exchanges are responsible for programming and budgeting the costs of supporting foreign exchange unit training in the United States. Exchanges involving Air Force Reserve or ANG units will be funded from their respective appropriations.

l. If the USAF does not receive reciprocal training and support within 12 months, the MAJCOM/Comptroller will bill the foreign air force for the training and related support provided by the USAF according to DODD 2020.11. If the USAF does not provide reciprocal training and support within 12 months after receiving it, the MAJCOM/Controller will reimburse the foreign air force for the training and services received. MAJCOM will ensure procedures for the review, reporting and, if required, billing or reimbursements are implemented for unit exchange programs within their areas of responsibility.

m. Exchange training for foreign personnel will be accomplished on an unclassified basis, unless classified information is specifically authorized on a case-by-case basis by /IAPD.

n. Access by foreign PME exchange students to USAF installations will be accomplished under self-invited visit procedures, according to AFI 16–201.

o. Personnel participating in unit exchanges will be briefed on the provisions of chapter 13 of this regulation and on customs inspections according to DOD 5030.49–R.

p. Foreign exchange students may participate in planned Field Studies Program activities at USAF bases at no additional expense to the Field Studies Program if the POC in the U.S. sponsoring unit concurs. The POC should contact the CONUS base IMSO to discuss the Field Studies Program if they desire to explore the program for the visiting foreign PME exchange students.

Appendix A
References

Section I
Required Publications

DOD 5105.38–M
Security Assistance Management Manual (Cited in paras 1–5, 3–9a, 3–22a, 3–26b, 3–33, 4–16b, 4–28a(3), 5–15, 6–8, 6–10, 6–12, 7–6e, 7–9c(1), 7–11a, 7–12c, 9–9a, 10–58, 11–2c, 11–4b, 11–19d, 12–11, and 12–17c(2).) (Available at http://www.dtic.mil/whs/directives/.)

Section II
Related Publications

A related publication is a source of additional information. The user does not have to read it to understand this publication. DOD publications are available at http://www.dtic.mil/whs/directives/. United States Codes are available at http://www.gpoaccess.gov/uscode/. Navy publications are available at http://doni.daps.dla.mil/default.aspx. Air Force publications are available at http://www.e-publishing.af.mil/. United States Marine Corps publications are available at http://www.marines.mil/news/publications/. CJCS publications are available http://www.dtic.mil/cjcs_directives/. DLIELC publications are available at https://www.dliflc.edu/.

AR 11–2
Managers' Internal Control Program

AR 12–1
Security Assistance, International Logistics, Training, and Technical Assistance Support Policy and Responsibilities

AR 12–7
Security Assistance Teams

AR 25–30
The Army Publishing Program

AR 25–51
Official Mail and Distribution Management

AR 25–55
The Department of the Army Freedom of Information Act Program

AR 25–400–2
Army Records Information Management System

AR 27–20
Claims

AR 30–22
The Army Food Program

AR 37–47
Representation Funds of the Secretary of the Army

AR 40–3
Medical, Dental, and Veterinary Care

AR 40–501
Standards of Medical Fitness

AR 55–46
Travel Overseas

AR 115–11
Geospatial Information and Services

AR 135–210
Order to Active Duty as Individuals for other than a Presidential Selected

AR 210–130
Laundry and Dry Cleaning Operations

AR 335–15
Management Information Control System

AR 360–1
The Army Public Affairs Program

AR 380–10
Foreign Disclosure and Contacts with Foreign Representatives

AR 381–12
Subversion and Espionage Directed Against the U.S. Army (SAEDA)

AR 420–1
Army Facilities Management

AR 550–1
Processing Request for Political Asylum and Temporary Refuge

AR 550–51
International Agreements

AR 600–8–22
Military Awards

AR 600–8–1
Army Casualty Program

AR 600–8–101
Personnel Processing (In-, Out-, Soldier Readiness, Mobilization & Deployment Processing)

AR 600–8–105
Military Orders

AR 601–210
Regular Army and Army Reserve Enlistment Program

AR 614–30
Overseas Service

AR 623–3
Officer Evaluation Reporting System

AR 670–1
Wear and Appearance of Army Uniforms and Insignia

AR 735–5
Policies and Procedures for Property Accountability

DOD 1000.11
Identification Cards for Members of the Uniformed Services, their Dependents, and other Eligible Personnel

DOD 1000.21–R
DOD Passport and Passport Agent Services

DOD 4515.13–R
Air Transportation Eligibility

DOD 5040.2
Visual Information (VI)

DOD 5220.22
National Industrial Security Program

DOD 7000–14–R, Volume 15
Financial Management Regulation

DODD 2000.11
Procedures for Handling Requests for Political Asylum and Temporary Refuge

DODD 4500.54E
DOD Foreign Clearance Program (FCP)

DODD 5030.49–R
DoD Customs Inspection Program

DODD 5132.03
DOD Policy and Responsibilities Relating to Security Cooperation

DODD 5132.10
Security Assistance Technical Assistance Field Teams

DODD 5410.17
A Field Studies Program for Foreign Military Trainees in the United States

DODD 5530.3
International Agreements

DODI 1000.1
Identity Cards Required by the Geneva Convention

DODI 1000.13
Identification (ID) Cards for Members of the Uniformed Services, their Dependents, and other Eligible Individuals

DODI 1015.10
Programs for Military Morale, Welfare, and Recreation (MWR)

DODI 1341.2
Defense Enrollment Eligibility Reporting System (DEERS) Procedures

DODI 5410.17
United States Field Studies Program (FSP) for International Military and Civilian Students and Military-sponsored Visitors

DODI 6000.11
Patient Movement

DODI 6055.7
Accident Investigation, Reporting, and Record Keeping

DODI 7230.08
Leases and Demonstrations and DOD Equipment

FAA, Section 506(a)(2)
Special Authority

FAA, Section 552
Authorization of Appropriations

FAA, Section 544
Exchange Training

FAA, Section 620(q)
Prohibitions Against Furnishing Assistance

FAA, Section 652
Limitation Upon Exercise of Special Authorities

FAA, Section 660
Prohibiting Police Training

8 USC 1302
Registration of aliens

8 USC 1182(a)(1)–(7)
Inadmissible aliens; Classes of aliens ineligible for visas or admission; Health-related grounds; Criminal and related grounds; Security and related grounds; Public charge; Labor certification and qualifications for certain immigrants; Illegal entrants and immigration violators; Documentation requirements

10 USC
Armed Forces

10 USC 112b
Department of Defense: seal

10 USC 166a
Combatant Command Budgets

10 USC 167b
Assignment of Forces

10 USC 168
Military-to-military contacts and comparable activities

10 USC 401
Humanitarian and civic assistance provided in conjunction with military operations

10 USC 1050
Latin American cooperation: payment of personnel expenses

10 USC 1051
Bilateral or regional cooperation programs: payment of personnel expenses

10 USC 1072
Definitions

10 USC 2011
Special operations forces: training with friendly foreign forces

10 USC 2166
Western Hemisphere Institute for Security Cooperation

10 USC 2350g
Authority to accept use of real property, services, and supplies from foreign countries in connection with mutual defense agreements and occupational arrangements

10 USC 2561
Humanitarian assistance

10 USC 2731
Definition

10 USC 2732
Payment of claims: availability of appropriations

10 USC 2733
Property loss; personal injury or death: incident to noncombat activities of Department of Army, Navy, or Air Force

10 USC 2734
Property loss; personal injury or death: incident to noncombat activities of the armed forces; foreign countries

10 USC 2735
Settlement: final and conclusive

10 USC 2736
Property loss; personal injury or death: advance payment

10 USC 2737
Property loss; personal injury or death: incident to use of property of the United States and not cognizable under other law

10 USC 2738
Property loss: reimbursement of members for certain losses of household effects caused by hostile action

14 USC 195
Admission of foreign nationals for instruction; restrictions; conditions

19 USC 1202, section 8, part 2, 820.40 and 822.20
Harmonized Tariff Schedule

22 USC
Foreign Relations and Intercourse

22 USC 2347
General authority

22 USC 2420(b)(3)
Exception; qualification with respect to assistance, including training, in maritime law enforcement and other maritime skills

22 USC 2420(b)(7)
Exception; qualification with respect to assistance provided to customs authorities and personnel, including training, technical assistance and equipment, for customs law enforcement and the improvement of customs laws, systems and procedures.

PL 101–510, Section 1004
Department of Defense Authorization Act, 1991

UCMJ, Art. 51
Voting and Rulings

NAVIPOINST 4950.1
Security Assistance Training Program, Contractor-Provided Training

OPNAVINST 1740.4C
U.S. Navy Family Care Policy

OPNAVINST 5710.27C
Chief of Naval Operations Counterpart Visit Program

SECNAVINST 4900.48
Transfer of U.S. Naval Vessels to Foreign Government and International Organizations

SECNAVINST 5212.5C
Navy and Marine Corps Records Disposition Manual

SECNAVINST 5510.34A
Disclosure of Classified Military Information and Controlled Unclassified Information to Foreign Governments, International Organizations, and Foreign Representatives

SECNAVINST 5710.34A
Political Asylum and Temporary Refuge

SECNAVINST 5710.25B
International Agreements

SECNAVINST 5720.44B
Department of the Navy Public Affairs Policy and Regulations

SECNAVINST 7042.14A
Funding of Visits of Foreign Dignitaries

AFI 11–401
Aviation Management

AFI 16–103
Managing the Defense English Language Program

AFI 16–107
International Personnel Exchange program

AFI 16–201
Foreign Disclosure of Classified and Unclassified Military Information to Foreign Governments and International Organizations

AFI 31–401
Information Security Program Management

AFI 32–6001
Family Housing Management

AFI 32–6005
Unaccompanied Housing Management

AFI 32–9003
Granting Temporary Use of Air Force Real Property

AFI 34–242
Mortuary Affairs Program

AFI 34–246
Air Force Lodging Program

AFI 36–2201
Training Development, Delivery and Evaluation

AFI 36–2903
Dress and Personal Appearance of Air Force Personnel

AFI 36–3002
Casualty Services (PA)

AFI 36–3026(I)/AR 600–8–14/BUPERINST 1750.10C/Marine Corps Order 5512.11D/ COMDINST M5512.1A
Identification Cards for Members of the Uniformed Services, their Eligible Family Members and other Eligible Personnel

AFI 36–3201
Professional Military Education

AFI 41–101
Obtaining Alternative Medical and Dental Care

AFI 41–115
Authorized Health Care and Health Care Benefits in the Military Health Services System

AFI 41–210
Patient Administrative Functions

AFI 41–305
Administering Aero medical Staging Facilities

AFI 48–123
Medical Examination and Standards

AFI 51–704
Procedures for Handling Requests for Political Asylum and Temporary Refuge

AFI 65–601, volume 1
Air Force Budget Policies and Procedures

AFMAN 16–101
International Affairs and Security Assistance Management

AFMAN 23–110
USAF Supply Manual

AFMAN 33–363
Management of Records

BUPERSINST 1750.10
Compliance with this Publication is Mandatory

CJCSI 3710.01
Chairman of the Joint Chiefs of Staff Instruction CJCSI 3710.01, Delegation of Authority for Approving Operational Support to Drug Law Enforcement Agencies and Counter-drug-Related Deployment of DOD Personnel

DFAS Guidance
Interim Guidance on Accounting for Obligations (Nov 2004, formerly DFAS–DE 7000.4–R and AFR 170–8)

DFAS Guidance
Interim Guidance of Accounting for Commitments (MS WORD Oct 2003, formerly DFAS–DE 7000.5–R and AFR 170–13)

DFAS Guidance
Interim Guidance on Procedures for Travel Accounting Operations (Formerly DFAS–DE 7010.3R and AFR 177–103)

DFAS–IN 37–1
Finance and Accounting Policy Implementation (Available at web site https://dfas4DOD.dfas.mil)

DLIELC Catalog
Catalog of American Language Course Materials for IMET and U.S. Government Agencies

DLIELC Catalog
Catalog of American Language Course Materials for Foreign Military Sales (FMS)

DLIELC Handbook
Handbook for the American Language Course Placement Test (ALCPT)

DLIELC Handbook
English Language Training Support for Security Assistance Officers

DLIELC Instruction 1025.7
Planning and Programming Security Assistance English Language Training

DLIELC Instruction 1025.15
English Comprehension Level (ECL) Test Guidelines

International Training Handbook (USCG G–C1)
(Available at http://www.uscg.mil/hq/g-ci/2000ith/ITHnew.htm.)

AECA
Arms Export Control Act

Section III
Prescribed Forms
Unless otherwise indicated, DA forms are available on the APD Web site at http://www.apd.army.mil; DD forms are available on the OSD Web site at http://www.dtic.mil.whs.directives/infomgt/forms/formsprogram.htm; Standard forms (SF) and Optional forms (OF) are available on the GSA Web site at http://www.gsa.gov; AF forms are available at http://www.e-publishing.af.mil.

DD Form 2285
Invitational Travel Order (ITO) for International Military Students (IMS) (Prescribed in para 9–3.)

DD Form 2496
International Student Academic Report (Prescribed in para 10–28.)

Section IV
Referenced Forms

AF Form 10
Unit Personnel Record Group (Folder)

AF Form 349
Receipt for Document Released to Accredited Representatives of Foreign Nations

AF Form 357
Family Care Certification

AF Form 475
Education/Training Report

AF Form 623 (Folder)
Individual Training Record Folder

AF Form 623A
On-the-Job Training Record-Continuation Sheet

AF Form 797
Job Qualification Standard Continuation/Command JQS

AF Form 1098
Special Task Certification and Recurring Training

AF Form 1122
Personal Property and Personal Effects Inventory

AF Form 1217
Informational Program (IP) Data Card

AF Form 1256
Certificate of Training

AF Form 1761
International Student Status Report

DA Form 2028
Recommended Changes to Publications and Blank Forms

DA Form 4186
Medical Recommendation for Flying Duty

DA Form 5304
Family Care Plan Counseling Checklist

DA Form 5305
Family Care Plan

DA Label 87
For Official Use Only Sheet

DD Form 7
Report of Treatment Furnished Pay Patients Hospitalization Furnished (Part A)

DD Form 7A
Report of Treatment Furnished Pay Patients Outpatient Treatment Furnished (Part B)

DD Form 652
Unified Services Meal Ticket (Available through normal form supply channels.)

DD Form 1172
Application for Uniformed Services Identification Card DEERS Enrollment

DD Form 1173
United States Uniformed Services Identification and Privilege Card (Dependent)

DD Form 1351
Travel Voucher

DD Form 1351–2
Travel Voucher or Subvoucher

DD Form 1588
Record of Travel Payments

DD Form 2765
DOD/Uniformed Services Identification and Privilege Card

DD Form 2807–1
Report of Medical History

DD Form 2808
Report of Medical Examination

NAVCOMPT Form 2275
Order for Work and Services (Available at http://navalforms.daps.dla.mil.)

NAVMED Form 2161
Referral For Civilian Medical Care (Available at http://www.dtic.mil.)

NAVMED Form 6410/2
Clearance Notice (Aeromedical) (Available at http://navalforms.daps.dla.mil.)

SF 1034
Public Voucher for Purchases and Services other than Personal

SF 1080
Voucher for Transfers between Appropriations and/or Funds

SF 1164
Claim for Reimbursement for Expenditures on Official Business

SF 1449
Solicitation/Contract/Order for Commercial Items

USCIS Form I–94
United States Citizenship and Immigration Services (USCIS), Arrival-Departure Record (Available at http://www.uscis.gov/portal/site/uscis/.)

Appendix B
Western Hemisphere Institute for Security Cooperation

The WHINSEC was established in public law with the signing of the National Defense Authorization Act for FY 2001, Section 2166, to provide professional education and training to eligible persons of the nations of the Western Hemisphere within the context of the democratic principles set forth in the Charter of the Organization of American States. WHINSEC toll-free number is 877–736–2512.

B–1. Western Hemisphere Institute for Security Cooperation/DOD facility

Operating under Army implementing agency at Fort Benning, GA. Oversight includes an independent, federally chartered Board of Visitors with members of Congress and eminent clergy, academicians, and business persons.

B–2. Western Hemisphere Institute for Security Cooperation's mission

To provide professional education and training to eligible personnel of nations of the Western Hemisphere within the context of the democratic principles set forth in the Charter of the Organization of American States, while fostering mutual knowledge, transparency, confidence, and cooperation among the participating nations and promoting democratic values, respect for human rights, and knowledge and understanding of U.S. customs and traditions.

B–3. Personnel that augment the U.S. military and DOD civilian workforce at the Western Hemisphere Institute for Security Cooperation

a. Foreign guest instructors. Officers, warrant officers, noncommissioned officers, civilian police agents, or government civilians serving in a foreign government's security force or government apparatus assigned to an authorized instructor position at a U.S. military school. Foreign guest instructors are afforded all the rights and privileges of their U.S. peers. In addition, foreign guest instructors are provided a daily per diem allowance for themselves and their authorized Family members, travel and moving expenses, as well as U.S. Government quarters, if available. Foreign guest instructors minimum tour of duty is 1 year. Foreign guest instructors usually serve 2–year tours of duty.

b. Volunteer foreign guest instructors. Officers, warrant officers, noncommissioned officers, civilian police agents, or Government civilians serving in a foreign government's security force or government apparatus that, through their government has offered to provide professional services to a U.S. military school at no cost to the United States. While the volunteer foreign guest instructors are afforded all the rights and privileges of their rank as U.S. peers, they do not receive a daily per diem allowance for themselves and their authorized Family members, or travel and moving expenses, or U.S. government quarters. If they desire they can stay in Government quarters and pay the housing costs for their rank. The volunteer foreign guest instructors can serve as members of the faculty or staff depending on the U.S. military school's needs and desires.

c. Fellows. Civilian academic or government officials in temporary residence at a U.S. military school to teach and assist in developing courses, study, and conduct research in support of the school's mission. The school invites fellows and provides a daily per diem allowance, travel, and lodging.

d. Interns. Undergraduate or graduate students providing short-term assistance to complete a project. Interns are provided a civil service salary dependent on their level of qualifications, but are not provided travel or lodging at government expense.

B–4. Commandant, Western Hemisphere Institute for Security Cooperation responsibilities

a. Develop and manage a Guest Instructor Program made up of officers, noncommissioned officers, law enforcement, and civilian government personnel from the democratic nations of the Western Hemisphere to bring regionally relevant security issues and views to the Institute.

b. Develop and manage a Fellows Program drawn from a broad spectrum of U.S. and foreign civilian universities, government, and non-government organizations to bring contemporary and regionally relevant views to enhance the academic environment of the Institute. Fellows will also be introduced to or increase their comprehension of U.S. defense security cooperation program goals and objectives. The nomination and selection of fellows candidates will be coordinated through the appropriate channels.

c. Recognize leaders in the promotion of democracy and human rights throughout the Western Hemisphere through an annual lecture series.

d. Develop and manage an Intern Program to involve U.S. university students in hemispheric relations through an understanding of the value of security cooperation.

e. Hire U.S. Title 10 civilian professors to develop courses and instruct at WHINSEC.

f. Conduct conferences, seminars, and symposiums to enrich the curriculum and expand student and staff learning.

g. Develop and conduct relevant courses that meet the challenges of the 21st Century in the primary languages of the hemisphere.

h. Develop and maintain a regionally-oriented faculty capable of developing and instructing the broad spectrum of joint, combined, and interagency course material in the Institute's curriculum listing. The faculty of the Institute will be composed of—

(1) Active duty U.S. military personnel, of all military departments, serving normal tours of duty in authorized joint manning slots and TDA instructor positions.

(2) Foreign guest instructors, serving at the request of the U.S. Government, filling authorized instructor positions, and provided travel and per diem through Army Operational and Maintenance Account funds. Foreign guest instructors are encouraged to bring their Family members to the U.S. under the Invitational Travel Order allowing them to travel to the Institute. The foreign guest instructors and Family members will be authorized Post Exchange and commissary privileges. Some foreign guest instructors are authorized routine medical care in accordance with Reciprocal Health Care Agreements, 10 USC 2559, and DODI 6015.23 agreement through Martin Army Community Hospital (MACH) or at any Military Treatment Facilities. Family members are authorized reciprocal care in military healthcare facilities. The foreign guest instructors must purchase private health insurance to cover the cost of dependent care and are encouraged to purchase private healthcare insurance for themselves for other than routine medical care expenses or if they are not covered by reciprocal health agreements. Dental care is emergency only and not routine care, per this regulation, chapter 10. The foreign guest instructors and Family members are not authorized use of any U.S. Government supplemental care program or medical care for preexisting conditions or elective surgery. Reciprocal agreements will not pay for prosthetic devices, eyeglasses, hearing aids, or orthopedic footwear. Selected foreign guest instructors for duty at WHINSEC will be vetted and coordinated with HQDA, the Director, SATFA, and the U.S. Embassy Country Teams.

(3) The volunteer foreign guest instructor, who serve as adjunct instructors to the TDA. The volunteer foreign guest instructors receive no remuneration or travel reimbursement from the U.S. government. Family members are encouraged to accompany the volunteer foreign guest instructor, but at no cost to the U.S. Government. The volunteer foreign guest instructors and Family members will be authorized post exchange and authorized use of U.S. military healthcare facilities, unless a reciprocal healthcare agreement is in place in accordance with the Reciprocal Health Care Agreements, 10 USC 2559, and DODI 6015.23, Delivery of Healthcare at Military Treatment Facilities. The volunteer foreign guest instructor must purchase private healthcare insurance to cover medical expenses for self and Family members. Dental care is not available to the volunteer foreign guest instructor when no reciprocal healthcare agreement exists. The volunteer foreign guest instructor selected for duty at WHINSEC will be vetted and coordinated with HQDA, the Director, SATFA, and the U.S. Embassy Country Teams. The volunteer foreign guest instructors can be moved from volunteer status to a funded status as long as the tour is for one year.

(4) U.S. Government civilian employees on the staff or serving in instructor positions at WHINSEC and/or another U.S. Executive Branch department or agency.

(5) Title 10, civilian professors to develop courses and instruct at WHINSEC.

(6) Contract civilian employees, either U.S. or foreign nationals, serving as adjunct, short-term instructors selected for their expertise in specified subject matter. Fellows may serve as guest lecturers to enhance teaching at WHINSEC when their expertise matches the requirements of a course.

(7) Guest lecturers from academia or business selected for their subject matter expertise.

(8) Ensure foreign guest instructors only have access to information approved for release to the foreign guest instructors's parent government and that is required in order to perform assigned duties.

B–5. Western Hemisphere Institute for Security Cooperation Fellows Program

Provides U.S. and foreign civilian personnel the opportunity to teach and work within the U.S. security cooperation apparatus and more fully understand U.S. goals and objectives for the Western Hemisphere. The Commandant, WHINSEC, manages the program and coordinates the selection process with HQDA and the U.S. Embassy Country Team.

a. Objectives. The objectives of the Fellows Program are the following:

(1) Enrich the educational environment of WHINSEC by teaching, assisting in the development of courses, and research that supports cooperative approaches to regional security issues.

(2) Offer a chance for civilian academics from both the U.S. and Western Hemisphere nations the opportunity to teach, study, research, and write on subjects of significance to the security interests of the U.S. and the nations of the Western Hemisphere.

(3) Establish mutual understanding and working relationships between the militaries of the region and civilian academic sectors.

(4) Improve the Fellows' first-hand knowledge of U.S. culture and institutions through study and travel in the United States.

b. Prerequisites. U.S. and foreign fellows selection should be governed by previously demonstrated professionalism and estimated potential to assist in teaching, course development, and to influence positive civilian-military relationships within their country of origin.

(1) Fellows should possess appropriate credentials in their field and be currently associated with civilian academic institutions of higher learning or with a government agency or ministry.

(2) Fellows must be motivated to undertake study and research on civil-military issues or issues dealing with achieving the goals of the U.S. security cooperation program among the nations of the Western Hemisphere.

(3) Fellows will have the opportunity to participate as guest lecturers in selected courses as well as serve as panel members during conferences and other forums hosted by the Institute.

c. Program description.

(1) The Fellows Program adds a dimension to the Institute that broadens the academic environment for both students and faculty members. The association of military students with civilian academics can improve mutual understanding of national security issues and bridge the gaps of misunderstanding and non-communication between the two sectors of society. The Institute also benefits by having civilian academics working within and promoting the role of the Institute in achieving security cooperation goals and objectives.

(2) Fellows may serve up to 179 days tours (including travel time) at WHINSEC. A successful fellow may reapply for additional tours, if warranted. The Institute will provide the fellow suitable lodging in guest quarters and reimburse the individual an appropriate per diem according to the JTR and a rental vehicle during the tour. Travel to and from WHINSEC will be provided at U.S. government expense. Healthcare and emergency health services will be at the individual's expense. The fellow will not be authorized post exchange and commissary privileges nor issued a U.S. Government identification card.

(3) The status of fellow, as opposed to student or foreign guest instructor makes individual initiative an essential part of the program. A large part of each program will be dedicated to individual study and research to produce a viable product for U.S. Government use and dissemination. A willingness to engage the local and national media is also part of the program's goals.

(4) WHINSEC is authorized to perform travel coordination with U.S. military installations to be visited by the Fellow.

d. Selection procedures. The Fellow's Program is advertised at United States and foreign universities to draw prospective candidates. The WHINSEC Fellows Selection Committee reviews potential candidates and recommends a candidate for selection by the Commandant, WHINSEC. In coordination with HQDA and the U.S. Embassy Country Team, a formal invitation is forwarded for the fellow to proceed to the United States. The U.S. Embassy Country Team does the vetting of each selected candidate. The Director, SATFA, will be notified of the selection of each fellow.

B–6. Western Hemisphere Institute for Security Cooperation Intern Program

Allows U.S. citizen university students the opportunity to work as government employees in a dynamic international environment, witness the implementation of U.S. foreign policy and understand the role of security cooperation in international relations. The Commandant, WHINSEC, manages the program.

a. Interns will provide short-term support for major conferences, forums, or special projects.

b. Interns will be hired as temporary general schedule government employees and must meet all the requirements for such employment. Travel and lodging costs are the responsibility of the selected Intern.

c. Interns will be selected from qualified applicants. Others may apply and be accepted as volunteer workers. Volunteer workers must register with WHINSEC and Fort Benning, GA volunteer services.

B–7. Foreign nationals serving on Western Hemisphere Institute for Security Cooperation's staff or faculty as guest instructors or fellows

May receive such training and retainable training materials, without reimbursement to the U.S. Government, as deemed necessary by the Commandant to prepare them to accomplish their duties.

B–8. Household goods shipment

Upon completion of the tour of the foreign guest instructors assigned to WHINSEC. Foreign guest instructors assigned to WHINSEC are authorized HHG under OMA funding. Shipment of household goods from CONUS to the instructors' home countries is authorized for foreign guest instructors who have completed a normal tour of duty at WHINSEC. The normal tour of duty for foreign guest instructors at WHINSEC is 2 years. Foreign guest instructors that have tours less than 2 years will be adjusted accordingly. The weight allowance will be as follows unaccompanied 1000 pounds, accompanied for one year tour 2000 pounds, over one year to 18 months 3000 pounds and over 18 months 4000 pounds. A net weight allowance of 6,000 pounds is authorized for the deputy commandant assigned to WHINSEC. In addition to net weights listed above, weight allowances are authorized for crating and packing materials on the same basis as for U.S. military personnel and according to the JTR. Shipment of HHG in excess of the authorized net weight will be at the expense of the foreign guest instructors or their governments. The above weights are absolute and no additional allowance is authorized for professional military material to be shipped at USG expense. The U.S. Government will not be responsible for insurance of the HHG shipment. The foreign guest instructors is encouraged to purchase private insurance to cover the damage of the HHG shipment. Shipment will be by surface common carrier.

B–9. Foreign guest instructors

Foreign guest instructors assigned to WHINSEC are authorized the following:

a. Foreign guest instructors are authorized a subsistence of $26 a day.

b. Basic allowance for housing based on the foreign guest instructors' rank.

c. Travel to WHINSEC for the foreign guest instructors and the authorized Family members and return to their country upon completion of the tour. If the military Family members do not travel with the military member, the military member will receive subsistence and rent cost at the "without Family members" rate. Also, they will not be eligible for on-post family housing. Once the military Family members arrive, the military member will begin receiving subsistence and rent cost at the "with Family members" rate and be eligible for on-post housing. If the military Family members do not arrive within 120 days after the military member's arrival, the military member will not be carried in an accompanied status for the remainder of the tour. They will be considered unaccompanied and paid at the "without Family members" rate, even if the Family arrives after the 120-day period. Also, if the military Family members do not arrive within the 120-day window, WHINSEC will not pay for their travel and household goods shipment will be paid at the unaccompanied rate. After the 120-day window, travel will become the responsibility of the host country and/or the military member. If the military Family members arrive with the military member or with the 120-day window, the military Family members are required to remain at Fort Benning, GA for at least 12 months of the military member's assigned tour. If the military Family members do not remain at Fort Benning, GA for at least 12 months, travel will not be authorized at WHINSEC/U.S. government expense. The military member and/or host country will be required to pay this travel expense.

B–10. Foreign guest instructor, volunteer foreign guest instructor, or foreign Family member employment
Neither fellows, foreign guest instructor', volunteer foreign guest instructor' nor their foreign Family members are permitted to seek or accept employment during their stay in the United States unless specifically approved and coordinated through the Department of Homeland Security, Bureau of Citizenship and Immigration Services.

B–11. Field Studies Program
WHINSEC staff and faculty (foreign guest instructors, volunteer foreign guest instructors, fellows, and interns) may attend a DOD Field Studies Program event in an unofficial, space-available capacity. Priority is 1) the student; 2) U.S. escorts; 3) student Family members. WHINSEC staff and faculty members will pay all expenses incurred including hotels, meals, air or bus travel, and fees to enter a venue.

Appendix C
Internal Control Evaluation

C–1. Function
The function covered by this evaluation is to ensure effective implementation of the SCETP.

C–2. Purpose
The purpose of this evaluation is to assist IMSO and SCO in implementing the SCETP.

C–3. Instructions
Answers must be based on the actual testing of key internal controls (for example, data analysis, direct observation, and sampling). Answers that indicate deficiencies must be explained and the corrective action identified in supporting documentation. These internal controls must be evaluated at least once every 5 years. Certification that the evaluation has been conducted must be accomplished on DA Form 11–2 (Internal Control Evaluation Certification).

C–4. Test questions
    a. Did the IMSO and SCO satisfactorily complete required training?
    b. Did the SCO perform required screening of IMS?
    c. Did the SCO prepare correct ITOs and documentation in DSAMS?
    d. Did the IMSO maintain current information in DSAMS?
    e. Did the IMSO perform designated responsibilities in support of IMS?

C–5. Supersession
Not applicable.

C–6. Comments
Help make this a better tool for evaluating internal controls. Submit comments to Deputy Assistant Secretary of the Army for Defense Exports and Cooperation (DASA DE&C), 103 Army Pentagon, Washington, DC 20310–0103.

Glossary

Section I
Abbreviations

ACOM
Army service component command

ACSC
Air Command and Staff College

AECA
Arms Export Control Act

AF
Air Force

AFB
Air Force base

AFI
Air Force Instruction

AFIT
Air Force Institute of Technology

AFM
Air Force manual

AFO
Accounting and Finance Officer

AIDS
Acquired Immune Deficiency Syndrome

ALCPT
American Language Course Placement Test

AMC
Army Materiel Command

AMEDD
Army Medical Department

AMEDDC&S
Army Medical Department Center and School

ANG
Air National Guard

APO
Army/Air Force Post Office

AR
Army regulation

ASA
Assistant Secretary of the Army

ASA (ALT)
Assistant Secretary of the Army (Acquisition, Logistics, and Technology)

ASCC
Army service component command

ASD (ISA)
Assistant Secretary of Defense (International Security Affairs)

ATRRS
Army Training Resource and Requirement System

AWC
Air War College

AWC
Army War College

BO
blanket order

BUMED
Bureau of Medicine and Surgery

BUPERS
Bureau of Naval Personnel

BY
budget year

CAO
case administering office

CBT
computer based training

CDR
commander

CD–ROM
compact disk-read only memory

CECOM
Communications-Electronics Command

CFS
contract field services

CG
commanding general

CGSC
Command and General Staff College

CJCS
Chairman, Joints Chiefs of Staff

CLO
country liaison officer

CMC
Commandant of the Marine Corps

CMI
classified military information

CNO
Chief of Naval Operations

COE
U.S. Army Corps of Engineers

COMPACFLT
Commander, Pacific Fleet

CONUS
continental United States

CRA
continuing resolution authority

CSA
Chief of Staff, Army

CTFP
Counterterrorism Fellowship Program

CUI
controlled unclassified information

CVS
cardiovascular screening

DA
Department of the Army

DAR
Defense Acquisition Regulation

DASA (DE&C)
Deputy Assistant Secretary of the Army for Defense Exports and Cooperation

DCS G–2
Deputy Chief of Staff, G–2

DCS G–3/5/7
Deputy Chief of Staff G–3/5/7

DELP
Defense English Language Program

DFAS
Defense Finance and Accounting Service

DFAS–DE
Defense Finance and Accounting Service - Denver Center

DIMO
Defense Institute for Medical Operations

DISAM
Defense Institute of Security Assistance Management

DL
disturbed/distance learning

DLIELC
Defense Language Institute English Language Center

DOD
Department of Defense

DODI
Department of Defense Instruction

DON
Department of Navy

DOS
Department of State

DRMI
Defense Resources Management Institute

DRU
direct reporting unit

DSAMS
Defense Security Assistance Management System

DSCA
Defense Security Cooperation Agency

DV
distinguished visitor

DVD
digital video disk

ea
each

ECL
English Comprehension Level

EE
extraordinary expenses

E–IMET
Expanded International Military Education and Training

ELT
English Language Training

ELTP
English Language Training Program

ETSS
Extended training service specialist

FAA
Foreign Assistance Act

FDME
flying duty medical examination

FDO
foreign disclosure officer

FLO
foreign liaison officer

FMF
foreign military financing

FMS
foreign military sales

FORSCOM
Forces Command

FOT
follow-on-training

FTD
field training detachment

FVS
Foreign Visits System

FY
fiscal year

GMAT
graduate management admission test

GPC
government purchase card

GRE
graduate record examination

GTR
Government transportation request

HIV
human immunodeficiency virus

HHG
household goods

HQ
headquarters

HQDA
Headquarters, Department of the Army

IAAFA
Inter-American Air Forces Academy

ID
identification

ILE
intermediate level education

IMET
International Military Education and Training

IMETP
International Military Education and Training Program

IMS
International military student

IMSO
International military student office

IPO
International Program Office

ITO
invitational travel orders

JCET
joint combined exchange training

JFTR
Joint Federal Travel Regulations

JTR
Joint Travel Regulation

LOA
letter of offer and acceptance

LTD
language training detachment

MAJCOM
Major Army Command (USAF)

MAP
military assistance program

MARFOR
Marine Corps forces

MARSOC
Marine special operations command

MASL
military articles and services list

MCCDC
Marine Corps Combat Development Command

MILDEP
military department

MOA
Memorandum of Agreement

MOD
Ministry of Defense

MOU
memorandum of understanding

MS
mission sustainment

MSC
Major Subordinate Commands (Army)

MTT
mobile training team

MWR
morale, welfare, and recreation

NATO
North Atlantic Treaty Organization

NAVMED
Navy medicine

NCO
Noncommissioned Officer

NDP
National Disclosure Policy

NDU
National Defense University

NLT
no later than

NPS
Naval Postgraduate School

NTE
not to exceed

OASD
Office of the Assistant Secretary of Defense

OASD (PA)
Office of the Assistant Secretary of Defense (Public Affairs)

OBT
observer training

OCONUS
outside continental United States

OJT
on-the-job-training

OMA
operations and maintenance, Army

OPI
oral proficiency interview

OPNAVINST
Chief of Naval Operations instruction

OPR
office of primary responsibility

OSD
Office of the Secretary of Defense

OT
orientation tours

P&A
price and availability

PA
public affairs

PCS
permanent change of station

PDO
Publishing Distribution Office

PFP
Partnership for Peace

PME
professional military education

POC
point of contact

POV
privately-owned vehicle

PT
physical training

QOL
quality of life

RIM
retainable instructional material

RST
requirements survey team

SAF
Secretary of Air Force

SAMM
Security Assistance Management Manual

SAT
Security Assistance Team

SAT
Security Assistance Training

SATFA
Security Assistance Training Field Activity

SATP
security assistance training program

SC
security cooperation

SCETP
Security Cooperation Education and Training Program

SECDEF
Secretary of Defense

SECNAV
Secretary of the Navy

SECNAVINST
Secretary of the Navy Instruction

SOCOM
Special Operations Command

SOF
Special Operations Forces

SOFA
status of forces agreement

SOW
Statement of Work

SSAN
Social Security Account Number

STANAG
standardized agreement

STL
standardized training listing

SYSCOM
Systems Command

TAD
Temporary Additional Duty

TAFT
technical assistance field team

TAT
technical assistance team

TB
tuberculosis

TCO
test control officer

TDA
table of distribution and allowances

TDY
temporary duty

TLA
temporary lodging allowance

TOEFL
Test of English as a Foreign Language

TPA
total package approach

TRADOC
Training and Doctrine Command

TRICARE
Tri-service medical care

TRM
team request memorandum

TSCP
Theater Security Cooperation Plans

TTAD
temporary tour of active duty

UA
unauthorized absence

UCMJ
Uniform Code of Military Justice

UPH
unaccompanied personnel housing

USAAMA
U.S. Army Aero-medical Activity

USAF
United States Air Force

USAFSOS
USAF Special Operations School

USAR
United States Army Reserve

USASAC
United States Army Security Assistance Command

USASCS
U.S. Army Security Cooperation Strategy

USASMA
United States Army Sergeants Major Academy

USASOC
United States Army Special Operations Command

USC
United States Code

USCIS
United States Citizenship and Immigration Services

USCG
United States Coast Guard

USD(P)
Under Secretary of Defense for Policy

USG
United States Government

USMC
United States Marine Corps

USN
United States Navy

VEQ
visiting enlisted quarters

VOQ
visiting officer's quarters

WCN
worksheet control number

WHINSEC
Western Hemisphere Institute for Security Cooperation

Section II
Terms
This section contains entries.

Section III
Special Abbreviations and Terms
This section contains no entries.

PIN 047393–000